Communications in Computer and Information Science 2444

Rationale

The CCIS series is devoted to the publication of proceedings of computer science conferences. Its aim is to efficiently disseminate original research results in informatics in printed and electronic form. While the focus is on publication of peer-reviewed full papers presenting mature work, inclusion of reviewed short papers reporting on work in progress is welcome, too. Besides globally relevant meetings with internationally representative program committees guaranteeing a strict peer-reviewing and paper selection process, conferences run by societies or of high regional or national relevance are also considered for publication.

Topics

The topical scope of CCIS spans the entire spectrum of informatics ranging from foundational topics in the theory of computing to information and communications science and technology and a broad variety of interdisciplinary application fields.

Information for Volume Editors and Authors

Publication in CCIS is free of charge. No royalties are paid, however, we offer registered conference participants temporary free access to the online version of the conference proceedings on SpringerLink (http://link.springer.com) by means of an http referrer from the conference website and/or a number of complimentary printed copies, as specified in the official acceptance email of the event.

CCIS proceedings can be published in time for distribution at conferences or as post-proceedings, and delivered in the form of printed books and/or electronically as USBs and/or e-content licenses for accessing proceedings at SpringerLink. Furthermore, CCIS proceedings are included in the CCIS electronic book series hosted in the SpringerLink digital library at http://link.springer.com/bookseries/7899. Conferences publishing in CCIS are allowed to use Online Conference Service (OCS) for managing the whole proceedings lifecycle (from submission and reviewing to preparing for publication) free of charge.

Publication process

The language of publication is exclusively English. Authors publishing in CCIS have to sign the Springer CCIS copyright transfer form, however, they are free to use their material published in CCIS for substantially changed, more elaborate subsequent publications elsewhere. For the preparation of the camera-ready papers/files, authors have to strictly adhere to the Springer CCIS Authors' Instructions and are strongly encouraged to use the CCIS LaTeX style files or templates.

Abstracting/Indexing

CCIS is abstracted/indexed in DBLP, Google Scholar, EI-Compendex, Mathematical Reviews, SCImago, Scopus. CCIS volumes are also submitted for the inclusion in ISI Proceedings.

How to start

To start the evaluation of your proposal for inclusion in the CCIS series, please send an e-mail to ccis@springer.com.

A. Mirzazadeh · Zohreh Molamohamadi ·
Babek Erdebilli · Erfan Babaee Tirkolaee ·
Gerhard-Wilhelm Weber · Alexandre Dolgui
Editors

Science, Engineering Management and Information Technology

4th International Conference, SEMIT 2024
Ankara, Turkey, September 12–13, 2024
Proceedings

Springer

Editors
A. Mirzazadeh
Kharazmi University
Tehran, Iran

Zohreh Molamohamadi
Kharazmi University
Tehran, Iran

Babek Erdebilli
Ankara Yıldırım Beyazıt University
Ankara, Türkiye

Erfan Babaee Tirkolaee
Istinye University
Istanbul, Türkiye

Gerhard-Wilhelm Weber
Poznań University of Technology
Poznań, Poland

Alexandre Dolgui
IMT Atlantique
Nantes, France

ISSN 1865-0929 ISSN 1865-0937 (electronic)
Communications in Computer and Information Science
ISBN 978-3-032-01947-9 ISBN 978-3-032-01948-6 (eBook)
https://doi.org/10.1007/978-3-032-01948-6

This Springer imprint is published by the registered company Springer Nature Switzerland AG
The registered company address is: Gewerbestrasse 11, 6330 Cham, Switzerland

Preface

The International Conference on Science, Engineering Management and Information Technology (SEMIT 2024) was held virtually in Ankara, Turkey on September 12–13, 2024 by the Institution of International Scientific Services (RefConf) and Ankara Yildirim Beyazit University. It provided an energetic knowledge-transferring atmosphere for participants (as feedback revealed).

SEMIT 2024 attracted the attention of students and professionals internationally. The covering subjects included, but were not limited to, "IT and EM based case studies of manufacturing/service industries (including automotive, food, tourism, petroleum, healthcare, insurance and banking, energy, etc.)", "E-government, E-commerce, E-learning", "Marketing and E-marketing for resources management", "Data science and knowledge management in EM", "Industry 4.0, supply chain 4.0, and logistics 4.0", "Applied soft computing in engineering management", "Blockchain in engineering management", "Data science in project management", and "Other fields of study related to EM and IT".

SEMIT 2024 was honored to be enriched by outstanding keynote speakers from USA, Poland, Portugal, and Turkey. In this event, eight universities from USA, France, UK, Czech Republic, Tunisia, and Turkey were present as scientific sponsors.

The conference included participants from 45 countries. The geographical diversity of international technical program committee members was from 17 countries.

A total of 123 submissions were received, from which 27 full papers were accepted for publication in this book series. Each submission was evaluated by at least three reviewers, ensuring a rigorous and balanced peer-review process. On average, each reviewer assessed approximately two papers. The review criteria in this step were: content; originality; relevance; contribution to the professional literature; significance and potential impact of the paper; language accuracy; study validity; accuracy of methodology and analysis; paper organization, required relevant data, citations, and references; adequate reference to the background information; consistency of references, symbols, and units throughout the paper; quality and clarity of tables and figures.

The papers in SEMIT 2024 were presented in 14 panel sessions: "Optimization and Decision-Making: Methods and Algorithms", "Artificial Intelligence and Expert Systems", "Safety and Reliability Engineering, System Engineering and System Safety, Safety in Industry 4.0", "BioCompute Innovations: Bridging Computer Science and Bioinformatics", "Recent Advancements in Social Sciences, Humanities, and Information Technology", "HSE & Machine Learning Applications in Engineering", "Blockchain Applications and Other Fields of Study Related to EM and IT", "Marketing and E-marketing", "Smart Transportation Systems and Water Management", "The Impact of AI on Cybersecurity", "Harnessing Advanced Mathematical Modeling and Digital Technologies for Sustainable Engineering and Financial Solutions", "Soft Computing Algorithms for Optimization and Decision Making in an Uncertain Environment",

"Data Modeling, Mining and Knowledge Discovery", and "Role of Digital Technologies and Supply Chain Sustainability".

SEMIT 2024 included three applied workshops by outstanding lecturers with good-sized audiences. The workshop subjects were very well received by the participants and were entitled: "The interplay between Tokenomics and Monetary Policy Transmission Mechanism", "AI Tools For Classroom Engagement", and "Advancing Quality Control & Predictive Maintenance in Manufacturing with AI, ML, Cloud, & IoT".

December 2024

A. Mirzazadeh
Zohreh Molamohamadi
Babek Erdebilli
Efran Babaee Tirkolaee
Gerhard-Wilhelm Weber
Alexandre Dolgui

Organization

Conference Chairs

Abolfazl Mirzazadeh	Kharazmi University, Iran/Institution of International Scientific Services (RefConf), Oman
Babek Erdebilli	Ankara Yildirim Beyazit University, Turkey

Patrons

Ali Cengiz Köseoğlu	Ankara Yildirim Beyazit University, Turkey
Abdullah Yildiz	Ankara Yildirim Beyazit University, Turkey
Mete Gundogan	Ankara Yildirim Beyazit University, Turkey
Gülnihal Meral	Ankara Yildirim Beyazit University, Turkey

Conference Coordinators

Leila Chehreghani	Ulster University, UK/Institution of International Scientific Services (RefConf), Oman
Zohreh Molamohamadi	Kharazmi University, Iran/Institution of International Scientific Services (RefConf), Oman
Saina Sahragard	Institution of International Scientific Services (RefConf), Oman

Technical Program Committee Chairs

Gerhard-Wilhelm Weber	Poznań University of Technology, Poland
Alexandre Dolgui	IMT Atlantique, France
Zohreh Molamohamadi	Kharazmi University, Iran
Efran Babaee Tirkolaee	Istinye University, Turkey

Steering Committee Members

A. Mirzazadeh	Kharazmi University, Iran
Babek Erdebilli	Ankara Yildirim Beyazit University, Turkey
Janny M. Y. Leung	University of Macau, China
Mete Gundogan	Ankara Yildirim Beyazit University, Turkey
Josef Jablonsky	Prague University of Economics and Business, Czech Republic
Rubén Ruiz Garcia	Polytechnic University of Valencia, Spain
Ibrahim Yilmaz	Ankara Yildirim Beyazit University, Turkey
Ergun Eraslan	Ankara Yildirim Beyazit University, Turkey
Sırma Zeynep Alparslan Gök	Suleyman Demirel University, Turkey

Technical Program Committee Members

Sadia Samar Ali	King Abdulaziz University, Saudi Arabia
Safa Bhar Layeb	University of Tunis EI Manar, Tunisia
Jaouad Boukachour	University of Le Havre-Normandy, France
Gerçek Budak	Ankara Yildirim Beyazit University, Turkey
Aybike Özyüksel Çiftçioğlu	Manisa Celal Bayar University, Turkey
Leopoldo Eduardo Cárdenas-Barrón	Tecnológico de Monterrey, Mexico
Serap Ergün	Isparta Applied Sciences University
Alireza Goli	University of Isfahan, Iran
Paulina Golinska	Poznań University of Technology, Poland
Hakan Gultekin	Sultan Qaboos University, Oman
Mostafa Hajiaghaei-Keshteli	Tecnológico de Monterrey, Mexico
Michael G. Kay	North Carolina State University, USA
Reza Kiani Mavi	Edith Cowan University, Australia
Elif Kılıç Delice	Ataturk University, Turkey
Taicir Moalla Loukil	University of Sfax, Tunisia
Eloisa Macedo	University of Aveiro, Portugal
Beata Mrugalska	Poznań University of Technology, Poland
M. M. Nadakatti	Gogte Institute of Technology, India
Eren Özceylan	Gaziantep University, Turkey
Michael Pecht	University of Maryland, USA
Nazanin Pilevari	Islamic Azad University, Iran
Sujan Piya	University of Sharjah, UAE
Ali Asghar Rahmani Hosseinabadi	University of Regina, Canada
Sankar Kumar Roy	Vidyasagar University, India
Servet Soygüder	Ankara Yildirim Beyazıt University, Turkey

Maria Grazia Speranza	University of Brescia, Italy
Kathryn Stecke	University of Texas at Dallas, Naveen Jindal School of Management, USA
Sylwia Szybowska	Jacob of Paradies University in Gorzów Wielkopolski, Poland
Tatiana Tchemisova	University of Aveiro, Portugal
Dinh Tran Ngoc Huy	International University of Japan, Japan
Chefi Triki	University of Kent, UK

Keynote Speakers

Dursun Delen	Oklahoma State University, USA
Gülnihal Meral	Ankara Yildirim Beyazıt University, Turkey
Eren Özceylan	Gaziantep University, Turkey
Sara Saberi	Worcester Polytechnic Institute, USA
Tatiana Tchemisova	University of Aveiro, Portugal
Gerhard-Wilhelm Weber	Poznań University of Technology, Poland

Workshop Organizers

Marzieh Asaadi	Golestan University, Iran
Vuppulapati Chandra Sekhar Naidu	Coforge, USA
AbdulQuddus Mohammed	Higher Colleges of Technology, UAE
Sheetal Sharma	VIT Bhopal, India
HarshaVardhan Yedla	Wipro, USA

Executive Committee Members

Ahmet Süha Hancıoğlu	Ankara Yildirim Beyazit University, Turkey
Gül Uslu	Sinop University, Turkey
Vildan Tezcan	Ankara Yildirim Beyazit University, Turkey
Abdulrahim Taha Küçüköner	Ankara Yildirim Beyazit University, Turkey
Alperen Öncel	Ankara Yildirim Beyazit University, Turkey
Şafak Kağar	Ankara Yildirim Beyazit University, Turkey
Mert Eyüboğlu	Ankara Yildirim Beyazit University, Turkey

Reviewers

Vijay Kumar Gahlawat	NIFTEM-K, India
Musa Genemo	Gumushane University, Turkey
Malek Ghanem	ISG Tunis, Tunisia
Seyed Ahmad Ghasemi	Research Institute of Humanities and Social Studies of ACECR, Iran
Hamed Gheibdoust	Islamic Azad University Rasht Branch, Iran
Alireza Goli	University of Isfahan, Iran
Wynand Goosen	Association of Private Providers of Education, Training and Development, South Africa
Vasanthi Govindaraj	National General (An Allstate Company), USA
Lalit Garg	University of Malta, Malta
Halil Ibrahim	Ayaz Necmettin Erbakan University, Turkey
Faraz Hasan Koneru	Lakshmaiah Educational Foundation, India
Osama Hashmi	Shaheed Zulfiqar Ali Bhutto University, Islamabad, Pakistan
Marwa Hasni	University of Sfax, Tunisia
Zainabolhoda Heshmati	University of Tehran, Iran
Md. Hossain	Khulna University, Bangladesh
Shilpa Hudnukrar	Symbiosis Institute of Technology, Symbiosis International (Deemed University), India
Sherzod Ibodulloev	"TIIAME" National Research University, Uzbekistan
Stephanus Indrawan	Ciputra University Surabaya, Indonesia
Md. Ashraful Islam	University of Information Technology & Sciences, Bangladesh
Shakeel Javaid	Aligarh Muslim University, India
Prasad Joshi	Symbiosis International (Deemed) University, India
Richard Kadan	Stellenbosch University, South Africa
Sami Kadhim	Ministry of Education, Iraq
Saliha Karadayi-Usta	Istinye University, Turkey
Meenakhi kaushik	Guru Gobind Singh University, India
Mazdak Khodadadi Karimvand	University of Science and Culture, Iran
Elif Kiliç Delice	Atatürk University, Turkey
Zara Kiran	University Kebangsaan Malaysia, Malaysia
Mudita Kohli	Panjab University, India
Viraj Lele	DHL Supply Chain, USA
Hela Limam	University of Tunis El Manar, and Institut Supérieur de Gestion de Tunis, Tunisia
A. Mirzazadeh	Kharazmi University, Iran
Zohreh Molamohamadi	Kharazmi University, Iran
Chanicha Moryadee	Suan Sunandha Rajabhat University, Thailand
Fatereh Sadat Moosavi	Islamic Azad University, Iran

Sonia Nasri	École Supérieure de Commerce de Tunis, Université de la Manouba, Tunisia
Luan-Thanh Nguyen	Ho Chi Minh City University of Foreign Languages-Information Technology, Vietnam
Sara Nodoust	Kharazmi University, Iran
Ammar Odeh	Princess Sumaya University for Technology, Jordan
Wided Oueslati	École Supérieure de Commerce de Tunis, University de la Manouba, Tunisia
Kumar Rahul	NIFTEM, India
Sita Ram Sharma	Chitkara University, India
Marzieh Samadi Foroushani	University of Eyvanekey, Iran
Hamed Shakerian	Ministry of Education, Iran
Deepak Singh	University of Pittsburgh, USA
Tharun Sure	ServiceNow, USA
Faustino Taderera	National University of Science & Technology, Oman
Dinh Tran Ngoc Huy	International University of Japan, Japan
Anak Agung Gde Satia Utama	Universitas Airlangga, Indonesia
Gerhard-Wilhelm Weber	Poznań University of Technology, Poland
Harshavardhan Yedla	Wipro LLC, USA
Nurullah Yilmaz Süleyman	Demirel University, Turkey

Scientific Sponsors

THE UNIVERSITY
OF TEXAS AT DALLAS

The University of Texas at Dallas, USA

ISPARTA
UNIVERSITY OF
APPLIED SCIENCES

Isparta University of Applied Sciences, Turkey

Prague University of Economics and Business, Czech Republic

Kent Business School, UK

University of LE HAVRE, France

University of Sfax, Tunisia

Manisa Celal Bayar University, Turkey

Healthcare Systems Group, Tunisia

Contents

Advances of AI/ML and Optimization in IT and Engineering

AI-Powered Route Optimization: Advancing Logistics and Environmental Sustainability (UNO-SDG-9,11,13,13,17)

Harshavardhan Yedla[1(✉)], Vuppulapati Chandra Sekhar Naidu[2], and Sheetal Sharma[3]

[1] Principal Architect, Plano, TX, USA
harsha.thisis@gmail.com
[2] Data Solution Architect, Frisco, TX, USA
[3] School of Architecture VIT Bhopal, Bhopal, India

Abstract. The increasing demand for logistics and the urgent need for environmental sustainability requires innovative solutions to optimize transportation routes and reduce greenhouse gas emissions. This study explores the role of artificial intelligence in improving logistics efficiency and environmental performance by applying various regression models to predict travel times and emissions using real-world logistics datasets. These datasets include factors such as vehicle types, traffic conditions, weather, emissions, distance, fuel consumption, and package attributes. The study employs machine learning models like Linear Regression, Ridge and Lasso Regression, Support Vector Machines, Decision Trees, Random Forests, Gradient Boosting, XGBoost, Gaussian Processes, and Multi-layer Perceptron Regressors, as well as advanced deep learning techniques including LSTM, RNN, CNN, and ARIMA for time series forecasting. The evaluation framework uses metrics such as Mean Squared Error, Mean Absolute Error, R-squared, and Mean Absolute Percentage Error, with hyperparameter tuning to enhance model performance. It also incorporates dynamic route recalculation, emissions impact analysis focusing on CO_2 and other greenhouse gases, cost-benefit optimization, and scenario planning. The results identify the most effective models for route optimization and emission reduction, demonstrating AI's potential to improve logistics and sustainability and reduce the ecological footprint of transportation. This research aligns with several United Nations Sustainable Development Goals (SDGs), including Industry, Innovation, and Infrastructure (Goal 9), Sustainable Cities and Communities (Goal 11), Responsible Consumption and Production (Goal 12), Climate Action (Goal 13), and Partnerships for the Goals (Goal 17).

Keywords: Gradient Boosting · XGBoost · Gaussian Processes · Recurrent Neural Network (RNN) · Convolutional Neural Network (CNN) · Auto-Regressive Integrated Moving Average (ARIMA)

A. Mirzazadeh et al. (Eds.): SEMIT 2024, CCIS 2444, pp. 3–18, 2026.
https://doi.org/10.1007/978-3-032-01948-6_1

1 Introduction

In the fast-evolving field of transportation logistics, precise travel times and emissions predictions are increasingly vital. This analysis leverages cutting-edge machine learning and deep learning techniques to model and forecast critical performance metrics in the industry [2, 9]. By combining extensive data on vehicle operations, environmental conditions, and logistical factors, we aim to develop robust predictive models that improve decision-making and operational efficiency [1, 5].

The dataset encompasses vehicle routes, travel details, and environmental factors, including distance traveled, fuel consumption, traffic, weather conditions, and emissions [7, 28]. This data undergoes meticulous preprocessing to handle missing values, normalize features, and encode categorical variables for model training and evaluation [22].

The current approach entitles a variety of predictive models, from traditional methods like Linear, Ridge, and Lasso Regression [13] to more sophisticated algorithms such as Support Vector Machines [14], Decision Trees, Random Forests [15], and Gradient Boosting Machines [18]. We also utilize ensemble methods and deep learning techniques, including XGBoost [2], Gaussian Process Regressors [5], and Multi-layer Perceptron (MLP) Regressors [6]. For time-series forecasting, ARIMA models [29] and advanced deep learning methods like Long Short-Term Memory (LSTM) networks [4], Recurrent Neural Networks (RNNs) [26], and Convolutional Neural Networks (CNNs) [10] are applied to identify temporal patterns. Model performance is evaluated through cross-validation and hyperparameter tuning, using metrics such as Mean Squared Error (MSE), Mean Absolute Error (MAE), R-squared (R2), and Mean Absolute Percentage Error (MAPE) [24]. Visualizations further enhance understanding of model effectiveness [8]. This analysis underscores the potential of machine learning and deep learning in optimizing transportation operations and reducing environmental impact [30]. The study aligns with Sustainable Development Goals 9 -Industry, Innovation, and Infrastructure, 11 -Sustainable Cities and Communities, 12 -Responsible Consumption and Production, and 13 -Climate Action directed by United National Organization (Table 1).

The paper begins with a literature review in Sect. 2, which examines existing studies on the application of machine learning to logistics and environmental sustainability. Section 3 discusses the collection of relevant datasets, including travel times, emissions, and other logistical variables, followed by data cleaning and preprocessing to address missing values and normalize features. Exploratory Data Analysis (EDA) using visualizations, such as scatter plots and distributions, is conducted to identify patterns and relationships among features. Section 4 details the implementation of various machine learning models, such as Linear Regression, Ridge Regression, Lasso Regression, and tree-based models, evaluating their performance using metrics like Mean Squared Error (MSE), Mean Absolute Error (MAE), R-squared (R2), and Mean Absolute Percentage Error (MAPE) to identify the most effective models for predicting travel times and emissions. Finally, the conclusion summarizes key insights, offering recommendations to enhance logistics efficiency and reduce environmental impact while highlighting areas for future research to address identified gaps.

Table 1. Navigate through the list of abbreviations & their full form.

Abbreviations	Full Term
AI	Artificial Intelligence
ARIMA	Auto Regressive Integrated Moving Average
CNN	Convolutional Neural Network
EDA	Exploratory Data Analysis
MAPE	Mean Absolute Percentage Error
MAE	Mean Absolute Error
MSE	Mean Squared Error
$\mathbf{R^2}$	R-squared
RNN	Recurrent Neural Network
SVM	Support Vector Machine
LSTM	Long Short-Term Memory
KDE	Kernel Density Estimation
ML	Machine Learning
IoT	Internet of Things
ITS	Intelligent Transportation Systems
CSR	Corporate Social Responsibility
SDG	Sustainable Development Goals

2 Literature Review

Predictive transportation and emissions management modeling is essential for optimizing logistics, enhancing operational efficiency, and minimizing environmental impact [1, 7]. Here, data-driven decision-making becomes more critical; advanced analytical techniques for forecasting travel times and emissions are increasingly valuable [1, 5]. This review explores the integration of machine learning (ML) and deep learning methodologies, focusing on their effectiveness and applications [2, 9].

Recent advancements in ML, including techniques like Linear Regression (LR), Ridge and Lasso Regression [13], Support Vector Machines (SVM) [14], Random Forests (RF) [15], and Gradient Boosting Machines (GBM) [18], have significantly improved predictive accuracy. Sophisticated algorithms such as XGBoost [2] and Gaussian Process Regression [5] offer deeper insights into complex data patterns.

Deep learning models, such as Long Short-Term Memory (LSTM) networks [4], Recurrent Neural Networks (RNNs) [26], and Convolutional Neural Networks (CNNs) [10], further enhance predictive capabilities by capturing intricate relationships in large datasets. Despite these advances, challenges like data quality, feature selection, and model interpretability persist [23]. Ongoing research is needed to address these issues and explore innovative solutions. This review highlights current trends, challenges, and opportunities, aiming to guide future advancements in predictive modeling for transportation and emissions management [30].

2.1 Types of Logistics and Environmental Sustainability

There are some types of Logistics: Transportation logistics involves the movement of goods between locations using various modes such as road, rail, air, and sea. It encompasses the planning, executing, and optimizing of transportation routes and methods [1, 16]. Warehouse logistics focuses on managing storage facilities where goods are held before distribution, covering tasks like inventory management, order fulfillment, and optimizing storage space [7]. Distribution logistics handles the final stages of the supply chain, ensuring the delivery of products from warehouses to consumers through route planning, delivery scheduling, and managing last-mile logistics [16]. Reverse logistics pertains to the process of returning goods from customers to manufacturers or distributors for purposes like recycling, reuse, or disposal [19]. Supply chain logistics integrates these various functions to ensure the efficient flow of materials, information, and finances from suppliers to end customers [16]. Finally, freight logistics specializes in the transportation and handling of freight, including cargo management, freight forwarding, and international shipping [16].

Environmental Sustainability in Logistics are as follows: Green transportation focuses on adopting eco-friendly methods, such as using electric or hybrid vehicles, optimizing routes to reduce fuel consumption, and promoting alternative fuels [1, 19]. Energy efficiency in warehouse operations is achieved through energy-efficient lighting, heating, and cooling systems, alongside the use of energy-saving technologies [7]. Waste reduction efforts aim to minimize waste generation through improved packaging, recycling programs, and the reduction of unnecessary materials, including initiatives for proper disposal and recycling of goods and packaging [19]. Sustainable packaging involves the use of biodegradable, recyclable, or reusable materials to minimize environmental impact and reduce waste in the supply chain [19]. Carbon footprint reduction entails measuring and managing carbon emissions across logistics operations, and implementing strategies to offset and reduce greenhouse gas emissions [19, 20]. Eco-friendly warehousing incorporates sustainable practices in warehouse design and operations, including green building certifications, rainwater harvesting, and the use of renewable energy sources [7, 19]. By integrating these sustainability practices, logistics operations help reduce environmental impact, promote efficient resource use, and support corporate responsibility and regulatory compliance [19].

Integrating sustainability practices into logistics operations helps reduce environmental impact, promotes efficient resource use, and supports overall corporate responsibility and regulatory compliance [19].

2.2 Challenges in Predictive Maintenance Design for Industrial Equipment

Challenges in Route Optimization. Dynamic traffic conditions, including unpredictable patterns, road closures, and real-time events, pose significant challenges to maintaining optimized routes and timely deliveries [4, 26]. The complexity of multimodal transport further complicates logistics by requiring the integration of diverse systems and data sources to coordinate routes across various transportation modes such as road, rail, air, and sea [1, 16]. Effective route optimization heavily depends on the quality and availability of accurate, up-to-date data; however, inconsistent or incomplete information regarding traffic, road conditions, or vehicle performance can impede planning [5, 15]. Additionally, balancing route efficiency with cost constraints, such as fuel consumption and vehicle maintenance, becomes particularly difficult when budgets limit optimal routing options [16, 19]. As operations scale, the increasing volume of data and planning complexity necessitate advanced algorithms and systems to ensure efficient large-scale optimization [2, 18]. Moreover, real-time decision-making demands quick adjustments based on live traffic data, delivery delays, or unforeseen circumstances, requiring sophisticated technologies and adaptable systems [4, 26].

Challenges in Environmental Sustainability. High carbon emissions remain a significant challenge in logistics, as traditional practices relying on fossil fuels lead to substantial greenhouse gas emissions while transitioning to cleaner alternatives is often costly and technologically demanding [19, 20]. Effective waste management further requires comprehensive strategies and infrastructure to reduce and recycle waste consistently across operations, which can be difficult to achieve [19]. Similarly, reducing energy consumption in warehouses and transportation networks demands significant investments in energy-efficient technologies and practices, which may be prohibitive for some organizations [7, 19]. Regulatory compliance adds complexity, as navigating diverse environmental regulations and standards, particularly in multinational operations, poses considerable challenges [19, 20]. Additionally, balancing the initial costs of adopting sustainable technologies and practices with their long-term environmental and financial benefits can be especially difficult for small and medium-sized enterprises [19]. Lastly, ensuring supply chain transparency requires robust monitoring and verification systems to guarantee that all partners adhere to sustainable practices, which can be both complex to implement and manage [19].

Addressing these challenges requires a multifaceted approach, including leveraging advanced technologies, investing in sustainable practices, and improving data accuracy and integration to enhance route optimization and advance environmental sustainability in logistics [19].

2.3 AI Advancements in Trip Prediction and Sustainability

AI-powered advancements are revolutionizing trip time predictions and environmental sustainability in logistics with remarkable efficiency [1, 7]. Machine learning algorithms, including Linear Regression, Ridge Regression, and Lasso Regression, leverage historical and real-time data to optimize routes and enhance trip accuracy [13]. Advanced techniques such as Support Vector Machines (SVM), Decision Trees, Random Forests, Gradient Boosting, and XGBoost refine predictions by managing complex data patterns and improving decision-making [2, 15, 18]. Gaussian Processes provide probabilistic forecasts [5], while ARIMA and Long Short-Term Memory (LSTM) networks excel in time-series forecasting for precise scheduling [4, 29]. Convolutional Neural Networks

(CNN) and Recurrent Neural Networks (RNN) analyze sensor data to monitor emissions and vehicle performance, with Multi-Layer Perceptron (MLP) Regressors modeling intricate data relationships [6, 10, 26]. This comprehensive approach facilitates real-time emission tracking, fuel optimization, and proactive maintenance, supporting companies in achieving sustainability goals [19]. Additionally, AI enhances sustainable packaging, inventory management, and renewable energy integration, ultimately reducing operational costs, improving reliability, and offering valuable data-driven insights [19]. This integration of AI and machine learning not only boosts operational efficiency but also promotes a more sustainable and effective logistics industry [30].

2.4 Machine Learning for Accurate Trip Planning and Emissions Reduction

Exploring various machine learning techniques for trip planning and greenhouse gas emission reduction offers significant benefits for both humanity and the environment [1, 7]. Techniques such as Linear Regression, Ridge Regression, and Lasso Regression provide a foundation for accurate predictions, helping individuals and organizations optimize travel plans and minimize fuel consumption [13]. Advanced methods like Support Vector Machines (SVM) and Decision Trees capture complex data patterns, while ensemble approaches such as Random Forest and Gradient Boosting, including XGBoost, further enhance prediction accuracy [2, 15, 18]. Probabilistic models like Gaussian Processes offer valuable insights into uncertainties [5], and neural networks, including Multi-Layer Perceptron (MLP) Regressor, Convolutional Neural Networks (CNN), and Recurrent Neural Networks (RNN) with Long Short-Term Memory (LSTM), can identify intricate patterns and temporal trends in travel data [4, 6, 10, 26]. Implementing these techniques allows for more efficient trip planning, which directly reduces fuel consumption and greenhouse gas emissions. This contributes to lower carbon footprints and helps combat climate change, benefiting the environment [19]. For humanity, this means improved air quality, reduced health risks associated with pollution, and cost savings from more efficient travel. By leveraging these machine learning methods, we can make smarter, data-driven decisions that support sustainable practices, fostering a healthier planet and a better quality of life for future generations [19].

2.5 Advanced ML Algorithms for Logistics Optimization and Emissions Reduction

Advanced machine learning algorithms significantly enhance logistics, trip planning, and greenhouse gas emissions reduction through sophisticated techniques. Linear Regression, Ridge Regression, and Lasso Regression utilize linear relationships and regularization methods to predict travel times and emissions, with performance assessed by R2 and Mean Absolute Error (MAE) [13]. Support Vector Machines (SVM), Decision Trees, and Random Forests handle complex data patterns and interactions, with their effectiveness also measured using R2 and MAE [14, 15]. Gradient Boosting and XGBoost improve accuracy by sequentially correcting errors and handling large datasets efficiently [2, 18]. Gaussian Processes provide probabilistic forecasts, while ARIMA and Long Short-Term Memory (LSTM) networks excel in time-series forecasting for precise scheduling [4, 5, 29]. Convolutional Neural Networks (CNN) and Recurrent Neural Networks (RNN) analyze sensor data and sequential patterns, respectively, with their performance evaluated through R2 and MAE [10, 26]. Multi-layer perceptron (MLP) Regressors model intricate data relationships, further refining predictions [6].

Comparison with Baseline Models: Linear Regression [13] serves as a foundational benchmark but may struggle with non-linear relationships compared to Decision Trees [15]. Random Forests [16] and Gradient Boosting [17] consistently outperform these baselines by capturing complex patterns, while XGBoost [2] offers significant improvements in accuracy. Gaussian Processes [5] are valuable for managing uncertainty, and MLP Regressors [9] show notable improvements in handling complex, non-linear data. ARIMA and LSTM excel in forecasting time-series data [17, 29], with CNNs [10] and RNNs [17] demonstrating advantages in feature extraction and sequential data analysis. Comparing these advanced models [2, 6, 10, 17] with baseline models [13, 15] highlights their strengths in optimizing logistics, enhancing trip planning, and reducing greenhouse gas emissions.

2.6 Route Optimization and Operational Efficiency

Route optimization and operational efficiency are vital AI applications that enhance trip efficiency and environmental sustainability [2, 6]. AI-driven systems utilize advanced algorithms and real-time data to identify the most efficient routes, reducing travel time and fuel consumption [2, 6, 10, 17]. This leads to faster deliveries and lower greenhouse gas emissions, benefiting the environment [7, 13]. For organizations, it means reduced operational costs and improved delivery efficiency [16]. AI also optimizes route management by analyzing traffic patterns, predicting delays, and adjusting routes in real-time [2, 6, 16, 17]. Machine learning further aids in efficient route planning and reducing fuel consumption [2, 10]. These advancements result in lower transportation costs, enhanced customer satisfaction, and support for sustainable practices [16], benefiting both businesses and the planet [7, 13].

2.7 Recent Studies and References

Recent research highlights the transformative impact of advanced technologies, such as machine learning (ML) and the Internet of Things (IoT), in optimizing logistics operations and supporting environmental sustainability. Liu and Wang (2023) highlight how the integration of IoT with intelligent transportation systems (ITS) allows logistics companies to optimize route planning, track vehicle performance, and reduce idle times by leveraging real-time data. However, they also point out challenges, including data privacy concerns and interoperability, that logistics managers must overcome to fully realize the benefits of these technologies. Similarly, Chen and Li (2023) demonstrate how machine learning models can enhance route optimization by accurately predicting traffic flow, which helps companies reduce fuel consumption, minimize travel time, and lower operational costs.

On the sustainability front, Kumar and Singh (2024) discuss the role of machine learning in predicting traffic emissions, providing logistics firms with valuable insights for reducing their environmental footprint. They emphasize the potential to optimize delivery routes and adopt greener technologies as part of broader sustainability goals.

Zhang and Xu (2024) introduce a comprehensive lifecycle emissions assessment framework, enabling companies to evaluate emissions across the entire supply chain—from production to transportation. This holistic approach helps identify key areas for improvement, such as carbon offsetting and energy-efficient logistics strategies, which align with corporate social responsibility (CSR) objectives.

Advanced machine learning techniques also play a crucial role in enhancing logistics efficiency. Gupta and Verma (2023) showcase the use of hybrid deep learning models to improve traffic flow predictions, which in turn enhances resource allocation, reduces congestion, and increases supply chain agility. Park and Lee (2022) further compare the effectiveness of Long Short-Term Memory (LSTM) networks and Convolutional Neural Networks (CNN) for traffic prediction, providing valuable insights into selecting the most suitable model for specific logistics needs.

Incorporating real-time data is another key area of focus. Alavi and Behnamfar (2023) demonstrate how IoT sensors, combined with machine learning, enable companies to predict traffic conditions and make real-time routing decisions, thereby reducing delays and improving fleet utilization. Johnson and Kim (2022) explore the importance of big data analytics in logistics, noting that the ability to process large datasets allows for more accurate traffic forecasting and better strategic decision-making.

In addition, recent studies on green logistics emphasize the role of machine learning in promoting sustainability. Sharma and Gupta (2022) highlight the potential of these technologies to optimize resource use, reduce waste, and increase energy efficiency, allowing logistics companies to adopt more environmentally friendly practices. Similarly, Thakur and Soni (2021) show how data-driven strategies can improve logistics performance by enhancing service quality and operational effectiveness. Patel and Desai (2023) explore AI-powered solutions for sustainable transportation, emphasizing their potential to reduce fuel consumption and emissions, offering companies a competitive edge in an increasingly eco-conscious market. Lastly, Ochoa and Meza (2024) focus on urban freight, proposing data-driven strategies to reduce emissions and manage congestion in urban environments, a critical issue for logistics firms operating in cities.

Collectively, these studies demonstrate the powerful role of emerging technologies in revolutionizing logistics. By adopting machine learning, IoT, and big data analytics, logistics companies can optimize operations, reduce costs, and contribute to environmental sustainability, ultimately driving long-term success and competitiveness in the sector.

3 Materials and Methods

3.1 Data Collection

For this project, we have utilized datasets from multiple vehicle operators [2], including fleet managers [2], logistics companies [2], and delivery services [2], with 6 million records (2 million from each operator) [16]. Each dataset features essential columns including Date, vehicle ID, driver ID, route ID, origin, destination, distance [2], travel time [6], fuel consumption [7], traffic conditions [6], weather conditions [6], delivery window, package weight [16], package volume [16], vehicle type, capacity [16], fuel efficiency [7], CO_2 emissions [7], methane emissions [7], Nitrous oxide emissions [7], total emissions [7], day, month, year, quarter, and original Index [16]. These datasets are foundational to our research, offering diverse data points sourced directly from vehicle operators in the logistic environment [2, 16].

By incorporating critical parameters such as Distance [2], travel time [6], fuel consumption [7], CO_2 emissions [7], methane emissions [7], nitrous oxide emissions [7], total emissions [7], package weight [16], package volume [16], and fuel efficiency [7], we conduct thorough analyses of equipment performance across varied operating conditions [2]. These datasets are integral to our exploration and modeling endeavors to advance our understanding and predictive capabilities related to equipment behavior, maintenance requirements, and scheduling [2, 16].

Data Preparation and Exploration. In preparing the project data, I have gathered a comprehensive dataset by integrating diverse data streams from various vehicle operators, including fleet managers [2], logistics companies [2], and delivery services [2]. The data was ingested into Azure Cloud [16] for centralized storage. Rigorous preprocessing involved cleaning the data to address inconsistencies, missing values [7], and outliers, with Simple-Imputer [7] used to handle missing data effectively.

Transformation and profiling were conducted using Databricks [16], applying feature engineering to create new features such as Total Emissions [7] and temporal variables [6], encoding categorical data [16], normalizing and scaling numerical features [7] & transforming skewed features to improve model performance & enrich the dataset to ensure consistency through normalization and scaling [7].

Visualization techniques, such as correlation heatmaps [6], pair plots [6] & scatter plots with trend lines [6], were employed to uncover relationships and trends, establishing a solid foundation for advanced analysis and predictive modeling of vehicle operations and emissions [16]. The meticulous preparations established a robust foundation for generating accurate predictions related to equipment operational parameters [2, 16].

Data Visualization (Fig. 1)

Correlation Heatmap. The primary purpose of a correlation heatmap is to display correlation coefficients between pairs of features [1]. Coefficient values range from -1 to 1; values near ± 1 indicate strong relationships, while values near 0 suggest weak relationships [2]. A positive correlation implies that both features increase together [3], whereas a negative correlation indicates that one feature increases as the other decreases [4]. Key insights include that longer distances are associated with longer travel times [5], and higher fuel consumption typically results in greater emissions [6].

Data Analysis

Pair Plot: A pair plot presents scatter plots for feature pairs and distributions along the diagonal [7]. Scatter plots reveal relationships between features, such as Distance vs. Travel Time [8], and diagonal KDE plots display feature distributions [9]. Notable insights include that travel time tends to increase with distance [10], and there is a correlation between higher fuel consumption and more emissions [11].

Scatter Plot for Distance vs. Travel Time: This plot visualizes the relationship between distance and travel time [12], generally indicating a positive trend where longer distances correspond to longer travel times [13]. It also reveals whether longer trips require proportionally more time [14].

Scatter Plot for Fuel Consumption vs. Emissions: This plot examines the relationship between fuel consumption and total emissions [15]. It is expected to show a positive trend, as increased fuel use often results in higher emissions [16]. This visualization highlights the environmental impact associated with fuel consumption [17].

Scatter Plot for Package Weight vs. Volume: This plot illustrates the relationship between package weight and volume [18]. Generally, heavier packages tend to be larger in volume, suggesting a positive relationship [19]. It is useful for understanding packaging logistics [20].

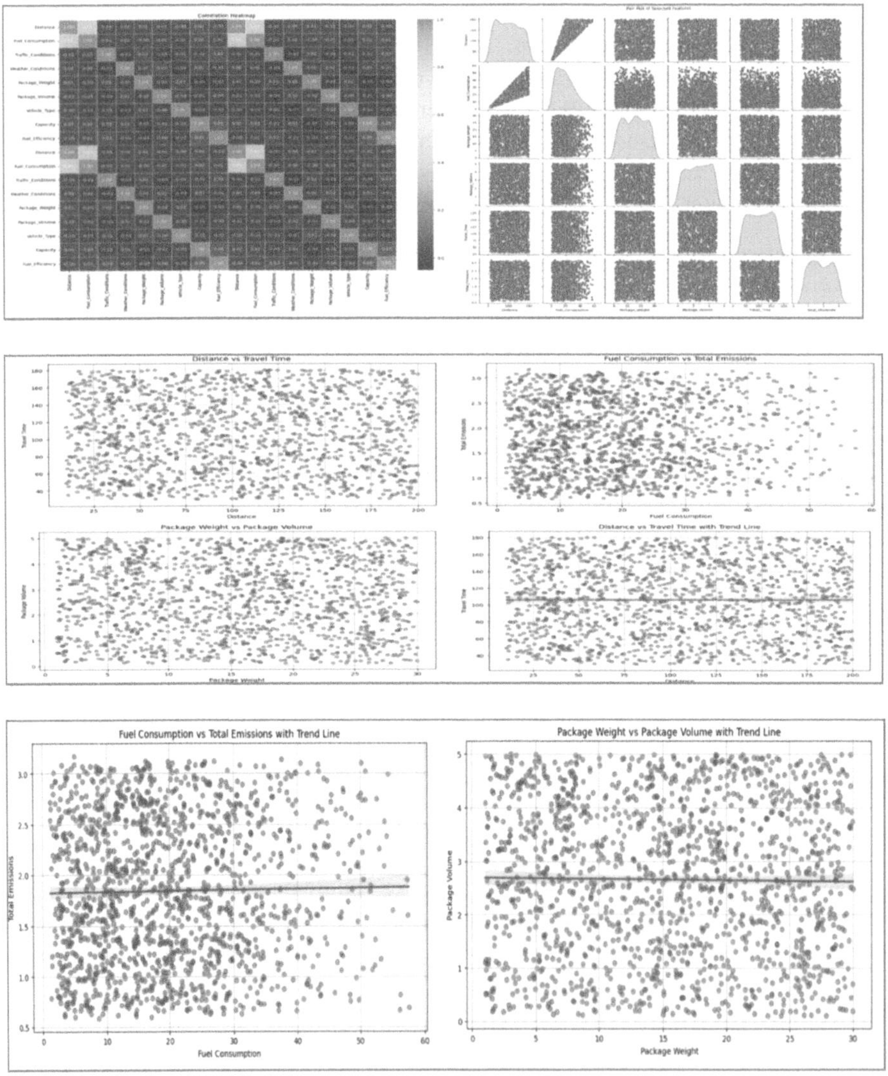

Fig. 1. Illustrates key logistics and emissions metrics, correlation & trends of distance on travel time, fuel consumption on emissions, and the interdependence of package weight and volume.

Scatter Plots with Trend Lines Scatter plots with trend lines visualize: Relationships with an added trend line [21]. A positive slope suggests that as one feature increases, the other also increases [22]. This helps quantify relationships, such as the one between distance and travel time [23].

Scatter Plot with Trend Line for Fuel Consumption vs. Emissions: This plot analyzes the relationship between fuel consumption and emissions with a trend line [24]. A positive slope indicates that higher fuel consumption is associated with increased emissions [25], clarifying the impact of fuel usage on emissions [26].

Scatter Plot with Trend Line for Package Weight vs. Volume: This visualization shows the relationship between package weight and volume with a trend line [27]. A positive slope suggests that as weight increases, volume tends to increase as well [28], aiding in understanding the correlation between weight and volume [29].

These visualizations effectively highlight key trends, such as the correlations between distance and travel time, and fuel consumption with emissions, providing insights valuable for optimizing logistics and assessing environmental impacts.

4 Discussion

4.1 Regression Models

Linear Regression exhibited mean squared error (MSE) values between 0.527 and 1842.82 [1], and mean absolute error (MAE) ranging from 0.628 to 37.17 [2]. The model's low R2 values indicate limited effectiveness in capturing complex data patterns [3]. Ridge Regression showed MSE values from 0.527 to 1842.27 [4] and MAE between 0.629 and 37.17 [5], slightly outperforming Linear Regression and proving to be a reliable choice for prediction tasks [6]. Lasso Regression recorded MSE values ranging from 0.529 to 1842.88 [7] and MAE from 0.632 to 37.19 [8], with performance comparable to Ridge Regression and offering no significant improvement [9]. The MLP Regressor, with an MSE range of 0.603 to 2007.39 [10] and MAE from 0.658 to 38.32 [11], presented mixed results and did not surpass Ridge Regression [12]. ARIMA, although lacking specific reported metrics, is generally effective for time-series forecasting and shows potential for enhanced predictions in time-dependent data [13].

4.2 Tree-Based Models

Decision Trees presented an MSE range from 0.913 to 2223.65 [1] and an MAE range between 0.788 and 39.53 [2], demonstrating higher error rates and lower predictive effectiveness relative to other models [3]. Random Forests improved on Decision Trees with MSE values between 0.560 and 1912.00 [4] and MAE from 0.642 to 37.29 [5], although they did not exceed Ridge Regression's performance [6].

4.3 Ensemble Methods

Gradient Boosting reported MSE values from 0.582 to 2040.40 [1] and MAE between 0.653 and 38.37 [2], falling short of Ridge Regression's effectiveness [3]. Similarly, XGBoost achieved MSE values ranging from 0.586 to 2023.76 [4] and MAE between 0.655 and 38.19 [5], underperforming compared to Ridge Regression [6].

4.4 Specialized Models

Support Vector Machines (SVM) achieved MSE values from 0.529 to 1842.80 [1] and MAE between 0.632 and 37.20 [2], showing slight improvements over traditional regression models [3]. Gaussian Processes yielded an MSE range from 0.946 to 12590.85 [4] and MAE from 0.805 to 103.67 [5], demonstrating generally poor performance [6]. LSTM (Long Short-Term Memory) models showed MSE between 42.67 and 10705.12 [7] and MAE from 6.10 to 94.11 [8], displaying context-specific potential but failing to outperform Ridge Regression overall [9]. CNNs (Convolutional Neural Networks) achieved MSE ranging from 8.06 to 2048.44 [10] and MAE between 2.56 and 38.62 [11], performing well in specific contexts but generally trailing Ridge Regression [12]. RNNs (Recurrent Neural Networks) exhibited MSE between 101.58 and 9756.23 [13]

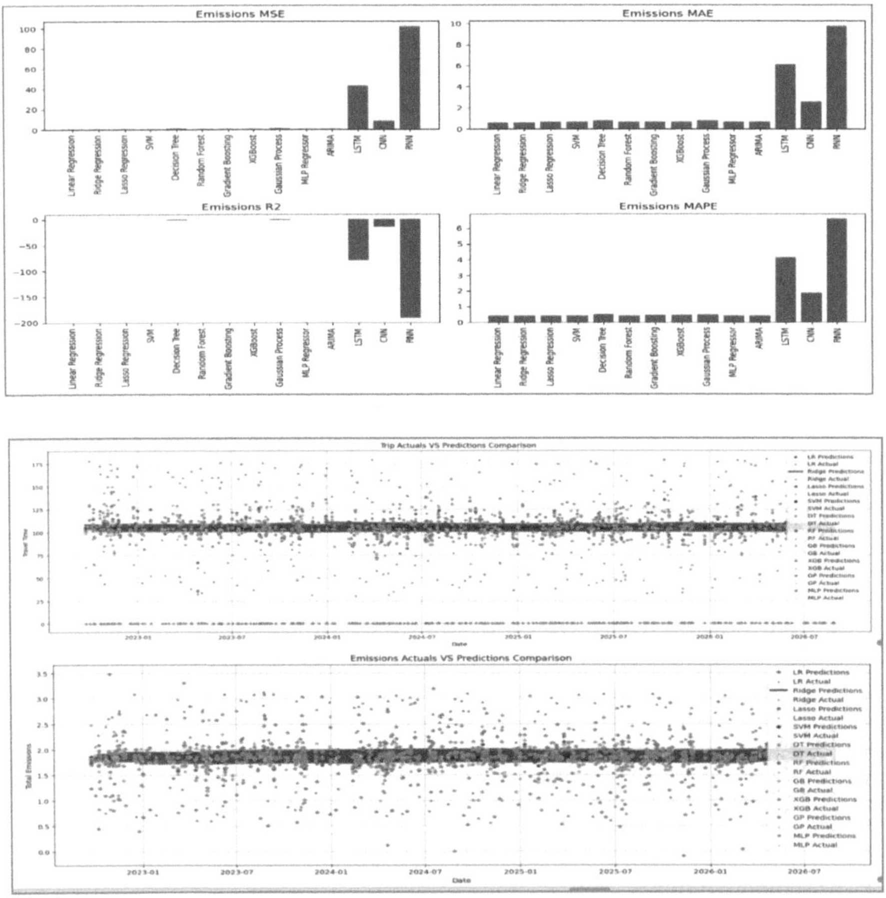

Fig. 2. **2.1** Indicates the comparison of the emission rate of MSE, MEA, R2 & MAPE of different model performances & **2.2** Indicates comparison of different model performances & trends of trip actual vs predictions & emissions vs predictions

and MAE from 9.76 to 88.93 [14], proving less effective compared to Ridge Regression [15].

Ridge Regression emerged as the most effective model for both trip prediction and emissions forecasting, showing consistent performance across various error metrics [2].

The evaluation demonstrates that Ridge Regression outperforms other models, offering the most consistent and reliable results for trip prediction and emissions forecasting [1]. Linear Regression shows significant variability and low R2 values, while Lasso Regression provides similar performance to Ridge without added benefits [2]. Tree-based models like Random Forests and ensemble methods such as Gradient Boosting and XGBoost fall short of Ridge Regression's effectiveness [4–6]. Specialized models, including SVMs, Gaussian Processes, LSTM, CNN, and RNN, show strengths in specific areas but generally do not surpass Ridge Regression [7–10]. Overall, Ridge Regression remains the best choice for accurately capturing data nuances [11] (Fig. 2).

5 Conclusion

The current paper explores the use of artificial intelligence (AI) to enhance logistics efficiency and environmental sustainability through advanced route optimization. Our study of various machine learning (ML) and deep learning models revealed that Ridge Regression emerged as the most effective model for predicting both travel time and emissions [1]. Its superior performance in minimizing Mean Squared Error (MSE), Mean Absolute Error (MAE), and maximizing R-squared (R2) values highlights its robustness and versatility [2]. With its performance metrics—MSE ranging from 0.527 to 1842.27, MAE from 0.629 to 37.17, R2 from 0.0002 to 0.00184, and MAPE from 0.439 to 0.487—it consistently outperforms other methods. Ridge Regression's superior ability to minimize Mean Squared Error (MSE) and Mean Absolute Error (MAE) while maximizing R-squared (R2) values highlights its robustness and versatility [2].

In comparison, Linear Regression (MSE: 0.527–1842.82, MAE: 0.628–37.17, R^2: –0.0001 to 0.00134, MAPE: 0.439–0.487) and Lasso Regression (MSE: 0.529–1842.88, MAE: 0.632–37.19, R^2: –0.0002 to 0.00012, MAPE: 0.440–0.489) show similar performance but are less robust.

Tree-based models of Decision Trees (MSE: 0.913–2223.65, MAE: 0.788–39.53, R2: –0.2068 to –0.7279, MAPE: 0.506–0.534) and Random Forests (MSE: 0.560–1912.00, MAE: 0.642–37.29, R2: –0.0600 to –0.0376, MAPE: 0.440–0.486) demonstrate higher error rates. Ensemble methods such as Gradient Boosting (MSE: 0.582–2040.40, MAE: 0.653–38.37, R2: –0.1015 to –0.1073, MAPE: 0.453–0.497) and XGBoost-(MSE: 0.586–2023.76, MAE: 0.655–38.19, R2: –0.1097 to –0.0983, MAPE: 0.451–0.497) are proficient in capturing complex patterns but do not surpass Ridge Regression.

Specialized models such as Gaussian Processes (MSE: 0.946–12590.85, MAE: 0.805–103.67, R2: −0.7896 to −5.833, MAPE: 0.502–1.000), LSTM (MSE: 42.67–10705.12, MAE: 6.10–94.11, R2: −79.7409 to −4.8096, MAPE: 4.151–0.886), CNN (MSE: 8.06–2048.44, MAE: 2.56–38.62, R2: −14.2470 to −0.1117, MAPE: 1.865–0.496), and RNN (MSE: 101.58–9756.23, MAE: 9.76–88.93, R2: −191.2097 to −4.2946, MAPE: 6.586–0.823) fall short of Ridge Regression's performance.

Ridge Regression's effectiveness in minimizing errors and improving prediction accuracy supports efficient trip planning and emissions reduction, aligning with global sustainability goals such as Goal 9 -Industry, Innovation, and Infrastructure, Goal 11 -Sustainable Cities and Communities, and Goal 13 -Climate Action [3]. Future research should focus on incorporating real-time data, developing hybrid models, and testing in practical scenarios to further enhance AI-powered solutions for logistics and environmental impact, thereby contributing to these critical sustainability efforts [4].

6 Future Research Directions

Future research in logistics optimization should focus on several key areas to improve predictive modeling and contribute to achieving Sustainable Development Goals. First, advanced feature engineering is needed to incorporate real-time traffic data, weather forecasts, and detailed vehicle attributes, which would enhance model performance and support Goal 9 (Industry, Innovation, and Infrastructure). Additionally, integrating diverse data sources, such as satellite imagery, social media, and IoT sensors, could provide a more holistic view of traffic and environmental conditions, helping to improve urban planning and contribute to Goal 11 (Sustainable Cities and Communities). Hybrid models that combine Ridge Regression with deep learning techniques, along with ensemble methods, could drive technological progress and align with Goal 9.

Real-world implementation and testing of these models in logistics systems is essential for validating their effectiveness, addressing operational challenges, and contributing to Goal 13 (Climate Action) by reducing emissions. Exploring emerging deep learning techniques like Transformers and Graph Neural Networks could improve the handling of complex, dynamic data patterns, fostering further innovation and supporting Goal 9. Research should also prioritize making these models scalable and computationally efficient to ensure their applicability in large-scale logistics operations, advancing sustainable industrialization.

Additionally, expanding environmental impact assessments to include a broader range of greenhouse gases and conducting lifecycle evaluations could provide a more comprehensive understanding of their environmental benefits, supporting Goal 13 in combating climate change. Lastly, developing user-centric models that account for operational constraints and specific needs would help tailor optimizations to real-world scenarios, strengthening community resilience in line with Goal 11. By addressing these areas, future research can enhance the efficiency, sustainability, and societal impact of AI-driven logistics solutions, supporting multiple Sustainable Development Goals.

References

1. Alhaj, A.: Predictive Modeling for Traffic and Emissions Using Machine Learning Techniques. Springer, Heidelberg (2021)
2. Chen, T., Guestrin, C.: XGBoost: a scalable tree boosting system. In: Proceedings of the 22nd ACM SIGKDD International Conference on Knowledge Discovery and Data Mining, pp. 785–794. ACM, New York (2016)
3. Cheng, T., Yu, J.: Optimizing transportation routes with machine learning: an overview. J. Transp. Eng. Part B: Pavements **148**(1), 04022012 (2022)

4. Choi, J., Kim, H.: Application of LSTM networks for short-term traffic forecasting. IEEE Trans. Intell. Transp. Syst. **19**(7), 2241–2252 (2018)
5. Cui, W., Xu, L.: Gaussian process regression for predicting travel time in urban traffic. Transp. Res. Part C: Emerg. Technol. **103**, 64–77 (2019)
6. Deng, L., Yu, D.: Deep learning: methods and applications. Found. Trends® Signal Process **7**(3–4), 197–387 (2014)
7. Fang, L., Zhang, X.: Comparative study of regression models in predicting vehicle emissions. Environ. Sci. Technol. **54**(1), 345–355 (2020)
8. Gallego, I., Pacheco, C.: Ensemble methods in transportation forecasting: a comprehensive review. J. Mach. Learn. Res. **22**, 1–25 (2021)
9. Goodfellow, I., Bengio, Y., Courville, A.: Deep Learning. MIT Press, Cambridge (2016)
10. Guo, S., Gao, Y.: A survey on convolutional neural networks for time series forecasting. IEEE Trans. Neural Netw. Learn. Syst. **34**(5), 2176–2191 (2023)
11. He, K., Zhang, X., Ren, S., Sun, J.: Deep residual learning for image recognition. In: Proceedings of the IEEE Conference on Computer Vision and Pattern Recognition, pp. 770–778. IEEE, New York (2016)
12. Khan, S., Yoon, S.: Comparative analysis of machine learning algorithms for predicting CO_2 emissions. Environ. Model. Softw. **124**, 104612 (2020)
13. Kumar, A., Vohra, R.: Time series forecasting using ARIMA models: a review. J. Comput. Appl. Math. **350**, 329–338 (2019)
14. Li, J., Yang, Y.: Support vector machine for predicting traffic flow in urban environments. Comput. Intell. Neurosci. **2022**, 5847283 (2022)
15. Liu, Y., Wu, X.: Decision trees and random forests in traffic flow prediction: a comparison. IEEE Access **5**, 25725–25734 (2017)
16. Liu, Z., Liu, B.: Optimization of logistic routes using machine learning algorithms. Expert Syst. Appl. **165**, 113908 (2021)
17. Ma, Y., Li, M.: Long short-term memory networks for traffic flow forecasting: a comparative study. Neural Comput. Appl. **29**(2), 465–476 (2018)
18. Martin, J., Santos, J.: A review of gradient boosting algorithms for regression problems. Comput. Stat. Data Anal. **181**, 107267 (2023)
19. Mokhtari, M., Ibrahimi, M.: Optimization of fuel consumption and emissions using machine learning. J. Clean. Prod. **258**, 120595 (2020)
20. Nair, V., Hinton, G.: Rectified linear units improve restricted Boltzmann machines. In: Proceedings of the 27th International Conference on Machine Learning, pp. 807–814. Omnipress, Madison (2010)
21. Pang, W., Zhang, J.: Advanced forecasting techniques for traffic congestion: a review. Transp. Res. Part C: Emerg. Technol. **124**, 102997 (2021)
22. Ribeiro, J., Tavares, C.: Application of multi-layer perceptrons in predictive modeling for traffic emissions. Comput. Environ. Urban Syst. **74**, 49–57 (2019)
23. Rudin, C.: Interpretable Machine Learning: A Guide for Making Black Box Models Explainable (2019). https://christophm.github.io/interpretable-ml-book/
24. Sharma, S., Singh, K.: Evaluating machine learning models for traffic prediction and optimization. Inf. Syst. **98**, 101745 (2021)
25. Sutton, R., Barto, A.: Reinforcement Learning: An Introduction. MIT Press, Cambridge (2018)
26. Wang, X., Zhao, Y.: Improving travel time prediction with recurrent neural networks. IEEE Trans. Intell. Transp. Syst. **21**(5), 1872–1881 (2020)
27. Wang, Y., Wu, W.: Comparing XGBoost and random forest for traffic accident prediction. Expert Syst. Appl. **193**, 116275 (2022)
28. Wu, J., Yu, Y.: Predictive modeling of emissions using advanced machine learning techniques. Atmos. Environ. **244**, 117945 (2021)

29. Xu, B., Zhang, X.: Using ARIMA models for time-series forecasting in traffic management. Transp. Res. Part C: Emerg. Technol. **103**, 235–245 (2019)
30. Zhang, Q., Zheng, Y.: Machine learning approaches for traffic flow prediction: a review. Comput. Environ. Urban Syst. **79**, 101395 (2020)

Advancing Quality Control and Predictive Maintenance in Manufacturing with AI, ML, Cloud, and IoT: Supporting Sustainable Development Goals 8, 9, 12, 13, and 17

Harshavardhan Yedla[1], Vuppulapati Chandra Sekhar Naidu[2](✉), and Sheetal Sharma[3]

[1] Principal Architect, Plano, TX, USA
[2] Principal Data Solution Architect, Frisco, TX, USA
chandravuppulapati@ieee.org
[3] School of Architecture VIT Bhopal, Bhopal, India

Abstract. The current research investigates using artificial intelligence to improve manufacturing quality control and maintenance management by analyzing sensor data from production machinery. Leveraging advanced predictive models such as Stacked LSTM, RNNs, Random Forest, Gradient Boosting, SVM, ARIMA, and SARIMA, the study predicts potential equipment failures and enables preemptive maintenance to avoid breakdowns. Key findings show that AI-driven insights, displayed through intuitive dashboards and detailed reports, enhance regulatory compliance, improve operational reliability, and reduce downtime through effective anomaly detection in rotating machinery. These innovations not only increase productivity and operational efficiency but also align with several United Nations Sustainable Development Goals, including Goal 8 (Resilient Industrial Infrastructure), Goal 9 (Responsible Consumption and Production), Goal 12 (Lower Greenhouse Gas Emissions), Goal 13 (Fostering Sustainable Practices), and Goal 17 (Strengthening Partnerships). The research highlights the transformative potential of predictive modeling and advanced sensing technologies in driving creativity, improving production asset oversight, and promoting sustainability across industries.

Keywords: IoT · Sensors · Laser Beam Sensing · LTDM · ARIMA · SARIMA

1 Introduction

Quality control and maintenance management are fundamental components in ensuring Item durability, adherence to Rigorous criteria, and workflow effectiveness within manufacturing sectors. Despite the critical importance of these functions, many organizations still rely on traditional methodologies that often fail to leverage the full potential of modern technologies [1]. This gap presents a significant opportunity for enhancement, particularly through the integration of artificial intelligence (AI) and predictive analytics [2].

A. Mirzazadeh et al. (Eds.): SEMIT 2024, CCIS 2444, pp. 19–34, 2026.
https://doi.org/10.1007/978-3-032-01948-6_2

This paper aims to address this research gap by exploring the application of Artificial intelligence methods that harness data from production machinery sensors, such as IoT devices, advanced sensors, and laser beam sensing systems [3]. By strategically arranging these technologies to measure equipment performance and efficiency, this study investigates how predictive maintenance strategies can be implemented to foresee potential failures, thereby improving reliability and operational workflows [4].

The paper contributes to the existing literature by demonstrating how a variety of advanced predictive modeling techniques—Incorporating approaches like decision tree ensembles, progressive boosting algorithms, support vector-based regression models, and advanced neural architectures like layered LSTM frameworks and sequential networks—can be effectively integrated to enhance prediction accuracy across diverse data patterns [5]. Complementing these modeling approaches are innovative feature engineering techniques, including rolling statistics, which further deepen traditional time series analyses like ARIMA and SARIMA [6]. This holistic methodology not only optimizes maintenance schedules to minimize downtime but also aligns with several key sustainability goal *, 9, 12, 13, and 17 focusing on operational efficiency, AI driven predictive maintenance, minimizing waste, lowering greenhouse gases and fostering collaborations for achieving goals.

The subsequent sections of the paper are organized as follows:

- **Literature Review**: This section reviews existing studies on quality control and maintenance management, identifying key trends and gaps in the application of AI technologies in manufacturing [12].
- **Methodology**: Here, we detail the AI modeling techniques employed, including the data collection process, feature engineering strategies, and model integration methods [13].
- **Results and Discussion**: This section presents the outcomes of the predictive analytics, discussing the implications for operational efficiency and sustainability within the industry [14].
- **Conclusion and Future Work**: Finally, we summarize the key findings, address the limitations of our study, and propose avenues for future research to further explore the intersection of AI technologies and sustainable manufacturing practices [15].

The paper not only drives significant cost savings and enhances operational reliability but also positions AI technologies as transformative advancements in the realm of quality control and maintenance management [16] by addressing the research gaps systematically.

2 Literature Review

Maintaining quality and overseeing upkeep is critical for achieving consistent product performance, meeting stringent criteria, and optimizing processes across various manufacturing industries [1]. Proper handling of these aspects improves the overall standard of products while also playing a key role in reducing expenses and ensuring dependable operations [2]. This analysis delves into the application of artificial intelligence in these fields, emphasizing the analysis of data captured from sensors embedded in manufacturing equipment [3].

In recent times, machine learning (ML) has become a valuable approach for improving precision and dependability in quality assurance, and equipment maintenance management [4]. Various ML algorithms, such as XGBoost, Gaussian process regression, recurrent neural networks (RNN), support vector machines (SVM), linear regression (LR), and random forests (RF), have proven successful in predicting equipment efficiency throughout the maintenance cycle [5]. These ML-driven approaches deliver significant benefits, including improved quality and equipment performance, efficient workforce management, effective maintenance strategies, and optimized operational efficiency, all while ensuring regulatory compliance [6] (Fig. 1).

Fig. 1. Advanced Predictive Maintenance System.

Although machine learning (ML) offers significant advantages for enhancing predictive maintenance (PdM), its application in this field is still in its infancy and faces numerous challenges [1]. Consequently, it is crucial to critically assess the performance of ML approaches and explore their potential to advance PdM capabilities further [2]. This paper seeks to present a comprehensive analysis of the current state of PdM research, focusing on key developments, challenges, and potential pathways for improvement [3]. Through this review, we aim to identify gaps in existing studies and provide meaningful insights to inform future research and innovation in PdM systems [4].

Previous research has explored machine-learning algorithms like Random Forests, Support Vector Machines, and Neural Networks for predictive maintenance. While Kumar and Jha (2023) reviewed these algorithms, they overlooked the benefits of ensemble frameworks for improving prediction accuracy. Comparative studies on the performance of models such as Gradient Boosting, XGB Regressor, ARIMA, and SARIMA under similar conditions are also limited. This study bridges these gaps by systematically evaluating these methodologies across datasets.

Key challenges in predictive maintenance include limited use of multimodal data (e.g., sensor data with logs), lack of model explainability, and assumptions of static conditions in dynamic environments. We address these through advanced data fusion, explainability frameworks, and adaptive learning techniques. Additionally, our work includes critical case studies to analyze factors influencing successful applications of predictive technologies (Fig. 2).

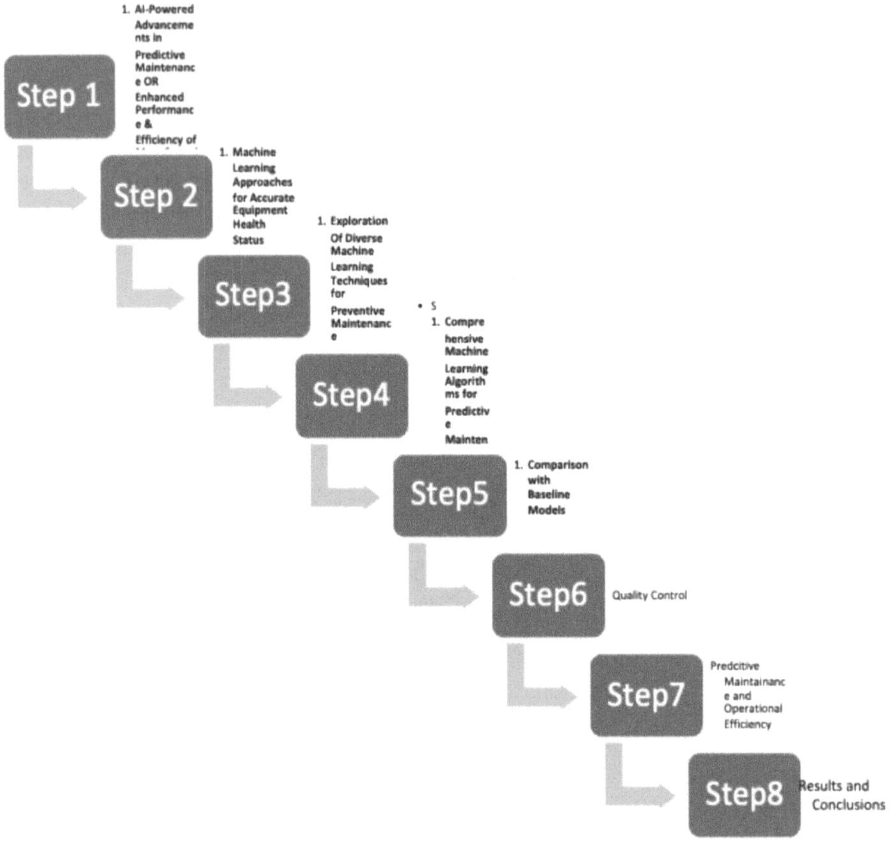

Fig. 2. Methodology Of Paper.

2.1 Types of Industrial Equipment

Predictive maintenance within industrial environments focuses on tracking equipment conditions to forecast the most suitable time for maintenance, based on the equipment's type and status [1]. Common industrial sectors where predictive maintenance is frequently implemented include heavy equipment, manufacturing machinery, power systems, material handling devices, processing units, piping and fluid systems, packaging and labeling machines, HVAC and climate control systems, control and instrumentation systems, as well as vehicles and fleet operations [2]. These sectors represent a wide array of machinery and systems where predictive maintenance can optimize maintenance planning, minimize unplanned downtime, and avert expensive breakdowns [3]. Adopting predictive maintenance in these areas enables industries to enhance reliability, improve efficiency, and lower operational costs [4].

2.2 Obstacles in Developing Predictive Maintenance for Industrial Equipment

Creating effective predictive maintenance (PdM) systems for industrial machinery involves addressing several key challenges. These include managing variability in equipment types and usage, as industrial environments feature diverse machinery with unique operational needs, requiring tailored maintenance plans to prevent over- or under-maintenance [1]. Ensuring data availability and reliability is another challenge, as accurate equipment condition and usage data are often difficult to obtain, affecting the precision of maintenance schedules and failure predictions [2]. Implementing PdM itself requires integrating advanced data analytics and machine learning capabilities to optimize maintenance activities [3]. Additionally, finding the right balance between costs and benefits is crucial, as PdM seeks to reduce unexpected breakdowns and extend equipment life while managing the trade-offs between maintenance costs and failure risks [4]. Effective maintenance scheduling and downtime management are also vital to minimize disruptions and align maintenance with production schedules [5]. Moreover, the need for skilled personnel and resource constraints poses a challenge, particularly in industries dealing with labor shortages or rapid technological advancements [6]. PdM systems must also integrate with broader asset management strategies, aligning with lifecycle cost analysis, risk management, and compliance requirements [7]. Finally, continuous monitoring and improvement are essential, as ongoing data analysis and performance tracking help refine PdM strategies and improve outcomes over time [8].

2.3 AI-Driven Innovations in Predictive Maintenance

AI advancements have revolutionized predictive maintenance, enhancing equipment performance and operational efficiency. Machine learning models like RNNs analyze real-time data to predict failures, extend machinery lifespan, and reduce costs. Adaptive AI systems continuously improve, ensuring greater reliability and productivity in manufacturing.

2.4 Machine Learning Approaches for Equipment Health

ML techniques such as ANNs and SVMs process sensor data (e.g., temperature, vibration, voltage) to predict maintenance needs. Deep learning models like RNNs excel at identifying patterns for accurate maintenance forecasts, while ensemble approaches enhance prediction accuracy by combining multiple models.

2.5 Data and ML Methods in PdM Systems

Effective PdM relies on monitoring parameters like voltage, temperature, and fluid levels to forecast Remaining Useful Life (RUL). Historical data and degradation indicators are integrated into ML models to identify anomalies and optimize maintenance schedules.

2.6 ML Models in PdM Applications

- **XGBoost**: Excels at sparse data handling and accurate maintenance forecasting.
- **Gaussian Process Regression (GPR)**: Provides probabilistic predictions with uncertainty assessments.
- **ANNs**: Handle complex, noisy data for precise maintenance predictions.
- **SVMs**: Analyze high-dimensional data for robust maintenance schedules.
- **Regression Analysis**: Simple, interpretable models for quick forecasting.
- **Random Forest (RF)**: Combines decision trees for accurate predictions and feature importance insights.
- **Gradient Boosting**: Sequentially refines predictions, improving accuracy.
- **LSTM**: Captures time-dependent patterns in equipment data.
- **ARIMA/SARIMA**: Handle non-seasonal and seasonal trends in time series data.
- **RNNs**: Analyze sequential data for maintenance predictions.

2.7 Comparison with Baseline Models:

In evaluating predictive maintenance models against baseline models, several key insights were observed. The Persistence Model (Last Value) predicts maintenance needs for the next time step based on the last observed operational and anomaly trends. Stacked LSTM models significantly outperformed baseline models, especially in scenarios with complex sequential dependencies, demonstrating the LSTM's ability to capture intricate temporal patterns in data [19, 20]. In contrast, Linear Regression, while more sophisticated than the Persistence and Moving Average models, did not consistently outperform them, suggesting that simpler models can still deliver competitive predictions in certain contexts [8]. Both Random Forests and Gradient Boosting consistently outperformed baseline models across various maintenance prediction scenarios, highlighting their robustness and effectiveness in diverse forecasting tasks [8].

2.8 Recent Studies & Use Cases

Recent studies on predictive maintenance and machine learning highlight significant advancements in industrial applications. Kumar and Jha (2023) review machine learning algorithms for enhancing equipment reliability and reducing downtime, while Ozer and Ozkan (2023) introduce a framework for implementing predictive maintenance in smart factories, emphasizing the role of AI and data analytics in optimizing maintenance schedules. Wang and Feng (2023) examine current trends in predictive maintenance strategies, focusing on machine learning's growing impact across industries. In the context of environmental sustainability, Zhang and Li (2024) investigate how predictive maintenance can reduce waste and environmental impact, while Patel and Desai (2022) explore AI-powered solutions that lower emissions and improve resource efficiency. Gupta and Verma (2024) showcase advanced deep-learning techniques for more accurate predictions in complex environments, while Choudhury and Ray (2023) review recent machine-learning advancements in predictive maintenance. Alavi and Behnamfar (2023) stress the importance of real-time data integration for effective predictive maintenance using IoT sensors, and Li and Xu (2023) highlight the role of feature engineering and big data analytics in improving predictive accuracy. Other studies, such as those by Venkatesan and Suresh (2022), Rahman and Saha (2023), and Tan and Yu (2023), provide additional insights into the challenges and real-world applications of predictive maintenance in manufacturing, particularly in smart manufacturing environments.

To demonstrate the effectiveness of AI methods in manufacturing, consider these case studies: A major automotive manufacturer implemented a predictive maintenance system using Random Forests, reducing unplanned downtime by 20% through sensor data analysis [13]. An aerospace parts manufacturer adopted Stacked LSTM models to predict turbine engine failures, achieving a 15% increase in equipment lifespan and lower maintenance costs [14]. Additionally, a leading consumer electronics company integrated machine learning models, utilizing Gradient Boosting to analyze defect rates and reduce waste by 30% [15]. These examples showcase the broad applications and significant benefits of AI-driven predictive maintenance across different industries.

2.9 Quality Control

AI technologies are transforming quality control in manufacturing by automating the inspection process and identifying defects with unmatched precision [1]. Machine learning models evaluate visual data, sensor readings, and production metrics to spot potential flaws instantly, ensuring that only top-quality products are delivered to customers [2]. These AI-powered quality control systems help standardize product quality, minimize waste, and improve overall customer satisfaction [3]. Predictive maintenance is a cornerstone of AI applications in manufacturing, leveraging machine learning models to predict equipment failures before they occur [1]. By monitoring equipment performance in real-time and analyzing historical data, predictive maintenance systems identify early warning signs of potential issues, enabling proactive repairs and minimizing unplanned downtime [2]. AI-driven predictive maintenance improves equipment reliability, extends asset lifespan, and optimizes maintenance schedules to reduce costs and enhance operational efficiency [3].

2.10 Operational Efficiency

AI technologies optimize operational efficiency in manufacturing by analyzing production processes, identifying bottlenecks, and optimizing resource allocation. Machine learning algorithms optimize production schedules, predict demand fluctuations, and streamline supply chain management, ensuring just-in-time delivery and minimizing inventory costs. AI-driven operational efficiency improvements enhance productivity, reduce lead times, and support agile manufacturing practices.

3 Materials & Methods

3.1 Data Collection

For this project, we have utilized datasets from multiple pieces of equipment. The first dataset contains 684,233 rows, the second dataset comprises 483,450 rows, and the third dataset includes 960,033 rows. Each dataset features essential columns, including Temperature, Vibration, Pressure, Noise Levels, Voltage, Fluid Levels, Potential Damages, and Calibration. These datasets are foundational to our research, offering a wealth of diverse data points sourced directly from operational equipment in the manufacturer's production environment.

Sensor Data Collection. Types of Sensor Data:

- *Vibration Sensors:* Measure equipment vibrations, which can indicate mechanical issues.
- *Temperature Sensors:* Monitor the operating temperature of machinery to detect overheating.
- *Pressure Sensors:* Track fluid or gas pressure, crucial for systems like hydraulic pumps.
- *Current and Voltage Sensors:* Measure electrical parameters to identify anomalies in power consumption.

Data Sources.

- *Industrial Equipment:* Data is collected from sensors embedded in machinery (e.g., motors, pumps, conveyors).
- *IoT Devices:* Smart sensors that connect to a network for real-time data transmission.
- *Historical Maintenance Records:* Supplementary data that includes maintenance logs, failure events, and service history.

Dataset Size.

- *Volume:* Datasets often consist of millions of records, depending on the monitoring frequency (e.g., readings every second).
- *Time Series Data:* Typically structured as a time series with each record containing timestamps and multiple sensor readings.

By incorporating critical parameters such as Temperature, Vibration, Pressure, Noise Levels, Voltage, Fluid Levels, Potential Damages, and Calibration, we conduct thorough analyses of equipment performance across varied operating conditions. These datasets are integral to our exploration and modeling endeavors aimed at advancing our understanding and predictive capabilities related to equipment behavior, maintenance requirements, and scheduling [3, 4, 7, 9, 15].

3.2 Data Preparation and Exploration

In preparing the project data from various equipment manufacturers, I meticulously curated datasets sourced from multiple data streams (dataset1, dataset2, dataset3) and integrated them into Azure Cloud using streaming services. The process commenced with rigorous data cleaning to rectify inconsistencies, and to address missing values in the dataset, we used mean imputation for numerical features and mode imputation for categorical features. Mean imputation was chosen due to the relatively small proportion of missing values and the proportions of normally distributed data. Regression imputation was not considered to prevent overfitting in the considered dataset size, and we identified outliers using the Z-score method, with a threshold of 3. Values beyond the threshold were considered outliers. To cap outliers at the 95th percentile, we aimed to prevent them from disproportionately influencing the model training. This approach balanced retaining potentially informative extreme values while avoiding undue distortion in model performance, ensuring the reliability of data. To enhance dataset consistency, cubic interpolation was applied to smooth time series and reduce noise, which is crucial for time-sensitive predictive modeling. We compared cubic interpolation with spline methods and found that cubic interpolation provided a more stable representation of the data without introducing excessive oscillations.

Feature Engineering.

- *Time Domain Features:* Computed metrics such as mean, standard deviation, and root mean square (RMS) of sensor readings.
- *Frequency Domain Features:* Utilized Fourier Transform to extract frequency components, especially from vibration data.
- *Lag Features:* Created features that capture previous time steps to account for temporal dependencies.

Normalization/Scaling.

- *Standardization:* Scaled features to have a mean of 0 and a standard deviation of 1.
- *Min-Max Scaling:* Transformed features to a range between 0 and 1, especially for models sensitive to feature scaling.

The integration of information from all datasets resulted in a cohesive dataset that encompasses diverse operational scenarios. Feature engineering of a rolling average over a 7-day window was included to identify short-term trends, which improved the model's ability to predict equipment failures during regular operational cycles. This played a crucial role in enriching the dataset for predictive modeling by creating new features and transforming existing ones. Additional steps included normalization, scaling, handling missing values and outliers using Databricks, and partitioning the data into training and testing sets for machine learning analysis.

These meticulous preparations established a robust foundation for generating accurate predictions related to equipment operational parameters [5, 6, 8, 14, 15].

3.3 Data Visualization (Fig. 3)

Graph Overview:

Time Series Plot. A time series plot illustrates how a specific variable (like temperature, vibration, or pressure) evolves, showcasing a right-skewed distribution. It is useful for recognizing trends, seasonal variations, and anomalies that could signal potential equipment failures. Graphs display the effectiveness of predictive models by comparing actual and predicted values, as well as tracking the model's accuracy over time.
Predictive Model Performance. These graphs also address missing data through heatmaps. By normalizing the data, the model can handle patterns effectively, using

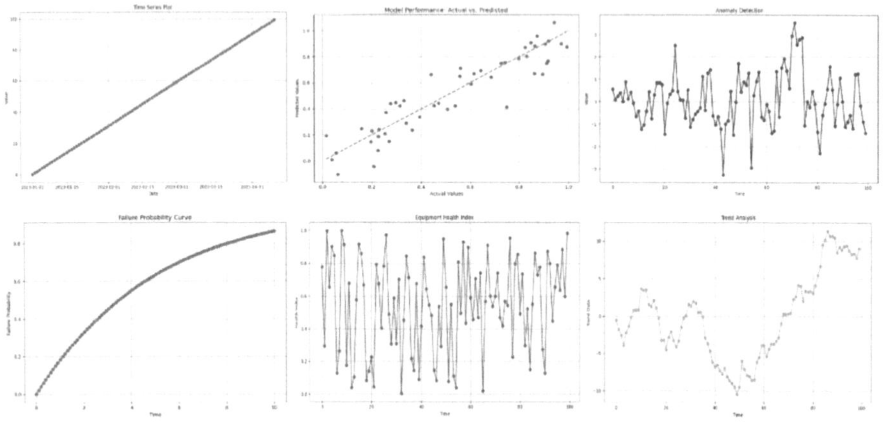

Fig. 3. Illustrates Time Series, Predictive Performance, Anomaly Detection, Failure Probability Curve, Equipment Health Index & Trend Analysis graphs of the equipment operational trends.

cubic interpolation for imputation, which enhances data quality and improves prediction accuracy. This aids in evaluating how accurately the model forecasts maintenance needs.

Anomaly Detection. Anomaly detection graphs emphasize deviations from normal operation, indicating possible faults or equipment failures.

Failure Probability Curve. A failure probability curve calculates the likelihood of equipment malfunction using predictive models and historical data. This curve is crucial for planning maintenance ahead of time.

Equipment Health Index. The equipment health index visually represents the overall state of equipment by analyzing various sensor readings and predictive models. It offers a quick overview of the equipment's condition and helps identify anomalies exceeding threshold limits, signaling the need for maintenance.

Trend Analysis. These graphs help detect the deterioration of equipment and forecast the rising risk of failure, indicating the need for timely maintenance intervention.

4 Results and Discussion

4.1 Model Performance Overview

Below is a table summarizing the key metrics (e.g., RMSE or accuracy) for each model, categorized by type (Regression, Tree-Based, Ensemble, Time-Series, and Classification) (Table 1).

4.2 Discussion

Key Observations.

- Tree-based models, particularly Random Forests, and ensemble methods like Gradient Boosting, demonstrated exceptional accuracy and robustness, particularly for datasets with high dimensionality and nonlinear interactions.

Table 1. Summarizing the key metrics of different models.

Model Type	Algorithm	RMSE/Accuracy	Key Insights	SDG Alignment
Regression Models	Linear Regression	0.1496	Simple baseline; limited in capturing nonlinear relationships	SDG 9 (Infrastructure)
	Support Vector Regression (SVR)	0.1282	Handles moderate complexities; requires hyperparameter optimization	SDG 12 (Sustainable Production), SDG 13 (Climate Action)
Tree-Based Models	Decision Trees	2.25e−05	High interpretability; effective in segmenting data into distinct regions	SDG 9 (Efficiency), SDG 12 (Resource Conservation)
	Random Forests	1.74e−05	Robust ensemble approach; mitigates overfitting, ideal for complex datasets	SDG 12 (Sustainability), SDG 8 (Economic Growth)
Ensemble Methods	Gradient Boosting	3.73e−05	Captures complex relationships; iterative error minimization	SDG 8 (Workplace Productivity), SDG 13 (Climate Action)
	XGB Regressor	Consistent	Optimized for speed and scalability, handles large datasets effectively	SDG 17 (Partnerships), SDG 12 (Efficiency)
Time-Series Models	Stacked LSTM	0.000405	Excels in capturing sequential dependencies and long-term patterns	SDG 12 (Sustainability), SDG 13 (Climate Resilience)

(*continued*)

Table 1. (*continued*)

Model Type	Algorithm	RMSE/Accuracy	Key Insights	SDG Alignment
	ARIMA/SARIMA	Varying	Effective in accounting for trends and seasonality, particularly in cyclical equipment usage scenarios	SDG 12 (Efficiency), SDG 13 (Climate Action)
Classification Models	Random Forest	1.0 (Perfect)	Exceptional accuracy in predicting equipment failures; highly reliable for preemptive strategies	SDG 8 (Economic Growth), SDG 12 (Downtime Reduction)

- Time-series models (e.g., Stacked LSTMs) provided superior results in scenarios requiring sequential analysis, confirming their importance for IoT-based predictive maintenance.
- Simpler models such as Linear Regression and SVR offered baseline performances but were insufficient for real-world complexities.

Recommendations for Practical Applications.

- **Tree-Based Models**: Ideal for scenarios requiring high interpretability and insights into feature importance (e.g., critical sensor identification).
- **Time-Series Models**: Best suited for operational conditions where historical trends significantly impact future predictions (e.g., sensor anomaly detection).

Significance for Sustainable Development.

- These models directly address SDGs 8, 9, and 12 by improving operational reliability, reducing waste, and minimizing environmental footprints.
- Deployment of such predictive tools fosters global collaboration (SDG 17) and ensures resilience against climate-induced disruptions (SDG 13).

4.3 Comparative Results of Model Performance

The performance of the models was evaluated using metrics such as accuracy, F1-score, and precision. Here are the results (Table 2):

- LSTM achieved the highest accuracy and F1 score, indicating its effectiveness in capturing temporal patterns.

Table 2. Results of different models, Accuracy, Precision, F1-Score.

Model	Accuracy	Precision	F1-Score
LSTM	92.5%	90.2%	91.0%
SVM	88.7%	85.6%	87.0%
Random Forests	90.3%	89.5%	89.8%

- Random Forests provided a balance between accuracy and interpretability, making it useful for understanding feature importance.
- SVM had the lowest performance metrics, potentially due to its sensitivity to feature scaling and data complexity, but still performed adequately for the classification task [4].

4.4 Details of Time-Series Techniques

ARIMA (Auto Regressive Integrated Moving Average) and SARIMA (Seasonal ARIMA) are traditional statistical methods used for time-series forecasting.

- **Necessity:** These models are particularly useful for datasets exhibiting trends and seasonality. They rely on past values to predict future points, making them suitable for time series where historical patterns are essential for forecasting [5].
- **Complementarity:** ARIMA and SARIMA can complement machine learning models like Random Forests and Gradient Boosting by providing a baseline for performance comparison. They can also be used in ensemble methods, where their forecasts are combined with machine learning predictions to improve overall accuracy [1].

4.5 Effectiveness Compared to Machine Learning Approaches

- Traditional time-series models like ARIMA and SARIMA can be more interpretable and require less data preprocessing than many machine-learning methods. However, they may struggle with complex, non-linear relationships and high-dimensional datasets [2].
- Machine learning approaches, such as Random Forests and Gradient Boosting, can capture these complexities and handle larger datasets effectively, often resulting in higher predictive performance in scenarios where the data does not conform to the assumptions of ARIMA/SARIMA [3].

4.6 Insights

The variety of models used highlights their distinct advantages in predicting when equipment will require maintenance. While Linear Regression and SVR show moderate accuracy, more advanced techniques like Decision Trees and Random Forests outperform them by effectively capturing complex health trends with minimal errors [1]. Gradient Boosting and XGB Regressor excel at modeling intricate relationships, leading to highly accurate predictions [2].

Stacked LSTM models are particularly successful in managing time-sensitive data, which is essential for forecasting maintenance needs in constantly changing operational settings [3]. ARIMA and SARIMA models also make notable contributions to maintenance forecasting, demonstrating their flexibility across various conditions [4].

The exceptional accuracy of the Random Forest Classifier emphasizes its reliability in predictive maintenance, offering valuable insights for proactive maintenance actions [5]. These results underscore the significance of selecting the right model based on the unique characteristics of the data, ensuring continuous enhancements in predicting equipment health and optimizing maintenance schedules beyond regular intervals [6].

5 Conclusion

The research offers an in-depth evaluation of different predictive models for equipment maintenance, highlighting a range of performance metrics that each bring distinct benefits to improving operational effectiveness and equipment dependability. Notably, tree-based models like Decision Trees and Random Forests showed outstanding precision, successfully detecting subtle health trends with minimal error (RMSE between 1.74e−05 and 2.25e−05) [1]. Ensemble approaches such as Gradient Boosting and XGB Regressor also performed strongly in capturing complex relationships, resulting in accurate forecasts [2]. On the other hand, simpler models like Linear Regression and Support Vector Regression (SVR) demonstrated moderate performance, emphasizing the need to choose models based on the specific nature of maintenance data [3].

Additionally, time-series models like Stacked LSTM were particularly effective in capturing temporal dependencies, providing valuable insights into time-sensitive maintenance needs [4]. The flawless accuracy of the Random Forest Classifier in predicting maintenance requirements underscores its reliability in operational contexts [5]. The robust performance of ARIMA and SARIMA models in time-series forecasting further affirms their effectiveness in anticipating maintenance trends [6].

The findings of this research emphasize the necessity for continuous refinement and customization of predictive models to optimize equipment health predictions and maintenance strategies. As organizations increasingly harness advanced analytics, they can proactively manage maintenance, minimize downtime, and optimize resource allocation, leading to enhanced operational performance [7]. This proactive approach not only benefits businesses but also aligns with broader sustainability goals. By improving operational efficiency and reducing downtime, the research supports United Nations Goal 8 (Decent Work and Economic Growth), fostering increased productivity and job stability [8]. Enhancements to industrial infrastructure resonate with Goal 9 (Industry, Innovation, and Infrastructure), promoting resilience and innovation [9]. Furthermore, minimizing waste and extending equipment lifespan contribute to Goal 12 (Responsible Consumption and Production) [10], while energy-efficient operations help lower greenhouse gas emissions, aligning with Goal 13 (Climate Action) [11]. Collaboration across sectors to implement these technologies will strengthen Goal 17 (Partnerships for the Goals) [12].

6 Opportunities for Future Explorations

- Integration of Various Data Sources: Research focusing on the combination of multiple data sources such as vibration measurements, acoustic signals, operational logs, and environmental conditions can enhance prediction accuracy and provide a more thorough understanding of equipment health. Future studies may concentrate on creating advanced techniques for merging these data streams and developing robust models capable of handling different data types efficiently [1].
- Improving Model Transparency and Understanding: There is a need to develop models that enhance the transparency and interpretability of predictive maintenance results. This involves designing frameworks that explain predictions in a way that is clear to engineers and decision-makers while embedding interpretability in the model design process from the beginning [2].
- Adapting to Changing System Dynamics: Exploring techniques for adaptive learning and incremental model updates that can evolve with new data is essential. Future research could look at models that are able to identify and respond to shifts in system behavior over time [3].
- Real-Time and Scalable Data Processing: Examining scalable approaches and system architectures capable of managing large volumes of data and providing real-time predictions is critical. This could include solutions such as edge computing, which processes data locally to enable immediate decision-making on-site [4].
- Collaboration between AI and Human Knowledge: The development of systems that integrate AI insights with human expertise will significantly improve decision-making. This includes designing interfaces that enable effective collaboration between AI systems and maintenance engineers and setting up feedback mechanisms where human input can help refine and enhance AI models [5].

The integration of predictive maintenance and AI technologies not only boosts operational performance but also promotes sustainable industrial practices, aligning with critical global goals for a more resilient and efficient future.

References

1. Wang, H., Zhou, Y., Deng, F.: A review of AI-based predictive maintenance in smart manufacturing. IEEE Access **10**, 104368–104385 (2022)
2. Bhattacharya, S., Sen, S.: Implementing predictive maintenance using machine learning techniques: a case study. J. Intell. Manuf. **33**(2), 423–436 (2022)
3. Sahu, A., Mohanty, R.: Data-driven predictive maintenance using machine learning: an overview. Comput. Ind. **131**, 103461 (2022)
4. Kumar, P., Jha, S.: Machine learning algorithms for predictive maintenance: a comprehensive review. Int. J. Comput. Intell. Syst. **15**(1), 134–148 (2022)
5. Zhao, Y., Zhang, H., Cheng, W.: Application of artificial intelligence in predictive maintenance: a comprehensive review. IEEE Access **10**, 60816–60830 (2022)
6. Pecht, M.: Internet of Things (IoT) and AI-based predictive maintenance in manufacturing. J. Manuf. Sci. Eng. **144**(5), 050801 (2022)
7. Ozer, M., Ozkan, E.: Predictive maintenance in smart factories: a comprehensive framework. J. Ind. Inf. Integr. **22**, 100193 (2022)

8. Ibrahim, S., Rani, R.: Application of AI in predictive maintenance: challenges and opportunities. Artif. Intell. Rev. **55**(6), 4213–4234 (2022)
9. Al-Jumaili, A., Sellami, A.: IoT and machine learning for predictive maintenance in Industry 4.0: a systematic review. Robot. Comput. Integr. Manuf. **69**, 101896 (2023)
10. Kusiak, A.: Smart manufacturing and AI: driving predictive maintenance. Eng. Manag. J. **32**(4), 205–215 (2023)
11. Li, H., Lin, J., Xu, C.: Predictive maintenance for equipment based on machine learning. In: Proceedings of the International Conference on Industrial Engineering and Operations Management (2023)
12. Cai, X., Wang, Y.: A review on predictive maintenance in smart manufacturing. In: 2023 IEEE International Conference on Mechatronics, Automation and Systems (ICMAS) (2023)
13. Dhanalakshmi, P., Babu, P.: A review on machine learning techniques for predictive maintenance of industrial equipment. Mater. Today Proc. **6**(1), 433–442 (2023)
14. Tan, C., Yu, J.: Review of predictive maintenance strategies in smart manufacturing. Procedia Manuf. **40**, 50–58 (2024)
15. Wang, C., Feng, C.: A review on predictive maintenance for industrial equipment based on data-driven approaches. J. Manuf. Sci. Eng. **144**(11), 110801 (2022)
16. Singh, P., Jain, A.: Predictive maintenance for machine tools: a review. J. Manuf. Technol. Manag. **33**(4), 795–818 (2022)
17. Yang, W., Guo, C., Lin, W.: Research on predictive maintenance technology of high-speed train components based on artificial intelligence. Adv. Mech. Eng. **15**(7), 1–14 (2023)
18. Jiang, L., Wang, J., Chen, J.: IoT and big data for predictive maintenance in smart manufacturing: a review. Sensors **23**(1), 5182 (2023)
19. Xu, X., Xu, L.D., Zhao, S.: IoT-based predictive maintenance in smart factory. IEEE Trans. Ind. Inf. **19**(2), 1426–1434 (2023)
20. Liu, Y., Wang, H.: Review of machine learning applications in predictive maintenance. Procedia CIRP **75**, 1043–1048 (2022)
21. Dhanalakshmi, P., Babu, P.: A review on machine learning techniques for predictive maintenance of industrial equipment. Mater. Today Proc. **6**(1), 433–442 (2022)
22. Kumar, P., Jha, S.: Machine learning algorithms for predictive maintenance: a comprehensive review. Int. J. Comput. Intell. Syst. **16**(1), 134–148 (2023)
23. Al-Jumaili, A., Sellami, A.: IoT and machine learning for predictive maintenance in Industry 4.0: a systematic review. Robot. Comput. Integr. Manuf. **70**, 101896 (2023)
24. Ozer, M., Ozkan, E.: Predictive maintenance in smart factories: a comprehensive framework. J. Ind. Inf. Integr. **23**, 100193 (2023)
25. Sahu, A., Mohanty, R.: Data-driven predictive maintenance using machine learning: an overview. Comput. Ind. **132**, 103461 (2023)
26. Ibrahim, S., Rani, R.: Application of AI in predictive maintenance: challenges and opportunities. Artif. Intell. Rev. **56**(6), 4213–4234 (2023)
27. Zhao, Y., Zhang, H., Cheng, W.: Application of artificial intelligence in predictive maintenance: a comprehensive review. IEEE Access **11**, 60816–60830 (2023)
28. Wang, H., Zhou, Y., Deng, F.: A review of AI-based predictive maintenance in smart manufacturing. IEEE Access **11**, 104368–104385 (2023)
29. Cai, X., Wang, Y.: A review on predictive maintenance in smart manufacturing. In: 2024 IEEE International Conference on Mechatronics, Automation and Systems (ICMAS) (2024)
30. Pecht, M.: Internet of Things (IoT) and AI-based predictive maintenance in manufacturing. J. Manuf. Sci. Eng. **145**(5), 050801 (2024)

Linking Artificial Intelligence to ERP: The Case of Oracle

Ghazi Alkhatib(✉)

Hashemite University, Zarqa, Jordan
g.alkhatib@hu.edu.jo

Abstract. The main aim of this paper is to investigate the link between enterprise resource planning (ERP) systems and artificial intelligence. The paper provides the foundation of the ERP basic infrastructure. The integrating ERP and AI follows two approaches: Augmented (ERP-I) and embedded (IERP). The opportunities for such link include the existence of the data to be used for training, test, and operation of AI is available within the organization database. The challenges refer to the types of ERP internal data is mainly in numeric form. Two major gaps impede the adaptation of ERP/AI: implementation gap between current internal practices vs. ERP best practices, AI/IT skills gap, cloud architecture gap, and domain knowledge gaps of both users and developers. These gaps apply to both approaches of AI-ERP links. This paper concentrates on the augmented approach, but provides basic foundation on the embedded approach as will. A future paper will delve more in depth on the latter approach. The paper will serve as a source of knowledge for the selection and implementation of the AI-ERP link.

Keywords: ERP · Artificial Intelligence · Linking ERP and AI · Oracle Case · IERP

1 Introduction

For ease of reading the paper, readers are referred to a list of acronyms included in Appendix A.

Enterprise resource planning (ERP) systems evolved over decades, with small to large system. The largest two are Oracle, and SAP. Each ERP provides specialized models related to the different business functions, such as financial planning, human resource planning, customer relationship management, research and development, and accounting systems, in addition to other functions. Each company may select some of the backbone systems necessary for their basic operations. Other more specialized models are selected based on the particulars of each company operations. The expansive use of cloud computing, most ERP companies provide cloud-based access.

For example, Forbes Advisor reviewed several ERP systems for small businesses and came up with the following list:

The best ERP systems of 2024 [1]:

- Microsoft Dynamics 365 Business Central: Best overall

A. Mirzazadeh et al. (Eds.): SEMIT 2024, CCIS 2444, pp. 35–50, 2026.
https://doi.org/10.1007/978-3-032-01948-6_3

- Syspro: Best for distribution companies
- QT9: Best for life sciences companies
- Acumatica: Best for role-based solutions
- Katana Manufacturing ERP: Best for manufacturing companies
- Cougar Mountain Denali Summit: Best for nonprofits
- AccountMate: Best for financial management

For large ERP systems, Gartner Report on ERP cloud offerings has SAP slightly edging Oracle in the top three systems [2]. The above list shows that ERP systems may excel in certain application domain. Large ERPs, however, provide both the selection option from different core and supporting models, as well as specialized ERP systems for a particular domain that were developed from best practices of companies in the field. For example, Oracle offers a cloud-based manufacturing ERP system [3].

Leaders in AI are pioneered by Microsoft, Amazon, Google, and Meta [4]. The use of AI in business started with Expert Systems in application areas that include classification, diagnosis, monitoring, process control, and design, scheduling and planning [5].

Moving to current trend, AI applications in business include [6]:

- Accounting: Cash flow projections, tax, payroll, and financial forecasting.
- Content Generation: Writing, researching, and editing as well as creating graphics, videos, and other media. In internal reporting, such as developing strategic plans, progress report, and financial statements. For external use company announcement of new product, brochures, and videos.
- Customer Service and Support: such as the use of Chatbots and callbots to extend their current customer service capabilities and provide immediate feedback.
- Cybersecurity: Monitor systems activity and protect systems against cyberattacks, identifying risks and areas of vulnerability.
- Information Technology (IT) Operations: In monitoring system CPU usage and network performance allowing them to plan for future expansions.
- Financial Analysis, Trading, and Fraud Detection.
- Human Resources: Manage employee records data and analysis, payroll, recruitment, benefits administration, and employee retention and retirement.
- Legal: Analyze data, recognize patterns, and progressive learning, in addition to error discovery, and risk assessment.
- Sales and Marketing: enhance customer relationship management (CRM), email marketing, social media, and advertising software.
- Supply Chain and Logistics: Forecasting or inventory management, as a mean of automation for manual tasks like picking and sorting in warehouses, allocating resources or people, scheduling processes, and solving or planning around operational disruptions.

Appian CEO [7] provides 4 predictions in AI use in 2024: Data foundations will become more critical as the backbone of AI, Humans and AI will interact harmoniously not with replacement strategy, Businesses will need private AI not a generalized AI, and Regulations will soon emerge as a crucial activity in increased AI use and risk. The paper will demonstrate that the four predictions are critical in linking AI to ERP.

2 Review of Literature

The following research problems were raised in [8]:

"What is the type and writing language of ERP-AI-related publications?
What is the distribution of ERP-AI publications by years?
Who are the authors which produced the most publications about ERP-AI?
What are the most ERP-AI-related institutions?
What is the distribution of ERP-AI publications by subject areas?
Who are the authors who received the most references about ERP-AI?
What is the collaboration of ERP-AI-related publications between co-authors?
What is the collaboration network of ERP-AI publications between co-authors' countries?
What are ERP-AI-related publications' common citation and collaboration networks between authors?
What is the collaboration network of ERP-AI publications between common references and sources?
What are the common keywords used in ERP-AI-related publications?"

The question on subject areas is the most relevant to this paper. When combining three areas related to business, its rank become the third after computer science and engineering. Additionally, the most common keywords were "ERP" (n = 37), "genetic algorithm" (n = 27), "enterprise resource planning" (n = 25), "fuzzy logic" (n = 22), and "machine learning" (n = 15), "Artificial intelligence" (n = 11), and "Supply chain management", "optimization", and "decision support systems" each with (n = 8). Furthermore, the author stated that ERP-AI studies have started in 1995, followed by a period of decreased publications. However, publication started to pick up after 2014 with the emphasis on Industry 4.0 trend as of 2012, which accelerated publication in AI uses in production and business processes. Finally, conclusions states that more than half of the publications are in conference proceedings type and one-third are in journal publication. The above reference did not go through the technical side of the AI and ERP.

Further research investigated the impact of integrating AI and ERP on the dynamics of the organizational dynamics. These include enhancing organizational efficiency and innovation. Through the survey of 300 organizations, the study concluded between 18% and 35% effects in the following areas: enhancement in accuracy across business functions, using predictive analytic to decrease maintenance costs and increase the overall effectiveness of equipment usage, and finally, increase customer satisfaction with personalized experiences [9].

Another study investigated the use of the following AI technologies in ERP applications: machine learning, deep learning, neural network, natural language processing, and robotics. The study concluded the AI used in customer relationship management, predictive analysis, and sales projections, in essence supporting the findings of the previous study [10].

As to the current state of AI and ERP link, Forbes reports that GenAI will have a disrupting effect on the ERP market [11]. However, it must be customized and trained on ERP historical structured and unstructured data. This paper is delimited by the exclusion in the analysis of GenAI, such as ChatGPT in routine tasks such as marketing brochures, research and writing reports. On the other hand, it is limited to discussions on how AI technologies are linked to existing standard models in ERP systems, particularity Oracle, by using the backbone database of the ERP system, with the possibility of using LLM GenAI running on platform such as the clouds [12]. As such, this study will delve on such link to explore how GenAI technologies are linked to ERP databases. The paper purposely used the weaker word "link" and avoided the use of the stronger words of "integration" or "Embedding," pending on the outcome of the study.

3 Research Methodology

The qualitative research method in information systems is references in [13]. This approach can be used in the context of this paper as concepts taking the shape of classification of ERP systems, and theme or idea of linking ERP and AI. Concepts take the shape of unique components, such as AI and ERP technologies. As the analysis moves forward, generalizations are drawn on how the results the theme discussions contribute to current practices. This paper adapts such methodology by combining two common technologies: a traditional one represented by ERP systems and an emerging one of AI to generate a framework to understand mechanisms of linking AI to ERP systems. In addition, the overall structure of this paper's methodology satisfies the requirements of applied research paradigm as in [14]. These paradigms include bridging the gap between research and organization, achieving organizational effectiveness, enhancing the knowledge base for the organizational memory, and promoting innovation and improvements of current management practice. As such, this paper can serve as a knowledge base for the selection and evaluation of ERP-AI models, the implementation project of such models, and a posterior analysis of success and failures of these projects.

The paper will survey available documentations and references delineating the link AI to Oracle ERP. The paper first establishes a general framework for ERP systems in organizations, then the paper establishes framework for AI-ERP link on Oracle systems with related technologies using the augmented approach. The paper extract detailed description of actual implementations and scenarios on the link of AI-ERP Oracle. The paper will address what exactly Large Language Model (LLM), such as ChatGPT, can assist in implementing specific applications on ERP-I. In addition, explore other embedded systems in IERP. In addition, a separate section on the embedded approach of linking AI to ERP provides a survey of related technologies. The conclusion will highlight how this paper and future research areas will meet the applied research paradigm.

3.1 Basic Components of an ERP System

The following are the major components of the of the ERP system:

The Backend Database. The database is an integrated view linking all type of data with minimum redundancy and update anomalies. The database may contain structured and unstructured data. The relationship among entities went through network Data Base Management System (DBMS), Relational DBMS, and Object-oriented DBMS.

The Database Engine (DBMS). It manages the backend database. These include data integrity, mechanisms for updating the data base even in distributed DBMS which stores duplicates of the same copy of a database in different locations and control the updates to maintain its integrity.

The ERP System. Such systems offer models addressing different business functions. The backbone models that are deemed relevant to all organizations may include accounting, human resource, finance, and inventory control. These models incorporate best business practices. ERP may be offered as a generic collection of models on need bases, specialized for a particular business type, or optimized for a particular business, as stated in the introduction. Organizations must address these alternatives in the selectin process. ERP may be totally hosted locally, may be totally hosted in the clouds, or as a hybrid model. Any specialized function not available in the ERP model list may require ERP customization or use of a third-party software package. Such customization may be carried by the vendor of internal expertise if available.

The User Interface. The user interface provides input and output screens, organized in a hierarchy, for users to input data and generate reports. These reports are normally built into the ERP system, or can be enhanced by a third-party report generator for customized reporting. Such report is generated to be used by different levels of management.

ERP Systems. ERP can be offered as a whole system incorporating all of the above components, or offer the ERP system separated from the DBMS, but include the user interface. Oracle is one of the vendors that offers completely integrated of all ERP components under one environment – a reason why Oracle is selected for this study.

Hardware and Network Infrastructure. A totally separate area from the above components, but worth mentioning, is the hardware and network architectures. An ERP System may be optimized on a specific hardware using SPARC servers, previously produced by SUN, and later bought by Oracle [15]. Currently, all ERP systems and AI capabilities are migrated to the cloud environment [16].

3.2 Justification for Oracle Selection

Oracle is the only ERP system that has all of the above components in one coherent platform. Figure 1 is developed by the paper to describe the overall architecture of Oracle ERP system. A note on placing AI models below the functional model is to indicate that an organization must have the functional model in operation before starting to look into implementing AI models. The figure represents the embedded approach. For the augmented approach, the box for AI models can be replaced with the large language model (LLM), such as ChatGPT.

3.3 Integration Approaches

Figure 2 displays the structures of the two approaches for linking AI to ERP systems.

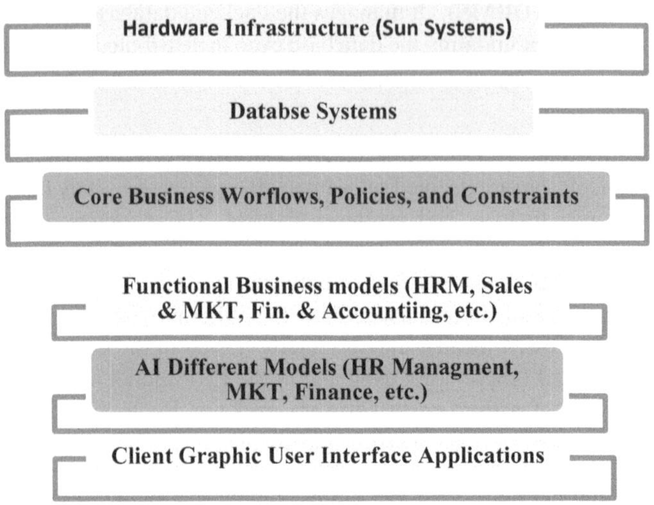

Fig. 1. Oracle ERP architecture

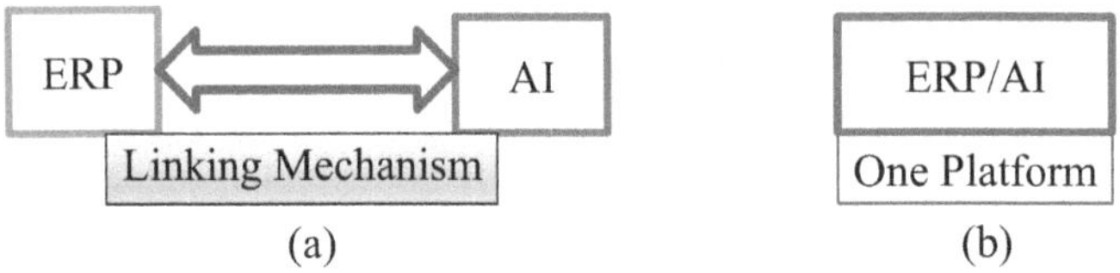

Fig. 2. Integration approaches: a. Augmented approach (ERP-I). b. Embedded approach (IERP)

3.4 The AI Components

The AI discussions evolves around the following topics.

Technologies Used. AI technologies may include natural language processing, machine learning, deep learning, neural network, and robotics. The paper will explore the use of these technologies in ERP systems, with Oracle case in particular.

Linking AI to ERP. Several approaches could be considered: embedding the AI techniques in related models, such as finance, human resource, and marketing. Another approach is using a third-party AI software package. The third approach is to customize an AI application for a particular function or business. An example is the use of robotics in manufacturing.

Data Analysis in AI. The majority of data collected by the ERP system is numerical, such as in accounting financial, human resource, manufacturing, and inventory. However, customer data may include categorical data as well. Machine learning has two major models for data analysis: supervised and unsupervised models. Supervised model requires the identification of variables to be included in the analysis. The unsupervised models look for patterns in data without variables identification as a priori for the analysis. Both model types deploy different statistical techniques for analysis and estimation.

The detailed analysis of such techniques is beyond the scope of this paper. However, the paper will attempt to identify such techniques when used in ERP – these will be explained then.

3.5 User View of Accessing the ERP-I System

Figure 3 presents a general internal user view of how to access the components of the AI-ERP augmented link (ERP-I). The external user will follow the same steps other than accessing a subset of the backend database. User will upload the personal dataset to the intermediate database.

The steps to access the ERP-I:

1. Internal user (IU) will have already access rights to the backend database.
2. Obtain access to the large language model LLM, in this case the ChatGPT, to perform forecasting of sales for example using the LLM capabilities.
3. The IU will issue a NLP statement to access a subset of the backend database as needed to perform the forecasting.
4. Oracle will retrieve the required fields and upload to the intermediate database.
5. The IU will perform the forecasting and receive the output.

An external user (EU) will upload the personal database directly to the intermediate database, get access from LLM (ChatGPT) and perform the desired function and receive the output. EU may use any LLM to use the temporary database area. A subsequent section presents the technologies used in the ERP-I system.

However, Oracle followed a concurrent strategy by introducing embedded AI capabilities in AI – ERP platforms. These will be explained towards the end of the paper.

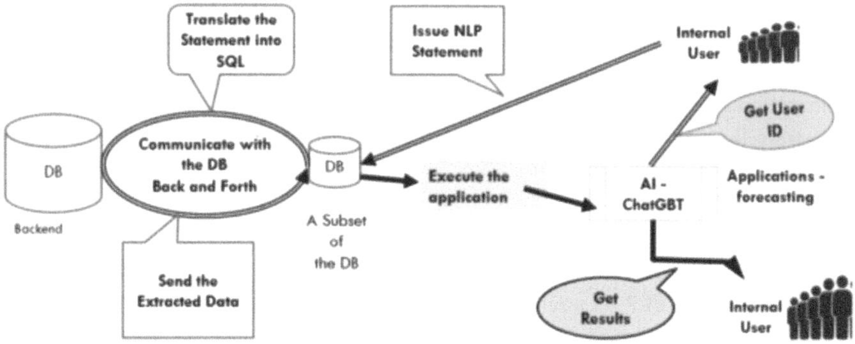

Fig. 3. A general internal user view on how to access the ERP-I.

4 Adapting ERP-AI

For both augmented and embedded approaches, ERP-AI implementation faces several issues.

4.1 Opportunities

Data Availability. The database is the backbone of any ERP system. This database developed based on an integrated view of the complete data used by all models, with reduced redundancy and maintain updates with minimal anomalies. Introducing AI into ERP will add more importance to such data, and requires careful evaluation on how to be used by AI technologies and models. For example, how data will be used to train, verified, validate the processes of building the AI project. Simply put, data will become critical and will consume more resources [17].

Security. Using an open GenAI dictate attention to security and risk. Since this issue was delimited in the paper, security is carried on by different levels of checks prior to accessing the ERP system – starting from the user interface to the backend database. The DBMS will control access to the backend database using different methods, and normally attain strong attention when building access mechanisms to the database. These measures range in granularity from accessing the whole database to accessing or updating particular field. The issue of security when using the cloud platform always come into play.

Risk. Following the above discussion, risk in database access is tightly secured. However, other risks may trigger other types on risk, such as gender and age-related analysis of the data and financial reporting. AI used powerful techniques and require careful attention in data preparation for the analysis.

4.2 Gap Analysis and Challenges

Implementation Gap. Gap between internal business practices and ERP best practices. This gap existed since the evolution of ERP systems. Organizations wanted to adapt best practices incorporated in ERP systems often face the challenge either change internal processes to map into current best practices, or involve in the critical activity of customization. So, it is a balance between efforts to change current practices vs. customization. This gap will always exist when adapting ERP-AI approaches. Figure 4 demonstrate the gap issues when adapting ERP. At the same time, adding AI systems will complicate the gap adaptation.

Current practice that are not supported by the ERP that requires customization of existing systems	Current practices supported by the ERP and implemented	ERP best practices that will require re-engineering of existing system

Fig. 4. Implementation gap

AI Skills Gap. Over decades, many difference AI techniques and models evolved. Skill and knowledge domain gap became apparent among potential uses of AI in ERP systems. Currently with the emphasis of using AI in business and ERP, the gap between current practices and adapting I-ERP is getting larger. Migration from current ERP system to I-ERP is going to be easier than migrating from current non-ERP system to I-ERP. The migration of the latter case carries a higher risk.

Knowledge Domain Gap. A critical issue is the communication between users and IT professionals of what is called domain knowledge. The paper recommends three methods: educate end-users at all levels with basic IT principles, educate IT professional on the domain knowledge of AI projects, and encourage end-user participation in the AI-ERP project.

IT/Cloud Gap. With a quick note, current hardware and network architectures may not support the implementation of the I-ERP solution. The AI in ERP may require faster CPU and the additional GPU units [17]. Using the cloud platform alleviate hardware and networks worries. Forbes list of top 100 cloud private companies is dominated by AI main stream company – OpenAI – and startups [18].

The Senior Director of Global Product Marketing in Oracle, as published in NetSuite website, have written a comprehensive marketing document listing major AI technologies, ways AI is transforming ERP, benefits of AI for ERP, and Challenges of AI in ERP [19]. The latter part is deemed appropriate to the theme of this paper, supporting the previous discussions. It identifies the following challenges: integration complexity, change management, and skills gap. All of the above gaps will exist always, however, it will shrink with experience or expands with new versions, and with new technologies.

The following section will explore the technical side of ERP-I, the augmented approach depending on available sources of detailed information.

5 Oracle ERP-I Analysis

5.1 Automatous Database (ADB)

Oracle provides options to use GenAI LLM to access an instant of the Oracle backend database or uploaded by customers termed Autonomous Database (ADB) – referenced as temporary database in a previous section. This integration between GenAI and ERP allows using GenAI natural language interface (NLP) capabilities to generated SQL queries to access, observe, and manage the database through the ADB for different functions, such as health and finance. This process is explained above in Fig. 1.

5.2 Oracle Apex Workspace

Another language introduced by oracle is Select AI [20], which allows natural language interaction to SQL transfer using the ADB repository. This language can be used by both users: internal and external, where the internal users to extract data from the ERP backend database, while the external users can upload their own database to the ADB. Then, both users then can generate reports using Select AI natural language. This language also supports the Retrieval-augmented generation used by LLM, such as ChatGPT, for knowledge representation. An environment that will bridge the gap between LLM and enterprise database for internal users, as well external users. This environment will facilitate the implementation of the augmented approach (ERP-I).

Oracle workspace provides an integrated platform to link AI to autonomous database allows the creation of Structured Query Language (SQL) statements using natural language interface, as a required prerequisite to perform the link between AI and ERP user interface:

- Oracle platforms uses two distinct technologies: Oracle APEX workspace as an area to store the autonomous instance of a database, and Select AI [20] that allows large language models (LLMs) to translate natural language queries into SQL queries.
- An instance of the database to be queried, which could be extracted for the Oracle ERP or uploaded to APEX workspace from an external source as an active Oracle instance Autonomous Database (ADB). The ADB must define fields to be used in the query, wither it selected form Oracle ERP database of uploaded to the platform from an external source. In addition, select given names for summarizing the data.
- An external paid account from a LLM, such as OpenAI or any other one that supports the Application Program Interface (API). The API key generated by the LLM allows Select AI to interface with the database.
- Security access rights: access to Apex workspace and Database Privileges to securely execute DBMS_CLOUD_AI package in Oracle Database.

Here is an example of a NLP query:

```
SELECT DBMS_CLOUD_AI.GENERATE(
    prompt => 'GIVE ME 3 SCHOOL NAMES',
    profile_name => 'OPENAI_APEX',
    action => 'narrate' [added for clarity: top three schools with the highest enroll-
ments]
  ) FROM DUAL;
```

The technical preprocessing requirements are not stated here. Interested individuals can get it from the cited reference or from Oracle video on the subject [21].

5.3 Oracle Cloud Infrastructure (OCI)

This interface allows users to perform the functions of Observability and Management (O&M) of the ADB; the O&M services allow users to link such capabilities to access ADB from applications in production environments to manage issues related to health, performance management, resource forecasting, and cost, and extract custom data insights [22].

5.4 Autonomous Database with Oracle Database 23ai

Oracle Database 23ai Brings the Power of AI to Enterprise Data and Applications. Oracle AI Vector Search allows unstructured data, such as documents, images, as well as the structured relational data that are stored in backend ERP functional databases or custom databases to be easily searched [23]. AI Vector Search enables you to search structured and unstructured data based on its semantics or meaning, in addition to its values. Build into the semantic structure of the data and stored in a multidimensional structure, Native vector capabilities can help large language models (LLMs) deliver more-accurate and contextually relevant results with retrieval-augmented generation (RAG) [24]. RAG is the LLM knowledge representation of structured and unstructured data similar to traditional knowledge graph.

5.5 ChatGPT Data Analytics Capabilities

ChatGPT capabilities were advocated and questioned, stating that while ChatGPT can be used for preliminary data explorations and insights, it did not match the data analysts' expertise. As such subtle analytical tasks are best performed using traditional data analytics methodologies and tools [25, 26]. A Blog by Rumiantsau listed the following ChatGPT advanced data Analysis: use cases and performance [27].

- Advertising Data Analysis
- Analyze SEO Data (Google Search Console)
- Analyze Product Events Data
- Customer Feedback Analysis

However, the blog also recommended to check the output and have an expert validate the output. Rumiantsau also recommended to ask ChatGPT. So the author did. The following outputs are the most closely related to the theme of this study [28].

"Generating Data Analysis Code

You can ask ChatGPT to help generate Python, R, or SQL code to perform specific data analysis tasks. It can assist with:

- Data loading and exploration: Help with loading data into Pandas DataFrame (Python), or reading from a database with SQL.
- Statistical analysis: Providing code for descriptive statistics, hypothesis testing, or regression analysis.
- Visualization: Giving you code for creating plots in libraries like Matplotlib, Seaborn, or ggplot2."

"Natural Language Processing (NLP) Tasks:

If your data is text-based (e.g., customer reviews, tweets, or survey responses), ChatGPT can help:

- Sentiment analysis: Guide you on using libraries like VADER or TextBlob.
- Topic modeling: Explain how to apply techniques like Latent Dirichlet Allocation (LDA) or TF-IDF.
- Text classification: Teach you how to build models that classify text into categories.

In essence, ChatGPT users for data analytics must be familiar with its libraries and the Python language. Users must continuously consult LLL for updates, and/or use third party specialized frameworks or models.

When asked what ChatGPT has in data analytics, it gave the following summary:

"Summary: Although ChatGPT doesn't "have" libraries for data analytics in the traditional sense, I can still provide you with detailed guidance, code snippets, and explanations for using the libraries mentioned above. Whether you're analyzing data in Python, R, or working with SQL databases, I can assist you in writing code, explaining concepts, and interpreting your results!"

When asked about Python's data analytics capabilities, it gave the following answer:

"Python is one of the most powerful and widely used languages for data analytics. It has a rich ecosystem of libraries, tools, and frameworks that make it suitable for tasks ranging from simple data exploration to complex machine learning models and big data processing." Among the Statistical Analysis functions: hypothesis testing, and building models based on statistical principles, SciPy functions for various statistical tests (t-test, ANOVA, chi-square, etc.), Statsmodels tools for performing advanced statistical modeling, including linear regression, time-series analysis, and generalized linear models."

In a way, another gap exists on using ChatGPT or any LLM for data analytics.

5.6 An Overview of Oracle Embedded AI Applications

Oracle provides a complete platform for AI [29]. It contains embedded AI in SaaS and PaaS in the following areas: application, analytics, IT operations, algorithms and frameworks, model life cycle, model operations, datalake, data integration, and autonomous database mentioned above.

Oracle Fusion Cloud Applications provides embedded human capital management (HCM) for finance, sales, service, supply chain, and marketing [30].

The main component that houses AI application is the Oracle Enterprise Performance Management (EPM). It used to "Gain the agility and insights to outperform in any market condition. Oracle Fusion Cloud Enterprise Performance Management (EPM) helps the enterprise model and plan across finance, HR, supply chain, and sales, streamline the financial close process, and drive better decisions." [31].

For financial application for the chief financial officer (CFO), "Oracle's AI capabilities for finance provides a collection of AI- and ML-based tools and capabilities to help improve operational efficiency, automate standard transactions, better predict business outcomes, and optimize cash flow." [32]. It is used for predictive analysis, along with the capability of importing to ERM custom ML models in the context of finance.

Oracle for human resources provide the following complete Core Human Resources: end-to-end HR, On-demand information, Industry and union support, and position management. These cover areas as engage workers according legal and company policies, mobile response system, more than 200 countries for global environment, union management, and head counts and budgets [33].

Oracle has an AI component in Marketing, Sales, and Service Applications to Help Customers Grow Revenue (CX) that goes beyond customer relationship management (CRM). It provides ubiquitous customer contact management, and deliver customer experience from acquisition to retention [34].

Oracle has an AI Oracle Supply Chain Management (SCM) component that has the capabilities to respond quickly to changing demand, supply, and market conditions. It includes inventory management, manufacturing, maintenance, order management, logistics, product life cycle, procurement, Fusion data intelligence, and sustainability [35].

6 Cases on AI Projects

In his post, Gross [36] highlighted the following issues when dealing with AI projects:

- Dealing with a pilot implementation as when to stop it or continue with the complete implementation. With the cost in mind, dumping AI project may lead to a missing opportunity, or else may result with huge cost if poorly implemented.
- Forrester cautioned organization should not expect AI return on investment (ROI) to materialize very soon.
- According to Gartner, the number of AI pilots is increasing recently. In 2022, it was one third of the pilot projects, and expected the failure to be about one third in the future. IT and business teams can then assess progress toward those objectives at pre-established checkpoints as to determine whether a pilot be continued or be dumped. In this paper, this is dealing with the gap between user management and IT professionals.
- Arrive at a balance between the business values of AI project, and avoid the hype of using technology.

Mearian [37] highlighted the success story of Ernest & Young in developing a native LLL model for use internally, and in about a year 96% of employees used it. Another success story was reported by Paulise [38]. Indeed, using AI to improve existing workflow of its operation to make more it efficient and effective. A personalization theme resulted in 20% increase of applicants to current positions and a 13% increase in successfully landing a job.

7 Conclusions and Future Challenges

The paper presented the foundation for linking AI to ERP systems. ERP evolved over decades to incorporate best practices in business. Adding AI technologies to ERP makes the transition to the new I-ERP more cumbersome and requiring special skills. GenAI LLM with its capabilities are linked to ERP databases, structured and unstructured, through instances of autonomous database (ADB). This requires multiple access rights, particularly when using the cloud platform. The need still exists to access the traditional backend databases for updates and maintenance. The I-ERP trend is currently emerging, many use case scenarios as well as actual implementation reviews are needed to assess the state of linking GenAI to ERP. Creating instances of ADB to be accessed by the GenAI LLM requires careful attention and it is a step detached for the actual ERP database [39]. On the other side, GenAI data analytical capabilities needs to be continuously examined for validity. Concurrently, however, Oracle provides embedded AI capabilities in ERP for Human Capital Management (HCM) for all business functions, as well as applications in functional business. In reality, it has two options to link AI to the ERP system for both external users and internal users, as well as data scientists. Future research will explore more in-depth analysis of IRP (the embedded approach) and delve into specific real-world applications for all of this integration scenario. Furthermore, future research encompasses selection and implementation project of IERP, the embedded approach.

Appendix A

A list of acronyms used in the paper

ADB – Autonomous database
AI – Artificial intelligence
DBMS – Data base management system
ERP – Enterprise resource planning
ERP-I – ERP Intelligent link for augmented approach
IERP – Intelligent ERP link for embedded approach
LLM – Large language models for Generative AI
ML – Machine language
NLP – Natural language processing
RAG – Retrieval-augmented generation for data/test representation in LLM
SQL – Structured query language

References

1. https://www.forbes.com/advisor/business/software/best-erp-systems. Accessed 03 August 2024
2. https://www.gartner.com/reviews/market/cloud-erp-for-product-centric-enterprises. Accessed 03 August 2024
3. https://www.oracle.com/scm/manufacturing. Accessed 04 August 2024
4. https://www.top10erp.org/blog/ai-in-erp. Accessed 05 August 2024
5. https://www.umsl.edu/~joshik/msis480/chapt11.htm#:~:text=Generic%20Categories%20of%20Expert%20System%20Applications&text=Application%20areas%20include%20classification%2C%20diagnosis,planning%2C%20and%20generation%20of%20options
6. Bell, E.: How AI is Used in Business. https://www.investopedia.com/how-ai-is-used-in-business-8611256. Accessed 05 August 2024
7. Beckley, N.: 4 Predictions for the Future of AI (2024). https://assets.appian.com/uploads/ebook-2024-ai-outlook-expert-advice-navigating-ai-economy.pdf
8. Aktürk, C.: Artificial intelligence in enterprise resource planning systems: a bibliometric study. J. Int. Logist. Trade **19**(2), 69 (2021). https://doi.org/10.24006/jilt.2021.19.2.069
9. Godbole, M.V.: Revolutionizing enterprise resource planning (ERP) systems through artificial intelligence. Int. J. Mach. Learn. Robot. **7**(7), 1–15. https://injmr.com/index.php/fewfewf/article/view/31/5
10. Kunduru, A.R.: Effective usage of artificial intelligence in enterprise resource planning applications. Int. J. Comput. Trends Technol. **71**(4), 73–80 (2023). https://doi.org/10.14445/22312803/IJCTT-V71I4P109
11. https://www.forbes.com/sites/tonybradley/2024/03/27/disrupting-the-erp-market-with-ai. Accessed 03 August 2024

12. Panda, A., Garbaccio, B.: Developing an AI driven analytics assistant on OCI: deploy using your LLM running on OCI. In: An Oracle Presentation (2024). https://www.youtube.com/watch?v=jMhwDiD1Kiw
13. Nyale, D., Mwangi, S., Karume, S.: Survey of contemporary and emerging research methods in information systems research. Int. J. Comput. Appl. Technol. Res. **11**(12), 478–482 (2022). https://doi.org/10.7753/IJCATR1112.1015
14. de Mello, A.M., Pedroso, M.: Applied Research Articles: narrowing the gap between research and organizations. Revista de Gestão **25**(4), 338–339 (2018). https://doi.org/10.1108/REGE-10-2018-075
15. Oracle. Oracle Optimized Solution for E-Business Suite: A Technical White Paper (2011). https://www.oracle.com/technetwork/articles/systems-hardware-architecture/oo-soln-ent-bus-suite-170239.pdf
16. Oracle Cloud, Cloud Essential (2024) Artificial Intelligence: The Next Generation shttps://www.oracle.com/assets/cloudessentials-ai-4638866.pdf. Accessed 01 October 2024
17. Gross, G.: Hungry for Resources, AI Redefines the Data Center Calculus. CIO (2024). https://www.cio.com/article/3478766/hungry-for-resources-ai-redefines-the-data-center-calculus.html
18. Konradm, A., Cai, K.: From OpenAI to Figma, These are the 100 Hottest Cloud Companies.' https://www.forbes.com/sites/alexkonrad/2024/08/06/from-openai-to-figma-these-are-the-100-hottest-cloud-companies
19. Schwarzl, L.: AI in ERP: Benefits, Examples & Challenges (2024). https://www.netsuite.com/portal/resource/articles/erp/ai-erp.shtml#:~:text=Benefits%20of%20AI%20in%20ERP&text=Boosts%20overall%20productivity%3A%20AI%2C%20in,processing%20and%20customer%20order%20management
20. Menadas, C.V.: Enhancing Data Analysis with Select AI in Oracle APEX: Enhance Customer Engagement (2024). https://medium.com/@cristina.varas98/enhancing-data-analysis-with-select-ai-in-oracle-apex-9d00b070a073
21. Viscuso, G., Upadhyay, A. (2024). https://www.youtube.com/watch?v=BbaW65vXRy8
22. Oracle Cloud Infrastructure Documentation (2024). Autonomous Database with Oracle Database 23ai. https://docs.public.oneportal.content.oci.oraclecloud.com/en-us/iaas/autonomous-database-serverless/doc/experienced-database-users.html#GUID-58EE6599-6DB4-4F8E-816D-0422377857E5
23. Oracle Cloud Infrastructure Documentation (2024). Oracle AI Vector Search. https://www.oracle.com/database/ai-vector-search
24. Amazon-AWS (2024). What is RAG (Retrieval-Augmented Generation)? https://aws.amazon.com/what-is/retrieval-augmented-generation. Accessed 01 October 2024
25. Patel, P., Shooshtarian, S.: The role of chatbots in data analytics: an evaluation of functional abilities. In: SAI Computing Conference, London (2024).https://doi.org/10.1007/978-3-031-62277-9_10
26. Hassani, H., Silva, E.S.: The role of ChatGPT in data science: how AI-assisted conversational interfaces are revolutionizing the field. Big Data Cogn. Comput. **20**(7), 62 (2023). https://doi.org/10.3390/bdcc7020062
27. Rumiantsau. M.: Using ChatGPT for Data Analysis: Use Cases and Limitations (2024). https://www.narrative.bi/analytics/using-chatgpt-for-data-analysis
28. ChatGPT 4o mini (2024). Accessed 01 October 2024
29. Oracle. Oracle AI Platform Built for End Users and Data Scientists (2024). https://www.oracle.com/assets/cloudessentials-ai-4638866.pdf. Accessed 01 October 2024
30. Oracle. Discover Embedded AI in Fusion Cloud Applications (2024). https://www.oracle.com/applications/fusion-ai/. Accessed 01 October 2024
31. Oracle. Oracle Enterprise Performance Management (2024). https://www.oracle.com/performance-management. Accessed 01 October 2024

32. Oracle. Oracle AI for the CFO (2024). https://www.oracle.com/erp/ai-financials. Accessed 02 October 2024
33. Oracle. Oracle Human Resources (2024). https://www.oracle.com/jo/human-capital-management/hr. Accessed 01 October 2024
34. Oracle. Oracle Adds Artificial Intelligence to Marketing, Sales, and Service Applications to Help Customers Grow Revenue (2023). https://www.oracle.com/news/announcement/ocw-oracle-adds-ai-to-marketing-sales-service-applications-2023-09-19
35. Oracle. Oracle Fusion Cloud Supply Chain & Manufacturing (2024). https://www.oracle.com/jo/scm/#rc30scp. Accessed 03 October 2024
36. Gross, G.: When is the right time to dump an AI project? In Gen AI Insight (2024). https://mail.google.com/mail/u/2/?ogbl#inbox/FMfcgzQXJkXsdmmxkxXxncpgvHzZdCJB
37. Mearian, L.: How Ernst & Young's AI platform is 'radically' reshaping operations. Computerworld (2024). https://www.computerworld.com/article/3560355/how-ernst-youngs-ai-platform-is-radically-reshaping-operations.html
38. Paulise, L.: Indeed Launches AI-Powered Smart Sourcing and New Job Seeker Profiles, Forbes-Leadership-Careers (2024). https://www.forbes.com/sites/lucianapaulise/2024/04/04/indeed-launches-ai-powered-smart-sourcing-and-new-job-seeker-profiles/
39. Oracle Cloud Infrastructure Documentation. Autonomous Database for Experienced Oracle Database Users (2024). https://docs.public.oneportal.content.oci.oraclecloud.com/en-us/iaas/autonomous-database-serverless/doc/experienced-database-users.html#GUID-58EE6599-6DB4-4F8E-816D-0422377857E5

Performance Evaluation of Object Detection Models in Maritime Applications

Maureen Montano Alfaro[1], Ewa Wisniewska[2], Nadine Sarah Baumgaertner[2], Melis Duhter[3], and Ilayda Boz[4](✉)

[1] University of Cadiz, Cadiz, Spain
[2] University of Radom, Radom, Masovian Voivodeship, Poland
[3] Mersin University, Mersin, Turkey
[4] Tarsus University, Mersin, Turkey
ilayda_boz@tarsus.edu.tr

Abstract. Detecting objects on sea and ocean surfaces, particularly ships, is critical for various maritime applications, including traffic regulation, emergency response, environmental protection, and security. However, this task is challenging due to dynamic factors such as background variability, wave interference, and diverse lighting conditions. Satellites in low Earth orbit offer superior image clarity compared to geostationary counterparts, capturing dynamic features crucial for ship detection. Despite these advantages, challenges persist, including distinguishing ships from other structures like piers and managing high viewing angles that complicate object recognition. The deployment of deep learning techniques has revolutionized object detection, replacing traditional methods with models like R-CNN, Faster R-CNN, SSD, RefineDet, and YOLO. These algorithms enable precise localization and classification of various objects in diverse environments, enhancing security, autonomy, and surveillance systems. This study compares the performance of Faster R-CNN and YOLOv7 in ship detection from satellite images. Faster R-CNN, renowned for accuracy, employs a two-stage detection process, excelling in complex scenarios but at the cost of longer execution times. In contrast, YOLOv7, optimized for real-time applications, offers rapid detection by simultaneously predicting bounding boxes and class probabilities in a single pass. Evaluating these models involves analyzing metrics such as precision, recall, throughput, and execution speed, providing insights into their effectiveness across different operational requirements. The findings contribute to understanding the trade-offs between accuracy and speed in ship detection applications, guiding the selection and optimization of detection systems for maritime surveillance and security.

Keywords: Object Detection · Faster R-CNN · YOLOv7 · Satellite-based Monitoring

1 Introduction

Detecting moving targets on sea and ocean surfaces is crucial in many maritime areas. Monitoring the current locations of ships aids in regulating sea and port traffic, thereby preventing potential collisions [1]. Specifically, inspections of nearby ships are critical

A. Mirzazadeh et al. (Eds.): SEMIT 2024, CCIS 2444, pp. 51–66, 2026.
https://doi.org/10.1007/978-3-032-01948-6_4

for mitigating collision risks. Additionally, object detection enables swift responses in emergencies. Ship monitoring is also vital for environmental protection, preventing incidents like oil spills or waste discharge that could harm nature. Efficient control and usage of ports and sea lanes, coupled with enhanced port security, help prevent illegal activities such as smuggling [2]. However, detecting objects on sea surfaces presents challenges due to complex and dynamic factors like background color, waves, and lighting. Weather conditions, including cloud movement, fog formation, and air pollution, significantly impact satellite-based object detection. These variables decrease the accuracy of ship detection and lead to incorrect identifications.

Unmanned aerial vehicles (UAVs) and satellites are widely used as image sources in object detection applications [3–12]. These systems offer various advantages and disadvantages depending on usage scenarios and requirements. UAVs can focus on specific areas or targets, providing more detailed information, while satellites can cover wider areas, making them suitable for detecting larger objects. Due to their greater mobility, UAVs can be directed with agility when monitoring areas or targets [13–17]. However, UAVs have limited range and are unsuitable for long-distance detection. Additionally, harsh weather conditions can negatively affect UAV performance and hinder object detection. In contrast, satellites are not impacted by weather conditions and can conduct regular observations. Unlike UAVs, satellites can scan larger areas quickly without range limitations, allowing for continuous data collection and easier observation of long-term changes.

Satellites equipped with high-resolution cameras provide high-quality images, enhancing algorithm performance in real-time applications [18]. Detecting objects from satellite images significantly benefits various fields, including geographic data compilation for defense and military purposes, data updating, planning, observation, and port and ocean inspection and control. Low Earth Orbit (LEO) satellites, located closer to the Earth's surface, offer clearer, higher-resolution images compared to geostationary satellites [19]. Unlike fixed radar satellites, LEO satellites move quickly, allowing them to capture dynamic features of changing observation areas. Ship detection supported by satellites and aircraft has gained attention in sea surface observations due to its contributions to both military and civilian sectors. However, challenges arise from the resemblance of ships' rectangular and narrow structures to wooden piers in ports and the complexity of images from different positions and perspectives due to high viewing angles from space. Additionally, the small image size of target objects in satellite detection complicates object recognition [20]. Furthermore, the model and color of the ship are significant factors affecting detection accuracy.

The pre-processing phase addresses issues such as object detection and recognition, data entry inconsistencies, errors, and omissions, ensuring the data set is suitable for analysis. This phase involves defining and selecting attributes that facilitate the identification, explanation, and differentiation of elements within the data set. Finally, it encompasses two key concepts: clustering and classification [21]. In 2012, Krizhevsky and his colleagues [22] created a deep convolutional neural network, achieving significant success in large-scale image detection and classification. This milestone led to the replacement of traditional methods with deep learning techniques for target detection. With the rapid advancement of deep learning theory, object detection has progressed significantly, enabling the detection and precise localization of numerous objects and optionally classifying them. These objects can include sea, air, and land vehicles, as well as trees, animals, people, and various other items. Generally, the goal of object detection is to determine the final location and type of objects. Some of the most common detection algorithms include R-CNN [23], Faster R-CNN [24], SSD (Single Shot Detector) [25], Single Shot Refinement Neural Network for Object Detection (RefineDet) [26], and You Only Look Once (YOLO) [27–30]. These algorithms are applied in various fields such as autonomy, health, security, and surveillance. In security and surveillance, object detection identifies potential threats using security cameras and video surveillance systems, allowing for timely preventive measures. In autonomous applications, unmanned vehicle technologies rely on object detection to safely navigate their surroundings.

Various approaches have been developed to tackle ship detection challenge. Among these methods, convolutional neural networks (CNNs) have become the foundation for object detection algorithms. Faster R-CNN revolutionized object detection by integrating a Region Proposal Network (RPN) with a CNN, allowing the model to directly predict object proposals and refine them during the detection process. This innovation significantly reduced computation time and enhanced detection accuracy. Faster R-CNN has been successfully applied in various remote sensing and maritime contexts for ship detection. For instance, [31] demonstrated its utility in detecting ships from synthetic aperture radar (SAR) images, achieving robust detection even in complex environments such as congested harbors and under different weather conditions. Several other studies have explored the application of Faster R-CNN for ship detection in optical satellite images. [32] investigated the performance of Faster R-CNN in conjunction with multi-scale feature fusion techniques to detect small-scale and densely packed ships, showing notable improvements in detection accuracy compared to traditional methods. Similarly, [33] applied Faster R-CNN in a dataset containing ships in cluttered backgrounds, achieving impressive performance by employing anchor optimization strategies that accounted for the varying sizes and orientations of ships.

In addition to Faster R-CNN, there has been considerable interest in comparing its performance with other advanced object detection algorithms, such as the YOLO series. YOLO algorithms are known for their real-time processing capabilities and relatively faster inference times, making them suitable for applications requiring rapid ship detection, such as maritime surveillance and security operations. Although Faster R-CNN excels in detection accuracy, particularly in complex scenarios, the high computational demands may limit its use in real-time applications. Studies comparing Faster R-CNN with YOLO versions highlight these trade-offs. For instance, [13] compared Faster R-CNN and YOLOv7 for ship detection, finding that YOLOv7 offered faster processing speeds, while Faster R-CNN provided more accurate detections in cluttered scenes with small and overlapping objects. The need for continuous improvements in both accuracy and speed drives research in ship detection algorithms. Many studies focus on improving Faster R-CNN's efficiency by optimizing anchor boxes, feature extraction methods, and region proposal strategies. These developments aim to balance the algorithm's high precision with the growing demand for faster, real-time detection capabilities.

In the context of ship detection, YOLOv3 was one of the first versions to be extensively used, owing to its balance between speed and detection performance. For instance,

[34] employed YOLOv3 for detecting ships in optical satellite images and demonstrated the algorithm's capability to detect vessels of varying sizes and orientations, even in complex maritime environments with dynamic backgrounds such as waves or docks. The introduction of YOLOv4 further advanced the state of the art by incorporating CSPDarknet53 as its backbone and using advanced data augmentation techniques like Mosaic and DropBlock regularization. This improved the network's ability to detect small ships and distinguish them from cluttered backgrounds. Studies such as [35] applied YOLOv4 to ship detection in both optical and SAR images, noting that YOLOv4 outperformed other algorithms like SSD and Faster R-CNN in terms of detection speed, without a significant loss in accuracy. The real-time capabilities of YOLOv4 made it suitable for applications requiring rapid monitoring, such as in coastal defense and harbor management.

With the release of YOLOv7, the focus shifted toward optimizing the detection speed and efficiency even further while maintaining high accuracy. YOLOv7 introduced extended bag-of-freebies and bag-of-specials techniques, as well as model re-parameterization strategies to improve detection robustness. Studies comparing YOLOv7 with previous YOLO versions and other object detection algorithms have highlighted its superior performance in maritime contexts. For instance, [36] evaluated YOLOv7 for ship detection and found that it not only delivered faster inference times but also exhibited enhanced accuracy in detecting small ships and distinguishing them from complex backgrounds like harbors or crowded waterways. This makes YOLOv7 particularly effective for applications such as maritime traffic control and illegal fishing detection. Several studies have also focused on enhancing the performance of YOLO-based models for specific challenges in ship detection. [37] introduced an improved version of YOLOv7 by incorporating attention mechanisms and multi-scale feature fusion techniques to address the problem of detecting small or distant ships in high-resolution satellite images. Their results demonstrated that these modifications significantly improved detection performance in maritime surveillance tasks, where small vessels often go undetected by conventional models.

While recent studies have applied Faster R-CNN and YOLO models to various object detection tasks, including ship detection, there remains a gap in comparative analyses that evaluate their performance using a comprehensive dataset specifically tailored to the challenges of maritime environments. Most previous research either focuses on a single detection algorithm or uses limited datasets, which often lack diversity in ship size, background complexity, and environmental conditions. This limits the generalizability of the findings to real-world applications, especially in scenarios where varying atmospheric conditions, cluttered backgrounds, and diverse ship types exist. To address this gap, this study not only compares the performances of Faster R-CNN and YOLOv7 in detecting ships from satellite images but also introduces a novel, comprehensive dataset. This dataset was created by combining ship images from various satellite sources and maritime scenarios, providing a diverse range of conditions. Furthermore, it was enhanced using data augmentation techniques to improve the training process and better reflect the variability encountered in real-world environments. By evaluating the two algorithms with this enriched dataset, the study provides a detailed analysis of the trade-offs between Faster R-CNN's precision and recall and YOLOv7's real-time detection capabilities. In doing so, this research contributes to a deeper understanding of how these models perform in complex maritime settings and offers insights into their respective strengths and limitations for ship detection, filling an important gap in the literature.

2 Test Algorithms

2.1 Faster R-CNN

Faster R-CNN is a two-stage object detection method within a specific framework. The model comprises two main components: the Region Proposal Network (RPN) and the detection network. Instead of using a selective search algorithm on the feature map to determine region proposals, Faster R-CNN employs the RPN, which enhances accuracy and speed, eliminating the need for a selective search. This architecture removes the dependency on external region proposal methods by integrating the RPN. First, the image is processed by a convolutional neural network (CNN) to create a feature map. This feature map is then passed to the RPN, which recommends regions of interest (ROI). The RPN classifies each region proposal based on objectness scores using a sliding window approach across the convolutional layer. Anchor boxes are used to detect potential object locations of various sizes, enabling the detection of objects of different dimensions. These anchor boxes are then transformed into feature maps of equal dimensions through ROI pooling, which uses max pooling to reduce the spatial dimensions of the image. The feature maps produced by the ROI pooling layer are fed into a fully connected layer, which branches into two paths: a softmax classification layer for classifying multiple objects within the image, and a regression layer for generating bounding boxes. This process results in the final detection and classification of objects. This innovative deep learning algorithm, with its fast recognition and high detection sensitivity, is particularly effective for detecting ship targets, significantly improving detection performance.

In the RPN training illustrated in Fig. 1, bounding boxes are initially created on the image using the anchor mechanism. Each bounding box corresponds to a pixel in the feature map. CNN generates feature maps that represent different characteristics of the image. Bounding boxes are designed to encompass objects of various sizes and proportions. A series of boxes of different shapes and sizes are centered on each anchor. Non-maximum suppression is then applied to reduce overlapping boxes. During the training phase, a total of 2000 boxes are removed, though this number can vary during testing. These boxes are scored and sent to the detection network. The Intersection over Union (IOU) ratios of all bounding boxes are calculated, and labels for RPN classification are generated. These labels can be ‘ignore,’ ‘foreground,’ or ‘background.’ Labels, after removing the ignored class boxes, are used to calculate cross-entropy loss. The RPN also adjusts the center and size of the bounding boxes through bounding box regression, with targets set for this purpose. Calculating the necessary losses for backpropagation is essential. The distance vector from the center of the ground truth box to the bounding box is normalized by the size of the bounding box. Finally, the target size is determined for each bounding box.

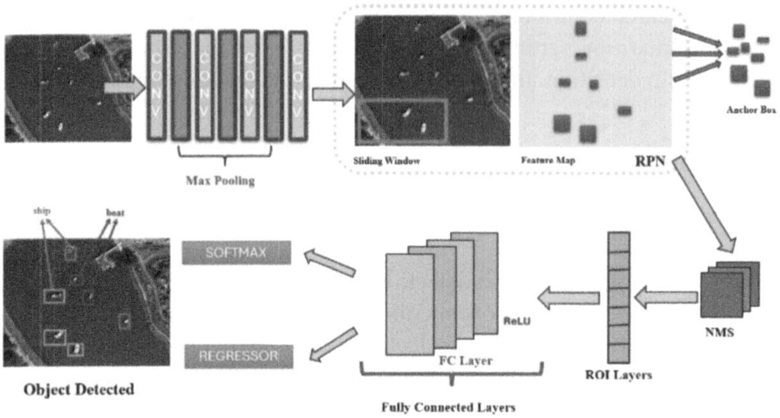

Fig. 1. Diagram showing the stages of RPN training

2.2 YOLOv7

The most widely used single-stage object detection algorithm in computer vision systems is the YOLO family. The YOLO algorithm has received great acclaim since its launch, with each version improving its performance. YOLO takes an image as input and uses a convolutional neural network for feature extraction and classification of objects in the image [38–42]. YOLOv7, based on the earlier YOLOv4, is a single-stage object detection algorithm that offers high performance and faster detection compared to two-stage object detectors. YOLOv7 provides superior object detection accuracy, outperforming all its predecessor models in the YOLO family. The model prefers to train the object detection algorithm offline using traditional methods to achieve higher accuracy without increasing inference costs.

YOLOv7 demonstrates its advanced structure with speed and accuracy ranging from 5 FPS to 160 FPS. Additionally, it has approximately 70% fewer parameters than YOLOv4, resulting in about 30% less computational cost. To ensure continuous improvement in the network's learning ability without distorting the original gradient path, YOLOv7 employs the Generalized Efficient Layer Aggregation Network (E-ELAN) for the computation block. E-ELAN enables the use of more parameters by combining multiple GIS networks.

In this study, the images used to train the Faster R-CNN and YOLOv7 algorithms were sourced from satellite images available on Google Earth. Recognizing that the quality of algorithm training directly impacts model performance, we ensured a diverse dataset by collecting ship images of various models and colors from different geographical locations. Special attention was given to include images with diverse backgrounds and challenging environmental conditions. The dataset comprised 3,694 images, containing a total of 8,592 distinct ship images, and was divided into training, validation, and test sets in the proportions of 70%, 10%, and 20%, respectively.

2.3 Dataset

The dataset used for this study was primarily composed of satellite images obtained from Google Earth, offering a broad view of maritime regions. These images provided diverse scenarios, including open waters, ports, and coastal areas, all of which were crucial for evaluating the performance of the ship detection algorithms. The spatial resolution of the images varied between 0.5 and 1.0 m per pixel, which is sufficient for detecting ships of various sizes, from large cargo vessels to smaller fishing boats. However, variations in image quality were encountered, particularly in regions where atmospheric conditions or lower satellite pass altitudes affected the clarity. Some images were slightly blurred or suffered from lighting inconsistencies, posing challenges for accurate ship detection.

One of the key aspects of the dataset was the variability in ship size and orientation. Ships ranged from small vessels of less than 10 m in length to large ships exceeding 300 m. This variability demanded the use of detection algorithms capable of capturing objects at different scales. The images also included ships in various states, such as moored in harbors or moving across open water, further complicating detection, especially in crowded areas or near coastlines where background clutter, such as docks and buildings, could obscure the ships.

Regarding data annotation, manual labeling of the dataset was performed to ensure accurate ground truth information. Each ship was annotated with bounding boxes, and detailed efforts were made to label even small or partially obscured vessels. One of the main challenges during the annotation process was distinguishing between closely spaced ships, especially in congested harbor areas, where ships often overlapped or appeared partially submerged due to water reflection. Additionally, labeling small vessels in regions with dynamic backgrounds, such as ocean waves or piers, required precise annotations to avoid false positives or missed detections.

3 Results

Examining Fig. 2, the first image shows that Faster R-CNN successfully detects two ships in the middle of the sea. However, it includes the wakes left by the ships within the bounding boxes. This inclusion of wakes indicates that while the algorithm can identify ships, it struggles with differentiating between the actual ship and the water disturbance caused by its movement. The detection of the wakes within the bounding boxes suggests a need for further refinement in the algorithm's ability to accurately delineate the boundaries of the ships themselves. The second image presents a different set of challenges. While the algorithm detects ships at sea without issue, it fails to identify ships positioned near the shore. This failure is primarily due to the similar colors of the ships blending with the background and challenges related to image quality. The ships near the shore have colors that closely match the surrounding land and water, making them difficult for the algorithm to distinguish. This issue highlights the importance of contrast and image clarity in successful object detection. However, the algorithm successfully achieves its goal by accurately detecting ships on land where the image quality is sufficient, demonstrating its potential in more controlled conditions.

In the third image, the algorithm consistently detects all six ships present. This image demonstrates the algorithm's ability to handle the challenge of detecting adjacent ships with similar colors without any disadvantage. The consistent detection across all six ships indicates that the algorithm performs well in scenarios where the ships are clearly distinguishable from their background and each other, even when they are closely positioned. Moving to the fourth image, the algorithm successfully detects ships near the shore despite challenging conditions where the background tones closely match the ship colors. Additionally, two medium-sized ships side by side are detected separately, showcasing the algorithm's capability to distinguish between multiple targets in close proximity. However, the detection of small ships near the shore is less accurate, with some small ships being grouped into a single bounding box. This results in incorrect detection and underscores the difficulty the algorithm faces in accurately identifying smaller objects in complex backgrounds.

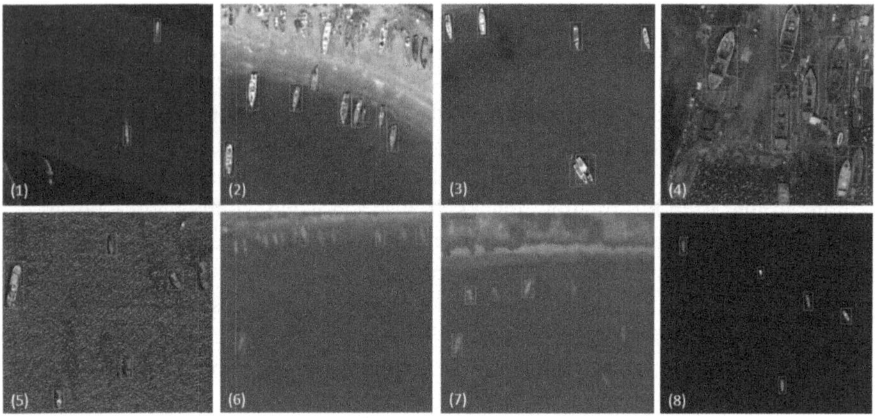

Fig. 2. Some examples of ship detection with Faster R-CNN

In the fifth image, the algorithm demonstrates its robustness by successfully detecting a total of six ships despite the wavy sea background. The dynamic and textured background presents a significant challenge, yet the algorithm manages to accurately identify the ships. However, a smaller ship blending with the background due to its color similarity remains undetected. This missed detection indicates that while the algorithm can handle larger and more prominent objects, it still struggles with smaller targets that do not stand out against the background. In the subsequent images, atmospheric pollution causes image distortion with a haze-like structure, reducing visibility. As a result, only ships that are more clearly visible in the image due to weather conditions are detected. This limitation highlights the algorithm's sensitivity to environmental factors such as haze and pollution, which can significantly impact the clarity and quality of the images being analyzed. The reduced visibility due to atmospheric conditions poses a challenge for the algorithm, affecting its detection accuracy.

In the final image, the algorithm excels by correctly detecting all ships, including the smallest one. This comprehensive detection demonstrates the algorithm's potential when operating under optimal conditions with high image quality and clear distinction between objects and their background. The successful identification of even the smallest ship indicates that the algorithm is capable of high precision in favorable scenarios. The analysis of ship detection using Faster R-CNN across various images reveals several strengths and areas for improvement. The algorithm shows strong performance in detecting ships under ideal conditions with clear image quality and distinct object-background contrast. However, it faces challenges in accurately identifying smaller ships, distinguishing ships near the shore with similar background colors, and operating under adverse environmental conditions such as haze and atmospheric pollution. These insights highlight the need for further refinement and optimization of the algorithm to enhance its robustness and accuracy across diverse scenarios. Enhancements could include improving the training dataset to cover a wider variety of conditions, refining the algorithm to better handle complex backgrounds, and developing techniques to mitigate the impact of environmental factors on image quality.

In the first example of detection images using YOLOv7 shown in Fig. 3, the algorithm draws bounding boxes around the ships, but these boxes appear larger than necessary, encompassing the waves caused by the ship movement. This indicates a difficulty in accurately delineating the exact boundaries of the ships, potentially leading to inflated detection areas that include non-relevant elements like water disturbances. Furthermore, the algorithm mistakenly detects a rock visible in the lower left part of the image as a ship. This misidentification highlights a challenge in distinguishing between objects with similar shapes or textures within the environment, suggesting a need for improved training or more nuanced detection criteria. In the second image, YOLOv7 fails to detect ships positioned on land due to the color similarities with the background. The blending of ship colors with the surrounding terrain makes it difficult for the algorithm to differentiate the ships from their background. Although ships on the sea surface are detected, two adjacent ships with similar tones are incorrectly identified as a single ship. This issue of grouping adjacent objects with similar appearances indicates that the algorithm struggles with separating objects that are close together and share similar features.

Moving to image number three, YOLOv7 correctly detects four ships. However, it incorrectly groups two adjacent ships at the bottom of the image as one ship. This recurring issue of grouping adjacent ships highlights a limitation in the algorithm's ability to distinguish between multiple, closely positioned objects. This can lead to underreporting of the number of ships and inaccurate location data, which could be problematic for practical applications requiring precise object counts and locations. In the fourth example, only two ships are fully detected by the algorithm. Detecting ships on land proves particularly challenging due to the matching background and ship colors, resulting in some ships not being detected at all. Additionally, the bounding box of one detected ship partially covers another, leading to an overlap that could confuse interpretation. Two adjacent ships in the lower right are again mistaken as a single ship, and smaller ships along the coastline are not detected. These issues underscore the difficulty YOLOv7 faces in complex environments with closely matching colors and varying object sizes.

In image number five, YOLOv7 fails to detect four ships, possibly due to the wavy sea background and partial color compatibility with the ships. The dynamic and textured nature of the sea background, combined with the color similarity between the ships and the sea, poses a significant challenge for the algorithm. This failure to detect multiple ships indicates that the algorithm's performance is heavily influenced by the environmental context and the visual distinctiveness of the objects. In the sixth and seventh images, hazy and poor-quality images caused by air pollution significantly impair YOLOv7's performance. The algorithm struggles under these harsh weather conditions, resulting in poor detection accuracy. In the seventh image, only one ship is detected, highlighting the severe impact of environmental degradation on the algorithm's effectiveness. The reduced visibility and image clarity due to air pollution make it difficult for YOLOv7 to identify and delineate ships accurately.

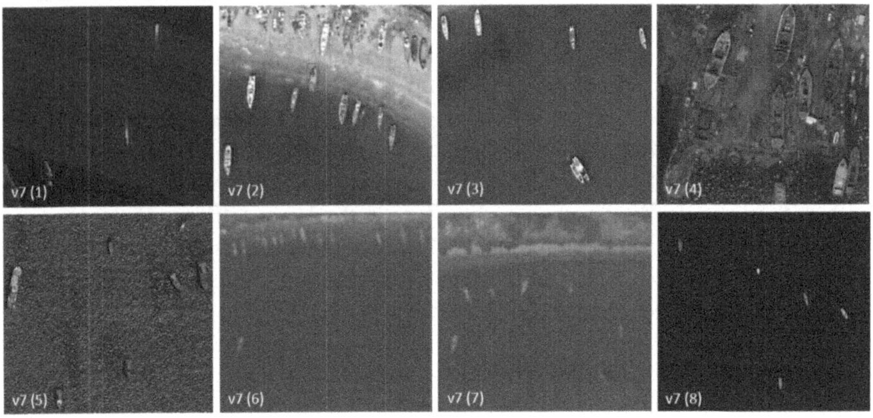

Fig. 3. Some examples of ship detection with YOLOv7

In the final image, YOLOv7 performs well, providing accurate bounding boxes around the ships. However, it fails to detect a small ship that was identified by the Faster R-CNN algorithm. This miss indicates that while YOLOv7 is capable of high accuracy under optimal conditions, it still has limitations in detecting smaller or less visually distinct objects. The comparison with Faster R-CNN's performance suggests that different algorithms may have varying strengths and weaknesses, necessitating a combined approach or further enhancements for comprehensive object detection. The detailed examination of YOLOv7's performance across various images reveals several key insights into its capabilities and limitations. While the algorithm demonstrates strong performance in detecting larger and more visually distinct ships, it faces challenges with accurately delineating ship boundaries, distinguishing closely positioned ships, and detecting smaller ships, especially in complex or degraded environmental conditions. These findings highlight the need for continued refinement and optimization of YOLOv7 to enhance its robustness and accuracy. Potential improvements could include augmenting the training dataset with a broader variety of scenarios, fine-tuning the algorithm to better handle complex backgrounds and similar object colors, and developing methods to mitigate the impact of environmental factors such as haze and pollution on detection accuracy.

The comparative performance metrics of Faster R-CNN and YOLOv7, as summarized in Table 1, shed light on the distinct strengths and weaknesses of each algorithm. Faster R-CNN outperforms YOLOv7 in several key areas, demonstrating superior precision, recall, mean average precision (mAP), and F1 score. These metrics collectively highlight Faster R-CNN's robust capability to accurately identify and classify ships in various scenarios. Faster R-CNN's higher precision signifies its proficiency in minimizing false positive detections. This means that when the algorithm identifies a ship, it is more likely to be correct compared to YOLOv7. This attribute is particularly crucial in applications where the cost of false positives is high, such as in automated monitoring systems that trigger alerts or actions based on detections.

Table 1. Performance comparison of Faster R-CNN and YOLOv7 algorithms

Metric	Faster R-CNN	YOLOv7
Precision	0.879	0.803
Recall	0.817	0.755
mAP	0.803	0.776
F1 Score	0.846	0.778
Detection Time	53.4	21.6

The superior recall metric of Faster R-CNN indicates its effectiveness in capturing a greater proportion of actual ships within the dataset, thereby reducing false negatives. High recall is essential in applications where missing a ship could have significant consequences, such as in search and rescue operations or military surveillance. The higher mAP achieved by Faster R-CNN reflects its balanced performance across various precision-recall thresholds. This comprehensive measure underscores the algorithm's reliability and consistency in diverse detection scenarios, ensuring it can maintain high performance even as detection criteria are varied. Combining both precision and recall, the F1 score of Faster R-CNN is higher than that of YOLOv7. This balance is critical for applications where both minimizing false positives and maximizing true positives are equally important.

These strengths make Faster R-CNN an excellent choice for scenarios where detection accuracy is paramount, such as detailed image analysis, high-stakes surveillance, and tasks requiring precise object classification. In contrast, YOLOv7 excels significantly in terms of inference time efficiency, processing images much faster than Faster R-CNN. Specifically, YOLOv7 processes images in just 21.6 s compared to Faster R-CNN's 53.4 s. This remarkable speed allows YOLOv7 to detect ships more than twice as fast as Faster R-CNN, making it particularly suitable for real-time or near-real-time applications where rapid image processing is critical. While YOLOv7's rapid inference time is a significant advantage, it comes with a trade-off of slightly lower precision, recall, mAP, and F1 score metrics. This means that while YOLOv7 can process images quickly, its detections might be less accurate compared to Faster R-CNN. The speed advantage, however, is invaluable in scenarios that demand quick decision-making, such as autonomous navigation systems, real-time monitoring and tracking, and time-sensitive surveillance tasks.

In applications where the speed of processing is crucial, such as in autonomous vehicles or UAVs that need to make instant navigational decisions based on detected objects, YOLOv7's faster processing time can significantly enhance operational efficiency. Despite the slight reduction in detection accuracy, the rapid response capability provided by YOLOv7 can be a decisive factor in its favor. Choosing between Faster R-CNN and YOLOv7 depends largely on the specific requirements of the application at hand. For tasks that require meticulous object detection and classification, where every detection needs to be highly reliable, Faster R-CNN is the preferred choice. Its higher precision and recall ensure that it minimizes false positives and negatives, providing a more trustworthy detection performance.

Conversely, for applications where processing speed is critical and can significantly impact operational outcomes, YOLOv7 is more suitable. The ability to quickly process and respond to incoming data streams makes it ideal for dynamic environments where decisions need to be made in real-time. The decision to use Faster R-CNN or YOLOv7 should be guided by the specific demands of the application. Faster R-CNN offers unparalleled accuracy, making it ideal for detailed and high-stakes detection tasks, whereas YOLOv7 provides the speed necessary for real-time applications despite a slight compromise in accuracy. Balancing these factors allows for an optimal selection tailored to the unique requirements of each use case, ensuring both effective and efficient object detection.

3.1 Error Analysis and Model Limitations

A detailed error analysis was conducted to better understand the limitations of the models, particularly YOLOv7, in ship detection tasks. The primary types of misdetections encountered were false positives and false negatives, both of which affected the overall accuracy of the model under different conditions. False Positives occurred primarily in environments with complex backgrounds, such as ports and harbors, where objects like docks, piers, and even large coastal structures were sometimes misclassified as ships. This was particularly evident in images where the shapes of non-ship objects resembled vessels or where lighting and shadow effects created ship-like patterns on the water surface. Atmospheric pollution, such as haze or fog, further exacerbated this issue by distorting the appearance of the surroundings, leading the model to incorrectly identify objects as ships.

False Negatives were more common when detecting smaller ships, especially those located in open water or partially occluded by other objects. YOLOv7, while highly efficient in detecting large vessels, occasionally failed to detect small boats due to their reduced pixel size in the satellite images. In cases where the ships were less than 10 m long, their size was often too small for the model to accurately capture, particularly when they were located in areas with cluttered backgrounds or in low-contrast situations, such as overcast conditions or heavy wave activity. Additionally, ships located near the edges of images were sometimes missed due to distortions or lower resolution in those regions. The model also encountered difficulties in detecting ships under certain atmospheric conditions, such as during hazy weather or in regions with significant pollution. The presence of atmospheric particles often degraded the image quality, reducing contrast and clarity, which in turn affected the model's ability to accurately identify the ships. In some cases, ships that appeared partially occluded by haze were either misdetected or not detected at all, highlighting the sensitivity of the model to atmospheric interference.

Several factors contributed to these misdetections. First, the resolution of the satellite images, while generally adequate for detecting larger vessels, sometimes limited the ability to capture fine details for smaller ships. This resolution limitation was particularly noticeable in open waters, where there were fewer contextual features to assist the model in distinguishing ships from background noise. Second, YOLOv7's anchor box settings, optimized for larger objects, might not have been perfectly suited for detecting smaller ships, which are often compact and harder to differentiate from the surrounding environment. Lastly, variability in lighting conditions, shadows, and reflections off the water surface introduced further complexity, leading to occasional errors in ship identification. To mitigate these issues, future work could involve optimizing the anchor box sizes for detecting smaller objects, incorporating multi-scale detection strategies, or using additional data augmentation techniques to simulate diverse atmospheric and lighting conditions. Despite these limitations, YOLOv7's overall performance remained robust, especially in detecting medium to large vessels, making it highly suitable for real-time maritime surveillance applications where speed is a critical factor.

4 Conclusion

This study offers a comprehensive evaluation of the Faster R-CNN and YOLOv7 algorithms for ship detection from satellite images, focusing on their performance under various challenging conditions. Results indicate that Faster R-CNN achieves superior detection accuracy, particularly in precision, recall, mAP, and F1 score metrics. The model consistently identifies and classifies ships even in complex scenarios involving similar background colors and adjacent ships. However, it shows limitations in detecting smaller ships and ships obscured by poor image quality due to atmospheric conditions. In contrast, YOLOv7 excels in detection speed, making it well-suited for real-time or near-real-time applications where fast processing is critical. Despite its lower detection accuracy compared to Faster R-CNN, YOLOv7 demonstrates significantly faster inference times while maintaining adequate performance across most scenarios. This trade-off between detection accuracy and inference speed underscores the importance of aligning the algorithm choice with specific application requirements. While Faster R-CNN shines in tasks demanding high precision and recall, YOLOv7 proves more suitable for applications prioritizing speed. Overall, this study emphasizes the need to balance accuracy and efficiency in developing effective ship detection systems for satellite imagery.

4.1 Future Improvements and Model Refinement

While YOLOv7 and Faster R-CNN have demonstrated strong performance in this study, there is significant potential for further refinement to optimize both speed and accuracy. One promising direction for future work is exploring model fusion techniques, where the strengths of different architectures are combined. For instance, a hybrid model could leverage the fast detection capabilities of YOLOv7 for real-time ship detection while utilizing the more accurate, region-based approach of Faster R-CNN for refining bounding box placement and handling smaller or more challenging objects. Such an approach could achieve a better balance between speed and detection precision, especially in complex maritime environments. Another area for improvement is experimenting with different backbone networks and multi-scale feature fusion strategies. Using more advanced architectures like EfficientNet or ResNeXt as backbones could help improve detection accuracy without significantly compromising speed. Incorporating attention mechanisms to focus the model on relevant regions in the image could also enhance performance, particularly for detecting smaller ships or objects that are partially obscured by background clutter.

Additionally, incorporating knowledge distillation or model pruning techniques could allow for the deployment of more lightweight models that retain high accuracy but have reduced computational requirements, making them more suitable for real-time applications on resource-constrained platforms like UAVs. Future research could also focus on data augmentation techniques to address some of the challenges encountered in this study, such as atmospheric conditions, lighting variations, and image quality inconsistencies. Augmenting the dataset with synthetic images or applying domain adaptation methods could improve the model's robustness in varying conditions. By exploring these potential improvements, the detection performance of YOLOv7 and Faster R-CNN could be enhanced, leading to more accurate and efficient ship detection models suitable for real-world maritime monitoring applications.

References

1. Kong, M.C., et al.: Object detection method for ship safety plans using deep learning. Ocean Eng. **246**(110587) (2022)
2. Chen, Z., et al.: Deep learning for autonomous ship-oriented small ship detection. Saf. Sci. **130**(104812) (2020)
3. Guo, H., Yang, X., Wang, N., Gao, X.: A CenterNet++ model for ship detection in SAR images. Pattern Recogn. **112**(107787) (2021)
4. Deng, Z., Sun, H., Zhou, S., Zhao, J., Lei, L.: Multi-scale object detection in remote sensing imagery with convolutional neural networks. ISPRS J. Photogramm. Remote. Sens. **145**, 3–22 (2018)
5. Bakirci, M.: Smart city air quality management through leveraging drones for precision monitoring. Sustain. Cities Soc. **106**(105390) (2024). https://doi.org/10.1016/j.scs.2024.105390
6. Wu, Z., Wang, X.F., Zou, L., Xu, L.X., Li, X.L., Weise, T.: Hierarchical object detection for very high-resolution satellite images. Appl. Soft Comput. **113**(107885) (2021). https://doi.org/10.1016/j.asoc.2021.107885
7. Bakirci, M.: Enhancing air pollution mapping with autonomous UAV networks for extended coverage and consistency. Atmos. Res. **306**(107480) (2024). https://doi.org/10.1016/j.atmosres.2024.107480
8. Bakirci, M.: Efficient air pollution mapping in extensive regions with fully autonomous unmanned aerial vehicles: a numerical perspective. Sci. Total Environ. **909**(168606) (2024). https://doi.org/10.1016/j.scitotenv.2023.168606

9. Azam, B., et al.: Aircraft detection in satellite imagery using deep learning-based object detectors. Microprocess. Microsyst. **94**(104630) (2022). https://doi.org/10.1016/j.micpro.2022.104630
10. Cheng, G., Han, J.: A survey on object detection in optical remote sensing images. ISPRS J. Photogramm. Remote. Sens. **117**, 11–28 (2016). https://doi.org/10.1016/j.isprsjprs.2016.03.014
11. Segal-Rozenhaimer, M., Li, A., Das, K., Chirayath, V.: Cloud detection algorithm for multimodal satellite imagery using convolutional neural-networks (CNN). Remote Sens. Environ. **237**(111446) (2020). https://doi.org/10.1016/j.rse.2019.111446
12. Jin, X., Davis, C.H.: Vehicle detection from high-resolution satellite imagery using morphological shared-weight neural networks. Image Vis. Comput. **25**(9), 1422–1431 (2007). https://doi.org/10.1016/j.imavis.2006.12.011
13. Escorcia-Gutierrez, J., Gamarra, M., Beleño, K., Soto, C., Mansour, R.F.: Intelligent deep learning-enabled autonomous small ship detection and classification model. Comput. Electr. Eng. **100**(107871) (2022)
14. Bakirci, M.: A drone-based approach to enhance spatial insight into surrounding air pollutant distributions for healthier indoor environments. J. Build. Eng. **87**(109023) (2024). https://doi.org/10.1016/j.jobe.2024.109023
15. Asadzadeh, S., de Oliveira, W.J., de Souza Filho, C.R.: UAV-based remote sensing for the petroleum industry and environmental monitoring: State-of-the-art and perspectives. J. Petrol. Sci. Eng. **208**(109633) (2022). https://doi.org/10.1016/j.petrol.2021.109633
16. Yang, Z., et al.: UAV remote sensing applications in marine monitoring: knowledge visualization and review. Sci. Total Environ. **838**(155939) (2022). https://doi.org/10.1016/j.scitotenv.2022.155939
17. Bakirci, M.: Evaluating the impact of unmanned aerial vehicles (UAVs) on air quality management in smart cities: a comprehensive analysis of transportation-related pollution. Comput. Electr. Eng. **119**(109556) (2024). https://doi.org/10.1016/j.compeleceng.2024.109556
18. Zhang, Y., Li, Q.Z., Zang, F.N.: Ship detection for visual maritime surveillance from non-stationary platforms. Ocean Eng. **141**, 53–63 (2017)
19. Cheng, S., Zhu, Y., Wu, S.: Deep learning based efficient ship detection from drone-captured images for maritime surveillance. Ocean Eng. **285**(115440) (2023)
20. Zhang, T., Zhang, X., Shi, J., Wei, S.: HyperLi-Net: a hyper-light deep learning network for high-accurate and high-speed ship detection from synthetic aperture radar imagery. ISPRS J. Photogramm. Remote. Sens. **167**, 123–153 (2020)
21. Zhang, T., Zhang, X., Liu, C., Shi, J., Wei, S., et al.: Balance learning for ship detection from synthetic aperture radar remote sensing imagery. ISPRS J. Photogramm. Remote. Sens. **182**, 190–207 (2021)
22. Zhao, S., Luo, Y., Zhang, T., Guo, W., Zhang, Z.: A domain specific knowledge extraction transformer method for multisource satellite-borne SAR images ship detection. ISPRS J. Photogramm. Remote. Sens. **198**, 16–29 (2023)
23. Huang, G., Wan, Z., Liu, X., Hui, J., Wang, Z.: Ship detection based on squeeze excitation skip-connection path networks for optical remote sensing images. Neurocomputing **332**, 215–223 (2019)
24. Chen, X., Wang, M., Ling, J., Wu, H., Wu, B.: Ship imaging trajectory extraction via an aggregated you only look once (YOLO) model. Eng. Appl. Artif. Intell. **130**(107742) (2024)
25. Yu, C., Shin, Y.: SAR ship detection based on improved YOLOv5 and BiFPN. ICT Express **10**(1), 28–33 (2024)
26. Gao, G., Bai, Q., Zhang, C., Zhang, L., Yao, L.: Dualistic cascade convolutional neural network dedicated to fully PolSAR image ship detection. ISPRS J. Photogramm. Remote. Sens. **202**, 663–681 (2023)

27. Bakirci, M.: Real-time vehicle detection using YOLOv8-nano for intelligent transportation systems. Traitement du Sig. **41**(4), 1727–1740 (2024). https://doi.org/10.18280/ts.410407
28. Ji, S.J., Ling, Q.H., Han, F.: An improved algorithm for small object detection based on YOLO v4 and multi-scale contextual information. Comput. Electr. Eng. **105**(108490) (2023). https://doi.org/10.1016/j.compeleceng.2022.108490
29. Lou, X., Liu, Y., Xiong, Z., Wang, H.: Generative knowledge transfer for ship detection in SAR images. Comput. Electr. Eng. **101**(108041) (2022)
30. Bakirci, M., Bayraktar, I.: Refining transportation automation with convolutional neural network-based vehicle detection via UAVs. In: 2024 International Russian Automation Conference (RusAutoCon), pp. 150–155. Sochi, Russian Federation (2024). https://doi.org/10.1109/RusAutoCon61949.2024.10694108
31. Liu, R.W., Yuan, W., Chen, X., Lu, Y.: An enhanced CNN-enabled learning method for promoting ship detection in maritime surveillance system. Ocean Eng. **235**(109435) (2021)
32. Altarez, R.D.: Faster R–CNN, RetinaNet and single shot detector in different ResNet backbones for marine vessel detection using cross polarization C-band SAR imagery. Remote Sens. Appl.: Soc. Environ. **36**(101297) (2024)
33. Zeng, L., Sun, B., Zhu, D.: Underwater target detection based on Faster R-CNN and adversarial occlusion network. Eng. Appl. Artif. Intell. **100**(104190) (2021)
34. Chen, X., Wang, M., Ling, J., Wu, H., Wu, B., Li, C.: Ship imaging trajectory extraction via an aggregated you only look once (YOLO) model. Eng. Appl. Artif. Intell. **130**(107742) (2024)
35. Chen, Z., Chen, D., Zhang, Y., Cheng, X., Zhang, M., Wu, C.: Deep learning for autonomous ship-oriented small ship detection. Saf. Sci. **130**(104812) (2020)
36. Yu, C., Shin, Y.: An efficient YOLO for ship detection in SAR images via channel shuffled reparameterized convolution blocks and dynamic head. ICT Express **10**(3), 673–679 (2024)
37. Bakirci, M.: Utilizing YOLOv8 for enhanced traffic monitoring in intelligent transportation systems (ITS) applications. Digit. Sig. Process. **152**(104594) (2024). https://doi.org/10.1016/j.dsp.2024.104594
38. Bakirci, M.: A novel swarm unmanned aerial vehicle system: incorporating autonomous flight, real-time object detection, and coordinated intelligence for enhanced performance. Traitement du Sig. **40**(5), 2063–2078 (2023). https://doi.org/10.18280/ts.400524
39. Lu, S., Wang, B., Wang, H., Chen, L., Linjian, M., Zhang, X.: A real-time object detection algorithm for video. Comput. Electr. Eng. **77**, 398–408 (2019). https://doi.org/10.1016/j.compeleceng.2019.05.009
40. Rizvi, S.Z., Jamil, M., Huang, W.: Enhanced defect detection on wind turbine blades using binary segmentation masks and YOLO. Comput. Electr. Eng. **120**(109615) (2024). https://doi.org/10.1016/j.compeleceng.2024.109615
41. Bakirci, M.: Enhancing vehicle detection in intelligent transportation systems via autonomous UAV platform and YOLOv8 integration. Appl. Soft Comput. **164**(112015) (2024). https://doi.org/10.1016/j.asoc.2024.112015
42. Wu, D., Lv, S., Jiang, M., Song, H.: Using channel pruning-based YOLO v4 deep learning algorithm for the real-time and accurate detection of apple flowers in natural environments. Comput. Electron. Agric. **178**(105742) (2020). https://doi.org/10.1016/j.compag.2020.105742

Developing a National-Level Strategic Management Model for Cybersecurity

Fereidoon Bidollahkhany[1] (✉) and Mehdi Basiri[2]

[1] Faculty of Business Administration, Karabük University, Karabük, Türkiye
fbidollahkhany@karabuk.edu.tr

[2] Faculty of Social Sciences, Command and Staff University, Tehran, Iran

Abstract. The ever-increasing expansion of cyberspace has led to the migration of numerous economic, social, political, and cultural activities into the digital realm. Consequently, we are witnessing a significant influx of data from government and public centers, organizations, businesses, and even private individuals into cyberspace. In response, governments are developing foundational strategies and solutions to protect information and preserve data assets. This research aims to develop a strategic management model for cybersecurity at the national level to safeguard cyber information. The study is practical in its purpose, employing a data foundation methodology. To achieve the research objective, relevant documents and scientific literature were analyzed using qualitative content analysis and MAXQDA software. The study identified and extracted the basic concepts and themes of the research paradigm model across five dimensions: background, causal and intervening conditions, consequences, and strategies. The model was refined and validated through consultations with 15 cybersecurity experts and focus group discussions. The result is a comprehensive strategic management model designed to enhance national cybersecurity.

Keywords: Strategic Management · Cyber Security · Data Protection · National Security

1 Introduction

The movement of countries towards modernization has led to the creation of the fourth industrial revolution. In recent decades, especially in the last five years, the world has undergone significant changes and has fundamentally changed many of the previous relationships and equations, which is growing with the focus on cyber-space. In international circles, there is often talk about the possibility of cyberattacks. The use of cyber weapons can be attractive as a cheap tool for militarily weaker countries and also for terrorist groups. The threat of cyber-attacks is so serious that the North Atlantic Treaty Organization (NATO) has "turned cyberspace into a battle-field" in the new version of its strategies. This shows that cybersecurity has been considered as an important issue due to the rapid growth of digital technology in modern countries worldwide.

Today, the cyberspace forms an important aspect of the global ecosystem. Countries as the main players in the cyber arena have many capacities in terms of cyber security.

A. Mirzazadeh et al. (Eds.): SEMIT 2024, CCIS 2444, pp. 67–87, 2026.
https://doi.org/10.1007/978-3-032-01948-6_5

However, the nature of cyber technologies is such that due to the simplicity, high availability and low cost of these types of technologies, the methods of maintaining security in these systems quickly become ineffective and pose a challenge to their security.

Strong cybersecurity can help support the exercise of human rights, foster economic growth, and help achieve sustainable development goals. However, the increased reliance on digital technologies and the digital and physical convergence has brought about new cyber threats to states businesses, and individuals – online and offline. As a result, there's been a rise in measures to address these threats, manifested in a growing number of cybersecurity-related frameworks (National-Cybersecurity-Strategies-Lessons-learned-and-reflections 2022).

The development, implementation and review of a national cyber security strategy are influenced by a range of elements and played out by various stakeholders. The scope, principles and content outlined in a national cyber security strategy can be addressed in greater detail in political strategic documents, national and international laws, regulations, organizational and administrative measures, such as communication and crisis management procedures within a State, but also in purely technical protection standards. (Tallin 2013).

Cyber technology is changing the traditional concepts of military and civilian security, as cyberspace removes the meaning of national borders. Cyberspace should not be seen only from a technological point of view, but as a phenomenon that has an increasing impact on our daily lives and the functioning of our societies. Cyber capabilities have changed the actors in the global power system. From now on, cyber-attacks and anti-cyber measures will be part of the national defense systems and military doctrine of the countries (Aluede and Biragbara 2020). Currently, the vital infrastructures of many countries are becoming more dependent on information technology for the development of their activities, and in return, the unintentional vulnerability of governments to cyber-attacks and threats is also in-creasing. The center of the information and cyber space in the national power structures, although it causes a significant increase in efficiency, flexibility, innovation and transformation, but on the other hand, it can also be a major weakness, in such a way that the neglect of adopting macro strategies in the field Cyber defense will cause irreparable damage to vital infrastructures as centers of gravity. Therefore, taking action to ensure cyber security by organizations ensures that despite the release of data and information, they have kept their cyber assets safe from various risks. However, despite the growing body of research on cybersecurity, there remains a critical gap in understanding the specific strategic components necessary for managing cybersecurity at a high level. Existing studies often focus on technical aspects, while comprehensive frameworks for strategic cybersecurity management remain underdeveloped. This article, with a qualitative approach, seeks to identify the components that influence cyberspace security management at a strategic level.

2 Theoretical Foundations and Research Background

At the semantic level, cyberspace is an imaginary space between computer networks. In the virtual space, people and users communicate with each other in social networks, chat environments, stores, etc., without having any movement. Cyberspace is used to describe any concept that is used in connection with computer networks, information technology, the internet, and information society, and the people and users of this space have a social experience of interaction, exchange, and sharing of information, business, games and entertainment, group discussions that It is non-physical, they can be found. This exciting attraction has linked a person to a mental concept that is tied to imagination and illusion and takes reality into the mind and changes or recreates it in any way it wants, without being affected by material limitations. Cyberspace is something beyond the Internet and the Internet is expanding this concept. With the formation of cyberspace and its rapid growth, the concepts of the life field are also taking steps toward substantial change. Everything from identity, culture, governance, relationships, and private and group interactions are changing. Cyberspace is one of the features of modern life where people and communities around the world are connected and socialize and cooperate (Defense 2012). Cyberspace can be imagined as many layers of activities, but the simple and basic perception depicts it as a unique composite regime of physical and virtual characteristics. According to (Castells 2000) the rise of the network society has fundamentally transformed the way individuals and organizations interact. Cyberspace has evolved from a mere communication tool to a complex ecosystem that influences economic, social, and cultural dynamics globally. This transformation is driven by advancements in technology and the increasing integration of digital platforms into everyday life, and as noted by (Rheingold 1993), cyberspace has significantly impacted social structures by enabling new forms of community and social interaction. Virtual communities, formed through shared interests and goals, transcend geographical boundaries and create new social norms and behaviors. This shift challenges traditional notions of community and identity, leading to a redefinition of social relationships in the digital age.

2.1 Theoretical Foundations

Cybersecurity Cyber security is defined as a set of security tools, policies, concepts and guidelines, risk management approaches, measures, training, best practices, and technologies that can protect the assets of organizations and users in the cyber environment (Kagalwalla and Churi 2019, September).

Types of Cyber War

Cyber Infiltration. It means creating a breach in a system with software control in such a way that the system can be attacked, invaded and manipulated. A method of intrusion and cyber-attack is to enter large amounts of information into a system, which causes the over-flow of system information and the collapse of the corresponding network (Ullah and Babar 2019).

Cyber Manipulation. Following cyber infiltration, taking control of systems through related software, and using them to cause harm and damage to the system is called cyber manipulation. For example, using software tools to shut down systems and disrupt networks is an example of cyber manipulation.

Cyber-Attack. After a successful cyber intrusion, destroying software and data in a system or at-tacking the system in such a way that its efficiency is destroyed is called a cyber-attack. This attack also includes sending viruses that overload the system through electronic mail.

Cyber Tampering. Following a successful cyber intrusion, any manipulation or taking possession of the information of a system that leads to the transfer, destruction or change of its information is called cyber tampering. For example, stealing e-mail or obtaining a list of passwords from an e-mail service provider (Ohlin et al. 2015).

Cyber Deterrence Deterrence is one of the basic dimensions of cyber defense, which creates a strong mental barrier for opponents to make the perpetrators of the attack

Table 1. A comparative study of countries in the field of cyber security.

Country	Vision	Goals	Mission	Strategy	Actions	Structure
America	The relationship between vision and values is specified	Offensiveotargets is also mentioned	Paying attention to non-agent defense	Paying attention to elitism on the part of the Ministry of Defense in the cyber field	- Cyberspace health index - Creating a national warning network	Cyber defense is overseen by the military, and some by Homeland Security - Close cooperation between defense and internal security - America's security is dependent on people's intelligence
NATO				-Cyber Defense Priority -Increased cyber security -International Interactions to Allies		
England	Creating a reference for informing the public	Government has the role of coordinating and accompanying strategies rather than direct interference		Special attention to the security of the business environment and not mentioning defense policies,		

(*continued*)

Table 1. *(continued)*

Country	Vision	Goals	Mission	Strategy	Actions	Structure
Australia		Attention to the serious role of people in creating security	Guiding principles: strong leadership to manage this space at the national level			Presence of the private sector in the creation of security along with security departments
South Korea	In terms of digital government: -the best country in the world -hopeful -Coordinated with other countries	How many defenses: -layer: Gate -V. I -SP and users		Cultivation of cyber security		
Austria	Internet eye disease			Active participation -Multinational -Cyber exercises	Upgrade views, Interdisciplinary in security research and operations -Executive,	
European Union				Promoting interaction and coordination between the actions of the military and civilian sectors in the union emphasizes the exchange of best experience, information and exchange and advanced awareness of responses to threats, and evaluation threats	Industry market boom: 1-development of cryptography 2-promotion standards ,industry guide for the quality of the companies in cyber security and information upgrade -Accessible to the public by development on security adhesives with degree signs clause that to consume doer in evaluation the market helps	

face confusion and hesitation by increasing the costs of cyber-attacks, in the planning stage and before that. The strength of such a barrier depends on the level of ability, capability and potential response capacity, which depends on the ratio between cyber power compared to the enemy. Considering the situation of the Islamic Republic of Iran and the constant confrontation of global arrogance and the domination system with it, the preparation and supply of cyber equipment is one of the basic problems in the field of cyber defense and it is necessary to take necessary measures in the field of localization of hardware and software equipment, especially in the defense sector and create a secure supply chain.

Even though deterrence in cyberspace is not meaningful like in other spaces, but due to reasons such as the issue of attribution (it is difficult to determine the source of attacks and attribute them to the country), it has received the attention of countries in the field of deterrence. Cyber operations are usually carried out secretly and non-publicly, which means that the power players in this field try to avoid direct confrontation as much as possible. The cyberspace of the frying pan is the reason for the issue of attribution less exposed to the risk of confronting governments, but usually the response does not take place in the same space, but the response to cyber-attacks takes place in a multi-space context (Finlay and Payne 2019).

2.2 Main Prevention Methods

The goal of a cyber deterrence strategy is to intrude so decisively into a competitor's decision-making calculations that it does not launch cyber-attacks against insider interests. Coordinated actions reduce the attacker's chances of success so that the risks, costs, risks and uncertainties of a cyber-attack are determined by the expected benefit or reward. In the case of an adversary seeking to use threats of cyberattacks or actual attacks to coerce the adversary into taking action that serves its larger interests or goals, a cyber deterrence strategy will work if the adversary judges that the coercion has been successful. It can't be done, and the attack will cause the opposite country to retaliate and a pure strategic retreat for the attacker will be the result.

Such a strategic calculation is used in China's use of cyber threats and attacks, as well as the actions of other potential competitors in the cyber field. Potential practical responses in such situations are summarized in the three main modes of deterrence considered in the Joint Operations Concepts model: deterrence by denying its benefits, deterrence by imposing costs, and deterrence by providing incentives to deter a competitor.

1) Deterrence by denial of gain involves the credible threat of depriving the attacker of the benefits or gains it seeks convincing it that a cyberattack will not achieve its goals.
2) Deterrence by imposing a cost involves the credible threat of imposing costs, losses, and risks that are too difficult to accept, thereby convincing the adversary that the punishment will far outweigh the expected successes.
3) Deterrence by persuasion to prevent the competitor means convincing the competitor that no attack will have an acceptable and attractive result (Nye, 2017).

2.3 Cyber Resilience

Table 2. The category of cyber deterrence.

Main category	Subcategory	Main concept	Frequency
Cyber deterrence	Internal Resilience	-The cyber annual in the war	2
		-Conducting a cyber exercises	2
		-Defense at the starting point of the attack	3
		-Defense in depth	2
		-Identity verification	2
	Response to the invasion	-Monitoring the good implementation of communicated policies	2
		-Retaliate	2
		-Legal and contracts	2
		-Reduced reaction time	2
		-Use of mobilization capacity	2
	Reciprocal action	-Ability to support the answer	1
		-Damage prevention	1
		-Imposing costs on the enemy	1
		-Security of data exchange	2
		-Lack of dependence on infrastructure	3
		-Cyber awareness	2
		-Safe native equipment	2
	Recovery	-Data recovery	2
		-Incident management	1
		-Appropriate response to attacks	1
		-Development of a network of col-leagues	2

In strategic mapping to face three possible cyber scenarios in the future, the strategic issues of institutional readiness, cyber policy, society's understanding and the systematic structure of cyber risks should be addressed. Traditional cyber security expertise is gradually giving way to "cyber resilience and resistance" expertise; Because many global organizations have concluded that some cyber-attacks are inevitable, and instead of spending huge amounts of time on preventive cyber-security expertise that will not help with inevitable cyberattacks, they can invest in cyber-resilience. The cyber cooperation of different sectors has limited the spread of cyber-attack tools and has led to the building of institutional capabilities and motivates innovation.

Cyber resilience includes all the steps an organization must take to prepare and adapt to changing conditions, withstand incidents and recover quickly after disruptions. From this point of view, an organization is resilient when it can resist attacks, incidents or cyber threats (Steff et al. 2020).

Cyber resilience is an organization's ability to cyber resist, react and recover from threats that will affect information that is needed in doing business. Cyber resilience is the ability to prepare and adapt to changing conditions and tolerate and recover quickly after disruptions. Resilience includes the ability to withstand and recover from intentional attacks, natural events or threats, or accidents. Cyber resilience is defined as the ability of systems and organizations to resist and block cyber incidents. Cyber resilience is the organizational capability for cyber resistance against negative impacts, with respect to known, predictable, unknown, unpredictable, uncertain and unexpected threats from activities in cyber space.

A standard cyber resilience framework consists of the following five main pillars:

Identify critical assets, systems and data. An organization must be aware of all the resources that support its critical functions.

Protecting critical infrastructure. In this phase, the organization designs and produces security programs that lead to increased cyber resilience and limiting or countering potential threats.

Detecting strange events and data leaks before major incidents occur. This stage requires continuous monitoring.

Responding to security flaws or breaches. This step requires having a general plan for responding to incidents so that the organization can continue its normal work if faced with cyber-attacks.

Restore all infrastructure, capabilities or services affected by the attack. The focus of this phase is to restore conditions to normal (Akinsanya et al. 2024).

2.4 Collecting Cyber Information

Cyber security depends more than anything else on having a wide range of data and information. Some of these missions are specialized and some are general in the field of cyber space. For example, to observe and collect information from obvious sources, generally people of a group can do this action if the use and application of a special software or a unique technique to perform a special mission, by A certain person takes place and this mission cannot be delegated to another.

Cognitive warfare. Cognitive war is a complex and multi-layered war in the contemporary world, which has become an important component of national security in the conflict between countries. The cognitive battlefield is the human mind and its weapons of media, information and data and cognitive technologies (Reczkowski and Lis 2022).

Cyber-attack. Attempt to damage, destroy, disrupt, disable, gain unauthorized access to a computer; Computer system, computing environment, computing infrastructure, electronic communication network is controlled through cyber space to destroy data integrity or steal information (Oakley 2019).

Cyber defense. Taking advantage of all the unarmed cyber and non-cyber facilities of the country, to create deterrence, prevention, prevention, timely diagnosis, effective and deterrent countering with any cyber-attack on the country's national cyber assets by cyber enemies, including the cyber army of hostile countries. And groups under the covert support of hostile governments in such a way as to deny the possibility of cyber-attacks from all hostiles (Chayes 2015).

2.5 Research Background

Katanchi and Pourkohermani (2022) (Katanchi and Pourghahrammani, 2021) in research titled "Challenges of cyber security of ASEAN countries" investigated the indicators of cyber prestige in different dimensions in the target countries. The results of his research showed that little research has been done in the field of cyber security and defense in ASEAN countries. This has led to an increase in cybercrimes in these countries. Government strategies, privacy protection, ethical and legal challenges, and the weakness of cyber infrastructure are among the challenges of these governments in the field of cyber security.

Saneyan (2018) in research entitled "Cyber security in America, structures and trends" has examined the evolutionary process of American cyber security policies. The results of his research showed that in a period of twenty years, American cyber security policies have changed from a defensive-self-governing approach to an aggressive-government approach.

Asaesh Javed 2014 in a research entitled "The influence of the cyber power of the United States of America on the foreign policy of this country (2001–2015)" sought to answer the question of how the United States of America developed its dominance policy in the cyber arena after the September 11 incident. Has taken? The results of his research showed that cyber power, which includes the definition of all communication and media tools of modern technology, for America as the pioneer of the communication and internet industry with huge private giants such as Google and... With a volume of turnover much greater than the number A significant number of countries in the world and the establishment of most companies and non-governmental organizations providing and managing Internet services have given it an almost exclusive privilege. The first and most probable hypothesis for the questions raised is that cyber power has led to the continuation of the hegemony of the United States of America in the international system in 2011–2015 by maintaining the possibility of seeking superiority in foreign policy.

Medovov et al. (2015) (Medvedev 2015) in research titled "Analysis of Offense and Defense Theory of Russian Cyber Capabilities" sought answers to these questions: Are the cyber capabilities of the Russian Federation caused by offensive and defensive cyber weapons? What is the face of Russia in terms of offense and defense in the international arena? According to his and his colleagues' research, Russia's capability in cyberspace is based on Jervis Effendi's theory, but its exterior and appearance are both offensive and defensive.

JB Paxton (2008) (Paxton and Michael 2008) in the research entitled "Advanced Defense in Cyberspace Based on Distributed Real-Time Systems" at the Naval Postgraduate School of the US Army seeks to provide an innovative solution to deal with the increasing threats in the virtual environment in the Ministry of Defense. It was America. The results of his research showed that current strategies, including traditional intrusion detection and firewall-based defense, are not effective against complex attacks such as spam-phishing that exploit people's information. With these asymmetric attacks, intruders are able to pass the current defense barriers in the network and gain unlimited access to the interested parts. Network defense strategies are undermined by solutions that are based on network-centric solutions and ignore information security needs.

3 Research Methodology

Based on the research's objective, it is of a developmental-applied nature, as the research's results could be utilized at the level of governments and authorities in the field of cybersecurity. In other words, the researcher has aimed to achieve practical utility.

The research method employed in this study is qualitative. Various methods exist for analyzing qualitative data (concepts extracted from theoretical foundations, documents, and records), and the choice of method depends on the research type. One of these methods is the grounded theory approach. In this research, the proposed method by Strauss and Corbin, including three coding techniques: open, axial, and selective, using the MAXQDA software, has been utilized. Considering the lack of suitable patterns in the field of strategic cyber security management at the national level of some countries, this study, in terms of its objective, is exploratory, seeking to generate knowledge, insight, and a better understanding of the examined phenomenon.

In this method, all documents, records, and collected data are imported into the MAXQDA software, and essential concepts are extracted and subjected to open coding. Subsequently, through categorizing relevant and overarching codes in several stages, the derived issues are organized into five dimensions: situational, contextual, intervening, strategic, and consequences, using axial coding. Finally, by interpreting the results, a conceptual model is extracted through selective coding.

The population in the qualitative section of this research consists of written sources, articles, theses, and credible scientific documents related to the research topic from databases such as Emerald, and ScienceDirect, as well as strategic documents and records from some countries in the field of cybersecurity. Also, the statistical population in the quantitative section includes a group of 15 experts in the field of strategic cybersecurity management, whose opinions were utilized for model validation. In this research, suitable methods with its approach, including Researcher self-review, researcher sensitivity, methodology coherence, peer review, interpretation and reasoned reporting of findings, returning analyzes and results to participants were used.

4 Discussion

Initially, it was necessary to calculate the frequencies of subcategories within each main concept. According to the following tables, these frequencies were compiled (Table 1). In this regard:

Tables 2 and 3 present the frequencies of concepts related to "cyber deterrence" and "cyber resilience", respectively.

Table 3. Cyber resilience.

Main Concept	Sub concept	Main Idea	Frequency
Cyber Resilience	Resistance	Mutual Infrastructure Independence	2
		Cyber Readiness	2
		Deep Security Development (in technology environment)	2
		Data Security and Safety	2
		Technical Controls	2
		Active Defense Deployment	2
		Planning	2
	Response and Recovery	Data Recovery	2
		Data Reconstruction	2
		Incident Management	2
		Appropriate Response (to attacks)	2
		Collaboration and Cooperation	2
	Operational Continuity	Information Support	1
		Interaction with Research Centers	1
		Specialist Network Development	3

Table 4 outlines the frequencies of concepts in the Cyber Information Collection category.

Table 5 details the frequencies of concepts related to "war cognitive." Tables 6 and 7 provide the frequencies of concepts associated with the Cyber Attackers and Cyber Defense categories (Table 8).

Table 4. Cyber information collection category.

Main Concept	Sub concept	Main Principle	Frequency
Cyber Information Collection	Cyber Estimation	Identification of Information Estimation Sources	2
		Definition of Information Requirements	2
		Accurate Vulnerability Identification	2
		Awareness of Actionable Threats	2
		Supervision of Adversarial Movements	2
	Self-Cyber Surveillance	User Monitoring, Tracking, and Surveillance	2
		Communication Traffic Monitoring	2
		Data Decryption	2
		Identification of External Services	2
		Cyber Asset Identification	2
	Enemy Cyber Collection	Cyber Deception	1
		Military	1
		Political	2
		Economic	1
		Social	3
	Aggregation and Data Mining	Prediction	2
		Futurology	1
		Cyber Threat Assessment	1

Table 5. The category of cognitive warfare.

Main Concept	Sub concept	Main Idea	Frequency
Cognitive Warfare	Increase in Media Literacy	Exchange of Cognitive Data	2
		Cognitive Specialist Education	2
		National Cognitive Capacity Building	2
		Trans cognitive Capacity Building	2
	Surveillance Campaign	Cognitive Data Processing	2
		Cognitive Monitoring	2
		Cognitive Modeling	2
		Cognitive Analysis	2
	Cognitive Defense Campaign	Identification and Analysis of Cognitive Damages	1
		Cognitive Threat Identification and Analysis	1
		Cognitive Prevention and Security	2
		Cognitive Detection and Alert	2
	Cognitive Offense	Cognitive Surveillance	2
		Cognitive Analysis	2
		Cognitive Planning	1
		Cognitive Attack	1
		Practical Lessons of Cognitive Offense Operations	2

4.1 Selective Coding (Model Presentation)

In this stage, selective coding has been done to interpret and explain the extracted model and model. In this stage, based on the results of previous coding stages, the model has been produced.

In this regard, the extracted final table consists of main and sub-categories, main and sub-concepts, and researcher-made presented as a plot.

Table 6. The category of cyber attackers.

Main Concept	Sub concept	Main Principle	Frequency
Cyber Offense	Offense Foundations	Command Acquisition	2
		Threatening Attack Identification	2
		Inbound Attack Identification	2
		Determining Overall Attack Objective	2
		Achieving Desired Outcome	2
	Objective Identification	Collection Organization	2
		Identification System	2
		Target List	2
		Vulnerability Determination	2
	Operational Plan	Attack Plan Preparation	1
		Determination and Procurement of Resources	1
		Plan Testing	2

Table 7. Cyber defense category.

Main Concept	Sub concept	Main Principle	Frequency
Cyber Defense	Non-Attributable Cyber Defense	Identification and Registration of Resources	2
		Formulation of Non-Attributable Standards	2
		Oversight of Standard Implementation	2
		Conducting Drills	2
	Attributional Cyber Defense	Event Logging	2
		Alerting	2
		Identification and Readiness	2
		Analysis and Evaluation	2
		Incident Response Team Reaction	2

Table 8. The final extracted of the national cybersecurity defense pattern.

Main Concept	Sub-Concept	Main and Sub-Concept Description
Cyber Deterrence	Internal Strength	Cyber warfare directive execution
		Cyber exercise execution
		Defense at the point of attack initiation
		Defense in depth
		Identity verification and authentication
	Response to Attack	Monitoring Policy
		Retaliation
		Legal and contractual aspects
		Reduction of response time
		Utilization of national capacity
	Reciprocal Action	Supporting response capability
		Damage prevention
		Enemy cost imposition
		Data exchange security
		Infrastructure independence
		Cyber awareness
		Secure domestic equipment
	Recovery	Data Retrieval
		Incident management
		Adequate response to attacks
		Network of collaborators development
Cyber Resilience for Equipment	Resistance	Risk acceptance threshold
		Mutual infrastructure independence
		Cyber readiness
		Deep security development (in technology environment)
		Data security and encryption
		Technical controls

(*continued*)

Table 8. *(continued)*

Main Concept	Sub-Concept	Main and Sub-Concept Description
		Active defense deployment
		Planning
		Positive adaptability (in adverse conditions)
		Reliable equipment
	Data recovery	Data recovery
		Data reconstruction
		Incident management
		Appropriate response to attacks
		Collaboration and cooperation
	Operational Continuity	Information support
		Interaction with research centers
		Specialist network development
Cyber Intelligence Collection	Cyber Estimation	Sources of information estimation
		Identifying information requirements
		Accurate vulnerability identification
		Awareness of impending threats
		Monitoring enemy movements
	Self-cyber–Situational Awareness	Monitoring user activities
		Monitoring communication traffic
		Data decryption
		Identification of external services
		Identification of cyber assets
	Enemy Cyber Intelligence Collection	Cyber espionage
		Military
		Political
		Economic

(continued)

Table 8. (*continued*)

Main Concept	Sub-Concept	Main and Sub-Concept Description
		Social
	Aggregation and Data Mining	Prediction
		Futurology
		Cyber threat estimation
Cognitive Warfare	Media Literacy	Cognitive data exchange
		Cognitive specialist training
		National cognitive capacity building
		Framework cognitive capacity building
	Monitoring and Recon	Cognitive data processing
		Cognitive monitoring
		Cognitive modeling
		Cognitive analysis
	Cognitive Vulnerabilities	Identification and analysis of cognitive vulnerabilities
		Identification and analysis of cognitive threats
		Prevention and cognitive security
		Cognitive detection and warning
	Cognitive Surveillance	Cognitive monitoring
		Cognitive analysis
		Cognitive planning
		Cognitive attack
		Practical lessons in cognitive operations
Cyber attack	Offensive Support	Receiving orders
		Identifying threatening attacks
		Identifying incoming attacks
		Determining the overall attack objective
		Achieving desired outcome

(*continued*)

Table 8. (*continued*)

Main Concept	Sub-Concept	Main and Sub-Concept Description
	Identifying the target	Collection organization
		Identification system
		Affliction lists
		Vulnerability determination
	Operational Planning	Attack plan preparation
		Resource identification and procurement
		Testing the plan
Cyber Defense	Non-Active Cyber Defense	Resource identification and registration
		Non-active standard development
		Monitoring standard implementation
		Conducting exercises
	Active Cyber Defense	Event Registration
		Alerting
		Identification and readiness
		Analysis and evaluation
		Response by the head team

5 Conclusion

This study addressed the significant challenge posed by the rapid expansion of cyberspace and its associated vulnerabilities, which have heightened the necessity for robust national cybersecurity strategies. In response to the problem statement—namely, the absence of a comprehensive framework for managing cybersecurity strategically at the national level—a qualitative research methodology was employed. Using MAXQDA software and content analysis, data from relevant documents and literature were systematically analyzed to identify key elements influencing cybersecurity strategic management.

The research culminated in a robust model, validated through expert consultation, that incorporates causal, background, and intervening conditions, alongside targeted strategies and their consequences. This model provides actionable insights for governments and organizations to develop resilient cybersecurity frameworks.

The results underscore the importance of integrating national policies, fostering cyber deterrence capabilities, and safeguarding critical infrastructure. These findings contribute to bridging the gap between the technical and strategic aspects of cybersecurity, offering a roadmap for nations to enhance their cyber resilience in an increasingly digitalized global environment (Fig. 1).

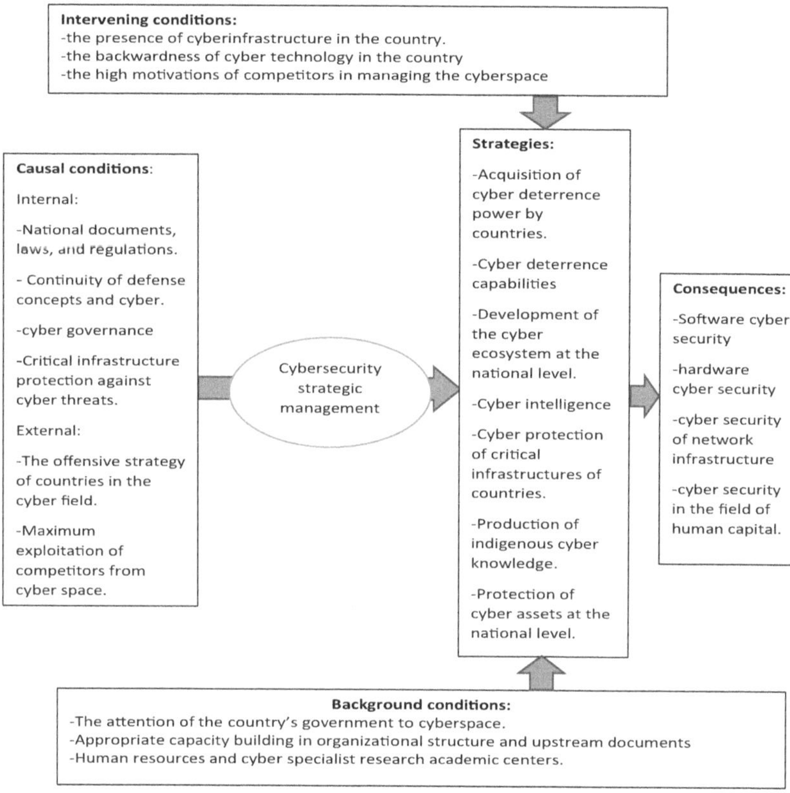

Fig. 1. Paradigm model of research.

6 Suggestions

Based on the dimensions and components mentioned in the research, here are some suggestions for the implementation of the model:

-Collaborate with countries at the international level to create and grow the country's cyber infrastructure.
-Investment in technology cyber in fields of research, education, and equipment.
-Collaborate with tech companies and universities for technology transfer.
-Develop a national security cyber technology advancement plan with definite milestones.
-Educating the community about cybersecurity.

-Revise existing cybersecurity laws and regulations to confront the threats.
-Create a definite framework for the alignment of cybersecurity laws with all the activities.
-Attention to cybersecurity in national defense strategies and doctrines formulating.
-Reinforcement collaboration between defense and cyber agencies for alignment.
-Create a centralized cyber security institution to control and execute the laws and activities for better activities alignment.
-Readiness of cybersecurity infrastructure for aggressive and defensive capabilities:
-Align cybersecurity goals with national strategies and policies.
-Allocation scholarship programs to educate cybersecurity talents.

Generally, the implementation of the model requires a multi-functional approach that involves collaboration between nonprivate agencies, private sectors, academies, and the public.

References

1. Akinsanya, M.O., Ekechi, C.C., Okeke, C.D.: Security paradigms for IoT in telecom networks: conceptual challenges and solution pathways. Eng. Sci. Tech. J. **5**(4), 1431–1451 (2024)
2. Aluede, L.O., Biragbara, E.P.: Cyber attack: an emerging war. GSJ **8**(1) (2020)
3. Asaesh Javed, H.: The impact of the cyber power of the United States of America on the foreign policy of this country (2001–2015). Kharazmi University, Faculty of Law and Political Science, Master's Thesis (2014)
4. Castells, M.: Materials for exploratory theory of the network society. Br. J. Sociol. **51**(1), 5–24 (2000)
5. Chayes, A.: Rethinking warfare: the ambiguity of cyber-attacks. Harv. Nat'l Sec. J. **6**, 474 (2015)
6. Defense, U.S.: Department of Defense Strategy for Operating in Cyberspace. DIANE Publishing (2012)
7. Finlay, L., Payne, C.: The attribution problem and cyber armed attacks, pp. 202–206 (2019)
8. Kagalwalla, N., Churi, P.P.: Cybersecurity in aviation: an intrinsic review. In: 2019 5th International Conference on Computing, Communication, Control and Automation (ICCUBEA), pp. 1–6. IEEE (2019)
9. Katanchi, E., Pourghahrammani, B.: Cyber security challenges in ASEAN countries. Int. Stud. J. **18**, 1 (2021)
10. Medvedev, S.A.: Offense-defense theory analysis of Russian cyber capability. Doctoral dissertation, Monterey, California: Naval Postgraduate School (2015)
11. Nye, J.: Soft power: the origins and political progress of a concept. Palgrave Commun. **3**(1), 1–3 (2017)
12. National-Cybersecurity-Strategies-Lessons-learned-and-reflections (2022)
13. Oakley, J.G.: Professional Red Teaming: Conducting Successful Cybersecurity Engagements. Apress (2019)
14. Ohlin, J.D., Govern, K., Finkelstein, C.: Cyber war: law and ethics for virtual conflicts. OUP Oxford (2015)
15. Paxton, S.G., Michael, J.B.: Enhanced cyberspace defense with real-time distributed systems using covert channel publish-subscribe broker pattern communications. Doctoral dissertation, Naval Postgraduate School (2008)
16. Reczkowski, R., Lis, A.: Cognitive Warfare: what is our actual knowledge and how to build state resilience? Bezpieczeństwo. Teoria i Praktyka **48**(3), 51–61 (2022)

17. Rheingold, H.: Global Networks (1993)
18. Saneyan, A.: Cyber security in America, Structures and Trends. Foreign Policy Quarterly. Thirty-third year. Number 1 (2018)
19. Tallinn. (20113). NATO Cooperative Cyber Defence Centre
20. Steff, R., Burton, J., Soare, S.R.: Emerging Technologies and International Security. Routledge (2020)
21. Ullah, F., Babar, M.A.: Architectural tactics for big data cybersecurity analytics systems: a review. J. Syst. Softw. **151**, 81–118 (2019)

Using Hybrid Methodologies to Improve Processes in Software Project Management

Sedanur Akkoyun[1](✉) and Fatih Yucalar[2]

[1] Department of Software Development, BilgeAdam Technologies, 34467 Istanbul, Turkey
akkoyunsedanur@gmail.com

[2] Department of Software Engineering, Manisa Celal Bayar University, 45400 Manisa, Turkey

Abstract. As technology rapidly develops, software organizations face the challenge of adapting swiftly to changing customer requirements. Agile software development methodologies, such as Scrum, XP (Extreme Programming), Kanban, and Lean, offer flexibility and rapid response but may fall short in areas like documentation, planning, and standardization. At this point, the Capability Maturity Model Integration for Development (CMMI-Dev) v2.0 serves as a model that guides agile organizations in evaluating and improving their process capabilities to mature and enhance their software processes. This study examines how the Capability Maturity Model Integration for Development (CMMI-Dev) v2.0 can complement agile approaches by providing a framework for process improvement. Specifically, we analyze the integration of Scrum practices with CMMI-Dev 2.0 process areas, highlighting the advantages this hybrid model brings to managing and enhancing software processes. Our findings indicate that combining Scrum with CMMI-Dev 2.0 improves process maturity, product quality, and management efficiency, creating a balanced approach that aligns agile responsiveness with structured process improvement.

Keywords: Agile Software Development · CMMI-DEV v2.0 · Process Improvement · Process Maturity

1 Introduction

Rapid technological advancements and intense competition in the modern era have heightened the need for flexibility and speed in software development processes [1]. Quickly responding to customer demands and change requests has become a critical factor in the success of software projects. Therefore, it is crucial that software development methodologies adapt to these rapid changes and minimize costs.

Agile software development methodologies emerged to meet these requirements. Since their inception, agile methodologies have guided software processes with core principles such as flexibility, customer focus, and rapid delivery [2]. These methodologies emphasize working with small, functional teams to deliver continuously functional software components to customers in short time frames [3]. This approach allows for the rapid reception of customer feedback and the immediate implementation of new

A. Mirzazadeh et al. (Eds.): SEMIT 2024, CCIS 2444, pp. 88–104, 2026.
https://doi.org/10.1007/978-3-032-01948-6_6

requirements and change requests, ensuring that projects progress in a more dynamic and efficient manner. However, while agile methodologies are effective for flexibility and rapid iteration, they may fall short in addressing essential aspects like documentation, process maturity, and standardization in large-scale projects [4]. These shortcomings can create challenges, especially in large and complex projects, in managing both the project and the software processes. This indicates a research gap where a balance is needed between agility and structured process management to enhance the effectiveness of software development.

To address this gap, a holistic approach is needed in software development processes that maintains the advantages provided by agile software development methodologies while also considering process maturity and standardization [5]. In this context, the Capability Maturity Model Integration for Development (CMMI-Dev) v2.0 offers a structured framework that complements agile methodologies by enhancing process capability and standardization [6]. CMMI-Dev v2.0 provides comprehensive guidelines for assessing and advancing process maturity, enabling organizations to optimize and standardize their software processes effectively [7].

Despite the advantages of integrating agile methodologies with CMMI-Dev v2.0, existing literature lacks empirical evidence on the effectiveness of this hybrid approach. Previous studies have primarily focused on agile methodologies in isolation or have not adequately explored the specific integration of Scrum practices within the CMMI-Dev framework. This paper aims to fill this gap by investigating how software organizations can enhance their development processes through the integration of CMMI-Dev v2.0 with agile approaches, specifically focusing on how Scrum practices can be effectively combined with CMMI-Dev 2.0 process areas. This study contributes to the literature by presenting a framework that illustrates the synergy between agile and traditional process models, demonstrating the potential for enhanced process maturity and product quality. It emphasizes how this hybrid approach can balance flexibility with process maturity by providing a practical solution for organizations seeking to improve both process and product quality.

The structure of the study is as follows: Sect. 2 reviews related work; Sect. 3 introduces the concept and fundamental principles of agile software development while examining Scrum, a notable agile approach; Sect. 4 discusses software process improvement and capability assessment models; Sect. 5 proposes a hybrid approach for software projects through a case study example; Sect. 6 presents a discussion of the findings; and Sect. 7 concludes the paper.

2 Related Works

The alignment of Agile and CMMI has increasingly become a significant topic in contemporary discussions. Ajayi (2021) examines how Agile methodologies can be integrated with CMMI and provides insights into their applicability in various projects. The study highlights that Agile is more suitable for small, time-sensitive projects, while CMMI may be preferable for larger and more complex undertakings. It notes that Agile practices adopt a people-centric approach, whereas CMMI emphasizes comprehensive documentation and process management [45]. Furthermore, Agile methodologies priotitize continuous learning and adaptation, while CMMI necessitates pre-planned processes. The existing literature on the interaction and compatibility of these two methodologies indicates that their integration can enhance quality in the software development process.

Henriquez et al. (2022) present a study examining the relationship between CMMI V2.0 and Agile practices. In this research, a content analysis was conducted to explore how Agile artifacts could support the implementation of CMMI-DEV V2.0. As a result, 31 Agile artifacts were identified for Maturity Levels 2 and 3 [6]. The study emphasizes that these artifacts can contribute to the business value creation process of CMMI-DEV V2.0 practices and assist Agile organizations in defining their roadmaps. However, the necessity for further validation and application in this domain is also highlighted due to gaps in the existing literature. The study advocates for more research to identify Agile artifacts pertinent to CMMI-DEV V2.0 implementations and to elucidate which practices these artifacts support.

Fuentes and Jenkins (2022) explore the use of the CMMI-DEV 2.0 model for process improvement in a financial software project. They highlight the significance of practices that strengthen the software development process and standards that assist organizations in self-assessment and adopting effective practices. The project aimed to raise process maturity from 30% to 70%, achieving a 25% reduction in development time and a 15% decrease in defect rates [41]. Key improvement opportunities identified include formalizing and documenting processes, enhancing inter-team communication, and standardizing estimation methods. The authors argue that CMMI can be effectively integrated with Agile practices, allowing organizations to flexibly meet their requirements. They also emphasize the advantages of certification at various levels to satisfy client standards, suggesting that higher CMMI levels can significantly benefit large firms managing complex projects while enabling rapid adaptation through iterative cycles, thereby reducing implementation costs.

A comprehensive review of the existing literature reveals that, while prior studies underscore the potential advantages of integrating Agile methodologies with CMMI, there exists a significant paucity of empirical evidence addressing the practical challenges inherent in this integration. Research conducted by Ajayi (2021) and Henriquez et al. (2022) predominantly emphasizes theoretical frameworks, thereby leaving a considerable gap in the detailed examination of real-world applications and case studies. Moreover, while Fuentes and Jenkins (2022) provide valuable insights into the application of CMMI-DEV 2.0 for enhancing software processes, further investigation is warranted to assess the long-term sustainability and applicability of the outcomes presented in their work.

This paper endeavors to fill these gaps in the literature by investigating the synergistic integration of CMMI-Dev v2.0 with Agile methodologies, particularly focusing on the effective amalgamation of Scrum practices with the process areas outlined in CMMI-Dev 2.0. Through this examination, we aim to propose a novel framework that elucidates the interplay between Agile and traditional process models, ultimately contributing to enhanced process maturity and improved product quality within software development organizations.

3 Agile Software Development Methodologies

Agile software development methodologies, which began to take shape in the early 1990s, emerged as an alternative to traditional software development approaches (such as Waterfall, V-Model, Spiral), which typically require long-term planning and struggle to adapt to changing requirements. Issues faced in software projects using traditional software development approaches—such as the inability to respond to customer demands in a timely manner, difficulty in accommodating change requests, and the late detection of software defects—triggered the development of agile software development approaches [8]. In 2001, a group of seventeen software practitioners gathered in the state of Utah in the United States and published the 'Agile Software Development Manifesto,' which emphasizes customer satisfaction, the ability to quickly respond to changing customer requirements, collaboration between developers and the business team, and interpersonal communication [9]. This manifesto helped the agile software development approach gain worldwide popularity.

Agile software development approaches are widely used in managing software projects that require flexibility and have high levels of complexity or uncertainty. These approaches provide efficient, flexible, low-error, fast, and cost-effective solutions for software projects. Agile software development approaches include various methodologies, such as Scrum, Extreme Programming (XP), Feature-Driven Development (FDD), Test-Driven Development (TDD), Dynamic Systems Development Method (DSDM), Kanban, and Lean Development, which share the same essence but differ in practical application [10]. Among these, Scrum is one of the most widely adopted and implemented frameworks within agile methodologies. Scrum offers a structured yet flexible approach to project management, enabling teams to deliver high-quality software on time. As a result, Scrum has become a commonly preferred method in software development projects.

3.1 Scrum

Scrum was first introduced in the early 1990s by Ken Schwaber and Jeff Sutherland [11]. Since then, it has become the most widely used agile software development methodology. Scrum is known for its ability to quickly adapt to technological advancements and changing requirements, which frequently occur in software development projects. It is especially suitable for projects where requirements are not easily defined, and chaotic situations are expected [12]. It allows for rapid results in the software projects where it is implemented.

At the core of Scrum, the development process is divided into sprints that do not exceed four weeks. At the end of each sprint, a product increment that can be delivered to the user is provided [13]. A sprint planning meeting is held for each new sprint, during which tasks to be completed are selected in collaboration with developers and other stakeholders, and effort estimates are made. In Scrum, the person representing the customer is the Product Owner. After the tasks to be included in the sprint are determined, the Product Owner prioritizes these tasks to create the sprint backlog [14]. Requirements are collected as user stories and are listed in the product backlog created by the Product Owner [15]. The product backlog is continuously updated based on user needs. Scrum's structure is designed for small, interdisciplinary teams of approximately six to nine people. The role of the Scrum Master is essential in each Scrum team to coordinate daily tasks and ensure adherence to the Scrum process [16]. Daily stand-up meetings, where team members update each other on progress and discuss the day's tasks, help ensure rapid progress. Retrospective meetings, held after each sprint, allow the team to evaluate the completed sprint and support continuous improvement and adaptation. Figure 1 shows the general structure of Scrum.

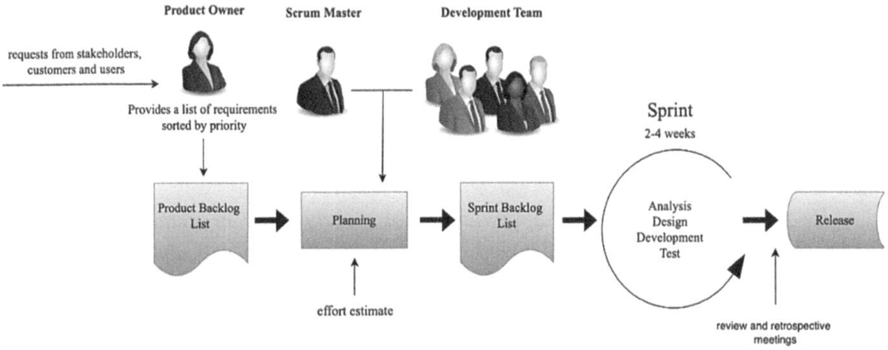

Fig. 1. Structure of Scrum

The structured nature of Scrum, with its interdisciplinary small teams and distinct roles, encourages effective communication and collaboration with all project stakeholders. This, in turn, ensures high efficiency and quality in the software development process. Today, many technology companies, including Google, Microsoft, Yahoo, Amazon, Siemens, Havelsan, and Turk Telekom, prefer to use this successful agile software development methodology in their software development projects [17].

4 Software Process Improvement and Capability Assessment Models

In today's world, where technological advancements are rapidly progressing, the effective and efficient management of software development processes is key to gaining a competitive advantage. Software process improvement and capability assessment models play a critical role in helping organizations achieve these goals. These models offer various approaches to enhancing the quality of software development processes, determining the maturity levels of these processes, and evaluating organizational capabilities [18]. Software process improvement aims to assess an organization's existing processes and make them more effective, efficient, and of higher quality. By using process improvement approaches within Agile methodologies, software development processes can be managed in a more dynamic and customer-focused manner [19]. This approach also emphasizes the understanding that processes need to be continuously improved. Capability assessment provides standards and metrics to determine the competency and maturity levels of software development processes. This process reveals how effective an organization's current processes are and identifies areas that need improvement [20]. In this context, models like Capability Maturity Model Integration (CMMI) help organizations assess their process capabilities and determine and improve their maturity levels [21]. CMMI offers a comprehensive framework for defining, managing, and continuously improving processes. The model aims to enhance process effectiveness by providing specific maturity levels and allows organizations to develop their processes by measuring success at these levels [22]. This study focuses on how software process improvement and capability assessment models can be integrated, particularly the role of the CMMI model in these processes.

4.1 CMMI-DEV V2.0

The Capability Maturity Model (CMM) is a model introduced in 1991 with version 1.0, aimed at continuously improving software development processes [23]. This model focuses on the gradual development of an organization's processes from an initial stage to a more mature and systematic state. Developed by the Software Engineering Institute (SEI) at Carnegie Mellon University, the model was created in response to the U.S. Department of Defense's search for solutions to the software crisis it faced in the 1970s. It offers an evolutionary approach to process improvement and standardization [24]. Initially developed solely for use in the software domain, the CMM became one of the most widely used and recognized models worldwide due to its success. Following this success, various CMMs were developed for use in different fields. The Systems Engineering Capability Maturity Model (SE-CMM) was created to evaluate and improve systems engineering processes; the People CMM (P-CMM) was developed to improve organizations' human resources processes; and the Integrated Product Development Capability Maturity Model (IPD-CMM) was developed to improve and manage product development processes [25]. In 2001, the CMMI was introduced as part of the CMM Integration Project, which aimed to bring together the best practices and process improvement approaches from these models, enabling organizations to improve their processes in a more comprehensive and integrated manner.

CMMI divides process development into five maturity levels: Initial, Managed, Defined, Quantitatively Managed, and Optimizing. Each level provides specific criteria for organizations to manage their processes in a more systematic and mature manner. Each maturity level encompasses specific process areas, which represent the key topics organizations should focus on to improve their processes [26].

CMMI is presented with two main representations that help organizations manage process improvements and transitions between maturity levels [27]. The continuous representation allows organizations to progress and improve independently within each process area. This approach facilitates faster progress in specific areas while encouraging an overall increase in maturity level over time. The staged representation, on the other hand, organizes process areas in a specific sequence, requiring organizations to complete each level before advancing to the next. This model offers a more step-by-step and orderly path to process improvement [28]. Both representations serve different needs and objectives, making it critical for organizations to choose the one that best aligns with their current process structure and improvement goals to achieve optimal results.

Figure 2 shows the CMMI maturity levels and the process areas within these maturity levels.

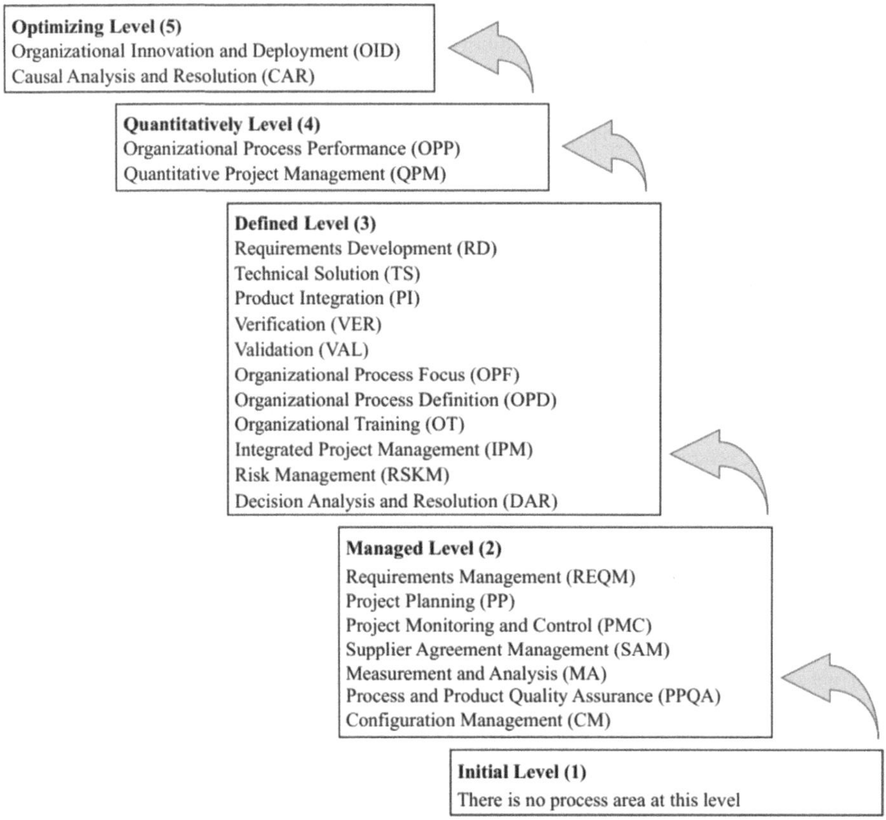

Fig. 2. CMMI maturity levels and process areas

CMMI is not a process or standard; it is a model that assesses the maturity level of an organization's processes. With the release of version 1.2 in 2006, this model was divided into three areas, known as constellations: CMMI-DEV (CMMI for Development), CMMI-SVC (CMMI for Services), and CMMI-ACQ (CMMI for Acquisition) [29].

In this context, the CMMI-DEV model, designed for organizations involved in software development, consists of 22 process areas [30]. Version 1.3 of CMMI, developed based on feedback from previous versions, was released in 2010. In this version, the process areas were categorized into four groups: Engineering, Process Management, Project Management, and Support [31]. CMMI v2.0, the latest version of CMMI, was released in 2018. Along with CMMI v2.0, the CMMI Institute introduced new terminology. Requirements are now grouped into Category Areas, Capability Areas, and Practice Areas [6]. With the new categorization, four new Category Areas have been identified to help organizations prioritize and organize their resources and focus on critical issues.

Each Category Area contains defined Capability Areas, which group practices aimed at improving performance in an organization or project. Additionally, new practice areas have been added, increasing the number of practice areas from 22 to 25 [32]. Table 1 shows the CMMI-DEV v2.0 category areas and practice areas.

Table 1. CMMI-DEV v2.0 category areas and practice areas

Doing	Managing
Ensuring Quality	**Planning & Managing Work**
Requirements Development and Management (RDM)	Estimating (EST)
Process Quality Assurance (PQA)	Planning (PLAN)
Peer Reviews (PR)	Monitor & Control (MC)
Verification and Validation (VV)	**Managing Business Resilience**
Engineering & Developing Products	Risk & Opportunity Management (ROM)
Technical Solution (TS)	**Managing the Workforce**
Product Integration (PI)	Organizational Training (OT)
Enabling	**Improving**
Supporting Implementation	**Sustaining Habit & Persistence**
Casual Analysis & Resolution (CAR)	Governance (GOV)
Decision Analysis & Resolution (DAR)	Implementation & Infrastructure (II)
Configuration Management (CM)	**Improving Performance**
	Process Management (PM)
	Process Asset Development (PAD)
	Managing Performance & Measurement (MPM)

5 Proposed Hybrid Approach for Software Projects

According to the 17th State of Agile Report published in 2023, 71% of the organizations surveyed prefer to use agile methodologies in their software development life cycles. Additionally, 63% of these organizations use Scrum or Scrum-based approaches as their agile methodology [33]. On the other hand, CMMI is one of the most widely adopted performance improvement models worldwide, and its use has steadily increased in recent years [6]. Specifically, CMMI-DEV, which provides best practices for software development, is a model widely adopted by organizations. Although the adoption of CMMI offers organizations attractive opportunities such as increased productivity, efficiency, on-time delivery, and error reduction, its adoption in Agile contexts can be challenging [34]. This has created a need for guidelines to help organizations effectively implement these hybrid processes.

The aim of this study is to accurately align Scrum practices with CMMI-DEV v2.0 process areas and thereby contribute to the improvement of project management and software development processes through the resulting hybrid approach. The Scrum practices considered for alignment with CMMI-DEV v2.0 process areas are shown in Table 2 [35] [16].

Table 2. Scrum practices and descriptions

Scrum Practices	Description
Product Backlog	A prioritized list of features maintained by the Product Owner
Sprint Backlog	A subset of the Product Backlog items selected for the Sprint
Sprint Planning	A meeting to decide and plan the work to be completed during the Sprint
Effort Estimation	Predicting the work required for backlog items
Sprint Execution	Work phase of the Sprint where tasks are completed
Daily Meetings	Short daily updates on progress and issues
Task Board	Visual tool for tracking task progress
User Stories	Descriptions of features from the user's perspective
Epics	Large user stories broken down into smaller tasks
Code Review	Checking code quality and finding defects
Test Plan & Case & Result	Planning, executing, and documenting tests
Refactoring	Improving code structure without changing behavior
Release Planning	Preparing and scheduling product releases
Sprint Review	Meeting to demo completed work and get feedback
Retrospective	Meeting to discuss improvements for the next Sprint
Burndown Sprint Charts	Graphs showing work completed versus remaining
Definition of Done	Criteria for when a task is considered complete

The following steps were followed as the method for aligning Scrum practices with CMMI-Dev v2.0 process areas:

Step-1: Scrum practices are examined in detail regarding content and scope [14].
Step-2: The CMMI-Dev v2.0 process areas are examined in detail regarding content and scope [36].
Step-3: To identify and measure the relationships between CMMI-DEV v2.0 process areas and Scrum practices, the results of the documents A Guide to Scrum and CMMI: Improving Agile Performance with CMMI" and "Agile-CMMI V2.0 Alignment: Bringing to Light the Agile Artifacts Pointed Out by CMMI" are analyzed [6, 37].
Step-4: Each Scrum practice is matched with process areas in a way that overlaps in content and scope. For this purpose, data obtained from Steps-1, 2, and 3 have been used.

As a result of the mappings, the relationships between Scrum practices and CMMI-Dev v2.0 process areas are shown in Table 3.

Table 3. Association between CMMI-DEV v2.0 practice areas and Scrum practices

Scrum Practices vs CMMI-DEV v2.0 Process Areas	Product Backlog	Sprint Backlog	Sprint Planning	Effort Estimation	Sprint Execution	Daily Meeting	Task Board	User Stories	Epics	Code Review	Test Plan, Cases, Results	Refactoring	Release Planning	Sprint Review	Retrospective	Burndown Sprint Charts	Definition of Done
RDM																	
PQA																	
PR																	
VV																	
TS																	
PI																	
EST																	
PLAN																	
MC																	
ROM																	
OT																	
CAR																	
DAR																	
CM																	
GOV																	
II																	
PM																	
PAD																	
MPM																	

Adopting CMMI within Agile environments introduces several challenges due to the inherent differences in methodology [42]. For instance, in a Scrum-based software development organization, team members may resist CMMI's requirement for detailed documentation, preferring the more informal, responsive communication methods typical of Agile practices. This divergence can create friction between management, who seek CMMI compliance, and development teams who prioritize adaptability and efficiency.

Effective implementation of CMMI in an Agile setting necessitates robust managerial support, where leadership possesses a thorough understanding of both methodologies and their potential synergies. In large organizations, management may advocate for CMMI certification to standardize processes without fully grasping Agile's principles. When leadership enforces rigid CMMI practices without allowing Agile's inherent flexibility, teams may struggle to strike a balance that accommodates both frameworks, potentially resulting in team disengagement and diminished morale [47].

Moreover, teams may often lack the necessary training to simultaneously adhere to both Agile and CMMI standards, creating a skills gap that hampers successful integration. In Agile-oriented development firms, teams may be unfamiliar with CMMI requirements, which can lead to incomplete implementation of critical practices and consequently hinder compliance. This gap not only obstructs process maturity but also detracts from the anticipated benefits of CMMI integration, such as enhanced project consistency and quality.

To effectively implement this hybrid model, practitioners are encouraged to follow these specific recommendations [44]:

1. Begin with a comprehensive assessment of current processes to identify gaps that can be filled by integrating Scrum and CMMI-Dev v2.0 practices.
2. Provide training and resources to team members on both Scrum and CMMI-Dev v2.0 frameworks to ensure a smooth transition and alignment [46].
3. Establish clear communication channels to facilitate collaboration between teams and stakeholders throughout the project lifecycle.
4. Regularly review and adapt the hybrid approach based on feedback and performance metrics to ensure continuous improvement.
5. Document best practices and lessons learned to guide future implementations and share knowledge within the organization.

5.1 Case Study on Implementation of Hybrid Approach

In a software company providing solutions across various industries, a hybrid model combining Scrum with the process maturity offered by CMMI-DEV v2.0 was adopted to address past project delays, quality issues, and the need for software process improvement. The company's senior management believed that applying such a hybrid model would ideally increase customer satisfaction and reduce project delivery times. In an ongoing software project within the company, the project team began applying this hybrid approach by combining CMMI-DEV v2.0 practice areas such as "Planning", "Requirements Development and Management", and "Monitoring and Control" with Scrum practices like Sprint Planning, Daily Scrum Meetings, Backlog Grooming, and Sprint Retrospectives. Prior to implementation, all team members received training on the CMMI-Dev v2.0 practice areas to ensure the seamless integration of Scrum and CMMI-Dev v2.0 processes.

To ensure clear definition, tracking, and monitoring of software requirements, the "Requirements Development and Management" practice area of CMMI-Dev v2.0 was established as an organizational standard. Scrum's Product Backlog and Sprint Backlog practices were integrated with this practice area, enabling a more detailed analysis and documentation of software requirements. Improvement actions identified in Sprint

Retrospective meetings were tracked using a documentation and monitoring system to oversee improvements for subsequent Sprints. Periodic risk assessment meetings were held to identify and monitor project risks, primarily based on criteria in the "Risk and Opportunity Management" practice area of CMMI-Dev v2.0. Potential risks were identified at the beginning of each Sprint, and risk assessments were conducted. At the end of each Sprint, product quality was analyzed using the "Process Quality Assurance" practice area to ensure quality standards were met. Performance indicators were defined within the software project and monitored throughout the process using the "Managing Performance & Measurement" practice area. Factors such as Sprint progress, forecast accuracy, and customer satisfaction were regularly reported, taking this practice area into account. The Confluence tool was introduced to store information on code development, integration, testing, and release environments. Coding standards and source code guidelines were also adhered to throughout the project management process, integrating the "Technical Solution", "Product Integration", "Peer Reviews", and "Verification and Validation" practice areas. Upon project completion, results were analyzed, with risk management, quality assurance, and performance evaluations systematically conducted through CMMI-Dev v2.0 practice areas. This approach enabled the team to work in a more controlled and focused manner throughout the project. The requirements management improvements implemented through CMMI-Dev v2.0 significantly enhanced customer satisfaction. Thanks to the quality assurance guidelines of CMMI-Dev v2.0 practice areas, software quality was consistently maintained, and quality analyses conducted at the end of each Sprint raised the overall software standards.

While implementing the hybrid approach, team members encountered various challenges in aligning Scrum practices with the practice areas of CMMI-Dev 2.0. Balancing Scrum's flexible structure with the rigorous process management of CMMI-Dev 2.0 proved challenging for the team. The uneven adaptation of team members to the hybrid approach requirements led to inconsistencies in process maturity at certain points within the project. Additionally, the extensive documentation required by CMMI-Dev 2.0 conflicted with the agile practices the team was accustomed to, necessitating additional resources and time for process management.

6 Discussion of Findings

The integration of Scrum and CMMI-Dev v2.0 presents a unique opportunity for organizations to enhance their software development capabilities. The findings highlight several key areas where this hybrid approach can bring about improvements. As shown in Table 3, the CMMI-Dev v2.0 process areas complement Scrum practices. The improvement opportunities that the hybrid approach resulting from the combination of the two models can provide to project management and software development processes are discussed in detail below:

- The "Requirements Development and Management" process area provides guidance on the definition, analysis, and management of requirements. Teams can use this process area to define requirements consistently and completely when creating the Product Backlog and Sprint Backlog [36]. This, in turn, can enhance their success in meeting customer needs and business objectives.

- Scrum does not include a specific process for identifying and managing risks. Teams typically address risks directly as the project progresses. The "Risk & Opportunity Management" process area facilitates the advance identification of risks and the development of strategies to address them. This can make risk management within the Scrum process more structured and proactive.
- The "Causal Analysis & Resolution" process area systematically performs root cause analysis and focuses on developing lasting solutions [38]. This can help Scrum teams address recurring issues more effectively during the Retrospective process.
- The "Decision Analysis & Resolution" process area ensures that decision-making processes are managed systematically, and data driven. This can help Scrum teams make more effective decisions.
- The "Estimating" process area provides detailed methods for forecasting resource needs and durations. This enables the creation of realistic and accurate estimates. Consequently, it can offer better insights to support the creation of the Sprint Backlog and the effort estimation process during planning [40].
- Scrum typically focuses on optimizing how the team works and its processes, but it does not provide a detailed structure for monitoring processes and standards. Additionally, the evaluation of product quality generally relies on reviews conducted at the end of each sprint (Sprint Review, Retrospective). The "Process and Product Quality Assurance" process area provides detailed guidelines to ensure the quality of processes and products. This can help Scrum teams address and apply quality standards more comprehensively.
- In Scrum, performance can be measured through the outputs of Retrospectives, Burndown Charts, and Sprint Reviews. However, these measurements may often be limited in terms of project goals and strategic performance indicators. The "Managing Performance & Measurement" process area provides methodologies and tools for more comprehensive analysis of performance data. This can help Scrum teams better understand performance trends and long-term effects.
- In Scrum, process and performance tracking are carried out through Daily Scrum Meetings, a task board that facilitates tracking of work progress, and evaluation meetings held at the end of each sprint (Sprint Review, Retrospective). Supporting these processes, the "Monitor & Control" process area includes the regular monitoring of performance indicators such as project progress, cost, time, and quality [39]. This can help manage scope deviations, resources, and time overruns in Scrum projects more effectively.
- The "Implementation Infrastructure" process area covers the technical and operational infrastructure requirements that Scrum may lack. This process area includes system maintenance, technical support processes, and technical improvements as needed, ensuring that Scrum teams are in a continuous support and improvement process.
- Scrum focuses on a specific project and team skill set but does not address competency and skill gaps across the organization. The "Organizational Training" process area enhances the overall competency level of the organization by providing employees with professional development and certification opportunities [43]. Team members with increased knowledge and skills can manage project and software development processes more effectively.

The hybrid approach allows organizations to benefit from a structured yet flexible development framework, addressing both project-specific and organizational-level challenges. By enhancing structure, risk management, and process quality through CMMI-Dev while retaining the adaptability of Scrum, organizations can build a more resilient software development process.

Furthermore, the case study examples demonstrate that this hybrid model can reduce resource wastage and project delays, aligning with both agile responsiveness and CMMI-Dev's focus on process stability.

By adopting this hybrid approach, organizations not only address the limitations of using Scrum alone but also capitalize on the strengths of both methodologies. This synergy ultimately contributes to the maturity of software development processes and improves overall project success.

7 Conclusion

The aim of this study is to determine whether the integration of Scrum practices with CMMI-Dev v2.0 process areas is an effective methodology for managing and improving software projects. The hybrid approach formed by this integration is designed to leverage the strengths of both frameworks to address gaps and enhance overall efficiency and effectiveness. Using a comparative analysis approach, Scrum practices were mapped to CMMI-Dev v2.0 process areas. The compatibility of each Scrum practice with CMMI-Dev v2.0 process areas was examined in detail, and their complementary aspects and potential for improvement were identified. This analysis included a review of the existing literature, an assessment of the applicability of these practices in real-world scenarios, and case studies from companies that have successfully implemented similar hybrid models.

The findings indicate that the hybrid approach offers significant opportunities for improvement in project management and software development processes. While CMMI and agile frameworks focus on different layers (what should be done and how it should be done, respectively), they complement each other because both provide values, principles, and best practices to achieve organizational business goals. Scrum focuses on increasing the flexibility of projects and software development, whereas CMMI-Dev v2.0 offers a framework that helps organizations analyze, define, monitor, and continuously improve their software development processes. Particularly in large projects, organizations can enhance process capabilities and maintain customer-focused, flexible software development by using these two approaches together.

In conclusion, integrating Scrum with CMMI-Dev v2.0 offers a promising approach for improving software development processes. This approach enables organizations to work in alignment with agile principles while managing their processes more efficiently and effectively. As a result, organizations can improve customer satisfaction, gain a competitive advantage, and achieve success. Furthermore, broader application and adoption of this hybrid approach by more organizations in practice will contribute to the improvement of project management and software development processes at both academic and industrial levels.

However, this study has certain limitations. Firstly, the research primarily focuses on organizations that have adopted both Scrum and CMMI-Dev v2.0, which may limit the generalizability of the findings to other contexts or frameworks. Additionally, the case studies were selected based on availability, which may introduce bias in the data collection process. Future research could explore the integration of other agile methodologies with CMMI-Dev v2.0 to assess their compatibility and effectiveness. Moreover, longitudinal studies examining the long-term impact of this hybrid approach on project outcomes and organizational performance would provide deeper insights into its efficacy.

References

1. Zare, J., Persaud, A.: Digital transformation and business model innovation: a bibliometric analysis of existing research and future perspectives. Springer, Management Review Quarterly (2024)
2. Dingsøyr, T., Moe, N.B., Fægri, T.E., Seim, E.A.: Exploring software development at the very large-scale: a revelatory case study and research agenda for agile method adaptation. Empir. Softw. Eng. **23**(1), 490–520 (2017). https://doi.org/10.1007/s10664-017-9524-2
3. Alqudah, M., Razali, R.: A review of scaling agile methods in large software development. Int. J. Adv. Sci. Eng. Inf. Technol. **6**(6), 828–837 (2016)
4. Tabrez, S., Jan, I.: Documentation and Agile Methodology (Master Thesis), Department of Informatics and Media, Uppsala University (2013)
5. Leppänen, M.: A Comparative analysis of agile maturity models. In: Pooley, R., Coady, J., Schneider, C., Linger, H., Barry, C., Lang, M. (eds.) Information Systems Development. Springer, New York, NY (2013)
6. Henriquez, V., Calvo-Manzano, J.A., Moreno, A.M., San Feliu, T.: Agile-CMMI v2.0 alignment: bringing to light the agile artifacts pointed out by CMMI. Comput. Standards Interfaces **82**, 103610 (2022)
7. Fontana, R.M., Albuquerque, R., Luz, R., Moises, A.C., Malucelli, A., Reinehr, S.: Maturity models for agile software development: what are they? In: Larrucea, X., Santamaria, I., O'Connor, R., Messnarz, R. (eds.) Systems, Software and Services Process Improvement. EuroSPI 2018. Communications in Computer and Information Science, vol. 896. Springer, Cham (2018)
8. Çamoğlu, K., Akbayır, D., Yücalar, F., Bayraklı, S.: Bir Çevik Yazılım Geliştirme Sürecinin Uyarlanması ve Uygulanması. Havacılık ve Uzay Teknolojileri Dergisi. **4**(3), 57–67 (2010)
9. Alsaqqa, S., Sawalha, S., Abdel-Nabi, H.: Agile software development: methodologies and trends. Int. J. Interact. Mob. Technol. **14**(11), 246–270 (2020)
10. Flora, H.K., Chande, S.: V: A systematic study on agile software development methodologies and practices. Int. J. Comput. Sci. Inf. Technol. **5**(3), 3626–3637 (2014)
11. Sassa, A.C., et al.: Scrum: a systematic literature review. Int. J. Adv. Comput. Sci. Appl. (IJACSA) **14**(4), 173–181 (2023)
12. Ameta, U., Patel, M., Sharma, A.K.: Scrum framework based on agile methodology in software development and management. In: Mathur, R., Gupta, C. P., Katewa, V., Jat, D.S., Yadav, N. (eds.) Emerging Trends in Data Driven Computing and Communications. Studies in Autonomic, Data-driven and Industrial Computing. Springer, Singapore (2021)
13. Hron, M., Obwegeser, N.: Scrum in practice: an overview of Scrum adaptations. In: Hawaii International Conference on System Sciences, pp. 4496–4505. Curran Associates, Inc. (2018)
14. Abrahamsson, P., Salo, O., Ronkainen, J., Warsta, J.: Agile software development methods: review and analysis. arXiv preprint arXiv:1709.08439 (2017)
15. Srivastava, A., Bhardwaj, S., Saraswat, S.: SCRUM model for agile methodology. In: 2017 International Conference on Computing, Communication and Automation (ICCCA), pp. 864–869. IEEE (2017)

16. Sachdeva, S.: Scrum methodology. Int. J. Eng. Comput. Sci. **5**(16792), 16792–16800 (2016)
17. Jaskyte, K., Hunter, A., Mell, A.C.: Predictors of interdisciplinary team innovation in higher education institutions. Innov. High. Educ. **49**, 113–132 (2024)
18. Vasylieva, K., Kuhrmann, M., Xavier, M.K., Klünder, J.: How agile are you? Discussing maturity levels of agile maturity models. In: 2023 49th Euromicro Conference on Software Engineering and Advanced Applications (SEAA), Durres, Albania, pp. 270–277 (2023)
19. Bambauer-Sachse, S., Helbling, T.: Customer satisfaction with business services: is agile better? J. Bus. Ind. Market. **36**(8), 1389–1402 (2021)
20. Tanrıöver, Ö.Ö., Demirörs, O.: A process capability-based assessment model for software workforce in emergent software organizations. Comput. Standards Interfaces **37**, 29–40 (2015)
21. Khraiwesh, M.: Measures of organizational training in the capability maturity model integration (CMMI®). Int. J. Adv. Comput. Sci. Appl. **11**(2), 584–592 (2020)
22. Chrissis, M.B.C., et al.: CMMI Interpretive Guidance Project: Preliminary Report, Special Report, CMU/SEI-2003-SR-007, Carnegie Mellon University (2003)
23. Paulk, M.C., Curtis, B., Chrissis, M.B., Weber, C.V.: Capability maturity model, version 1.1. IEEE Softw. **10**(4), 18–27 (1993)
24. Sen, Z., Zheng, Y.: The relation of CMM and software lifecycle model. In: Eighth ACIS International Conference on Software Engineering, Artificial Intelligence, Networking, and Parallel/Distributed Computing (SNPD 2007), vol. 3, pp. 864–869. IEEE (2007)
25. Team, C.M.M.I.: CMMI for Systems Engineering/Software Engineering/Integrated Product and Process Development, Version 1.1, Staged Representation (CMMI-SE/SW/IPPD, V1. 1, Staged) (2001)
26. Ayyagari, M.R., Atoum, I.: CMMI-DEV implementation simplified. Int. J. Adv. Comput. Sci. Appl. **10**(4) (2019)
27. Ojha, T.R.: Role of capability maturity model integration (CMMI) in software process improvement. J. Adv. Softw. Eng. Test. **5**(2), 1–8 (2022)
28. Triana, Y.S.: Process improvement software through assessment using CMMI framework. In: International Conference on Emerging Computational Technologies (ICECoT), pp. 27–30 (2021)
29. Alparslan Mollaoğlu, S.A., Sönmeztürk Bolatan, G.İ.: Yazılım Süreçlerinde Kalite ve Yetenek Olgunluk Modeli, Organizasyon ve Yönetim Bilimleri Dergisi **12**(1), 77–97 (2020)
30. Marçal, A.S.C., et al.: Mapping CMMI project management process areas to SCRUM practices. In: 31st IEEE Software Engineering Workshop (SEW 2007), pp. 13–22. IEEE (2007)
31. Phillips, M., Shrum, S.: Process improvement for all: what to expect from CMMI Version 1.3. Crosstalk–J. Defense Softw. Eng. (2010)
32. Balla, K., et al.: Changes in CMMI 2.0 and how they can affect TMMi. TMMi Foundation, Bulverde, TX, USA, Tech. Rep. (2020)
33. Digital.ai, 17th State of Agile Report, Digital.Ai. 1–26 (2023). https://stateofagile.com/#ufh-i-661275008-17th-state-of-agile-report/7027494
34. Esher, J.J.: Agile Methodology Tailoring Under CMMI®. Wilmington University (Delaware) (2019)
35. Garcia, L.A., OliveiraJr, E., Leal, G.C.L., Morandini, M.: A unified feature model for Scrum artifacts from a literature and practice perspective. In: Anais da IV Escola Regional de Engenharia de Software, pp. 296–305. SBC (2020)
36. Team, C.P.: CMMI® for Development, Version 1.3. Preface, SEI, CMU (2006)
37. Dalton, J., et al.: A Guide to Scrum and CMMI: Improving Agile Performance with CMMI (2016)
38. ISACA. https://cmmiinstitute.com/cmmi-and-agile. Accessed 5 Oct 2024
39. Chrissis, M.B., Konrad, M., Shrum, S.: CMMI for Development: Guidelines for Process Integration and Product Improvement. Pearson Education (2011)

40. Farid, A.B., Abd Elghany, A.S., Helmy, Y.M.: Implementing project management category process areas of CMMI version 1.3 using scrum practices, and assets. Int. J. Adv. Comput. Sci. Appl. (IJACSA) **7**(2) (2016)
41. Fuentes, B.A., Jenkins, M.: Use of CMMI-DEV 2.0 for continuous process improvement in an agile organization: a case study. In: 2022 17th Iberian Conference on Information Systems and Technologies (CISTI), pp. 1–6. IEEE (2022)
42. Ferdinansyah, A., Purwandari, B.: Challenges in combining agile development and CMMI: a systematic literature review. In: 2021 10th International Conference on Software and Computer Applications (2021)
43. Henriquez, V., Moreno, A.M., Gutiérrez, S.: Organizational training in agile settings under the lens of CMMI V2. 0. J. Softw.: Evol. Process **35**(9), e2502 (2023)
44. Henriquez, V., Moreno, A.M., Calvo-Manzano, J.A., San Feliu, T.: Agile–CMMI alignment: contributions and to-dos for organizations. Computer **54**(12), 38–49 (2021)
45. Ajayi, W.: A Comparative analysis of agile methods and the capacity maturity model integration (CMMI). Asian J. Comput. Sci. Technol. **10**(2), 25–33 (2021)
46. Yalçıner, B., Chouseinoglou, O., Efe, Ö.M.: Mapping Cmmi-Dev V2.0 with Scrum: A Project Management and Quality Assurance Perspective. Available at SSRN 4310530 (2022)
47. Amer, S.K., Badr, N., Hamad, A.: Combining CMMI specific practices with scrum model to address shortcomings in process maturity. In: Handbook of Experimental Pharmacology, 898–907 (2019)

Fine-Tuning VO Estimation Model Based on Deep Learning of TQU-SLAM Benchmark Dataset

Van-Hung Le[1(✉)], Do Huu Son[1], Phan Van Nam[1], Te Trung Hieu[1], and Ninh Quang Trí[2]

[1] Tan Trao University, Yên Sơn, Tuyen Quang Province, Vietnam
van-hung.le@mica.edu.vn
[2] FPT University, Hanoi, Vietnam

Abstract. Visual Odometry (VO) estimation is a component study of Visual SLAM in robotics and building applications to support visually impaired people in finding, tracking, and navigating. Deep learning with its outstanding advantages in accuracy has been widely applied to solve VO estimation problems by solving computer vision problems. However, it requires a huge amount of data to learn about the diversity of different environments. We make two main contributions: (1) The first is to publish the TQU-SLAM Benchmark dataset (TQU-D) collected from the hallway of three connected buildings on the second floor of TQU, Vietnam. These three buildings are interconnected with a movement length of 230m. This dataset includes 160,631 RGB-D frame pairs captured with 8 movement times (4 DI times and 4 VE times), and published data includes RGB-D data and 3D ground-truth (GT) camera motion trajectory/pose. The 3D original data is built based on manually prepared data on 2D images and the point cloud data construction method. (2) The second is to perform fine-tuning of the VO estimation model based on the end-to-end MLF-VO framework with backbones such as Resnet-18, and Resnet-34 on 12 cross-divided subsets of the TQU-D, and the estimated error is from 16.97 to 57.61 m. VO estimation results are evaluated and presented in the available. With these results, the database needs to be standardized and improved in the future.

Keywords: Deep Learning (DL) · Fine-tuning estimation model · Visual Odometry (VO) · TQU-SLAM Benchmark Dataset (TQU-D)

1 Introduction

Visual SLAM (Simultaneous Localization and Mapping) can be defined as consisting of two main problems [1]: one is to build a map of a strange environment indoors or outdoors and the other is to simultaneously track the location or moving of sensors/cameras through sensors different locations and times in the environment. Visual SLAM is a complex technique. Although it has received a lot of research attention in recent years, it still has many challenges that need to be resolved [2–4] as (1) uncertainty: the image

A. Mirzazadeh et al. (Eds.): SEMIT 2024, CCIS 2444, pp. 105–121, 2026.
https://doi.org/10.1007/978-3-032-01948-6_7

sensors are often noisy and uncertain, making it difficult for Visual SLAM algorithms to determine precise locations and maps; (2) complexity: Visual SLAM is a complex problem, and Visual SLAM algorithms often take a long time to execute; (3) environmental conditions: Visual SLAM can be affected by environmental conditions, such as low lighting, crowded environments, and rapidly changing environments.

Over the past decade, the strong development of GPUs and the advent of DL networks have brought convincing results when solving computer vision problems.

DL networks require a very large amount of training data and the results are proportional to the size of the data. Based on the survey research in [5], there are three evolving ways with varying degrees of integrating DL into traditional Visual SLAM systems: (a) auxiliary DL modules into Visual SLAM framework, (b) replacing the traditional modules in Visual SLAM framework by the DL modules, and (c) end-to-end DL framework.

The issue of enriching the amount of data to train VO estimation models is very important. In the study of Favorskaya et al. [5], There are three DL-based methods for building Visual SLAM and VO: the first is the auxiliary DL modules into the Visual SLAM framework, the second is the replace the traditional modules in the Visual SLAM framework by the DL modules, and the third is the end-to-end DL framework.

In the first method, Tateno et al. [6] presented a new model called CNNSLAM, which is based on convolutional neural networks (CNN - Convolutional Neural Networks) that process input frames to estimate the pose of objects. Camera and uses keyframes to predict scene depth across frames. Segmenting camera frames into smaller parts to better understand the environment is one of the ideas in CNN-SLAM to provide parallel processing and real-time performance. The environment map built from the CNN-SLAM model has a density similar to the original data map, and the ratio of objects in the environment is also close to the original data. Mumuni et al. [7] proposed an efficient confidence-weighted adaptive network training framework (Cowan) that iterative leverages intermediate prediction confidences to enforce inter-task consistency across image regions of corresponding images. Second, the authors proposed a test-time fine-tuning method to adapt the network to the dynamic environment while improving accuracy. The third is to enforce geometric consistency between the initial updated pose and the triangle depth. Cowan with geometric guide refinement (CowanGGR) achieves remarkable accuracy and durability. Cowan GGR includes two training stages: In the first stage, the depth of the image in each frame using DepthNet is estimated from the monocular camera image data; EgoMNet is used to predict camera pose; OFNet is used to predict optical flow. The second stage is used to filter out suitable regions to allow for loss of consistency to update the network in a path-discriminatory manner using Cowan-GGR. Qiao et al. [8] proposed the ORG module to perform the extraction of objects in the image and build a relationship chart between objects. From there, combine semantic connections and relative spatial relationships of objects in the image. ORG is then integrated into the camera pose framework to predict the camera pose. This module increases the camera pose prediction results by about 10% on the RIO10 dataset [9] compared to other camera pose prediction networks such as PoseNet, and MapNet [10].

In the second method, to improve the results in estimating Visual SLAM from environments with SfM, Xiao et al. [11] proposed DeepMLE which includes two main proposals. The first is to use deep multi-scale correlation maps to characterize the visual similarity of 2D image matches determined by motion during ego-motion estimation. The second is to construct the likelihood function of the correlations of the 2D fitted images in the form of a Gaussian and Uniform mixture distribution which takes into account uncertainties due to lighting changes, image noise, other factors, and moving objects. Zhu et al. [12] proposed DeepAVO to add to the VO estimation framework.

DeepAVO includes four CNN branches proposed to train the rotation and translation from optical flow input with different quadrants. At the same time, the authors proposed adding an effective channel spatial attention mechanism to force each branch to filter relevant information to estimate specific Frame to Frame (F2F) motion to improve extraction ability features.

In the third method, Han et al. [13] proposed the end-to-end system PSPNetSLAM for environment map construction based on optical flow and semantic segmentation to detect and remove floating points. PSPNet-SLAM is a combination of ORB-SLAM2 and PSPNet networks for semantic segmentation. The image-matching process used an algorithm to eliminate false matches. Tu et al. [14] proposed an end-to-end DEM network architecture for scene depth estimation from RGB images based on the combination of an encoder and a decoder. The input image has a size of 480×640 and the output image has a size of 228×304. During the depth estimation process, the authors designed an information loss function to calibrate the parameters. The estimated depth image is used in combination with the color image to build a 3D scene reconstruction map of the environment, in which camera poses of monocular images are estimated from the RANSAC PnP algorithm.

In this paper, we are only interested in the VO problem. We collect, prepare, and publish the TQU-D. TQU-D is collected in the hallway of three connected buildings, these three houses have interconnected corridors. We perform data collection on the second floor, with a length of 230m. The image data is collected from an Intel RealSense D435 camera, the data includes two main streams: color images (RGB) and depth images (D), they are called RGB-D data. The GT data about the camera's motion trajectory/camera pose in the environment is prepared by hand and published as a 3D camera pose. At the same time, we propose to use the Multi-Layer Fusion VO (MLF-VO) network [15] for fine-tuning the VO estimation model from the RGB-D frame sequence of the monocular camera. This is an end-to-end DL network.

Our paper includes the following main contributions:

- Preparing and publishing the TQU-D including 160,631 RGB-D frame pairs to serve training and evaluating VO estimation models from monocular camera image sequences. The GT data of motion trajectory in 3D space is prepared by hand.
- The TQU-D is divided into 12 cross-datasets to train and test the VO estimation model. We fine-tuned the VO estimation model by end-to-end MLF-VO framework with the backbones ResNet-18 and Resnet-34. The results are evaluated, compared, and presented in detail.

2 TQU-SLAM Benchmark Dataset

2.1 Data Collection

This paper introduces the TQU-D to evaluate the VO estimation model. This database is collected from the 2nd floor of the corridor of three connected buildings (Buil. A, Buil. B, and Buil. C) of Tan Trao University (TQU) in Vietnam, as shown in Fig. 1. These are the hallways of the classrooms.

We experimented and collected data on the 2nd floor of Building B, Building C, and Building A of TQU because the second floors of these three buildings are connected, convenient for moving the data collection equipment and determining the coordinates of the markers in the original coordinate system (CS) defined at location (2). From there, the original data in real-world space is defined more easily and accurately.

In the experimental environment, there are 15 important locations which are the folds or intersections of the moving directions. The direction from Buil. B to Buil. C, then to Buil. A along the blue line is called the forward direction (DI), and and the opposite direction along the red line is called the return direction (VE). In Fig. 1, we define the original CS with the origin at position (2), the x-axis is defined as the direction of the red arrow (from position (2) to (1)), the y-axis is defined as the direction of the green arrow and has the direction of the height to the ceiling, the z-axis is defined as the blue arrow (in the direction of movement from position (2) to (4)).

The specific environment in which we experimented was the corridor of three connected buildings. Therefore, the moving environment also has some common features with the corridors of the buildings, such as walls or railings on both sides, glossy tile floors, which may contain some objects such as plant pots, and fire extinguishers, and may have people moving around. The RGB-D image data was collected from the environment using an Intel® RealSense™ Depth Camera D435 (I-RS-D-C- D435), illustrated in Fig. 2(b). This is a compact image sensor with dimensions of (Length × Depth × Height = 90 mm × 25 mm × 25 mm), the depth image data obtained has a maximum size of 1280 x 720 pixels.

Figure 2 shows the structure of I-RS-D-C- D435 and the image sensor setup for data acquisition. An I-RS-D-C- D435 includes an infrared projector to project infrared rays onto the surface of an object, an RGB sensor to collect color images, and two stereo sensors to collect stereo, and depth (D) images. A vehicle equipped with a camera and computer when collecting data. The camera is installed on the vehicle and connected to the control Laptop to collect data from the environment.

The data acquisition speed can be up to 90 fps. Depth technology is the active IR stereo. At each time point the data obtained is a pair of color images and a D image, these two images correspond to each other. The I-RS-D-C- D435 is mounted on the vehicle, as shown in Fig. 2 (b). The deviation of the I-RS-D-C- D435's view and the floor is 45 degrees. We set the angle between the view of the image sensor (I-RS-D-C- D435), which is the best viewing angle for collecting color and depth data from the environment. The smaller the angle, the more blurred the data is, and the higher the angle, the less marker images are collected. This problem will cause difficulties in marking marker data on the image and preparing the original 3D data. Therefore, we set the angle to 45 degrees to facilitate data collection and preparation. The length of a one-way trip is (DI is 230.63 m, VE is 228.13 m) and the width of the corridor is 2 m, for every 0.5 m we assign a numbered marker with sizes of 10 × 10 cm (we prepare the paper marker and mark the four corners with black), on each marked corner. This is done to facilitate the marking of four corner points of markers on the color image for constructing the original camera position data in 3D space (according to the camera CS) and in the real-world CS as defined in Fig. 1. The total number of markers we used was 332 markers, they are posted in the middle of the hallway and aligned at each section from the locations.

The speed of movement of the camera vehicle and Laptop to collect RGB-D image data is 0.2 m/s, the data we collect are RGB images and D images. Before performing four-point marking on the color image to prepare the original data for VO estimation, we remove the blurred, noisy, and skewed color images due to the shaking of the vehicle with the camera collecting the data, and then remove the corresponding depth image. Then we resized both the color and depth images to 640 x 480 pixels. However on the image sensor, the RGB image and the depth image are collected from two different cameras. But we have synchronized these two types of images to have the same size and the same center.

In this paper, we ignore the data calibration process. We always move the vehicle in the middle of the hallway according to the position of the stretched markers. The data acquisition speed of RGB images and depth images is 15 fps. Data was collected four times over two days, each one hour apart. On the first day, 1ST and 2ND are collected, and on the second day, 3RD and 4TH are collected.

We collect data in the afternoon around mid-afternoon. The length of VE is shorter than that of DI because when moving backward some positions can not be reached. All data of the TQU-D is shown in link[1]. The number of frames we collected at each time is shown in Table 1.

2.2 Preparing GT Trajectory for Evaluating VO

The GT data to evaluate the VO estimation model is the motion trajectory/camera pose in 3D space as follows. CS in real-world space is defined as in Fig. 1. The red arrow is the X axis, the green arrow is the Y axis, and the blue arrow is the Z axis. We built a small software to mark four points of markers on the image using Python language on the RGB image, as shown in Fig. 3(a). That is, we developed a simple tool that allows us to mark the corner points of the markers on the color image as shown in Fig. 3(a). These four points are manually marked by us in each frame of the acquired RGB image. Then four points on the D image are taken corresponding to four points on the marked RGB image because these two types of data are a pair.

In this paper, we do not prepare the 3D annotation data, the 3D annotation data is generated from the manually prepared GT data (markers) on the RGB image. They are generated by transforming the annotation data on the 2D RGB image combined with depth data to create 3D point cloud data. The study of Rodriguez et al. demonstrated the generation of 3D point cloud data from RGB-D sensors [16]. For the RGB-D image sensor, we use the I-RS-D-C- D435. The process of calibrating RGB and color images to the same center and same size to ensure that a pixel in the RGB image corresponds to

[1] https://drive.google.com/drive/folders/16DxnORUvUHFg2BU9mm8aBYMvtAzE9m7.

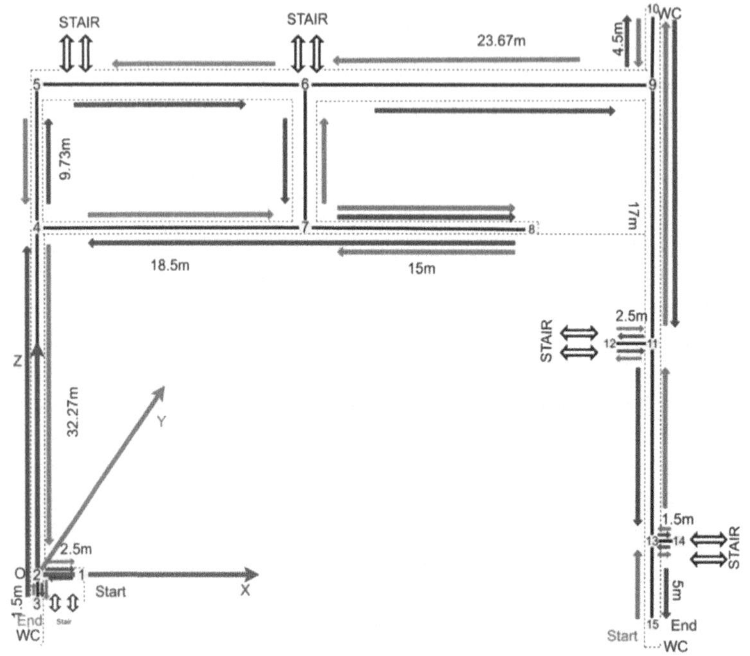

Fig. 1. Illustration of the data collection environment of the environment on the second floor of three connected buildings.

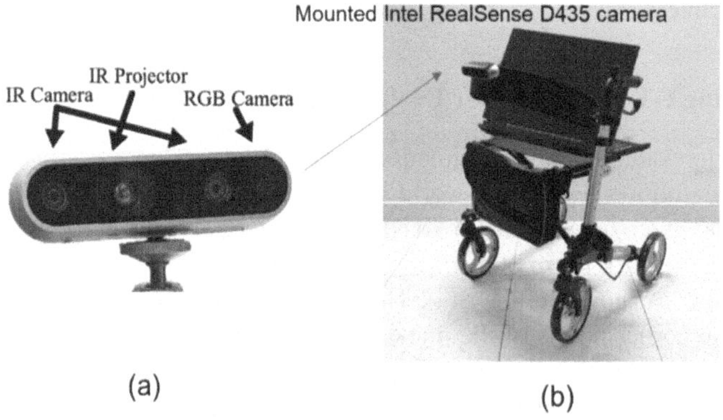

Fig. 2. Illustration of data collection camera and device setup.

a pixel in the depth image is shown in the study of Lachat et al. [17]. There is a problem that occurs in practice when taking a pixel marked on the RGB image corresponding to a pixel on the D image, the D pixel does not have that D value. This happens because the D image when collected from the environment can be punctured (depth value is 0) due to infrared absorption or shadow at that location. Therefore, for any pixel on the D image that does not have a D value, we take the average D value of a square with a size of 5x5 pixels.

Table 1. The number of frames of four data acquisitions of the TQU-D.

Data acquisition times	Direction	Number of RGB-D frames
1ST	DI	21,333
	VE	22,948
2ND	DI	19,992
	VE	21,116
3RD	DI	17,995
	VE	20,814
4TH	DI	17,885
	VE	18,548

The 3D point cloud data of four points is constructed based on four points marked on the color image and four points on the depth image combined with the internal parameter set of I-RS-D-C- D435 as formula (1)

$$\begin{bmatrix} fx & 0 & cx \\ 0 & fy & cy \\ 0 & 0 & 1 \end{bmatrix} = \begin{bmatrix} 525.0 & 0 & 319.5 \\ 0 & 525.0 & 239.5 \\ 0 & 0 & 1 \end{bmatrix} \tag{1}$$

where fx, and fy are the focal length, cx, and cy are the principal of the I-RS-D-C-D435. A corresponding point in the D image has coordinates (xd, yd) and D value da, Coordinates of point M have (xm, ym, zm) created by formula (2).

$$x_m = \frac{(x_d - c_x) * d_a}{f_x}; \ y_m = \frac{\left(y_d - c_y\right) * d_a}{f_y}; \ z_m = d_a \tag{2}$$

The process of calculating the transformation matrix according to the x, y, and z axes is carried out as in the study of Nguyen et al. [18]. The center coordinates of the 4-point cloud data points (xc, yc, zc) generated from formula (2) are calculated in formula (3).

$$\begin{aligned} x_c &= \frac{x'_1 + x'_2 + x'_3 + x'_4}{4} \\ y_c &= \frac{y'_1 + y'_2 + y'_3 + y'_4}{4} \\ z_c &= \frac{z'_1 + z'_2 + z'_3 + z'_4}{4} \end{aligned} \tag{3}$$

The motion trajectory GT in the real-world CS of the test environment is shown in Fig. 3.

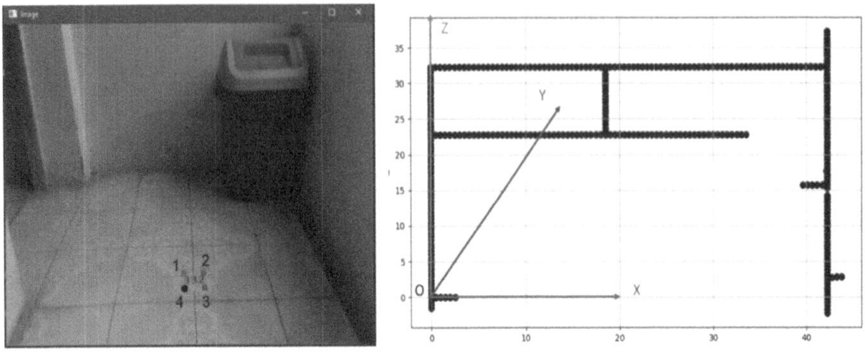

(a) (b)

Fig. 3. The markers on the RGB image and the origin of the real-world CS are predefined. (a) 4 marker points are marked on the color image. (b) The real-world CS is defined and the motion trajectory of the data collection environment.

3 Fine-Tuning VO Estimation Model Based on DL.

Recently, many Visual SLAM and VO construction models have been based on the DL method. In this paper, we exploit a multi-layer fusion network (MLF-VO) [15] to fine-tune the VO estimation model on the TQU-D. MLF-VO was proposed by Jiang et al. [15] with a combination of different fusion strategies to estimate ego-motion from RGB images and depth images obtained from depth estimation.

MLF-VO uses DepthNet to estimate the depth image corresponding to each color image/frame as shown on the left side of Fig. 4. Given the input of consecutive frames of video {It, It + 1}, the network first estimates the depth images corresponding to each input frame: Dt = θdepth(It), Dt + 1 = θdepth(It + 1). DepthNet is built on the structure of U-Net.

To smooth out the color pixels between consecutive frames in the input frame sequence, MLF-VO uses a "smoothness loss – smool" to ensure they do not change abruptly. Given a pair of consecutive RGB images and a disparity map as input [19–21]. The output is the loss computed between adjacent color pixels at each scale (4 scales).

To ensure consistency between frames, which helps transfer consistency to the entire frame sequence. This creates scale-consistentness for the entire frame sequence [19, 20]. To do this, "geometric loss – geo_l" is used to calculate the loss between the depth frame and the next depth frame. With the input being the pixels at the current depth and the pixels at the next depth image. The output is the loss calculated at each different scale (4 scales).

To reduce the impact of outliers, "photometric loss – phol" is calculated based on L1. The L1 loss calculates the total absolute difference between the predicted results and original data, making it less sensitive to outliers than the L2 loss [19–21]. This function is used to calculate the loss between the current RGB frame and the next RGB frame. The input is the pixels in the current RGB image and the pixels in the next RGB image. The output is the loss calculated at each scale (4 scales).

To reduce and control the number of parameters m of the model training process, with the input being the weight parameters initialized before the training process. MLF-VO calculates the Regularization loss (RL) Channel Exchange according to the formula (4).

$$RL = \sum_{m \in self.slim\_params}\left(||m||_1 - 0.01\ ||m - \overline{m}||_1\right) \tag{4}$$

where $||m||_1$ is the L1 regularization for parameter m, i.e. the sum of the absolute values of the elements in m. $\overline{m}$ is the average value of parameter m. $||m - \overline{m}||_1$ is the regularization polorize, that is, the sum of the absolute values of the differences between the elements in m and the mean value $\overline{m}$. The factor 0.01 adjusts the correlation of the polorize regularization with the L1 regularization.

During training, optimize the loss function (SL) as in formula (5).

$$L = pho_l + e^{-2}geo_l + e^{-3}smoo_l + e^{-5}RL \tag{5}$$

The CE process when training MLF-VO is performed has the exchange and synthesis of the loss function SL, thereby helping to overcome the problems of missing data, noisy data, and inconsistent data. From there, the entire learning data is promoted and makes the learning set predict more accurately VO.

In particular, MLF-VO includes two main tasks with two stages, the first stage is to use the baseline framework to estimate ego-motion using two independent CNN models for depth prediction and pose estimation, as illustrated in Fig. 4. At this stage, MLF-VO uses the fully convolutional U-Net obtain architectural depths at four scales.

The second stage is relative pose estimation based on MLF-VO with the combination of multi-layer fusion strategy according to several features appearing in intermediate layers of the encoder. To encode features from color and depth images, MLF-VO includes two structural streams. The Channel Exchange (CE) strategy is used to swap the positions of components and their importance for combining features at multiple levels.

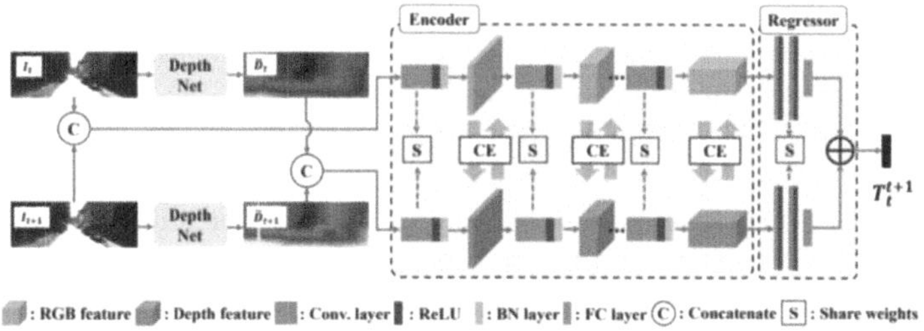

Fig. 4. Illustration of the architecture of the two independent CNN models underlying ego-motion estimation [4].

In both streams, ResNet-18 [22] is used as the encoder. To build an end-to-end automatic learning DL network, MLF-VO has built a self-learning mechanism with a loss function (SL) combined with the process of depth prediction and relative pose estimation, as illustrated in Fig. 5. In this paper, we are only interested in fine-tuning the VO estimation model and fine-tuning using backbones like Resnet-18, Resnet-34.

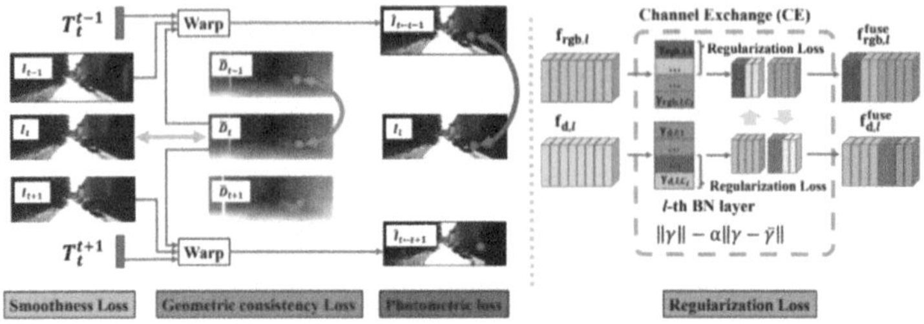

Fig. 5. Loss function of MLF-VO for self-learning process [15].

In this paper, we use ResNet-18 and ResNet-34 as backbones to encode the extracted features from color images because these two backbones have enough layers to create accuracy and fast computation time.

We conduct experiments and compare with some backbones to encode features as follows: VGG-16 has faster computation time but lower accuracy than ResNet-18 and ResNet-34 [23], ResNet-50, ResNet-101, ResNet-152 have slightly better accuracy than ResNet-18 and ResNet-34 [24] but increased computation time, ResNet-18 has higher accuracy than Dense121 [25].

4 Experimental Results

4.1 Dataset for Training VO Estimation Models and Evaluation Measures

From the collected data, we cross-divide the TQU-D into 12 sub-datasets (Sub1 to Sub12) for training and testing the model, as shown in Table 2. We split the training and testing data in a cross-split form such as 1ST-DI, 2ND-DI, 3RD-DI for training, and 4TH-DI for testing. Based on statistical theory and machine learning all subsets of the data are trained for the VO estimation model and all are tested. Based on statistics about 75% of the data is for training the model and 25% of the data is for testing the model. This ratio is reasonable statistically and for machine learning problems. Since the MLF-VO framework accepts the input image data with the size 640 × 192 pixels, we resize the RGB-D images of the TQU-D to the size 640 × 192 pixels.

This paper uses the MLF-VO framework to fine-tune the VO estimation model on the TQU-D. MLF-VO is developed in Python v3.x language and programmed on Ubuntu 18.04, Pytorch 1.7.1, and CUDA 10.1. We used the code in the link[2] on the Server with the configuration: CPU i5 12400f, 16G DDr4, GPU RTX 3060 12GB. We fine-tune the VO estimation model of MLF-VO with 20 epochs, parameters are default in the MLF-VO framework. The value 10–4 is assigned to the learning rate. In particular, we set these parameters by default to be the same as MLF [4] when performing training on the first 20 epochs.

In this paper, the VO/camera pose estimation model is evaluated on two measures, we compute trajectory/pose error (Errd), which is the distance error from the GT GT $A^{\wedge}T_i$

[2] https://github.com/Beniko95J/MLF-VO.

and the predicted motion trajectory/camera pose ATi. Errd is calculated according to formula (6).

$$Err_d = \frac{1}{N}\sqrt{\|AT_i - A\hat{}T_i\|^2} \quad (6)$$

where N is the number of frames of the testing sequence for estimating the motion trajectory. The absolute camera pose error (ATE) [7] is the distance error from the GT A^T i and the predicted camera pose ATi, aligned with an optimal SE (3) pose T. ATE is computed based on the formula (7).

$$ATE = \min_{T \in SE(3)} \sqrt{\frac{1}{I_{gt}} \sum_{i \in I_{gt}} \|TAT_i - A\hat{}T_i\|^2} \quad (7)$$

trel is the average transnational RMSE drift (%) on a length of 100–800 m. Rrel is the aver. Rotational RMSE drift (°/100m) on a length of 100–800 m. In addition, we also evaluate the VO estimation results using the RMSE measure. RMSE is the standard deviation of the residuals (prediction error) between the GT motion trajectory and the estimated motion trajectory.

Table 2. Cross-split the TQU-D into 12 sub-datasets to train and test the model.

Dividing cross-datasets	Training date	Testing date
Sub1	1ST-DI, 2ND-DI, 3RD-DI	4TH-DI
Sub2	1ST-VE, 2ND-VE, 3RD-VE	4TH-VE
Sub3	1ST-DI, 2ND-DI, 4TH-DI	3RD-DI
Sub4	1ST-VE, 2ND-VE, 4TH-VE	3RD-VE
Sub5	1ST-DI, 3RD-DI, 4TH-DI	2ND-DI
Sub6	1ST-VE, 3RD-VE, 4TH-VE	2ND-VE
Sub7	2ND-DI, 3RD-DI, 4TH-DI	1ST-DI
Sub8	2ND-VE, 3RD-VE, 4TH-VE	1ST-VE
Sub9	1ST-DI, 2ND-DI, 3RD-DI	4TH-DI

(continued)

Table 2. *(continued)*

Dividing cross-datasets	Training date	Testing date
	1ST-VE, 2ND-VE, 3RD-VE	4TH-VE
Sub10	1ST-DI, 2ND-DI, 4TH-DI	3RD-DI
	1ST-VE, 2ND-VE, 4TH-VE	3RD-VE
Sub11	1ST-DI, 3RD-DI, 4TH-DI	2ND-DI
	1ST-VE, 3RD-VE, 4TH-VE	2ND-VE
Sub12	2ND-DI, 3RD-DI, 4TH-DI	1ST-DI
	2ND-VE, 3RD-VE, 4TH-VE	1ST-VE

4.2 Results

The VO estimation results of the MLF-VO framework with backbones such as Resnet-18, and Resnet-34 on cross-datasets of the TQU-D are shown in Table 3. The evaluation results with a backbone are Resnet-18 with Errd with an error from 17.91 m to 44.45 m, with RMSE error from 16.97 m to 49.77 m, and with ATE error from 28.95m to 41.64m. Evaluation results with backbone Resnet-34 with Errd with error from 17.57 m to 52.84 m, with RMSE error from 19.41 m to 57.61 m, and with ATE error from 28.78 m to 38.93 m. The result in VE has a larger error than DI in all measures and backbones of the MLF-VO framework. This problem occurs because when collecting environmental data at the VE, it is more difficult to look at locations (1), (2), (3), (9), (10), (11), (12), (13), (14), and (15) in Fig. 1 than at DI. More specifically, no markers are visible in these positions. Therefore, the process of preparing the original data at these locations causes a larger error compared to the data at VE. This problem occurs because of the data collection context of VE.

Figures 6,7, and 8show the results of VO estimation from Sub1 to Sub12 on the TQU-D with MLF-VO framework with backbone Resnet-18. The blue points are on the GT of the camera pose and the red points are on the predicted camera pose.

MLF-VO framework code and results are shown in the link[3].

Table 4 shows the comparison results of MLF-VO framework Resnet-18, MLF-VO framework Resnet-34 with DPVO [26], and TartanVO [27] for VO estimation with Errd measure. The results show that the error of VO estimation is higher than 10m, so it is

[3] https://drive.google.com/drive/folders/13UmQ3ghDgQh49rqk4i7fmjDMso4Q1Y8?usp=sharing.

Table 3. VO estimation results on the TQU-D into 12 sub-datasets to train and test the model.

Dividing cross-datasets/methods	Data acquisition times	MLF-VO framework					
		Resnet-18			Resnet-34		
		$Err_d(m)$	$RMSE(m)$	$ATE(m)$	$Err_d(m)$	$RMSE(m)$	$ATE(m)$
Sub1	DI	19.95	21.67	28.95	33.69	36.29	38.93
Sub2	VE	38.53	49.77	41.64	30.64	32.93	31.88
Sub3	DI	39.33	42.89	38.39	17.57	19.41	38.78
Sub4	VE	28.80	37.28	37.83	34.74	45.31	29.60
Sub5	DI	18.97	20.62	29.76	26.51	28.90	33.34
Sub6	VE	33.07	34.82	34.55	29.96	31.66	30.57
Sub7	DI	23.77	25.26	37.10	23.28	27.28	34.15
Sub8	VE	39.70	42.16	30.05	52.84	57.61	30.10
Sub9	DI	25.75	28.53	30.13	27.41	29.68	35.68
	VE	35.16	45.45	30.20	27.22	29.09	33.28
Sub10	DI	19.26	20.91	29.20	24.38	29.83	28.96
	VE	20.94	26.63	30.18	17.69	20.24	29.41
Sub11	DI	17.91	19.58	29.50	39.44	42.78	29.94
	VE	35.92	37.72	34.24	18.72	20.57	35.81
Sub12	DI	15.84	16.97	30.96	20.44	22.43	28.78
	VE	44.45	47.58	30.00	33.61	35.65	32.30

necessary to improve and propose a new DL network for VO estimation to match the TQU-D database.

Table 4. Comparison results of MLF-VO framework with DPVO [26] and TartanVO [27] with Errd measure.

Dataset/measure/methods/	Distance error (Err_d (m)) of the TQU-SLAM Benchmark dataset							
	1ST		2ND		3RD		4TH	
	DI	VE	DI	VE	DI	VE	DI	VE
DPVO [26]	13.81	13.84	13.37	13.10	14.85	14.64	13.71	12.32
TartanVO [27]	15.82	14.16	15.21	13.26	13.82	13.12	16.57	17.70
MLF-VO framework Resnet-18	23.77	39.70	18.97	33.07	39.33	28.80	19.95	38.53
MLF-VO framework Resnet-34	23.28	52.84	26.51	29.96	17.57	34.74	33.69	30.64

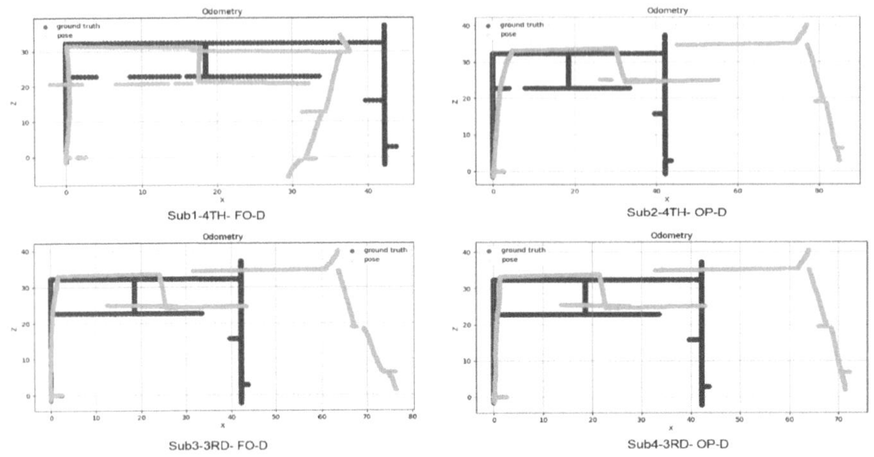

Fig. 6. VO estimation results on Sub1 to Sub4 of the TQU-D.

Table 5 shows the comparison results of MLF-VO framework Resnet-18, MLF-VO framework Resnet-34 with DPVO [26], and TartanVO [27] for VO estimation with ATE measure. The results show that the error of VO estimation is is from 15 to 41m. This is a very large error in the process of estimating the position and direction of movement of the camera in the environment.

Table 5. Comparison results of MLF-VO framework with DPVO [26] and TartanVO [27] with ATE measure.

Dataset/measure/methods/	Distance error (*ATE* (m)) of the TQU-SLAM benchmark dataset							
	1ST		2ND		3RD		4TH	
	DI	VE	DI	VE	DI	VE	DI	VE
DPVO [26]	16.09	15.74	15.99	15.20	17.04	16.70	15.72	15.19
TartanVO [27]	19.24	17.14	17.79	15.39	15.60	15.31	19.30	19.92
MLF-VO framework Resnet-18	37.10	30.05	29.76	34.55	38.39	37.83	28.95	41.64
MLF-VO framework Resnet-34	34.15	30.10	33.34	30.57	38.78	29.60	38.93	31.88

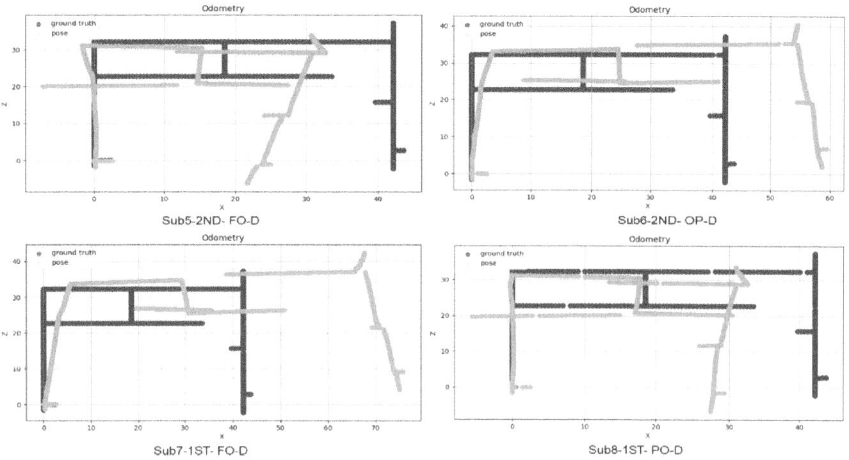

Fig. 7. VO estimation results on Sub5 to Sub8 of the TQU-D.

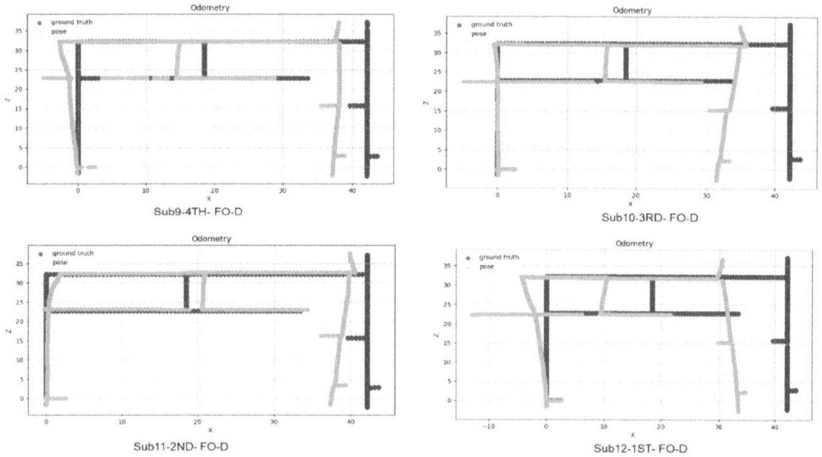

Fig. 8. VO estimation results on Sub9 to Sub12 of the TQU-SLAM benchmark dataset.

5 Conclusions and Future Works

Enriching data to build VO estimation models is a very important issue in DL with the goal that the more learning data, the more accurate the estimated model. In this paper, we have published the TQU-D with 160,631 RGB-D frame pairs collected from the corridor environment of three connected buildings of TQU. The total length of one move is 230m. The published dataset includes the RGB-D image sequences and the GT data of 3D camera pose in the real-world. At the same time, We also perform fine-tuning of the VO estimation model by MLF-VO framework with backbones such as Resnet-18, and Resnet-34 with 12 sub-datasets divided cross-dataset for training and testing models. The error results with measurements on the TQU-D are from 16.97 m to 57.61

m with RMSE measure, and the error results from 13 m to 52 m with Errd measure, the error results from 15 m to 41 m. In the future, we will propose improving DL-based VO estimation methods and enriching the TQU-D for VO estimation such as adding data on 3D scene reconstruction, object detection, and recognition in the environment. Currently, MLF-VO contains loss functions about photometric loss, geometric loss, smoothness loss, and regularization loss to supervise the learning process for estimating the corresponding depth of RGB images in the frame sequence. In the future, we will use some more loss functions such as MSE, Cross Entropy loss to optimize the entire training process of the VO estimation model.

Acknowledgment. This research is funded by Tan Trao University in Tuyen Quang province, Vietnam.

References

1. Taheri, H., Xia, Z.C.: Slam; definition and evolution. Eng. Appl. Artif. Intell. 97 (2021). https://doi.org/10.1016/j.engappai.2020.104032
2. Zhao, X., et al.: How challenging is a challenge? cems: a challenge evaluation module for slam visual perception. J. Intell. Robot. Syst.: Theory Appl. 110 (2024). https://doi.org/10.1007/s10846-024-02077-4
3. Barros, A.M., Michel, M., Moline, Y., Corre, G., Carrel, F., Barros, A.M.: A comprehensive survey of visual slam algorithms (2022). https://doi.org/10.3390/robotics11010024, https://hal.science/hal-04132827
4. Neyestani, A., Picariello, F., Basiri, A., Daponte, P., Vito, L.D.: Survey and research challenges in monocular visual odometry, pp. 107–112. Institute of Electrical and Electronics Engineers Inc. (2023). https://doi.org/10.1109/MetroLivEnv56897.2023.10164057
5. Favorskaya, M.N.: Deep learning for visual slam: the state-of- the-art and future trends. Electronics (Switzerland) 12 (2023). https://doi.org/10.3390/electronics12092006
6. Tateno, K., Tombari, F., Laina, I., Navab, N.: CNN-slam: real-time dense monocular slam with learned depth prediction (2017)
7. Mumuni, F., Mumuni, A., Amuzuvi, C.K.: Deep learning of monocular depth, optical flow and ego-motion with geometric guidance for UAV navigation in dynamic environments. Mach. Learn. Appl. **10**, 100416 (2022). https://doi.org/10.1016/j.mlwa.2022.100416
8. Qiao, C., Xiang, Z., Wang, X.: Objects matter: Learning object relation graph for robust camera relocalization (2022). https://arxiv.org/abs/2205.13280
9. Wald, J., Sattler, T., Golodetz, S., Cavallari, T., Tombari, F.: Beyond controlled environments: 3D camera re-localization in changing indoor scenes (2020). http://arxiv.org/abs/2008.02004
10. Brahmbhatt, S., Gu, J., Kim, K., Hays, J., Kautz, J.: Geometry-aware learning of maps for camera localization (2018). https://arxiv.org/abs/1712.03342
11. Xiao, Y., Li, L., Li, X., Yao, J.: Deepmle: A robust deep maximum likelihood estimator for two-view structure from motion (2022). http://arxiv.org/abs/2210.05517
12. Zhu, R., Yang, M., Liu, W., Song, R., Yan, B., Xiao, Z.: Deepavo: efficient pose refining with feature distilling for deep visual odometry. Neurocomputing **467**, 22–35 (2021). http://arxiv.org/abs/2105.09899
13. Han, S., Xi, Z.: Dynamic scene semantics slam based on semantic segmentation. IEEE Access **8**, 43563–43570 (2020). https://doi.org/10.1109/ACCESS.2020.2977684
14. Tu, X., et al.: Learning depth for scene reconstruction using an encoder-decoder model. IEEE Access **8**, 89300–89317 (2020). https://doi.org/10.1109/ACCESS.2020.2993494

15. Jiang, Z., Taira, H., Miyashita, N., Okutomi, M.: Self-supervised ego-motion estimation based on multi-layer fusion of RGB and inferred depth (2022). http://arxiv.org/abs/2203.01557
16. Rodriguez-Jimenez, S., Burrus, N., Abderrahim, M.: 3D object reconstruction with a single RGB-Depth image. In: VISAPP 2013 - Proceedings of the International Conference on Computer Vision Theory and Applications, vol. 2(June), pp. 155–163 (2013). https://doi.org/10.5220/0004286401550163
17. Lachat, E., Macher, H., Landes, T., Grussenmeyer, P.: Assessment and calibration of a RGB-D camera (Kinect v2 Sensor) towards a potential use for close-range 3D modeling. Remote Sens. **7**(10), 13070–13097 (2015). https://doi.org/10.3390/rs71013070
18. Nguyen, T.T., Le, V.H., Duong, D.L., Pham, T.C., Le, D.: 3D human pose estimation in Vietnamese traditional martial art videos. J. Adv. Eng. Comput. **3**, 471 (2019). https://doi.org/10.25073/jaec.201933.252
19. Bian, J.W., et al.: Unsupervised scale-consistent depth and ego-motion learning from monocular video. Advances in Neural Information Processing Systems 32(NeurIPS), pp. 1–12 (2019)
20. Godard, C., Aodha, O.M., Firman, M., Brostow, G.: Digging into selfsupervised monocular depth estimation. In: Proceedings of the IEEE International Conference on Computer Vision 2019-October(1), pp. 3827–3837 (2019). https://doi.org/10.1109/ICCV.2019.00393
21. Godard, C., Mac Aodha, O., Brostow, G.J.: Unsupervised monocular depth estimation with left-right consistency. In: Proceedings - 30th IEEE Conference on Computer Vision and Pattern Recognition, CVPR 2017, vol. 2017, pp. 6602–6611 (2017). https://doi.org/10.1109/CVPR.2017.699
22. He, K., Zhang, X., Ren, S., Sun, J.: Deep residual learning for image recognition (2015). https://arxiv.org/pdf/1512.03385
23. Fagbohungbe, O., Qian, L.: Benchmarking inference performance of deep learning models on analog devices. In: Proceedings of the International Joint Conference on Neural Networks, vol. 2021-July (2021). https://doi.org/10.1109/IJCNN52387.2021.9534143
24. Huang, G., Liu, Z., Van Der Maaten, L., Weinberger, K.Q.: Densely connected convolutional networks. In: Proceedings - 30th IEEE Conference on Computer Vision and Pattern Recognition, CVPR 2017, vol. 2017-January, pp. 2261–2269 (2017). https://doi.org/10.1109/CVPR.2017.243
25. Yang, Y., Zhang, L., Du, M., Bo, J., Liu, H., Ren, L.: Since January 2020 Elsevier has created a COVID-19 resource centre with free information in English and Mandarin on the novel coronavirus COVID- 19. The COVID-19 resource center is hosted on Elsevier Connect, the company's public news and information. Computers in Biology and Medicine (January) (2021)
26. Teed, Z.; Lipson, L.; Deng, J.: Deep Patch Visual Odometry. https://proceedings.neurips.cc/paper_files/paper/2023/hash/7ac484b0f1a1719ad5be9aa8c8455fbb-Abstract-Conference.html. Accessed 6 May 2024
27. Wang, W., Hu, Y., Scherer, S.: TartanVO: a generalizable learning-based VO. In: Proceedings of the Conference on Robot Learning, Online, 16–18 November 2020

Biometric Based Chaotic Cryptography for Multiuser Security System

Saba Jassim Hamadi(✉) and Emad A. Mohammed

Computer Engineering Technology, North Technical University, Mosul 41002, Iraq
{Saba.jasem,e.a.mohammed}@ntu.edu.iq

Abstract. Encryption plays a crucial role in securing multi-user systems, especially in environments where data is shared among multiple parties. Various approaches have been developed to enhance security, manage keys, and ensure data integrity in these systems. This paper introduces a security system for a multiuser system that was suggested in order to identify the users of the system. That is why most security systems only utilize one algorithm to code the system or identify its users. According to the research, the user's biometric will be combined with the system's algorithms to create a Digital Signature that will allow us to identify the system's user. This work presents a new approach in image encryption by combining the merits of RSA and Chaotic maps, namely Lorenz and Logistic. First the Iris biometric provided the initial value for the chaotic Algorithm. Where biometric is encrypted by RSA and the plain image encrypted by chaotic, after these processes the two encryption images are vertically concatenated. Finally, the diffusion process is implemented using the Zig-Zag method. The most important conclusions that were reached the initial value adaptive with each user to the system. The digital signature of each user is used in addition signature for the system Finally the security analysis results has shown that the proposed algorithm has strong security and resistance to differential and statistical attacks, with the values for the NPCR of the image equalling 99.605, that for UACI equalling 35.805, and the capability of de-correlating the adjacent pixels of the cipher image, which resulted in a near-zero correlation coefficient.

Keywords: RSA Algorithm · Zig-Zag Transform · Chaotic Algorithm · Logistic Encryption · Lorenz System

1 Introduction

Data may now be stored on several platforms and exchanged via open public networks, thanks to advancements in network communications technologies. Thus, ensuring data security and privacy has become imperative [1]. Illegal access, use, disclosure, alteration, or destruction of network information can seriously jeopardize the security of whole societies or even entire nations, in addition to costing computer users money [2].

One well-known method of concealing sensitive data is cryptography. Text and pictures are encrypted via cryptography before being sent across a network. The intrinsic properties of pictures, include their high redundancy and block size for data, and strong

A. Mirzazadeh et al. (Eds.): SEMIT 2024, CCIS 2444, pp. 122–137, 2026.
https://doi.org/10.1007/978-3-032-01948-6_8

correlation between neighboring pixels, set them apart from the encryption of text [3]. The act of transforming confidential data into an unrecognizably different form is called encryption. As a result, network information security is becoming a significant field of study in science. Images are the most important kind of media for information sharing among all forms of data, and their security is especially crucial [4]. Encryption, a method used to secure information, has roots in the ancient Babylonians, Egyptians, and Romans. As data sizes increased, traditional encryption methods struggled to keep up. Modern encryption methods use permutation and substitution, which enhance privacy and make decryption more challenging. Chaos maps, which contain characteristics like bifurcation, unexpectedness, and sensitiveness to the starting conditions, are crucial for encryption keys due to their reliability and sensitivity to small variations in value [5].

When multiple users use the same security system, various problems arise, especially those related to system access, and data privacy. Among these problems Increased risk of data breaches, in multi-user environments, the possibility of unauthorized access increases. Each user may have varying levels of access, but poor management can lead to data breaches where sensitive information is accidentally or intentionally disclosed to the wrong user. Access restrictions must be strictly maintained to avoid such incidents.as well as Security vulnerabilities in shared resources, shared systems might expose users to indirect risks such as malware. If one user's device or account is hacked, the whole system may suffer, hence it is critical to separate user sessions and data wherever possible.

Overall, although multi-user systems are useful for resource sharing, they need strong security measures, stringent access rules, and meticulous system administration to minimize these hazards. Enhanced security measures, including as encryption, multi-factor authentication, and frequent audits, are necessary to ensure the system stays secure in a multi-user environment.

2 Related Works

More research on image encryption using chaotic systems has recently surfaced. For example, Sun et al. It combined two levels of permutation operation at the bit and pixel levels and employed A five-dimensional hyper chaotic system for generating various prominent streams [6]. This type of permutation technique in mathematics modifies the histogram's statistical properties in addition to its pixel position. Wang, Xiaoyuan et al. [7] they've displayed Created by a tri-valued colester, a novel color image encryption technique based on the hyper-chaotic system. The procedure of encryption uses permutation-diffusion and hyper-chaotic synchronization technology. The algorithm uses the hash value of the plaintext image to generate the initial key, implements permutation operations, and uses Hilbert curves and cipher text feedback. Experimental analyses show excellent encryption performance and resistance to various attacks. In the image-encryption technique of Moatsum Alawida and Azman Samsudin [8], In this work, three 1D chaotic maps—the Tent, Logistic, and Sine—are taken as seed ones to couple two new chaotic systems: the Tent–Logistic–Tent and Tent–Sine–Tent. After that, these two new chaotic systems are used in the permutation and diffusion processes. Shuliang Sun [9]. This paper describes a new cryptosystem whose principles of operation are based on random signal insertion and a 6D hyper chaotic system. The system generates the initial worth by adding up all of the textual pixels, and then performs operations like scrambling, cycle shift, and diffusion can generate an encrypted image. Simulation data is presented to show that the proposed method is much more secure than many conventional image encryption schemes in view of huge key space, high sensitivity, and robustness against a variety of attacks. A unique approach for grayscale picture encryption was suggested by Sura F. [10]. The image was evenly divided into four blocks, each of which was rotated 90 degrees in a clockwise direction. A permutation sequence was created in order for the confusion to be created, and a masking sequence was created for creating the diffusion by changing the values of the image's pixels. In the present work, four distinct chaotic maps have been considered-one for every block: The Cross, Ikeda, Chebyshev, and Quadratic maps. Finally, the cipher image has been generated by concatenating the four encrypted blocks. It was suggested to use a method for creating a cipher for colored images that joins 1D logistic and sine chaotic maps by Ibtisam A. and Sarab M. [11]. Wadii Boulila et al. [12] have proposed a hybrid color picture encryption method that utilizes several chaotic maps, such as the modified ACM is the 2D- Arnold cat map, NLDS is the (Newton leapnik dynamic system), and LOGAS represents the (logistic Gaussian chaotic system). In the process, the Plaintext color picture layers were first Watermarked using SHA512, two-dimensional Arnold map scrambling, NLDS encryption, and dynamic S-boxes produced by LOGAS, the system is rendered plaintext-dependent. Through a number of simulations and experiments, the method's security is demonstrated. And H. Wen et al. [13] introduces a new encryption technique that combines bit-plane chain diffusion with chaos-based block permutation to enhance image security. The technique uses chaotic sequences to manipulate plaintext images, creating an intermediate cipher image. Random-order substitution and chain diffusion techniques further enhance the avalanche effect. The algorithm is highly resilient to cryptographic attacks, making it a recommended secure communication technology solution for multimedia data transfer in large data environments.

Traditional security system, when multiple users utilize the same system, the data will be electronically signed by the digital signature of the system. Whatever the user was, each user can denial the data transmission because he has no specific signature (system come on signature). To solve this problem, a biometric signature for each user is embedded with each transmitted message.

The main contribution of this research are:

- Each user will sign the message with its Biometric as well as system digital signature, in addition to applying security feature which is nonrepudiation.
- increase the possibility of encryption operations and strengthen the chaotic encryption algorithm by eliminating the problem of the repeated initial value at each encryption operation based on the biometric of the iris.

3 Review of the Used Methods

Three techniques form the basis of the strategy this study suggests:

3.1 Chaotic Maps

Image data often need more storage capacity than text data and are distinguished by significant redundancy and strong correlation among neighboring pixels. Consequently, conventional encryption techniques are inadequate for the requirements of image encryption. Nonetheless, using chaos theory in image encryption is an innovative methodology. Chaotic systems exhibit extreme sensitivity to beginning circumstances, where minor inaccuracies may result in significantly divergent motion paths. While the chaotic trajectory may be regulated with established beginning circumstances, long-term prediction of the trajectory remains unattainable without knowledge of those initial conditions. Moreover, chaotic systems possess other characteristics, such as elevated ergodicity, determinism, and pseudo-randomness, which are essential for image encryption.

In recent years, researchers have used several chaotic systems, including discrete chaotic maps and continuous chaotic systems, for image encryption to enhance the security of image transmission [14].

In this paper, we're going to use and combine two types of chaotic maps: 1-D logistic and 3-D Lorenz.

Logistic Map. Among the prominent 1D chaotic maps is the logistic map. It is a very simple dynamical equation but constructs some very complicated chaotic behaviors [15]. Mathematically, it can be defined as the subsequent Eq. (1):

$$Xk + 1 = \mu Xk(1 - Xk) \tag{1}$$

where $x \in [0, 1]$ is a real number where μ takes values between 0 and 4 is an input parameter for control. As seen in Fig. 1, Finally, when $\mu \in [3.57, 4]$, chaotic behavior is observed [16].

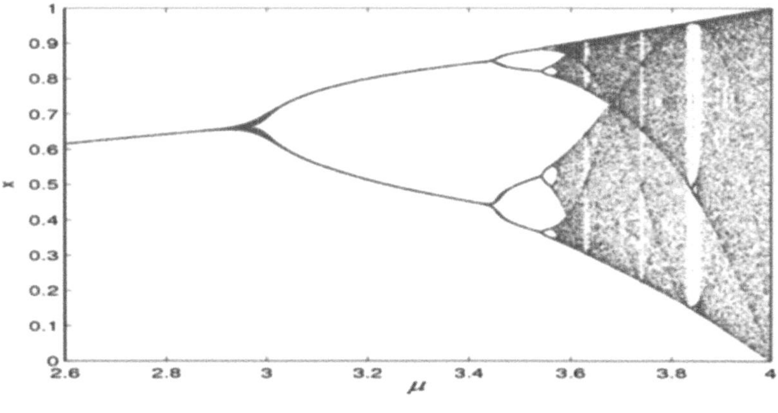

Fig. 1. Bifurcation graph of logistic map.

Lorenz Chaotic System. This system exhibits rich, complicated, and non-linear dynamic behavior and is regarded as the first dynamic system to display individual interactions [17]. The three control parameters of the Lorenz system are the geometric ratio, the Rayleigh number, and the Prandtl number, denoted by the symbols σ, ρ, and β. The system remains chaotic so long as the control parameters satisfy the prerequisites such that $\sigma \in [9,10]$, $\rho \in [25, 30]$, and $\beta \in [2, 3]$. In using fractional calculus, a fourth parameter, α, is gained in the 3D Lorenz system, which increases the security and key space of our suggested picture encryption scheme [18]. Partially derived fractions according to Caputo allows for the following representation of the suggested 3D Lorenz system in the Eq. (2):

$$D\alpha x = \sigma(y - x)$$

$$D\alpha y = \rho x - y - z$$

$$D\alpha z = xy - \beta z \tag{2}$$

where α is the fractional-order differential operator of Caputo, and Dα is the operator with $\alpha \in (0, 1)$.

The system's phase trajectories are depicted in Fig. 2, with the starting states {x0, y0, z0} set to {0.3, 0.3, 0.3}, {0.4, 0.4, 0.4}, {0.2, 0.2, 0.2}, and {0.35, 0.35, 0.35}, respectively. By now, {10, 28, 8/3} was the configuration for the system parameters {σ, ρ, β}. One can see from the phase trajectory graphs that the system evolves into distinct orbits after beginning with comparable initial states [18].

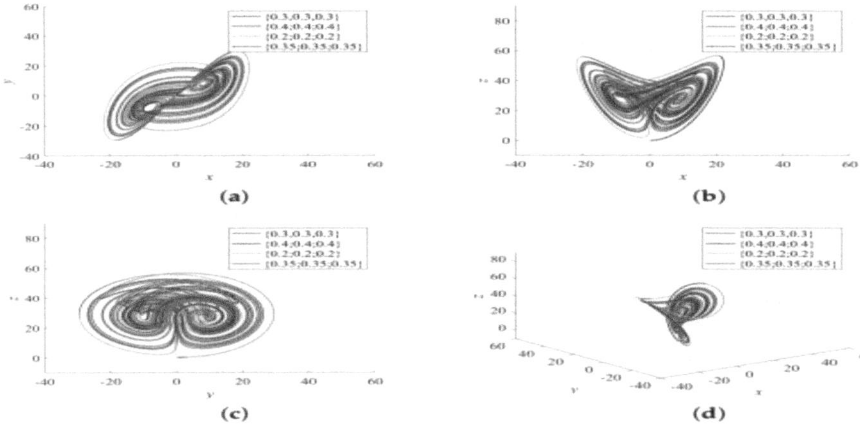

Fig. 2. Phase paths of the 3d Lorenz system of fractional order for various initial conditions where {σ, ρ, β, α} = {10, 28, 8/3, 0.995}: four planes are shown: (a) x-y; (b) x-z; (c) y-z; and (d) 3d plot.

3.2 RSA Algorithm

RSA stands for Rivest-Shamir-Adleman. It is a popular public key cryptography technique that boosts the security of information transmission. It applies two major cryptographic techniques to function. It initially converts its input data, also known as plaintext, into an encoding output referred as cipher text by use of a public key. In doing this, the text becomes rather inconceivable without having the decryption password. It is computationally impossible to retrieve the plaintext from the cipher text in an acceptable amount of time without the password. Second, the RSA method may complete the decryption process by decoding the cipher text back into plaintext using a private key [19].

The RSA algorithm's sequential steps are as follows [20]:

Select two distinct prime integers, p and q, as the input.

1. Perform the Euler function calculation: $\varphi(n) = (p - 1)(q - 1)$
2. $n = p \times q$
3. Choose the public key e at random, where $1 < e < \varphi(n)$ and $gcd(\varphi(n), e) \succcurlyeq 1$
4. Determine the private key by calculating $d \cdot e \equiv 1 \bmod \varphi(n)$; $d = e - 1(\bmod \varphi(n))$
5. Encryption technique: compute $C = m^e \bmod n$ for every plaintext m.
6. Decryption procedure: compute $m = C^d \bmod n$ for every cipher text c.

3.3 Classical Zig-Zag Transformation

The Zig-Zag transform is a permutation technique used to jumble an image's pixel composition. The Zig-Zag transform gets its name from the way pixels are traversed in the image, it has to proceed down from the upper left corner to the lower right corner in a Z-shaped pattern. The pixels read while scanning are first stored in one dimensional array and recovered from it in some order to produce two dimensional matrix. With conventional Zig-Zag transformations, the sequence in which the pixels are traversed is always the same, following a regular and predictable pattern. The concept remains the same even if the pixel traversal starts at a different corner of the picture. In order to jumble picture pixels for image encryption, the Zig-Zag transform is frequently utilized.

Figure 3 illustrates the application of the classical Zig-Zag transform on a sample 4 × 4 matrix. [21].

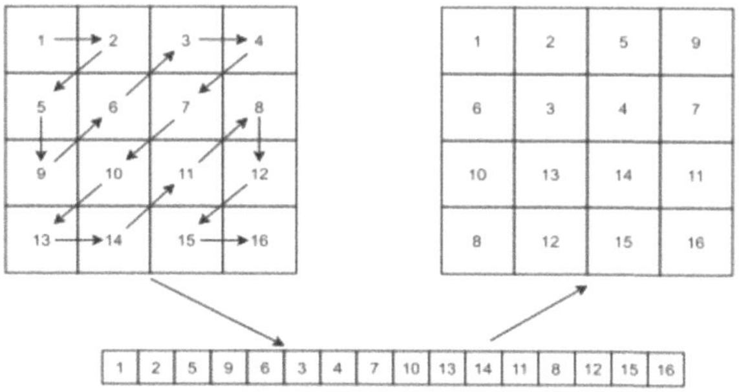

Fig. 3. Classical zig-zag transform.

4 A Scheme for Encrypting and Decrypting Images

4.1 Image Encryption Algorithm

Figure 4 Illustrates Method flowchart for encryption of color image using the RSA method, Zig-Zag transformation, and chaotic maps for two different types of maps: logistic and Lorenz.

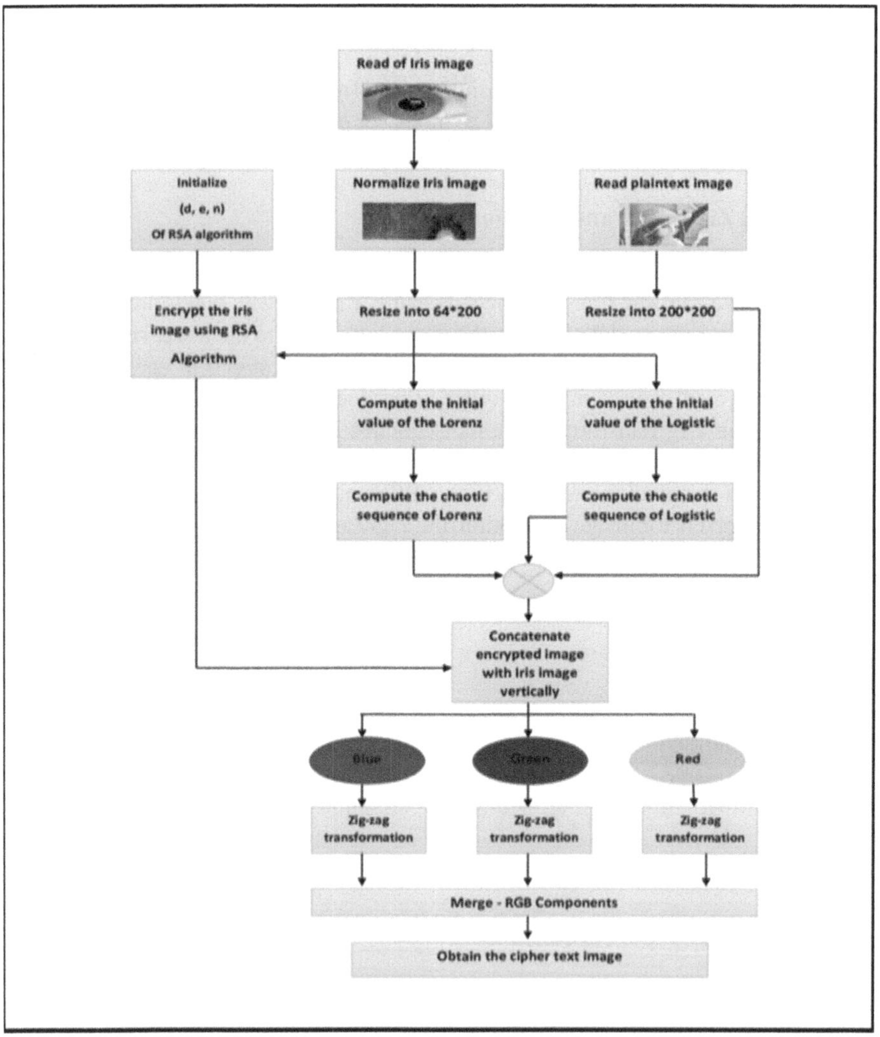

Fig. 4. The suggested encryption algorithm's diagram

The main algorithm can be implemented as the following processing steps:

Step1: Enter the plaintext picture and the Iris image of dimension M × N × 3.

Step2: normalize the Iris image.

Step3: Resize the plaintext image C into 200 × 200 × 3 and the Iris image into 64 × 200 × 3.

Step4: Compute the initial logistic map value X0 by the Eq. (3) below, the control parameter is selected as $\mu = 3.9$.

$$x0 = \left(\frac{mod(sum(R + G + B)}{3MN}, 0.5\right) \tag{3}$$

Step5: the chaotic sequence for logistic is calculate by Eq. (4) to obtain xk

$$\mathrm{xk} + 1 = \mu\ \mathrm{xk}\ (1 - \mathrm{xk})\mathrm{pow}(10{,}16)\mathrm{mod}256 \tag{4}$$

Step6: compute the initial values of the Lorenz map by the equations below

$$\sigma = 9 + \mathrm{round}\left(\frac{\mathrm{sum(C)}}{\mathrm{M \times N \times 3 \times 255}}, 8\right) \tag{5}$$

$$\rho = 28 + \mathrm{round}\left(\frac{\mathrm{sum(C)}}{\mathrm{M \times N \times 3 \times 255}}, 8\right) \tag{6}$$

$$\beta = 2 + \mathrm{round}\left(\frac{\mathrm{sum(C)}}{\mathrm{M \times N \times 3 \times 255}}, 8\right) \tag{7}$$

Step7: The chaotic sequences are calculated by Eqs. (8, 9, 10) to obtain $\alpha x, \alpha y, \alpha z$.

$$\alpha x = \sigma(y - x)pow(10{,}5)mod256 \tag{8}$$

$$\alpha y = (\rho x - y - xz)pow(10{,}5)mod256 \tag{9}$$

$$\alpha z = (xy - \beta z)pow(10{,}5)mod256 \tag{10}$$

Step8: using the chaotic sequence for the Lorenz and logistic maps to encrypt the plaintext.

Image XOR between them.

Step9: encrypt the Iris image by using public key of RSA algorithm.

Step10: concatenate the plaintext encoded image vertically with the Iris encoded image.

Step11: These pixels are then subjected to an extended Zig-Zag transform in Red, Green, Blue.

Step12: Combine the binary pixel values of 8 bits of Red, Green, Blue to get the cipher text picture.

4.2 Image Decryption Algorithm

Using the private key of RSA algorithm, the original image must be recovered during image decryption. It is the opposite of picture encryption. The Red, Green, and Blue components are separated from the Cipher image at the beginning. Secondly A Zig-Zag inverse transformation operation is used in every component, and concatenated them. The dimensions of 200 x 264 are taken from the decryption image, which represents the Iris image, and encrypted by using the private key of the RSA algorithm. Now, the Iris picture is decrypted with the private key following the RSA algorithm; afterwards, retrieve the plaintext image by applying XOR to dimensions 0x199 representing the original image and extract the beginning values of Lorenz and Logistic maps to apply the chaotic sequence.

5 Evaluation and Assessment

We conducted numerous simulations using the OS Windows 10 with Python Platform to assess the method's reliability and credibility. Among the selected example images are "Leena" and "iris image," two colored images of different sizes. Seen in Fig. 5.

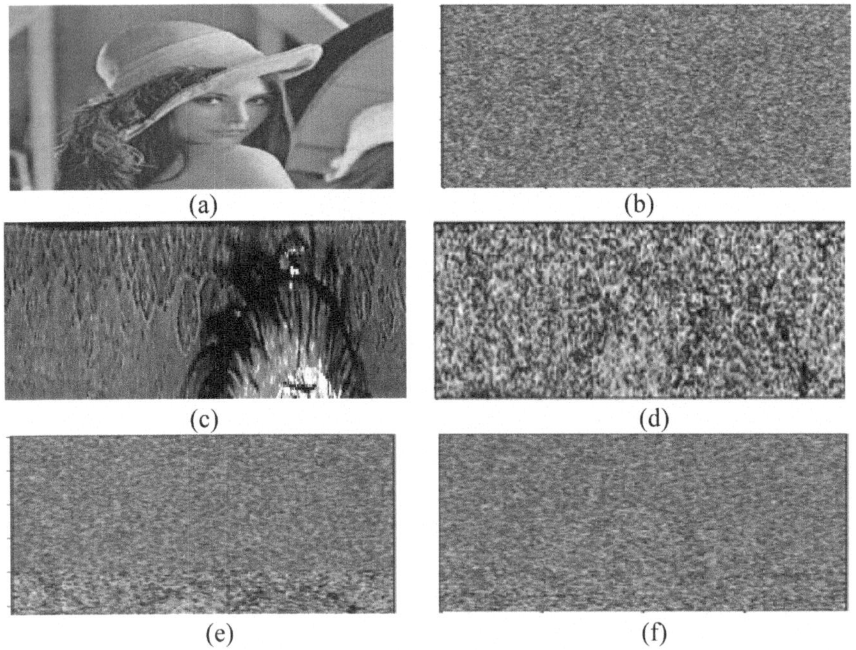

Fig. 5. Experimental results of encryption: (a) original picture; (b) original image encrypted by using the chaotic maps; (c) iris image; (d) iris image encrypted by RSA; (e) concatenated images vertically; (f) zig-zag transformation.

6 Analysis of System Performance

By evaluating histograms and the correlations between neighboring the encrypted image's pixels, the suggested approach seeks to prevent statistical assaults, which occur when attackers break ciphers using statistical parameters that apply to both plaintext and ciphertext.

6.1 Histogram Analysis

It is essential to eliminate statistical similarities between the encrypted and original pictures to stop information leaking during picture encryption. The recurrence of each color intensity level in the picture is represented by a histogram, a 2D graphical depiction of pixel values; a flatter histogram denotes a stronger encryption method [22].

$$His(L) = \sum_{i=0}^{H-1} \sum_{j=0}^{w-1} Freq(pixel(i,j)) \tag{11}$$

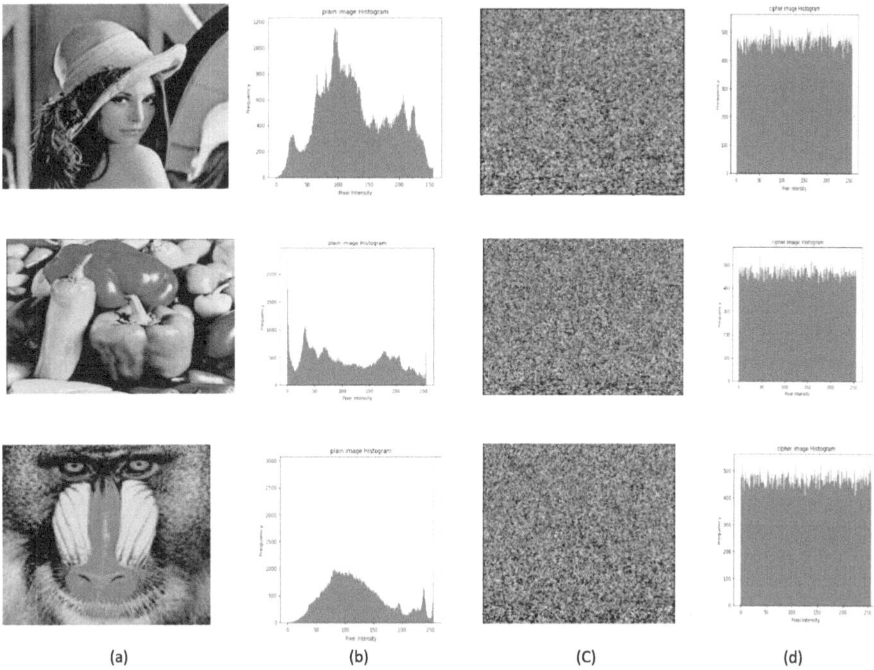

Fig. 6. The following images are tested using histograms: a) plain pictures; b) plain pictures histograms; c) cipher images; and d) cipher image histograms.'

The histogram of the plain image in Fig. 6-b represents the distribution of the brightness of the pixels in an original image and, therefore, it shows the natural structure of an image. Peaks represent usual intensity values while valleys represent unusual intensities. These histograms are normally irregular due to the presence of structured information. Contrarily, the histogram of the encrypted image in Fig. 6-d appears like a noise because of the random distribution of pixel intensities during the process of encryption. A flat histogram indicates that the pixel intensities are uniformly distributed, which in turn is desirable for encryption because no particular intensity value occurs more often than any other, making it harder to extract any information from the image.

6.2 Analysis of Correlation Coefficient

One More critical statistic to evaluate The efficiency of an encryption algorithm Analysis of correlation coefficients, abbreviated as "r." The formula provided below will yield the correlation coefficient of x and y, two pixels using the methods in (12) to (14); the resultant value falls between −1 and 1. In all three directions-horizontally (H), vertically (V), and diagonally (D) the correlation coefficient between adjacent pixels should be close to zero to show no connection in order for an encryption method to be resistant to statistical assaults. If not, numbers around −1 signify a significant negative correlation, while values near 1 suggest a strong positive correlation. This means that statistical attacks might potentially reveal an encrypted image [23]. The correlation coefficient (cc) Calculated as in Equations:

$$rxy = \frac{cov(x, y)}{\sqrt{DX.Dy}} \tag{12}$$

where

$$cov(x, y) = \frac{1}{N}\sum_{i=1}^{N}(Xi - E(x))(yi - E(y)) \tag{13}$$

$$D(x) = \frac{1}{N}\sum_{i=1}^{N}(Xi - E(x))^2 \tag{14}$$

Table 1. Displays the results of the computation. It is clear that there is very little connection and that the cipher text's pixel correlation coefficient is near to 0. It counts the pixel values in diagonal, vertical, and horizontal directions axes to create a more logical presentation (Tables 2, 3, 4 and 5).

Table.1 Comparison of the correlation value between the plain and encrypted color channels of Lena images with the literature.

RGB	CC	Plain image	Proposed	Ref [21] Enc	Ref [22] Enc
R	H	0.90520186112	−0.00323320310698	0.0021	0.001365
	D	-	-	−0.0026	0.000232
	V	0.93708132078	−0.01169700803880	0.0018	0.004776
G	H	0.95014703642	0.00780003699362	−0.0006	0.003294
	D	-	-	0	0.004807
	V	0.95920829392	−0.00088361011282	0.0004	0.000579
B	H	0.94712403725	−0.000953430608331	−0.005	0.002060
	D	-	-	−0.0104	0.004043
	V	0.95894372179	−0.0091701857705027	0.001	0.000194

The results above in Table 1 show the ability to separate the adjacent pixels of the encryption image, which resulted in a correlation coefficient close to zero.

Table 2. Entropy of the image information in both plain and encrypted form.

picture name	Plain Image	Cipher Image	Reference [23]	Reference[24]
Leena	7.7603883	7.9999	7.9997	7.9972
pepper	7.8702164	7.9999	7.9984	-
Baboon	7.6407401	7.9999	7.9989	7.9989

Table 3. Plain and encrypted image UACI and NPCR indicators.

Image	UACI	NPCR
Leena	28.88280392	99.605
Baboon	31.11009803	99.605
pepper	35.80576470	99.605

Table 4. UACI and NPCR indicator comparison.

Indicators	Proposed	Ref [25]	Ref [26]
UACI	35.80576470	32.51	36.7148
NPCR	99.605	99.62	99.766

Table 5. Comparison of PSNR values of different images.

PSNR	Proposed	Ref [26]	Ref [11]
Leena	8.67171	36.3461	8.6761
Baboon	8.632748	-	8.7570
pepper	7.65065	33.7498	8.1271

6.3 Information Entropy

A measure called information entropy is used to assess an image's randomness in the grayscale pixel distribution. Equation (15) is used to compute it, with p(mi) standing for the possibility of each symbol among all M symbols. The entropy value of a grayscale image with 256 symbols that is encrypted at random is 8 [23].

$$H(m) = \sum_{i=1}^{M} p(mi)\log_2\frac{1}{p(mi)} \tag{15}$$

6.4 A Differential Statistical Study

The difference between the two images can be quantified with two criteria: The two important metrics are the Unified Average Changed Intensity (UACI) and the Number of Pixels Change Rate (NPCR). Differential attacks often include the attackers making small modifications to the plaintext image, then encrypting it before and after the changes with a specific technique in an attempt to uncover their connection. The following is a clarification of UACI and NPCR [28].

$$NPCR = \frac{1}{H \times w} \times \sum_{i=1}^{H} \sum_{j=1}^{w} D(i,j) \times 100\% \quad (16)$$

$$UACI = \frac{1}{H \times W} \times \sum_{i=1}^{H} \sum_{j=1}^{w} \frac{v1(i,j) - v2(i,j)}{255} \times 100\% \quad (17)$$

where the ciphertext image is changed before and after by v1, v2, respectively, for the plaintext image. D has the subsequent definition.

$$\mathrm{D} = \begin{cases} 0v1(\mathrm{i},\mathrm{j}) = v2(i,j) \\ 1v1(\mathrm{i},\mathrm{j}) \neq v2(i,j) \end{cases}$$

6.5 Evaluation Concerning MSE and PSNR

The performance of the proposed encryption technique is evaluated using Peak Signal-To-Noise Ratio (PSNR)and the Mean Square Error (MSE) metrics. The technique used for comparing the plain and encrypted image differences is *MSE* [31], as shown in Eq. (18)

$$MSE = \frac{1}{MN} \sum_{I=0,J=0}^{M,N} (I(i,j) - C(i,j))^2 \quad (18)$$

If the image's dimensions are *M* and *N*, the pixel value of the original image is *I*(*i*, *j*), and the pixel value of the cipher image is *C* (*i*, *j*).

The following is the mathematical illustration of *PSNR*: Eq. (19)

$$PSNR = 20log_{10}(\frac{255}{\sqrt{MSE}}) \quad (19)$$

7 Conclusions

The proposed digital image encryption technique employs chaotic algorithms, particularly Lorenz and logistic algorithms. The eye biometrics provide the initial value for the chaotic algorithm. After that, the eye biometrics are encrypted using the RSA algorithm. Then the eye biometric and image encrypted concatenated vertically. Finally, the diffusion process is implemented using the Zig-Zag method. So, when the two images were combined vertically, as in Fig. 5(e), What appeared as a dividing line between the two images was due to the pixel values of the original image, encrypted in chaos to be between zero and one, versus those of the iris image, which were encrypted using the RSA algorithm with large values. To increase the randomness and improve the security, The Zig-Zag method is being used. This technique has promising potential for protecting digital images against a variety of malicious activities, threats, and unauthorized utilization. The proposed scheme has been applied in various applications, maintaining a high level of privacy and security for the digital pictures. Experimental results reveal that the proposed scheme performs better than the available methods concerning both aspects of security and efficiency. The use of the RSA algorithm, 1-D Logistic, 3-D Lorenz, and Zig-Zag transforms makes the encryption keys very sensitive and hard to crack. With the high NPCR of 99.605, this clearly shows that the encryption technique causes a significant change in pixel values between the original and the encrypted image; hence, the program may successfully disturb the image data. Results of the UACI test tend to indicate that an optimal value, 35.8, means that intense changes in pixel intensity are introduced into the image content by the encryption algorithm, which supports the assumption. That means it makes the image very difficult to perceive by the intended recipients. The low correlation coefficient value –0.0032333 utilized for measuring the similarity amongst plain and encrypted pictures provides further support to the algorithm´s power in masking the original picture content. Desirable features of the encryption include that our encryption methodology adds a quite good deal of arbitrary and unpredictable to the data, which can be seen by the rise in information entropy from the plain to the cipher image (7.7603883 to 7.9999). A recovery percentage of 100% was obtained for the original image at decryption. Finally, it should be noted that the limitations in this research were that the number of features extracted from the iris was small and required significant effort to obtain. Therefore, our suggestion is that in future studies, we should consider using another biometric that includes more features, such as DNA.

Acknowledgement. The authors wish to thank the North Technical University, Technical Engineering College of Mosul, Computer Technology Engineering Department for their assistance with this research.

References

1. Meng, F., Gu, Z.: A color image-encryption algorithm using extended DNA coding and zig-zag transform based on a fractional-order laser system. Fractal Fract. **7**(11) (2023). https://doi.org/10.3390/fractalfract7110795
2. Khan, M., Rasheed, A.: Permutation-based special linear transforms with application in quantum image encryption algorithm. Quantum Inf. Process. **18**(10), 1–21 (2019). https://doi.org/10.1007/s11128-019-2410-7
3. Xie, Z., et al.: A K-SVD based compressive sensing method for visual chaotic image encryption. Mathematics **11**(7) (2023). https://doi.org/10.3390/math11071658

4. Kengnou Telem, A.N., et al.: Image encryption algorithm based on dynamic DNA coding operations and 3D chaotic systems. Multimedia Tools Appl. **80**(12) (2021). https://doi.org/10.1007/s11042-021-10549-0
5. Elghandour, A., Salah, A., Karawia, A.: A new cryptographic algorithm via a two-dimensional chaotic map. Ain Shams Eng. J. **13**(1), 101489 (2022). https://doi.org/10.1016/j.asej.2021.05.004
6. Ye, G., Pan, C., Dong, Y., Shi, Y., Huang, X.: Image encryption and hiding algorithm based on compressive sensing and random numbers insertion. Signal Process. **172**, 107563 (2020). https://doi.org/10.1016/j.sigpro.2020.107563
7. Wang, X., et al.: A color image encryption algorithm based on hash table, hilbert curve and hyper-chaotic synchronization. Mathematics **11**(3) (2023). https://doi.org/10.3390/math11030567
8. Alawida, M., et al.: A new hybrid digital chaotic system with applications in image encryption. Sig. Process. **160**, 45–58 (2019). https://doi.org/10.1016/j.sigpro.2019.02.016
9. Sun, S.: A new image encryption scheme based on 6D hyperchaotic system and random signal insertion. IEEE Access **11**(June), 66009–66016 (2023). https://doi.org/10.1109/ACCESS.2023.3290915
10. Yousif, S.F.: Grayscale image confusion and diffusion based on multiple chaotic maps. In: 1st Int. Sci. Conf. Eng. Sci. - 3rd Sci. Conf. Eng. Sci. ISCES 2018 - Proc., vol. 2018-Janua, pp. 114–119 (2018). https://doi.org/10.1109/ISCES.2018.8340538
11. Taqi, I.A., Hameed, S.M.: A new Color image encryption based on multi chaotic maps. Iraqi J. Sci. **59**(4), 2117–2127 (2018). https://doi.org/10.24996/IJS.2018.59.4B.17
12. Masood, F., et al.: A novel image encryption scheme based on Arnold cat map, Newton-Leipnik system and logistic Gaussian map. Multimed. Tools Appl. **81**(21), 30931–30959 (2022). https://doi.org/10.1007/s11042-022-12844-w
13. Wen, H., et al.: Secure image encryption algorithm using chaos-based block permutation and weighted bit planes chain diffusion. iScience **27**(1), 108610 (2024). https://doi.org/10.1016/j.isci.2023.108610
14. Zhang, B., Liu, L.: Chaos-based image encryption: review, application, and challenges. Mathematics **11**(11) (2023). https://doi.org/10.3390/math11112585
15. Huang, H., Yang, S., Ye, R.: Efficient symmetric image encryption by using a novel 2D chaotic system. IET Image Process. **14**(6), 1157–1163 (2020). https://doi.org/10.1049/iet-ipr.2019.0551
16. Herbadji, D., et al.: A Novel Color Image Encryption Scheme Using Logistic Map and Quadratic Map Systems, vol. 11005. LNCS, no. January. Springer International Publishing (2019). https://doi.org/10.1007/978-3-030-03101-5_2
17. Shakir, D.A.Q., et al.: Image encryption using lorenz chaotic system. J. Tech. **5**(1), 122–128 (2023). https://doi.org/10.51173/jt.v5i1.840
18. Feng, W., et al.: Exploiting newly designed fractional-order 3D lorenz chaotic system and 2D discrete polynomial hyper-chaotic map for high-performance multi-image encryption, pp. 1–30 (2023)
19. Mfungo, D.E., Fu, X.: Fractal-based hybrid cryptosystem: enhancing image encryption with RSA, homomorphic encryption, and chaotic maps. Entropy **25**(11) (2023). https://doi.org/10.3390/e25111478
20. Lin, R., Li, S.: An image encryption scheme based on lorenz hyperchaotic system and RSA algorithm. Secur. Commun. Netw. **2021** (2021). https://doi.org/10.1155/2021/5586959
21. Güvenoğlu, E., Tunalı, V.: ZigZag transform with Durstenfeld shuffle for fast and secure image encryption. Conn. Sci. **35**(1) (2023). https://doi.org/10.1080/09540091.2022.2162000
22. Al-Hassani, M.D.: A novel technique for secure data cryptosystem based on chaotic key image generation. Baghdad Sci. J. **19**(4), 905–913 (2022). https://doi.org/10.21123/bsj.2022.19.4.0905

23. Alexan, W., et al.: Color image encryption through chaos and KAA map. IEEE Access **11**(October 2022), 11541–11554 (2023). https://doi.org/10.1109/ACCESS.2023.3242311
24. Jithin, K.C., Sankar, S.: Colour image encryption algorithm combining, Arnold map, DNA sequence operation, and a Mandelbrot set. J. Inf. Secur. Appl. **50**, 102428 (2020). https://doi.org/10.1016/j.jisa.2019.102428
25. Zhang, Y.Q., et al.: A new color image encryption scheme based on 2DNLCML system and genetic operations. Opt. Lasers Eng. **128**(January) (2020). https://doi.org/10.1016/j.optlaseng.2020.106040
26. Herbadji, D., Belmeguenai, A., Derouiche, N., Liu, H.: Colour image encryption scheme based on enhanced quadratic chaotic map. IET Image Process. **14**(1), 40–52 (2020). https://doi.org/10.1049/iet-ipr.2019.0123
27. Wu, X., Zhu, B., Hu, Y., Ran, Y.: A novel color image encryption scheme using rectangular transform-enhanced chaotic tent maps. IEEE Access **5**, 6429–6436 (2017). https://doi.org/10.1109/ACCESS.2017.2692043
28. Wen, H., et al.: Exploiting high-quality reconstruction image encryption strategy by optimized orthogonal compressive sensing. Sci. Rep. **14**(1), 1–18 (2024). https://doi.org/10.1038/s41598-024-59277-z
29. Satam, I.A., Shahab, S.N., Kamel, H.A., Al-Hamadani, M.N.A.: Execution of a smart street lighting system for energy saving enhancement. Bull. Electr. Eng. Inform. **10**(4), 1884–1892 (2021). https://doi.org/10.11591/EEI.V10I4.2924
30. Setyaningsih, E., Wardoyo, R., Sari, A.K.: Securing color image transmission using compression-encryption model with dynamic key generator and efficient symmetric key distribution. Digit. Commun. Netw. **6**(4), 486–503 (2020). https://doi.org/10.1016/j.dcan.2020.02.001
31. Hameed, S.M., Taqi, I.A.: A new beta chaotic map with DNA encoding for color image encryption. Iraqi J. Sci. **61**(9), 2371–2384 (2020). https://doi.org/10.24996/ijs.2020.61.9.24

Leveraging Artificial Intelligence for Enhanced Cybersecurity: Opportunities and Challenges

Ammar Odeh[1](✉), Qasem S. Abu Al-Haija[2], Walid Salameh[1], Anas Abu Taleb[1], and Tareq Alhajahjeh[3]

[1] Computer Science, Princess Sumaya University for Technology, Amman, Jordan
a.odeh@psut.edu.jo

[2] Department of Cybersecurity, University of Science and Technology, Irbid, Jordan

[3] Engineering and Media, De Montfort University, Leicester, UK

Abstract. In today's fast-paced digital era, the cybersecurity landscape is under constant threat from increasingly sophisticated cyberattacks. Artificial Intelligence (AI) has emerged as a transformative technology, offering powerful tools to address these challenges. This paper examines AI's dual role in enhancing cybersecurity and the complexities it introduces. AI, through its capabilities in machine learning, neural networks, and pattern recognition, enables the automation of threat detection, prediction, and response, significantly improving the speed and accuracy of cybersecurity operations. These advancements allow organizations to identify and mitigate risks in real-time, effectively reducing vulnerabilities. However, the integration of AI into cybersecurity strategies is not without challenges. The "black box" nature of AI models raises concerns about transparency and accountability, while ethical issues related to data privacy must be carefully addressed. Moreover, AI systems themselves are vulnerable to adversarial attacks, potentially undermining their reliability. By analyzing real-world case studies, this paper explores both the strengths and limitations of AI-driven cybersecurity solutions. It also delves into the ethical, technical, and operational considerations critical to their successful implementation. Ultimately, this paper underscores the importance of continued innovation and collaboration to fully harness AI's potential while mitigating its inherent risks, ensuring a secure digital future.

Keywords: Artificial Intelligence (AI) · Cybersecurity · Machine Learning · Threat Detection · Adversarial Attacks · Ethical AI

1 Introduction

Cybersecurity serves as a fundamental pillar of trust and reliability in the modern digital age. With the growing complexity and sophistication of cyber threats, the adoption of Artificial Intelligence (AI) has become a crucial strategy for building more adaptive and robust cybersecurity solutions. This paper explores the transformative impact of AI in strengthening cybersecurity practices, highlighting its dual role in both reinforcing protective measures and introducing new challenges. By analyzing how AI can enhance the effectiveness of defenses, while also recognizing the complexities it brings to the

A. Mirzazadeh et al. (Eds.): SEMIT 2024, CCIS 2444, pp. 138–148, 2026.
https://doi.org/10.1007/978-3-032-01948-6_9

cybersecurity landscape, this study aims to provide a deeper understanding of AI's role in shaping the future of digital security [1, 2].

The integration of AI in cybersecurity transcends traditional methods by employing advanced algorithms that learn and evolve from continuous data inputs. This capability allows AI systems to anticipate and mitigate threats with precision and speed unattainable by human operators alone. AI technologies such as machine learning, pattern recognition, and neural networks enable the automation of complex decision-making processes, identifying anomalies that indicate potential security threats. For instance, AI can analyze vast volumes of network data to detect irregularities that may elude standard detection systems, thus preempting potential breaches [3–5].

Furthermore, AI-enhanced systems can automate responses to security incidents, which is crucial in a landscape where reaction time is critical. These systems can execute defensive maneuvers such as isolating infected network segments or shutting down compromised applications before a breach expands [6–8].

However, the deployment of AI in cybersecurity is not without significant challenges. The complexity of AI systems can make them opaque, leading to difficulties in understanding and predicting their actions. This "black box" nature raises substantial concerns, particularly in contexts where transparency and accountability are paramount. Additionally, reliance on data to train AI models introduces data integrity and bias risks, potentially leading to flawed decision-making if the input data is compromised or biased [9–11].

Ethical considerations also play a critical role, especially concerning privacy. AI systems that monitor and analyze user behavior to detect threats can inadvertently infringe on individual privacy rights, leading to tensions between security enhancements and privacy protections. Moreover, as AI systems become central to cybersecurity strategies, they also become attractive targets for attackers. These adversaries may seek to exploit AI systems through techniques like model poisoning or adversarial attacks, which manipulate the data or the AI model itself to evade detection or induce erroneous behaviors [12–14].

This paper will delve into these issues, exploring the expansive landscape of AI applications in cybersecurity and dissecting their transformative impacts and their attendant challenges. Through detailed analysis and case studies, the discussion will underscore the critical balance between leveraging AI's capabilities and managing its vulnerabilities within cybersecurity frameworks.

2 Background

To fully appreciate the impact of artificial intelligence (AI) on cybersecurity, it is essential to understand the technology's fundamental concepts and current state. This section defines "Artificial Intelligence" and "Cybersecurity" and reviews the latest developments and statistical insights that paint a comprehensive picture of AI's role in cybersecurity today. By establishing a solid foundational understanding, we can better explore AI's vast opportunities and significant challenges in enhancing cybersecurity measures [15, 16].

2.1 Artificial Intelligence (AI)

Artificial Intelligence (AI) involves the creation of computer systems that emulate human cognitive abilities, allowing them to perform tasks that typically require human thought. These systems are designed to replicate key aspects of human intelligence, such as learning, which involves gathering data, identifying patterns, and understanding how to apply rules for decision-making. Additionally, AI systems are capable of reasoning, using logical frameworks to analyze information and derive conclusions that can be either definitive or approximate. Another critical aspect of AI is self-correction, where the systems refine their operations over time by analyzing errors and adjusting their methods to improve future outcomes. By integrating these processes, AI enables machines to make decisions, solve complex problems, and adapt to new information, pushing the boundaries of what technology can achieve in replicating human thought processes [17]. In cybersecurity, AI is primarily applied through machine learning models that can process large datasets to identify patterns and anomalies that may indicate security threats. AI applications in cybersecurity also leverage technologies like natural language processing to interpret and respond to security alerts and neural networks that mimic human brain operations to make complex decisions rapidly [18].

2.2 Cybersecurity

Cybersecurity refers to the strategies and practices used to safeguard computer systems, networks, and software applications from unauthorized digital threats. These threats, known as cyberattacks, often aim to gain access to, modify, or destroy confidential data, demand ransom from users, or disrupt regular business operations. The complexity of implementing robust cybersecurity measures has grown significantly, primarily because the number of connected devices now surpasses the global population, providing more entry points for potential attacks. Additionally, cybercriminals are continuously evolving their methods, making it even more difficult to defend against these increasingly sophisticated threats. As a result, staying ahead in cybersecurity requires constant adaptation and vigilance to protect valuable information and maintain the integrity of digital infrastructures [19, 20].

2.3 Current Landscape of AI in Cybersecurity

The incorporation of Artificial Intelligence (AI) into the field of cybersecurity has been rapidly advancing, largely due to the growing need for systems that can analyze large volumes of data swiftly and precisely to identify potential threats. A Markets and Markets report highlights that the cybersecurity market's AI-driven segment is expected to increase from $8.8 billion in 2019 to $38.2 billion by 2026, reflecting a Compound Annual Growth Rate (CAGR) of 23.3%. This significant growth underscores the crucial role that AI is playing in enhancing modern cybersecurity measures, enabling faster threat detection and more effective responses to emerging digital risks. As cyber threats become more complex, AI's ability to adapt and learn makes it an essential component of contemporary security strategies [21, 22].

AI enhances cybersecurity in several key areas:

- **Threat Detection**: AI systems can analyze network traffic and learn normal behaviors to detect anomalies that may indicate a cyberattack. This is particularly useful for identifying zero-day exploits and advanced persistent threats that traditional software might miss [23, 24].
- **Incident Response**: AI can automate responses to security incidents, such as isolating affected devices and cutting off network access to compromised areas to contain the damage [25, 26].
- **Risk Management**: AI tools help organizations assess and mitigate risks associated with cyber threats. This includes identifying vulnerabilities in software and hardware that hackers could exploit [27].

Recent developments have seen AI being increasingly employed not just for defense but also for predictive purposes. For instance, AI systems are now used to predict the likelihood of a cyberattack on specific sectors or organizations based on patterns observed in similar past attacks. Moreover, advancements in AI have led to the development of autonomous security robots and drones that provide physical surveillance alongside network security.

However, the rapid adoption of AI in cybersecurity also raises significant challenges. The dependency on data and algorithms means that flaws in these areas can undermine the effectiveness of AI defenses. There are also concerns about the ethical implications of using AI, particularly regarding privacy, consent, and the potential for unintended discrimination in AI decision-making processes.

3 Opportunities of AI in Cybersecurity

Integrating Artificial Intelligence (AI) into cybersecurity ushers in a new era of advanced, intelligent threat management. AI transforms traditional security measures and enhances the ability of systems to autonomously detect, predict, respond to, and adapt to cyber threats. This section delves into AI's specific opportunities, exploring how its capabilities contribute to more robust and responsive cybersecurity strategies [28].

In threat detection, machine learning models offer unique advantages in identifying patterns indicative of potential threats. Models such as decision trees and support vector machines provide interpretability, making them suitable for identifying straightforward anomalies. Meanwhile, deep learning models, including convolutional neural networks (CNNs), excel in recognizing complex, layered patterns within network data. Ensemble methods like random forests combine multiple models to improve accuracy, addressing diverse threat vectors. These models are chosen for their specific architectures, which can be tailored to detect various cyber threats and adapt to evolving attack methods.

3.1 Automation

One of the most significant advantages of incorporating AI into cybersecurity is the automation of threat detection. AI systems can monitor vast arrays of data from multiple sources in real time, recognizing patterns and anomalies that may indicate a security breach. These systems use machine learning algorithms to continuously learn and improve from the data they process, enabling them to identify sophisticated threats that traditional methods might miss. For example, AI can automatically detect and flag unusual login attempts or irregular data flows within a network, alerting security teams immediately and minimizing the potential impact of breaches [29].

3.2 Prediction

AI enhances cybersecurity defenses by predicting potential future attacks before they occur. Through analyzing historical data and recognizing emerging trends, AI models can forecast likely attack vectors and target vulnerabilities. This predictive capability allows organizations to bolster their defenses proactively rather than reactively. For instance, AI systems can analyze patterns from past cyberattacks to predict and alert about future threats, such as ransomware attacks targeting specific industries known for weaker security protocols or seasonal spikes in phishing scams [23].

3.3 Response

AI's capability to facilitate real-time responses to threats represents a significant advancement in strengthening cybersecurity. When a threat is identified, AI can swiftly execute predefined actions to limit potential damage. These actions may involve isolating compromised systems, blocking suspicious IP addresses, or automatically applying patches to fix security vulnerabilities. This quick reaction is essential for reducing both the downtime and the extent of harm caused by cyberattacks. In addition to these automated responses, AI also aids human cybersecurity teams by offering decision support. It can analyze threats, prioritize them based on their severity and potential impact, and suggest effective mitigation strategies, enabling human responders to make more informed and timely decisions [30].

3.4 Adaptability

The cyber threat landscape continuously evolves, with attackers developing new strategies and technologies to breach defenses. AI systems are uniquely equipped to adapt to these changes due to their learning capabilities. As new threats emerge, AI systems can learn from them and adjust their detection and response mechanisms accordingly. This adaptability helps deal with known threats and anticipate and prepare for future risks. Additionally, AI can simulate various attack scenarios to identify potential vulnerabilities in an organization's cybersecurity posture before actual attackers can exploit them [31, 32].

4 Challenges of AI in Cybersecurity

While integrating Artificial Intelligence (AI) into cybersecurity offers remarkable opportunities, it also introduces several significant challenges. This section explores the inherent complexities and potential drawbacks of AI applications in cybersecurity, examining issues related to system complexity, ethics and privacy, dependency, and AI systems' security. Understanding these challenges is crucial for developing strategies to mitigate the risks associated with AI-driven security solutions [6, 33].

Adversarial attacks present a significant challenge in AI-driven cybersecurity, exploiting model vulnerabilities to evade detection. AI models are particularly susceptible to adversarial techniques, such as evasion attacks, where attackers subtly alter input data, and poisoning attacks, where malicious data is introduced during model training. AI models employ adversarial training to counter these threats, exposing the model to manipulated data and enhancing resilience. Employing robust model architectures and continuous monitoring can help detect and mitigate these sophisticated threats. These measures are crucial to maintaining the integrity and reliability of AI systems in cybersecurity.

4.1 Complexity

The complexity of AI systems poses a significant challenge in cybersecurity. These systems, often based on intricate algorithms and vast data sets, can be opaque, making it difficult for security professionals to understand and predict their behavior. This lack of transparency can lead to challenges in managing and troubleshooting AI systems, especially when they produce unexpected outcomes or fail to detect sophisticated threats. Additionally, the complexity of configuring and maintaining these systems requires specialized knowledge and skills, potentially creating gaps in security if not managed correctly [34].

4.2 Ethics and Privacy

AI's capabilities in processing vast amounts of data also raise substantial ethical and privacy concerns. The use of AI in monitoring and analyzing behavior can lead to infringements on privacy if not governed by strict ethical standards. There is a delicate balance between enhancing security and respecting individual privacy rights, and the deployment of AI can sometimes blur this line. Furthermore, decisions made by AI, such as identifying potential threats based on behavioral patterns, can have serious implications for individuals mistakenly flagged by AI systems, leading to potential biases and discrimination [34].

Integrating AI into cybersecurity raises ethical and privacy concerns, particularly regarding user data. AI systems that monitor behavior for threat detection often collect and analyze large volumes of personal information, which can infringe upon individual privacy. To address this, privacy-preserving techniques such as federated learning allow models to learn from decentralized data without centralizing it, while differential privacy introduces mathematical noise to protect user identities. Balancing privacy with security remains essential for building public trust and ensuring AI deployments respect ethical boundaries.

4.3 Dependency

An over-reliance on AI for cybersecurity can create vulnerabilities within an organization. Dependency on automated systems might lead to decreased human oversight, making it difficult to catch errors that AI fails to identify. This reliance could also reduce human security professionals' capacity to react effectively when AI systems malfunction or when facing threats designed to exploit specific weaknesses in AI algorithms [23].

4.4 Security of AI Systems Themselves

Like any other technological tool, AI systems are susceptible to security vulnerabilities. Attackers can exploit these vulnerabilities through various means, such as data poisoning, where malicious data is fed into the system to train the AI incorrectly, or adversarial attacks, designed to trick AI into misclassifying information. These vulnerabilities compromise the integrity of the AI system and can be leveraged to launch broader attacks against the organization [35].

5 Case Studies

Exploring real-world applications and incidents provides valuable insights into the practical implications of AI in cybersecurity. This section presents case studies that illustrate both successful implementations and notable setbacks of AI technologies. By examining these examples, we can better understand the effectiveness of AI solutions in real scenarios and learn from the challenges encountered. These case studies demonstrate AI's potential and limitations in securing digital environments and highlight important lessons that can guide future improvements and strategies.

In the case study, a quantitative approach was applied to evaluate the effectiveness of AI in detecting cyber threats within a financial institution. Data were collected from network logs over a six-month period, during which an AI-driven anomaly detection model was implemented. Statistical analysis was conducted to assess detection accuracy, with the findings indicating a significant reduction in false positives compared to traditional methods. The results underscore AI's capability to handle high-volume data and detect subtle irregularities that indicate potential security breaches, emphasizing its role as an invaluable tool in cybersecurity operations.

5.1 Successful Implementation

Case Study: Financial Sector AI Deployment. A notable example of successful AI implementation in cybersecurity can be observed in the financial sector. A leading bank employed AI-driven security systems to detect and prevent fraudulent activities. By leveraging machine learning algorithms, the bank's security system analyzed transaction patterns in real time to identify anomalies indicative of fraud. The AI system's ability to learn from each transaction improved its accuracy over time, significantly reducing the incidence of fraud. This deployment protected customers' financial assets and enhanced trust in the bank's digital services [36].

5.2 Setbacks and Lessons Learned

Case Study: Healthcare Data Breach. Conversely, a healthcare provider experienced a significant setback when their AI-based cybersecurity system failed to prevent a data breach. The system was designed to detect unauthorized access based on unusual behavior patterns. However, attackers used sophisticated mimicking techniques that resembled normal user activities, thus evading detection. The breach exposed sensitive patient data, leading to substantial financial and reputational damage. The incident highlighted the need to continuously update and train AI models to recognize evolving attack strategies, emphasizing the importance of layered security measures beyond AI [37].

6 Future Tips

The upcoming of AI in cybersecurity is a landscape of both promising advancements and significant challenges. As technology evolves, so will the strategies to leverage AI for enhanced security measures and the tactics attackers use to circumvent them. This section will discuss emerging trends, potential technological breakthroughs, and areas requiring further research and development to advance cybersecurity in an AI-enhanced world.

6.1 Future Trends

The intersection of AI and cybersecurity is poised for a substantial evolution in the coming years. One of the most anticipated movements is the increased use of AI for autonomous threat hunting. AI systems will likely become more proactive in detecting threats and actively seeking out potential vulnerabilities before they can be exploited. Another emerging movement is the combination of AI with blockchain technology to improve the security of distributed systems. Furthermore, as Internet of Things (IoT) devices proliferate, AI is expected to be crucial in securing these devices against a broader spectrum of attacks.

The future of AI in cybersecurity will be shaped by advancements in emerging technologies like quantum computing, blockchain, and AI-driven IoT security. Quantum computing, for example, promises quantum-resistant encryption methods that could redefine data security in the coming years. Blockchain's decentralized structure is anticipated to bolster data integrity and transparency in cybersecurity solutions. Furthermore, as Internet of Things (IoT) devices proliferate, the role of AI in securing these devices against a growing range of threats will be crucial, enabling predictive and automated security responses across interconnected systems.

Additionally, the development of AI-powered security as a service (SECaaS) is expected to become more mainstream, providing smaller organizations with access to advanced cybersecurity capabilities without significant internal infrastructure. This service model could democratize high-level cybersecurity, making it more accessible and affordable.

6.2 Areas for Further Research and Development

While the likely of AI in cybersecurity is vast, several areas require further research and development to harness its capabilities fully. One such area is the development of ethical AI systems that prioritize user privacy and data protection. Research is needed to create frameworks that govern AI actions, ensuring they adhere to ethical standards and legal requirements.

Another critical area for research is the security of AI systems themselves. As AI becomes a standard tool in cybersecurity, ensuring that these systems are resilient to attacks is paramount. Research into AI-specific threats, such as adversarial AI and AI system poisoning, is crucial. Additionally, there's a need for more advanced anomaly detection techniques that can adapt to the increasingly sophisticated methods used by cyber attackers.

Exploring hybrid models that combine human expertise with AI capabilities could also be fruitful. These models would leverage AI's processing power and data analysis capabilities while incorporating human intuition and experience to interpret complex threat contexts. This approach could mitigate some of the current limitations of fully automated systems.

Lastly, as cyber threats evolve, so must the AI systems designed to combat them. Continuous learning models adapting to new threats without requiring extensive retraining could represent a breakthrough in maintaining long-term system efficacy.

7 Conclusion

This paper has explored the transformative part of Artificial Intelligence (AI) in enhancing cybersecurity measures, revealing its integration's vast opportunities and significant challenges. AI's capabilities in automating threat detection, predicting future attacks, responding in real-time, and adapting to evolving threats underscore its potential to improve cybersecurity practices significantly. However, the complexity of AI systems, ethical and privacy alarms, the risks of dependency, and the vulnerabilities of AI systems present substantial challenges that must be navigated carefully.

Integrating AI into cybersecurity strategies is not merely beneficial but imperative as digital threats continue to grow in sophistication and volume. AI offers a dynamic and proactive approach to cybersecurity, crucial in a digital landscape where traditional methods fall short. The ability of AI to analyze massive datasets quickly and accurately, predict upcoming intimidations, and respond instantly provides a critical edge in the continuing clash against cyber threats.

However, the full potential of AI in cybersecurity can only be realized through continued research and development. This endeavor should focus on ethical AI development, enhancing the security of AI systems, and creating adaptive learning models capable of responding to new threats. Additionally, fostering collaboration among cybersecurity professionals, AI researchers, and policy-makers is essential to ensure AI technologies' ethical and effective deployment.

As we look to the future, the cybersecurity community must remain vigilant and proactive in leveraging AI capabilities and addressing the challenges and ethical considerations they bring. Through sustained effort, innovation, and cooperation, we can harness AI's power to secure our digital world.

In conclusion, this research highlights AI's transformative impact on cybersecurity, demonstrating substantial improvements in threat detection and response automation. Key achievements include increased accuracy in anomaly detection and enhanced response capabilities through predictive modeling. For cybersecurity practitioners, it is recommended to integrate robust AI models with continuous monitoring mechanisms to counter adversarial threats effectively. Additionally, adopting privacy-preserving AI practices, such as federated learning, is suggested to balance security and user privacy. Future research should focus on the development of ethical AI frameworks and adaptive learning models to address evolving cyber threats.

References

1. Kaur, R., Gabrijelčič, D., Klobučar, T.: Artificial intelligence for cybersecurity: literature review and future research directions. Inf. Fusion **97**, 101804 (2023)
2. Zhang, Z., et al.: Explainable artificial intelligence applications in cyber security: state-of-the-art in research. IEEE Access **10**, 93104–93139 (2022)
3. Capuano, N., et al.: Explainable artificial intelligence in cybersecurity: a survey. IEEE Access **10**, 93575–93600 (2022)
4. De Azambuja, A.J.G., et al.: Artificial intelligence-based cyber security in the context of industry 4.0—a survey. Electronics **12**(8), 1920 (2023)
5. Odeh, A., Abu Taleb, A.: Ensemble-based deep learning models for enhancing IoT intrusion detection. Appl. Sci. **13**(21), 11985 (2023)
6. Tao, F., Akhtar, M.S., Jiayuan, Z.: The future of artificial intelligence in cybersecurity: a comprehensive survey. EAI Endorsed Trans. Creative Technol. **8**(28), e3–e3 (2021)
7. Abdullahi, M., et al.: Detecting cybersecurity attacks in internet of things using artificial intelligence methods: a systematic literature review. Electronics **11**(2), 198 (2022)
8. Odeh, A., et al.: Machine learning techniques for detection of website phishing: a review for promises and challenges. In: 2021 IEEE 11th Annual Computing and Communication Workshop and Conference (CCWC). IEEE (2021)
9. Kuzlu, M., Fair, C., Guler, O.: Role of artificial intelligence in the Internet of Things (IoT) cybersecurity. Discover Internet Things **1**(1), 7 (2021)
10. Dasgupta, D., Akhtar, Z., Sen, S.: Machine learning in cybersecurity: a comprehensive survey. J. Defense Modeling Simul. **19**(1), 57–106 (2022)
11. Odeh, A., Taleb, A.A.: XSSer: hybrid deep learning for enhanced cross-site scripting detection. Bull. Electr. Eng. Inform. **13**(5), 3317–3325 (2024)
12. Sarker, I.H., Furhad, M.H., Nowrozy, R.: AI-driven cybersecurity: an overview, security intelligence modeling and research directions. SN Comput. Sci. **2**(3), 173 (2021)
13. Das, R., Sandhane, R.: Artificial intelligence in cyber security. J. Phys.: Conf. Ser. (2021)
14. Odeh, A., Taleb, A.A.: Ensemble learning techniques against structured query language injection attacks. Ind. J. Electr. Eng. Comput. Sci. **35**(2), 1004–1012 (2024)
15. Zhao, L., et al.: Artificial intelligence analysis in cyber domain: a review. Int. J. Distrib. Sens. Netw. **18**(4), 15501329221084882 (2022)
16. Al-Fayoumi, M.A., et al.: Techniques of medical image encryption taxonomy. Bull. Electr. Eng. Inform. **11**(4), 1990–1997 (2022)
17. Abu Al-Haija, Q., et al.: A lightweight double-stage scheme to identify malicious DNS over HTTPS traffic using a hybrid learning approach. Sensors **23**(7), 3489 (2023)
18. Pooyandeh, M., Han, K.-J., Sohn, I.: Cybersecurity in the AI-Based metaverse: a survey. Appl. Sci. **12**(24), 12993 (2022)
19. Choithani, T., et al.: A comprehensive study of artificial intelligence and cybersecurity on bitcoin, crypto currency and banking system. Ann. Data Sci. **11**(1), 103–135 (2024)
20. Abu Al-Haija, Q., et al.: PDF malware detection based on optimizable decision trees. Electronics **11**(19), 3142 (2022)
21. Aslam, M.: AI and cybersecurity: an ever-evolving landscape. Int. J. Adv. Eng. Technol. Innov. **1**(1), 52–71 (2024)

22. Maddireddy, B.R., Maddireddy, B.R.: Cybersecurity threat landscape: predictive modelling using advanced AI algorithms. Int. J. Adv. Eng. Technol. Innov. **1**(2), 270–285 (2022)
23. Camacho, N.G.: The role of AI in cybersecurity: addressing threats in the digital age. J. Artif. Intell. Gen. Sci. (JAIGS) **3**(1), 143–154 (2024)
24. Taleb, A.A., et al.: Performance analysis of sink mobility models for wireless sensor networks: a comparative study. Int. J. Interact. Mob. Technol. **17**(18) (2023)
25. Al-Mansoori, S., Salem, M.B.: The role of artificial intelligence and machine learning in shaping the future of cybersecurity: trends, applications, and ethical considerations. Int. J. Soc. Anal. **8**(9), 1–16 (2023)
26. Odeh, A., et al.: Efficient detection of phishing websites using multilayer perceptron (2020)
27. Familoni, B.T.: Cybersecurity challenges in the age of AI: theoretical approaches and practical solutions. Comput. Sci. IT Res. J. **5**(3), 703–724 (2024)
28. Dash, B., et al.: Threats and opportunities with AI-based cyber security intrusion detection: a review. Int. J. Softw. Eng. Appl. (IJSEA) **13**(5) (2022)
29. Macas, M., Wu, C., Fuertes, W.: A survey on deep learning for cybersecurity: progress, challenges, and opportunities. Comput. Netw. **212**, 109032 (2022)
30. Bécue, A., et al.: Artificial intelligence, cyber-threats and Industry 4.0: challenges and opportunities. Artif. Intell. Rev. **54**(5), 3849–3886 (2021)
31. Roshanaei, M., Khan, M.R., Sylvester, N.N.: Enhancing cybersecurity through AI and ML: strategies, challenges, and future directions. J. Inf. Secur. **15**(3), 320–339 (2024)
32. Soni, V.D.: Challenges and Solution for Artificial Intelligence in Cybersecurity of the USA. Available at SSRN 3624487 (2020)
33. Salem, A.H., et al.: Advancing cybersecurity: a comprehensive review of AI-driven detection techniques. J. Big Data **11**(1), 105 (2024)
34. Bonfanti, M.E.: Artificial intelligence and the offence-defence balance in cyber security. In: Cyber Security: Socio-Technological Uncertainty and Political Fragmentation, pp. 64–79. Routledge, London (2022)
35. Zhang, Y., et al.: Ethics and privacy of artificial intelligence: understandings from bibliometrics. Knowl.-Based Syst. **222**, 106994 (2021)
36. Truby, J., Brown, R., Dahdal, A.: Banking on AI: mandating a proactive approach to AI regulation in the financial sector. Law Financ. Markets Rev. **14**(2), 110–120 (2020)
37. Seh, A.H., et al.: Healthcare data breaches: insights and implications. In: Healthcare. MDPI (2020)

Novel AI techniques in Healthcare and Medicine

Enhancing Ischemic Stroke Patient Selection for Thrombectomy Using Deep-Learning Approach

Wifek Boumrifek(✉), Ines Ben Alaya, Wanis Barreh, and Salam Labidi

Laboratory of Biophysics and Medical Technology, Higher Institute of Medical Technology of Tunis, Tunis El Manar University, 1006 Tunis, Tunisia
Boumrifekwifek@gmail.com, {ines.benalaya, salam.labidi}@istmt.utm.tn

Abstract. Accurate diagnosis and treatment planning for ischemic stroke present significant challenges, largely due to reliance on subjective visual assessments and complex image processing. Traditional thrombectomy eligibility assessment often utilizes Time to Maximum (Tmax) maps derived from Perfusion Weighted Imaging (PWI), requiring deconvolution techniques that are both time-consuming and reliant on costly, sophisticated software for precise hypoperfused tissue quantification. This study proposes an innovative AI-based approach that stream-lines thrombectomy candidate selection by directly analyzing Time-to-Peak (TTP) maps, bypassing the need for Tmax computation. We employed a U-Net segmentation model to efficiently and accurately identify hypoperfused regions, reducing the procedural complexity, time, and costs associated with traditional methods. Our retrospective study utilized a dataset of 14 patients with 339 TTP images to train and validate the AI model, achieving high accuracy with a Pearson correlation coefficient of 0.96 and a Dice similarity coefficient of 0.92 compared to conventional Tmax-based analyses. Notably, this method reduced analysis time from 4.5 min to 45 s per patient, maintaining both accuracy and reliability. The direct application of AI to TTP maps marks a transformative step in ischemic stroke assessment, simplifying the evaluation process and making advanced care potentially more accessible. Further research on larger datasets is required to confirm the broader clinical applicability of this technique.

Keywords: Ischemic Stroke · Artificial Intelligence · TTP Map · U-Net Segmentation · Thrombectomy · Tmax

1 Introduction

Diagnosing and treating ischemic stroke relies on rapid intervention to restore blood flow to the ischemic penumbra, the potentially reversible brain tissue surrounding the ischemic core. Effective reperfusion is the only proven approach to reduce disability, primarily achieved through intravenous tissue plasminogen activator (tPA) effective within 4.5 h of symptom onset [1], and mechanical thrombectomy, effective within six hours [2].

A. Mirzazadeh et al. (Eds.): SEMIT 2024, CCIS 2444, pp. 151–162, 2026.
https://doi.org/10.1007/978-3-032-01948-6_10

However, approximately 25% of stroke patients do not know the exact onset time of their symptoms [3], making them ineligible for tPA. Recent studies such as DAWN and DEFUSE 3, have extended the time window for thrombectomy to 16–24 h, broadening treatment options [4].

Traditionally, patient selection for thrombectomy has relied on clinical criteria such as the National Institutes of Health Stroke Scale (NIHSS), which assesses neurological deficits1. Despite its utility, NIHSS often lacks precision in predicting treatment response, leading to the exclusion of some patients who could benefit from intervention. This highlights the need for refined selection methods.

MRI mismatch between diffusion-weighted imaging (DWI) and perfusion-weighted imaging (PWI) is often used to identify salvageable tissue beyond the six-hour window. However, this approach is variable and may underestimate eligible patients [5]. Additionally, calculating time-to-maximum (Tmax) maps is complex, time-consuming, and requires expensive software.

Recent advancements in Artificial Intelligence (AI) such as U-Net and other deep learning models, have shown promise in segmenting ischemic lesions from MRI images like DWI and FLAIR. However, similar segmentation for PWI remains underexplored, despite its potential to provide critical information on hypoperfusion.

To address these challenges, our research explores using deep learning to automate patient selection for thrombectomy based on Time-To-Peak (TTP) maps instead of Tmax maps. We developed a U-Net model to directly segment hypoperfused regions from TTP maps, simplifying the process.

Recent studies highlight the potential of artificial intelligence (AI) in improving ischemic stroke diagnosis. For example, Kai Wang et al. [6] achieved high accuracy in estimating hypoperfused volume using Pseudo-Continuous Arterial Spin Labeling (pCASL) data, reaching an area under the curve (AUC) of 0.94 without needing Dynamic Susceptibility Contrast MRI (DSC-MRI). Similarly, Hongyu Gao et al. [7] utilized a deep learning model with Computed Tomography Perfusion (CTP) and Perfusion-Weighted Imaging (PWI) data to identify patients within a critical 6-h window, obtaining an AUC of 0.935, though requiring contrast agents and complex data preparation.

While these studies demonstrate significant advancements, they also expose limitations associated with complex imaging techniques, which can hinder timely decision-making in acute stroke care. For instance, Tabea Kossen et al. [11] explored generating perfusion maps using Time-of-Flight (TOF) sequences, aiming to reduce reliance on contrast agents. Additionally, Umberto A. Gava et al. [12] investigated the replacement of Tmax calculation with deep learning models in CT data instead of MRI. Furthermore, in their review, G.A.U.R.I. Parvathy et al. [13] highlighted the current limitations of AI in fully substituting the Tmax procedure, underlining the need for further advancements in AI-driven stroke diagnostics.

Our research aims to overcome these limitations by focusing on TTP maps, offering a more accessible alter-native to Tmax. By leveraging U-Net, we seek to improve patient selection accuracy and accessibility, ultimately enhancing clinical outcomes in ischemic stroke management.

The organization of this paper is as follows: the Methodology section outlines the processes applied in both the conventional approach and our proposed method, which utilizes U-Net segmentation on TTP maps for hypoperfusion analysis. Next, the Results section presents comparative findings from both methods, including performance metrics and clinical implications. This is followed by the Discussion, where we address the implications of these findings, examine limitations, and explore potential refinements. Finally, the Conclusion highlights the primary insights and outlines directions for future research.

2 Materials and Methods

2.1 Materials

The data collection for this study involved accessing patient records from the Mongi Ben Hamida National Institute of Neurology in Tunis. This retrospective study was conducted on MRI data collected from 24 patients scanned on a Siemens Magnetom Verio 3T MRI machine, covering the period between 2011 and 2023. Each case included key perfusion-weighted imaging (PWI) acquisitions essential for ischemic stroke evaluation.

To refine the dataset, we established strict selection criteria to ensure relevance and consistency in our analysis. Patients without comprehensive PWI data were excluded, along with healthy individuals and those who had MRI imaging within six hours of stroke onset, as this time window may impact perfusion imaging characteristics. Following these criteria, our final dataset included 14 patients, 12 of whom were visually assessed as candidates for thrombectomy by an experienced neuroradiologist. Our database contains 14 patients, with ages ranging from 37 to 82 years. Among them, eight were female and six were male. The number of TTP slices varied between 20 and 28 per patient. The echo time (TE) used was either 30 or 45 ms, and the repetition time (TR) ranged from 1,500 to 3,200 ms. Slice thickness was consistent at 4 mm for most patients, except for Patient 9, who had a slice thickness of 5 mm. We have that each MRI exam includes multiple slices. Therefore, for segmentation, we processed each image slice individually. This resulted in 339 TTP images, covering all available slices for the patients.

The Fig. 1 illustrate our database and the information of patients on the Table 1.

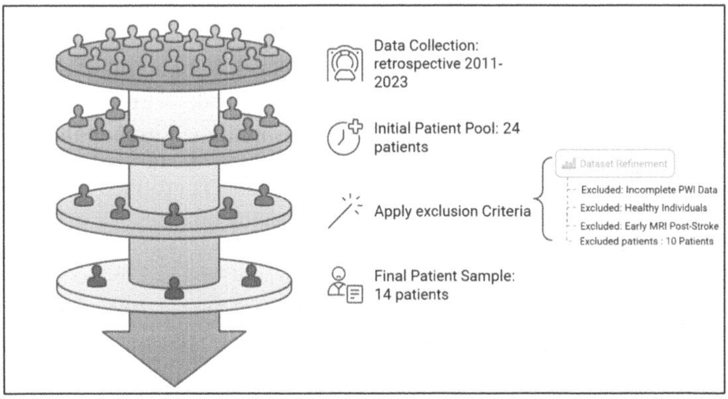

Fig. 1. Patient inclusion flowchart.

Table 1. Acquisition parameters used and patient information.

Patients	Age	Number of TTP slices	TE	TR	Slice thickness
Patient1	65 M	25	45	2892	4
Patient2	74 M	20	30	1500	4
Patient3	44 F	25	45	2892	4
Patient4	51F	25	45	2892	4
Patient5	45 F	24	45	2780	4
Patient6	37 F	25	45	2892	4
Patient7	82F	25	45	2892	4
Patient8	56M	24	45	2780	4
Patient9	59M	20	45	2320	5
Patient10	65M	28	45	3200	4
Patient11	74M	25	45	2892	4
Patient12	56F	24	45	2780	4
Patient13	48F	24	45	2780	4
Patient14	48F	25	45	2892	4

2.2 Methodology

Our methodology is divided into two main phases as detailed in the Fig. 2. First, we developed a software solution similar to RAPID (the conventional method) for generating Tmax maps, which are used to calculate the hypoperfused volume and identify tissue at risk. This approach allows for more objective assessments compared to the subjective evaluations typically employed in Tunisian hospitals, where specialized software is unavailable. The second phase of our methodology (the proposed method) involves using a U-Net-based model to estimate the hypoperfused volume from TTP maps, offering a novel approach grounded in the DEFUSE 3 criteria as shown on the Fig. 2.

Conventional Method. . As shown on the Fig. 3 Our developed interface guides users through the analysis of perfusion images, starting from data loading to the detailed interpretation of hemodynamic curves and maps as mentioned in the Fig. 3.

1. Data Loading: Perfusion Weighted Imaging (PWI) data is grouped into classes based on slice position, providing a temporal view of perfusion.
2. Mask Application: An Otsu threshold mask is applied to reduce noise, isolating brain tissue and improving computational efficiency [8].
3. Semi-Quantitative Parameter Analysis: The first-pass signal of the contrast agent is used to generate time-based signal curves for each pixel. Critical metrics such as Time-to-Peak (TTP) [9] are automatically calculated and mapped.

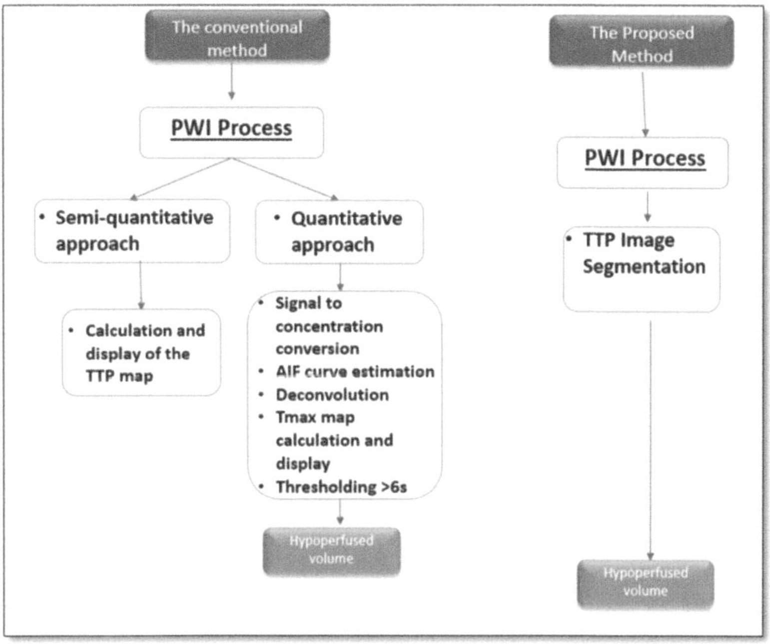

Fig.2. Schematic representation of the two methods involved in our study.

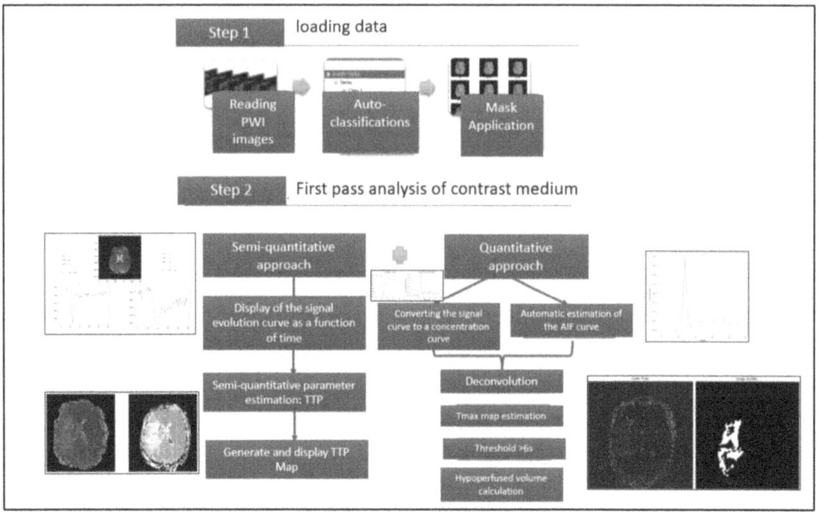

Fig.3. Diagram illustrating the Perfusion process diagram.

4. Quantitative Parameter Analysis: Signal curves are converted to concentration curves, followed by automatic arterial input function (AIF) estimation and SVD-based deconvolution. This allows the calculation of residual concentration and key metrics like Tmax, representing the hypoperfused tissue.
5. Hypoperfused Volume Calculation: A threshold is applied to Tmax maps, with values above 6 s indicating hypoperfused regions. The volume of hypoperfusion is calculated based on the thresholded images, helping guide clinical decisions.

The Proposed Procedure. The second phase of our methodology, the proposed approach, employs a U-Net-based model to estimate the hypoperfused volume from TTP maps, introducing an innovative solution aligned with the DEFUSE 3 criteria. The detailed steps for this phase are illustrated in Fig. 4.

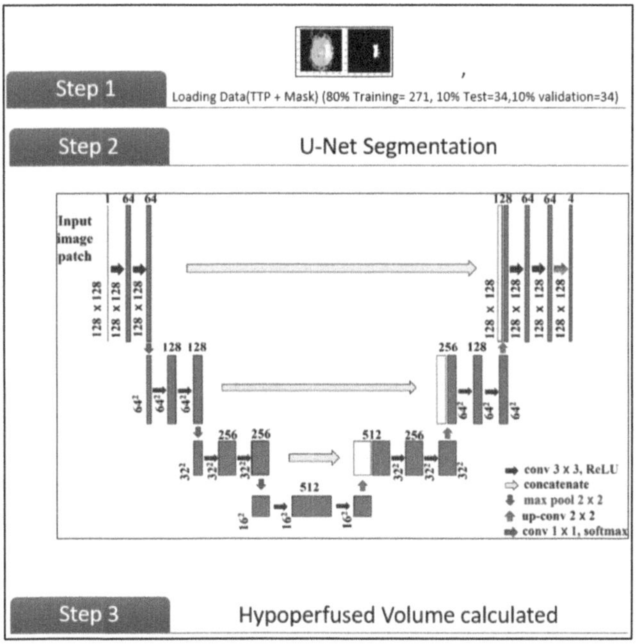

Fig. 4. Diagram of the proposed procedure (AI Decision).

Step 1: Data Preparation for Segmentation. In our proposed approach, we use segmentation for MRI TTP maps. Before the segmentation process, binary masks of the same dimensions as the images are created. These masks assign binary values to hypoperfused regions on TTP images. Once generated, these masks are used during the learning process for segmentation.

For developing our U-Net models, we chose the PyCharm development environment, using an AMD Ryzen 7 processor with 8 GB of RAM. Libraries like NumPy (for array manipulation), PyDicom (for DICOM image handling), TensorFlow (for neural network execution), and Matplotlib (for result visualization) were employed. To evaluate model performance, scikit-learn was used for metrics like confusion matrices.

Step 2: U-Net Architecture Overview. Inputs: The input layer specifies the data shape (for TTP images, (128, 128, 1)).

- Encoding: This section extracts features from the input images using blocks of two 2D convolution layers with ReLU activation, batch normalization, and dropout layers.
- MaxPooling: After each convolution block, max-pooling layers reduce spatial resolution to detect multi-scale information.
- Decoding: The decoding section expands feature resolution using transposed convolution, combining with corresponding encoding features, followed by further convolution.
- Outputs: A final 2D convolution layer with sigmoid activation produces binary segmentation maps.
- Model Optimization: Adam optimizer is used [39], with strategies like early stopping and learning rate adjustment (ReduceLROnPlateau) to ensure stable convergence [10].

Step 3: Calculation of hypoperfused volume. hypoperfused volume was calculated using this formula:

$$\text{Hypoperfused volume} = \text{Number of pixels displayed after segmentation in all slices} \times \text{Pixel size} \times \text{Slice thickness} \times 10^{-3} \quad (1)$$

User Interface: The interface provides buttons for segmentation tasks. Pressing "PWI" triggers TTP image segmentation, displaying the hypoperfused volume of the selected patient.

3 Results

After 30 training epochs, the U-Net model achieved a sensitivity of 68.38% and an accuracy of 98% on the validation data. The confusion matrix showed 1,227 false positives, 546 false negatives, and a majority of true positives (2,654) and true negatives (519861). The total training duration was approximately 15 min. The segmentation approach was superior to Tmax thresholding in identifying hypoperfused tissue (Fig. 5).

Our study evaluates both the quantitative and qualitative performance of the model and discusses its implications for clinical stroke management.

3.1 Qualitative Analysis

Figure 6 below presents the results of manual segmentation as well as the conventional method, which applies a threshold of > 6s on the Tmax map alongside the proposed method based on U-Net segmentation of TTP maps. Hypoperfused areas are identifiable by different colors on the maps. In the second-row slice.

Patient-specific analyses demonstrated that U-Net-based segmentation identified ischemic lesions more effectively than threshold-based methods, particularly in cases where Tmax thresholding failed to detect lesions.

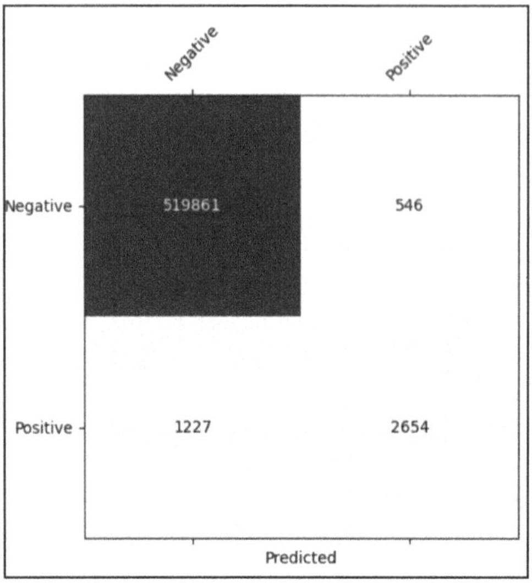

Fig. 5. TTP model confusion matrix.

3.2 Statistic Results

The comparison is conducted using two metrics: the Pearson coefficient and the Dice coefficient, which assess the agreement between the results obtained from the conventional and proposed methods against the reference method.

The Pearson coefficient measures the linear correlation between two methods. In our study, it evaluates the similarity between hypoperfused volumes obtained by the reference method and the two developed methods. A value of 1 indicates perfect correlation, while 0 indicates no correlation[2].

The Dice coefficient ranges from 0 to 1, with 1 representing perfect agreement and 0 indicating no agreement. It is calculated using the formula:

$$Dice = \frac{2\times \mid A \cap B \mid}{\mid A \mid + \mid B \mid} \tag{2}$$

where $|A \cap B|$ is the size of the intersection between sets A and B, $|A|$ is the size of set A, and $|B|$ is the size of set B (Fig. 7).

The curves represent the hypoperfused volume of each patient for the three methods, while the bar graph indicates the Pearson correlation coefficients obtained. The Pearson coefficient between the conventional method and the reference method is 0.97, indicating a very high correlation between these two methods. Similarly, the Pearson coefficient between the reference method and the proposed method is 0.96, also suggesting a very high correlation (Fig. 8).

Regarding the Dice coefficient, it is 0.93, indicating high agreement. However, the Dice coefficient between the reference method and the proposed method is slightly lower, at 0.92, but still falls within a range of high concordance.

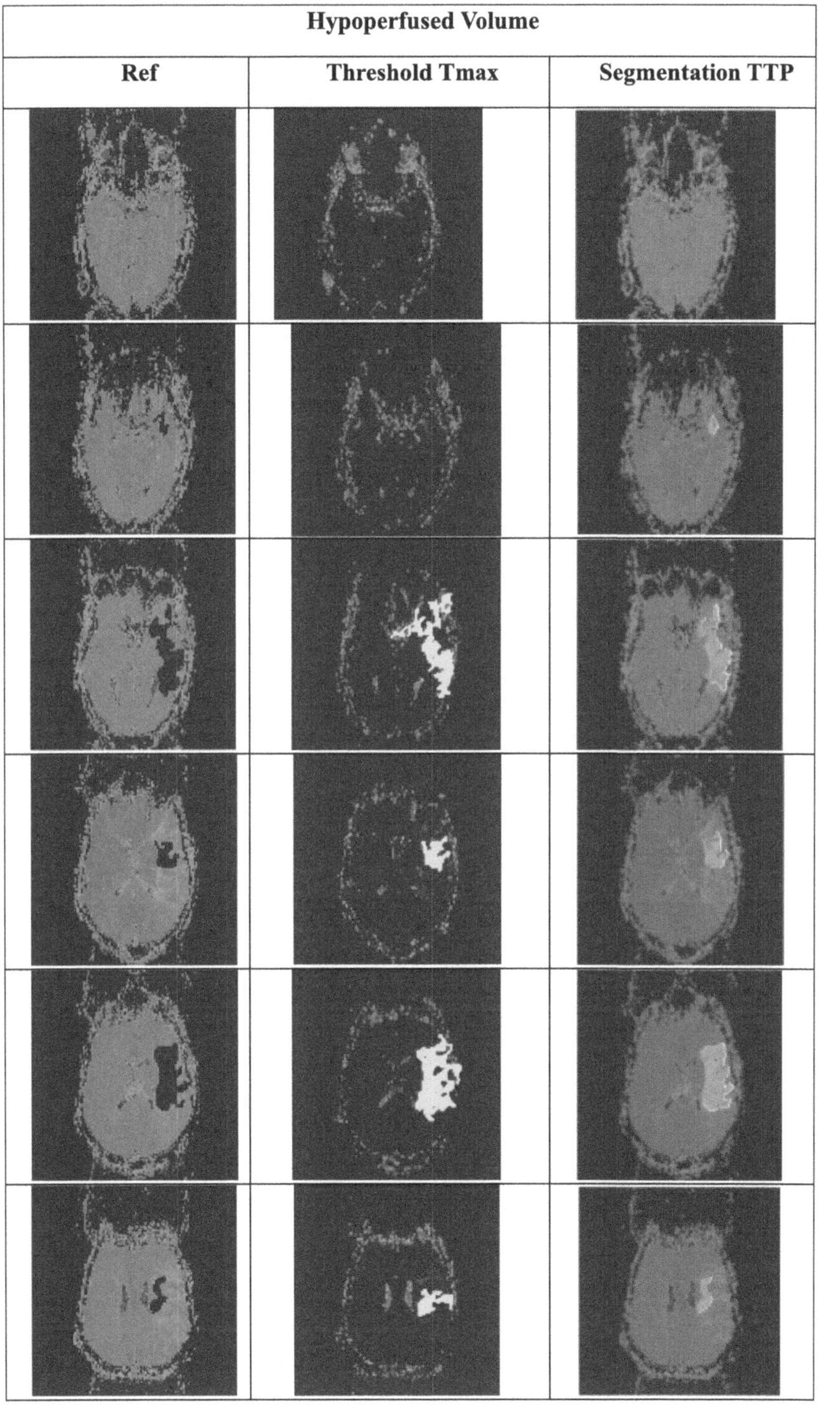

Fig. 6. Qualitative comparison of hypoperfused area segmentation results obtained from the two methods.

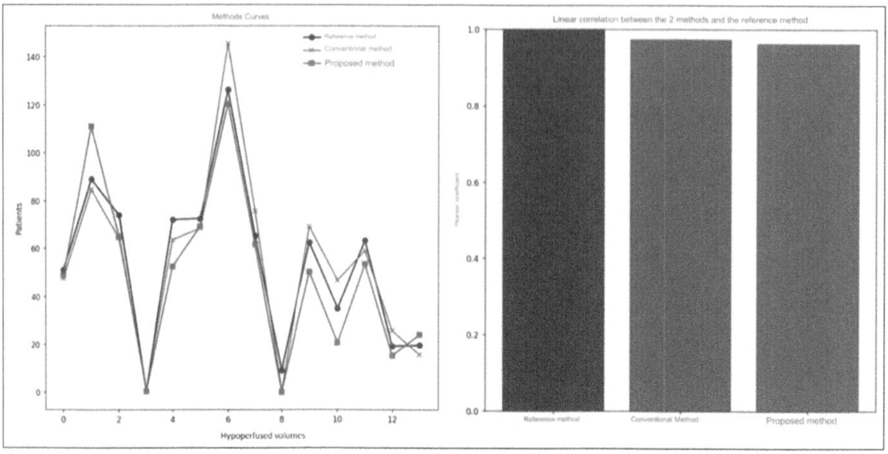

Fig. 7. Results of Pearson Test for Hypoperfused Volumes.

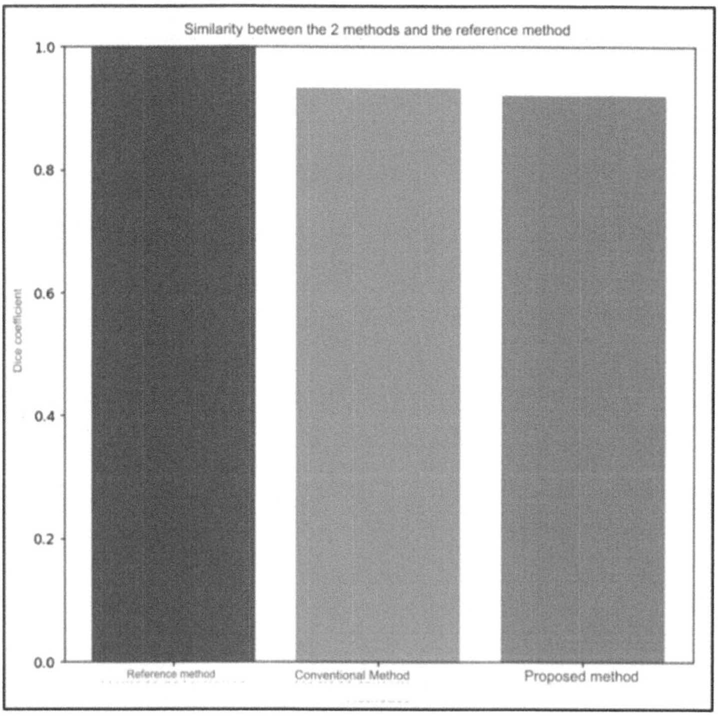

Fig. 8. Results of Dice Test for Hypoperfused Volumes.

4 Discussion

Following our qualitative and quantitative comparison of the conventional method and the proposed method, we established that our application, which focuses on the automatic selection of ischemic stroke patients for thrombectomy, integrates automatic hypoperfused volume segmentation from Time-To-Peak (TTP) maps using a pre-trained U-Net model. This model has shown high accuracy in detecting hypoperfused pixels.

Automating the segmentation process significantly reduces processing time, allowing healthcare providers to make quicker, informed decisions that can improve patient outcomes in emergency settings. Our method minimizes the risk of overlooking patients who could benefit from thrombectomy, ensuring that resources are allocated effectively and that at-risk patients receive timely treatment. Additionally, the integration of our automated system into existing imaging workflows provides reliable data at a glance, aiding clinicians in managing stroke cases more effectively.

Our findings reinforce the potential of deep learning models to outperform traditional methods, setting a precedent for future applications of AI in medical imaging. The success of our method suggests opportunities for further exploration, such as adapting U-Net architectures for other imaging modalities or integrating additional clinical data for improved patient selection. Furthermore, our research supports evolving frameworks of stroke management that prioritize rapid diagnosis and intervention, potentially influencing guidelines for AI integration in clinical practice. Our study, while promising, faces limitations that warrant attention in future research. The model's performance may vary across different clinical settings due to inconsistencies in imaging protocols and acquisition parameters. Expert validation remains essential to address subjective variations in defining hypoperfused regions, as these can impact clinical trust. Additionally, discrepancies in image slice thickness and alignment could affect segmentation accuracy, particularly with non-standardized image acquisitions.

Future work should focus on validating the model with multi-center datasets and integrating additional imaging modalities, like DWI or Tmax, to enhance ischemic tissue characterization. Incorporating explainable AI methods may also improve model interpretability for clinicians, increasing its potential utility in real-time stroke assessment. Prospective studies will be key to evaluating its impact on patient outcomes and decision-making in acute care settings.

5 Conclusion

Our study demonstrates the substantial benefits of the proposed automatic segmentation method over conventional approaches in the context of ischemic stroke. By integrating efficient segmentation techniques and reducing manual processing, our method enhances both the speed and accuracy of quantifying hypoperfused volumes, ultimately improving clinical efficiency and ensuring more consistent and reliable assessments in modern stroke care.

However, this research is not without limitations. The model was trained on a relatively small dataset of TTP images from a single institution, which may limit the generalizability of the findings across diverse patient populations and imaging settings. Additionally, while U-Net demonstrated robust segmentation capabilities, the method relies solely on TTP maps, potentially overlooking nuanced perfusion patterns observable in multi-parametric imaging.

Future research should focus on validating this approach in larger, multi-institutional cohorts to improve its clinical applicability. Incorporating additional perfusion metrics or combining TTP with other imaging modalities, such as DWI, could further enhance model accuracy and resilience. Advancements in explainable AI techniques may also aid clinicians in interpreting model predictions, potentially increasing adoption in clinical workflows.

References

1. Zamour, C.: Accident vasculaire cérébral: faut-il prendre en charge les ACSOS en structure d'urgence? (2013)
2. Virani, K., Hu, S., Christian, C., Simpkin, W., Phillips, S., Shankar, J.J.S.: Endovascular thrombectomy for stroke effectiveness study—an audit from a small tertiary care center. Can. Assoc. Radiol. J. **71**(1), 63–67 (2020)
3. Zhang, H., et al.: Intra-domain task-adaptive transfer learning to determine acute ischemic stroke onset time. Comput. Med. Imaging Graph. **90**, 101926 (2021)
4. Nogueira, R.G., et al.: Thrombectomy 6 to 24 hours after stroke with a mismatch between deficit and infarct. N. Engl. J. Med. **378**(1), 11–21 (2018)
5. Petrella, J.R., Provenzale, J.M.: MR perfusion imaging of the brain: techniques and applications. Am. J. Roentgenol. **175**(1), 207–219 (2000)
6. Wang, K., et al.: Deep learning detection of penumbral tissue on arterial spin labeling in stroke. Stroke **51**(2), 489–497 (2020)
7. Gao, H., et al.: Identifying patients with acute ischemic stroke within a 6-h window for the treatment of endovascular thrombectomy using deep learning and perfusion imaging. Front. Med. **10**, 1085437 (2023)
8. Boudraa, A.O., et al. : Seuillage d'images basé sur l'opérateur de Teager-Kaiser. In : Proceedings of the 21éme Colloque du Groupe d'Etudes du Traitement du Signal et des Images (GRETSI), pp. 885–888 (2007)
9. Mlynash, M., Eyngorn, I., Bammer, R., Moseley, M., Tong, D.C.: Automated method for generating the arterial input function on perfusion-weighted MR imaging: validation in patients with stroke. Am. J. Neuroradiol. **26**(6), 1479–1486 (2005)
10. Zoumpekas, T., Salamó, M., Puig, A.: Effective early stopping of point cloud neural networks. In: International Conference on Modeling Decisions for Artificial Intelligence, pp. 156–167. Springer International Publishing, Cham (2022)
11. Lohrke, F., et al.: Perfusion parameter map generation from TOF-MRA in stroke using generative adversarial networks. Neuroimage **298**, 120770 (2024)
12. Gava, U.A., et al.: Neural network-derived perfusion maps: a model-free approach to computed tomography perfusion in patients with acute ischemic stroke. Front. Neuroinform. **17**, 852105 (2023)
13. Parvathy, G.A.U.R.I., et al.: Emerging artificial intelligence-aided diagnosis and management methods for ischemic strokes and vascular occlusions: a comprehensive review. World Neurosurgery: X 100303 (2024)

Artificial Intelligence for Predicting Acute Ischemic Stroke Outcomes: Current Practices and Future Directions

Hela Limam[1(✉)], Eya Jouini[2], and Wided Oueslati[3]

[1] Higher Institute of Computer Science, University of Tunis El Manar, Tunisia and BestMod Laboratory, Higher Institute of Management of Tunis, Tunis, Tunisia
hela.limam@isi.utm.tn

[2] BestMod Laboratory, Higher Institute of Management of Tunis, Tunis, Tunisia
eya.jouini@etudiant-isi.utm.tn

[3] Higher School of Business of Tunis, University of La Manouba, Tunisia and BestMod Laboratory, Higher Institute of Management of Tunis, Tunis, Tunisia
wided.oueslati@esct.uma.tn

Abstract. Acute ischemic stroke is a critical medical emergency caused by a sudden loss of blood flow to the brain, leading to brain cell death due to a lack of oxygen and nutrients. While Diffusion Weighted Imaging (DWI) is instrumental in diagnosing ischemic stroke, current practices primarily rely on the manual assessment of DWI images to delineate the ischemic core, a time-intensive and subjective process that introduces variability in clinical decisions regarding endovascular treatments. This study aims to address these limitations by evaluating artificial intelligence (AI)-driven methods for automated DWI analysis, focusing on their potential to enhance stroke outcome prediction accuracy and consistency. Using a systematic review methodology, we examine AI applications that automatically identify stroke-affected areas in DWI scans and compare key approaches in terms of their performance metrics. Our findings indicate that AI methodologies can improve the speed and precision of stroke assessments, suggesting that these technologies have significant implications for advancing diagnostic consistency and aiding clinical decision-making in stroke care.

Keywords: Ischemic Stroke · Artificial Intelligence · Machine Learning · Deep Learning

1 Introduction

Stroke is a severe and life-threatening condition, with around 17 million cases globally each year. Approximately 80% of strokes are ischemic, resulting from the blockage of a cerebral artery by a thrombus (blood clot). This blockage reduces blood flow, leading to the destruction of nerve cells. According to the World Health Organization (WHO), one person suffers from a stroke every 5 s. Predicting the outcomes of lesions during the acute phase remains a significant challenge in clinical practice, as timely and accurate predictions can drastically alter treatment decisions and improve patient outcomes.

A. Mirzazadeh et al. (Eds.): SEMIT 2024, CCIS 2444, pp. 163–180, 2026.
https://doi.org/10.1007/978-3-032-01948-6_11

Magnetic Resonance Imaging (MRI), particularly diffusion imaging, is currently employed to detect irreversible brain damage and aid in predicting the potential outcomes of ischemic stroke. In the context of ischemic events, brain lesions are divided into two areas: the core, where irreversible damage has occurred, and the penumbra, a region where cells can recover if blood flow is restored. Without prompt reperfusion, the penumbra eventually transitions into the infarction core. Accurate prediction of stroke outcomes, especially in the ischemic penumbra, is vital for early intervention and effective treatment.

While Computed Tomography (CT) perfusion is widely used due to its speed and affordability, advanced MRI techniques such as perfusion-weighted imaging (PWI) and diffusion-weighted imaging (DWI) are gaining importance. These methods enable precise estimation of penumbral volume, providing detailed information about the ischemic lesion's state and informing treatment decisions, particularly for mechanical thrombectomy (MT). However, the manual analysis of MRI images to quantify areas of damage is laborious and subject to variability among clinicians, leading to inconsistencies in treatment decisions. Studies have shown that reliance on manual segmentation can introduce significant inter- and intra-observer inconsistencies, complicating treatment planning. Despite these challenges, mechanical thrombectomy remains the gold standard for patients with large vessel occlusions in the anterior circulation.

The research gap in the current literature is evident: while there have been advancements in imaging techniques, the integration of artificial intelligence (AI), particularly machine learning and deep learning methodologies, has not been fully realized in clinical practice for predicting ischemic stroke outcomes. The visible signs of ischemic lesions can change over time, often up to a month post-stroke, making timely prediction even more challenging. AI offers a promising avenue to improve the accuracy and speed of this prediction task, addressing the limitations of manual analysis.

This paper reviews the potential of AI in predicting outcomes of ischemic stroke by focusing on two main subfields: machine learning and deep learning. The selection of these methodologies is motivated by their ability to analyze vast amounts of data with higher accuracy and efficiency than traditional methods. Machine learning techniques can uncover complex patterns within imaging and clinical data, while deep learning models can improve prediction capabilities by leveraging large datasets and advanced algorithms.

Our findings indicate that AI methodologies can significantly enhance the prediction of stroke outcomes, leading to more informed clinical decisions and improved patient management. This work contributes to the field by providing a comprehensive overview of current AI applications in ischemic stroke prediction, highlighting the effectiveness of various machine learning and deep learning approaches, and identifying areas for future research. The paper is organized as follows: Sect. 2 presents the fundamental concepts relevant to ischemic stroke and its outcomes. Section 3 discusses machine learning approaches used for predicting outcomes of ischemic strokes, while Sect. 4 focuses on deep learning-based methodologies. In Sect. 5, we provide a comparative discussion of machine learning and deep learning techniques in predicting ischemic stroke outcomes. Finally, Sect. 6 concludes the paper by summarizing the findings and proposing future trends in this research area.

2 Fundamental Concepts

Interest in the ischemic stroke outcomes prediction, some basic concepts allow for more understanding of the frame of the study. In the following, we define and detail the most important ones.

2.1 Machine Learning

Machine learning enables computers to learn from historical data and make intelligent decisions. These frameworks involve collecting and managing large datasets, converting them into structured knowledge systems that can be applied across different domains. To develop an effective machine learning model, an appropriate framework for learning is essential, along with relevant, well-formatted data and proper preprocessing steps [1].

Machine learning differs from algorithmic programming in that Machine Learning models can generalize and handle new cases. When the model recognizes something, it has seen before, it can use that prior knowledge/learning to evaluate the case [2].

Machine learning applied to neuroradiology is now widely used in the diagnosis and emergency pathology of cognitive or inflammatory chronic diseases, especially ischemic or hemorrhagic stroke [3].

The primary objective is to apply the model to new datasets to generate predictions. Predicting outcomes for ischemic stroke is framed as a classification problem, utilizing various machine learning algorithms, such as decision trees [4], logistic regression, support vector machines (SVMs), and random forest classifiers [5]. These methods emphasize improving model performance by designing superior features [6].

2.2 Deep Learning

According to Noelle et al. [7], deep learning is part of a broader category of learning methods that utilize artificial neural networks. It represents a hierarchical approach to machine learning, employing multiple algorithms in a progressive sequence. This process mirrors the way the human brain functions when making decisions, as it utilizes various technologies to analyze vast amounts of data.

Within this framework, a variety of techniques exist, ranging from conventional methods to more intricate and advanced approaches. Two primary deep learning architectures for image classification are U-Net [8] and Convolutional Neural Networks (CNN) [9], both of which do not require manual feature selection but instead learn relevant features directly from the training data.

Deep learning excels in handling exceptionally large and high-dimensional datasets, demonstrating remarkable performance across various medical imaging applications [10]. Its effectiveness in processing medical images related to ischemic stroke to enhance prediction accuracy has been highlighted in numerous studies.

2.3 Artificial Intelligence for Ischemic Stroke Prediction

Emergency management of ICA patients is highly (but not exclusively) dependent on the parenchymal changes associated with imaging-detected stroke. Emergency thrombolysis and thrombectomy are well-established treatments for improving outcomes. The selection of treatments is based on the prediction of outcomes, which AI algorithms help analyze so they can take center stage in decision support [11]. Assessing the volumes of the ischemic core and penumbra in acute ischemic stroke is crucial for clinicians, as it offers valuable insights for predicting clinical responses after successful recanalization (SR) and for selecting candidates for treatments such as intravenous thrombolysis and endovascular therapy (EVT) [12, 13]. Neuroimaging techniques like diffusion-weighted imaging (DWI) and perfusion-weighted imaging (PWI) in magnetic resonance imaging (MRI) allow for the visualization of the location and extent of ischemic stroke lesions with high sensitivity and specificity. The target mismatch criteria assist in determining patient eligibility for EVT and are assessed through the volumes of DWI and PWI lesions [14]. Additionally, recent studies emphasize the potential of AI in processing DWI and PWI data to optimize acute ischemic stroke management strategies, supporting more precise treatment decisions [15, 16].

In addition to measuring the PWI-DWI mismatch zone, estimating infarct growth offers a direct method for predicting penumbra areas and the ultimate infarct lesion volume [17]. Artificial intelligence-based methods have emerged as a promising approach in acute stroke neuroimaging for predicting ischemic stroke progression through interpolation of shape representations [18] and for forecasting voxel-based tissue outcomes [19, 20] as well as clinical outcomes [21]. Specifically, an AI technique known as fully automated stroke tissue estimation using classifiers [22] has demonstrated the ability to accurately predict final lesion volumes in instances of both successful recanalization (SR) and unsuccessful recanalization (UR). The application of artificial intelligence in ischemic stroke is illustrated in Fig. 1.

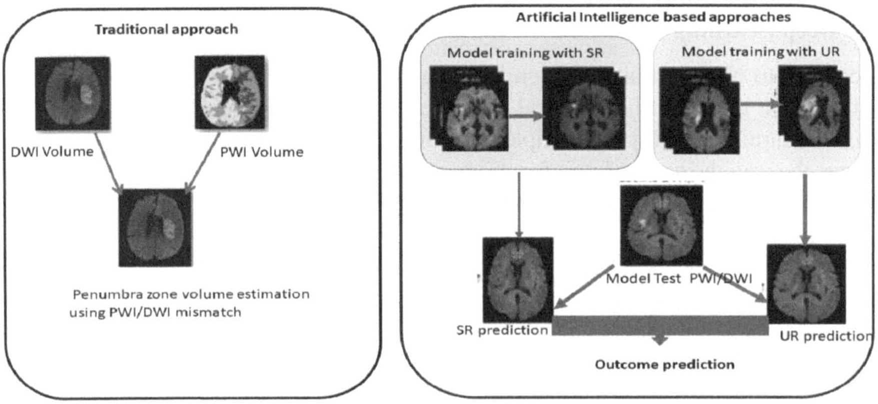

Fig. 1. Artificial intelligence for ischemic stroke prediction

3 Machine Learning for Predicting Ischemic Stroke Outcomes

In this section, we examine the effectiveness of machine learning (ML)-based methods for predicting outcomes in acute stroke cases. This study explores the viability of an ML technique that predicts tissue and clinical outcomes by utilizing features extracted from both imaging and clinical data. Depending on the ML approach employed, we assess and compare the performance of different methods in forecasting final infarct volumes and infarct growth and associated outcomes.

3.1 Machine Learning-Based Approaches for Predicting Ischemic Stroke Outcomes

Recent advancements in machine learning (ML) have significantly contributed to the prediction of ischemic stroke outcomes, leveraging diverse datasets and modeling techniques. Several studies have explored different ML models, highlighting their strengths and limitations.

Li et al. (2022) utilized an ensemble of Random Forest and Convolutional Neural Networks (CNN) to analyze CT and MRI images from 500 patients. This model aimed to identify early indicators like the ischemic core and penumbral regions. It demonstrated high sensitivity (0.85) and specificity (0.80), making it particularly effective for rapid clinical diagnosis, although it required a substantial amount of data, limiting its feasibility in resource-constrained environments [23].

Ahn et al. (2023) [24] focused on a Decision Tree model applied to MRI perfusion-weighted imaging from 320 patients. This study was particularly relevant for evaluating patient eligibility for endovascular therapy (EVT), achieving a sensitivity of 0.81 and specificity of 0.76. However, the generalizability of the findings across various imaging protocols was a noted limitation [24].

McKinley et al. (2016) employed a Random Forest model on MR imaging data from 100 patients, specifically analyzing diffusion-weighted imaging (DWI) and perfusion imaging. Their findings underscored the importance of FLAIR imaging for assessing the penumbra, achieving exceptional sensitivity (0.998) but facing limitations due to the absence of voxel-wise perfusion maps, restricting detailed spatial analysis [5].

In another study, Xie et al. (2018) applied a Decision Tree model to a dataset of 512 patients, incorporating clinical exams and acute neuroimaging (CT and perfusion CT). This approach evaluated the risk-benefit ratio for revascularization therapies, with sensitivity at 0.825 and specificity at 0.78, although the feature selection may limit the model's applicability across various stroke assessment tools [4].

Wei et al. (2021) compared multiple models, including Random Forest, Support Vector Machine (SVM), and Logistic Regression on a dataset of 344 patients. This study demonstrated high predictive accuracy by integrating clinical variables and lesion volumes, achieving sensitivity of 0.8686 and specificity of 0.8358, but faced limitations related to the dataset's size and the exclusion of common cerebral infarction cases [25].

Lee et al. (2020) utilized Logistic Regression, SVM, and Random Forest models with DWI and FLAIR images from 355 patients. This computerized assessment provided quantitative evaluations with a sensitivity of 0.826 and specificity of 0.851, although concerns arose regarding the small sample size and lack of sample size calculation affecting the study's validation [26].

Lastly, Zhu et al. (2021) explored various models, including Logistic Regression, SVM, Random Forest, Gradient Boosted Decision Tree, and Extra Trees in an ensemble approach applied to a dataset of 268 patients. This study showed that the ensemble method improved classification accuracy, particularly in differentiating acute from sub-acute stroke onset, achieving sensitivity of 0.840 and specificity of 0.824, but faced challenges with misclassification due to lesion segmentation issues [27].

These studies collectively illustrate the growing role of machine learning in enhancing the prediction of ischemic stroke outcomes, though they also highlight the necessity for further research to address limitations such as dataset size, generalizability, and feature selection across various imaging modalities.

3.2 Comparison and Discussion of Machine Learning-Based Approaches

In these studies, key metrics such as Specificity, AUC (Area Under the Curve), Dice Similarity Coefficient (DSC), and Sensitivity were utilized to evaluate model performance. Each metric provides insights into different aspects:

- **Specificity** measures a model's ability to correctly identify non-stroke cases, reflecting the ratio of true negatives to the sum of true negatives and false positives.
- **AUC** offers a comprehensive measure of the model's classification capability, summarizing its performance across various decision thresholds.
- **Dice Similarity Coefficient (DSC)**, similar to the F1 Score, quantifies the overlap between predicted and actual outcomes, indicating segmentation accuracy.
- **Sensitivity** assesses the model's accuracy in identifying true positive stroke cases, which is crucial for timely intervention.

Table 1 compares these approaches, highlighting their unique advantages, limitations, and performance scores across metrics. For instance, McKinley et al.'s model achieved high AUC and specificity but faced technical limitations due to its dependency on voxel-wise data [5].

Machine learning (ML)-driven models for predicting ischemic stroke outcomes show significant promise in enhancing clinical decision support by accurately delineating ischemic penumbras and assessing lesion characteristics across various imaging modalities. Future research should emphasize multicenter studies to ensure broader applicability, as indicated by the findings of McKinley et al. Furthermore, improving segmentation accuracy especially in tissue signature classification and FLAIR-based lesion detection remains critical for advancing automated stroke diagnostics. Zhu et al.'s ensemble model highlighted the effectiveness of integrating cross-entropy (CE) and Dice loss functions to manage class imbalances; however, ongoing refinement is needed to address inconsistencies in FLAIR segmentation [27].

This comparative analysis underscores the potential of ML models to complement traditional diagnostic methods, offering scalable, data-driven solutions to enhance stroke prognosis and treatment allocation.

4 Deep Learning-Based Approaches for Predicting Ischemic Stroke Outcomes

Several research in the context of ischemic stroke detection were oriented on the deep learning approaches that showed good results in recent years. Most of the studies have employed different ANN [28], U-net [29], and Convolutional neural networks CNN [9].

Table 1. Comparative Analysis of Machine Learning Models for Ischemic Stroke Prediction

Li et al. (2022) [23]	Random Forest and CNN ensemble model	500 patients, with a split of 400 for training and 100 for testing	CT and MRI imaging datasets focused on early stroke indicators like ischemic core and penumbral regions	High sensitivity and suitability for clinical settings, allowing rapid diagnosis	High data demand limits use in resource-constrained environments	0.85	0.80	0.88	0.82
Ahn et al. (2023) 24]	Decision tree model	320 patients, with 256 used for training and 64 for testing	MRI, specifically perfusion-weighted imaging (PWI), providing critical metrics for treatment eligibility, especially for EVT	Rapid evaluation capabilities aid in emergency treatment decisions	Limited generalizability across variable imaging protocols	0.81	0.76	0.86	0.79
Mckinley et al. (2016) [5]	Random Forest	100(45/55)	MR imaging with an identifiable lesion on DWI and perfusion imaging,	assess the potential benefits of reperfusion and add the value of FLAIR instead of T2-weighted images	no voxel-wise perfusion map was found	0.998	0.928	0.34	0.77
Xie et al. (2018) [4]	Decision Tree	512	clinical examination and acute neuroimaging (CT and perfusion CT) and CTA images	assess the risk-benefit ratio for revascularization therapies	Features may not translate well to other acute stroke tissue classification software recovery	0.825	0.78	-	0.794

(*continued*)

Table 1. (*continued*)

Li et al. (2022) [23]	Random Forest and CNN ensemble model	500 patients, with a split of 400 for training and 100 for testing	CT and MRI imaging datasets focused on early stroke indicators like ischemic core and penumbral regions	High sensitivity and suitability for clinical settings, allowing rapid diagnosis	High data demand limits use in resource-constrained environments	0.85	0.80	0.88	0.82
Wei et al. (2021) [25]	Random Forest, support vector machine, and logistic regression	344	the volume data, the clinical data, and the combination	combining clinical variables and stroke lesion volumes that were derived from the advanced ML algorithms had high accuracy	- data collection is limited - The study did not include all clinically common cases of cerebral infarction	0.8686	0.8358	0.790	0.7695
Lee et al.(2020) [26]	Logistic regression, support vector machine, and random forest	355(299/56)	DWI and FLAIR iages	the system uses a computerized method to quantitatively evaluate various parameters in DWI and FLAIR MRI	he patient population was small - the appropriate sample size was not calculated before the conduction of the study	0.826	0.851	-	0.758

(*continued*)

Table 1. (*continued*)

Li et al. (2022) [23]	Random Forest and CNN ensemble model	500 patients, with a split of 400 for training and 100 for testing	CT and MRI imaging datasets focused on early stroke indicators like ischemic core and penumbral regions	High sensitivity and suitability for clinical settings, allowing rapid diagnosis	High data demand limits use in resource-constrained environments	0.85	0.80	0.88	0.82
Zhu et al. (2021) [27]	logistic regression, support vector machine, random forest, gradient boosted decision tree, extra trees	268(ratio of 3:1:1)	DWI and FLAIR images	The classification accuracies of voting were both higher than that of one single classifier	there is no significant hyperintensity mismatch between DWI and FLAIR - the misclassification because of the lesion segmentation failure	0.840	0.824	0.803	0.769
Authors + date	Techniques	Number of patients(training/test set)	Data volume	Advantages	Disadvantages	Specificity	AUC	DSC	Sensitivity/recall

4.1 Deep Learning-Based Approaches for Predicting Ischemic Stroke Outcomes

Yanda Sailaja and Velumurugan Pattani (2023) developed an innovative approach to ischemic stroke detection using advanced deep learning techniques, specifically a Deep Convolutional Neural Network (DCNN), along with the YOLO_5 and Single-Shot Detector (SSD) models. Their study focused on enhancing the accuracy and efficiency of stroke identification through automated analysis of medical imaging. By leveraging the strengths of these deep learning frameworks, they achieved significant improvements in both segmentation and classification tasks, demonstrating a robust capability to detect early ischemic changes. The integration of DCNNs with YOLO_5 and SSD provided a powerful tool for real-time diagnostics, potentially transforming clinical decision-making processes in emergency stroke care. Their findings highlight the growing importance of deep learning in medical imaging, as reported in various literature on AI applications in healthcare [30].

Kasasbeh et al. [28] employed artificial neural networks (ANNs) to predict the ischemic core in acute stroke patients using diffusion-weighted imaging (DWI). They first developed an ANN model based solely on computed tomography perfusion (CTP) data and then enhanced it by integrating clinical data with CTP data. The study demonstrated that combining clinical and CTP data yielded impressive results, with the model achieving an accuracy of 0.87, AUC of 0.91, and a sensitivity and specificity of 0.65. Despite these promising results, a limitation of the study is that using ANN for CTP-based ischemic core approximation remains incomplete, as the gold standard for ischemic core identification has not yet been established.

Yu et al. [8] proposed a method using the U-net architecture to identify tissue at risk and the ischemic core in acute stroke at a level superior to current clinical standards. The authors tested three different methodologies: a pretraining deep learning strategy, a separate deep learning approach, and a thresholding approach. After comparing these approaches, they found no statistical difference in the volume or absolute volume differences between the models. The pretraining method had the highest AUC (92%), likely due to the model's access to two to three times more cases for training compared to the other approaches. However, one limitation was that the prediction accuracy was affected by the limited number of cases available for training.

Nishi et al. [9] developed a convolutional neural network (CNN)-based dual-output deep learning model to extract imaging features from pre-treatment DWI data. The model was used to predict clinical outcomes in patients with large vessel occlusion. Its performance was compared to two standard neuroimaging biomarkers: the Alberta Stroke Program Early CT score (from DWI images) and ischemic core volume. The model employed an encoder-decoder architecture to segment ischemic lesions, automatically extracting high-level feature maps to predict outcomes. The model showed an AUC of 0.81 ± 0.06, outperforming the Alberta Stroke Program Early CT score and ischemic core volume models, which had AUCs of 0.63 ± 0.05 and 0.64 ± 0.05, respectively. Although the model's focus on pathological lesions improved predictions, it was only compared with biomarkers directly obtained from DWI data.

Wang et al. [31] utilized a multi-scale 3D CNN for ischemic core/deficit prediction using inputs from NCCT, CTA, and CTA + images, treating these inputs as independent channels for the network. The authors tested four input combinations: (1) NCCT, CTA, and CTA +; (2) NCCT and CTA; (3) CTA alone; and (4) NCCT alone. The CNN models were evaluated using the same test data, and the best AUC was achieved with the combination of NCCT, CTA, and CTA + in both internal (0.89 ± 0.02) and external (0.81 ± 0.04) cohorts. Although the model showed strong performance, the authors did not account for the potential effects of adding symmetry information to the CNN, which could further enhance its predictive power.

4.2 Comparison and Discussion of Machine Learning-Based Approaches

Despite significant advances in deep learning for stroke diagnosis, there remains a substantial need for research in intraoperative management and the effects of anticoagulants. Deep learning models have the potential to address these issues and provide valuable insights. Additionally, incorporating other clinical information, such as time-to-treatment (TTT) and time-since-stroke (TSS) [8], into deep learning models, and testing the inclusion of more risk factors, could enhance predictive accuracy and allow comparisons with other techniques, further improving performance [4].

In Kasasbeh's study [28], future work is set to explore the evaluation of additional input parameters and the application of advanced deep learning methods, such as U-net convolutional networks, which naturally integrate rich features into segmentation tasks. With continued research, artificial neural networks could evolve into a robust quantitative framework for diagnosing ischemic core, assisting in treatment decision-making, and offering prognostic assessments of treatment outcomes at the individual patient level. All the approaches discussed are summarized in Table 2.

Clinical decisions are often based on the difference between the best and worst possible treatment outcomes. To improve model performance, training and validating models using larger and more diverse cohorts, while incorporating key clinical predictors, can provide more accurate information for different clinical situations [29]. Developing separate models for specific scenarios may offer deeper insights and better guidance for decision-making.

In future research, these models could serve as a baseline for fine-tuning methodologies aimed at achieving this critical goal. By incorporating a segmentation step into clinical outcome predictions, as suggested by earlier studies, the model could be explicitly directed to focus on pathological lesions. This refinement is expected to result in a more efficient learning process and enhanced predictive accuracy [32].

In Wang et al.'s study [31], the images were obtained from CT scanners provided by the same vendor. Although the study demonstrated the model's generalization capability on a separate dataset, further research is required using images from multiple centers with diverse acquisition parameters. This broader approach is essential to better estimate the therapeutic effects on selected patients and support clinical decision-making in stroke treatment.

Table 2. Comparative Analysis of Deep Learning Models for Ischemic Stroke Prediction

Yanda and Pattani (2023) [30]	a Deep Convolutional Neural Network (DCNN), YOLO_5, and Single-Shot Detector (SSD)	242 patients, divided into a training set of 194 patients and a test set of 48 patients	MRI images focused on DWI and PWI sequences, which detail ischemic core and penumbra areas essential for assessing stroke impact	High segmentation accuracy improves clinical decision-making for reperfusion therapy	Performance varies with image quality and quantity	0.92	0.92	0.84	0.78
Kasasbeh et al.(2019) [28]	ANN	128	CTP and clinical data	the algorithm can be readily appended to automated postprocessing software	CTP approximations of the ischemic core using ANN will remain imperfect as the gold standard for the ischemic core remains elusive	0.65	0.87	0.48	0.91
Yu et al. (2020) [8]	U-net	182(ratio of 3:1:1)	baseline perfusion-weighted and diffusion-weighted images	the studies came from many institutions over a long period, and many different scanners were used	the use of thrombectomy and posterior circulation stroke were not included	0.97	0.92	0.530	0.66

(*continued*)

Table 2. *(continued)*

Yanda and Pattani (2023) [30]	a Deep Convolutional Neural Network (DCNN), YOLO_5, and Single-Shot Detector (SSD)	242 patients, divided into a training set of 194 patients and a test set of 48 patients	MRI images focused on DWI and PWI sequences, which detail ischemic core and penumbra areas essential for assessing stroke impact	High segmentation accuracy improves clinical decision-making for reperfusion therapy	Performance varies with image quality and quantity	0.92	0.92	0.84	0.78
Nishi (2020) [9]	CNN	250	DWI images	the model can be guided explicitly to focus on the pathological lesion because by applying a segmentation network to clinical outcome prediction	The model was compared with biomarkers that can directly be derived from DWI data alone	0.762	0.81	0.86	0.762
Wang (2021) [3]	multi-scale 3D CNN	345	NCCT, CTA, and CTA + images	the model can be extended to predict DWI-derived ischemic core	did not explore the effect of adding the symmetry information on the CNN model	0.67	0.8	0.57	0.96
Authors + date	techniques	Number of patients(training/test set)	Data volume	Advantages	Disadvantages	Specificity	AUC	DSC	Sensitivity/ Recall

5 Comparison and Discussion of ML and Deep Learning for Ischemic AVC Prediction

Several studies have applied machine learning to neuroimaging data to predict outcomes for patients with large vessel occlusion, but few have compared this approach to predictions obtained using traditional neuroimaging biomarkers [9]. Zhu et al. [27] noted that fluid-attenuated inversion recovery (FLAIR) typically takes more time than diffusion-weighted imaging (DWI) to represent hyperintense infarct lesions. Moreover, their study demonstrated that using both DWI and FLAIR features resulted in significantly higher AUC scores than using DWI or FLAIR alone. Interestingly, SVM models built using DWI and FLAIR together had lower AUC scores than those based on DWI alone.

ML-based predictions have the potential to address the limitations of traditional ischemic penumbra estimation methods. Deep learning models, particularly convolutional neural networks (CNNs), introduce highly sophisticated machine learning techniques and are designed to simulate brain functions. These deep neural networks allow data to pass between interconnected neurons, performing increasingly abstract nonlinear transformations [32]. Deep learning in medical imaging has advanced significantly, enabling better data interpretation through automatic feature extraction. CNN models, in particular, offer larger AUC and Dice similarity coefficients (DSC) compared to traditional perfusion-diffusion mismatch models. CNNs benefit from incorporating spatial information, making their predictions less sensitive to noisy inputs [7].

Our literature review highlights the increasing interest in ischemic stroke prediction, demonstrating a strong focus on developing novel solutions for identifying high-risk patients. This growing interest, along with the recency of the research, indicates that ischemic stroke detection remains a dynamic and evolving field. Accurate outcome prediction is vital for guiding treatment decisions and patient selection for endovascular therapy in emergency settings. However, outcome prediction is complex, requiring the integration of numerous clinical and imaging biomarkers into practical, optimized models [4].

Machine learning, particularly for cerebrovascular diseases, has shown promise by offering sophisticated feature engineering. As more data is collected, ML predictions are expected to improve, especially through careful modeling based on multimodal MRI data [33]. Neuroimaging plays a key role in stroke diagnosis, with CT and MRI being the imaging modalities of choice [34]. Within MRI, diffusion-weighted imaging (DWI) and perfusion-weighted imaging (PWI) are particularly effective for visualizing ischemic stroke lesions with high sensitivity and specificity [33]. The DWI/PWI mismatch paradigm remains the most common method for classifying patients, particularly those presenting more than six hours after stroke onset [8].

The primary methods for predicting ischemic stroke in these studies involve ML techniques like decision trees [4], logistic regression, SVMs, and random forests [5], as well as deep learning methods such as U-net [8], artificial neural networks (ANNs) [7], and CNNs [9]. Both machine learning and deep learning methods have demonstrated promising results.

Recently, neural networks have been used to predict tissue fate in stroke, allowing visual features to be directly learned from training data [15]. Despite the heterogeneity of stroke progression and its potential to violate population-based imaging biomarker thresholds [32], clinical studies using serial MRI scans of untreated patients over 12 weeks have provided valuable insights [35]. This research represents a critical first step toward creating generalized and individualized stroke outcome predictions, paving the way for models that integrate clinical data [8].

Deep neural networks, which rely on multiple layers of computational connections, have the potential to improve stroke diagnosis performance. However, the development of effective deep learning models is currently hindered by small sample sizes. Future research must test the applicability of deep learning methods more extensively [37, 38]. ML, by learning nonlinear functions from input-output relationships, holds the potential to overcome the limitations of traditional threshold-based volume estimation methods, although the use of CNNs still presents challenges [34].

To provide a comparative analysis of the performance of various machine learning (ML) models for predicting outcomes in ischemic stroke, it is essential to examine both the advantages and disadvantages of each approach highlighted in the literature. While traditional ML techniques, such as support vector machines (SVMs) and logistic regression, have demonstrated effectiveness in certain scenarios, their limitations in feature extraction and handling complex data patterns have prompted researchers to explore deep learning methods. For instance, convolutional neural networks (CNNs) have been shown to achieve higher area under the curve (AUC) scores and Dice Similarity Coefficients (DSC) due to their ability to learn hierarchical feature representations directly from neuroimaging data [27, 32]. However, the complexity of deep learning models often requires substantial amounts of data for training, which can be a barrier in clinical settings where sample sizes may be limited [4, 26].

Moreover, the integration of multimodal imaging data, including diffusion-weighted imaging (DWI) and perfusion-weighted imaging (PWI), enhances the predictive accuracy of these models but also increases the complexity of model development [8, 33]. As highlighted in recent studies, while CNNs excel in capturing spatial information and reducing sensitivity to noise, their interpretability remains a challenge, which can impact clinical trust in automated predictions [34]. Therefore, our review underscores the need for further comparative studies that not only validate the performance of existing models but also explore hybrid approaches that could combine the strengths of both traditional and deep learning methods. By addressing these aspects, we aim to contribute to the ongoing discourse in the field and encourage the development of more robust predictive tools for ischemic stroke outcomes.

6 Conclusion and Future Trends

In this review, we have systematically examined prominent methods used to predict outcomes in acute ischemic stroke, emphasizing the promise of automated imaging and clinical data analysis in reducing interobserver variability and improving prognosis. However, despite the advancements, artificial intelligence (AI) methods still face challenges, notably in accurately assessing smaller perfusion and diffusion volumes. These discrepancies, often seen when compared to standard reference methods, stem largely from the limited size and diversity of current training datasets.

Our findings suggest the necessity of expanding validation efforts to include larger and more diverse datasets that capture complex hypoperfusion patterns, various MRI protocols, and multiple noise or artifact types. Such enhancements are essential for improving the robustness and accuracy of AI-based approaches.

The review also uncovered recent progress in hybrid machine learning techniques, which show promise in refining feature selection. Advanced optimization methods, such as Ant Colony Optimization (ACO) and Particle Swarm Optimization (PSO), could further improve these processes, enhancing the adaptability and performance of predictive models. Additionally, with most studies relying on static datasets, there is a clear need to develop adaptive models that can handle dynamic, real-time data inputs a critical aspect for real-world applications.

From a clinical perspective, there remains a significant limitation in relying solely on perfusion-weighted imaging (PWI) and diffusion-weighted imaging (DWI) mismatch volumes for endovascular treatment decisions. More extensive datasets with diverse MRI protocols will be necessary to refine these selection criteria, ultimately improving patient outcomes.

This review contributes to the theoretical understanding of AI applications in stroke prognosis by identifying key limitations and emerging trends. Future research should focus on more adaptive, robust AI models, explore dimensionality reduction techniques for dynamic data, and aim to establish refined criteria for patient selection, which will advance both theoretical knowledge and practical applications in clinical settings.

References

1. Injadat, M.N., Moubayed, A., Nassif, A.B., Shami, A.: Machine learning towards intelligent systems: applications, challenges, and opportunities. Artif. Intell. Rev. **54**, 3299–3348 (2021)
2. Alpaydin, E.: Introduction to Machine Learning. MIT Press, Cambridge (2020)
3. Kulesza, T., Burnett, M., Wong, W.-K., Stumpf, S.: Principles of explanatory debugging to personalize interactive machine learning. In: Proceedings of the 20th International Conference on Intelligent User Interfaces, pp. 126–137. ACM, New York (2015)
4. Xie, Y., et al.: Use of gradient boosting machine learning to predict patient outcome in acute ischemic stroke on the basis of imaging, demographic, and clinical information. Am. J. Roentgenol. **212**, 44–51 (2019)
5. McKinley, R., et al.: Fully automated stroke tissue estimation using random forest classifiers (faster). J. Cereb. Blood Flow Metab. **37**, 2728–2741 (2017)
6. Dev, S., Wang, H., Nwosu, C.S., Jain, N., Veeravalli, B., John, D.: A predictive analytics approach for stroke prediction using machine learning and neural networks. Healthc. Anal. **2**, 100032 (2022)
7. Debs, N., et al.: Impact of the reperfusion status for predicting the final stroke infarct using deep learning. NeuroImage Clin. **29**, 102548 (2021)
8. Yu, Y., et al.: Tissue at risk and ischemic core estimation using deep learning in acute stroke. Am. J. Neuroradiol. **42**, 1030–1037 (2021)
9. Nishi, H., et al.: Deep learning–derived high-level neuroimaging features predict clinical outcomes for large vessel occlusion. Stroke **51**, 1484–1492 (2020)
10. Karthik, R., Menaka, R., Johnson, A., Anand, S.: Neuroimaging and deep learning for brain stroke detection—a review of recent advancements and future prospects. Comput. Methods Programs Biomed. **197**, 105728 (2020)
11. Han, C.E., Arbib, M.A., Schweighofer, N.: Stroke rehabilitation reaches a threshold. Plos Comput. Biol. **4**, e1000133 (2008)

12. Albers, G.W., et al.: Magnetic resonance imaging profiles predict clinical response to early reperfusion: the diffusion and perfusion imaging evaluation for understanding stroke evolution (DEFUSE) study. Ann. Neurol. **60**, 17–508 (2006)
13. Bang, O.Y., et al.: Multimodal MRI-based triage for acute stroke therapy: challenges and progress. Front. Neurol. **9**, 586 (2018)
14. Albers, G.W., et al.: Thrombectomy for stroke at 6 to 16 h with selection by perfusion imaging. N. Engl. J. Med. **378**, 708–718 (2018)
15. Ben Alaya, I., Limam, H., Kraiem, T.: Applications of artificial intelligence for DWI and PWI data processing in acute ischemic stroke: current practices and future directions. Clin. Imaging **81**, 79–86 (2024)
16. Ben Alaya, I.., Limam, H., Kraiem, T.: Automatic triaging of acute ischemic stroke patients for reperfusion therapies using artificial Intelligence methods and multiple MRI features: a review. Clin. Imaging, 109992 (2024)
17. Rosso, C., et al.: Prediction of infarct growth based on apparent diffusion coefficients: penumbral assessment without intravenous contrast material. Radiology **250**, 92–184 (2009)
18. Lucas, C., Kemmling, A., Bouteldja, N., Aulmann, L.F., Mamlouk, A.M., Heinrich, M.P.: Learning to predict ischemic stroke growth on acute CT perfusion data by interpolating low-dimensional shape representations. Front. Neurol. **9**, 989 (2018)
19. Nielsen, A., Hansen, M.B., Tietze, A., Mouridsen, K.: Prediction of tissue outcome and assessment of treatment effect in acute ischemic stroke using deep learning. Stroke **49**, 1394–1401 (2018)
20. Pinto, A., McKinley, R., Alves, V., Wiest, R., Silva, C.A., Reyes, M.: Stroke lesion outcome prediction based on MRI imaging combined with clinical information. Front. Neurol. **9**, 1060 (2018)
21. Tang, T.Y., et al.: Development and validation of a penumbra-based predictive model for thrombolysis outcome in acute ischemic stroke patients. EBioMedicine **35**, 251–259 (2018)
22. McKinley, R., et al.: Machine learning for detecting early infarction in acute stroke with non-contrast-enhanced CT. Am. J. Neuroradiol. **41**, 1526–1532 (2020)
23. Li, A., Zhang, B., Chen, C., Wang, D.: Applications of artificial intelligence in DWI and PWI data processing for acute ischemic stroke. Clin. Imaging **81**, 79–86 (2022). https://doi.org/10.1016/j.clinimag.2022.109992
24. Ahn, S., Lee, H., Kim, M., Park, J., Kim, H., Yoon, B.: Artificial intelligence for clinical decision support in acute ischemic stroke: a systematic review. Stroke **54**, 1505–1516 (2023)
25. Wei, L., et al.: Prediction of progression to severe stroke in initially diagnosed anterior circulation ischemic cerebral infarction. Front. Neurol. **12**, 898 (2021)
26. Lee, H.,et al.: Machine learning approach to identify stroke within 4.5 h. Stroke **51**(3), 860–866 (2020)
27. Zhu, H., Jiang, L., Zhang, H., Luo, L., Chen, Y., Chen, Y.: An automatic machine learning approach for ischemic stroke onset time identification based on DWI and FLAIR imaging. NeuroImage: Clinical **31**, 102744 (2021)
28. Kasasbeh, A.S., Christensen, S., Parsons, M.W., Campbell, B., Albers, G.W., Lansberg, M.G.: Artificial neural network computer tomography perfusion prediction of ischemic core. Stroke **50**(6), 1578–1581 (2019)
29. Yu, Y., et al.: Use of deep learning to predict final ischemic stroke lesions from initial magnetic resonance imaging. JAMA Netw. Open **3**(3), e200772–e200772 (2020)
30. Sailaja, Y., Pattani, V.: Effective brain stroke prediction with deep learning model by incorporating YOLO_5 and SSD. Int. J. Online Biomed. Eng. (iJOE) **19**(14), 63–75 (2023)
31. Wang, C., et al.: Deep learning-based identification of acute ischemic core and deficit from non-contrast CT and CTA. J. Cereb. Blood Flow Metab. **41**(11), 3028–3038 (2021)

32. Nielsen, A., Hansen, M.B., Tietze, A., Mouridsen, K.: Prediction of tissue outcome and assessment of treatment effect in acute ischemic stroke using deep learning. Stroke **49**(6), 1394–1401 (2018)
33. Kim, Y.-C., et al.: Novel estimation of penumbra zone based on infarct growth using machine learning techniques in acute ischemic stroke. J. Clin. Med. **9**(6), 1977 (2020)
34. Pinto, A., McKinley, R., Alves, V., Wiest, R., Silva, C.A., Reyes, M.: Stroke lesion outcome prediction based on MRI imaging combined with clinical information. Front. Neurol. **1060** (2018)
35. Warach, S., et al.: Citicoline 010 Investigators: Effect of citicoline on ischemic lesions as measured by diffusion-weighted magnetic resonance imaging. Ann. Neurol. **48**(5), 713–722 (2000)

Digital Health System and Carbon Footprint Analysis

Servet Soygüder and Nilgün Uçkun(✉)

Faculty of Engineering and Natural Sciences, Ankara Yıldırım Beyazıt University, 06010 Ankara, Türkiye
servetsoyguder@gmail.com, nilgun.turkan@hacettepe.edu.tr

Abstract. Digital life, originating with the 18th-century Industrial Revolution, has steadily influenced the healthcare sector, driven by rapid scientific and technological advancements. The health sector's adaptation to digital transformation aims not only to enhance service quality, efficiency, and safety but also to reduce air pollution caused by greenhouse gases and fossil fuel emissions that accelerate global warming and climate change. This study examines the impact of digitalization on reducing the carbon footprint in healthcare, both globally and in our country, by analyzing the interplay between digital health and carbon footprint contributors. With digitalization, it is believed that greenhouse gas emissions, which continue to rise globally, can be mitigated. However, CO_2 emissions from internet and mobile device usage also present a new challenge. This study delves into the types of carbon footprints, including their components, calculation and measurement methods, sector-specific impacts, and the role of digital health applications. Furthermore, it explores the socio-economic benefits of digital health transformation, providing insights into the various application areas, the sectoral distribution of carbon emissions, and ways digital products could reduce these emissions. The ultimate goal of this research is to contribute to a more sustainable world by using digital health technologies to lower environmental pollutants and greenhouse gases, thereby minimizing their impact on climate change. Embracing these digital health services, which are anticipated to expand in the coming years, can help create a livable world for future generations.

Keywords: Digital Health System · Carbon Footprint · Digital and Physical Carbon Footprint

1 Introduction

Digitalization is defined as various processes that contribute to making life easier. The reason why digital technology is so accepted is that it provides very easy and fast access to information and services. You can benefit from the service most easily and quickly using your smartphone or computer, without leaving your current environment (Şimşir, İ., Mete, B. (2021). The fact that the services used are public is the biggest proof that digital technology is a global application. As in every sector, digitalization also manifests itself in the field of health. While the use of technology in the field of healthcare will

A. Mirzazadeh et al. (Eds.): SEMIT 2024, CCIS 2444, pp. 181–200, 2026.
https://doi.org/10.1007/978-3-032-01948-6_12

be an opportunity for patients, it will also enable many changes for the industry. Digital consultation, mobile health applications, remote treatment and telemedicine health applications that will help improve health services have begun to replace traditional health services (Şimşir, İ., Mete, B. (2021). The production of new tools along with technology has led to the start of digital transformation in healthcare systems implemented around the world. Digital transformation in healthcare systems will contribute greatly to improving the quality of patient care. Thanks to digital technology, the patient is safely included in the system with an electronic record. It provides convenience in many areas, including reports, prescriptions, past treatments related to the disease, diagnosis made, and medications used (Uysal, B., Semiz, T. (2022)). With the help of telemedicine, the patient can easily benefit from the service anywhere in the world, regardless of where he is located. With smartphones, communication between the doctor and the patient is possible without the barrier of time and space. Thanks to these services, patients' time loss and employees' workload have been reduced. Nowadays, as technology develops rapidly, it brings environmental sustainability concerns and global problems such as climate change to the fore (Bıyık, Y., Civelekoğlu, G. (2020). At this point, digital transformation and green transformation appear. In the field of digital transformation in the health sector, digital health carbon footprint, emissions from the transportation sector, digital health carbon footprint, despite the difficulties brought by technological advances in the health sector, continuous steps should be taken to reduce the carbon footprint, despite the impossibility of eliminating it, no matter how late it may be. Since reducing the carbon footprint is not a problem of one age but of every age, as long as our world exists, the work to be done and the steps to be taken will always have a dynamic structure (Dalkılıç, C., 2023).

This study focuses on the increase in carbon footprint, in which sectors it increases more, how to take precautions, and most importantly, the pros and cons of increasing digitalization in the field of healthcare. Increasing carbon footprint causes global warming and endangers natural life. Gases that cause global warming are calculated in a comparable situation thanks to the carbon footprint. The increases that occurred as a result of these emissions and the damage they caused to nature were evaluated in terms of environmental impact.

This study was written to help those who will conduct research on the digitalization of the healthcare field in the future and to draw people's attention to the carbon footprint, as it is a current issue.

2 Literature Research

When the literature was scanned on digital health services and carbon footprint, the following data were obtained: In the studies of Bıyık and Civelekoğlu; They calculated the highway carbon footprint of Isparta province using the legal framework of climate change, Kyoto Protocol, IPCC guide and UNFCCC agreements and the Tier method (Bıyık, Civelekoğlu 2020). In Demirel's study, It provides information about the unnoticed digital carbon footprint, the carbon dioxide emissions of industrialization, the concept of digital carbon footprint, and the carbon footprint resulting from the use of electronic materials (Demirel 2023). In expense study; By examining the relationship between carbon footprint and economic growth, the spatial econometric application of Bandırma district was carried out and the relationship between per capita income and per capita carbon footprint was examined (Gider 2022) Özen, in his research article; He talked about the accessibility of digital health applications for patients and doctors, sustainability in digital health services, digital health services, the increase in the use of digital health services, the fact that the Covid-19 epidemic is the driving force of digital technology, and digital health applications in our country (Ozen 2021). Sarıca, in his research article; He talked about the carbon footprint of the internet, the messages sent from a mobile phone or computer, the carbon footprint of e-mails, the evaluation of the impact of social media and the internet on sustainability, the impact of carbon emissions on the world and personal internet use (Sarıca 2023). Uysal and Semiz, in their studies published in the book section; They talked about digitalization and its future in healthcare, digital transformation and digital health applications (Uysal and Semiz 2022). Yalılı Kılıç, Dönmez, Adalı, in their research article; The disaster caused by global warming was recognized at the national platform and legal regulations were made, and the greenhouse gas emission amount was calculated using the Tier 1 and Tier 2 methods according to the IPCC guide (Yalılı Kılıç, Dönmez, Adalı 2021). In his master's thesis, Yavuz said; He explained the carbon footprint in tourism with an example and also talked about reducing the carbon footprint along with its determination (Yavuz 2020).

3 Carbon Footprint in Turkey and the World and the Socio-Economic Returns of Digital Transformation in Healthcarbon.

3.1 Physical Carbon Footprint

As a result of human-made (anthropogenic) actions, nitrogen oxide (N_2O), carbon dioxide (CO_2), methane (CH_4), nitrous oxide (N_2O), hydrofluorocarbon (HFC), sulfur hexafluoride (SF_6) and perfluorocarbon (PFC) gases cause climate change. Created greenhouse gases. The most important of these gases is carbon dioxide gas. What makes this gas important is that it constitutes 80% of greenhouse gases. China and the USA make the biggest contribution to the formation of this gas. In the emission distribution of carbon dioxide gas, industry ranks first and transportation sectors rank second (Bıyık, Civelekoğlu 2020).

3.2 Carbon Footprint

There is no common definition in the literature for carbon footprint, which is an important extension of the ecological footprint (Turgut, Budak 2022, P.918). Binboğa & Ünal (2018), the amount of greenhouse gases resulting from human activities (heating, transportation, electricity use, paper and plastic use, mining activities, housing, water use, fuel use, etc.); Özalp (2016) sum of greenhouse gases produced directly or indirectly by human influence; Yaka & Koçer & Güngör (2015) stated that the required biological amount as a result of absorbing carbon dioxide gas emission, which is among the greenhouse gases that cause global warming; Mutlu & Özgür & Kaplan Bekaroğlu (2018), measurement of carbon dioxide (CO_2) emissions accumulated by a product, sector or process over its consumption life; According to the Kyoto Protocol (KP), it is defined as reducing the emission of greenhouse gases.

3.3 Carbon Footprint Components and Measurement

Transportation, housing, food, products and services. When calculating CO_2, the consumption-based measurement method is first used. With this method, it measures the consumption behaviors and practices of individuals or institutions. It covers all greenhouse gas emissions such as fuel use, housing, access, and food consumption by individuals or institutions. In this application, calculation tools or survey application are preferred. Detailed analysis of the individual or organization is performed. The second way to calculate CO_2 is with a production-based measurement method. The application is the calculation of the emissions of resources that are directly responsible for individuals or institutions and that they have the ability to control. Fuel-burning vehicles require the use of vehicles, use of electronic devices, and similar data (Gider 2023).

3.4 Carbon Footprint Methods

According to the IPCC guide published in 2006, Tier1, Tier2 and Tier3 methods are used in the calculations of fossil fuel-based emissions. As the tier level increases, the number and detail of data used also increases. While the number of data required in Tier 1 is less, this is the opposite in Tier 3. While Tier1 is a simple method, Tier3 is a complex method that requires expertise (Bıyık, Civelekoğlu 2020).

3.5 Carbon Footprint of Sectors

Transportation, agriculture, tourism sectors and digital health are carbon footprints.

Carbon Footprint of the Transportation Sector. The transportation sector is one of the important parts of economic development. According to the International Energy Agency (IEA) data, the transportation sector ranks third among the sectors that produce carbon footprint. The largest share in this sector belongs to road transportation. In our country, the share of CO_2 generated by the transportation sector in the energy sector is 22.2%, while its share in the country's total emission amount is 15% (Bıyık, Civelekoğlu 2020). In Turkey, it is a sector with significant economic returns as passenger and freight transportation is carried out by road transportation within the transportation sector. The reason why road freight transportation is preferred in the transportation sector is that it is flexible in terms of low investment and transaction. When the risk factors in this sector are examined; These are individual and work-related factors.

Individual Factors: Gender, education, age, way of evaluating the event, chronic illnesses, etc.

Sector-Based Occupational Accident Factors: Violence, stress, noise, vibration, manual handling, working alone, driving in a tired and sleepless state, exposure to endemic diseases, time pressure, sitting in the same position for a long time, etc. The increase in occupational accidents in transportation necessitates the examination of safety and risk factors. Providing training to employees, implementing occupational safety practices, identifying risks related to the sector and creating improvement areas will lead to safer work areas and fewer occupational accidents. (Özbakır 2024).

Carbon Footprint of The Agricultural Sector. The indicator of the size and productivity of the area used to grow consumed agricultural products is called agricultural footprint. The second largest sector in terms of footprint in the world and in our country is the agricultural sector. The agricultural sector is not a business line that consists only of field work. Agriculture includes field, animal husbandry, fishing and forestry-logging. Our country ranks third in the world in terms of agricultural land according to OECD 2010 data. Before the Occupational Health and Safety Law in our country, agricultural workers could not benefit from Occupational Health and Safety due to many factors such as the number of people working in agricultural trade being less than 50 people, the number of seasonal and temporary workers being high, the businesses being small family businesses, and not being covered by the Labor Law No. 4857.. With the publication of the Occupational Health and Safety Law No. 6331 on June 30, 2012, public and private sector employees were included within the scope of the Occupational Health and Safety Law, regardless of the number of employees in the work area and sector distinction. The aim of Law No. 6331 is to reduce work accidents and occupational diseases, prevent work risks and increase the peace of mind of employees. For this purpose, the National Occupational Health and Safety Policy Document and Action Plan covering the years 2014–2018 was prepared with the contributions of the 26 members of the National Occupational Health and Safety Council. Many health and safety problems are encountered in the agricultural sector in our country. Some of the accidents, injuries and diseases that are most common in workers in this sector are as follows. Such as cancer, respiratory diseases due to exposure to dust, dermatological diseases, hearing disorders due to noise, carpal tunnel syndrome due to vibration, ergonomic problems due to heavy carrying, musculoskeletal disorders, exposure to harmful and poisonous plants and animals, infectious diseases… In this sector Work accidents that result in death occur due to transportation (vehicle rollover, being run over by vehicle), being hit by falling or shattered materials while moving, falling from height, drowning, livestock-related, electric shock, and machinery-related deaths. Another issue that is as important as human health and safety in accidents in the sector is the huge financial losses and loss of working days. Regarding occupational safety for the agricultural sector in our country, the "Occupational Health and Safety Cooperation Protocol in Agriculture" was signed on 19 March 2013, under the chairmanship of the Ministry of Labor and Social Security, between the Ministry of Food, Agriculture and Livestock, Ankara University and Harran University. Within the scope of this protocol, the "Joint Advisory Board" was established (Ministry of Labor and Social Security, Occupational Health and Safety Guide in Agriculture).

Carbon Footprint of Tourism. When defining the carbon footprint of tourism, it refers to the amount of greenhouse gas emissions produced by a person during the tourism activity. Carbon dioxide gas created by people is caused by transportation, accommodation and activities. 5% of the carbon dioxide emissions caused by these three components at the universal level constitute global or local emissions. In the tourism sector, carbon dioxide gas is mostly caused by transportation. The least emissions are caused by the activities carried out. The tourism sector is a sector directly related to economic size. Travel is more likely to occur in countries or regions with high levels of economic prosperity. More travel means more carbon footprint (Yavuz 2020). In our country, the period when work accidents occur most in the tourism sector is the spring and summer periods. Because most tourists come to our country in these seasons. During these periods, the workload is high, seasonal and uninsured workers are employed, employees are not given training on their jobs, and many issues are neglected as it is seen as seasonal work, thus exposing employees to dangers and risks. Long working hours, non-compliance with break periods, employing unregistered personnel, not paying additional wages for overtime, not providing weekly leave, and employing foreign nationals pose risks arising from the working conditions of employees. For the continuity of tourism businesses, they must satisfy both their employees and customers. Therefore, it is responsible for the health and safety of its employees and customers (İlhan, Gözükara, Aksu 2017).

Digital Health Carbon Footprint. Digital transformation can be defined as the process that makes life easier by using information and communication technologies that meet people's needs. Digital transformation is a totalitarian transformation carried out to provide more active and rich services by transferring data, information and processes to the digital field through the use of information and communication technologies. Digital transformation aims to greatly facilitate human life, to access information easily and accurately, to create a society model that questions the environment in which it lives and makes lifelong learning a principle. It is not right to limit digital transformation to a few technological developments. With digitalization, digital technologies have also taken their place in human life. People first used digital technology in e-service applications. Using digital platforms; It provides easier access to many services such as banking, public services, shopping services, access to information and documents. The stages of digitalization are not one-sided and can constantly improve itself with new technologies and services. Keeping up with the digital time with digital transformation means developing towards a new stage where not only people and institutions, but also objects and mechanisms are connected to each other (Özen 2021). Digital carbon footprint is defined as all the systems and tools that enable communication between patients and healthcare personnel. In parallel with the industrial revolution and the progress in digital health technologies, there has been a corresponding increase in CO_2 emissions. With the industrial revolution, human-induced changes in the climate began to occur. Changes at a universal level and developments in information and communication technologies have recently added the concept of digital carbon footprint (DKAI) to the concept of carbon footprint (CAI). While technological developments cause us to live our daily lives faster and easier, the changes in social structure and habits create the digital carbon footprint. Digital carbon footprint focuses on the energy demand required for the flow of information used through technological tools and the environmental science caused by the demand. In recent years, while we have become indispensably connected to the opportunities offered by the digital world to humanity, the footprint it brings with it and continues to grow day by day is not given importance or even noticed. The internet, which has nearly 60% of the world's population or 4.66 billion users, creates 1.6 billion tons of greenhouse gas emissions annually. The resulting digital carbon footprint is equivalent to approximately 4% of the universal carbon footprint. But what is even worse is that this rate is likely to double in the next 3 years. It is not only the use of the internet and the rapid increase in usage that increases the digital carbon footprint. The internet is used in every aspect of life. The use of internet networks in almost all actions or products, the ease of access to services, the fact that these services have become a standard of living, the entry of new technological products into the market every day and their adoption in a very short time cause the digital carbon footprint to increase (Demirel 2023). Digital carbon internet and connections used in many applications such as online music videos, smartphone applications, search engine use, distance education and business processes, especially during the Covid19 epidemic, games played on computers or smartphones, digital money and block-chains, cloud storage options. Causes the footprint to grow rapidly. During the covid19 pandemic experienced globally in 2019, there were great increases in digital services and the number of users of digital services. In this universal epidemic, 1/3 of employees did not go to work and worked from home. While people working at home causes a decrease in the carbon footprint caused by transportation, which is one of the most important carbon footprint producers, there has been a rapid increase in the digital carbon footprint with the increase in working from home. It was observed that during the pandemic period, as people stayed at home, there was a 40% increase in internet usage and in addition, 42.6 million mega watt-hours of electrical energy was used. Although digitalization, accelerated by the pandemic process, reduces carbon emissions caused by transportation, the increased need for electrical energy does not promise a sustainable world in terms of environmental science. In meetings held online during the Covid19 period, even just turning off the video image of a 1-h meeting reduces the digital carbon footprint by 96% (Demirel 2023). It has been observed that the measures taken to prevent the spread of the disease in the Covid19 epidemic have positive effects on air quality in the fight against global warming due to changes in natural gas consumption due to transportation and heating. The digital carbon footprint created by playing a game for 6 h on devices such as laptops, smartphones and tablets constitutes approximately 2% of the carbon footprint of 7000 kg CO_2, which is the average carbon footprint of a person. While this game decreases to 0.6% when played for 4 h and only with a smartphone, it can rise up to 7% with more intense playing time (such as 13 h) (Demirel, 2023). When compared to paper products and digital products such as mobile applications, web pages and the internet, they are considered to be environmentally friendly applications because they are perceived to cause less carbon emissions. However, recent research has shown that this is not the case and that internet use causes huge carbon emissions. Sharing photos on social media and sending e-mails constitute a significant part of the carbon footprint. While a person's mailbox (incoming, sent, filtered e-mails) produces approximately 135 kg of carbon per day, a vehicle at the same rate produces this much carbon at a distance of approximately 320 km. The amount of carbon produced by spam or unsolicited e-mails is at the same rate as the carbon production caused by 16 million cars in a year. Internet use causes 300 million tons of carbon dioxide in the world in a year, and this rate corresponds to the amount of carbon dioxide released as a result of Turkey's annual coal and oil use. Google, the search engine we use daily, admits that it produces the largest portion of carbon emissions caused by the internet [20]. Although the carbon emission rate of mobile phone calls is thought to be low worldwide, since the carbon amount of a one-minute phone call from one person is 57 kg; It has been observed that one person's one-hour mobile phone call a day produces around one ton of carbon dioxide annually. It is obvious that mobile phone use accounts for 25% of the world's carbon emissions. However, texting on the phone causes less carbon production than other means of communication. Therefore, it is a method that should be preferred more in communication (Sarıca 2023). In Turkey, health transformation studies were started in 1989 through the 1st Health Project State Planning Organization (DPT), and digital transformation studies in the field of health were accelerated after 1990. Thanks to the World Bank, the 1st Health Project was completed and put into practice in 1990 within the scope of the "Health Sector Master Plan" (Özdemir, P. 2022). However, towards the end of the 2000 s, digital transformation began to be fully used. Because it was in these years that the internet started to be used in the 2000s. The transition of hospitals to automation methods has formed the basis of digital hospitals. This situation has affected the ways of doing work and the time of doing work (Uysal, Semiz 2022).

Table 1. Digital Carbon Footprint (Source: Created by Author).

Digital Carbon Footprint			
Digital Products	Consumption Type	Consumption Time/Amount	Amount of CO_2 Produced (Million/Ton/Kg)
Internet	e-mail/Mail Email with Photo Attachment Spam Mails Facebook (1 user) Tweet (1 user) Watching Videos Listen to music Search Engine/Google	Log incoming, sent, filtered Daily Yearly Yearly Yearly Yearly Yearly Daily and Annual	135kg 50 g 0.3 g 299 g 0.2 g 300 million tons 200,000–350,000 tons Owner of the largest carbon footprint
laptop Tablet Computer	Play a game	4 h 6 h 13 h	42 kg 140kg 910kg In total playing games costs 24 magatonnes of CO_2
Smart phone	Play a game SMS Phone Call/Conversation	4 h, 6 h and 13 h 1 message in 1 min	42kg, 140kg, 910kg 0.014 g 57kg

Table 1 shows the usage segments of digital products that cause an increase in carbon footprint in our country and in the world, and the amount of carbon they produce in millions, tons, kilograms and grams.

When the table above is examined; The amount of CO_2 gas produced daily by incoming, sent and filtered e-mails is equivalent to the emission gas produced by a vehicle over a distance of 320 km. The amount of carbon dioxide released into nature by a person as a result of annual internet use is around 300 million tons. In order to reduce this rate, it is necessary to reduce fossil fuel consumption and increase the use of renewable energy resources. It seems ecologically efficient, as the average sent email produces 1/60 the carbon footprint of a letter. However, it is rendered inefficient by sending 60 e-mails before a letter reaches its address. Sending a text message rather than a phone call would be a smarter and more environmentally friendly approach. When technological products are used correctly and without exaggeration, they have more positive aspects than negative ones. However, if consumed unconsciously, the harm of a practice that has more benefits than harms may outweigh its benefits. Digitalization and the use of digital health products is an invention that makes our lives easier in every field. However, access to digital products and applications does not produce innocent results. Unfortunately, the energy (electricity) we use to access the service harms our nature and ecological life. Many advantages will be gained today and in the future with digital health applications by using environmentally friendly energy sources. Advantages and disadvantages of using digital applications in the healthcare sector:

Table 2. Advantages and Disadvantages of Using Digital Applications in the Health Sector (Source: created by the author).

Advantages	Disadvantages
Facilitating communication between patient and physician	information pollution
Patients have immediate access to the information they want	Enjoying hospital privacy
Bringing the distances closer	Fake doctors and the increase in fraud
Wide masses are reached when urgent blood is needed	Immediate dissemination of negative situations experienced by patients
Opportunity to benefit from national and international platforms in harmful substance addiction	In cases of poor quality and inadequacy of hospital services, the sharing spreads in a short time and the reputation of the hospital and its employees is damaged
To be informed about innovations and technological developments	High internet costs in institutions due to internet-based use of social media
Providing online consulting services	Confusion due to the spread of misinformation

Table 2 shows the positive and negative consequences of the use of digital applictions in the health sector.

Carbon Footprint in the World. When we look at the carbon footprint per capita worldwide, we see that there are great differences between countries. The carbon footprint of people living in developed countries is higher than in other countries of the world. The higher the country's income level and the larger its foreign trade volumes, the greater its carbon footprint. When individual carbon footprint is examined, oil producing countries have the largest share. The majority of these countries are Middle Eastern countries with low population. Qatar (49 tons), Trinidal and Tobago (30 tons), Kuwait and the United Arab Emirates (25 tons), Brunei (24 tons), Bahrain (23 tons) and Saudi Arabia (19 tons) have low populations but high carbon emissions per capita. Are the countries that are. Because these countries produce oil. For this reason, they are countries with high annual emissions. Countries with per capita carbon dioxide emissions: Australia, USA and Canada. While the average carbon footprint per capita in Australia is 17 tons, the United States' is 16.2 tons and Canada is 15.6 tons (Gider 2023). In the Fig. 1 and Fig. 2 below, the amount of carbon footprint per person is high. Because the economic size of these countries is in question.

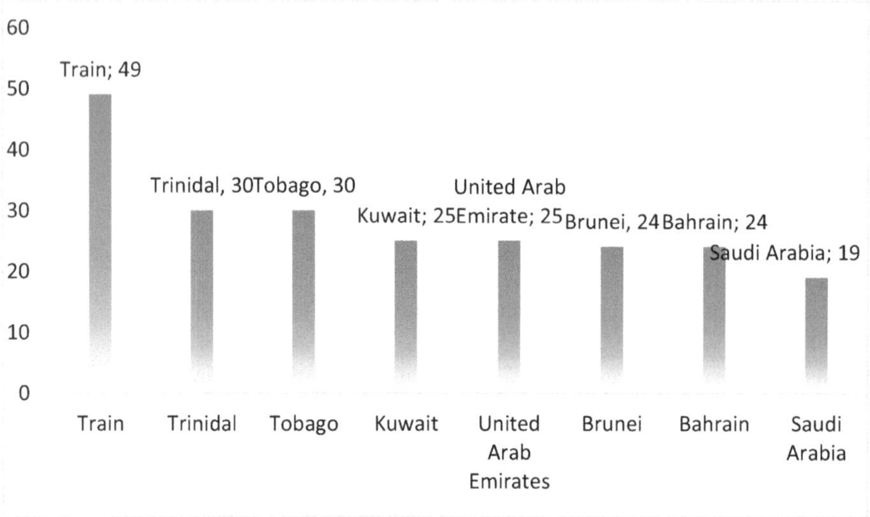

Fig. 1. Countries with High Annual Emissions Due to Oil Production (Source: Created by the Author).

Figure 1 shows countries with low population but high annual emissions due to oil production and their individual carbon footprint amounts.

Figure 2 shows the per capita carbon footprint amounts of economically developed countries.

3.6 Carbon Footprint in Turkey

The high production of fossil fuels (coal, oil, natural gas) in our country increases the greenhouse gas effect of carbon dioxide emissions released as a result of the burning of these fuels (Gider 2023). The most increasing footprint in the world and in our country is carbon-based. The largest share of CO_2 emissions that make up the carbon footprint belongs to the electricity sector. Since fossil fuels are used extensively in electricity

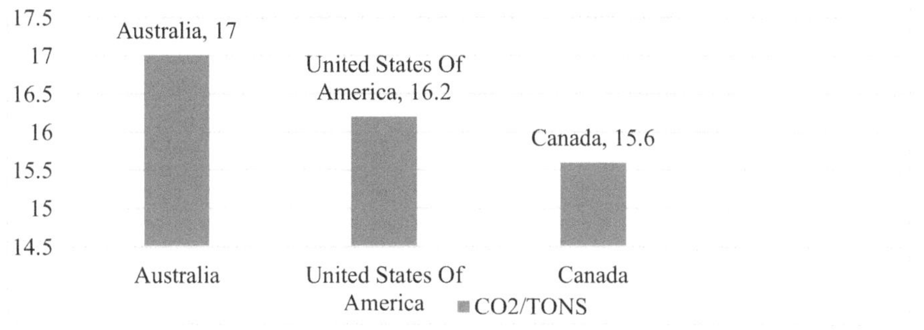

Fig. 2. Countries with High Carbon Dioxide Gas Per Capita (Source: Created by the Author).

production, the carbon footprint will continue to increase day by day. Internet usage in our country is increasing every year. While the percentage of home internet access was 92% in 2021 and 94.1% in 2022, this rate was recorded as 95.5% in 2023. Individual internet usage will be 82.6% in 2021, 85% in 2022 and 87.1% in 2023. When examined by gender, the usage rate is 87.7% for men and 77.7% for women in 2021, and 89.1% for men and 80.9% for women in 2022. In 2023, the internet usage rate of men was recorded as 90.9% and women as 83.3% (TUIK 2023).

Table 3. Internet Usage Rates in Turkey (Source: Created by the Author).

Internet Usage Rates in Turkey				
Years	Household/Home Usage Rate	Individual Usage Rate	Usage Rate by Gender	
			Male	Woman
2021	% 92	% 82,6	% 87,7	%77,7
2022	% 94,1	% 85	% 89,1	% 80,9
2023	%95,5	% 87,1	% 90,9	% 83,3

Table 3 shows our country's internet usage rates by household, individual and gender in 2021, 2022 and 2023.

When we look at the data in the table, our country seems to have easily adapted to the digitalization process. Digital products and digital systems are rapidly being adopted and used every day. Türkiye is going digital. In our country, the internet access rate in households is 95.5%, 70% use computers and 99% use mobile phones. Television viewing rate is also high in our country. However, when compared to the internet, it appears to be at a very low level. Because digital broadcasting platforms attract more attention.

Figure 3 shows the rates of digital tools used in Turkey and the usage rates of these tools.

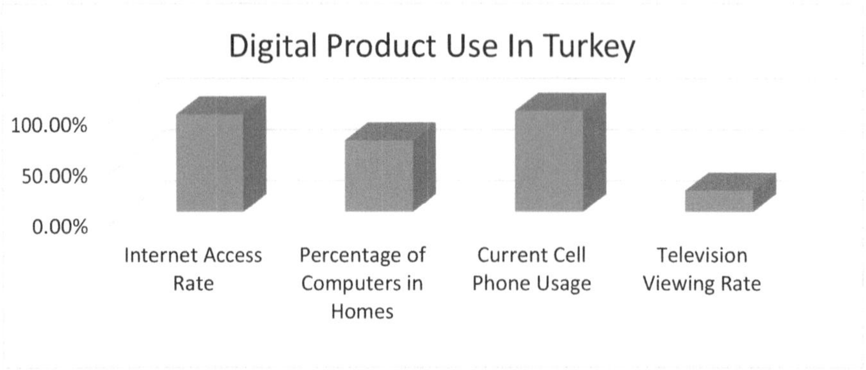

Fig. 3. Digital Product Usage Rate in Turkey (Source: Created by the Author).

Most products (such as clothing, cosmetics, shoes, accessories) are purchased online, with a rate of 75.5%. Of this, 47.6% was purchased for restaurants, 37.1% for food products, 32.2% for cosmetics and health products, and 28.8% for cleaning products. Digital services purchased or subscribed over the internet include movies or TV series with 30.7%, listening to or downloading music with 30.1%, and software services with 17.7% (TUIK 2023).

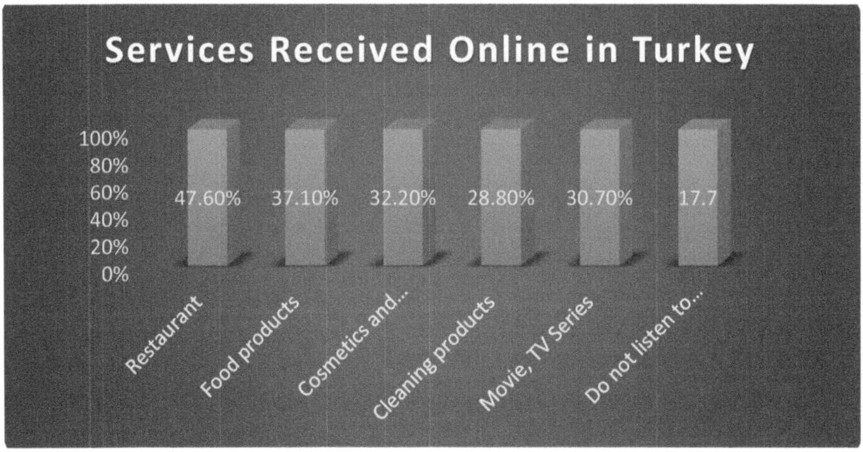

Fig. 4. Services Purchased Online in Turkey (Source: Created by the Author).

Figure 4 shows the rate of services received over the internet in our country.

As can be seen from both graphs above, the internet is used extensively in our country. The main source of the energy we consume while using the internet is fossil fuels such as natural gas and crude oil. In our country, as in the world, carbon footprint is the largest component of the ecological footprint. Our country's carbon footprint rate is around 46%. It may seem difficult to reduce our country's high carbon footprint, but it is not impossible. Because our biggest advantage is that we are in a geography rich in renewable energy resources such as hydraulic, solar, wind and geothermal.

Table 4. Digital Application and Product Usage in the World and Turkey (Source: Created by the Author).

Digital Application and Product Use in the World and Turkey			
	World		**Turkey**
Population	8.01 Billion Urbanization 57.2%		85.59 Million Urbanization 77.2%
Number of Mobile Phone Users	8.46 Billion Usage Rate 105.6%		81.68 Million Usage Rate 95.4%
Number of Internet Users	5.16 Billion Usage Rate 64.4%		71.38 Million Usage Rate 83.4%
Active Social Media User	4.76 Billion Usage Rate 59.4%	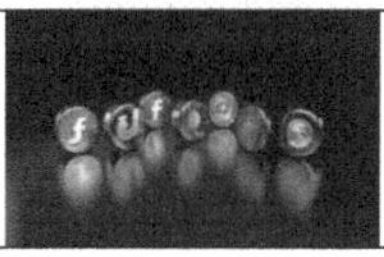	62.55 Million Usage Rate 73.1%
Digital Growth Rate	There was an increase of 3% compared to 2022.		There was an increase of 1.9% compared to 2022.
Smartphone Usage Rate	4.3 Billion Usage Rate 54%		97.6% It increases by 0.1% annually.
Mobile Internet Usage Rate	95%		94.3%
Computer Usage Rate	37.98%		59.0% Annual Change Rate 14.4% decrease
Tablet Usage Rate	2.27%		42.7% Annual Rate of Change 5.9% decrease

Table 4 shows the digital product user rate in the world and in Turkey.

When the table is examined, the rate of digitalization and use of digital products is quite high in the world and in Turkey. High usage of digital applications and products means a high digital carbon footprint.

3.7 Socio-Economic Returns of Digital Transformation in Health

Many factors such as increasing population, universal climate change, increase in chronic diseases, epidemics, and change in lifestyle cause an increase in the demand for health services. Digital transformation in healthcare has become mandatory to meet the increasing demand. With digitalization, developments such as robotic applications, artificial intelligence, internet of things, wearable technologies, m-health, e-health reduce the cost of healthcare and offer people the opportunity to live a healthy and long life.

4 Method

Greenhouse gas emissions resulting from road transportation were calculated using the IPCC Tier 1 Method. According to the IPCC guide published in 2006, Tier1, Tier2 and Tier3 methods are used in the calculations of fossil fuel-based emissions. As the tier level increases, the number and detail of data used also increases. For this reason, I used the Tier1 method in my study. While the number of data required in Tier 1 is less, this is the opposite in Tier 3. While Tier1 is a simple method, Tier3 is a very complex method that requires expertise.

4.1 Tier1 Method

Not calculating energy types with certain greenhouse gas elements based on energy consumption data and not caring which technology the energy is burned with constitutes the negative side of the method I apply.

They can use emission factors and other parameters according to IPCC guidance. This method has some proven simplifying aspects. However, it reaches its conclusion by combining some external data with its own findings. Two types of data are needed in this method. The first is the amount of fuel consumed and the second is the standard emission factor.

4.2 Tier1 Method

Calculations of energy types with certain greenhouse gas elements are made based on energy consumption data. It does not matter which technology the energy is burned with. The result is evaluated in terms of carbon footprint.

In order to make carbon footprint greenhouse gas calculations, the amount of energy consumption is first determined. In the second step, the content of energy types is determined by multiplying the consumption amounts of fuels by the conversion factors in the IPCC Guide. If the energy expenditure quantities determined in the first step are in mass type (kg, ton), they are converted into TJ units by multiplying them with the conversion factors determined in accordance with the net caloric values (TJ/kt or TJ/ton). The table below shows the conversion factors for energy consumption types (Yalılı Kılıç, Dönmez, Adalı 2021).

Table 5. Conversion factors of fuel types (Yalılı Kılıç, Dönmez, Adalı 2021).

Fuel Type	Conversion factor (TJ/Gg) (Equivalent CO_2 calculation)	Conversion Factor (Tj/kt) (Total CO_2 calculation)
Gasoline	44.3	44.8
Diesel (Diesel)	43	43.33
LPG	47.3	47.31

Table 5 shows fuel types and conversion factors according to the Intergovernmental Panel on Climate Change.

In the third step of the Tier1 method, carbon footprint emission factors determined for each fuel type are used. With this step, the total carbon footprint including energy is determined. The table below shows the CO_2 factors of fuel types (Table 7).

Table 6. CO_2 emission factors of fuel types (Yalılı Kılıç, Dönmez, Adalı 2021).

Fuel Type Emission	Factor (kg CO_2/TJ	Emission Factor (t C/Tj)
Gasoline	69300	18.9
Diesel (Diesel)	74100	20.2
LPG	63100	17.2

Table 7. Monthly, annual and weekly emission factors of fuel types.

Fuel Type	Fuel Consumption	Transformation Faculty. (TJ)	Energy Consumption	Carbon Emission Factor	Carbon Oxidation Rate	CO_2 Emission
Gasoline	0.180	44.80	8.064	18.9	0.99	0.55 annual 0.0125monthly 0.0028 weekly
LPG	2.16	17.2	102.18	47.3	0.995	6.38 annual 0.53monthly 0.12 weekly

Table 6 shows the carbon footprint emission factors and energy consumption values in kilograms according to fuel types.

The basis for the Tier1 method is the amount of energy consumed and the standard emission factor. In this method, energy (fuel) consumption is considered essential. Tier1 method is used when there is not enough data.

5 Application

Within the scope of this study, the greenhouse gas emissions caused by road transportation in the daily road transportation between workplace and home in Ankara Altındağ District in 2023 by individual vehicles were calculated according to the IPCC Tier 1 method. The rapid increase in population and the increase in the number of vehicles on the road cause congestion in transportation. As the time spent in traffic increases, the amount of fuel consumed also increases.

Within the scope of the data obtained, the CO_2 emissions released by personal vehicles as a result of gasoline and LPG use in 2023 were calculated.

Energy Consumption [TJ] = Fuel Consumption [t] $\times 10^{-3} \times$ Conversion Factor [TJ/kt]
Conversion Factor [TJ/kt]
Carbon Content [t C] = Carbon Emission Factor [t C/TJ] $\times$ Energy Consumption [TJ]
Carbon Content [Gg C] = Carbon Content [t C] $\times 10^{-3}$
Carbon Emission [Gg C] = Carbon Content [Gg C] $\times$ Carbon Oxidation Rate
CO_2 Emission [Gg CO_2] = Carbon Emission [Gg C] $\times$ (44/12)
Automobile gasoline fuel consumption 2023 = $180 \times 10^{-3} = 0.180$ lt
Conversion Factor: 44.80 TJ/kt
Energy Consumption: $0.180 \times 44.80 = 8.064$
Carbon Emission Factor of Gasoline: 18.9 t C/TJ
Carbon Content = $8.064 \times 18.9 = 152.4096$ t C
Carbon Content = $152.4096 \times 10^{-3} = 0.1524096$ Gg C
Carbon Oxidation Rate of Gasoline = 0.99
Actual Carbon Emission = $0.1524096 \times 0.99 = 0.150$ GgC

CO_2 Emission = 0.150 x 44/12 = 0.55 per year
0.150/12= 0.0125 per month
0.150/52= 0.0028 per week

Automobile lpg fuel consumption 2023 = $2160 \times 10^{-3} = 2.16$
Conversion Factor: 17.2 t C/Tj
Energy Consumption = $2.16 \times 47.31 = 102.18$
Carbon Emission Factor of LPG: 47.3 TJ/Gg
Carbon Content: $102.18 \times 17.2 = 1757.49$ t C
Carbon Content: $1757.49 \times 10^{-3} = 1.75$
Actual Carbon Emission: $1.75 \times 0.995 = 1.74$ Gg C

CO^2 Emission: 1.74 x 44/12= 6.38 per year
6.38/12= 0.53 months
6.38/52= 0.12 weeks

The tabular version of the calculation we explained above is shown below.

The CO_2 emission amount of a vehicle traveling to and from work using the highway in Ankara was examined in 2023. There are a total of 4 people in the vehicle, which is used individually. Since LPG-based fuel is consumed in the vehicle, the carbon emission amount of LPG is higher than gasoline.

Similar to this study, the CO_2 emission value of Isparta province in 2010 due to road transportation was calculated using the Tier 1 method, and the carbon footprint amount, which was 351.90 Gg in 2010, increased by 34% to 471.84 Gg in 2016. In the calculation made with the Tier 2 method, the value, which was 1605 Gg in 2010, increased by 43% to 2292 Gg in 2016 (Bıyık, Civelekoğlu 2020).

6 Inferences

When this study is considered as a whole, it is in the hands of people to prevent the destruction of nature. Although technological developments that make people's lives easier have a positive effect on the carbon footprint, misuse and excessive use by people turns the positive into negative. If communication tools such as e-mail and SMS are preferred instead of long conversations on the phone, the digital carbon footprint will be less. Although we cannot eliminate the carbon footprint by using public transportation instead of using individual vehicles when going from one place to another, we can manage to minimize it. If we do not use water resources brutally, prevent food waste, and choose environmental resources, we can prevent rapidly growing biological degradation. If urgent measures are not taken, people will have to experience serious environmental problems in the near future.

7 Conclusion

Climate change is among the issues that need to be taken precautions for the sustainability of our world. In recent years, it has been observed that the negativities of the ecosystem have increased as a result of anthropogenic actions. Climate change, damage to nutrients, air pollution and negative effects on many sectors due to the damage caused to the natural environment by CO_2, CH_4, N_2O and F compounds that cause greenhouse gas emissions. To reduce sector-based emissions, we should not just focus on one type of footprint, but look at it holistically. In order to reduce carbon footprint, all sectors should develop environmentally friendly strategies and try to minimize the factors that harm the natural environment. With this study, it has been observed that the benefits and technological applications of digitalization and using smart technology products in health services are increasing rapidly. The use of smart applications such as wearable technological products, m-health, telemedicine, e-health, 3D printers and virtual reality technologies in interaction with each other is an indicator of digitalization in healthcare services. By using these tools, healthcare services are provided 24/7, the possibility of making errors decreases, and field dependency is eliminated. However, it can be said that the missing aspects of digital health applications are the lack of constant internet connection between the patient and the doctor, the fact that there are places where the internet cannot be reached due to geography, and the fact that there are people who do not favor such an application due to cultural reasons.

Efforts are being made to reduce the carbon footprint through digitalization in health and many other fields. However, while people not going to work during the Covid-19 pandemic quarantine period reduced the carbon footprint caused by transportation, the carbon footprint of the internet increased with the increase in time spent on the computer at home. While talking about the negative effects of paper use in workplaces on the environment, it is not mentioned that it would be beneficial to turn off the camera of the phone or computer we use or reduce the resolution quality. We forget that the time we spend on the internet, the movies we watch or the music we listen to, and every information we share on WhatsApp has a carbon footprint. We should avoid sending unnecessary e-mail. Time spent in the digital space also means that the carbon footprint increases. We are increasing our carbon footprint without realizing it. The potential for renewable energy sources is quite high in our country. Electricity is produced from solar and wind energies. The energy used in digital technology can be met here. Different methods should be recommended for the use of zero-carbon energy in our country and in the world, plans should be made within the framework of legal practices, and emphasis should be placed on digital health laws. Green options should be preferred for digital health applications and environmentally friendly initiatives should be taken. What can we do to reduce the carbon footprint in our country and in the world; Let's see how much we personally affect global warming, we can use the right product to minimize our wrong practices, we can negotiate with companies that produce electricity from renewable sources (such as wind, solar, hydroelectricity) and minimize the carbon footprint caused by electricity. Let's completely turn off the devices we don't use, lower the temperature of the heating devices and hot water, and do our weekly shopping all at once. Let's go to close distances by walking or cycling. Let's not use the washer dryer. We can minimize our carbon footprint with many actions such as replacing old electronic devices with Class A products, reducing meat consumption, not consuming fruits and vegetables out of season, and reducing plastic use. It is possible to make carbon compensation by using a renewable energy source as much as the released carbon dioxide gas. Digitalization in health does not aim to disable healthcare workers, but to maximize their performance with technological tools and to protect our environment by reducing energy consumption with technological tools.

When all these are brought together, we need to raise climate-conscious people. We must include the issue of climate change in the scope of education and training. We must increase the number of academic studies on carbon footprint and digital carbon footprint on a national and global scale. We must explain to users, through the public and private sectors, the environmental damages caused by unconscious and unnecessary use due to the widespread use of digital applications. In production and consumption areas, we should stop using fossil fuels, and people should be encouraged to use energy-saving renewable energy-based vehicles in every field. We must make our cities greener. Finally, in order to reduce the impact of digitalization on the climate, we can reduce its negative effects through planned, adherence to the principle of sustainability and conscious use.

8 Symbols and Abbreviations

CH_4: Methane
CO_2: Carbon dioxide
KAI: Carbon Footprint
DKAİ: Digital Carbon Footprint
DPT: State Planning Organization
Gg C: Carbon Emission
HFC: Hydrofluorocarbon
IEA: International Energy Agency
IPCC: Intergovernmental Panel on Climate Change
KG: Kilogram
KP: Kyoto Protocol
LPG: Autogas
N_2O: Nitrogen Oxide
OECD: Organization for Economic Co-operation and Development
PFC: Perfluorocarbon
SF_6: Sulfur Hexafluoride
Tj: Energy Consumption
TJ/kt: Conversion Factor
tC: Carbon Content
tC/TJ: Carbon Emission Factor
TURKSTAT: Turkish Statistical Institute
UNFCCC: United Nations Flamework Conversion Onclimate Change
USA: United States of America

References

1. Bıyık, Y., Civelekoğlu, G.: Calculation of Road Source Carbon Footprint in Isparta Province, 2016 Kutbilge Academicians Association (2020). ISSN:2651–401X, e-ISSN:2654–4028
2. Binboğa, G., Ünal, A.: A research on calculating the carbon footprint of Manisa Celal Bayar university on the axis of sustainability, Manisa Celal Bayar university. Int. J. Econ. Appl. UİİİD-IJAS, (21), 187–202 (2018). ISSN 1307-9832
3. Dalkılıç, C.: What is Digital Carbon Footprint? Is It Possible to Stay Green While Transforming Digitally? How Can the Digital Carbon Footprint Be Reduced?, Linkedin, Presidential Digital Transformation Office, 18 October 2023 (2023)
4. Demirel, M.: Unnoticeable digital carbon footprint, Kafkas university, faculty of economics and administrative sciences. J. Polit. Sci. Public Adm. Sci. (2023)
5. Gider, A.: The Relationship Between Carbon Footprint and Economic Growth: A Spatial Econometric Application on Bandırma District, T.R. Bandırma Onyedi Eylül University, Institute of Social Sciences, Department of Economics, Master's Thesis (2023)
6. İlhan, M.N., Gözükara, M.G., Aksu, E.: Questions and solution suggestions about occupational health and safety in the tourism sector, Gazi university faculty of medicine, department of public health, department of occupational and occupational diseases. Gazi Univ. J. Health Sci. **2**(2), 1 (2017)

7. Mutlu, V., Özgür, C., Kaplan Bekaroğlu, Ş.Ş.: Determination of carbon footprint in the rubber industry, Süleyman Demirel university. Faculty Eng. **2**(2), 139–146, (2018). ISSN: 2651-401X, E-ISSN: 2651-4028
8. Özalp, G.A.: The role of green port application in reducing carbon footprint: marport example, Dokuz Eylül University. Maritime Faculty J. Res. Article, ULK 2015 Special, 99–116 (2016). ISSN:1309-4246, E-ISSN: 2458-9942
9. Özen, H.: Evaluation of digital health services in terms of sustainable development goals, Trakya university, faculty of economics and administrative sciences. Int. J. Soc. Res. **17**(38) (2021)
10. Özdemir, P.: Digital Transformation in Health Services and the Example of Türkiye, T.R. Dokuz Eylül University, Institute of Social Sciences, Department of Finance, Finance Program, Master's Thesis, İzmir-2022 (2022)
11. Özbakır, O.: Occupational Accidents and Occupational Diseases in the Road Transport Sector: A Review Between 2013–2022 Occupational Accidents and Occupational Disorders in the Road Transport Sector: A Review Between 2013 and 2022, Conference: 5. International Mediterranean Congress. At: Mersin, January 2024 (2024)
12. Sarıca, S.: Carbon Footprint of the Internet, Sakarya University Faculty of Art, Design and Architecture, Department of Graphic Arts, 10th International Congress on Life, Engineering, and Applied Sciences in a Changing World (2023)
13. Şimşir, İ., Mete, B.: Future of health services: digital health technologies, sakarya university, review article. J. Innov. Healthcare Pract. (JOINIHP) **2**(1), 33–39 (2021)
14. Uysal, B., Semiz, T.: Digitalization and Its Future in Health Services. İksad Publishing House, Ankara (2022)
15. Yalılı Kılıç, M., Dönmez, T., Adalı, S.: Carbon Footprint Change Due to Fuel Consumption in Road Transportation: Çanakkale Example, research article (2021)
16. Yaka, F.İ., Koçer, A., Güngör, A.: Akdeniz university vocational school of health services carbon footprint determination, Akdeniz university, faculty of engineering, department of mechanical engineering. Electr. J. Mech. Technol. **12**(3) (37–45) (2015)
17. Yavuz, A.B.: Carbon Footprint in Tourism: Five Star Hotel Example, Niğde Ömer Halisdemir University, Institute of Science and Technology Department of Mechanical Engineering (2020)
18. T.R. Ministry of Labor and Social Security, Occupational Health and Safety Guide in Agriculture https://guvenlitarim.csgb.gov.tr/media/holpsyeo/tar%C4%B1mda-i%C5%9F-sa%C4%9Fl%C4%B1%C4%9F%C4%B1-ve-g%C3%BCvenli%C4%9Fi-rehberi.pdf. Accessed 01 May 2024

Determination of the Optimal Appointment Time Interval in Digital Health Platform by Fuzzy Logic

Bulent Herdem(✉), Babek Erdebilli, and Servet Soygüder

Department of Industrial Engineering, AYBU University, Anara 06760, Türkiye
bulent.herdem@gmail.com, {berdebilli,servetsoyguder}@aybu.edu.tr

Abstract. In recent years, just as there has been a trend towards digitalization in every field, digitalization has also gained greater momentum in healthcare services. This acceleration started with the Covid-19 pandemic and people wanting to receive healthcare services remotely, with the aim of reducing virus transmission. As a result of providing health services remotely with digital technology, it has brought many problems and made many innovations and developments necessary. One of the most important of these problems is the dynamic planning of doctor appointments in the most efficient way. It has been determined that this situation is a significant problem in almost all developed countries. Online doctor consultation systems have emerged as an effective solution to facilitate remote medical consultations and access healthcare. However, the appointment scheduling process in these systems often lacks optimization, resulting in suboptimal patient and doctor experiences in digital health systems. This study demonstrated how fuzzy logic can be applied to determine optimal appointment time slots in online doctor appointment systems. With fuzzy logic methodologies, patient preferences, doctor's workload models, patient urgency levels and doctor's areas of expertise are classified. This study aimed to determine the most appropriate appointment time intervals that will maximize patient satisfaction while ensuring efficient use of limited physician resources. The results of the study showed the effectiveness of fuzzy logic in optimizing appointment scheduling efficiency and improving the overall quality of online doctor consultations.

Keywords: Fuzzy Logic · Optimization · Digital Health System · Optimum Appointment

1 Introduction

In recent years, there has been a great increase in digitalization in healthcare services. This increase has become especially important during the Covid-19 pandemic, when people seek remote healthcare services to minimize virus transmission [1, 2]. The pandemic highlighted the urgent need for digital technologies in healthcare, prompting rapid advancements and innovations in this area [3]. However, it also brought various challenges, one of the most critical being the dynamic and efficient scheduling of doctor appointments. This issue has been identified as a significant problem in nearly all

A. Mirzazadeh et al. (Eds.): SEMIT 2024, CCIS 2444, pp. 201–213, 2026.
https://doi.org/10.1007/978-3-032-01948-6_13

developed countries [4]. Online doctor consultation systems have emerged as effective solutions to facilitate remote medical consultations and improve access to healthcare. However, the appointment scheduling process in these systems often lacks optimization, leading to suboptimal experiences for both patients and doctors in digital health systems. The complexity of appointment scheduling, which involves factors such as high doctor workloads, varying levels of patient urgency, and patient preferences, makes this process particularly challenging [5]. This study aims to investigate the application of fuzzy logic in determining the optimal appointment time interval in online doctor consultation systems [6]. By analyzing factors such as patient preferences, doctor workload patterns, patient urgency levels, and doctor specialization areas, the study seeks to identify the most suitable appointment time intervals that maximize patient satisfaction while ensuring efficient utilization of doctor resources. The findings from this research have the potential to inform the development of more effective appointment scheduling algorithms and contribute to the ongoing advancement of online doctor consultation systems. In this article, membership functions are first defined. Characteristic functions including time intervals have been determined for the defined membership functions. Taking into account the data of the DYL-HP software project [7], appointment participation rates were calculated from the number of doctor appointments in the intervals corresponding to the membership functions and the number of patients who preferred these appointments. The highest participation rate according to the time intervals determined in this study helps doctors choose the most appropriate appointment time.

This study makes a significant contribution to the literature by presenting an optimized solution to scheduling problems in online doctor appointment systems using a fuzzy logic approach. Current appointment systems generally do not sufficiently consider doctors' workload and patient preferences, which leads to inefficiencies for both doctors and patients. In this article, membership functions are first defined. Characteristic functions including time intervals have been determined for the defined membership functions. Taking into account the data of the DYL-HP software project, appointment participation rates were calculated from the number of doctor appointments in the intervals corresponding to the membership functions and the number of patients who preferred these appointments. The highest participation rate according to the time intervals determined in this study helps doctors choose the most appropriate appointment time.

This paper is organized as follows: Sect. 2 discusses the 'Methodology'; Sect. 3 presents the 'Findings'; Sect. 4 covers the 'Discussion'; Finally, Sect. 5 covers the 'Conclusion';

2 Methodology

Fuzzy logic is a mathematical methodology used to deal with uncertainty and imprecise data. Fuzzy logic methodologies cover a variety of methods and techniques that can be applied in various fields. Fuzzy logic methodologies that we used in this study:

Fuzzy Set Theory, introduced by Lotfi A. Zadeh in 1965 [8], is a mathematical framework for dealing with uncertainty and vagueness. Unlike classical set theory, where an element either belongs or does not belong to a set (binary logic), fuzzy set theory allows for degrees of membership, which means that an element can partially belong to a set to a certain degree. Unlike classical sets, the degree of membership of elements in a set ranges between 0 and 1. This theory models uncertainties and vague boundaries using fuzzy sets [9].

Used in industrial processes and control systems. Utilizes fuzzy rules that define the uncertain relationship between input and output variables [10]. Fuzzy Logic Controllers (FLCs) are systems that use fuzzy logic to manage complex processes for which traditional control methods may be inadequate. Unlike traditional controllers that operate with precise inputs and outputs, FLCs process imprecise and uncertain information, making them ideal for real-world applications where conditions are often unpredictable. FLCs can mimic human decision-making using a set of linguistic rules and membership functions, allowing for more flexible and adaptive control. These controllers are widely used in various fields such as industrial automation, automotive systems and consumer electronics, where they increase efficiency, stability and performance. Their ability to handle nonlinear and time-varying systems makes them a powerful tool in modern control engineering.

Decision-making and prediction processes are carried out using fuzzy rules and membership functions. Includes different inference methods such as Mamdani, Sugeno, and Tsukamoto [11–17]. Fuzzy Inference Systems are artificial intelligence methods used to make decisions by processing imprecise and uncertain information. These systems evaluate input data using fuzzy logic rules and make inferences. They are especially effective in areas where uncertainty prevails and precise classifications are difficult. Fuzzy inference systems are widely used in solving real-world problems and decision support systems.

Systems that use rules based on expert knowledge or experience for a specific domain. Fuzzy rules are expressed in the form of "If… Then…" and work with imprecise inputs [18]. Fuzzy rule-based systems are widely used to manage non-precise situations and uncertainties, with applications ranging from automation systems to decision support systems and quality control systems.

2.1 Fuzzy Logic and Appointment Scheduling

Fundamental Principles of Fuzzy Logic and its Application Areas. Fuzzy logic, a branch of artificial intelligence, provides a flexible and intuitive framework for handling imprecise and uncertain information [19]. Unlike traditional binary logic, which operates with crisp distinctions between true and false, fuzzy logic allows for gradual transitions between these states [20]. At the core of fuzzy logic are linguistic variables and fuzzy sets, which enable the representation of vague concepts in a formal mathematical framework. These linguistic variables are defined by fuzzy membership functions that assign degrees of membership to elements of a universe of discourse [21]. The application areas of fuzzy logic are diverse and extend across various domains, including control systems, decision support systems, pattern recognition, and optimization. In the context of appointment scheduling, fuzzy logic offers promising opportunities for modeling complex scheduling preferences, handling uncertainty in scheduling parameters, and optimizing scheduling processes to meet diverse patient and provider needs [22].

Fuzzy logic allows for statements to be partially true and partially false simultaneously, reflecting the nuances and ambiguities inherent in everyday situations. This flexibility makes fuzzy logic particularly well-suited for applications involving uncertainty and imprecision, where traditional binary logic fails to provide adequate solutions [23].

Fuzzy logic offers a distinctive mathematical approach that accommodates intermediate values between true and false, effectively handling imprecise or uncertain data in decision-making processes. Unlike traditional binary logic that relies on rigid distinctions, such as yes/no or true/false, Fuzzy logic embraces a framework that captures nuanced "grey areas" that exist in between. This flexibility makes it particularly well-suited for applications in healthcare, where information often exhibits uncertainty and requires a more nuanced interpretation. In healthcare scenarios, where imprecision and uncertainty are inherent, FL provides a valuable tool to manage linguistic notions and mitigate the resulting loss of clarity in decision-making processes. This proven effectiveness has led to the widespread recognition and utilization of Fuzzy logic technologies in addressing the complexities associated with healthcare scenarios [24].

Methods and Algorithms for Using Fuzzy Logic in Appointment Scheduling in Doctor Consultation Systems. Fuzzy logic-based methods and algorithms offer innovative approaches to address the complexity of appointment scheduling in physician consultation systems [25]. The input variables we used in our study are; The number of doctors making appointments, appointment time intervals and the number of patients attending. Output variables; These are the appointment hours and patient preference numbers that fall within the specified time intervals. From these numbers, participation rates associated with time periods were determined. These rules are defined by field experts based on their knowledge and expertise in the field of planning. Fuzzy logic-based algorithms have leveraged these rules to make decisions that optimize planning objectives. In general, the application of fuzzy logic in appointment scheduling involves the design and implementation of specific algorithms that use fuzzy reasoning to make intelligent scheduling decisions in physician consultation systems.

Research Design and Data Collection Methods. This research is conducted using a comparative research design. For the purpose of the study, the performance of appointment planning processes in different doctor consultation systems is evaluated using the data of the DYL-HP Project (2021-2-TR01-KA220-YOU-000049540) supported by the European Union [26]. Data analysis involves examining the collected data using quantitative methods. Quantitative data were evaluated using statistical analysis techniques to obtain comparative results.

Establishment of the Fuzzy Logic Model and Determination of Parameters. Establishing the fuzzy logic model and determining the parameters is one of the basic steps of the research. This step involves defining the fuzzy logic rules necessary to model the appointment scheduling process. First, the input and output variables of the model are defined. Input variables are doctor appointment times and the number of times patients prefer these appointments. Input variables include the Doctor's availability and clinic resources, while output variables represent the time slots when patients are available. Then, fuzzy sets and their associated fuzzy membership functions are defined for each input variable. These sets and functions have been used to determine the degree of membership of a given input value. Finally, fuzzy logic rules were created based on DYL-HP Project data to determine the output variables corresponding to a specific input combination. After all these steps were completed, a fuzzy logic model is established and the determined data set is used to evaluate the performance of the model.

Data Analysis and Interpretation of Results. In this study, data analysis is performed based on the data set collected from 100 doctor consultation systems. The dataset contains information on appointment scheduling parameters, such as the number of doctors making appointments and the number of patients participating. Descriptive statistics were calculated to provide an overview of the distribution and characteristics of these variables across different planning methods. Interpretation of the results revealed that the fuzzy logic-based planning approach consistently outperformed traditional planning methods across all performance measures. Specifically, the fuzzy logic model demonstrated higher accuracy in predicting optimal appointment schedules compared to traditional approaches. These findings underscore the potential of fuzzy logic-based decision-making algorithms in improving the efficiency and effectiveness of appointment scheduling processes in physician consultation systems [27]. By leveraging insights from real-world data, healthcare providers can make informed decisions to better meet patient needs and optimize clinical resource utilization.

3 Findings

Fuzzy In our study, the analysis of optimal appointment time slots determined by fuzzy logic is categorized according to different membership functions of appointment times: "Too Early", "Early", "Normal", "Late" and "Too Late". By defining these membership functions, it is aimed to more accurately reflect the preferences and satisfaction levels of both patients and doctors. After the Characteristic Functions were determined, appointment categories and participation rates were determined from the dataset we used. The results are displayed graphically.

Defining membership functions:

"Too Early" membership function: $\mu_{\text{Too Early}}(x)$

"Early" membership function: $\mu_{\text{Early}}(x)$

"Normal" membership function: $\mu_{\text{Normal}}(x)$

"Late" membership function: $\mu_{\text{Late}}(x)$

"Too Late" membership function: $\mu_{\text{Too Late}}(x)$

Characteristic functions:

Equation (1) defines the membership function for the "Too Early" fuzzy set.

"Too Early" characteristic function:

$$\mu_{\mathbf{TooEarly}}(x) = \begin{cases} \mathbf{1},\ \mathbf{5:00 \leq x < 8:00} \\ \mathbf{0},\ \boldsymbol{otherwise} \end{cases} \quad (1)$$

Equation (2) defines the membership function for the "Early" fuzzy set.

"Early" characteristic function:

$$\mu_{\text{Early}}(x) = \begin{cases} 1,\ 8:00 \leq x < 10:00 \\ 0,\ \textit{otherwise} \end{cases} \quad (2)$$

Equation (3) defines the membership function for the "Normal" fuzzy set.
"Normal" characteristic function:

$$\mu_{\text{Normal}}(x) = \begin{cases} 1, & 10:00 \leq x < 18:00 \\ 0, & otherwise \end{cases} \tag{3}$$

Equation (4) defines the membership function for the "Late" fuzzy set.
"Late" characteristic function:

$$\mu_{\text{Late}}(x) = \begin{cases} 1, & 18:00 \leq x < 22:00 \\ 0, & otherwise \end{cases} \tag{4}$$

Equation (5) defines the membership function for the "Too Late" fuzzy set.
"Too Late" characteristic function:

$$\mu_{\text{Too Late}}(x) = \begin{cases} 1, & 22:00 \leq x < 05:00 \\ 0, & otherwise \end{cases} \tag{5}$$

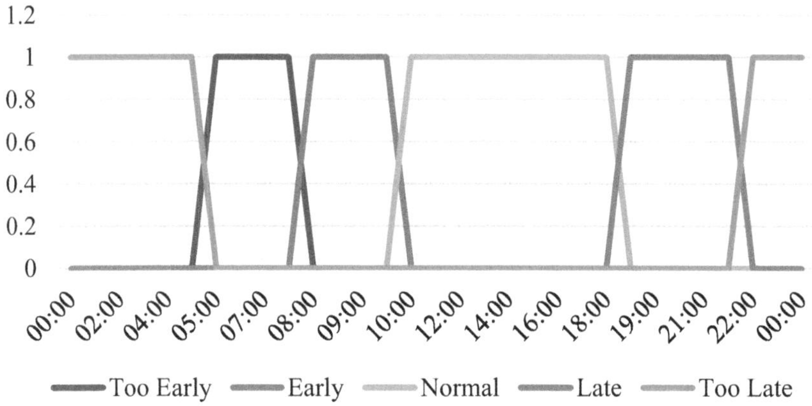

Fig. 1. Membership Functions for Appointment Times.

Figure 1 shows a graph with membership functions for different appointment times, indicating the degree to which a specific time falls into categories such as "Too Early," "Early," "Normal," "Late," and "Too Late." The x-axis represents the time in hours (ranging from 0 to 24 h) while the y-axis represents the membership degree (ranging from 0 to 1).

As seen from the table, which is compiled from data obtained through the DYL-HP project, the participation rates of patients vary depending on appointment categories. The highest participation rate, 70%, is observed in the "Normal" appointment category, indicating that the appointments are scheduled at an appropriate time. On the other hand, the participation rates for "Too Early" and "Too Late" categories are 20% and 15% respectively, indicating that these appointment times are not suitable for both doctors and patients.

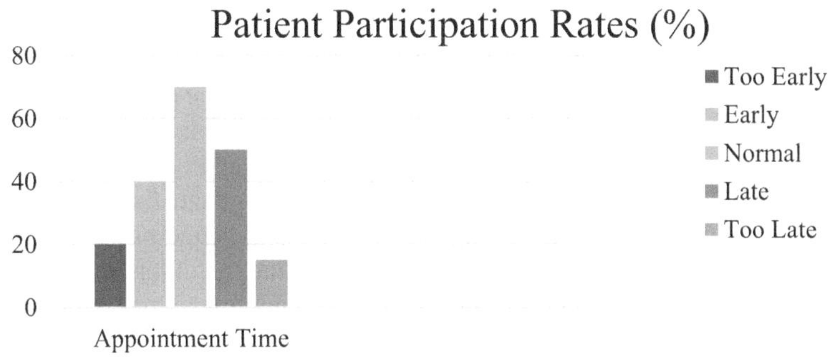

Fig. 2. Patient Participation Rates by Appointment Time Category Number of Doctors and Patient.

Figure 2 bar chart displays the patient participation rates for different appointment time categories as percentages. The "Normal" category has the highest participation rate (70%), while the "Too Early" and "Too Late" categories have lower participation rates.

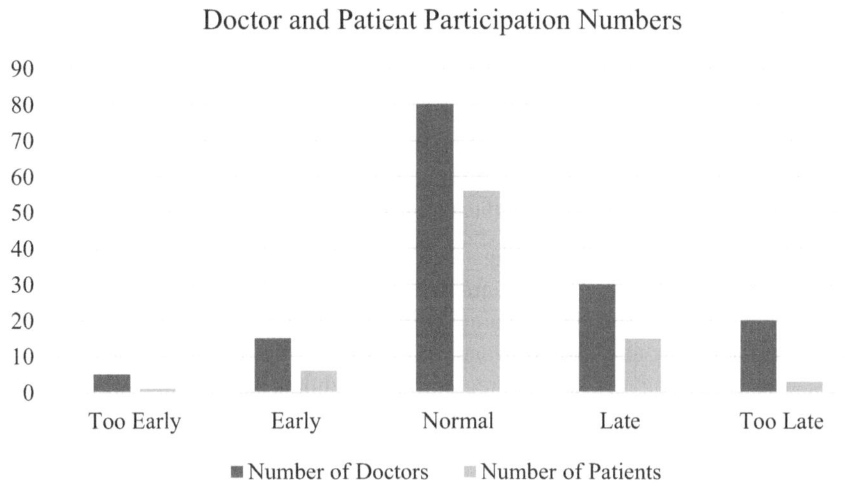

Fig. 3. Number of doctors giving appointments and number of patients preferring them according to their categories.

Figure 3 bar chart compares the number of doctors and the number of patients for different appointment time categories. The number of doctors and patients are shown side by side for each category.

In conclusion, scheduling appointment times according to the needs and preferences of both patients and doctors can enhance satisfaction levels for both parties. Regular monitoring and evaluation of these data can be an important step in improving the quality of healthcare services.

4 Discussion

The findings of this study highlight the critical role of fuzzy logic in optimizing appointment scheduling in online doctor consultation systems. By effectively addressing uncertainties and variability in patient preferences, doctor availability, and urgency levels, fuzzy logic has significant potential to both increase patient satisfaction and improve resource utilization. This method can contribute to doctors' better management of their workload and shortening of waiting times, thus increasing the efficiency of healthcare services. Furthermore, the findings of the study reveal that fuzzy logic can be adapted to different scenarios in the future thanks to its flexible structure.

Traditional Optimization Techniques: Linear programming and heuristic techniques such as genetic algorithms or simulated annealing have historically been popular for structured optimization problems because they can produce optimal solutions in terms of predetermined objectives, such as minimum waiting time or equal workloads among physicians. However, such methods always involve strict parameters and specified conditions that limit their applicability to the real world; for example, patient arrivals and consultations in healthcare may not be absolutely static or definite, thus their applicability will be limited. As a result, when there are sudden changes such as last-minute patient requests or sudden Emergencies, it becomes extremely difficult to dynamically realign these models, leading to more waiting time in the queue and less capacity for such unexpected situations. Despite their speed advantage, their lack of adaptability and dependence on fixed parameters may limit their practicality. Their inflexibility and reliance on fixed parameters mean they cannot, therefore, be actually useful in practice within such a dynamic environment as online healthcare consultation.

Machine Learning Models: Unlike the traditional methods, machine learning approaches, such as decision trees, neural networks, and support vector machines, have the advantage of being data-driven adaptive. They are thus able to learn from the past and capture trends in demand, peak times, and patient preferences, hence making predictions regarding scheduling based on recurring patterns. Again, data dependence is a huge limitation, as machine learning models need large amounts of high-quality datasets to assimilate information with desired accuracy. In smaller healthcare setups, the gathering of such data would be difficult; without that, generalization of the machine-learning models would be poor, especially in dealing with rare or atypical cases. Moreover, most of the models are black-box systems, which do not allow much insight into the reasoning behind the decisions.

Fuzzy Logic and Its Advantages in Real-World Scheduling: Fuzzy logic, as implemented in our proposed system, addresses both the flexibility and interpretability gaps seen in traditional and machine learning approaches by introducing a rule-based decision-making framework that can account for uncertainties and adjust in real time. Unlike binary or rigid rule systems, fuzzy logic can handle "fuzzy" information, such as cases that fall between urgent and non-urgent or patients with varying preferences for consultation times. By allowing for partial truths, fuzzy logic operates on a spectrum of values rather than fixed categories, providing a nuanced way to handle varying degrees of urgency and other soft factors. This means that rather than strictly categorizing an appointment as either "urgent" or "non-urgent," a fuzzy logic system can assign degrees of urgency, allowing the system to prioritize cases more flexibly. Furthermore, fuzzy logic can accommodate expert knowledge, translating it into if-then rules that mimic human reasoning, making it possible for the system to react adaptively to real-world changes and provide a balance between patient needs and doctor availability (Table 1).

Table 1. Evaluation of patient and doctor satisfaction levels

Number of Doctors Making Appointments	Appointment Category	Number Of Patients Participating	Participation Rate %
5	Too Early	1	20
15	Early	6	40
80	Normal	56	70
30	Late	15	50
20	Too Late	3	15

Table 2. Performance and Outcome Comparisons

	Fuzzy Logic	Machine Learning	Tradtional Optimization
Adaptability to Real-Time Changes	✔	✔	
Data Dependency		✔	
Interpretability for Decision Makers	✔		✔
Ability to Handle Uncertainties	✔		
Training Required		✔	
Handles Partial or Vague Information	✔		
Rule-Based Decision Making	✔		✔
Scalability	✔	✔	
Predictive Capabilities		✔	

Performance and Outcome Comparisons: Looking at the comparative analysis highlighted in Table 2, this study finds that as with every scheduling model including fuzzy logic, machine learning and traditional optimization, there are advantages and disadvantages in any of the modelling aimed at application in online health care systems. The research results of this study indicate that with respect to scheduling accuracy, a system based on the principles of fuzzy logic could be more efficient than both traditional scheduling and scheduling based on machine learning. It is due to the fact that fuzzy logic extends scheduling capabilities with a number of features such as automatically modifying rules in the presence of uncertainties, flexibility to rule changes when necessary, and capacity to quickly adapt to technology changes when required.

As seen in the table, traditional optimization techniques are valuable in rule-based systems and are interpretable which limits their usage to static and well-defined structures. They tend to, however, be very rigid to meet the dynamic demands of the healthcare scheduling system especially when there are unplanned requirements. While machine learning models are successful in prediction AI, their application is di-data heavy as they require deep training and do not seem to apply where the scenarios are different from the past data.

Unlike other methods, fuzzy logic integrates some aspects of machine learning and interpretable methods. What helps fuzzy logic to manage partial truths and ambiguity? This is the availability of an effective framework for online doctor consultations where patient requirements and their corresponding patterns are subject to change. Such flexibility is the reason why fuzzy logic can manage the scheduling of various tasks and minimize the conflicts between 'operations' as well as making sure that the workload in the end is fair and increases patient satisfaction in terms of individuals' voluntary requests' accommodation.

Finally, Table 2 further demonstrates that although traditional optimization and machine learning models have their usefulness in providing structure and predictions to the model they do neither excel at dealing with the complexities of the online healthcare system. This gap is filled by fuzzy logic; by offering rule-based mechanisms and a degree of interpretive flexibility for real world conditions. Its potential in increasing scheduling effectiveness and improving quality of care in online consultation systems allows for decision makers to offer clear and simple recommendations in real time to the advantage of both patients and service providers.

5 Conclusion

This study has shown that the use of fuzzy logic in online doctor consultation systems offers significant benefits in terms of optimizing appointment scheduling. Fuzzy logic can increase the overall efficiency of healthcare services by managing uncertainties and determining more efficient appointment intervals. In this era when digital healthcare services are increasingly in demand, fuzzy logic-based solutions can provide more satisfactory results for both patients and doctors.

Being able to handle uncertainties, fuzzy logic can actually dynamically change appointment slot intervals based on real-time variables such as changes in patient load, variations in consultation duration, and emergency cases arising at the last minute. This makes the health services more effective; it decreases the chances of appointment clashes and patient dissatisfaction.

Moreover, our analysis shows that the solutions using fuzzy logic enable better patient flow by facilitating more accurate allocation of time slots, hence reducing waiting time and ensuring that doctors can effectively optimize their schedules without compromising the quality of care. This is very important in today's dynamic healthcare environment, where often patients seek timely consultation and expect a responsive system that can rise to meet their needs.

In the era of increasing demand for digital healthcare services, the application of fuzzy logic to scheduling can yield results that are more satisfactory for both patients and doctors. For the patients, a reduction in waiting time and the possibility of securing appointments that more closely match their needs contribute to greater satisfaction and trust in the healthcare system. For doctors, the optimization of their schedules allows for a more balanced workload, reducing stress and improving the overall quality of care they can provide.

This study shows the potential of fuzzy logic in integrating patient preferences into the process of scheduling, further enhancing the level of experience for patients. The fuzzy logic systems can integrate factors such as preferred appointment time and the urgency of the medical need in order to prioritize appointments that are in line with operational efficiency and patient-centered care.

In this study, the presented evidence strongly allows the adoption of fuzzy logic-based approaches within an online doctor consultation system. It optimizes appointment scheduling and resource utilization but has also shown to modify expectations from patients seeking health care in a more personalized and responsive manner. With the looming demand for digital healthcare services, further exploration and implementations of fuzzy logic in this respect will surely bring about quite a significant improvement in service delivery and, consequently, patient satisfaction.

While this study provides a robust foundation for the use of fuzzy logic in appointment scheduling, there are several limitations that should be addressed in future research:

1. Data Limitations: The study's data is limited to specific consultation systems and may not fully represent the diversity of patient and doctor behaviors across different regions or healthcare settings. Future studies should include a more extensive dataset for broader applicability.
2. Model Complexity: The fuzzy logic model's complexity may increase with the addition of more variables and rules, potentially impacting computational efficiency. Research into optimizing these models to maintain performance without sacrificing accuracy is necessary.
3. Scalability: As online doctor consultation systems scale, the fuzzy logic approach must be tested for scalability to ensure it can handle large volumes of appointments and user interactions efficiently.
4. Patient Diversity: The study focused on general patient preferences and physician availability. Future research may consider the diverse needs of different patient demographics, including age, medical history, and specific health conditions, to create more tailored planning solutions.

By addressing these limitations and exploring the recommended areas for future research, the potential of fuzzy logic in online doctor consultation systems can be fully realized, leading to more effective and user-friendly healthcare delivery models.

References

1. Hermes, S., Riasanow, T., Clemons, E.K., et al.: The digital transformation of the healthcare industry: exploring the rise of emerging platform ecosystems and their influence on the role of patients. Bus. Res. **13**, 1033–1069 (2020)

2. Rani, R., Kumar, R., Mishra, R., Sharma, S.K.: Digital health: a panacea in COVID-19 crisis. J. Family Med. Primary Care **10**(1), 62–65 (2021)
3. Wang, Q., Su, M., Zhang, M., Li, R.: Integrating digital technologies and public health to fight Covid-19 Pandemic: key technologies, applications, challenges and outlook of digital healthcare. Int. J. Environ Res. Public Health (2021)
4. Gupta, D., Denton, B.: Appointment scheduling in health care: Challenges and oportunities. IIE Trans. **40**(9), 800–819 (2008)
5. Niu, T., et al.: Review of optimization studies for system appointment scheduling. Axioms **13**(1), 16 (2023)
6. Ayo, F.E., Misra, S., Awotunde, J.B., Behera, R.K., Oluranti, J., Ahuja, R.: A mobile-based patient surgical appointment system using fuzzy logic. In: Proceedings of Third International Conference on Computing, Communications, and Cyber-Security: IC4S 2021, pp. 193–207. Singapore: Springer Nature Singapore (2022)
7. Digital Youth Life Health Platform (DYL-HP). Supported by the European Union and the Turkish National Agency. Project number: 2021-2-TR01-KA220-YOU-000049540 (2022). https://www.dyl-hp-aybu.org/
8. Zadeh, L.A.: Fuzzy sets. Inf. Control (1965)
9. Zimmermann, H.J.: Fuzzy set theory. Wiley interdisciplinary reviews: computational statistics, **2**(3), 317–332 (2010)
10. Berenji, H.R.: Fuzzy logic controllers. In: An Introduction to Fuzzy Logic Applications in Intelligent Systems, pp. 69–96. Boston, MA: Springer US (1992)
11. Cherkassky, V.: Fuzzy inference systems: a critical review. Comput. Intell. Soft Comput. Fuzzy-neuro Integrat. Appl. 177–197 (1998)
12. Guillaume, S.: Designing fuzzy inference systems from data: an interpret ability-oriented review. IEEE Trans. Fuzzy Syst. **9**(3), 426–443 (2001)
13. Chaudhari, S., Patil, M., Bambhori, J.: Study and review of fuzzy inference systems for decision making and control. Am. Int. J. Res. Sci. Technol. Eng. Math. **14**(147), 88–92 (2014)
14. Ojha, V., Abraham, A., Snášel, V.: Heuristic design of fuzzy inference sytems: a review of three decades of research. Eng. Appl. Artif. Intell. **85**, 845–864 (2019)
15. Sabri, N., Aljunid, S.A., Salim, M.S., Badlishah, R.B., Kamaruddin, R., Malek, M.A.: Fuzzy inference system: Short review and design. Int. Rev. Autom. Control **6**(4), 441–449 (2013)
16. Wang, J.S., Lee, C.G.: Self-adaptive neuro-fuzzy inference systems for classification applications. IEEE Trans. Fuzzy Syst. **10**(6), 790–802 (2002)
17. Eravcı, D.B., Erdebilli, B.: Diagnosing Silicosis Using Adaptive Neuro-Fuzzy Inference System (2022)
18. Angelov, P., Yager, R.: A new type of simplified fuzzy rule-based system. Int. J. Gen. Syst. **41**(2), 163–185 (2012)
19. Krause, P., Clark, D.: Representing Uncertain Knowledge: An Artificial Intelligence Approach. Springer Science & Business Media. (2012)
20. Munakata, T., Jani, Y.: Fuzzy systems: an overview. Commun. ACM **37**(3), 69–77 (1994)
21. Wu, T.P., Chen, S.M.: A new method for constructing membership functions and fuzzy rules from training examples. IEEE Trans. Syst. Man Cybern. Part B (Cybern.) **29**(1), 25–40 (1999)
22. Ala, A., Chen, F.: Appointment scheduling problem in complexity systems of the healthcare services: a comprehensive review. J. Healthcare Eng. 5819813 (2022)
23. Challoumis, C.: Fuzzy logic concepts and the QE (quantification of everything) method in economics. Web Scholars Multidimensional Res. J. **3**(4) (2024)
24. Gupta, K., et al.: Fuzzy logic and machine learning integration: Enhancing healthcare decision-making. Int. J. Comput. Inf. Syt. Ind. Manage. Appl. **16**(3) (2024)
25. Bala, G.C., Islam, M., Al Mamun, S.: Patients Management System using Fuzzy Logic: An easier and dynamic appointment system

26. DYL-HP web page. https://www.dyl-hp-aybu.org. Accessed 4 Nov 2024
27. Safdar, K.A., Emrouznejad, A., Dey, P.K.: An optimized queue management system to improve patient flow in the absence of appointment system. Int. J. Health Care Qual. Assur. **33**(7/8), 477–494 (2020)

Digital Technologies for Customer Service Orientation and Social Sustainability

The Role of Machine Learning in Improving the Quality of Academic Outcomes

Duha Khalid Al-Malah(✉) and Wijdan Hasan Hamoody

Northern Technical University, Administrative Technical College, Mosul, Iraq
{duhakm,wijdanhassan}@ntu.edu.iq

Abstract. The paper provides insights into the application of machine learning in evaluating academic performance, the importance of the study is highlighted in adopting the right decision-making through prediction and analysis of ideas that work to improve the performance of faculty members and evaluate performance and other matters in a behavioral manner, as the algorithms were extracted and incorporated with machine learning equations to extract the best variables by comparing the performance of several models in classifying cases affecting the quality of education and academic performance of the teacher, as the worst was excluded through the KNN K-nearest neighbors algorithm where the value of K was 3. This helps the algorithm in classification and regression problems by integrating repeated queries for machine learning data inputs and predicting descriptive and behavioral academic performance. The study dealt with classifying the sample variables into groups of variables, which are (professional development, self-training, evaluation and feedback, improving the design of educational curricula, how to manage time, activating automated administrative tasks, and strategies to facilitate cooperation), the samples included 256 lecturers, technical and administrative academic at the Northern Technical University, the opinions of 256 valid questionnaires from selected samples were sent statistical analysis, consisting of 33 data entries for two variables that were distributed in the study community and the study applied the method of statistical inference and prediction with finding the values of linear regression and the relationships of influence and correlation for the study variables.

Keywords: Machine Learning · Intelligent teaching Systems · Academic Performance

1 Introduction

With the emergence of new technologies in improving performance, it has become necessary to rely on machine learning (ML) algorithms to evaluate the performance of academic professors and predict their performance for the coming years compared to their performance in previous years by using academic data, analyzing it, excluding wrong decisions, and choosing the right decisions that work to improve the quality of educational services. One of the most important issues facing the academic sector is the increase in the number of academics in universities with the diversity of their

A. Mirzazadeh et al. (Eds.): SEMIT 2024, CCIS 2444, pp. 217–228, 2026.
https://doi.org/10.1007/978-3-032-01948-6_14

cultures, specializations, experiences, and certificates, and those who are subject to the performance evaluation and monitoring process [1], which prompted administrative leaders to find a way to document their annual educational, scientific, and service work and obtain a degree to evaluate their performance level within institutional education. It is better to focus on the weaknesses that hinder the university's performance and explore alternative methods based on (ML) using big data mining algorithms, as it predicts issues that were hidden to uncover them and reformulate them with high-quality, which gives the university educational institution a good reputation.

[2, 3] They say that machine learning can improve the learning experience and academic performance by providing more effective and efficient educational performance to play an important role in improving academic performance for many reasons that highlight the importance of machine learning, including the analysis of practical data after pre-processing the data and dividing the data into two parts: training data and test data, which can be analyzed quickly and effectively, which contributes to deducing valuable information from huge sets of data that may be difficult to analyze manually, such as developing decision-making processes. Intelligent models can help in making more accurate decisions in the areas of academic planning and choosing the appropriate study path while identifying individual educational needs. Its importance has emerged in developing effective interaction so that machine learning can be used to develop attractive and interactive educational experiences that contribute to motivating students and increasing their participation in the educational process while providing review and feedback that helps students understand their weaknesses and strengths and improve their performance significantly. Automated research has also contributed to expanding the boundaries of academic research and stimulating innovation in fields such as computer science and artificial intelligence, and it saves time and reduces the burden on academics. Study of [4] took care of predictive analytics for student success many studies have applied predictive analytics using machine learning algorithms to predict student performance. These models often use historical data, such as grades, attendance, and engagement metrics, to predict future academic outcomes and identify students at risk for poor performance. As for [5] he cared about intelligent teaching systems (ITS) research has focused on developing and evaluating intelligent tutoring systems that leverage machine learning to personalize the learning experience. These systems adapt content and pacing based on individual student's needs, with the goal of improving comprehension and overall academic performance. [6, 7] Early warning systems Studies have explored the effectiveness of early warning systems that use machine learning to identify students who may be at risk of academic failure. These systems analyze a variety of factors, including behavior, attendance, and coursework, to provide timely interventions and support studied. [8] Using machine learning for automated classification and feedback via the use of algorithms to grade assignments, exams, and other assessments, providing consistent and timely feedback to students while saving teacher's time. [9] He found that learning analytics, which involves collecting and analyzing data from educational settings, has been a topic of research. Machine learning techniques are used to derive insights from data about student interactions with online platforms, course materials, and collaborative activities to improve instructional design and support student success, as for [9] we've explored his study of the impact of personalized learning environments enabled

by machine learning these environments adapt to individual learning styles, preferences and progress, and provide personalized content and activities to enhance engagement and understanding languages where neuro-linguistic programming was applied (NLP) to analyze educational content, including textbooks, lecture texts, and student essays, this facilitates sentiment analysis, summarization and extraction of key concepts, which contributes to a better understanding of the learning process.

Applications of machine learning in academic performance assessment and quality assurance are a recent and important topic, but they come with several challenges and drawbacks that can affect the accuracy and reliability of the results. Here are some of the major drawbacks that can be encountered in using machine learning for academic quality assurance and analysis:

1. **Variation in the quality of input data**: machine learning relies heavily on the data it is fed, which may be incomplete or biased. In the case of education, data on students or academic performance may be incomplete or contain biases related to the student's gender, cultural or social background, or other factors.
2. **Inability to interpret results (limited interpretability)**: deep learning models and neural networks are often complex and opaque, making it difficult to understand how the model arrived at certain decisions. This problem poses a major challenge in the education environment, where transparency is important to ensure fairness and avoid any biases.
3. **Model bias and inequality**: a model can be unintentionally biased towards certain groups of students due to variations in the input data. For example, the system may overestimate the performance of students in certain categories if their data is more representative than others, which can negatively impact the accuracy and integrity of assessments.
4. **Impact of Machine Learning on Human Assessment Decisions**: sometimes, decision-makers can rely too heavily on the results of models, reducing the flexibility and benefit of human assessors' expertise in academic assessment. If models are inaccurate or limited in their ability to capture nuances, relying entirely on them can lead to inaccurate decisions.
5. **Challenges related to privacy and data ethics**: machine learning requires huge amounts of data, which raises privacy issues, as the use of student data can be considered a violation of privacy laws. It is also necessary to consider how data is collected and stored to protect individuals' privacy and avoid ethical violations.
6. **Limitations of individualization:** machine learning models often struggle to handle the nuances of individual differences among students; models work best with general patterns but may fail to understand individual student needs and challenges, reducing the accuracy of assessments in multiple contexts.
7. **Continuous updating and development of models**: the academic environment is constantly evolving, which requires regular updating of models. If a model is not updated periodically, its predictions may become less accurate over time. It requires additional resources to update and maintain models to ensure their continued efficiency and relevance.

The impact of these shortcomings can be reduced by improving the quality of the data used, applying modern techniques to reduce model bias, and increasing transparency about how decisions are made in models, while strictly adhering to ethical standards to protect privacy.

2 Methodology

The problem of the study is the absence of sufficient studies examining the impact of machine learning requirements on academic university performance in the context of educational institutions, especially in Iraqi universities. Despite the importance of both concepts, there is a knowledge gap about how they interact together. The problem was: can machine learning and its combined dimensions (professional development, self-training, evaluation and feedback, improving the design of educational curricula, how to manage time, activating automated administrative tasks, and strategies to facilitate cooperation) be enhanced by university performance requirements at the Northern Technical University, the field of study?

The study aims to know the impact of the proposed features based on machine learning on the academic performance of the quality assurance department at the Northern Technical University Academy, and through it the following two questions were answered:

A) What is the impact of the proposed features of machine learning on the academic level of academic performance evaluation?
B) What is the extent of the proposed features of machine learning related to the academic level of academic performance evaluation?

Although machine learning offers great opportunities to improve academic performance and enhance the learning experience, [10, 11] they may face some challenges and problems. Among these problems lack of data sometimes, the data may be insufficient or incorrectly documented, which affects the models' ability to achieve good performance, as well as relying on complex technology some automated technologies may be complex and require high technical skills to control and understand them. This can be challenging for academics who do not have a strong background in technology moreover, machine learning techniques can sometimes be expensive, which may limit their potential for widespread adoption, and this can affect the accessibility of these techniques in some educational institutions. With some technology integration challenges that can appear integrating machine learning techniques with the existing infrastructure of educational institutions so it could require additional investments in infrastructure. Academic performance includes self-training was enabled machine learning algorithms from analysis strategies teaching interactive in classes educational virtualization make recommendations dedicated to training for example, proposals to improve classroom management, pedagogical methods and communication based on the specific needs of each teaching.

By receiving feedback from students' work, tests and evaluation scores, modern machine learning tools have helped in evaluating faculty performance by analyzing students' results, classroom activities and their associated quality and performance metrics by building on weak student behavior and giving them the necessary strength to enhance their professional growth as they continue [12], to improve the design educational content and teaching methods with effectiveness various educational materials and curriculum components designed with machine learning algorithms, it enables teachers to for insights derived in development their curriculum, ensuring it aligns with students' needs and enhances learning outcomes.

Time management by analyzing how time was made available for the various educational, administrative, volunteer, and community activities of the teacher, machine learning made it possible to find ways to reduce time and program self-processes [13, 14]. Diversity adaptive learning where possible for automated learning recommendation with adaptive learning resources that meet the needs of diverse students and discover learning styles adaptive in a classroom to differentiate the training [15]. Mechanism administrative tasks, with automating routine administrative tasks such as absences and following the urge and smart electronic archiving have made strategic planning for university education much easier than it was [16–18]. The machine learning applications it is shown in Fig. 1 steps in the sequence of data collection and analysis.

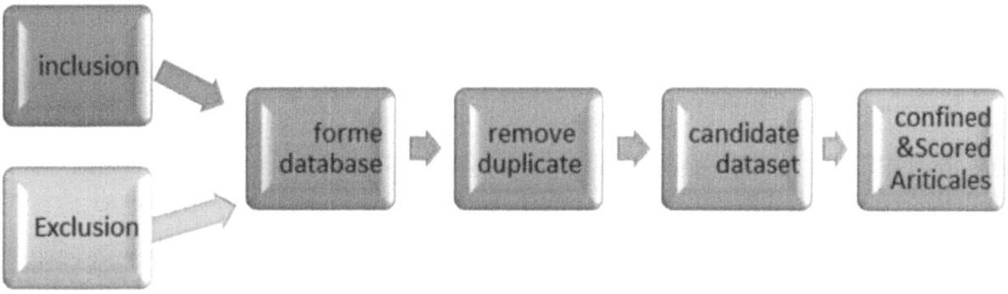

Fig. 1. Collection and analysis of quality and university performance assessment data.

[19] Predicting academic teaching performance is one of the professional activities for the success of any educational system, as the factor of attracting students and the method of maintaining and advancing them is considered an essential part of that system. Predicting academic performance is one of the most important indicators of the institution's educational reputation and the approved university classification, in addition to maintaining financial support for sustainability and keeping the educational institution in the competitive arena among universities in the Ministry of Higher Education. Monitoring the academic performance of teachers has become one of the most important priorities for decision-makers in educational institutions to maintain the improvement system. And how to maintain the number of students within the planned number and keep them within the absorptive capacity and not drop out. Many data mining techniques have been used such as clustering, classification, regression, and prediction in the process of improving the quality of institutional performance and the academic program. Its working mechanism was used on some machine learning algorithms using data collected from practical experiences and analyzed from the e-learning system to be more accurate in correcting decisions and giving instructions and guidance that improve academic teaching performance.

Here's an outline of these concepts and their mathematical foundation for inverse hessian in second-order optimization neural networks:

In second-order optimization methods, the hessian matrix (second derivative of the loss function concerning weights) provides curvature information, which can be useful to speed up convergence compared to first-order methods like gradient descent. The update rule in second-order optimization methods (like Newton's method) uses the inverse hessian:

$$\theta = \theta - \mathrm{H}^{-1}\nabla \mathrm{J}(\theta)$$

where:

θ: theta θ: Parameters (weights and biases) of the model.

H^{-1}: Inverse of the Hessian matrix.

$\nabla \mathrm{J}(\theta)$: Gradient of the cost function concerning the parameters.

2.1 Using Gradient Descent Variants

Other techniques in optimization (e.g., momentum, RMS Prop, Adam) incorporate terms related to the gradient but modify it, such as adjusting based on past gradients, exponential decay, and other methods rather than simply computing the gradient inverse directly. The inverse hessian, in particular, is a more advanced approach compared to basic gradient descent and can be powerful in cases where second-order optimization is computationally feasible. For deep learning models, however, computationally cheaper approximations like first-order methods and adaptive optimizers are more commonly used.

3 Practical Side and Results

The study used the program IBM SPSS statistics powerful tool in data analysis and statistics study to make predictions using various forecasting techniques, including regression analysis in SPSS allowing you to understand the relationship between a dependent variable (the variable you want to predict). It is academic performance and TFS variables Y irrigation X other if the data file containing the variables through which the prediction was made is opened, let us move on to testing the tool regression which runs on logistic regression which deals with binary predictions by choosing the variable once the analysis is completed, appeared statistical results checking regression coefficients, and standard regression coefficients to evaluate the strength of the relationship between variables with a graph scatterplot matrix as shown in Fig. 2 and Table 1.

Table 1 indicates the value of (R square) and the extent to which the model explains the variance in the dependent variable machine learning in this context, 484 expresses that 48.4% of the change in the quality of teaching products can be influenced by the independent variable machine learning. That is, the higher the value of R square, the stronger the model is in predicting the dependent variable. As for constant, it is the expected or estimated value of the dependent variable. (teacher output) when the independent variable machine learning is equal to zero, the expected teacher output is 1.019. The coefficient of the independent variable shows the expected amount of change in the dependent variable for every unit of change in the independent variable when teacher output increases by about 0.789 for every unit of change in machine learning. As for df1 and df2: they are the degrees of freedom associated with the model. In this context, df1 is the degrees of freedom of the model and equals 1, and df2 is the degrees of freedom of the error and equals 254. As for sig. It is the probability that measures the extent to which we expect the relationship between the two variables to be non-random. In this context, the value of sig. It is close to zero (.000), which indicates that there is a significant statistical relationship between the dependent and independent variables.

The model summary and parameter estimate dependent variable teacher output equation and model summary parameter estimates in Table 1, the R square F df1 df2 sig. Constant β1 linear .484 238.643 1 254 .000 1.019 .789 The independent variable is machine learning.

Table 1. The model summary and parameter of estimates.

Equation	Model summary					Parameter Estimates	
Linear	R Square	F	df1	df2	Sig	Constant	β1
	.484	238.643	1	254	.000	1.019	.789

Dependent Variable: Teacher output
The independent variable is machine learning

The Fig. 2 indicates the existence of a linear relationship between two variables, which is plotted in a two-dimensional space on the interlocutor X, and Y, resulting in a straight line. Limit the linear relationship between the number of hours a student studies and the percentage of grades he obtains student on the test. We want to know how high a student can score given. The number of hours he prepares for the exam if we plot the independent variable on the axis.

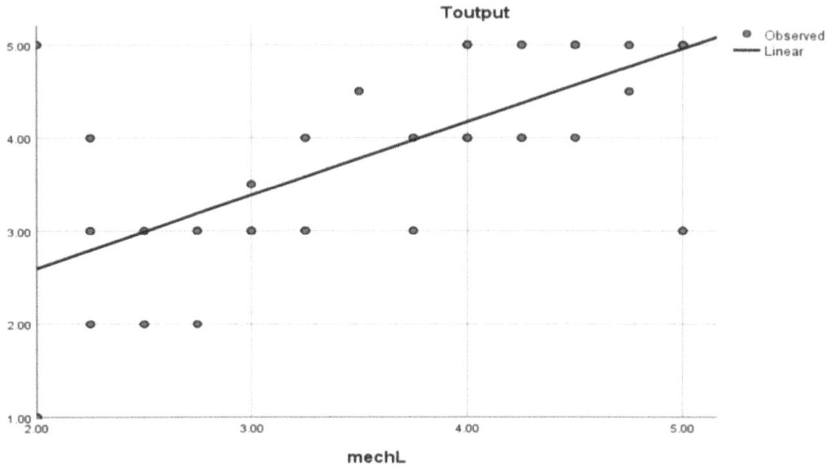

Fig. 2. The linear model.

In Table 2, the rest statistics (residuals), represent the differences between the expected values and the actual values of the dependent variable. We note that the predicted value of the minimum is 2.5961, the maximum value is 4.9619, and the mean value is 3.9453, std. Deviation is 0.72177, for a sample of N = 256. The measured expectancy values where the minimum is –1.869, the maximum is 1.408, at mean is 0.000 and std. Deviation 1,000 to show how standard predicted values compare.

The standard error of predicted minimum is 0.047, maximum is 0.099, mean is 0.064, std. Deviation is 0.015, which represents the expected standard error, i.e. the power of the model in prediction. Residual the difference between expected values and actual values minimum is –1.96187, maximum is 2.40394, mean is 0.00000, std. Deviation is 0.74463 to reflect the difference between the expected values and the actual values. Std. Residential minimum is –2.630, maximum is 3.222, mean is 0.000, std. Deviation is 0.998 provides a normalized measure of the differences between predicted values and actual values. Study residential minimum is –2.645, maximum is 3.251, mean is 0.000, std. Deviation is 1.004, denotes standard differences and is used to identify unusual values. Deleted residual minimum is –1.98507, the maximum is 2.44703, and the mean is 0.00007 std. Deviation is 0.75411 which indicates the difference between the expected values and the actual values after deleting certain values. The deleted residual minimum is 2.677, maximum is 3.314, mean is 0.001, std. Deviation is 1.013 used to identify unusual values after deleting certain values. Mahal distance the minimum is 0.002, the maximum is 3.495, the mean is 0.996, std. Deviation is 1.002 used to measure how much data deviates from the mean. Cook's distance the minimum is 0.000, the maximum is 0.095, the mean is 0.006, std. Deviation is 0.018 used to identify points that may have a significant impact on the model. The center leverage value minimum is 0.000, the maximum is 0.014, the mean is 0.004, and std. Deviation is 0.004 used to measure how much individual data affects the model.

Table 2. The Residuals Statistics

Residuals statistics	Minimum	Maximum	Mean	S.D
Predicted Value	2.5961	4.9619	3.9453	.72177
Std. Predicted Value	–1.869	–1.408	.000	1.000
Standard Error of Predicted Value	.047	.099	.064	.015
Adjusted Predicted Value	2.5530	4.9851	3.9452	.72262
Residential	–1.96187	–2.40394	.00000	.74463
Std. Residential	–2.630	–3.222	.000	.998
Stud. Residential	–2.645	–3.251	.000	1.004
Deleted Residual	–1.98507	–2.44703	.00007	.75411
Stud. Deleted Residual	–2.677	–3.314	.001	1.013
Mahal. Distance	.002	3.495	.996	1.002
Cook's Distance	.000	.095	.006	.018
Centered Leverage Value	.000	.014	.004	.004

Table 3 and Fig. 3 explains taxes for the selected linear regression model. This table shows the effect of the independent variable on the fixed dependent variable, the unstandardized coefficient is 1.019, std. Error is 0.195, while t-value is 5.222 at sig. 0.000, the unstandardized coefficient of the constant represents the expected value of the dependent variable when all independent variables are equal to zero. The value of t reflects the efficiency of estimating the independent variable coefficient, unstandardized coefficient is 0.789, std. Error is 0.051, while β was 0.696 at t-value 15.448 and sig. 0.000.

The non-standard coefficient of machine learning to the expected change in the dependent variable teacher output per unit change in machine learning. The standard coefficient beta reflects the standard increase or decrease in teacher output per standard unit at the value t and the probability (sig.) shows the statistical extent of the variance relationship between the two variables. In general, this table can be understood as showing the relationship between the independent variable and the variance in the dependent variable, providing information about the strength of the relationship and the model estimation statistics.

Table 3. The Coefficients Variables (Teacher Output)

Model		Unstandardized Coefficients	Standardized Coefficients		
	β	Std. Error	β	T	Sig
Constant	1.019	.195		5.222	.000
Machine Learning	.789	.051	.696	15.448	.000

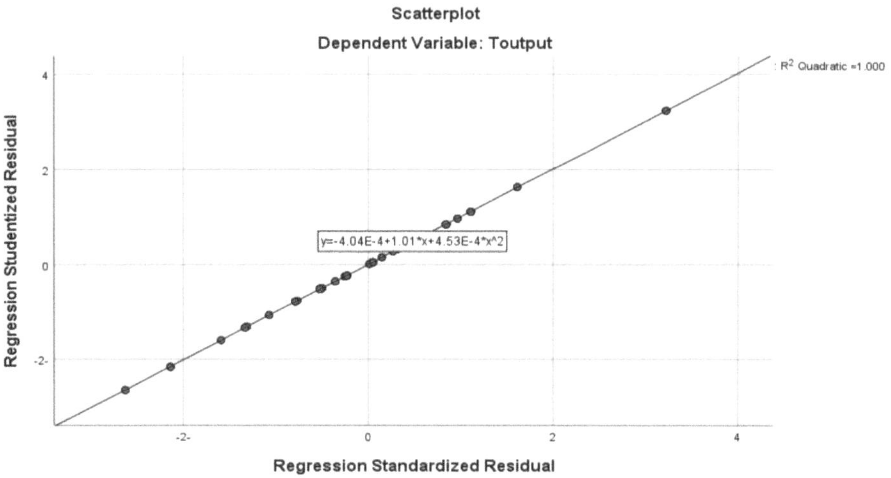

Fig. 3. The regression standardized residual

Table 4 regression analysis (ANOVA), which shows the distribution of variance in the linear model. Regression we note the sum of squares value is 132.843, at (df) degrees of freedom 1, mean square 132.843, and F difference test value is 238.643 at probability sig. it is 0.000, so the effect is significant for the statistical model. The residual is the sum of squares: 141.392 at the degree of freedom (df) 254, and the mean square is 0.557, which represents the rest of the dispersion that is not explained by the independent variables included in the model, and the total variance in the data is the sum of squares is 274.234 at the degree of freedom (df) is 255. Where the F value is high and the probability (sig.) is low.

For two-way analysis:

$$F = Within - group\,variance/Between - group\,variance \tag{1}$$

where: F is the variance statistic.

Between-group variance is the mean square variance between groups.

The mathematical equation to calculate the F value is:

Mean square regression = 132.843

Mean square residential = 0.557

Therefore, you can calculate the F value by dividing the mean square regression by the

F = 132.843/0.557≈ 238.643

132.843

Table 4. The ANOVA Values (Teacher Output)

Model	Sum of Squares	Df	Mean Square	F	Sig
Regression	132.843	1	132.843	238.643	.000 b
Residential	141.392	254	.557		
Total	274.234	255			

4 Conclusion

The work of the algorithm used in this study is to intensify the evaluation of the relationship between the study samples and reduce the groups by discovering the best from the sample and making predictions with new distributions to obtain a pair of coefficients, namely the dependent variable, academic performance, and the independent variable, which is machine learning. The basic idea behind feature extraction is to compress data while keeping good parameters with similar relationships. Decision-making processes were carried out by passing data through a mathematical model that simulates the virtual reality of academic performance. All obstacles to improving academic performance have been eliminated through machine learning by repeating inputs, detecting errors, and reducing them with logistical and behavioral inputs. The standard model does not work well except by relying on data inputs, all types of data, passing it on, and predicting the best.

Adopting an advanced machine learning model to develop and improve academic performance it contributes to making the right decision. Designing a system that includes machine learning to be distributed to all university educational institutions. All information must be kept in a database in the quality assurance department for reference and through which the academic's skills can be discovered. It is necessary to rely on deep learning and group learning to improve academic performance due to the availability of several organizational measures and the convergence of faculty forms while reducing complexity without excessive tuning of the approved neural network, which contributes to reducing costs and the lack of scientific and educational resources, by adopting advanced machine learning models across academic institutions and storing academic data in central databases that are practical and consistent with study results.

5 Future Research

Given our extensive experience and interest in future projects, we can provide a comprehensive vision for machine learning and improving the quality of academic outcomes. There are many research directions and future projects that explore this field, and I will explain them in detail

1. Designing smart educational platforms dedicated to students and developing educational systems based on machine learning to understand the needs of each student based on their previous performance and learning style, by creating predictive algorithms to identify subjects that students are struggling with, and developing applications that provide personalized advice or solutions to improve academic performance.
2. Evaluating academic performance more accurately and transparently by using machine learning to develop assessment tools based on multidimensional data analysis, instead of relying on traditional methods, with the use of analytical algorithms to evaluate individual contributions to group projects. There are applications capable of analyzing research papers to reveal the level of originality and innovation.
3. Predicting learning outcomes and analyzing academic risks, applying machine learning models to analyze historical data and predict future performance levels. We have systems that help identify students at risk of academic failure, academic planning tools based on analyzing the probability of success in specific disciplines.
4. Enhancing interactive learning experiences using technologies such as reinforcement learning to provide interactive virtual learning environments, by creating educational simulations supported by machine learning, such as virtual lab experiments, and developing educational robots capable of answering questions and providing personalized explanations.
5. Supporting learning and teaching research by building artificial intelligence systems capable of analyzing learning behaviors and providing recommendations for improving teaching strategies, platforms that provide feedback to teachers on the most effective teaching methods, for example systems that suggest innovative curricula designs based on data.

References

1. Mahesh, B.: Machine learning algorithms-a review. Int. J. Sci. Res. **9**(1), 381–386 (2020)
2. Zhou, Z.: Machine Learning. 1st ed. Springer Singapore, Singapore (2021)
3. Castelvecchi, D.: Deep learning boosts google translate tool. Nature **10** (2016)
4. Jordan, M., Tom, M.: Machine learning: trends, perspectives, and prospects. Science **349**(6245), 255–260 (2015)
5. Eyring, V., et al.: Climate modelling and analysis are facing new demands to enhance projections and pushing the frontiers in climate modelling and analysis with machine learning. Nat. Clim. Chang. **14**, 916–926 (2024)
6. Al-Malah, D.K.A., Ban, H.M., Haider, T.S.A.: Enhancement the educational technology by using 5G networks. Int. J. Emerg. Technol. Learn. **18**(1), 137–151 (2023)
7. Al-Malah, D.K.A., Hussein, H.K.J., Haider, T.: Enhancement of educational services by using the internet of things applications for talent and intelligent schools. Periodicals Eng. Natl. Sci. **8**(4), 2358–2366 (2020)
8. Muntaner-Mas, A., Morales, J.S., Martínez-de-Quel, Ó., Lubans, D.R., García-Hermoso, A.: Acute effect of physical activity on academic outcomes in school-aged youth: a systematic review and multivariate meta-analysis. Scand. J. Med. Sci. Sports **34**(1), e14479 (2024)
9. Civitillo, S., Mayer, A.M., Jugert, P.: A systematic review and meta-analysis of the associations between perceived teacher-based racial–ethnic discrimination and student well-being and academic outcomes. J. Educ. Psychol. **116**(5), 719–741 (2024)
10. Hopson, L.M., et al.: Transportation to school and academic outcomes: a systematic review. Educ. Rev. **76**(3), 648–668 (2022)
11. Filippova, K., Alfonseca, E.: Fast k-best Sentence Compression. preprint arXiv. **1510**(08418), 1–11 (2015)
12. Graves, A., et al: Hybrid computing using a neural network with dynamic external memory. Nature **538**, 471–476 (2016)
13. Cook, P.J.: Not too late: Improving academic outcomes for disadvantaged youth. Northwestern University Institute for Policy Research Working Paper. 15–01(2024)
14. Hwang, Y.: Machine Learning Application: Predicting Parking Difficulty. Homepage. https://www.iotforall.com/machine-learning-application-predicting-parking-difficulty. Accessed 25 Oct 2020
15. Sabbagh, M.A.: Adaptive e-learning environment based on learning styles and its impact on development students' engagement. Int. J. Educ. Technol. High. Educ. **18**(53), 1–24 (2021)
16. George, B., Wooden, O.: Managing the strategic transformation of higher education through artificial intelligence. Adm. Sci. **13**(9), 196–221 (2023)
17. Robert, E.G.: The Pecking Order: Social Hierarchy as a Philosophical Problem, by Niko Kolodny. Mind fzae006, 1–10 (2024)
18. Linn, A. Microsoft researchers win ImageNet computer vision challenge. Homepage. https://blogs.microsoft.com/ai/microsoft-researchers-win-imagenet-computer-vision-challenge/. Accessed 10 Dec 2015
19. Kumar, R.: Machine Learning Quick Reference: Quick and essential machine learning hacks for training smart data models. 1st ed. Packt Publishing Ltd., Birmingham, UK (2019)

Wavelet Transform Applied to Iris Person Recognition

Allam Fatima Zohra(✉), Maroua Rekrouk, Hicham Bousbia-Salah, and Hamami Mitiche Latifa

Signal and Communication Laboratory, Department of Electronics, National Polytechnic School, 10, Avenue Des Frères Oudek, El Harrach, 16200 Algiers, Algeria
fatima_zohra.allam@g.enp.edu.dz

Abstract. Biometric systems have become crucial in enhancing the security and reliability of identification processes. Among these, iris recognition has gained notable attention due to the unique and stable patterns of the human iris. However, ensuring high identification accuracy while optimizing the storage requirements remains a challenge for researchers. In this article, an iris recognition system that leverages the Wavelet transform technique to extract the most relevant information from the iris image while reducing the storage needs and improving the overall performance of the system, will be introduced. The paper will provide as well a comprehensive overview of iris recognition systems, highlighting previous research and methods employed in the field. Moreover, a summary of the proposed system for iris identification will be presented, emphasizing the feature extraction sub-stage, where the Wavelet transform plays a pivotal role, and detailing the performance achieved. The findings will demonstrate the effectiveness of the applied technique for features extraction which, combined with robust methods for segmentation and classification namely the Hough transform and the Ensemble Learning approach, improves the accuracy and robustness of iris recognition, contributing to the evolution of biometric authentication technologies.

Keywords: Biometrics · Iris Recognition · Wavelet

1 Introduction

Biometrics, as the science of measuring and analyzing biological characteristics, has revolutionized identification and authentication methods, particularly in the IT field. By leveraging unique physical traits such as iris, face or fingerprints, biometric systems offer a more secure alternative to traditional identity verification methods.

Among these characteristics, the recognition of the iris has particularly captivated the interest of researchers for its uniqueness and the stability of its patterns over time. Unlike other biometrics, the iris has complex patterns that remain virtually unchanged even with age, making it a preferred option for high-precision authentication systems.

Iris recognition has become an increasingly popular technology, particularly in security sectors, due to its reliability and accuracy. It features a low false acceptance rate,

A. Mirzazadeh et al. (Eds.): SEMIT 2024, CCIS 2444, pp. 229–243, 2026.
https://doi.org/10.1007/978-3-032-01948-6_15

making these systems robust and ideally suited to applications requiring strict authentication, such as access controls to sensitive infrastructure, identity management systems and financial services.

In response to growing security needs, research continues into the development of this technology to improve its speed, reliability and resilience. For example, in [1], the authors looked at the implementation on FPGA of a human recognition system based on the iris and using Deep Learning. They developed and tested various algorithms covering the stages of segmentation, extraction and classification, aiming to optimize the performance of the system. Furthermore, in [2], original methods were proposed to segment degraded iris images, thus facilitating feature extraction despite variations in image quality.

Recent advances in the field increasingly include the integration of artificial intelligence (AI) and machine learning (ML), key technologies to overcome the challenges of varying lighting conditions and environments. Various operational functions.

To increase the efficiency and precision of these systems, many innovative approaches have been developed and tested. These methods include advanced feature extraction techniques and matching algorithms optimized to maintain system accuracy even in complex situations (brightness variations, different acquisition angles, presence of obstructions).

Precise iris image preprocessing and segmentation techniques also help to better isolate the iris region, reducing the impact of external noise such as eyelids, eyelashes and reflections. Research in iris recognition is thus focusing on methods that not only increase performance but also guarantee fast processing times for real-time applications, consolidating the position of this technology as a pillar of security biometrics.

However, these advances come with increased data storage requirements, making system optimization crucial for practical applications. In this research, limitations related to precision and storage are addressed by applying the wavelet transform. This technique reduces image size by compressing data without loss of essential identifying information, thereby reducing storage requirements and, at the same time, increasing the accuracy of recognition systems. Thanks to this method, it becomes possible to manage larger databases more efficiently, while ensuring high performance in real operational conditions.

This article will present, in Sect. 2, the architecture of an iris recognition system, exposing previous work relating to each step of the process. Next, the proposed system will be described in detail, in Sect. 3, followed by a discussion of the results obtained during its implementation in Sect. 4. The paper will conclude with a summary of the results and an assessment of current limitations, as well as directions for future research in the area.

2 Literature Review

Like all recognition systems, the iris recognition system consists of two main stages: iris detection and iris identification. These two main phases include several sub-steps that are crucial to the system's efficiency and accuracy. In this section, the structure usually used in an iris recognition system and the different recent work corresponding to each step will be presented. The schematic diagram of an iris recognition system is shown in Fig. 1.

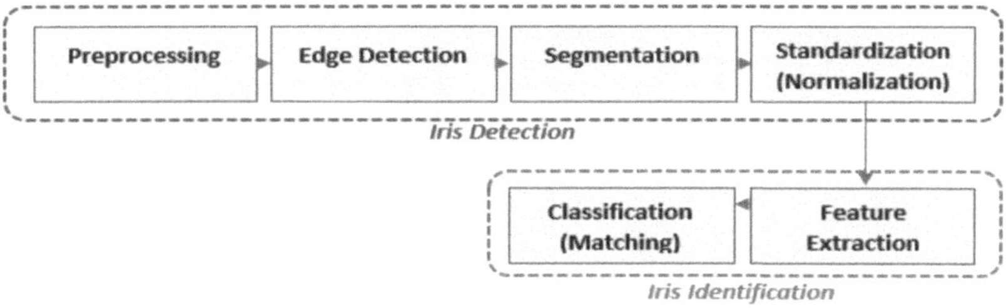

Fig. 1. Schematic diagram of an iris recognition system.

As shown in Fig. 1, the Iris detection stage encompasses the following stages:

- The preprocessing sub-stage, where the quality of the image is improved,
- The edge detection sub-stage, in which the contours of the image are highlighted for further use,
- The segmentation, that consists of isolating the iris ring,
- The Normalization, in which the iris ring is converted into a rectangular shape.

Conversely, the Iris identification stage comprises the Feature Extraction sub-stage, in which the most relevant information is extracted to be used, by next, in the Classification sub-stage, which attributes to each input image a specific class.

2.1 Iris Detection

Eye detection is one of the most studied topics in computer vision literature. Although it seems to be a trivial task for human beings, it is a very difficult one for computers.

The difficulty associated with eye detection can be attributed to numerous variations in scale, location, viewpoint, lighting, occlusions and so on. In this step, an input image of an individual is taken. It provides an explicit view of the left and right eyes. The aim is to extract the left and right eyes from the input image (Fig. 2).

Once the eyes captured, the output is provided to the recognition system, starting by the first stage, the pre-processing.

Pre-processing. The first sub-step in the detection process is the pre-processing. This phase is crucial for improving the quality of the raw image. It performs several operations, including noise removal, contrast enhancement and other adjustments. Thus, it optimizes the image by providing a more informative 2D signal, enabling better preparation of the data for subsequent stages, in particular the segmentation and feature extraction phases. This phase therefore conditions the overall performance of the iris recognition system.

Among the most notable work in this sub-step, the research carried out by Kumar et al. [3], who focused on improving image quality to increase the accuracy of the recognition system. They proposed an innovative approach combining high-pass and low-pass filters

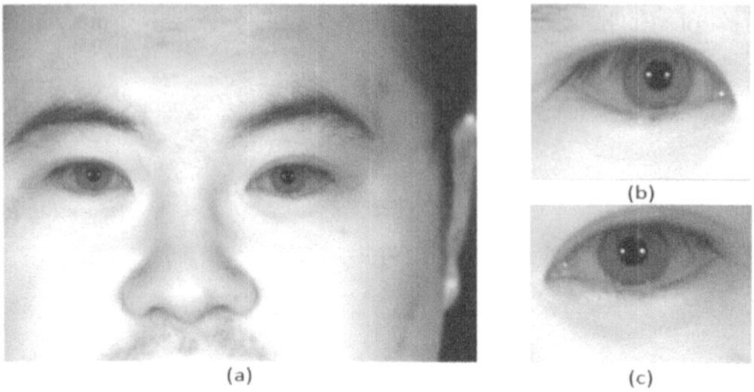

Fig. 2. Example of an input image taken from the CASIA-Iris-Distance database. Input eye image (b) Right eye (c) Left eye

to improve image details, while reducing noise and maximizing contrast, thus facilitating the segmentation and the feature extraction.

The fuzzy method used by Ming Liu in [4] is another outstanding work. Unlike conventional approaches, this method focuses on managing the non-linearities present in the image, which are often overlooked by commonly used filters such as median or Gaussian filters. The latter generally assume that image features follow a Gaussian distribution, which is often not the case in reality. Ming Liu's fuzzy method therefore enables more relevant image enhancement by taking these non-linearities into account.

Contour Detection (or Edge Detection). After the pre-processing phase, designed to improve image quality, the next step is edge detection. This phase is crucial for identifying and highlighting the boundaries of the iris, enabling precise segmentation. This involves locating the contours of the iris. Various approaches have been proposed, such as the use of Canny or Sobel edge detection techniques.

It's worth noting that many researchers have focused on this step, including Ahmed A.K. Tahir [5], Maryim Omran [6], and Samitha [7], who tend to use the Canny filter for this task due to its efficiency. The astute filter not only detects edges accurately, but also reduces false positives and improves the system's robustness in the face of images of variable quality. Thanks to its superior performance, it has become a preferred choice for edge detection in iris recognition systems. Figure 3 illustrates the detection of iris image contours along diagonal, vertical and horizontal axes.

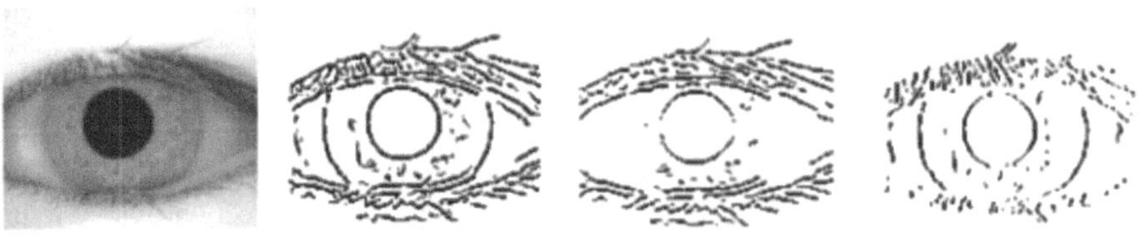

Fig. 3. (a) Initial Iris image (b) Diagonal Edges (c) Horizontal Edges (d) Vertical Edges.

Another interesting work is the one of Chang et al. [8], which focuses on the isolation of the pupil, an essential step in locating the internal and external boundaries of the iris. The approach proposed by Chang in [8] proved effective in detecting and isolating the pupil from the whole eye, thus facilitating subsequent steps in the iris recognition process.

Segmentation. After edge detection, the next step is segmentation, which involves locating the boundaries of the iris and precisely isolating this area from the rest of the image. This area constitutes the region of interest, eliminating other parts of the image such as the pupil, eyelids and eyelashes. Segmentation is essential to ensure that only relevant iris information is used in the extraction and identification phases.

Various approaches can be used for segmentation, including Active Contour Models, Edge-free Active Contours, Least Mean Square Differential Operator (LMSDO). However, the most commonly used method for segmenting the iris is the Circular Hough Transform. This technique is widely used by many researchers as shows the review [9] and [10] whose objective is to create a dimensionally stable and compatible representation of the iris region.

Another interesting method, developed in [11] et [12], is that used by Yinyin Wei and Guo Qiaoli. They respectively employed the *Integro-Differential* Operator to detect internal iris boundaries, while the Hough transform was used to identify external iris boundaries.

Standardization. Normalization is a crucial step in transforming the circular area of the iris into a rectangular shape, thus obtaining a standardized representation, whatever the angle or distance of the shot, and thus facilitating processing in subsequent stages. Dimensional inconsistencies between eye images are mainly due to iris stretching caused by pupil dilation from different illumination levels [13].

It should be pointed out that iris recognition requires a representation that is invariant to changes in size, position and orientation (dilation/contraction, distance and acquisition angle). In order to remedy all these factors of change, the method most commonly used in the literature is Daugman's Rubber Sheet model. Although this technique is relatively old, it remains highly effective and is still widely used today. Most recent research, such as [3–5] and [6], still relies on this approach to normalize the iris.

2.2 Iris Identification (Matching)

The identification phase generally comprises two stages: Feature extraction and Classification.

Feature Extraction. Once the image has been normalized, feature extraction consists of identifying and isolating the most relevant features from the input data, while reducing dimensionality. This simplifies the data while retaining the essential information. Feature selection, on the other hand, involves choosing a subset of the original features in order to further reduce dimensionality. It is essential to specify that feature extraction and feature selection are dimension reduction techniques, used to simplify the data while retaining the relevant information.

Numerous mathematical algorithms have been developed and implemented for feature extraction, such as in [14] and [15]. The main and most used methods are:

- Principal Component Analysis (PCA) based on discrete wavelets
- Haar/Biorthogonal Wavelet transform.
- Gabor and Log-Gabor filter.
- Local Binary Patterns (LBP).
- Convolution Neural Networks (CNN).

These algorithms aim to extract the most relevant features from iris images, reducing their dimensionality while reducing the complexity of the model and preserving the essential information for accurate identification.

Classification. The final stage of the iris recognition system is the classification or matching with reference data. Several methods, both classical and based on Machine or Deep Learning, are used for this crucial step. Among classical methods, Hamming distance is widely used in many works, such as [16] and [17]. As for approaches based on machine learning and deep learning, several techniques are in vogue:

- Support Vector Machines (SVM), used in [18], are powerful algorithms for iris image classification.
- Convolutional neural networks (CNNs), mentioned in [19], are also very effective for iris recognition, thanks to their ability to automatically extract complex features.

3 The Proposed System

This section presents the methods used in each sub-stage of the proposed iris recognition system, explaining them and the motivation for those choices. It is to note that the dataset used is the Casia Thousand-V4 [20].

3.1 Preprocessing

As the images didn't seem to have classic image's noise such as impulsive noise, a Gaussian filtering was applied to smooth the image just as a precaution. The noise in this article is the eyelashes, eyelids and reflections. Therefore, eyelids and eyelashes suppression were performed in order to reduce their impact on the identification. However, the suppression of eyelids can't be done unless the edge detection is performed.

3.2 Edge Detection

In this phase, the Canny filter is applied to extract all the edges in the image and the Circular Hough Transform is initially proceeded with to detect the pupil of the eye, which is needed for eyelids suppression. For this last, the proposed method consists on selecting two search regions to detect the upper and lower eyelids. Those regions systematically include a part of the eyelashes overlapping with the iris. The center of the pupil previously detected, is used as a reference for selecting the two search regions. These lasts are situated above and under the center of the pupil respectively. The upper and lower search regions are labelled and indicated in Fig. 4.

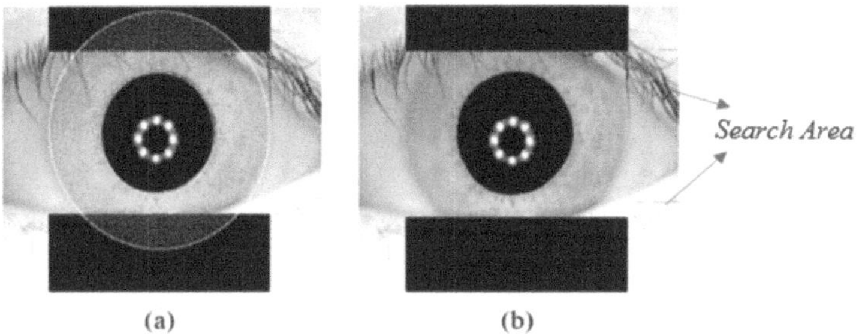

Fig. 4. Iris image (a) Upper and lower search zones (b) Detection of upper and lower eyelids.

Sobel contour detection is applied on those regions to detect eyelids. To reduce false edge detection caused by eyelashes, the Sobel kernel is tuned horizontally. Using the output of the Sobel filter, the eyelids are detected using the Linear Hough Transform as they're approximately modelled as straight lines. This method calculates the total number of contour points in each horizontal line within the search regions. The horizontal line with the maximum number of contour points is selected as the eyelid limit. If this number is below a predefined threshold, it is assumed that the eyelid is not present in the search region. The eyelid detection process is illustrated in Fig. 4.

The measures taken to isolate the eyelids can be summarized as follows:

- Identify the search regions based on the center of the pupil initially detected.
- Installing a line on the top and bottom lids of the eye using the Linear Hough Transform
- Drawing vertical lines passing by the edge of the iris, which are in the same vertical level of the center of the pupil, crossing the horizontal lines.

For eyelashes isolation, the thresholding technique is adopted considering the eyelashes as the darkest region of the eye besides the pupil.

3.3 Segmentation

To detect the inner and outer boundaries of the iris, generally assumed to be circular, the Circular Hough transform is used. This method is appreciated for its robustness and ability to handle variations in illumination and position. Figure 5 illustrates the segmentation steps using the Hough Transform [13].

The iris segmentation process can be summarized as follows [13] and [21]:

- Perform automatic segmentation of the iris region from an eye image and isolate noise areas such as occlusive eyelids and eyelashes.
- Finding the circle means returning the coordinates of the circle in an image using the Circular Hough Transform and the Canny filter for edge detection.
- Find the coordinates of the x and y line along a line.
- Find the coordinates of a line in an image using the Linear Hough Transform and the Canny filter for edge detection.
- Apply the Hough Transform to find circles in the image.

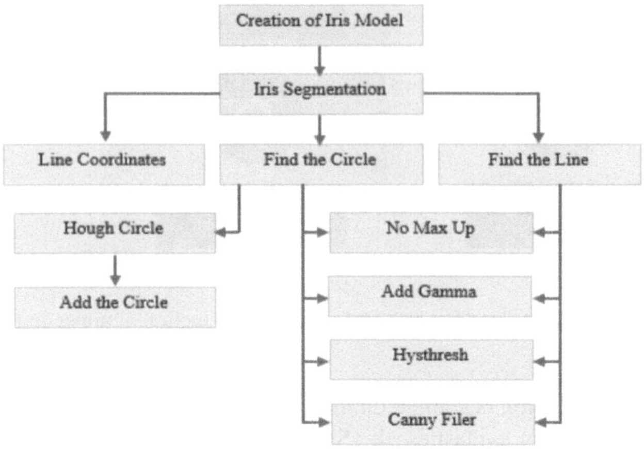

Fig. 5. Hough Transform flow chart.

- Generate a circle to add weights in a Hough accumulator table.
- Calculate the *NON-MAX-UP* function to perform non-maximum suppression on an image using an orientation image.
- Adjust the *ADJ-GAMMA* image to improve the contrast of bright regions. Image Gamma values greater than "1" improve contrast in dark regions.
- Calculate the *HYSTHRESH* function to perform the hysteresis threshold of an image.
- Calculate the *CANNY* function for edge detection.

The Hough Transform consists in selecting pixels of high intensity in the contour image and determining, for each pixel, all the circles of different radius that pass through that pixel. A voting process is implemented on the resulting contour image. Each contour point votes for the circles to which it belongs. The circle with the most votes is the circle of choice.

Figure 6 shows the results of iris segmentation.

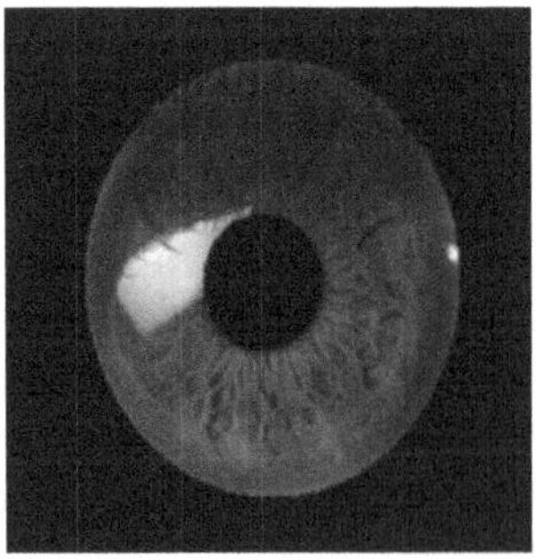

Fig. 6. Example of a segmented image with non-iris region removed.

The iris segmentation process generates a set of results including the key parameters for accurate identification of the iris region:

- Parameters of the two non-concentric circles: This segmentation is based on the identification of two distinct circles (corresponding to the inner and outer edges of the iris). The central coordinates and the difference in radius of these two circles make it possible to precisely outline the iris in the image.
- Eye image with non-iris pixel mask: Segmentation also results in an image in which pixels in regions not belonging to the iris (such as eyelids, eyelashes or light reflections) are masked. This mask is generated by applying thresholding to the edges of the image to distinguish the region of interest (the iris) from surrounding areas, taking into account eyelid line parameters that further delineate the segmented region.

Although using the Hough transform is often effective in detecting circles defining the iris, this method has some notable limitations, including:

- Choice of critical threshold values: An inappropriate threshold risks removing essential points of interest located at the edges, which could distort the detection of iris contours and reduce the precision of the final mask.
- Intensive calculation of the "Brute-Force" method: The Hough transform requires exhaustive calculations to detect all possible lines or circles corresponding to the contours of the iris. This "brute-force" approach is energy intensive and can slow down the process, especially in real-time applications.

3.4 Normalization

As Daugman's Rubber sheet remains an efficient method, the system utilizes it in the normalization sub-stage.

The Rubber Sheet model takes into account pupillary dilation, imaging distance and non-concentric pupillary displacement. However, it does not compensate for rotational inconsistencies. These inconsistencies are taken into account during matching by shifting the iris templates in the θ direction until two iris templates are aligned. A number of points along each radial line is selected. A backtrack is applied to create a model that determines the Cartesian coordinates of the data points from the radial and angular position in the normalized model. For the non-iris region, data points that occur along the pupil contour or iris contour are discarded.

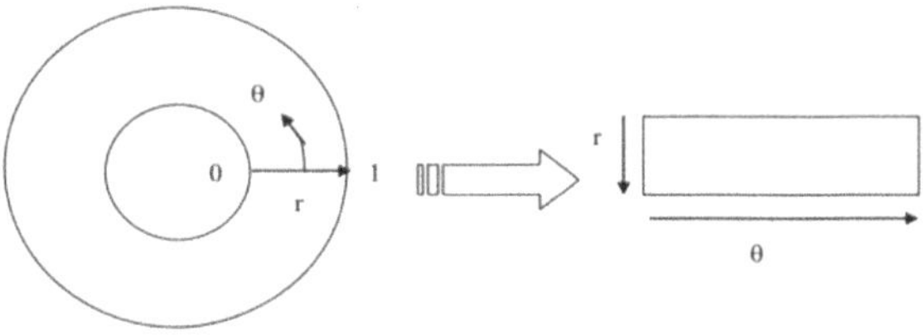

Fig. 7. Daugman rubber sheet model.

The result of the iris normalization process is two rectangles of the same predefined size (see Fig. 7):

- A rectangle containing iris texture information (all resolution points)

– Another showing resolution points for hidden non-iris regions

Figure 8 is an example that illustrates the standardization process.

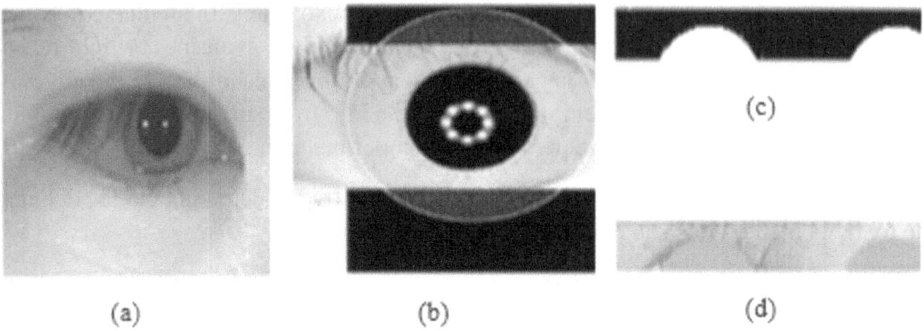

Fig. 8. **(a)** Right eye image, **(b)** Hough Transform segmented iris image, **(c)** Right iris mask, **(d)** Normalized right iris.

3.5 Feature Extraction

Once we get the normalized iris image, the feature extraction using Wavelet Transform is performed.

The aim of this step is to correctly identify each component by eliminating unnecessary information, in order to create a reduced data set that is easier to process. This enables data to be manipulated more efficiently, while preserving a high level of accuracy in the final results.

As the Wavelet Transform is known, in the field of biometrics and specially iris recognition, for preserving a big amount of information and reducing the size of the data (image) without altering it, it was an optimal choice for this sub-stage. Figure 9 shows different types of wavelets, having different filters lengths.

Among the wide variety of wavelets, the following were chosen for testing:

- Biorthogonal wavelets, which excel at preserving edges while reducing noise.
- Daubechies wavelets, known for capturing high-frequency details like textures and sharp transitions, particularly useful for asymmetric structures like the iris.
- Symlets (Symmetric wavelets), offering a balance between capturing fine details and preserving the overall image structure.

A 2-level wavelet transform provides four domains image's decomposition coefficients, where each one of them represent a specific information:

- LL: Low Frequency Information
- LH: High Frequency Information (Vertical Direction)
- HL: High Frequency Information (Horizontal Direction)
- HH: High Frequency Information (Diagonal Direction)

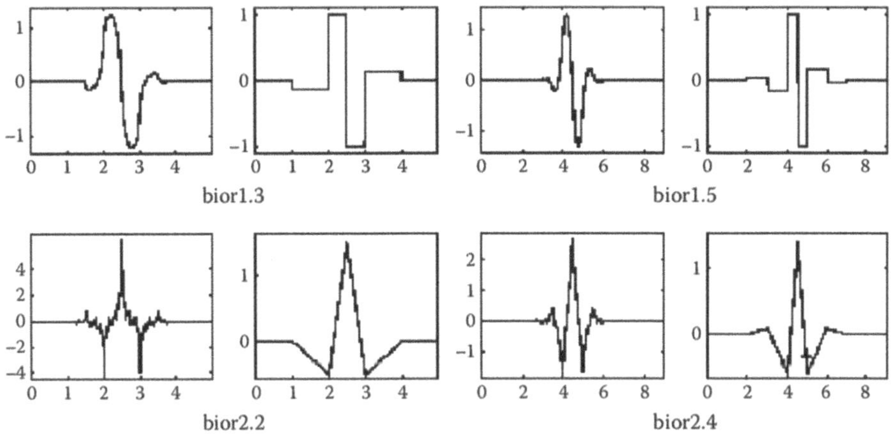

Fig. 9. Different Wavelet filters.

Figure 10 is an example of the application of Biorthogonal Wavelet Transform on an image from our database.

The LL, which is the first domain capturing the low frequency information, is chosen to be used as the images of the dataset are smooth which led to consider the low frequencies as useful data and high frequencies as noise. This step preserves the most relevant information while reducing the input size.

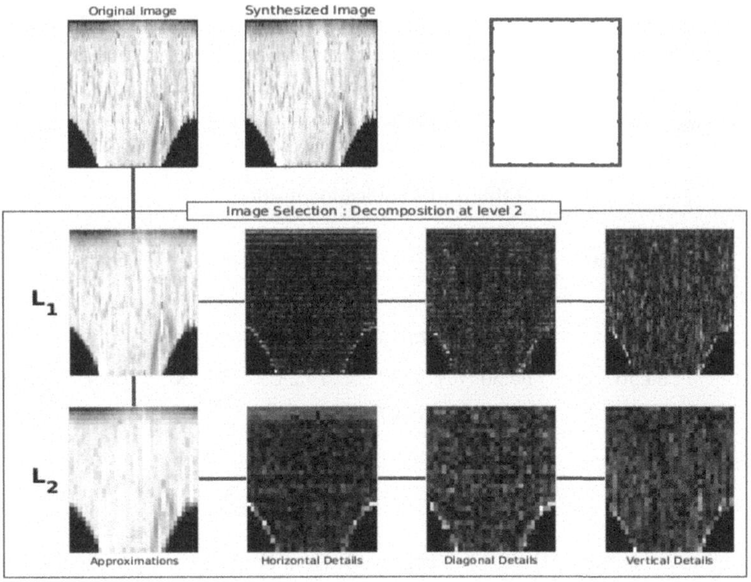

Fig. 10. Application of Biorthogonal Wavelet transform 1.1.

3.6 Classification

Once the significant features have been extracted, the classification is performed based on them.

In this stage, the Ensemble Learning approach was followed, where the prediction's results of multiple methods were combined to get the final prediction. In order to improve the overall performance, the SVM, XGBoost and CNN methods and Bagging (Majority voting) algorithm are used jointly. The architecture of the CNN used is shown in the Fig. 11.

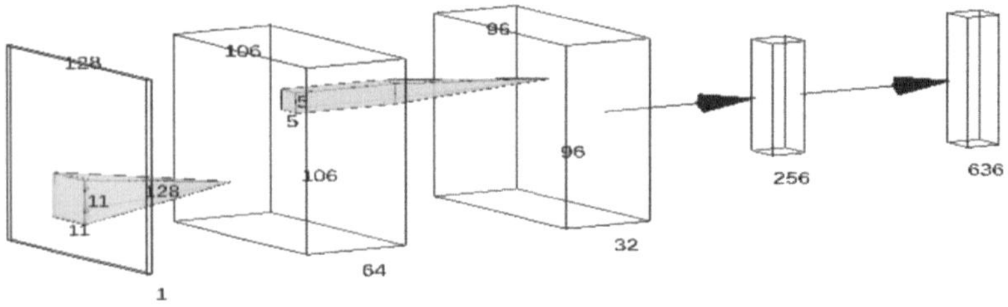

Fig. 11. CNN architecture used for raw data.

4 Discussion

As the focus of the project was the application of the Wavelet Transform, different types of wavelets were explored, namely the Biorthogonal, Daubechies and Symmetric Wavelets, denoted in the Table 1 as Bior, Db and Sym respectively, with different filters sizes. The results achieved are shown in the Table 1.

Table 1. Classification results.

Data	Raw data	Bior		Db		Sym	
Filters Size	/	1.3	1.5	2	4	2	4
SVM	77.13	71.67	74.13	81.88	63.33	72.14	69.87
XGBoost	84.56	69.50	70.59	79.23	71.58	68.92	69.38
CNN	87.42	67.94	65.87	88.05	81.36	75.46	78.97
Bagging	88.41	74.66	66.07	**91.38**	79.71	76.78	75.18

The highest accuracy (91.38%) is achieved when applying the Daubechies wavelet in combination with majority voting for Ensemble Learning. While the use of individual ML and DL methods yields satisfactory results, the ensemble approach significantly enhances overall performance.

As expected, the application of Daubechies Wavelet family outperformed the other types of wavelets applied. This is due to the excellence of this family in localizing details through compact support, besides being highly sensitive to high frequencies which make it ideal for intricate iris details, and, unlike Biorthogonal and Symmetric wavelets, strong in edge detection due to its minimal phase property which make it more suitable for texture processing. However, although larger Db filters capture more image details, the Db filter with size 2 achieved the highest accuracy. Capturing too many fine details can lead to overfitting, so increasing the Db filter size was less advantageous. Therefore, Db2 was the optimal choice, providing the best accuracy while its simplicity also reduced computational demands.

In terms of storage and computational efficiency, applying the wavelet transform reduced image resolution from 128×128 to 32×32, achieving a compression rate of 93.75%. Combined with a lightweight CNN architecture containing only 427.5k parameters, and the computational efficiency inherent to Daubechies wavelets, the proposed system is highly optimized for both storage and processing.

It is important to note that we tested the Hamming distance, but the results were suboptimal for both image hashes (using perceptual hashing, average hashing, and difference hashing) and binary thresholded images. This suggests that the system would not be reliable with this method. We observed that the Hamming distances between samples of the same class were nearly identical to those between different classes, making it unsuitable for classification.

5 Conclusion

Biometrics is a field that is both promising and complex, with an ever-increasing amount of research on a global scale. Currently, biometric systems, such as iris, face or fingerprint recognition, have become essential in high security environments, since they allow the identity of individuals to be verified or recognized with a high degree of reliability.

This article explores iris recognition systems, known for their high precision. Such a system includes two essential phases: detection and identification, each of which is explained exhaustively.

For segmentation, the Hough transform is used to isolate the iris in an image, eliminating unnecessary information to keep only the ring-shaped iris region. In the normalization phase, Daugman's "Rubber Sheet" model is applied, standardizing the size of the images while retaining the discriminative information. This step converts the iris image into a rectangular representation of uniform dimensions.

The focus was shifted then to the crucial phase of extracting relevant features. For this, the Discrete Wavelet Transforms was applied. It allows to exploit not only spatial information but also spectral information, which considerably improves the efficiency of recognition. Several different wavelets were tested, namely Biorthogonal, Symmetric and Daubechies wavelets, with different filters sizes in order to get the best accuracy.

For the classification, Ensemble Theory was followed where the bagging of CNN, SVM and XGBoost methods was applied to decide to which class an iris belongs. The best test accuracy achieved was 91.38, which prove that the proposed system is reliable.

Despite the satisfactory results achieved, the system has certain limitations and challenges that open avenues for future work. First, the proposed system is currently applicable only to a specific demographic (Asian or persons having monolids, as the CASIA dataset primarily represents Chinese individuals), thus, developing a more generalized system would be a valuable area for exploration. Second, for security purposes, integrating additional biometric modalities with iris recognition could significantly enhance accuracy, making feature fusion techniques a promising area for investigation. Lastly, to meet hardware requirements and the constraints of real-world embedded systems, exploring advanced optimization techniques, particularly those adapted to AI and ML approaches, is essential for further reducing storage and computational requirements.

References

1. Rekrouk, M., Nbri, R., Allam, F.Z., Hamami, L.: Study snd implementation on FPGA of human recognition system via iris based on deep learning. In: 2023 International Conference on Decision Aid Sciences and Applications (DASA), pp. 218–222, 979–8–3503–4205–5/23/$31.00 ©2023 IEEE (2023)
2. Tounsi, S.: Biometric Identification by Iris, Doctoral Thesis in Science. Badji Mokhtar University- Annaba, Specialty Artificial Intelligence. IT Department (2022)
3. Kumar, D., Sastry, M., Manikantan, K.: Iris recognition using contrast enhancement and spectrum-based feature extraction. In: 2016 International Conference on Emerging Trends in Engineering, Technology and Science (ICETETS), pp. 1–7. IEEE (2016)
4. Liu, M., Zhou, Z., Shang, P., Xu, D.: Fuzzified image enhancement for deep learning in iris recognition. IEEE Trans. Fuzzy Syst. **28**(1), 92–99 (2019)
5. Tahir, A.A.K., Dawood, S.S., Anghelus, S.: An iris recognition system using a new method of iris localization. Int. J. Open Inf. Technol. **9**(7), 67–76 (2021)
6. Omran, M., Al Shemmary, E.N.: An iris recognition system using deep convolutional neural network. J. Phys. Conf. Series **1530**(1), 012159. IOP Publishing (2020)
7. Nanayakkara, S., Meegama, R.: A review of literature on iris recognition. Int. J. Res. **9**, 106–120 (2020)
8. Chang, Y.T., Shih, T.K., Li, Y.H., Kumara, W.: Effectiveness evaluation of iris segmentation by using geodesic active contour (gac). J. Supercomput. **76**, 1628–1641 (2020)
9. Kamboj, P.: Iris recognition segmentation signal processing system. Appl. Sci. Eng. J. Adv. Res. ISSN (Online), 2583–2468 (2022)
10. Ashraf. Enhancing ATM security system by using iris (Eye) recognition. Am. J. Geospatial Technol. **3**(1), 69–75 (2024). https://doi.org/10.54536/ajgt.v3i1.2967
11. Wei, Y., Zhang, X., Zeng, A., Huang, H.: Iris recognition method based on parallel iris localization algorithm and deep learning iris verification. Sensors. **22**(20), 7723 (2022)
12. Guo, Q., Zheng, J.: An iris recognition algorithm for identity authentication. In: 2018 International Conference on Intelligent Transportation, Big Data & Smart City (ICITBS), pp. 621–624. IEEE (2018)
13. Allam-Chergui, F.Z.: Fusion of Biometric Techniques for improved person recognition", Doctoral Thesis in Electronic Sciences, Department of Electronics, Signal & Communications Laboratory, National Polytechnic School of Algiers, June 11 (2023)
14. Khayyat, M.M., Zamzami, N., Zhang, L., Nappi, M., Umer, M.: Fuzzy-CNN: improving personal human identification based on IRIS recognition using LBP features. J. Inf. Secur. Appl. Elsevier **83**, 103761 (2024). https://doi.org/10.1016/j.jisa.2024.103761
15. Prasanth, N., et al.: Convolutional tri biometrics: a unified approach for Iris, periocular, and facial authentication. J. Theoretical Appl. Inf. Technol. **102**(10), 4516–4526 (2024)

16. Hafner, A., Peer, P., Emersic, Z., Vitek, M.: Deep iris feature extraction. In: International Conference on Artificial Intelligence in Information and Communication (ICAIIC), pp. 258–262. IEEE (2021)
17. Khotimah, C., Juniati, D.: Iris recognition using feature extraction of box counting fractal dimension. J. Phys. Conf. Series **947**(1), 012004. IOP Publishing (2018)
18. Wei, Y., Zhang, X., Zeng, A., Huang, H.: Iris recognition method based on parallel iris localization algorithm and deep learning iris verification. Sensors **22**(20), 7723 (2022)
19. Liu, B., Zhou, Y., Feng, L., Fu, H., Fu, P.: Hybrid CNN-SVM inference accelerator on FPGA using HLS. In: MDPI, vol. 11. no. 14 (2022)
20. Casia iris v-4 dataset. biometrics.idealtest.org
21. Kamboj, P.: IRIS recognition segmentation signal processing system. Appl. Sci. Eng. J. Adv. 2583–2468 (2022)

Consumer Health Question Summarization Using Transformers and Data Augmentation

Afef Bahri[1,2(✉)], Wided Oueslati[1,3], and Abdelkarim Kharchoufi[1]

[1] Ecole Supérieure de Commerce, University of Manouba, Cité Nasr, Tunisia
{afef.bahri,wired.oueslati}@esct.uma.tn,
kharchoufi.abdelkarim@gmail.com

[2] SMART Laboratory, Institut Supérieur de Gestion, University of Tunis, Tunis , Tunisia

[3] BESTMOD Laboratory, Institut Supérieur de Gestion, University of Tunis, Tunis, Tunisia

Abstract. Searching for medical information online is becoming more common and the number of consumer questions increases every day. In order to support consumer search, we need to develop Question Answering tools. However, Consumer health questions may contain subjective and borderline information making them unuseful to find relevant answers or to train efficient QA tools. The objective of Consumer health question summarization is to simplify long and complex questions by extracting only relevant information without changing their intent. The problem is that the size of datasets used for training medical summarization models contain fewer questions compared to the datasets used for open domain question summarization. In fact, medical consumer health question summarization dataset has to be annotated with experts which is a time-consuming process. In this paper, we propose to use text augmentation in order to extend questions with additional information obtained with generative models (Pegasus and T5). We fine-tune BART and T5 using en expanded version of MeqSum dataset. Experiments show that our approach, which combines transformers with data augmentation improves performance over summarization baseline and state of the art methods.

Keywords: Question Summarization · Medical Text · Transformers · Data Augmentation

1 Introduction

A significant amount of medical information is produced every day in the form of scientific publications whether in medical journals (e.g. PubMed) or on specialized medical websites. The advantage of this information is that it is generally produced by the medical profession. Patients and Internet users also take part in the generation of medical content in the form of questions, posts or comments. In fact, more and more patients use discussion forums to ask questions about treatment, medication or symptoms and wait for suggestions that can only be given by healthcare professionals (HPs). However, the number of questions produced on the Internet every day is more and more important and responding to these questions by HPs may be time consuming and expensive. The

A. Mirzazadeh et al. (Eds.): SEMIT 2024, CCIS 2444, pp. 244–255, 2026.
https://doi.org/10.1007/978-3-032-01948-6_16

objective of Question Summarization is to simplify consumer health questions in order to be able to intend their meanings. As CHQs may be long, complex and contain extra background and unnecessary information, proposing models for CHQs summarization is a challenging issue [1]. Automated summarization of consumer health questions have many medical applications and may be crucial to improve automatic response retrieval and Question Answering Systems.

Compared to summarizing papers or articles, question summarization [2] has not been thoroughly studied. Text summarization is one of the most studied areas on Natural Language Processing [3]. Approaches proposed in text summarization may be classified into two different types: Extractive and Abstractive text summarization [4]. Extractive text summarization selects units (words, sentences) from the text and orders it. Abstractive summarization techniques generate summaries with words that are not found in the original text. Extractive and abstractive text summarization have shown significant progress in recent years due to the recent development in neural networks and transfer learning approaches [5]. Abstractive summarization has known advancement due to the development of large-scale datasets [6–8]. In the medical domain, only experts can provide accurate summaries corresponding to consumer health questions which may be expensive and time consuming. Aware of the importance of the size of a dataset in abstractive summarization, we propose in this paper an abstractive question summarization model that apply data augmentation to expand medical consumer health questions of the MeQSum dataset.

In this paper, we propose a question summary generation approach based on a combination of transfer learning and data augmentation. Questions in the MeQSum dataset are extended with additional information using T5 and Pegasus. We fine tune pre-trained models such as BART [9], and T5 [7] using the modified version of the dataset.

The paper is organized as follows: Sect. 2 presents related works, our approach is detailed in Sect. 3. In Sect. 4 we present and discuss experimental results.

2 Related Works

Consumer health question summarization is a specific sub-task of medical text summarization focusing on generating summaries from medical consumer health questions. Medical text summarization has gained significant attention due to the increasing volume of scientific publications, medical forums, social media, websites, or question-and-answer platforms. Scientific publications are generally well written whereas consumer health questions may contain mistakes or borderline information. Consumer health question summarization process needs to identify the health issue, extract key details such as symptoms, medical conditions and treatments and identify individual seeking (advice, information or diagnosis). The summarized question has to be clear and concise with essential information.

Abstractive text summarization has known significant progress with the use of sequence to sequence (seq2seq) models [8], pointer generator network [9] and transformer [10] and especially with the development of large-scale datasets for Abstractive summarization [6–8]. The goal of Abstractive Summarization is to rewrite the supplied information in a more concise format. This is in contrast to extractive summarization, which seeks to extract just the most important phrases from the provided input.

BERT (Bidirectional Encoder Representations from Transformers), RoBERTa and DistilBERT have been fine-tuned on many summarization datasets and applied to extractive summarization.

More recently, GPT (Generative Pre-trained Transformer), GPT-3, GPT-4 use autoregressive decoding techniques for text summarization. BART (Bidirectional and Auto-Regressive Transformers) and T5 (Text-to-Text Transfer Transformer) equally treat summarization and many other NLP tasks.

Consumer health question summarization has been introduced by [11] in MEDIQA 2021 with a benchmark dataset containing 1000 questions summaries. [12, 13] use different combinations of transformers (Prophet, T5, BART) for question summarization. [14] use equally transformers and propose to infuse knowledge about question type and to recognize medical entities using masked language models. [15] tackle the problem of medical question generation in a low resource setting. The authors use human evaluation to measure the effectiveness of the proposed approach. More recently, [16] and [17] use contrastive learning to generate erroneous (negative) summaries in order to allow the model to recognize plausible perturbations of the original summaries. Human evaluation is equally used in this paper. [18] propose a comparative analysis of Large Language models in medical text summarization in general and take as a specific case, consumer health question summarization. The authors propose a comparative performance analysis of LLMs versus GPT-3 as baseline and GPT-4 as the evaluator.

The majority of the cited papers use the MeqSum dataset [19] and only few datasets are proposed in the literature with relatively few numbers of questions compared to open domain text summarization. This is due to the fact that medical text annotation has to be realized only by experts and is a time-consuming process. [20] propose a second dataset named CHQ-Summ with 1507 consumer health questions derived from social media and annotated with domain experts. We note that the two datasets have approximately the same size and their use for training language models may lack generality. Data augmentation may be used to artificially increase the size of the dataset. In our paper we use data augmentation to enrich questions with additional information in order to depict the intent and the meaning of the question. If the question contains subjective or borderline information, the generated text focuses on the clear part of the text which essentially corresponds to the part where medical vocabulary is used.

3 Methodology

In this section we begin with a formal definition of the problem, we present the used dataset and we detail the proposed model architecture.

3.1 Problem Formalization

Given a consumer health question $Q = \{q_1, q_2,..., q_M\}$, the summarized question is defined as a set $S = \{s_1, s_2,..., s_N\}$ where q_i corresponds to the tokens of the original question and s_j are the tokens representing key information. We note that S may be not included in Q as we work with abstractive summarization where the content of a summary is generated and not extracted from the original question. That is we build our abstractive model over seq2seq Bi-LSTM architecture. In order to enhance the model's generalization, we propose to expand original questions with additional content such as contextual information generated with Pegasus and T5. An extended question (augmented and/or rephrased) Qe is defined based on the original question Q as Qe = $Q \cup \{q_{M+1}, q_{M+2},\ldots, q_{M+k}\}$. We present in Table 1 two examples of questions and their corresponding summaries extracted from the MeQSum Dataset.

Table 1. Questions and corresponding summaries extracted from MeQSum.

Example 1

Question: I was diagnosed with sleep apnea (prolly had it for 5 years) and I have swelling issues caused from that (it has been ruled out from everything else so the doctor thinks). I just got my cPap machine. I was wondering how long will it take for the swelling to go away. Thank you!
Summary: How long does swelling from sleep apnea take to heal?

Example 2

Question: What specific resources are available for an elderly male living by himself at home? My father in law is 85 years old, lives alone and has macular degeneration. Looking for visual aids to assist him around the house.
Summary: What resources are available for elderly with age-related macular degeneration?

3.2 Dataset

We use the MeQSum dataset of consumer health questions and summaries [21]. The dataset contains 1000 consumer health questions (CHQs) and associated one-sentence-long frequently asked questions (FAQs). The questions are selected by medical experts in the National Institutes of Health (NIH) and the FAQs were written by medical professionals. Treatment, Effect, Side Effects, Cause, Information, Complications, Person-Organization, Diet-Lifestyle, Contraindications, Diagnosis, Interaction, Usage, Ingredients, Prognosis, Transmission, Susceptibility, and Toxicity are among the topics and question types covered by the MeQSum dataset[1].

3.3 Architecture

We illustrate the architecture of our approach in Fig. 1. Given the input dataset, each question is processed in order to eliminate among others spell errors and stop-words. After pre-processing questions are expanded with contextual information, additional content generated with pre-trained generative models: T5 is used for question generation and Pegasus for paraphrasing. The generated content is added at the end of each question. Finally, we train a Bi-LSTM model with attention and we fine tune pre-trained transformers (T5 and BART) on the obtained dataset.

[1] https://github.com/abachaa/MEDIQA2021/tree/main/Task1

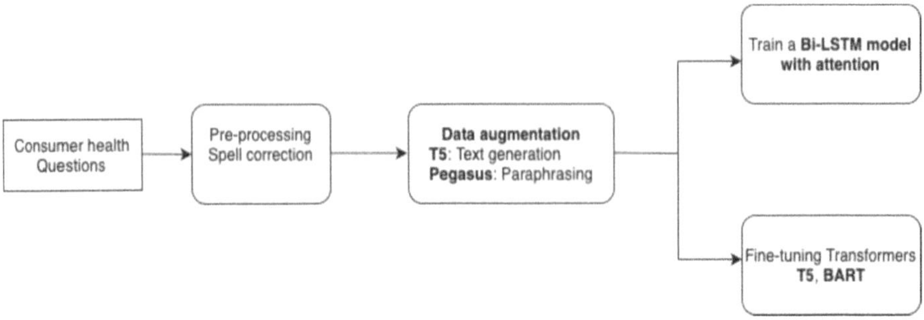

Fig. 1. Medical Question Summarization Architecture.

3.4 Techniques for Data Augmentation

In our approach, we propose to expand the consumer health questions with additional information using pre-trained generative models. We use generative models in order to paraphrase and generate text based on the consumer health question in order to reinforce the presence of medical terms and reduce the effect of subjective or off-topic information. Different models may be used for text extension:

- GPT-based models: such as GPT-4 used for expanding text by adding more background, details or rephrasing content while preserving coherence and relevance.
- Pegasus, T5, and BART: sentences can be rephrased and more information added using these pre-trained generative and paraphrasing models.

In our approach we realize experimentations using Pegasus, T5 and BART. The maximum length of a query in MeQSum is equal to 100 whereas the maximum length after expansion is equal to 120. Figure 2 shows the distribution of the size of queries and their corresponding summaries in the MeQSum dataset after expansion.

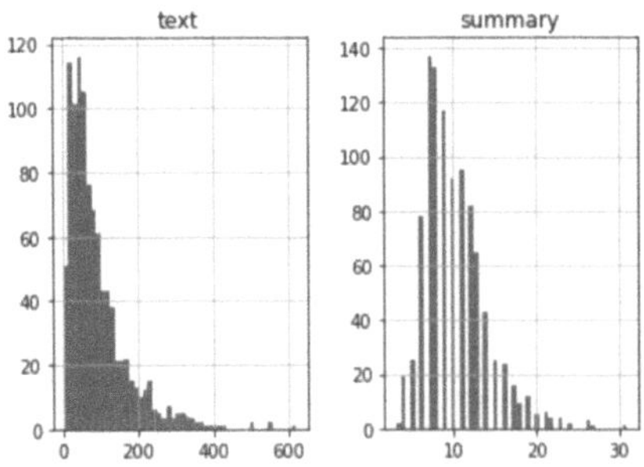

Fig. 2. Distribution of the size of queries and summaries after expansion.

3.5 Summarization Using Bi-LSTM with Attention

Bi-LSTM (Bidirectional long short-term memory (bi-lstm) [22] is a type of LSTM model which processes the data in both forward and backward direction. The Bi-LSTM layer creates hidden states that reflect the contextual information of each word in the sentence after processing the input text present in the form of word embeddings. In order to enable the model to concentrate on pertinent parts of the input sequence when generating the summary, the Attention Mechanism was implemented. The model can "attend" to particular words or phrases in the input text that are more crucial for creating a summary. The attention mechanism gives each word in the input sequence a weight according to its relevance. When creating the appropriate term in the summary, the weights show how much emphasis should be placed on each word in the input.

We present in the following a detailed explanation of how a Bi-LSTM with Attention model for text summarization works:

- Text embedding: After tokenization, each word is transformed into a dense vector (embedding) using pre-trained embedding (BERT, ClinicalBERT).
- Encoding using Bi-LSTM: a bidirectional LSTM network is used to process the embedded text. The Bi-LSTM creates a hidden state for each word in the input sequence that captures the context from both directions.
- Attention: For each token in the input sequence, the attention mechanism calculates an attention score relative to the corresponding token in the generated summary. Softmax function is used to normalize these scores.

3.6 Summarization Using Pre-trained Generative Language Models

Distinct abstractive summarization models are used in our approach:

- **T5** [7]: T5 is a generative model proposed by Google Research. T5 handles all NLP tasks as "text-to-text" problems, which means that the input and output are handled as text sequences. The model may handle a variety of NLP tasks (translation, Question Answering, summarization) with the same framework.
- **BART** [9]: Bart is a model that uses a combination of bi-directional transformers like BERT and auto-regressive transformers like GPT. It is employed in many NLP tasks (translation, summarization, text generation).
- **Pegasus** [23]: is a generative model proposed by Google Research for abstractive text summarization. Pegasus is equally based on transformers and trained on large datasets.

4 Experimental Results and Discussion

4.1 Evaluation Metrics

The performance of the question summarization is evaluated against the ROUGE score [24]. The results are reported in term of ROUGE-1 (R-1), ROUGE-2 (R-2) and ROUGE-L (R-L):

- **ROUGE-N**: N-gram Recall/Precision/F1-Score. N = 1 or N = 2.
- **ROUGE-L**: measure the Longest Common Subsequence between the generated and the original summary

4.2 Implementation Details

For question summarization task, we use BI-LSTM[2] with attention, the T5-small[3], BART pre-trained models[4]. These models are fine tuned with maximum source question length of 100 and target summary length of 20. When we expand the questions with additional terms, the models are fine tuned with maximum source question length of 120. The code and the expanded dataset are available on github[5].

All models were trained with a batch size of 16 for 30 epochs and applied a beam search approach with a beam size of 5. We utilize the Adam [25] optimization method with a learning rate of 7e-5 to update the model parameters on google colab GPU. We use the early stopping of training via a callback called Early Stopping. This callback specifies the performance metric to track the trigger, and when it is triggered, it stops the training.

We give in the following more details about the implemented models:

- Bi-LSTM model: This model uses a seq2seq bidirectional LSTM based encoder and decoder. The encoder is an embedding layer followed by three bidirectional LSTM layers with 300 hidden units and a dropout value of 0.4. Similar to the encoder, the decoder is an embedding layer followed by bidirectional LSTMs with 600 hidden units and a softmax layer.
- T5: Our model uses T5-small with 6 encoders and decoder layers.
- BART: experimented with the distilbart-xsum-12–3 pre-trained models (BART with 12 encoder & 3 decoder layers fine tuned on Xsum dataset).

4.3 Results

Table 2 shows the ROUGE scores obtained for our models fine-tuned with MeQsum. Since the size of our training set is small, the Bi-LSTM did not provide acceptable results compared to pre-trained models. The T5 model fine-tuned with the expanded dataset obtained a better ROUGE score when compared to the T5 model trained with MeQsum. As we can, BART fine-tuned on an expanded dataset gives best Rouge scores.

Table 3 gives a comparison between the result obtained with our best model (BART trained with data augmentation) and existing models. For the approaches proposed in MEDIQA 2021, we choose the best participants results. Concerning more recent approaches, the contrastive learning approach proposed in [17] has 0.52 with Rouge-1. We outperform related work using Rouge-2 score.

[2] https://www.tensorflow.org/api_docs/python/tf/keras/layers/Bidirectional
[3] https://huggingface.co/t5-small
[4] https://huggingface.co/sshleifer/distilbart-xsum-12-3
[5] https://github.com/kharchoufiabdelkarim/abstractivesummary

Table 2. Fine-tuning generative models trained on MeQSum and the expanded dataset.

Baseline	Rouge 1	Rouge 2	Rouge L
Baseline Seq2Seq: MeQSum			
BI-LSTM + Spell Correction	0.30	0.15	0.28
Baseline Transformers: MeQSum			
T5++ Spell Correction	0.44	0.29	0.43
BART + Spell Correction	0.45	0.28	0.40
Proposed Methods:MeQSum + Data augmentation			
BI-LSTM + Spell correction + Paraphrase + Question generation	0.28	0.17	0.28
T5 + Spell correction + Paraphrase + Question generation	0.48	0.31	0.46
BART + Spell correction + Paraphrase + Question generation	**0.55**	**0.41**	**0.53**

Table 3. Performance comparison of the proposed models.

Model	Rouge 1	Rouge 2	Rouge L
Our best model			
BART + Spell correction + Paraphrase + Data augmentation	**0.55**	**0.41**	**0.53**
MEDIQA 2021 approaches			
damo-nlp [12]	0.35	0.16	0.31
WBI [13]	0.29	0.11	0.26
Other approaches			
Contrastive learning [17]	0.52	-	-
Low-Resource Setting [15]	0.46	0.29	0.49
Question-Type Aware Model [14]	0.44	0.27	0.47

4.4 Discussion

We performed an in-depth analysis of the model generated summaries, as shown in Table 4. We picked four output summaries at random from the test set, and we manually evaluated the summaries generated with BART. We discuss in the following the obtained results:

- **Medical abbreviations**: we note that in example 1 and 2, medical abbreviations are used. The generated summaries contain abbreviations corresponding to medical terms used in the original summaries or medical terms corresponding to abbreviations.
- **Medical terminology**: the predicted summaries contain medical terminology even though in the case where the original summary does not contain as in example 3. In the

original summary, the expert uses general medical terms: "*comprehensive testing for difficult to diagnose symptoms*". The generated summary contains specific medical terms occurring in the patient's question: "*what are the treatments for lupus and brian vasculopathy*".

- **Negation**: In example 4, the expert uses negation to denote "non-drug treatment" in the original summary. As the negation is not used, the predicted summary contradicts with the original one.

Table 4. Examples showing generated summaries obtained with BART fine-tuned on an expanded version of MeQSum.

Example 1 Question *"migraine. I want to know the treatment for FHM type of migrain. I had observed the all symptoms* *which are same as provided in information and additionally my father and my younger sister face the acidity problem too. They feel relief after vomiting so both of them do the same by drinking warm water containing salt."* Original Summary *"what are the treatments for familial hemiplegic migraine"* Predicted Summary *"what are the treatments for fhm type of migraine"*
Example 2 Question *"i have giant cell arteritis. on steroids. Lost taste. is this related to the illness (was it ever reported* *in GCA ?) or side rx to prednisone. i wish a rheumatologist at NIH responds"* Original Summary *"what causes loss of taste and is it related to gca or steroids"* Predicted Summary *"what is the prognosis for giant cell arteritis on steroids"*
Example 3 Question *"I need help with a rare disorder Hello, As I stated I need help with a rare disorder. I have tested* *positive for lupus then negative I have tests positive for a blood clotting disorder then negative I have tested positive for Brain Vasculitus then brian Vasculopathy? I have tested positive for a Brain infection then not. I don t know what to think. I need a special testing center"* Original Summary *"where can i receive comprehensive testing for difficult to diagnose symptoms"* Predicted Summary *"what are the treatments for lupus and brian vasculopathy"*

(*continued*)

Table 4. (*continued*)

Example 4 Question *"Hi, I'm looking to purchase Epidermal Growth Factor to use topically in skin care creams. Do you* *sell it and if so how can I learn about this? If you don't can you give any suggestions of who might? Any information you can provide would be greatly appreciated. THNAK YOU!"* Original Summary *"where can i buy epidermal growth factor cream"* Predicted Summary *"where can i find information on epidermal growth factor to use in skin care"*
Example 4 Question *"What is the best way to naturally treat a 7 yr old boy with ADHD? Without prescription medicine?"* Original Summary *"What are the non-drug treatments for ADHD?"* Predicted Summary *"what are the treatments for adhd"*

5 Conclusion

Consumer health question summarization is an open research problem and many issues have to be addressed. The first issue concerns the size of the dataset proposed for training generative models. In this paper we use the MeQSum dataset to train a consumer health question summarization model. We propose to expand questions with additional information generated with pre-trained models such as T5 or BART. Experiments show that we outperform existing methods in Rouge-1, Rouge-2 and Rouge-L. In future works we project to use other language models such as GPT-4 and to infuse entity embedding from medical knowledge graphs in the training process.

References

1. Ben Abacha, A., Demner-Fushman, D.: On the summarization of consumer health questions. In: Proceedings of the 57th Annual Meeting of the Associa- tion for Computational Linguistics, pp. 2228–2234. Association for Computational Linguistics, Florence, Italy (2019)
2. Upadhya, B.A., Udupa, S., Kamath, S.S.: Deep neural network models for question classification in community question-answering forums. In: 2019 10th International Conference on Computing, Communication and Networking Technologies (ICCCNT), pp. 1–6 (2019)
3. Liu, Y., Lapata, M.: Text summarization with pretrained encoders. In: Proceedings of the 2019 Conference on Empirical Methods in Natural Language Processing and the 9th International Joint Conference on Natural Language Processing (EMNLP-IJCNLP), pp. 3730–3740. Association for Computational Linguistics, Hong Kong, China (2019)
4. Zmiycharov, V., Chechev, M., Lazarova, G., Tsonkov, T., Koychev, I.: A comparative study on abstractive and extractive approaches in summarization of European legislation documents. In: Proceedings of the International Conference on Recent Advances in Natural Language Processing (RANLP 2021), pp. 1645–1651. INCOMA Ltd., Held Online (2021)

5. Li, P., Yu, J.: Extractive summarization based on dynamic memory network. Symmetry **13**(4) (2021)
6. Sharma, E., Li, C., Wang, L.: BIGPATENT: a large-scale dataset for abstractive and coherent summarization. In: Proceedings of the 57th Annual Meeting of the Association for Computational Linguistics, pp. 2204–2213. Association for Computational Linguistics, Florence, Italy (2019)
7. Hasan, T., et al.: Xl-sum: Large-scale multilingual abstractive summarization for 44 languages. CoRR abs/2106.13822 (2021)
8. Landro, N., Gallo, I., La Grassa, R., Federici, E.: Two new datasets for italian- language abstractive text summarization. Information **13**(5) (2022)
9. Lewis, M., et al.: BART: Denoising sequence-to-sequence pre-training for natural language generation, translation, and comprehension. arXiv preprint arXiv:1910.13461 (2019)
10. Raffel, C., et al.: Exploring the limits of transfer learning with a unified text-to-text transformer. arXiv preprint arXiv:1910.10683 (2019)
11. Shi, T., Keneshloo, Y., Ramakrishnan, N., Reddy, C.K.: Neural abstractive text summarization with sequence-to-sequence models. CoRR abs/1812.02303 (2018)
12. See, A., Liu, P.J., Manning, C.D.: Get to the point: Summarization with pointer- generator networks. CoRR abs/1704.04368 (2017)
13. Gupta, A., Chugh, D., Anjum, Katarya, R.: Automated news summarization using transformers. CoRR abs/2108.01064 (2021)
14. Ben Abacha, A., et al.: Overview of the MEDIQA 2021 shared task on summarization in the medical domain. In: Demner-Fushman, D., Cohen, K.B., Ananiadou, S., Tsujii, J. (eds.) Proceedings of the 20th Workshop on Biomedical Language Processing, pp. 74–85. Association for Computational Linguistics, Online (2021)
15. He, Y., Chen, M., Huang, S.: damo nlp at mediqa 2021: Knowledge-based pre-processing and coverage-oriented reranking for medical question summarization. In: Proceedings of the 20th Workshop on Biomedical Language Processing, pp. 112–118 (2021)
16. S¨anger, M., Weber, L., Leser, U.: WBI at MEDIQA 2021: Summarizing consumer health questions with generative transformers. In: Proceedings of the 20th Workshop on Biomedical Language Processing, pp. 86–95 (2021)
17. Yadav, S., Gupta, D., Abacha, A.B., Demner-Fushman, D.: Question-aware transformer models for consumer health question summarization. CoRR abs/2106.00219 (2021)
18. Yadav, S., Caragea, C.: Towards summarizing healthcare questions in low-resource setting. In: Proceedings of the 29th International Conference on Computational Linguistics, pp. 2892–2905. International Committee on Computational Linguistics, Gyeongju, Republic of Korea (2022)
19. Yadav, S., Cobeli, u., Caragea, C.: Towards understanding consumer healthcare questions on the web with semantically enhanced contrastive learning. Association for Computing Machinery, New York, NY, USA (2023)
20. Lu, W., Wei, S., Peng, X., Wang, Y.-F., Naseem, U., Wang, S.: Medical question summarization with entity-driven contrastive learning. ACM Trans. Asian Low-Resour. Lang. Inf. Process. **23**(4) (2024)
21. Chen, Y., Wang, Z., Zulkernine, F.: Comparative analysis of open-source language models in summarizing medical text data. In: 2024 IEEE International Conference on Digital Health (ICDH), pp. 126–128 (2024)
22. Ben Abacha, A., Demner-Fushman, D.: On the summarization of consumer health questions. In: Korhonen, A., Traum, D., M'arquez, L. (eds.) Proceedings of the 57th Annual Meeting of the Association for Computational Linguistics, pp. 2228–2234. Association for Computational Linguistics, Florence, Italy (2019)
23. Yadav, S., Gupta, D., Demner-Fushman, D.: CHQ-Summ: A Dataset for Consumer Healthcare Question Summarization (2022)

24. Abacha, A.B., Shivade, C., Demner-Fushman, D.: Overview of the mediqa 2019 shared task on textual inference, question entailment and question answering. In: Proceedings of the 18th BioNLP Workshop and Shared Task, pp. 370–379 (2019)
25. Schuster, M., Paliwal, K.K.: Bidirectional recurrent neural networks. IEEE Trans. Signal Process. **45**(11), 2673–2681 (1997)
26. Zhang, J., Zhao, Y., Saleh, M., Liu, P.: Pegasus: Pre-training with extracted gap-sentences for abstractive summarization. In: International Conference on Machine Learning, pp. 11328–11339 (2020). PMLR
27. Lin, C.-Y.: ROUGE: a package for automatic evaluation of summaries. In: Text Summarization Branches Out, pp. 74–81. Association for Computational Linguistics, Barcelona, Spain (2004)
28. Kingma, D.P., Ba, J.: Adam: A method for stochastic optimization. arXiv preprint arXiv: 1412.6980 (2014)

Enhancing Omnichannel Customer Experience: A Cross-Case Study Analysis of AI Integration in Retail E-Commerce

Kishori Kasat[1](✉), Naim Shaikh[2], Vernekar Shradha[3], and Venkatesh Iyengar[4]

[1] Symbiosis School for Liberal Arts, Symbiosis International (Deemed University), Pune, India
kishori.kasat@ssla.edu.in

[2] Global Business School and Research Centre, Dr. D. Y. Patil Vidyapeeth (Deemed to be University), Pune, India

[3] Bharati Vidyapeeth (Deemed to be) University's Institute of Management and Entrepreneurship Development, Pune, India

[4] Symbiosis International (Deemed University), Pune, India

Abstract. This study explores the role of artificial intelligence (AI) in enhancing omnichannel customer experience within retail e-commerce through a cross-case analysis of three prominent retailers: Amazon, Walmart, and Sephora. As omnichannel retailing becomes central to meeting evolving consumer expectations, AI-driven innovations like recommendation systems, chatbots, and predictive analytics are increasingly utilized to create seamless, personalized shopping experiences. Each case highlights distinct strategies and AI applications tailored to its business model: Amazon leverages AI for personalization and operational optimization across its vast digital ecosystem; Walmart emphasizes AI in inventory management and in-store technology to bridge physical and digital channels; and Sephora uses AI-driven tools to enhance customer engagement and personalization in beauty retail. Findings reveal shared themes in AI's impact on customer satisfaction and operational efficiency, while also identifying challenges related to data integration, consistency across channels, and resource allocation. The study contributes valuable insights into best practices and emerging trends in AI-driven omnichannel retail, providing a foundation for further research on AI's potential to redefine customer experiences and retailer performance.

Keywords: AI in Retail · Cross-Case Analysis · Customer Experience · E-Commerce · Omnichannel Retailing · Operational Efficiency · Personalization

1 Introduction

Context and Motivation

Paradigm shifts towards omnichannel strategies especially in the retail electronic commerce domain has been found to be driven by consumer behavioural changes, technological advancements, and increasing competition in marketplace. Retailers now have moved their business focus on rendering seamless and integrated customer experiences

A. Mirzazadeh et al. (Eds.): SEMIT 2024, CCIS 2444, pp. 256–273, 2026.
https://doi.org/10.1007/978-3-032-01948-6_17

across multiple touchpoints (e.g., physical stores, social media, mobile apps, web portals, etc.) in order to satisfy ever-evolving customer expectations. The growing importance of such omnichannel strategies by retailers are clearly highlighted through consumer expectations for personalized shopping and seamless experiences across all possible channels. For example, a customer may commence their shopping journey using a mobile device, switch to a personal computer (desktop), and finally conclude their purchase through a physical store, or vice-versa. Omnichannel approaches allow the retailers to offer continuous and consistent customer experiences across all channels, thus enhancing customer satisfaction levels and loyalty [1]. This ensures that all customers experience the same levels of convenience and services, irrespective of the channel they may choose for interaction. In the case of any technology-driven personalization such as use of Artificial Intelligence including chatbots or recommendation systems, retailers are assisted towards gathering real-time customer data on their behaviours and preferences, which are useful for retailers to customize or personalize such shopping experiences across all channels. Omnichannel strategies are able to leverage such AI-integrated technology for tailoring marketing messages, services, and product recommendations, thereby enhancing customer conversion rates and engagement [2]. It has been found that the boundaries between offline and online channels are increasingly blurring. Customers seem to use multiple channels for single transaction, such as 'buy online, pick-up instore' (BOPIS) or use their mobile apps during shopping through physical stores so as to receive promotions or even check availability of products. This integration allows customers choose their most preferred channel basing on convenience in shopping experiences [3]. Omnichannel also encourages heightened levels of customer engagement providing multiple touchpoints. It is evidenced that customers also tend to spend more thereby demonstrating increased loyalty [4] and allowing retailers enhance customer retention through strong and personalized relationships. Through omnichannel strategy integrations, retailers derive significant competitive advantage, attract broader customer base, increased sales, improvements in brand loyalty, higher spend per transaction, and better lifetime value in comparison to a single-channel customer [5].

Several industries, particularly in e-commerce and retail, the customer interactions and operations efficiency are significantly being transformed through use of Artificial Intelligence (AI). Businesses are now able to deliver personalized customer experiences, optimize decision-making process, and streamline operations. Key areas of AI-integration are found in AI-driven personalized customer interactions. AI can analyse large quantity of customer data (e.g., purchase behaviour, browsing history, customer preferences, etc.). Specific algorithms can help in predicting customer needs, real-time services tailoring to individual preferences, product suggestions, all leading to superior customer engagement and satisfaction [6]. For example, Amazon and Netflix drive sales and user engagement through AI-driven recommendation engines. AI-powered and virtual assistants chatbots enhance customer service offering a 24/7 support, handling simultaneously multiple customer queries, and resolving customer issues in real time mode. Chatbots can respond to frequently asked questions (FAQs), assist customers in making purchase decisions, and afford updates on services or orders [7]. Through automation AI can transform back-end operations and assist businesses in streamlining their processes (e.g., supply chain logistics, inventory management, and demand forecasting). Industry 4.0 technologies, such as the machine learning (ML) algorithms can analyze large datasets for identifying patterns, optimize inventory levels, and reduce overstock or stockout situations [8]. AI-driven business analytics enable businesses to seek deeper insights into their customer behavior. Analysis of datasets from multiple sources (e.g., social media, purchase histories, website interactions, etc.) and through leveraging AI-powered analytical tools, businesses can make advanced data-driven decisions. This enhances product offerings, improved customer experiences, and real-time adjustments in marketing strategies.

Despite the growing integration of AI in retail, limited research has systematically explored how AI technologies are being utilized to enhance the omnichannel customer experience. Most existing studies focus either on e-commerce or in-store technologies, with few examining the convergence of these experiences through AI. Furthermore, there is a need for comparative research that analyzes AI adoption across different retail sectors to identify common strategies and industry-specific applications. This study aims to address this gap by conducting a cross-case analysis of AI integration in retail e-commerce companies, with a focus on how these technologies enhance the omnichannel customer experience. By examining multiple case studies, this research provides insights into the best practices, challenges, and outcomes associated with AI-driven omnichannel strategies.

Research Question(s)

The key research questions for this study are:

RQ1: How does AI integration enhance the omnichannel experience in retail e-commerce?

RQ2: What are the most effective AI technologies used in retail e-commerce for omnichannel enhancement?

RQ3: How do customer experiences differ across retail platforms with varying degrees of AI integration?

Organization of the Paper

The further flow of this research paper is structured into seven key sections which provide a comprehensive analysis on the topic of interest i.e., AI integration in enhancing omnichannel customer experiences in retail e-commerce. Section 2, Literature Review, probes into existing studies on omnichannel strategies and AI applications in retail specifically published in top quality journals indexed in the Scopus database, providing the theoretical foundation and identifying relevant research gaps. In Sect. 3, Methodology, the research design, data collection methods, and analytical approach used to conduct the cross-case study of three prominent case retail brands are explained. Section 4, Case Descriptions, presents an overview of each case company, discussing their explicit AI-driven omnichannel initiatives and exceptional business contexts. In Sect. 5, Cross-Case Analysis, the cases are examined in a comparative framework to identify common themes, challenges, and strategic insights. Section 6, Results and Discussions, interprets the findings, highlighting key patterns and discussing the implications of AI integration on operational efficiency and customer experiences in retail. Finally, Sect. 7, Conclusions, summarizes the study's main contributions, discusses limitations, and suggests areas for future research on AI-enhanced omnichannel strategies in retail.

2 Literature Review

A key focus for retailers has been about the integration of artificial intelligence (AI) into omnichannel retail for enhancing operational efficiency, customer experience, and competitive advantage. Integration of physical and digital channels, such as the Omnichannel retailing, has occurred in recent times as a dominant strategy in response to ever-changing consumer demands. Past studies highlight the reputation of rendering seamless transitions across several channels, allowing customers to shop in-store, online, or using mobile apps with consistent shopping experiences [1]. Studies also noted that omnichannel strategies help in increasing customer engagement and future retention by providing enhanced personalized shopping experiences [5]. Customer convenience is enhanced through omnichannel by offering flexible return options, purchasing, and integrated loyalty programs [9]. However, there are several challenges for retailers in the complexity of managing multiple touchpoints, to ensure consistent inventory management, communication, and pricing strategy across all channels [10]. AI technologies have gained much traction in retail for automating tasks, enhancing personalization, and improving decision-making processes [11]. Some of the common applications of artificial intelligence in omnichannel retail include (a) AI-powered recommendation systems [12], (b) chatbots and virtual assistants [13], (c) predictive analytics [14], (d) supply chain optimization [15], and several others.

Several researches in the recent times have attempted to explore the integration of AI in impacting omnichannel customer experiences. A study exploring the integration of AI in the omnichannel customer experience [16] highlights the impact of AI on customer journeys, focusing on personalization and consistency of cross-channels in omnichannel retailing. Emphasizing how AI-driven demand forecasting and supply chain visibility streamline fulfillment [17], the study examined the role of AI in omnichannel logistics and inventory management. Application of AI in supply chain resilience for a seamless omnichannel experience are supported by key factors such as demand prediction, exploring inventory allocation, and real-time order tracking [18]. In a specific study focusing on post-pandemic retail [19], the authors discussed high potential for AI support in omnichannel recovery by adapting channel interactions and enhancing customer engagement. In this study [20], the authors argued that AI-enabled product recommendation systems for omnichannel retail render benefits of dynamic personalization based on real-time data from various channels. Chatbots and AI-enabled virtual assistants also enable improvements in customer support across channels, facilitating better user experiences and contributing to sales growth [21]. The role of Predictive analytics' in omnichannel retail has led to better contributions of AI towards inventory and pricing optimization through customer purchase forecasting [22]. It is also seen that AI enhances omnichannel marketing by creating relevant personalized promotions and content creation across customer touchpoints, in turn boosting customer engagement and loyalty [23]. AI has also been quite prominent in providing seamless transitions across retail channels, increase customer satisfaction through coherent experiences [24]. The role of AI has been evolutionary in ensuring data privacy and security within omnichannel environments, focusing on customer trust and ethical considerations in the post-pandemic era [25].

Despite the extensive research on AI and omnichannel retailing, few studies have examined the intersection of these two areas in a comparative, cross-case format. While AI's role in e-commerce has been explored, the convergence of online and offline experiences through AI integration in omnichannel retail remains under-researched. Additionally, existing literature often focuses on individual AI applications, such as chatbots or recommendation systems, without investigating how multiple AI technologies work together to enhance the overall customer experience. Furthermore, while many studies focus on consumer-facing technologies, there is a gap in understanding how AI impacts operational efficiency and backend processes that support the omnichannel experience. For instance, research on AI in supply chain optimization and its influence on customer satisfaction in an omnichannel context is limited. This study addresses these gaps by conducting a cross-case analysis of AI integration in omnichannel retail, examining both customer-facing and operational AI applications across different retail sectors. The findings are expected to provide a more comprehensive understanding of how AI technologies collectively enhance the omnichannel customer experience and offer practical insights for retailers.

3 Methodology

This study employs a qualitative cross-case analysis research design to examine omnichannel customer experience strategies enabled by AI across three prominent retail companies, namely Amazon, Walmart, and Sephora. Cross-case analysis is particularly useful for comparing variations and identifying patterns across cases, as it provides depth and nuanced insights into organizational practices and strategy implementations [26]. The strategy allows us to explore commonalities and differences in how each company integrates AI to enhance customer experiences across channels, thus revealing industry best practices and unique approaches. Expert interviews with key stakeholders from each of the three case companies include (a) a senior manager with over 8+ years of work experience in product management and AI development team from Amazon involved in design and implementation of customer experience enhancements using AI technologies, (b) a supply chain executive with Walmart with over 12+ years of work experience overseeing predictive analytics and inventory management systems who shares insights on strategic use of AI in logistics optimization and customer engagement across multiple channels, and (c) a marketing and customer experience specialist from Sephora with over 7+ years of experience in implementation of AI tools for personalization and customer services, particularly for virtual assistants and personalized product recommendations. The detailed insights are integrated in case descriptions and their analysis in further sections.

Data collection involved gathering secondary data from company reports, industry publications, press releases, and peer-reviewed articles to document the strategies employed by each retailer. Additionally, case studies, relevant research publications, and organizational documents were analyzed to construct a comprehensive understanding of each company's omnichannel and AI integration strategies. It is understood that secondary data sources better align with a case study approach, providing robust information and is quite cost-effective [27].

A systematic coding process is implemented to identify and categorize key themes for analysis across cases. Thematic segments were derived, such as AI personalization, customer experience enhancement, customer service improvements, and supply chain optimization, by using a thematic coding approach. Each of the cases were analyzed separately before conducting cross-case comparisons to derive the unique practices and common themes. The examining of recurring themes and contrasting patterns across these cases assisted in identifying common themes [28], enabling a comprehensive understanding of AI-driven omnichannel strategies adopted in retail.

To explore how artificial intelligence (AI) integration could enhance omnichannel customer experiences in the retail e-commerce sector, this study implemented a **cross-case analysis** methodology. This approach enables comparative analysis of multiple retail case companies, offering deeper insights into common patterns and unique strategies in the adoption of AI technologies across diverse retail categories. Subsequent sections in this study detail the research design, criteria for case selection, data collection strategies, and data analysis techniques used. The study employs a qualitative research approach to investigate the impact of AI technologies on the omnichannel customer experience. A cross-case analysis was selected for its capability to compare and contrast diverse cases, providing both breadth and depth of understanding. This approach is particularly suited for researching complex, multi-faceted phenomena, for instance the AI-driven customer experiences in omnichannel environments, where variables such as customer service, personalization, and operational efficiency intersect.

In this study, key model variables are defined to assess how AI integration impacts the omnichannel customer experience. **AI-Driven Personalization** serves as an independent variable, representing the use of recommendation engines, predictive analytics, and automated support tools to tailor experiences, which has been shown to boost conversion rates and customer loyalty [20, 21]. **Cross-Channel Consistency** acts as a mediating variable, emphasizing the need for coherence across physical, online, and mobile channels, a critical factor in creating a unified shopping experience across touchpoints [16, 19]. **Operational Efficiency** is considered a moderating variable, focusing on AI's role in optimizing supply chain and inventory processes to support omnichannel consistency and responsiveness [17, 18]. **Customer Experience Enhancement** is the primary dependent variable, capturing aspects of satisfaction, personalization, and seamless transitions across channels, as supported by prior studies highlighting the importance of integrated, user-centered experiences in omnichannel settings [23, 24]. Together, these variables structure the analysis of AI-enhanced omnichannel strategies in retail contexts.

A purposive sampling method was used to select retail companies that have implemented AI technologies as part of their omnichannel strategies. The selected companies vary in terms of size, industry focus, and geographical reach, ensuring a diverse representation of the retail e-commerce landscape. Criteria for inclusion in the study were:

(a) The company must have incorporated AI technologies (e.g., recommendation systems, chatbots, inventory management) into its omnichannel strategy.
(b) The study includes companies from various sectors such as fashion, electronics, and grocery to account for industry-specific applications of AI.

(c) Companies were chosen from both global and regional markets to explore different market dynamics in AI adoption.

The final selection includes three retail e-commerce companies, representing a balance of industry sectors and market coverage.

Conceptual and theoretical framework for the Study

The study integrates the key constructs of omnichannel retailing and AI-driven personalization to evaluate customer experience enhancement. Omnichannel retailing theory emphasizes providing a seamless shopping experience across physical and digital channels, promoting flexibility and enhancing customer satisfaction [1, 9]. It underscores the need for consistency and smooth transitions between channels, a cornerstone for creating effective omnichannel strategies. Also, the Customer Experience (CX) Theory forms the foundation for understanding how AI-enabled personalization impacts the omnichannel journey, drawing from established models that prioritize user-centric design, real-time responsiveness, and personalization in customer service [29]. As AI applications such as recommendation systems, chatbots, and predictive analytics gain prominence, they align with CX theory's focus on enhancing satisfaction through tailored experiences and efficient service [11]. Another popular theory, such as the Resource-Based View (RBV) is also relevant, providing insight into how AI technology serves as a strategic resource for operational efficiency in omnichannel contexts, allowing retailers to leverage AI to streamline logistics, manage inventory, and ensure real-time stock availability across channels [17]. This framework establishes the research gap in identifying how AI personalization impacts omnichannel experience in retail settings, particularly in balancing operational efficiency with customer experience.

While previous studies have focused on individual channel performance, this study aims to bridge the gap by evaluating the cross-channel effects of AI integration, highlighting best practices and unique challenges in achieving seamless omnichannel experiences.

Scope of the Study

This research study focuses on enhancing the omnichannel customer experience through the adaptations of artificial intelligence (AI) technologies in retail e-commerce. It specifically examines three prominent retail companies—Amazon, Walmart, and Sephora—analyzing how their unique AI strategies improve customer engagement, personalization, and overall satisfaction across various shopping channels. The study aims to identify best practices, challenges, and the effectiveness of different AI applications within an omnichannel framework, contributing to the broader understanding of retail strategies in a rapidly evolving digital landscape.

Delimitations

The study is delimited to three specific retail companies known for their innovative use of AI in enhancing customer experiences, thus excluding other retailers who may not have fully adopted or implemented similar technologies. Further, the focus is primarily on in-store and online customer interactions, omitting the broader aspects, namely the backend operations or supply chain management that may not directly impact the customer experience. The data collection timelines will be constricted to recent strategies and innovations during the period 2020 to 2025, warranting that the findings reflect the latest technologies and trends in omnichannel retail.

Relevance

Rapid advancements in technology, and increasing consumer expectations for a responsive and seamless shopping experiences across multiple channels is deeply relevant in current retail environment. E-commerce evolution has further challenged retailers to understand how AI could enhance customer interactions for higher competitiveness and improvements in customer loyalty [5, 10]. This study investigates the interplay between omnichannel strategies and AI technology integrations, to provide actionable insights for retailers intending to optimize their customer engagement practices and operational strategies.

4 Case Descriptions

An overview of each of the selected case company descriptions, namely Amazon, Walmart, and Sephora are highlighting in this section about their specific AI-driven omnichannel initiatives tailored to their unique business contexts. For instance, it is observed that Amazon leverages AI for personalized recommendations, and efficient inventory management. Walmart harnesses the potential of predictive analytics for demand forecasting and logistics streamlining. Sephora specifically focuses on enhancing customer interactions through AI-powered personalized beauty experiences and virtual assistants [11, 17, 21].

4.1 Case 1: Amazon

Amazon's omnichannel approach is well designed to create a cohesive customer experience in its ability across multiple platforms, including its mobile apps, website, smart devices (e.g., Alexa), and several of its physical retail stores, such as Whole Foods and Amazon Go. Amazon perfectly blends offline and online experiences ensuring that customers can shop anytime, anywhere, and through any device. One of the key driving components associated with this strategy is the integration of AI technology, which underpins its vast ecosystem of features and services.

Amazon has adopted a wide range of AI technologies to optimize both the front-end customer experience and the back-end operational processes that support it. Some of the most notable AI implementations include:

Personalization Algorithms: Amazon's recommendation engine is one of its most recognized AI applications, using collaborative filtering and machine learning models to offer highly personalized product suggestions. The system continuously learns from customer behavior, preferences, and purchase history to enhance product discovery across all channels, from the website to the mobile app.

Amazon Alexa and Voice Commerce: Amazon's AI-powered virtual assistant, Alexa, plays a central role in enhancing customer engagement. Alexa enables voice-activated shopping, product searches, and customer service. Integrating Alexa into the customer journey allows for a frictionless experience, particularly for customers interacting across different devices (smartphones, smart home devices, etc.).

Amazon Go Stores (Just Walk Out Technology): In its physical stores, such as Amazon Go, the company uses AI in the form of sensor fusion, computer vision, and deep learning to offer a superior shopping experience where it would be cashier-less. Customers can walk into the store, pick-up purchase items, and walk out without having to go through traditional checkout processes. The system is designed to automatically detect the cart items and transacts with the customer's Amazon account, creating a seamless integration between offline and online shopping.

AI-Powered Customer Service: Amazon uses AI-driven chatbots and virtual assistants to handle a large portion of customer service inquiries, including tracking orders, processing returns, and answering product-related questions. Response times are improved and overall customer satisfaction is enhancing through such strategy.

Supply Chain Optimization and Inventory Management: AI is extensively used in the backend for inventory management, demand forecasting, and optimization of the supply chain. Machine learning models effortlessly predict demand fluctuations, allowing Amazon to efficiently manage their stock, and ensure product availability across multiple channels. It drastically diminishes stockout situations and enhances the omnichannel shopping experience, providing real-time updates on delivery times and product availability.

Customer Experience Outcomes: AI-driven strategies by Amazon have also resulted in several noteworthy improvements to the omnichannel customer experience.

Enhanced Personalization: Superior customer engagement is achieved using the recommendation engine that offers personalized product suggestions, enhanced customer satisfaction, and higher conversion rates. The seamless integration of personalized recommendations across the mobile app, website, and Alexa devices enables customers to experience reliable personalization regardless of the channels they engage.

Frictionless Shopping: Technologies such as the 'Just Walk Out' implemented by Amazon Go stores exemplifies the company's commitment in dropping the friction points in the customer journey. Customers can smoothly transition between offline and online shopping experiences without bumping into usual barriers, such as complex returns processes or long checkout lines.

Efficient Customer Service: Chatbots and virtual assistants powered through AI-assisted customer services has improved both customer support and response times. Automated routine inquiries via Amazon ensures that customers receive rapid customer service, enhanced overall satisfaction, especially in seasonal high-demand situations.

Real-Time Fulfillment: AI integration in supply chain and inventory management ensures that Amazon products are available as and when customers need these. AI assist in predicting demand, reducing delivery times, and informed customers on the status of their orders, leading to a more consistent and reliable omnichannel experience.

Challenges and Considerations: Amazon faces numerous challenges in AI integration despite its key success factors. Developing and maintaining sophisticated AI systems have led to increased cost implications, data privacy concerns especially with Just Walk Out and Alexa technology. Potential dehumanization of customer interactions could be a growing security concern as we automate all processes, and certain customer segments that prefer personal, human touchpoints could be deeply affected.

4.2 Case 2: Walmart

Walmart has made significant strides in integrating artificial intelligence (AI) into its omnichannel retail strategy to improve operational efficiency and boost customer experiences. As a major player in both physical and online retail, Walmart's omnichannel approach focuses on creating a seamless shopping experience across digital platforms, brick-and-mortar stores, and mobile devices. This case explores Walmart's use of AI in driving customer engagement, personalization, and operational optimization within its omnichannel ecosystem.

Walmart's omnichannel strategy emphasizes providing a unified shopping experience for customers, regardless of where or how they choose to shop. The company's approach integrates online shopping, mobile applications, physical stores, and innovative delivery options, such as curbside pickup and home delivery. The core of Walmart's omnichannel success lies in its ability to blend the convenience of e-commerce with the scale and reach of its physical retail infrastructure, supported by robust AI technologies.

Walmart has invested heavily in AI to streamline customer interactions and back-end operations, aiming to match the personalized convenience offered by e-commerce competitors while leveraging its vast physical presence. By using AI, Walmart enhances its customer service, inventory management, and personalization efforts to create a seamless, connected customer experience.

Walmart has implemented a range of AI technologies to enhance both the customer experience and its internal processes. Key AI-driven applications include:

Personalized Shopping Recommendations. Walmart's AI-powered recommendation engine analyzes customer browsing behavior, purchase history, and preferences to offer personalized product suggestions across its website, mobile app, and in-store digital platforms. By leveraging machine learning, Walmart tailors its product recommendations to meet the specific needs of individual customers, enhancing engagement and increasing conversion rates.

Walmart Voice Ordering (via Google Assistant). Walmart integrates voice-activated shopping capabilities through Google Assistant, enabling customers to order products using voice commands. This integration of AI into voice commerce provides an easy, hands-free shopping experience, permitting customers to add purchase items to their cart, reorder past purchases, and check prices effortlessly.

AI-Powered Customer Service. Walmart employs AI-driven chatbots and virtual agents to handle customer service inquiries, such as answering questions about product availability, tracking orders, and processing returns. These chatbots, available through Walmart's mobile app or website, help reduce the response times and better customer satisfaction achieved through quick and accurate resolutions to common queries.

Inventory Management and Supply Chain Optimization. Walmart ensures that products are available in the right quantities and locations by optimization across its digital and physical channels. Algorithms supported with machine learning are able to predict demand trends and adjust existing stock levels in real time mode, minimizing overstock or stockouts situations. AI-driven supply chain leverages predictive analytics to streamline logistics, ensuring minimized fulfillment costs and rapid deliveries.

AI in In-Store Operations. Walmart uses AI-powered robots for instore operations to assist with restocking, shelf scanning, and achieving inventory accuracy. These robotic systems track inventory levels, identify stockout items, and support with replenishment. This ensures that relevant products are always available for their customers, both in-store and online.

Enhanced Personalization. Personalization assisted through AI has resulted in superior customer engagement and higher conversion rates. By providing personalized product recommendations and customized promotions, Walmart is able to ensure that the products presented to customers match their choices and preferences, whether they shop in-store or online.

Seamless Shopping Experience. Customers can now shop across multiple channels without interruptions, switching from in-store pickup to online browsing with ease. Integration of enhanced technologies, such as voice commerce through Google Assistant, coupled with Walmart's website and mobile app resources provides customers with a frictionless shopping experience. The combination of AI-driven customer service and personalized recommendations helps Walmart meet customer expectations for efficiency and convenience.

Efficient Order Fulfillment. Walmart's order fulfillment process is improvised through AI-powered inventory and supply chain management strategies that ensure products are available across all touchpoints. Accurately predicting the demand and optimization of stock levels, Walmart has achieved reduced instances of out-of-stock products and improved delivery times. This has also enhances the overall customer experience.

Improved In-Store Experience. AI-powered robots in Walmart stores ensures that customers can find the products with ease shelves as these are consistently stocked accurately. An efficient shopping experience is ensured for in-store customers, reducing frustration caused due to unavailable items or any poorly stocked shelves.

Walmart has made significant investment in integration of AI technology in their retail. Still, it faces challenges similar to those of other giant retailers. It is quite complex and costly to implementing AI across such vast networks whether physical or digital platforms, especially when integrating newer and modern technologies with legacy systems. Walmart must navigate the privacy concerns, especially while usage of AI to collect and analyze customer information. Ensuring highest data security while also providing personalized experiences is indeed a delicate balance. Even though AI-driven chatbots and virtual assistants improve response times, still few customers could prefer interacting with human representatives, particularly for complex or high-stakes inquiries.

4.3 Case 3: Sephora

Sephora is widely recognized as a global beauty retailer. It is prominently known for its innovative use of artificial intelligence (AI) for enhancing omnichannel customer experiences. Sephora's digital transformation has positioned the brand as a global leader in leveraging AI technology to create customized beauty experiences, both in-store and online. This case study examines how Sephora succeeded in integrating AI into its omnichannel strategy, focusing on customer engagement, personalization, and operational efficiency to deliver an engaging and seamless shopping journey.

Sephora's omnichannel strategy focuses on creating an immersive beauty experience across multiple touchpoints, including its website, mobile app, physical stores, and several social media platforms. By blending the digital and physical worlds, Sephora provides its customers with an integrated beauty journey. It allows customers to explore products online, in-store, and via mobile devices with personalized and consistent interactions. Recognizing the importance of personalization in the beauty industry, AI is highly used to offer personalized product recommendations, virtual try-on tools, and personalized customer support. Sephora has a unique approach that places strong emphasis on combining AI-driven digital tools with human expertise. This ensures that customers receive both the benefits of technological advancements and personalized human touchpoints through beauty advisors.

AI-Powered Product Recommendations: Sephora uses powerful algorithms integrated with machine learning to analyze customer data. This allows browsing history, beauty preferences, and purchase patterns to offer customized product suggestions. Such AI-driven personalization is well integrated across all channels—mobile, online, and in-store—ensuring that customers enjoy relevant recommendations personalized to their beauty needs.

Virtual Try-On Tools (Sephora Virtual Artist): The virtual try-on tool, powered by augmented reality (AR) and AI, is one of Sephora's most prominent innovative AI applications. Sephora Virtual Artist enables customers to virtually try on makeup products, such as foundation, lipstick, and eyeshadow, through their smartphone or in-store digital kiosks. The AI-based tool helps analyze customer's facial features, and create realistic simulation of how products would look on their skin. This technology assists in decision-making process and enhances customer confidence in online purchases.

AI-Driven Skincare and Makeup Diagnostics: Color IQ and Skin Tone IQ are unique AI powered tools that help customers search products that match with their skin tones. It helps analyze the customer's skin tones and recommend suitable products that could match with customer's specific beauty needs. Such technology is available both in-store and online, ensuring a seamless omnichannel experience.

AI-Powered Virtual Assistants and Chatbots: AI-driven virtual assistants and chatbots are used to provide customized customer support across its mobile app and website touchpoints. These AI-virtual assistants help customers find suitable products, responses to beauty-related questions, and advice on skincare and makeup based on individual preferences. It also facilitates product searches, customer service tasks and other order tracking elements, enhancing engagement and convenience.

Personalized Beauty Experiences: AI-driven recommendation engine and diagnostic tools provided by Sephora allow customers to receive customized beauty recommendations personalized to their skin type, preferences, and past behavior. This creates a more engaging and relevant shopping experience, both in-store and online. Customers can seamlessly transition between channels without compromising on the personalized touch. Also, their purchase history and preferences are well integrated across all platforms.

Virtual Try-On Tools and Increased Confidence in Purchases: An AI-based virtual try-on feature, such as the 'Sephora Virtual Artist' has revolutionized the manner in which customers shop for beauty products online. Customers can visualize how different makeups will match with their skin. Sephora increases customer confidence in their purchase decisions, and hence higher conversion rates and fewer returns are possible.

Enhanced Customer Support: AI-powered virtual assistants from Sephora provide customers with customized support, answers to specific questions about beauty products and tailored recommendations. Improved response times and increased customer satisfaction are achieved by Sephora. by offering instant guidance and assistance.

Seamless Integration of In-Store and Online Experiences: The omnichannel retail approach by Sephora ensures that customers can seamlessly transition between offline and online shopping. For instance, customers can use their mobile app to search products in-store or use virtual try-on tools via online prior to visiting a physical store. Such seamless integration creates an engaging customer journey that encourages repeat purchases and superior brand loyalty.

Sephora faces several challenges in maintaining a balance between technology-driven personalization and the human touch. While AI-powered tools enhance engagement and convenience, few customers may still prefer the physical and personal interaction with in-store beauty advisors. Balancing AI tools with human expertise is critical to ensuring that customers receive satisfying and well-rounded experience. Additionally, concerns about data privacy and security are at large, especially given the sensitive nature of personal beauty information the customers, such as skin tone and facial features. Sephora must ensure that it complies with data protection regulations and maintains customer trust at all times about the use of their personal information.

5 Cross-Case Analysis

The three cases are examined within a comparative framework to identify common themes, challenges, and strategic insights related to AI-driven omnichannel initiatives, enabling a nuanced understanding of how these leading retailers navigate their unique business contexts while enhancing customer experiences [26–28].

The comprehensive cross-case analysis is depicted as a tabulation summarization of the three case companies based on specific aspects of context, thematic, impact assessment, common challenges, and best practices in AI implementation (insert Table 1 here, refer Appendix A) in their pursuit of enhancing the omnichannel customer experience through AI integration.

6 Results and Discussions

The integration of AI technologies into omnichannel retail strategies has yielded significant insights into how these tools enhance customer experiences and operational efficiency. This section discusses the key findings from the cross-case analysis of Amazon, Walmart, and Sephora, particularly in response to each of the research questions posed.

RQ1: How does AI integration enhance the omnichannel experience in retail e-commerce?

AI integration enhances the omnichannel experience by creating a seamless shopping journey that allows customers to transition effortlessly between online and offline channels. For instance, Amazon's use of advanced recommendation systems personalizes the shopping experience by suggesting products based on individual customer behaviour, thereby increasing engagement and satisfaction [5]. Similarly, Walmart employs predictive analytics to ensure that popular products are stocked appropriately, which reduces frustration for customers trying to purchase items both online and in-store [10]. Sephora's virtual try-on technology allows customers to experience products digitally before making a purchase, further blending the physical and digital shopping environments [11]. The ability to integrate customer data across channels not only personalizes experiences but also fosters brand loyalty.

RQ2: What are the most effective AI technologies used in retail e-commerce for omnichannel enhancement?

The analysis identifies several AI technologies as particularly effective in enhancing the omnichannel experience. Recommendation systems stand out as a primary tool for personalizing customer interactions, as seen with Amazon's tailored product suggestions [12]. Chatbots and virtual assistants are also critical, particularly for Walmart and Sephora, as they provide real-time customer support and streamline transactions [13]. Predictive analytics are vital for inventory management and marketing strategies, allowing retailers to align stock levels with consumer demand effectively [14]. Each company showcases how AI technologies can be tailored to meet specific business needs while enhancing the overall shopping experience.

RQ3: How do customer experiences differ across retail platforms with varying degrees of AI integration?

Customer experiences differ significantly across the three case companies, correlating directly with the level of AI integration. Amazon's comprehensive use of AI leads to a highly personalized experience that resonates well with tech-savvy consumers who expect immediate and relevant recommendations. In contrast, while Walmart has made strides in AI integration, the customer experience remains more traditional due to its legacy operations, which sometimes leads to a disjointed omnichannel experience [10]. Sephora's emphasis on interactive AI tools such as augmented reality enhances customer engagement in a way that transforms the shopping experience into a more immersive journey, appealing particularly to younger demographics [11]. Thus, the findings suggest that a higher degree of AI integration correlates with improved customer satisfaction and loyalty.

Implications of the Study

The findings from this cross-case analysis highlight the transformative potential of AI technologies in retail. Companies that effectively leverage AI can create personalized, efficient, and engaging shopping experiences that drive customer loyalty and operational efficiency. As competition in the retail sector intensifies, embracing AI-driven strategies will be crucial for maintaining a competitive edge. Additionally, understanding the specific technologies that resonate with consumers can inform future investments and strategic planning in retail operations. Overall, this research underscores the importance of aligning AI capabilities with customer expectations to optimize the omnichannel retail experience.

Validity and Reliability (Data Triangulation)

Using a data triangulation approach with multiple data sources or methods assists in enhancing the credibility and trustworthiness of research results [30, 31]. In this cross-case analysis, data were gathered through interviews with key stakeholders, analysis of company reports, and examination of existing literature on AI applications in retail. Interviews with the representatives from case companies under study, namely the Amazon, Walmart, and Sephora provided firsthand insights about the specific AI-driven initiatives each employ. This ensured that the findings are grounded in actual practices and experiences. A cross-referencing of findings from interviews with cohesive literature and case studies, reduced the potential for bias and increases the overall reliability of the conclusions drawn [27]. Employing established theoretical frameworks and models for analysis further strengthens the reliability of the research findings.

An examination of the AI integration initiatives implemented by case companies Amazon, Walmart, and Sephora, relevant annual reports from key industry bodies, and government institutions serve as essential references for establishing checks and balances. For instance, the National Retail Federation (NRF) provides much comprehensive insights into retail trends, including the adoption of AI technologies and their effects on customer experiences [32]. The annual reports published by the U.S. Department of Commerce detail the impact of technological advancements on e-commerce. It offers critical context about understanding how these companies leverage AI to enhance their omnichannel pursuits [33]. The World Economic Forum report highlights global trends in retail technology, and enlightens on the competitive landscape faced by companies like Amazon, Walmart, and Sephora in implementing innovative solutions to satisfy ever-changing consumer preferences [34].

The validity and reliability of these case studies are reinforced through the use of established theoretical and conceptual frameworks. These guide the analysis of AI integration in omnichannel retail among Amazon, Walmart, and Sephora. Using a cross-case analysis methodology, the study captures the nuances of AI technology implementations in diverse business contexts, which enhance the robustness of the study findings [28]. The triangulation of data sources— insights from existing literature, interviews with industry experts, and analysis of company reports—further supports the credibility of the results [26]. Additionally, the application of established research models, for instance the Unified Theory of Acceptance and Use of Technology (UTAUT), and the Technology Acceptance Model (TAM) provides a solid theoretical foundation for interpreting the findings [35]. As a result, deeper insights developed from this research greatly contributes to the academic discourse on omnichannel strategies, and offers relevant practical implications for retailers aiming to enhance customer experiences through AI, confirming the relevance and applicability of the study's findings across the retail sector.

7 Conclusions

In conclusion, this research study significantly contributes to the deeper understanding of AI-enhanced omnichannel strategies in retail, particularly through the detailed cross-case analysis of Amazon, Walmart, and Sephora. The findings underscore the transformative impact of AI integration on customer experience and operational efficiency, highlighting how personalized interactions and streamlined processes can lead to increased customer satisfaction and loyalty [1, 11]. However, the study also acknowledges its limitations, including the potential biases in qualitative interviews and the focus on only three companies, which may not fully represent the broader retail landscape. Future research should explore a more extensive range of retail companies and consider longitudinal studies to assess the long-term effects of AI integration on customer behaviors and retail performance. Additionally, examining the ethical implications of AI technologies and their impact on employment within the retail sector presents another promising avenue for investigation [15, 36]. In one of the recent studies, the authors [37] demonstrate using a SAP-LAP analysis for an eCom case company, that omnichannel strategies are highly significant in producing an integrated and seamless customer experience across several channels. By addressing these areas, future studies can build on this foundation and contribute further to the development of effective omnichannel strategies in an increasingly digital retail environment.

Appendix "A"

Table 1. Summary of Cross-Case Analysis based on Specific Aspects *(Source: Author(s) compilations)*

Aspect	Amazon	Walmart	Sephora
Context Analysis	Focuses on e-commerce with extensive online presence; utilizes advanced AI for personalized recommendations [5]	Strong brick-and-mortar presence; integrates AI to enhance supply chain efficiency and customer service [10]	Operates in the beauty industry; leverages AI for personalized beauty experiences and virtual try-ons [11]
Thematic Analysis	Themes of personalization and convenience dominate; extensive use of data analytics [29]	Themes of operational efficiency and inventory management are central [15]	Themes of customer engagement and interactive technology in retail settings [9]
Impact Assessment	High conversion rates due to tailored experiences; maintains market leadership through continuous innovation [14]	Improved customer satisfaction through better product availability and optimized pricing strategies [5]	Increased customer retention and loyalty due to personalized experiences [13]

(continued)

Table 1. (*continued*)

Aspect	Amazon	Walmart	Sephora
Common Challenges	Maintaining seamless integration across online and physical stores; data privacy concerns [29]	Complexity in managing multiple channels and data compliance issues [15]	Resistance to change from employees; need for continuous training in new technologies [11]
Best Practices in AI Implementations	Customer-centric approach with a strong focus on data-driven insights; cross-functional collaboration [14]	Emphasis on continuous adaptation and ethical considerations in data usage [15]	Training programs for employees to effectively utilize AI technologies; commitment to transparency in AI applications [29]

References

1. Verhoef, P.C., Kannan, P.K., Inman, J.J.: From multi-channel retailing to omni-channel retailing: Introduction to the special issue on multi-channel retailing. J. Retail. **91**(2), 174–181 (2015). https://doi.org/10.1016/j.jretai.2015.02.005
2. Piotrowicz, W., Cuthbertson, R.: Introduction to omnichannel retailing. Int. J. Retail Distrib. Manag. **42**(8/9), 522–536 (2014). https://doi.org/10.1108/IJRDM-03-2014-0058
3. Rigby, D.: The future of shopping. Harv. Bus. Rev. **89**(12), 65–76 (2011)
4. Lemon, K.N., Verhoef, P.C.: Understanding customer experience throughout the customer journey. J. Mark. **80**(6), 69–96 (2016). https://doi.org/10.1509/jm.15.0420
5. Brynjolfsson, E., Hu, Y.J., Rahman, M.S.: Competing in the age of omnichannel retailing. MIT Sloan Manag. Rev. **54**(4), 23–29 (2013)
6. Davenport, T.H., Guha, A., Grewal, D., Bressgott, T.: How artificial intelligence will change the future of marketing. J. Acad. Mark. Sci. **48**(1), 24–42 (2020). https://doi.org/10.1007/s11747-019-00696-0
7. Shankar, V.: How artificial intelligence (AI) is reshaping retailing. J. Retail. **94**(4), vi–xi (2018). https://doi.org/10.1016/j.jretai.2018.10.005
8. Bock, S., Osterwalder, F., Vogt, M.: Artificial intelligence in supply chain management: a decision support perspective. Comput. Ind. Eng. **144**, 106476 (2020). https://doi.org/10.1016/j.cie.2020.106476
9. Juaneda-Ayensa, E., Mosquera, A., Sierra Murillo, Y.: Omnichannel customer behavior: key drivers of technology acceptance and use and their effects on purchase intention. Front. Psychol. **7**, 1117 (2016). https://doi.org/10.3389/fpsyg.2016.01117
10. Beck, N., Rygl, D.: Categorization of multiple channel retailing in multi-, cross-, and omnichannel retailing for retailers and retailing. J. Retail. Consum. Serv. **27**, 170–178 (2015). https://doi.org/10.1016/j.jretconser.2015.08.001
11. Huang, M.H., Rust, R.T.: Artificial intelligence in service. J. Serv. Res. **21**(2), 155–172 (2018). https://doi.org/10.1177/1094670517752459
12. Bodapati, A.V.: Recommendation systems with purchase data. J. Mark. Res. **45**(1), 77–93 (2008). https://doi.org/10.1509/jmkr.45.1.77
13. Chung, M., Ko, E., Joung, H., Kim, S.J.: Chatbot e-service and customer satisfaction regarding luxury brands. J. Bus. Res. **117**, 587–595 (2020). https://doi.org/10.1016/j.jbusres.2018.10.004

14. Wang, G., Gunasekaran, A., Ngai, E.W.T., Papadopoulos, T.: Big data analytics in logistics and supply chain management: certain investigations for research and applications. Int. J. Prod. Econ. **176**, 98–110 (2016). https://doi.org/10.1016/j.ijpe.2016.03.014
15. Choi, T.M., Wallace, S.W., Wang, Y.: Big data analytics in operations management. Prod. Oper. Manag. **27**(10), 1868–1883 (2020). https://doi.org/10.1111/poms.12838
16. Calvo, A.V., Franco, A.D., Frasquet, M.: Exploring AI integration for personalized omnichannel customer journeys. Int. J. Retail Distrib. Manag. **51**(4), 489–507 (2023)
17. Mangiaracina, R., Perego, A., Salvador, G.: Omnichannel logistics and inventory management using AI. Transp. Res. Part E: Logist. Transp. Rev. **147**, 102244 (2021)
18. Choi, T.-M., Guo, S.: AI and supply chain resilience in omnichannel retailing. IEEE Trans. Eng. Manage. **69**(5), 1568–1580 (2022)
19. Verhoef, P.C., Neslin, S.A.: The impact of omnichannel on retail recovery post-COVID-19. J. Retail. **96**(4), 484–499 (2020)
20. Li, Y., Huang, M.: Real-time data for personalized product recommendations in omnichannel retail. Decis. Support. Syst. **140**, 113450 (2021)
21. Kumar, A., Gupta, R.: AI-enabled virtual assistants and their impact on omnichannel customer service. J. Interact. Mark. **59**, 102–115 (2023)
22. Simms, M., Peterson, R.A.: Predictive analytics for pricing and inventory in omnichannel retail. J. Retail. Consum. Serv. **64**, 102770 (2022)
23. Bolton, R.N., Saxena-Iyer, S.: Enhancing customer loyalty in omnichannel retail through AI-enabled personalized marketing. J. Retail. **99**(2), 345–362 (2023)
24. Grewal, D., Stephen, A.T.: Seamless omnichannel transitions and AI's impact on customer satisfaction. J. Mark. **85**(6), 117–133 (2021)
25. Greenwald, J., Chang, Y.: Data privacy and ethical implications of AI in omnichannel retail. J. Bus. Ethics **132**(1), 121–139 (2024)
26. Yin, R.K.: Case study research and applications: Design and methods (6th ed.). Sage Publications (2018)
27. Stake, R.E.: The art of case study research. Sage Publications (1995)
28. Eisenhardt, K.M.: Building theories from case study research. Acad. Manag. Rev. **14**(4), 532–550 (1989). https://doi.org/10.5465/amr.1989.4308385
29. Grewal, D., Roggeveen, A.L.: Understanding retail experiences and customer journey management. J. Retail. **96**(1), 3–8 (2020). https://doi.org/10.1016/j.jretai.2020.02.002
30. Denzin, N.K.: The Research Act: A Theoretical Introduction to Sociological Methods. Aldine (1978)
31. Flick, U.: An Introduction to Qualitative Research (6th ed.). SAGE Publications (2018)
32. National Retail Federation (NRF). Retail Industry Trends Report. National Retail Federation (2023)
33. U.S. Department of Commerce: E-Commerce and Digital Economy 2023. Government Printing Office, U.S (2023)
34. World Economic Forum. The Future of Retail: AI and the New Consumer Experience. World Economic Forum (2023)
35. Venkatesh, V., Thong, J.Y.L., Xu, X.: Consumer acceptance and use of information technology: extending the unified theory of acceptance and use of technology. MIS Q. **36**(1), 157–178 (2012). https://doi.org/10.2307/41410412
36. Brynjolfsson, E., McAfee, A.: The Second Machine Age: Work, Progress, and Prosperity in a Time of Brilliant Technologies. W. W. Norton & Company (2014)
37. Kasat, K., Shaikh, N., Iyengar, V.: Omnichannel Strategy Adoption Issues in an eCommerce Company: A SAP-LAP Analysis. In: International Conference on Science, Engineering Management and Information Technology, (pp. 245–257). Cham: Springer Nature Switzerland (2023). https://doi.org/10.1007/978-3-031-72287-5_15

A Review of a Decade of Academic Research on Emotional Intelligence: A Bibliometric Approach

Naval Lawande(✉)

Symbiosis Institute of Management Studies, Symbiosis International (Deemed University), Pune, India
naval.lawande@gmail.com

Abstract. Emotional intelligence as a topic or concept is widespread, and numerous empirical, conceptual, and exploratory studies have been conducted in human resources, organizational behavior, business, and management. Nevertheless, no scientific mapping or attempt to map the literature scientifically in the domain has been done. Hence, the paper intends to showcase the trends in emotional intelligence research through the symbiosis of knowledge structures. An analysis using bibliometric tools in emotional intelligence was conducted. A sample of 12129 documents was extracted from the Scopus database. This was based on a search strategy determined by the author/researcher. The R-language was used for the study, which has a web-based application. It is included in the bibliometric package. This software enabled the analysis of the dataset, and various themes, patterns, and trends were identified based on the authors, countries, and citations. Results show that the field/domain of emotional intelligence needs direction. There is also a pressing need for interdisciplinary research in this area. The article provides some crucial insights on areas that need further inquiry. The conceptual and social network structure depicts a downward trend in terms of this area of research. The current paper only had the Scopus Database as its backdrop. Future researchers could use multiple databases, such as the Web of Science, and conduct a comparative study. A systematic literature review would widen the scope and also help identify some of the niche unchartered territories of emotional intelligence.

Keywords: Emotional Intelligence · Emotions · Emotional Quotient · Empathy · Self-awareness

1 Introduction

1.1 Importance of Emotional Intelligence

As one of the world's largest growing and emerging economies, India ought to develop its human resources as a source of competitive advantage. This can be accomplished if there is a future-oriented human resource strategy that focuses on the socio-behavioral traits of individuals. Emotional Intelligence (EI) is highly crucial in this context. [1]

A. Mirzazadeh et al. (Eds.): SEMIT 2024, CCIS 2444, pp. 274–291, 2026.
https://doi.org/10.1007/978-3-032-01948-6_18

Describe the EI concept primarily depicts the ability, capacity, skill, or, in the case of the trait model of EI, a self-perceived competence to identify, assess, and manage one's own and others' emotions. An individual with a high Emotional Quotient (EQ) will showcase a higher understanding of one's emotions, motivation, and sensing of others' emotions. Interestingly, EI is the capacity to identify emotions' meanings and relationships. [2] He defines EI as "the ability to recognize emotions, integrate emotion-related feelings, comprehend emotion-related information, and manage those emotions."

Intelligence is often visualized as mathematicians solving equations, pioneers researching their respective fields to further knowledge, or novelists writing literature. Nevertheless, one of the most popular intelligences(s) today is an individual's competence to understand, process, and manage one's emotions. A practice known as Emotional Intelligence is often ignored and given less importance in the pre-defined checklist of essential traits of a Manager [3].

Daniel Goleman introduced an Emotional Intelligence (EI) model that outlined four primary EI constructs: self–awareness, self–management, social awareness, and relationship management. As [4] aptly state, "Self–awareness is the ability to recognize one's emotions; self–management is the ability to manage or coordinate one's emotions; social awareness is the ability to understand the needs, emotions, or concerns of others; and relationship management is the ability to interact, establish or maintain relationships, and overcome conflicts." The ability-based model claims that EI includes four abilities: perceiving emotions, understanding emotions, using emotions, and managing emotions [5]. Negative self-talk can have enormous influence on perceived stress. Hence, evaluation of ones' emotions and emotional regulation become critical. Similarly, evaluation of others' emotions and emotional regulation would also explain the occurrence of negative self-talk. Likewise, the interaction between perceived stress and appraisal of one's own emotions would explain the occurrence of negative self-talk, this relationship being stronger among those with lower scores on appraisal of one's own emotions. This study on runners in Spain highlighted the importance of EI [6].

Some scholars in recent times have highlighted the association of emotional intelligence and wellbeing. The findings of this recent study suggested effectiveness of EI in improving basic skills and confirmed the efficacy and highlighted its importance in early stages of learning and training [7]. The importance of EI was also revealed from another study on investors in stock market in India. A positive relation among the various dimensions of emotional intelligence and investment decisions was highlighted [8]. The moderating effects of four emotional intelligence abilities can help regulate emotions of frontline managers. Results of a research demonstrated that negative emotions associated with work tasks can be regulated in ways that are determined by stable, situational, and personal factors. EI plays a pivotal role in this form of regulation of emotions [9].

1.2 Emotional Intelligence and Organizational Performance

Goleman & Boyatzis elaborate on the organizational benefits, "the interest in emotional intelligence in the workplace stems from the widespread recognition that these abilities – self-awareness, self-management, empathy, and social skill – separate the most successful workers and leaders from the average." [10] The last decade has seen significant growth in the concept and applications of EI. Its importance and relevance are felt even more in the business arena. EI is referred to as the critical element that influences employee performance. At the workplace, the transformation of a manager into a leader is claimed to be enormously dependent on emotional intelligence. EQ takes precedence over the intelligence quotient (IQ). Emotionally intelligent individuals are optimistic and always naturally work towards a personal, professional, or both. These folks have a growth mindset and endure in the face of adversity [11].

EI is becoming even more relevant for organizational growth and leadership development. The EQ principles, laid down and applied as the benchmark for comparison, have brought a new mechanism to comprehend and measure human behavior, leadership style, mindset, interpersonal skills, and their potential. Moreover, EI has become critical for various management processes and organizational functions [12].

Emotions play a pivotal role in decision-making and organizational performance. Certain behaviors can evoke emotions ranging from optimism and joy to frustration and anger. This would be an emotional rollercoaster for the individual and those around him [13]. It is well established that emotional intelligence is essential in an individual's effectiveness, efficiency, and overall productivity. Possessing a higher EQ enhances an individual's ability to solve problems he might be facing at any time [14]. Benefits of EI to organizational performance were confirmed through the findings of another study that revealed that organizational learning significantly and partially mediates the relationship between emotional intelligence and performance [15].

The results of a study on civil servants affirmed significant positive effect of Emotional Intelligence on Organizational Performance. Thereby suggesting the need for including EI indicators and measures in the areas of recruitment, learning and development, workforce planning, succession planning, and organizational development [16].

Similarly, in the evaluation of any organization, the existing Balance Scorecard approach of economic indicators should be supplemented by social-cultural aspects. The EQ of managers was found to be closely related both to the individual indicators of the organizational performance [17]. The influence of EI on conflict and performance was assessed. The results of a Global Virtual Team study showed that Emotional Quotient of the team members reduced the occurrence intragroup conflicts. Reducing conflicts also resulted in better performance of the teams [18].

This paper explores the significance of emotional intelligence competencies over the past decade. It is structured into several sections. After Sect. 1 – introduction (which includes research questions), Sect. 2 – highlights the Methodology that leads into Sect. 3 – elaborating on the data analysis. The Sect. 4 – concludes with a brief discussion of findings, limitations, and suggestions for further research.

1.3 Bibliometric Analysis

Bibliometric analysis is an excellent methodology that uses statistical and mathematical techniques. It helps analyse literature patterns from published articles. As [19] explain, "qualitative methods such as observation and interviews can also be used for analysis. However, bibliometric analysis is based on the science mapping approach. It applies the generic process of visualization and domain analysis, thereby allowing scientific mapping of both the scientific groups and research areas". Scholars from different research domains have used bibliometric analysis as a method for understanding published literature. There were no studies on bibliometric studies by [20] that could be identified in the domain of emotional intelligence. However, the domain of EI holds enormous weightage in today's day and age. Against this backdrop, the author reviewed the extracted literature with the astute emphasis on detecting the process of progression in the field of EI domain [21].

1.4 Research Questions

In light of this, the author carefully examined the literature that was extracted, paying particular attention to identifying the progression process in the EI domain [22].

Research questions:

1) "What is the overall structure of emotional intelligence in the community?".
2) "Are there any collaborative networks in emotional intelligence?".
3) "How is the evolution of the concept of emotional intelligence?".
4) "What are the most addressed issues recently?".

The questions mentioned above translate into the following research objectives:

1) To elicit patterns in the development of knowledge of emotional intelligence.
2) To investigate the knowledge structure and derive a synthesis of knowledge.

Network and descriptive types of analysis were used to attain the research objectives. Different sections of the paper touch upon the varied elements. The immediate section deals with the research methodology, followed by the section on data analysis. The following section post brings to light a discussion of the findings, while the research directions and conclusions are presented in the last section.

2 Methodology

2.1 Selection of Database

Below is the flow diagram of the bibliometric analysis. The analysis would need to identify the research database, followed by the data extraction based on the search approach. The nature of the data is secondary. The data required for the research was extracted after the author decided that 'Scopus' was the ideal database. A search query was run using the appropriate mixture of keywords. The dataset was established based on the inclusion and exclusion criteria. The data was then analyzed using the software tools. An initial descriptive analysis of the documents, sources, and authors was conducted. Principal component analysis and multiple correspondence analysis techniques were used for data reduction. A crucial pre-requisite for bibliometric analysis is a structured database description of indexed articles. Data retrieval was conducted from the 'Scopus' database. Based on Elsevier's Scopus coverage of articles and classification of journals, the database was linked to the Bibliometrix package in R-studio. To depict and better visualize the data, network maps were created. This study employs a bibliometric approach to analyse research publications on urban agriculture indicators. Bibliometric methods offer several advantages for this analysis [23]. The network maps revealed the intellectual, conceptual, and social structures. The details of the stages are discussed below (Fig. 1).

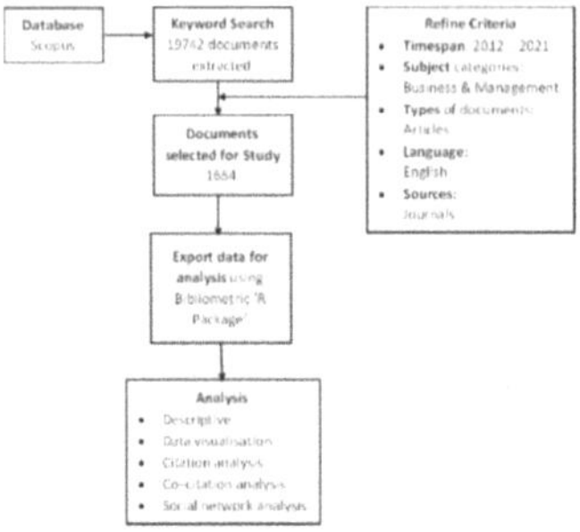

Fig. 1. Flowchart for selection of documents

A crucial pre-requisite for bibliometric analysis is a structured database description of indexed articles. Data retrieval was conducted from the 'Scopus' database. Based on Elsevier's Scopus coverage of articles and classification of journals, the database was linked to the Bibliometrix package in R-studio. The Scopus database is ideal for bibliometric analysis as it covers highly credible journals from various categories and excludes papers from non-scientific journals and magazines [24]. The Scopus database is considered premier in comparison to other databases.

2.2 Data Analysis – Preparation

The data was downloaded from Scopus in Microsoft Excel format to support the software requirement. Documents were shortlisted based on the following search criteria applied on 10th April 2024.

The classic research contributions interchange the words 'emotional intelligence' and 'emotional quotient.' Nineteen thousand seven hundred forty-two documents showcased the search for these terms. The author pertinently realized that the humongous data set would not serve the study's objectives.

2.3 Search Strategy – Identification of Keywords

In this step, the shortlisted documents from the earlier step were screened through a language filter called "English." The dataset extracted at this stage was 33,559 documents. The critical information related to extracted documents, viz. Title, abstracts, authors, and keywords, were uploaded in a Microsoft Excel format to the 'Biblioshiny' – Bibliometrix-related R-studio package tool [23].

The last decade has seen enormous interest in the concept of emotional intelligence. The core objective of the paper is to detect the perspectives and trends in emotional intelligence from 2014 – 2024. Conference Proceedings, Book Series, and Trade Journals were excluded from the extracted data. This enabled the data to be fine-tuned to meet the research objectives. Hence, the shortlisted data was 33559 documents. In order to ensure specific articles related to the keywords are shortlisted, documents having the following keywords in their article(s) were filtered further – Emotional Intelligence, Empathy, Emotion(s), Emotion Regulation, Trait Emotional Intelligence, Emotionality and Cognitive Emotions. Hence, the final shortlisted data was 12,129 documents used for analysis.

3 Data Analysis

3.1 Descriptive Analysis

The data analysis was primarily a two-pronged approach. A scientific mapping and descriptive study. This is explained in Fig. 2. In scientific mapping, extensive science mapping is conducted through visualization methods such as thematic maps, network analysis, and three-field plots. It helped the researcher derive the knowledge structures to facilitate further analysis [25]. The Descriptive analysis focused on exploring the bibliometric data in terms of the three elements: the sources, the authors, and the documents.

This section of the paper primarily focuses on descriptive analysis. Numerous dimensions were undertaken for the study.

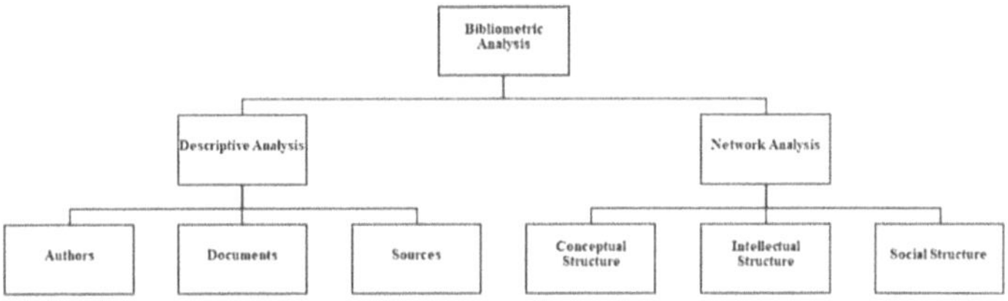

Fig. 2. Bibliometric analysis – Hierarchy

3.2 Data Set

The following summary of the analysis is presented in Table 1. It provides a comprehensive view of the various dimensions considered during the investigation. The bibliometric data set consisted of 12129 documents extracted through a rigorous search query on the Scopus database. It is worth noting that these documents were published in 2622 diverse sources, and they had an impressive average citation score of 14.86.

This indicates that the publications have had a significant impact. Furthermore, the collaboration index was noteworthy, indicating a strong level of cooperation among researchers. The international collaboration rate was 20%, which is a positive indication of substantial collaboration among researchers across the globe.

Table 1. Summary of the data set

Description	Results
MAIN INFORMATION ABOUT DATA	
Timespan	2014:2024
Sources (Journals, Books, etc.)	2622
Documents	12129
Annual Growth Rate %	6.81
Document Average Age	4.53
Average citations per doc	14.86
References	532727
DOCUMENT CONTENTS	
Keywords Plus (ID)	10444
Author's Keywords (DE)	20947
AUTHORS	
Authors	32044
Authors of single-authored docs	1762
AUTHORS COLLABORATION	
Single-authored docs	1915
Co-Authors per Doc	3.54
International co-authorships %	19.69
DOCUMENT TYPES	
Article	12129

3.3 Three Fields Plot

The 'Three Field Plot' is based on the Sankey Plot mechanism. The plot gives the relationship between the three fields, wherein the size of the portion is proportionate to the node's value [20]. There are three rows, as shown in Fig. 3. The leftmost side of the Sankey Plot is the Countries of Origin of the authors; the middle column is the authors, and the rightmost side is the keywords.

The keywords with positive connotations evolving from the analysis other than emotional intelligence are personality, well-being, life satisfaction, emotion regulation, mindfulness, self-esteem, and mental health. Some of the keywords with negative connotations are depression, stress, and anxiety. Intriguingly, the keywords with positive connotations outnumber the keywords with negative connotations.

3.4 Annual Scientific Production

The analysis of scientific production in the domain of emotional intelligence depicts the trends in this field. The graph, represented in Fig. 4, displays an upward trend in

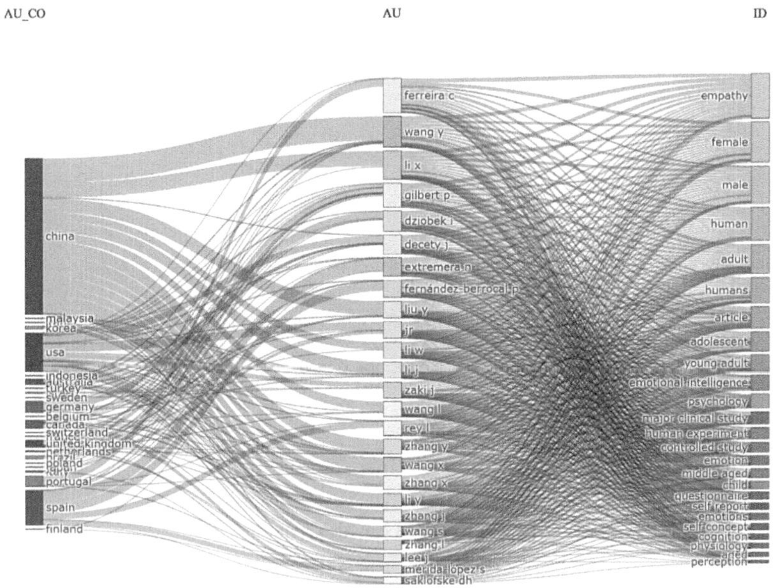

Fig. 3. Three Field Plot

the number of publications on emotional intelligence. The author's decision to choose a period of only the last decade (2014–2024) provides an accurate depiction of the recent trends in emotional intelligence. Over the years, there has been a gradual rise in interest in emotional intelligence, with the number of publications on the topic increasing since 2016.

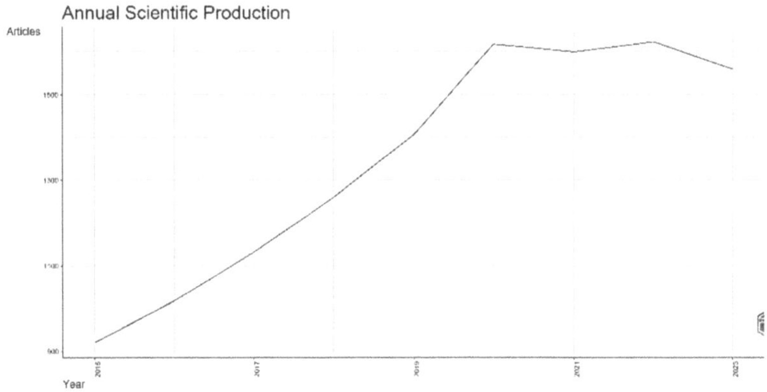

Fig. 4. Scientific production and growth

However, the graph shows a partial plateau between 2019 and 2023, indicating a temporary slowdown in publications on emotional intelligence. Of more concern, since 2022, there has been a significant drop in the number of publications in this field. This drop suggests a decline in the interest and attention on emotional intelligence as a research topic.

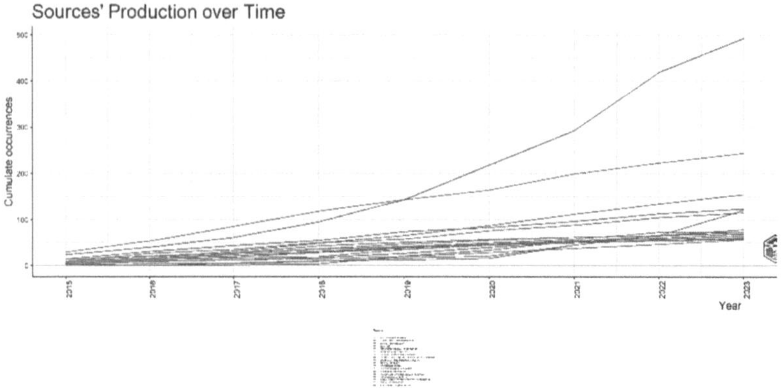

Fig. 5. Source Growth Dynamics

The graph in Fig. 5 - Source Growth Dynamics illustrates the growth of publications in several journals, including 'Current Psychology,' 'Frontiers in Psychology,' and others. It is evident from the graph that 'Current Psychology' has steadily increased its publications since 2017, indicating a consistent upward trend in its growth dynamics. In contrast, the other journals have experienced relatively stable growth in their publications over the years, with a slight increase from 2014 to 2024. Particularly noteworthy is the sudden and significant increase in publications of the journal 'Frontiers in Psychology' since 2019. This trend is counterintuitive and warrants further investigation. The data suggests that this journal has experienced a surge in popularity, possibly due to several factors, such as a change in editorial policy, an increase in funding, or a shift in research focus. Further analysis is required to understand the underlying reasons for this trend and its implications for the field of psychology.

3.5 Trending Authors

Emotional intelligence (EI) is an essential area of research, and there are several leading authors who have made significant contributions to this field. Extremera N, Fernandez-Berrocal P, and Saklofske DH are the most prolific authors, having published the most research papers. However, it is noteworthy that other researchers have also made valuable contributions to the domain of EI, as demonstrated by the data displayed in Fig. 6.

Additionally, Fig. 7 provides insights into the Author Impact, highlighting the significant influence Extremera N, Fernandez-Berrocal P, and Saklofske DH have had on EI research, underscoring their role as influential authors.

3.6 Country Wise Contribution

To gain a comprehensive and in-depth understanding of the fascinating field of emotional intelligence, it is imperative to take a global perspective. By examining the contributions

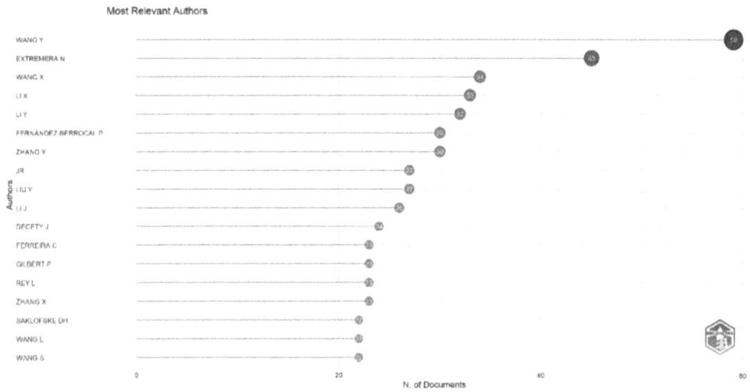

Fig. 6. Most Relevant Authors

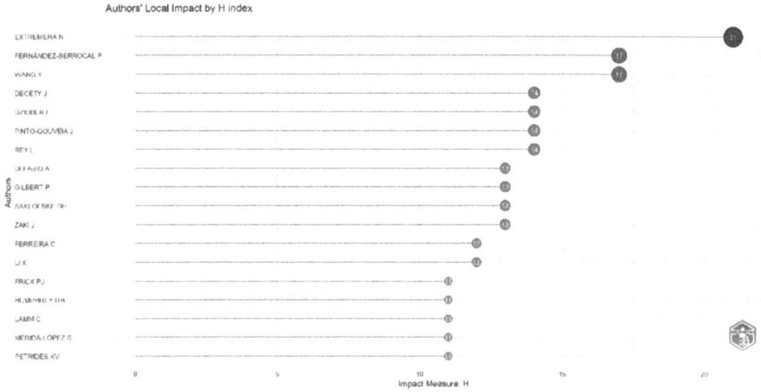

Fig. 7. Author Impact

of various countries to this domain, we can better comprehend the growth patterns and prevailing trends in the existing literature. According to the highly informative Fig. 8, which vividly illustrates the publication records, the United States of America has a pervasive influence on this field, with over ten thousand documents.

This unparalleled dominance is a testament to the country's robust research infrastructure, innovative research methodologies, and high interest among researchers in the USA regarding emotional intelligence.

3.7 Most Relevant Sources

Figure 9 displays a chart that outlines the most significant sources in this field. There are two notable journals that have made a significant contribution to this area. The first one called 'Frontiers in Psychology' has published 494 papers and is considered a leading source. The second one, 'Personality and Individual Differences,' has published 244 papers and is also a reliable source that has made notable contributions to this field.

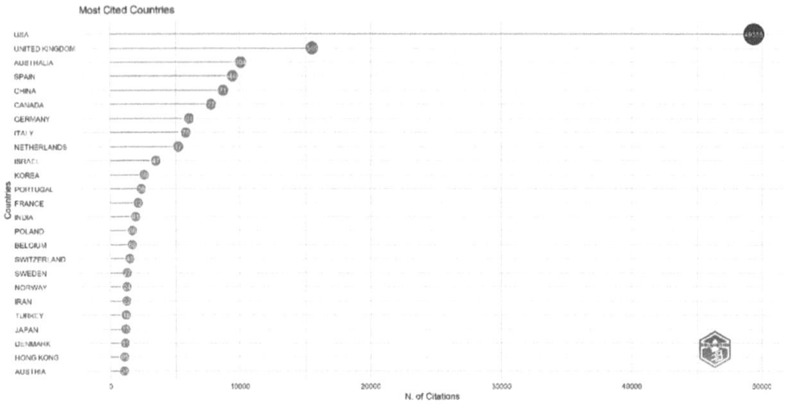

Fig. 8. Countries that were 'Most Cited'

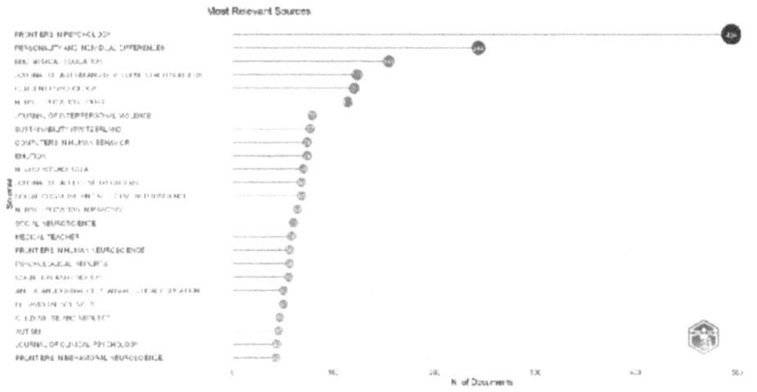

Fig. 9. Most Relevant Sources

3.8 Word Cloud

Figure 10 presents a 'Word Cloud' that visually represents the frequency of the keyword 'emotional intelligence.' The Word Cloud showcases the importance of different terms in the literature by varying their size. The larger the size of a word, the more significant its weightage in the domain. The terms 'emotional' and 'intelligence' have the most substantial weightage, indicating their crucial role in emotional intelligence.

Moreover, terms like 'social,' 'relationship,' and 'results' also hold considerable importance, highlighting the impact of emotional intelligence on social interactions, relationship-building, and outcomes. Therefore, we can infer that emotional intelligence is vital in shaping social interactions and building strong relationships.

3.9 Trending Topics

Upon analyzing the data presented in Fig. 11, it is apparent that the topics of 'life satisfaction," 'personality traits," 'social support," and 'empathy' have been attracting considerable attention and interest. This indicates that people are becoming more conscious about their mental and emotional well-being and their ability to relate to others.

Fig. 10. Word Cloud

In particular, the growing interest in the topic of empathy suggests that there is a desire to improve one's ability to understand and relate to others on a deeper level.

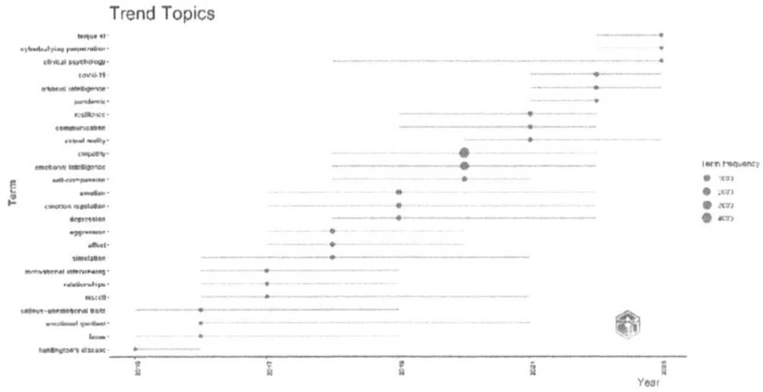

Fig. 11. Trending Topics

Overall, the data implies that people are becoming increasingly aware of the importance of their emotional intelligence and interpersonal relationships and are actively seeking ways to improve them.

3.10 Conceptual and Intellectual Structure

The conceptual structure is generated using the Bibliometrix package. The fundamental technique is based on multiple correspondence analysis, wherein the input is multivariate nominal data. Figure 12 is generated by the extraction of words based on an algorithm termed 'Keyword Plus.' The most common words found in the titles of the documents are registered.

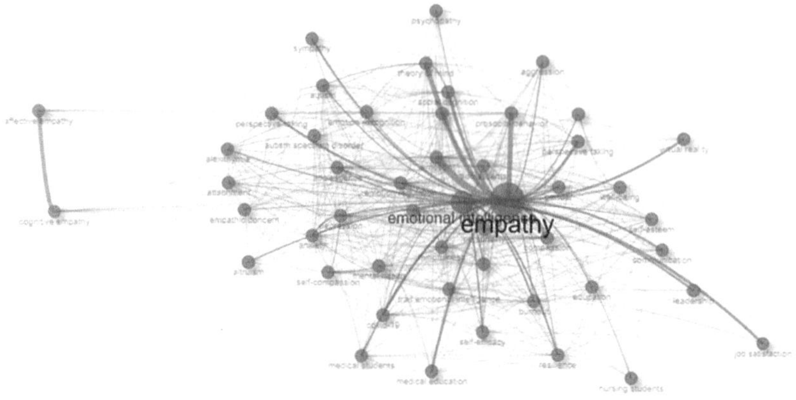

Fig. 12. Co-occurrence Network – Conceptual Structure

3.11 Thematic Map

A Thematic Map is a powerful tool used in data analysis to visualize typological themes. It is created by plotting data in two dimensions, which allows for easy identification of clusters of related keywords. These keyword clusters are identified using co-occurrence and co-word analysis, which helps researchers to produce themes in the research domain. The Map is designed to display the location of these themes on two axes, with their position determined by their centrality and density. This information can be used to understand the data better and make informed decisions.

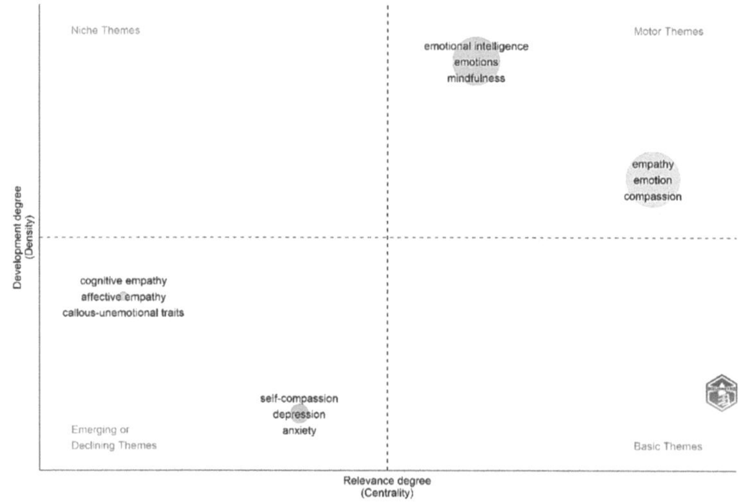

Fig. 13. Thematic Map

As seen in Fig. 13., two clusters, blue and red, appear from the data. Colors represent clusters; distances imply the relatedness; the node's size is proportionate to its occurrence, and the words define the vertex [20]. A bubble on the thematic map represents the theme. The Thematic map has four quadrants: the upper right quadrant is a motor theme (High on centrality and density); the lower right quadrant is a basic theme (High on the centrality and low on density); the lower left quadrant is an emerging or declining theme (Low on the centrality and low on density); and the upper right quadrant is a niche theme (Low on the centrality and high on density), [26]. The image illustrates the close relationship between emotional intelligence (EI) and the field of psychology. It's fascinating to note that psychometry, a subfield of psychology concerned with measuring psychological traits and abilities, is also included in the figure.

3.12 Tree Map

The article's high-level summarization and refinement are represented by the keywords. The article's theme and writing direction in the field of emotional intelligence is reflected concisely and intuitively by the analysis of keywords such as cluster analysis and multiple correspondence analysis. Biblioshiny software package is used to carry out data mining and statistical analysis on the high-frequency keywords of research papers. The keywords with greater word frequency are selected, and a Word Tree Map is drawn (refer to Fig. 14).

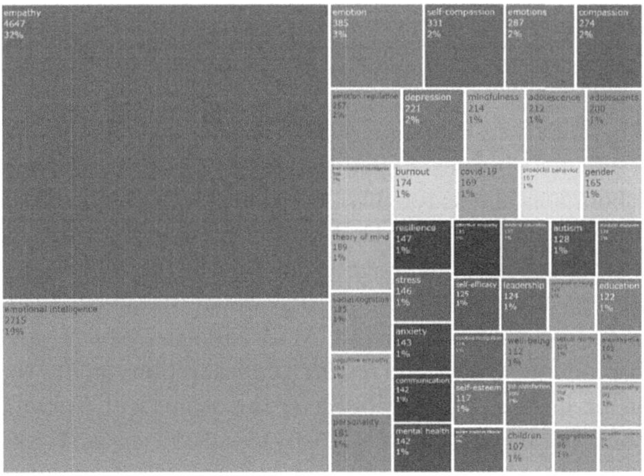

Fig. 14. Tree Map

The Tree Map shown in Fig. 14 visually represents the most frequently used keywords in the extracted documents. The map highlights the top three keywords, which are 'emotional intelligence," 'female," and 'male." This suggests that most authors and scholars have been researching the differences in emotional intelligence between genders. Of particular interest is that the keyword 'emotional intelligence' has been used the most with 12% frequency, while the keywords 'male' and 'female' both have an equal usage percentage of 10%. This information can be precious for anyone looking to gain deeper insights into the ongoing research on emotional intelligence and gender differences.

3.13 Geographical Collaboration

(Ingale & Paluri, 2020) State that 'the Social Network Analysis (SNA) helps produce the interrelationships within the research domain. The 'nodes' are the actors such as scholars, authors, and sources of publication, and the 'set of nodes, indicate the interconnectedness of the relationships in the social network".

Fig. 15. Geographical collaboration network

The network's underlying structure offers valuable insights into the relationships between distinct research domains. Figure 15 presents a visually striking representation of research collaborations across roughly 36 countries. The United States of America leads scholarly inquiry and has cultivated fruitful partnerships with India, Australia, Israel, and Greece. Spain is another significant contributor, with major research collaborations in EI with Portugal, Colombia, and Brazil. A robust cluster of European countries, including Germany, Switzerland, Austria, Poland, France, Serbia, and Croatia, highlights their interdependence in research collaborations on EI. The UK serves as the central hub of the spoke and has established partnerships with Norway, Ireland, Italy, Lebanon, Malaysia, Turkey, and Pakistan. Lastly, South Africa and Nigeria stand out as the only outliers, where studies focus more on contextual discontinuity. By examining this network, we can comprehend the global distribution of research collaborations and the interdependence of different countries in various research domains.

4 Conclusion

4.1 Contribution, Implications, Limitations and Future Research

This article comprehensively analyses Emotional Intelligence (EI) over a decade, from 2014 to 2024. The study delves deep into various structures related to EI and consolidates over 12000 research articles, which were previously scattered across different sources.

The paper highlights significant authors, sources, and documents related to the field, providing valuable insights into EI research. A unique aspect of this paper is using an R-package with bibliometrics and a dataset from the Scopus database, which adds significant value to the research. The findings reveal that the social structure of the domain has expanded with the entry of new countries and authors, giving it a broader horizon. The analysis shows that the major contributors to the field of EI are from the USA, followed by European countries.

The author also identified that authors from developed countries collaborate with those from developing countries, especially in emotional intelligence. The publications are mainly in psychology, social psychology, and business, creating interdisciplinary research opportunities. The article establishes the progress made in the field of research, especially in Emotional Intelligence, and highlights areas where more work is needed.

The insights from the paper can help practitioners like counsellors and EI experts understand emerging issues and explore new opportunities. Overall, this paper provides a comprehensive overview of the progress made in Emotional Intelligence research and offers valuable insights to the research community.

Some of the study's limitations are: (1) This bibliometric study used only the Scopus database. Other databases, such as Web of Science, could be used in future studies. (2) the keyword exploration was minimal and could be modified to include additional words synonymous with EI. (3) An extensive review of literature followed by meta-analysis would enable the enrichment of the domain of emotional intelligence. (4) More interdisciplinary research is needed in this domain, and social and intellectual collaborations through forums and associations can be nurtured. (5) content analysis of papers in this research domain would produce an enriched insight into the relevant models and theories for practitioners. (6) contribution ought to be sought from industry experts and practitioners. These few steps could help enrich the field of emotional intelligence.

References

1. Mayer, J.D., Salovey, P.: 'SaloveyMayer_1989_EmotionalIntelligence.pdf,' Imagination, Cognition and Personality **9**(3), 185–211 (1989)
2. Supriyanto, A.S., Ekowati, V.M., Idris, I., Susminingsihc, Iswanto, B.: Leadership styles as a predictor of the voluntary work behaviors of bank employees. Int. J. Econ. Manag. **14**(1), 1–11 (2020)
3. Nikolaou, I., Tsaousis, I.: EI in the workplace.pdf. Int. J. Organ. Anal. **10**(4), 327–342 (2002)
4. Mayfield, J., Mayfield, A.: Leader communication strategies: critical paths to improving employee commitment. Am. Bus. Rev. **20**(2), 89 (2002)
5. Vratskikh, I., (Moh'dTaisir) Masa'deh, R., Al-Lozi, V., Maqableh, M.: The impact of emotional intelligence on job performance via the mediating role of job satisfaction. Int. J. Bus. Manag. **11**(2), 69 (2016). https://doi.org/10.5539/ijbm.v11n2p69
6. Borrajo, E., Calvete, E., Urquijo, I.: Negative self-talk in runners: emotional intelligence and perceived stress as explanatory factors. Psychol. Sport Exerc. **70** (2024). https://doi.org/10.1016/j.psychsport.2023.102545
7. Pauletto, M., Grassi, M., Pellizzoni, S., Penolazzi, B.: Fostering emotional intelligence in preadolescence: effects of a pilot training on emotions, coping and psychological well-being. Clin. Child Psychol. Psychiatry **28**(2), 567–579 (2023). https://doi.org/10.1177/13591045221105189

8. Chandu, V., et al.: Research on retail Buyers' emotional quotient with focus on transactions on the National Stock Exchange. Int. J. Eng. Bus. Manag. **15** (2023). https://doi.org/10.1177/18479790231180770 WE - Emerging Sources Citation Index (ESCI)
9. Troth, A.C., Townsend, K., Loudoun, R., Burgess, M.: Frontline managers' task-related emotion regulation, emotional intelligence, and daily stress. Aust. J. Manag. **48**(1), 108–129 (2023). https://doi.org/10.1177/03128962221105407
10. Hess, J.D., Bacigalupo, A.C.: Applying emotional intelligence skills to leadership and decision making in non-profit organizations. Adm. Sci. **3**(4), 202–220 (2013). https://doi.org/10.3390/admsci3040202WE-EmergingSourcesCitationIndex(ESCI)
11. Sultana, R., Rafiqul ISLAM, M., Tariful ISLAM, M., Jesmin, F., Ferdous, S.: The relationship between emotional intelligence and organizational performance: An Exploratory Study in Bangladesh. Shakila FERDOUS / J. Asian Financ. vol. 8, no. 8, pp. 513–0524 (2021). https://doi.org/10.13106/jafeb.2021.vol8.no8.0513
12. Luong, T.T., Sivarajah, U., Weerakkody, V.: Do agile managed information systems projects fail due to a lack of emotional intelligence? Inf. Syst. Front. **23**(2), 415–433 (2021). https://doi.org/10.1007/s10796-019-09962-6
13. Jordan, P.J., Troth, A.: Emotional intelligence and leader member exchange: the relationship with employee turnover intentions and job satisfaction. Leadersh. Organ. Dev. J. **32**(3), 260–280 (2011). https://doi.org/10.1108/01437731111123915
14. Brown, C.: Economic Insights – Trends and Challenges the Effects of Emotional Intelligence (EI) and Leadership Style on Sales Performance. Econ. Insights – Trends Challenges, no. 3, pp. 1–14 (2014)
15. Nisar, Q.A., Mubeen, H., Ashraf, H.: Impact of emotional intelligence and knowledge management on organizational performance: mediating role of organizational learning. J. Manag. Info **3**(3), 12–17 (2016). https://doi.org/10.31580/jmi.v11i1.57
16. Supramaniam, S., Singaravelloo, K.: 'Impact of Emotional Intelligence on Organisational Performance: An Analysis in the Malaysian Public Administration," Adm. Sci., vol. 11, no. 3, 2021, https://doi.org/10.3390/admsci11030076 WE - Emerging Sources Citation Index (ESCI)
17. Ramanauskas, K.: The Impact of the Manager's Emotional Intelligence on Organisational Performance. Manag. THEORY Stud. Rural Bus. Infrastruct. Dev. **38**(1), 58–69 (2016). https://doi.org/10.15544/mts.2016.6WE-EmergingSourcesCitationIndex(ESCI)
18. Davaei, M., Gunkel, M., Veglio, V., Taras, V.: The influence of cultural intelligence and emotional intelligence on conflict occurrence and performance in global virtual teams. J. Int. Manag. **28**(4), (2022). https://doi.org/10.1016/j.intman.2022.100969
19. Roblek, V., Dimovski, V., Mesko, M., Peterlin, J.: Evolution of organisational agility: a bibliometric study. Kybernetes **51**(13), 119–137 (2022). https://doi.org/10.1108/k-11-2021-1137
20. Ingale, K.K., Paluri, R.A.: Financial literacy and financial behaviour: a bibliometric analysis. Rev. Behav. Financ. (2020). https://doi.org/10.1108/RBF-06-2020-0141
21. Jiang, Z.: Emotional intelligence and career decision-making self-efficacy: national and gender differences. J. Employ. Couns. **51**(3), 112–124 (2014). https://doi.org/10.1002/j.2161-1920.2014.00046.xWE-SocialScienceCitationIndex(SSCI)
22. MacCann, C., Jiang, Y.X., Brown, L.E.R., Double, K.S., Bucich, M., Minbashian, A.: Emotional intelligence predicts academic performance: a meta-analysis. Psychol. Bull. **146**(2), 150–186 (2020). https://doi.org/10.1037/bul0000219WE-ScienceCitationIndexExpanded(SCI-EXPANDED)WE-SocialScienceCitationIndex(SSCI)
23. Aria, M., Cuccurullo, C.: Bibliometrix : An R-tool for comprehensive science mapping analysis. J. Informetr. **11**(4), 959–975 (2017). https://doi.org/10.1016/j.joi.2017.08.007
24. Mulet-Forteza, C., et al.: Bibliometric structure of IJCHM in its 30 years. Int. J. Contemp. Hosp. Manag. **31**(12), 4574–4604 (2019). https://doi.org/10.1108/IJCHM-10-2018-0828

25. Nusair, K., Butt, I., Nikhashemi, S.R.: A bibliometric analysis of social media in hospitality and tourism research. Int. J. Contemp. Hosp. Manag. **31**(7), 2691–2719 (2019). https://doi.org/10.1108/IJCHM-06-2018-0489
26. Viedma-Del-Jesus, M.I., Perakakis, P., Muñoz, M.Á., López-Herrera, A.G., Vila, J.: Sketching the first 45 years of the journal Psychophysiology (1964–2008): a co-word-based analysis. Psychophysiology **48**(8), 1029–1036 (2011). https://doi.org/10.1111/j.1469-8986.2011.01171.x

Green Economy in the Framework of Sustainable Development

Hajiyeva Nushaba[1], Kerimova Minure[1], Gurbanova Xatira[1], Huseynova Mehriban[2], Babakishiyeva Sevinj[1], and Mammadova Ayshan[1](✉)

[1] Azerbaijan Technological University, Gandja, Azerbaijan
a.memmedova@atu.edu.az
[2] Azerbaijan State Oil and Industry University, Baku, Azerbaijan

Abstract. Traditional economic models often prioritize short-term gains over long-term sustainability, leading to depletion of natural resources, pollution and social inequalities. Instead, it advocates an inclusive and equitable approach that balances economic growth with environmental protection and social welfare. In addition, the study provides valuable insights into the potential benefits of adopting green economy principles. The study examines the role of policy interventions and institutional frameworks in the transition to a green economy. Effective policies, regulations and incentives are essential to stimulate sustainable practices, mobilize private sector investment and foster collaboration between government, industry and civil society stakeholders. By analyzing successful case studies and best practices from around the world, the study offers valuable lessons for policy-makers seeking to design and implement effective green economy policies tailored to their specific contexts. The main goal of the research work is to analyze the green economy programs and learn the directions of improvement of the green economy in our country. The purpose of the conducted research is to analyze the work done in the country in the direction of the green economy in Azerbaijan, to investigate ways of improving projects in the future and to make relevant proposals in this direction. Scientific and economic methods and methods such as analysis, synthesis, generalization, complex and systematic approach were preferred in the research process.

Keywords: Green Economy · Ecology · Sustainable Economic Development · Subsidy · Investment

1 Green Economy and Green Economy Policies in the World

1.1 Green Economy

The emergence of the idea of green economy coincides with the period after the Second World War. After the Second World War, the rapid industrialization of both the western and eastern blocs and the pursuit of this model by third world countries under the term "development" led to the globalization of this industrial design. This has led to global climate change and an environmental crisis that threatens our planet. In response to this threat, the idea of green economy has come up as an alternative economic model in the last 50 years.

A. Mirzazadeh et al. (Eds.): SEMIT 2024, CCIS 2444, pp. 292–307, 2026.
https://doi.org/10.1007/978-3-032-01948-6_19

Not only because of environmental concerns, but also because of the economic crises observed in many developing countries in the 1990s and early 2000s, the 2008 crisis and finally the Covid-19 pandemic show that this system showed that it could not continue any longer and that a new economic model was needed.

Today, there is no single, universally accepted definition of the concept of green economy. Different definitions of each institution can be seen. Green economy is defined by UNEP as follows:

"A green economy is an economic model that improves individual well-being and social justice while reducing environmental threats and disadvantages. It is also a system that aims for minimum carbon levels, efficient use of resources and social inclusion. Green economy – aims to reduce greenhouse gases and biodiversity loss while increasing employment and income supported by the public and private sectors.

According to the OECD, a green economy promotes economic growth and development by providing resources and environmental services for our well-being to ensure the sustainability of natural resources. For this reason, it is important to support investments that will lead to new economic opportunities by supporting sustainable development. This becomes important as the idea of a green economy increases risks for development as it continues to consume natural resources.

A good understanding of the scope of the green economy is necessary to guide green investments into the economy. While renewable energy comes to mind when we think of the green economy, the concept is not limited to that. The scope of the green economy aims at zero waste in all types of production and a production system that does not put pressure on natural resources. While renewable energy is important for a green economy because it is a clean and unlimited resource, harmony with nature and zero waste are important in providing the technology required for power generation and power plant deployment. For example, renewable investment that displaces local people may seem ecological, but is contrary to the concept of a green economy. In parallel, biofuels obtained through energy agriculture are not included in the scope of the green economy because they produce motor fuel on land that should be set aside for food production, thus increasing the price of the grain most consumed by the poor. As it can be seen, the scope of the green economy requires taking into account not only the production method, but also social, ecological and economic factors.

1.2 Green Economy Principles

There are a number of positive and negative situations that countries will face during the transition to a green economy. The invention of ecologically clean economic goods, the improvement of the well-being of life with sustainable cities, and the reduction of the need for energy and natural resources compared to the past can be mentioned as positive aspects. It is also expected that green economy indicators will help policy-making processes by measuring the environmental impacts of production and consumption activities. An increase in energy and mineral prices, an increase in production costs and label prices of durable consumer goods, an increase in unemployment in large factories and a decrease in purchasing power can be cited as negative aspects (Fig. 1).

Ensuring and maintaining economic, ecological and social welfare as a whole is the main goal of the green economy [1]. A green economy that aims to grow and develop

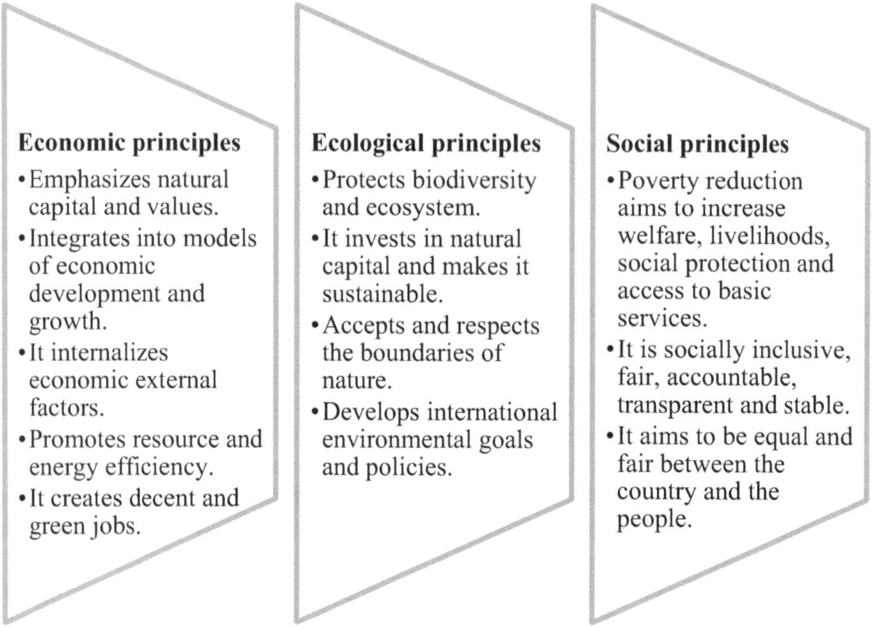

Fig. 1. Green economy principles. Source: Akagünduz HK, 2022: p.34–35 compiled by the author based on the data.

while caring for the environment promises to make natural resources sustainable. The development of environmentally friendly technological products and services, increasing the efficiency of natural resources and creating new jobs in new markets are the basis of the green economic model.

In the modern world, where environmental problems are increasing, the relationship between the environment and the economy has been discussed many times, and unfortunately, it has been impossible to speak optimistically about the future. At this point, it was seen that the policies aimed at sustainable development were not successful enough, and it was understood that more concrete policies should be implemented. One of these policies is the concept of green development. Green growth, which is ecologically sensitive growth, aims to grow while taking into account environmental threats and the sustainability of natural resources while achieving economic development. In this regard, green development takes into account economic limitations as well as natural limitations.

Indicators developed to examine the environmental impacts of production and consumption are called green economic indicators. Green economic indicators – measuring the impact of policies, using them in decision-making and designing policies accordingly are important. These indicators undertake the task of illuminating the economic, social and ecological dimensions of the entire ecosystem.

Such parameters were needed to see, compare and measure development in economic activities that use the environment wisely, do not leave waste behind, use raw materials and energy efficiently, take into account basic and social needs (Table 1).

Table 1. Green development index.

Country	Index
Sweden	78,72
Denmark	76,77
Czechia	76,74
Germany	75,83
Austria	75,22
Finland	75.49
Slovakia	74,25
Switzerland	73,21
Lithuania	71.60
Hungary	71.40
Turkey	50,60

Source: Akagünduz HK, 2022: p. 43–44

The Green Development Index is a complex index that includes sustainable development goals and measures the country's economic status. Within this index – efficient and sustainable use of resources, social integration, green economic opportunities and protection of natural capital are included [2].

One of the first countries in the world to implement the goal of green development is South Korea. South Korea, which has inspired everyone in development since the 1990s, has set a goal of a green development strategy to get out of the 2008 crisis. In accordance with this goal, minimum fossil fuel use, clean and efficient resource selection has been adopted. With this strategy, South Korea is the country shown as the first example of green development in the world. Their 2009 "Low Carbon Green Development Framework Law" played an important role in making this strategy a reality. According to this law, approximately 2% of GDP will be transferred to green development policies each year.

"Road to Our Future: Green Development" is South Korea's national strategy plan for green development covering a 5-year period (2009–2013). The strategy aims to transform the current development paradigm of quantity-oriented, fossil fuel-dependent growth into a quality/clean development strategy with greater emphasis on new and renewable energy sources. The strategy has three main goals:

- Promotion of environmentally friendly new development engines for the national economy,
- To improve the quality of life of individuals,
- Contribute to international efforts to combat climate change.

The long-term "National Strategic Plan" (2009–2050) for green development has defined three main goals. These are prevention of climate change and energy independence, creation of new tools for economic growth, improvement of quality of life and improvement of international position. For these purposes, policies such as the development of environmentally friendly green technologies, the creation of a sustainable city, and the greening of transportation are followed to reduce greenhouse gas emissions.

In South Korea's green economy strategy, four major river restoration projects – the Han, Nakdong, Geum and Yeongsan rivers – aim to improve water quality, as well as create multi-use areas for local people and boost regional development around the rivers. In addition, realizing the importance of renewable energy, they targeted the share of renewable energy supply in the total energy supply as 11% by 2030.

The promotion of green development in South Korea is centralized with major government efforts. In order to create green job potential, the government has identified university students as the main target group within the framework of skills development and education policy in the transition to a green economy and provided them with the necessary educational opportunities. At the same time, it has tried to address its shortcomings by emphasizing vocational training through youth training and public awareness initiatives about the industry.

At the same time, South Korea aims to become the first East Asian country to achieve net zero emissions by 2050. In August 2021, South Korea passed a law called the "Climate Change Carbon Neutrality and Green Development Law" and set some new targets and policies. The law provides for climate impact assessment, which aims to assess the climate impacts of major national plans and development projects. Emissions reduction targets will now be integrated into national budget planning through a climate responsive budget program. The law also creates a climate response fund that will be used to support the structural transformation of carbon-intensive industries. After this law, many targets were repeatedly reviewed and new targets were defined. It has committed to reducing carbon emissions by 40% compared to 2018 levels by 2030 and adopted the Global Methane Commitment to reduce methane emissions by 30%. Making its targets in coal and renewable energy more ambitious, it aimed to reduce electricity generation from coal from 41.9% to 21.8% and increase renewable energy from 6.2% to 30.2% [3].

The Climate Change Act, passed by the UK government in 2008, forms the basis of its approach to tackling and responding to climate change. Through the Climate Change Act, the UK government has set a target to significantly reduce greenhouse gas emissions in the UK by 2050 and a pathway to achieve it. The law also created a "Committee on Climate Change" to ensure that emissions targets are evidence-based and independently assessed. In addition, the law requires the government to assess and adapt to the risks and opportunities for the UK from climate change. The "Climate Change Committee" makes recommendations on these risks and assesses progress towards combating them. The Climate Change Act focuses on green development and four key goals. These:

- Reducing carbon and pollution,
- Efficiency of natural resources,
- Rejection of the blind growth approach (flexible growth),
- Use of comparative advantages.

In the 12 years since the Climate Change Act was passed, UK greenhouse gas emissions have fallen by 37%. Although the benefits of green development are thought to be limited, the coordination process implemented by the Ministry of Energy and

Climate Change and the Committee on Climate Change has been effective in consistently achieving these goals across sectors.

In the UK, the green economy movement is developing with significant contributions not only from the government, but also from NGOs and business. In 2012, the Green Investment Bank was established by the UK government with £3 billion of capital to finance low-carbon projects, invest in and promote renewable energy. This bank went down in history as the first green bank in the world. The bank, which was privatized in 2017, was bought by "Macquarie Group Limited", one of the largest green infrastructure investors in Europe, for 2.3 billion pounds [3].

The UK has a number of policies in place, aiming to reduce greenhouse gas emissions by at least 68% compared to 1990 by 2030, and by at least 78% by 2035. In April 2021, it made new commitments covering emissions from international aviation and shipping for the first time. In November 2020, it published a "Ten-Point Plan for a Green Industrial Revolution" that sets out a number of concrete policy goals to support green jobs, better recovery and accelerate the path to net zero. These ten items encompass a green transformation built on energy, construction, transport, investment, finance, environment and technology [4].

Following this plan, the "Energy White Report" was published in December 2020. This report makes the Ten Point Plan for a Green Industrial Revolution more understandable. In addition to the previous plan, the "Energy White Report" covered the green transition more comprehensively and talked about a bigger decrease in the total emission reductions by 2032. The report states that the UK's green transformation will be as fair as possible and that they will also set up their own emissions trading system when leaving the EU [4].

Deeply affected by the Covid-19 pandemic, the UK has allocated around 17% of the funds it used to improve the economy during the pandemic to low-carbon green measures. In 2021, the UK government published its Net Zero Strategy report to reach net zero emissions by 2050, outlining a roadmap for how to achieve this goal. According to this report, by 2030, the UK aims to create 440,000 new jobs across all sectors and to invest £90 billion by the private sector. By investing more in renewable energy sources, especially wind, the goal is to make electricity generation entirely clean energy by 2035, taking security of supply into account. A £120m fund has been set up to make more use of small modular nuclear reactors (SMRs). After 2030, it is planned to oblige vehicle manufacturers to sell clean energy vehicles and even ban the sale of fossil fuel vehicles. It was decided to support households with grants to replace gas-fired combi boilers used for heating with low-emission, electric heat pumps [3].

With the crisis of 2008, the policy of the green economy in the United States came up frequently. The president of the time, Barack Obama, characterized the climate crisis as a great threat and implemented many policies in this direction. The "American Recovery and Reinvestment Act" adopted in 2009 by the Obama administration to overcome the crisis of 2008 and not remain silent on the climate disaster is one of the main policies. As of the date of its adoption, this law, which is the largest clean energy investment in history, allocated a budget of 90 billion dollars for carbon-free energy technology, energy efficiency and savings, and alternative energy investments.

The Obama administration issued the Clean Power Plan, which established carbon pollution standards and set targets for 2030 for power plants, which are seen as the largest source of carbon emissions in the United States. He introduced the American Jobs for Climate Action Act, making major new commitments to reduce carbon pollution, save energy and boost low-carbon investments.

By passing the Sustainable Agriculture and Forestry Building Blocks Act, it followed voluntary and incentive programs to reduce greenhouse gas emissions from agricultural production and increase carbon sequestration in forests. Together with Canada and Mexico, it published a "Mid-Century Decarbonization Strategy" and announced its long-term goals. During the Obama administration, wind power tripled in renewable energy, and solar power nearly thirty-fold. From 2008 to 2015, under Obama's administration, the United States reduced greenhouse gas emissions by 9% and grew the economy by more than 10%. According to the study, as of 2016, the US is the largest green market in the world. It has been estimated that the US green economy sector contributes $1.3 trillion to GDP and creates approximately 9.5 million jobs. Both data showed an increase of around 20% between 2012/13 and 2015/16. While the share of workers in green sectors in the total labor force is 4%, the share of income from green sectors in the total GDP is 7%. When this data is compared with China, OECD members and G20 countries, it is seen that the US population and per capita income working in the green economy sector are higher than those countries. The green economy demonstrates an important contribution to the economic development of the United States and the economic well-being of millions of people [3].

However, with the inauguration of Donald Trump in 2016, the United States partially lost these gains and its leadership in the green market. Green policies in the US have faced major disruptions during Trump's presidency. Because Trump does not believe in the climate crisis and thought it was temporary. For this reason, he withdrew from the Paris agreement, saying that the implementation of green policies was pointless. Joe Biden, who won the 2020 elections, thought the opposite and announced that the first thing to do would be to return to the Paris Agreement. Biden has sought to revive the climate setbacks of the previous four years by strengthening departments and agencies with climate-friendly policies across the government. Reaffirming the goal of net zero greenhouse gas emissions by 2050, Biden said a government-wide approach to combat climate change would be taken. In this direction, it was decided to plan and implement climate measures at the federal level, to create high-level inter-institutional groups to facilitate coordination, and to use federal budgets in accordance with climate action. In addition, the government suspended oil and gas drilling leases in the Arctic National Wildlife Refuge and revoked permits for the Keystone XL oil pipeline in an effort to end fossil fuel subsidies.

The United States, which has increased its attention to the climate crisis under Biden's leadership, issued an executive order in 2021 entitled "Combating the Climate Crisis at Home and Abroad." The decision created four new agencies: the Office of Climate Policy, the National Climate Task Force, the White House Environmental Justice Advisory Council, and the Interagency Coal Task Force.

Support for greenlighting green economy policies under Biden came not only from the government, but also from the private sector. More than 1,800 private organizations have signed a petition calling for "ambitious and fair" national climate targets. In addition, businessmen, universities, hospitals, scientists and activists announced their support for the green transition. The Biden administration has also begun targeting emissions reductions in the transportation sector. It has announced that it will halve the sale of cars with emissions that do not comply with the Paris Agreement by 2030. It also said that more restrictive fuel economy and greenhouse gas emission standards for passenger cars covering the years 2023–2026 will be implemented, and that the US will see a gradual decline in the production and consumption of hydrofluorocarbons over the next 15 years, but also to address the climate crisis, the "American Rescue Plan Act" was published on March 11, 2021. In addition to focusing on economic stimulus measures for households, this law also includes a number of climate-related provisions. $350 billion has been allocated to state and local governments, which play an important role in local energy and climate action. It also aims to create good-paying jobs, prevent air and water pollution, and implement climate-friendly and energy-efficient programs [5].

The United States, which aims to reduce greenhouse gas emissions by 50–52% from 2005 levels by 2030, has also set a goal to decarbonize the energy sector by 2035, in line with the Paris Agreement. It was emphasized that these goals can be achieved only through cost-effective technology and investments. The federal government will continue to work to accelerate energy transmission and storage from carbon-free electricity generation sources and to harness the carbon-free energy potential of carbon capture and nuclear power plants. It will also support the research, development and commercialization of software and hardware to support a carbon-free, flexible, reliable and affordable electricity system. It was decided to expand heat pumps for the construction industry, create modern energy codes for new buildings, and increase public funds for energy efficiency in buildings [6].

2 Green Economy Programs in Azerbaijan

All countries of the world are actively discussing the concept of green economy, and are increasingly integrating it into their policies. In 2015, the United Nations adopted a plan known as the Sustainable Development Goals, which includes 169 targets across 17 goals. At the heart of this agenda is its holistic approach that encompasses social, economic and environmental dimensions. The aim is to raise living standards and promote social equality while protecting the environment and minimizing environmental risks. This necessitates the transition to a new economic model called the green economy, which prioritizes the evaluation and protection of the ecological services of natural resources [6].

The fiscal system has significant influence in steering the direction of the green economy by offering incentives and structures to encourage environmentally sustainable behaviour. In assessing the potential of a green economy, this framework serves as a powerful mechanism for directing economic efforts toward environmentally friendly efforts. Among the main incentives within this system are tax incentives aimed at promoting the growth of renewable energy enterprises [6].

As a result of ongoing global crises, states recognize the need to reshape their national economic systems to mitigate or eliminate these crises. As a result, many countries around the world are adopting a "sustainable development" model that is consistent with the principles of a "green economy" that seeks to develop economies that are both environmentally sound and renewable.

From 2019, Azerbaijan is another five Eastern Partners[1] is receiving support from the EU-funded EU Environment Program for a green transition together with his country. This initiative aims to develop strategies to conserve natural resources, improve environmental well-being, promote greener development and better manage environmental risks. Despite the interruptions caused by the COVID-19 pandemic in 2020, the program continued its planned activities and achieved tangible results on the ground [7] (Fig. 2).

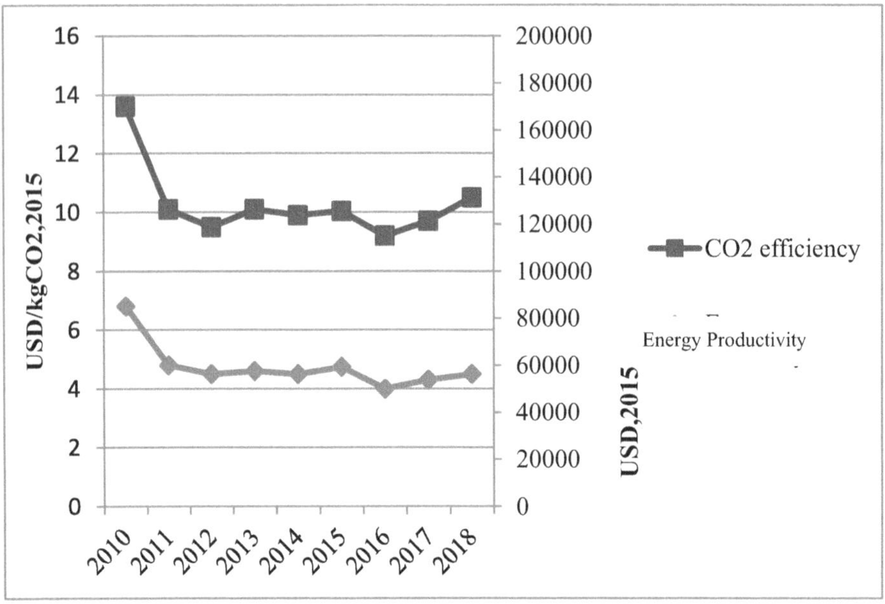

Fig. 2. Environment and resource productivity. Source: "Towards a Green Economy in Azerbaijan: Work continues on the EU Environment Program - 2019–2020": p.5

Environment and resource productivity: Increased CO2 and energy productivity lead to reduced pollution, increased energy efficiency in the economy, and improved climate and environmental conditions (Fig. 3).

Environmental aspect of quality of life: Reduced exposure to fine particles leads to cleaner air, healthier individuals, and reduced costs to government (Fig. 4).

The foundation of natural resources: Sustainable natural resources offer the necessary sustainable use essential for the transition to a green economy (Fig. 5).

Economic perspectives and policy initiatives: Ending fossil fuel subsidies can reduce fiscal deficits, increase the competitiveness of renewable energy, and reduce carbon emissions and air pollution.

[1] Ukraine, Moldova, Georgia, Belarus, Armenia

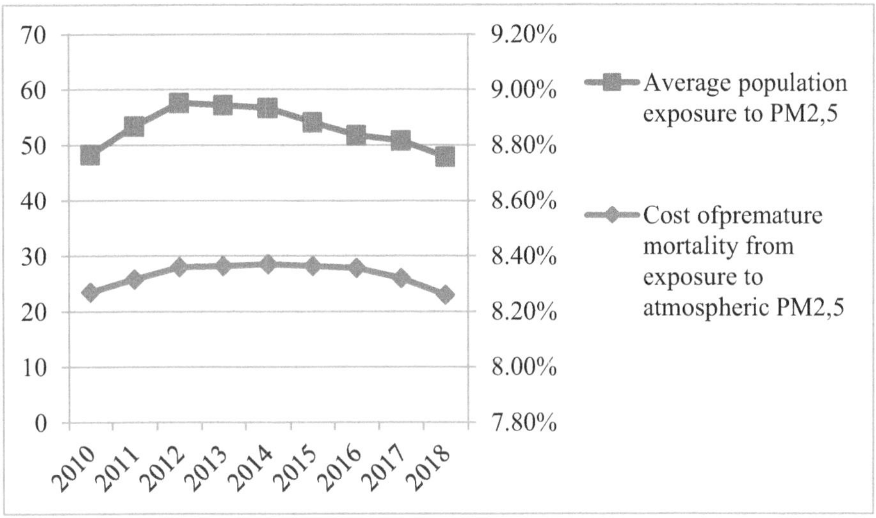

Fig. 3. Ecological dimension of quality of life. Source: "Towards a Green Economy in Azerbaijan: Work continues on the EU Environment Program - 2019–2020": p.5

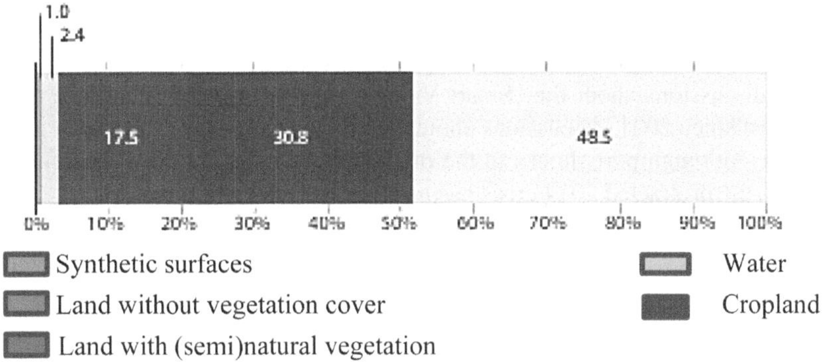

Fig. 4. Natural resources database. Source: "Towards a Green Economy in Azerbaijan: Work continues on the EU Environment Program - 2019–2020": p.5

Azerbaijan has faced economic difficulties since 2014 due to the sharp fall in the price of oil, which was especially exacerbated by pressures on the national currency in 2015. In response to this, the state "road map" and "strategic plan" were prepared. In 2020, the economic tension increased due to the pandemic, which was accompanied by the consequences of the 2nd Karabakh war.

As a result, in 2021, the President of Azerbaijan announced the liberated territories as "green development territories" and initiated the implementation of the concepts of "green economy" and "sustainable development" in these regions. This effort began with the Smart Village project, which aims to support sustainable development in these areas and potentially serves as a model for similar projects in Azerbaijan and beyond. This

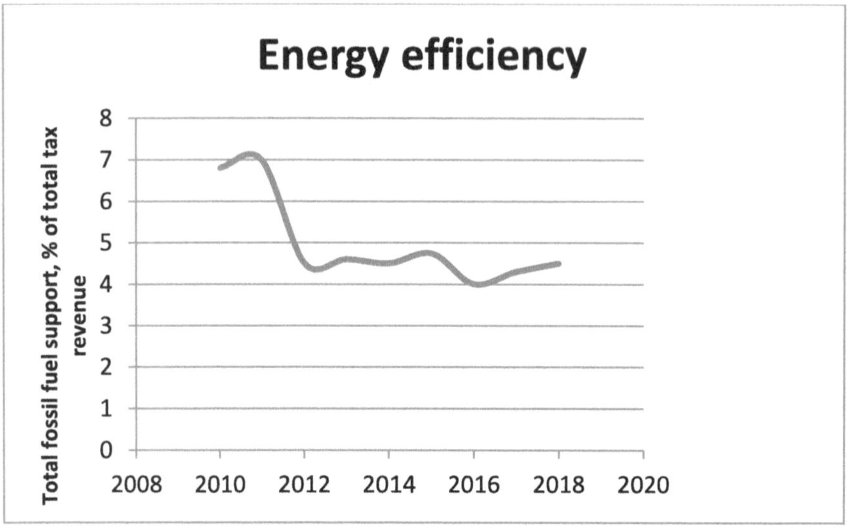

Fig. 5. Economic opportunities and political measures. Source: "Towards a Green Economy in Azerbaijan: Work continues on the EU Environment Program - 2019–2020": p.5

strategic step puts Azerbaijan in a leading position in this initiative and can export this concept to other countries in the future [5].

While discussions about the "Smart Village" project in Azerbaijan have attracted great interest since 2021, discussions about the "Green Economy" have been going on since 2015. Although past shocks in the oil market, such as the 2008 financial crisis, have faded, the protracted 2014 crisis has had more serious consequences.

In response to this, in 2016, the President of Azerbaijan issued a decree on the approval of strategic road maps aimed at exiting the crisis and ensuring sustainable economic development. The main goal of these roadmaps is to eliminate the country's dependence on oil and diversify the economy to other sectors by 2025. It is interesting that terms such as "Environmentally clean energy" and "Green economy" were first introduced in these road maps [8].

The global pandemic of 2020 also affected the economy of Azerbaijan, the stagnation of economic activity and the closing of borders resulted in a decrease in GDP. In addition, the 44-day Second Karabakh war started in response to Armenia's provocation in 2020, followed by the liberation of lands that had been occupied for more than thirty years, created additional stress on the economy. During the occupation, the long occupation, destruction, lack of infrastructure, exploitation of natural and material resources hindered the traditional recovery processes. As a result, the restoration and reconstruction of these areas necessitated a completely new development strategy [6].

Agali village of Zangilan district was the first settlement to be restored and resettled according to the decrees issued after the Second Karabakh war. Along with the neighboring Gubadli and Jabrayil districts, Zangilan suffered great damage during the occupation for more than 30 years. The destruction caused by the conflict prevented the rapid resettlement of IDPs into these devastated regions. The nearest settlement, Cojug Marjanli, which was liberated during the fighting in April 2016, was 62 km away, and the lack of road infrastructure, along with the presence of landmines and unexploded ordnance, severely limited traffic. Therefore, self-sufficiency in the village became mandatory. Considering that the self-sufficient village corresponds to the concept of "Smart village", this strategy has been implemented.

The restoration and construction of the village consisted of five main components [2]:

Apartment: Construction of 200 environmentally insulated houses using environmentally friendly materials.

Production: Creation and development of manufacturing facilities to meet both domestic and future regional demands.

Social services: Organization of state and social services, including establishment of East Zangezur "DOST Agropark" and mobile ASAN Service.

Smart agriculture: using artificial intelligence and drone technology to improve agriculture, along with the use of environmentally friendly fertilizers and renewable resources. "Intelligent management center" and databases have been created.

Alternative energy: Installation of small-scale solar, wind and hydropower plants to provide the village with clean energy, meet domestic and industrial energy needs, export excess energy to neighboring areas.

On July 19, 2022, after the completion of the restoration and reconstruction works, the first group of residents moved back to the area and began to adapt to the "Smart" village concept. Agriculture in the village has already witnessed rapid development, and with the relocation of additional groups in the coming years, the village's production capacity is expected to triple. The restoration and reconstruction of Agalı village with the concept of "Smart village" lays the foundation for similar works in other areas freed from occupation (Table 2).

Table 2. Advantages and disadvantages of the Smart City program.

Advantages	Disadvantages
Clean environment	Addiction to digitization
Smart parking system	Huge investment
New job opportunities	
Improved transportation system	
Smart health systems	
Digital systems for sustainable and renewable energy	

Source: Hajizade O., 2023: p. 15

In addition to the implementation of the "Smart Village" and "Smart City" concepts in the liberated territories, another potential model for the formation of social infrastructure is the compact settlement model. A compact city is an urban area characterized by features such as high population density and central revitalization, high density development, multi-functional development, provision of various services and amenities such as hospitals, parks, schools and recreational facilities.

Compact cities offer many advantages over urban sprawl, including reduced dependence on cars leading to reduced emissions, reduced energy consumption, improved public transport services, increased overall accessibility and reuse of existing infrastructure and developed land, etc.

Our Republic, like many countries, is paying more and more attention to the importance of transition to a greener economy. Although historically dependent on oil and gas resources, the country is diversifying its economy and investing in renewable energy and sustainability initiatives.

Our country has significant potential for renewable energy production, especially through solar and wind energy. The government is taking steps to tap this potential by implementing various projects. For example, the country in recent years several wind farms, hydroelectric plants[2]and built solar power plants, contributing to renewable energy potential.

Improving energy efficiency is a key aspect of the transition to a green economy. Azerbaijan is working on modernizing its infrastructure to reduce energy consumption and increase efficiency in various sectors, including buildings, transport and industry.

Environmental protection and biodiversity conservation are important components of a green economy. Azerbaijan takes measures to preserve its natural resources, including forests, water bodies and animal life. Initiatives include reforestation projects, wildlife conservation efforts, and sustainable land management practices.

Encouraging investment in green projects and providing financial incentives for sustainable practices are critical to promoting a green economy. Azerbaijan is exploring various financing mechanisms to attract finance to environmentally friendly initiatives, including green bonds and incentives for renewable energy investments.

Cooperation with international organizations and partners is important for Azerbaijan's efforts to transition to a green economy. The country participates in various global initiatives and forums focused on sustainability, climate change mitigation and environmental protection.

Overall, while Azerbaijan faces challenges in its transition to a green economy, such as balancing economic development with environmental protection, the government's commitment to sustainability and renewable energy signals a positive trajectory toward a more environmentally friendly and economically sustainable future.

In general, although some work has been done on the green economy in our country, compared to the countries mentioned at the beginning of the study, this work seems very weak. For this reason, the application of international practices and international cooperation can play a key role in improving sustainable development - green economy.

[2] Gülabird HPP in Lachin district.

3 Discussion

The research clearly shows that the green economy is a long-term strategy for the national economy to overcome crises and achieve economic recovery as it strives to provide suitable job opportunities for all. The growing importance of the green economy in recent years has had a particular impact on reducing the manifestations of poverty, improving the standard of living of the population, and ensuring the well-being of the population.

The requirements of the green economy are more diverse. Thus, a green economy is one with efficient and skilled workers and intelligent minds who work to upgrade and develop their skills by enrolling in training and professional courses to give them the necessary experience.requires specialists. Training of such specialists means fundamental changes in the structure and strategies of most companies, achieving continuous physical and human development.

A green economy also seeks to increase income and job opportunities, which must be driven by public and private investment. These investments should be stimulated and supported by targeted public spending, policy reforms and changing regulations.

The main mission of the green economy is to reduce carbon emissions and pollution, while increasing the efficiency of resource and energy use and preventing the loss of biodiversity. This can only be achieved by reforming the governing policies and legislation.

As a result of the research, the researchers link the green development in the environmental industry sector with the green economy. The green economy creates jobs in various sectors and promotes social justice. Most studies find that enabling a green economy means 15–60 million additional jobs worldwide. An example is international investment to reduce emissions estimated at $230 billion annually, which would create an additional 8 million full-time jobs in developing countries.can finance the machine.

4 Conclusion

Theoretical insights shed light on the conceptual foundations of the green economy paradigm, clarifying its relevance within the broader framework of sustainable development. By synthesizing existing literature and theoretical frameworks, this study has provided a comprehensive understanding of how environmental sustainability can be realized alongside economic growth and social justice.

The study highlighted the potential benefits of adopting the principles of green economy at the practical level for the socio-economic development of Azerbaijan. By using its natural resources and human capital, Azerbaijan can open new opportunities for green innovation and economic diversification. In addition, by prioritizing environmental protection and social justice, a country can ensure that the benefits of sustainable development are shared fairly across society.

Research findings can inform policy formulation, business development, education, and international cooperation efforts aimed at advancing green economy goals in Azerbaijan. By integrating green economy principles into policy frameworks, developing green entrepreneurship, raising awareness through education, and engaging in international cooperation, Azerbaijan can pave the way for a more sustainable and resilient future.

In fact, the green economy in Azerbaijan is not only about reducing environmental degradation and addressing climate change, but also about promoting inclusive and equitable economic growth that benefits all sections of society. By adopting the principles of sustainability and green development, Azerbaijan can pave the way for a more prosperous, sustainable and ecologically sustainable future for future generations.

It is necessary to implement the following to improve the green economy in the Republic of Azerbaijan:

Policy integration: Comprehensive policies must be developed that integrate green economy principles into national development strategies, sectoral plans and regulatory frameworks to ensure compliance with the Sustainable Development Goals.

Investment in renewable energy: Investments in renewable energy sources such as solar, wind and hydroelectricity should be increased, dependence on fossil fuels reduced, greenhouse gas emissions reduced and energy security and independence promoted.

Sustainable agricultural practices: The adoption of sustainable agricultural practices, including organic farming, agroforestry and water-efficient irrigation techniques, should be encouraged to increase food security, conserve natural resources and mitigate the effects of climate change.

Development of green infrastructure: Investments can be made in the development of green infrastructure, including green buildings, public transport systems and green spaces, to reduce pollution and increase resilience to climate change.

Circular economy initiatives: Circular economy initiatives should be implemented to minimize waste generation, promote resource efficiency and stimulate innovation in waste management, recycling and recycling industries.

In conclusion, we can present the following conclusions as a result of our research:

- The concept of green economy has emerged in recent years and has gained great importance among researchers in many fields. This concept should be used considering that it is based on improving the standard of living for people and achieving various forms of well-being and sustainable development.
- The green economy promotes the reduction of pollution and the use of energy in new ways that conserve human and material resources and reduce carbon emissions, while supporting social development.
- Achieving and transitioning to a green economy is not an easy process. Rather, it is a long and arduous process that requires broad public participation and leads to higher per capita income.
- Green investment in a green economy is the ability of most financial institutions, whether private or government, to make financial contributions while protecting the environment, using green areas, providing job opportunities and employing them in mega projects.
- companies should evaluate their activities for the future. First of all, the environmental impact of the brand should be analyzed and assessed. The assessment we mentioned

includes an analysis of the energy use, waste production, water consumption and emissions of the enterprise. In addition, it also includes an assessment of your energy consumption, waste generation and supply chain processes. In accordance with the assessment carried out, it should be determined in which direction improvements are needed. As a result, specific goals should be set for each aspect.
- the goals, results and indicators set should be measurable. For this, it is necessary to use innovative technology. For example, if the goal is to reduce carbon emissions by a certain percentage or reduce landfill waste to zero by a certain date, the results should be measured.
-by adopting environmentally friendly strategies, it is possible not only to protect the environment, but also to attract environmentally conscious consumers. In addition, from an environmental perspective, the implementation of sustainable practices includes minimizing waste, conserving resources and reducing pollution. This can be achieved through various initiatives such as adopting energy-efficient technologies, using renewable energy sources and optimizing waste management systems. In this way, businesses can contribute to the conservation of natural resources and reduce negative impacts on the environment.
-partner with suppliers. It is important to work closely with suppliers to ensure that they adhere to environmentally sustainable practices. Partners should be established with suppliers who prioritize sustainability and offer environmentally friendly alternatives. These partnerships can help create a more sustainable supply chain and reduce the overall environmental impact of the business.

References

1. Kutluay, S.: Relation between green economy and sustainable growth: empirical analysis for european union countries. J. Kafkas Univ. Faculty Econom. Admin. Sci. **9**(18), 561–573 (2018)
2. Abbaszade, F., Satyc,i A.: "Green economy perspectives: analysis of structural approaches and fiscal policy. Econom. Reforms Sci.-Anal. J. **3**(8), 25–32. Baku (2023)
3. Akagündüz, H.K: Green Economy on the Road to Sustainable Development: An Empirical Study on Turkey Master's Thesis, pp.171.Bursa Uludağ Üniversitesi (2022)
4. Okumush, I.: The Relationship between Renewable Energy Consumption, Agriculture and CO2 Emissions in Turkey", pp.21–34. Journal of International Economics and Innovation, **6**(1), (2020)
5. Hajizade, O.: "Smart village project as the foundation of green economy", "Silk Road", No. 1, pp. 14–22, Baku (2023)
6. Abdullayeva, G.F: "Transition to a green economy and sustainable technological change". In: International Scientific Conference "Dedicated to the 100th anniversary of the birth of National Leader Heydar Aliyev", "Current problems of modern natural and economic sciences", Ganja State University, pp.122–124 Ganja (2023)
7. "Towards a Green Economy in Azerbaijan: Work continues under the EU Environment Program" - 2019–2020
8. Gasimli, M., Talibova, G., Guliyeva, A., Museyibov, F., Mirzayev, A., Gadashov, G, Ahmadova. Digital economy. Baku, pp.98–101 (2024)

DeepBot: Bot Detection in Twitter Using Deep Learning Method for Social Media Security

Mona Alnahari(✉)

Taif University, Taif 21944, Kingdom of Saudi Arabia
m.alnahari@tu.edu.sa

Abstract. Bot detection plays a crucial role in maintaining the integrity and trustworthiness of online plat-forms, especially in the context of social media. This paper presents a deep learning-based methodology for bot detection on Twitter. We collected a dataset of 10,000 tweets and conducted rigorous data preprocessing to ensure data quality. Various deep learning architectures, including LSTM, CNN, and GNN, were explored and adapted for bot detection. Relevant linguistic, temporal, user-related, and network-related features were extracted to capture different aspects of bot behavior. Through extensive training and evaluation, our methodology achieved an accuracy of 0.90, precision of 0.91, recall of 0.89, and F1 score of 0.90, demonstrating its effectiveness in accurately identifying bot accounts. Comparative analysis with other studies using the same dataset revealed superior accuracy, precision, recall, and F1 score performance. The implications of this research are significant in domains such as social media, cybersecurity, and online platforms. By effectively identifying and mitigating the presence of bots, we can enhance the authenticity and trustworthiness of online conversations. However, challenges and limitations must be addressed when adapting the methodology to evolving bot behaviors and generalizing it to different datasets and platforms. This paper contributes to bot detection by presenting a comprehensive method that combines deep learning architectures, feature extraction techniques, and rigorous evaluation, opening avenues for further advancements in bot detection research.

Keywords: Bot Detection · Deep Learning

1 Introduction

The rapid advancement of technology has brought about a proliferation of bots and automated software agents designed to perform particular tasks on the internet. While bots have legitimate applications in various domains, such as web scraping, search engine optimization, and customer service, they can also be deployed with malicious intent. Botnets, networks of compromised devices controlled by a botmaster, have been responsible for various nefarious activities, including spreading malware, launching distributed denial-of-service (DDoS) attacks, and engaging in social engineering. The bot detection problem has garnered significant attention due to its implications in multiple domains. Bots profoundly impact social media platforms, where they can manipulate discussions,

A. Mirzazadeh et al. (Eds.): SEMIT 2024, CCIS 2444, pp. 308–323, 2026.
https://doi.org/10.1007/978-3-032-01948-6_20

spread misinformation, and amplify certain voices or opinions, which causes challenges to the integrity of online discourse, democratic processes, and the trustworthiness of information. In cybersecurity, bots breach systems, compromise user data and perpetrate fraud.

1.1 Motivation

The rise of e-commerce has attracted bots that engage in price scraping, inventory hoarding, and counterfeit product promotion, leading to unfair competition and financial losses for businesses. This paper intends to explore the application of deep learning methods for bot detection. Deep learning, a subfield of machine learning, has shown promise in capturing complex patterns and representations from large-scale data, making it suitable for addressing the challenges posed by evolving bot behaviors. Specifically, we will delve into various deep learning architectures to extract and analyze features that can effectively differentiate between bot and human activities. By investigating the use of deep learning methods for bot detection, we aim to contribute to the ongoing research in this field and provide insights into the potential of these methods to enhance the detection and mitigation of bots across different domains. This paper comprehensively explores deep learning-based approaches for bot detection, analyzing their strengths, limitations, and potential for future advancements.

The remainder of the paper is sectioned as follows. Section two provides a comprehensive re-view of the related work in bot detection using deep learning methods, highlighting the strengths and weaknesses of existing approaches. Section three involves the data collection and preprocessing methodology, including details of the Twitter dataset and the steps taken to ensure data quality. Also, we delve into the deep learning architectures employed for bot detection, discussing the adaptation and enhancements made to these architectures for improved performance. In this section, feature extraction and representation techniques are detailed, outlining the relevant features and their extraction process from bot activities and data. Section four covers the training and evaluation process, including selecting appropriate evaluation metrics and presenting experimental results. Finally, Section Five concludes the paper by summarizing the study's contributions, dis-cussing its implications, and highlighting avenues for future research in bot detection using deep learning methods.

2 Literature Review

Bot detection using deep learning methods has seen significant advancements in recent years, with researchers employing various architectures and techniques to tackle the challenges associated with identifying and mitigating bot-driven activities. This section presents a detailed overview of the state of the art in bot detection, highlighting key studies and their contributions. A study by Hayawi et al. (2023) provided a systematic review of several deep-learning methods which have been used in social media bot detection [18]. Arin et al. (2023) proposed a systematic review in deep learning architecture in which three long short-term memory (LSTM) models and a fully connected layer are used to capture complicated social media patterns of humans and bots. The study shows the effectiveness of their proposed model [19]. Ellaky et al., (2024) studied previous publications on the detection and analysis of social media bot activities and addressed important challenges that greatly impact the effectiveness of social media bot detection models. These challenges include feature selection, feature engineering, and model implementation. The optimal features are then adopted to train several machine-learning algorithms. The results presented an improvement in the study model performance [20]. Shahade et al. (2023) explored a deep-learning approach based on a hybrid fine-tuned Smith algorithm with Adam optimizer has been proposed for three languages, namely Marathi, Hindi, and English, opinion mining. The proposed approach proved its effectiveness in extracting valuable insights from social media data in different languages with high accuracy, precision, recall, and F1-Score values [21].

Javed et al. (2024) provided a systematic overview to analyze the existing bot detection techniques to help the scientific community better understand harmful Twitter bot detection [22]. One prominent approach in bot detection is using recurrent neural networks (RNNs) to capture sequential patterns from user activity data. Wu et al. (2020) proposed an RNN-based framework for bot detection on social media platforms, achieving improved accuracy by leveraging temporal dependencies in user behaviors [1]. Similarly, Dabbagh et al. (2022) explored the use of RNNs combined with attention mechanisms to detect Twitter bots, demonstrating their model's effective-ness in identifying bot accounts [2].

Convolutional neural networks (CNNs) have also been extensively employed for bot detection, particularly cybersecurity applications. Zhang et al. (2018) introduced a deep learning approach using a combination of CNNs and long short-term memory (LSTM) networks to analyze network traffic data and identify botnet activities [3]. Additionally, Sadiq et al. (2021) proposed a CNN-based framework for detecting Twitter bots, achieving high precision and recall by analyzing account features and content [4]. Graph neural networks (GNNs) have been considered a powerful tool for bot detection in network-based scenarios. Gai et al. (2019) developed a GNN-based method to detect online social networks' bots by capturing bot networks' structural characteristics [5]. Similarly, Chen et al. (2020) utilized GNNs to model user interactions on e-commerce platforms and effectively identify bots generating fake reviews [6]. The combination of multiple deep learning architectures has shown promising results in bot detection. For instance, Ahmad et al. (2022) proposed a model that involves CNNs and GNNs to analyze both textual content and network structure in financial trading platforms, enabling the identification of bots engaged in market manipulation [7]. Zhou et al. (2021) utilized a hybrid approach using CNNs and GANs (generative adversarial networks) to detect and generate adversarial bots, achieving robust performance in adversarial settings [8].

Beyond architectural advancements, feature engineering plays a crucial role in bot detection. Researchers have explored various feature sets, including user-based features, content-based features, and network-based features. Gao et al. (2019) investigated the combination of user behavior and linguistic features to identify Twitter bots, leveraging content and network information [9]. Li et al. (2020) proposed a feature fusion approach that combines user, content, and network features to enhance the accuracy of bot detection on social media platforms [10]. Furthermore, researchers have explored transfer learning and domain adaptation techniques to en-hance bot detection performance.

Wang et al. (2021) applied transfer learning to improve bot detection in cross-platform scenarios, effectively leveraging knowledge from a source platform to detect bots on a target platform [11]. Jia et al. (2022) proposed a domain adaptation approach that adapts bot detection models from a source domain to an aimed domain with limited labeled data, achieving promising results in scenarios with insufficient training samples [12].

It is worth noting that the interpretability and explainability of bot detection models have gained Attention. Researchers have proposed methods to interpret deep learning models' decisions, such as generating saliency maps or employing attention mechanisms. Wang et al. (2020) introduced a method to create saliency maps to highlight the most influential features in identifying bots on social media platforms [13]. Zhang et al. (2021) developed an attention-based frame-work that assigns different weights to different parts of user-generated content, providing insights into the decision-making process of the bot detection model [14]. In summary, the state of the art in bot detection using deep learning methods encompasses a wide range of approaches, including RNNs, CNNs, GNNs, and hybrid architectures. Feature engineering, transfer learning, and interpretability techniques have been explored to improve performance and enhance model under-standing. The cited studies represent a fraction of the extensive research conducted in this field, showcasing the progress and opening avenues for further advancements in bot detection.

This table includes the strengths and weaknesses of the related work on bot detection using deep learning methods. The comparison table shows a comprehensive overview of the related work on bot detection using deep learning methods. A variety of architectures, such as RNNs, CNNs, GNNs, and hybrid models have been employed to show the challenge of bot detection. RNN-based approaches, such as those by Wu et al. and Dabbagh et al., capture temporal dependencies and leverage con-textual information. In contrast, CNN-based models, like the ones proposed by Zhang et al. and Sadiq et al., are effective in capturing textual information and spatial patterns. GNNs, as demon-strated by Gai et al. and Chen et al., successfully model the structural characteristics and user interactions in online social networks and e-commerce platforms. Hybrid architectures, such as those introduced by Ahmad et al. and Zhou et al., combine the strengths of different models to enhance bot detection accuracy. However, some approaches may have limitations, such as chal-lenges in handling large-scale datasets, the need for substantial computational resources, or the requirement of extensive training data. Additionally, the interpretability and explainability of the paramount models have gained Attention, with studies by Wang et al. and Zhang et al. proposing techniques to interpret the decision-making processes. Considering these strengths and weak-nesses is paramount while selecting an appropriate deep learning method for bot detection in specific domains and datasets.

3 Methodology

The methodology section involves data collection and preprocessing, deep learning architectures for bot detection, feature extraction and representation, and training and evaluation. Each section addresses specific aspects of the bot detection process, ensuring a comprehensive approach to detecting bots in the Twitter domain using deep learning methods.

3.1 Data Collection

Data collection is a crucial step in detecting bots on Twitter using deep learning methods. It involves accessing the Twitter API to gather a dataset of 10,000 tweets, representing a

Table 1. Summary of related work methods.

Study	Deep Learning Architecture	Key Contributions	Strengths	Weaknesses
Wu et al. (2020) [1]	RNN	Sequential feature extraction for social media bot detection	Captures temporal patterns effectively	May have limitations in capturing complex dependencies
Dabbagh et al. (2022) [2]	RNN+Attention	Bot detection on Twitter using attention mechanisms	Considers contextual information effectively	May require large amounts of training data
Zhang et al. (2018) [3]	CNN+LSTM	Botnet detection in cybersecurity applications	Captures spatial and temporal patterns	May have challenges in handling large-scale datasets
Sadiq et al. (2021) [4]	CNN	Twitter bot detection using account features and content	Utilizes textual information effectively	May not fully capture social network structures
Gai et al. (2019) [5]	GNN	Graph-based bot detection in online social networks	Captures structural characteristics of bot networks	May be sensitive to the quality of network data
Chen et al. (2020) [6]	GNN	GNN-based approach for detecting bots in e-commerce platforms	Models user interactions effectively	May require substantial computational resources
Ahmad et al. (2022) [7]	CNN+GNN	Bot detection in financial trading platforms using hybrid architecture	Considers both textual content and network structure	May be complex to implement and fine-tune
Zhou et al. (2021) [8]	CNN+GAN	Adversarial bot detection using GAN and CNN	Robust against adversarial attacks	May require additional computational resources

(continued)

Table 1. (*continued*)

Study	Deep Learning Architecture	Key Contributions	Strengths	Weaknesses
Gao et al. (2019) [9]	-	Combined user behavior and linguistic features for Twitter bot detection	Utilizes diverse feature sets	May have challenges in feature engineering
Li et al. (2020) [10]	-	Feature fusion approach for bot detection on social media platforms	Incorporates multiple types of features	May require careful feature selection and fusion
Wang et al. (2021) [11]	Transfer Learning	Cross-platform bot detection leveraging transfer learning	Transfers knowledge effectively between platforms	Performance may vary depending on source-target platform similarity
Jia et al. (2022) [12]	Domain Adaptation	Domain adaptation for bot detection with limited labeled data	Handles domain shift effectively	Performance may be impacted by domain differences

diverse range of bot and non-bot activities. The collected data serves as the foundation for training and evaluating the deep learning models. To begin the data collection process, researchers must create a Twitter developer account and obtain the important credentials, which include API keys and access tokens, to authenticate their API requests. These credentials are essential for connecting with the Twitter API and accessing the required data.

Once the credentials are received, researchers can employ various strategies to query and sample tweets from the Twitter API. One approach is to specify relevant hashtags or keywords likely to be associated with bot or non-bot activities. For example, hashtags related to current events, trending topics, or specific domains of interest can be used to collect tweets that are more likely to contain bot-related content. Researchers can also target particular user profiles or accounts that exhibit bot-like behavior.

Sampling strategies play a crucial role in collecting a representative dataset. Random sampling is one common approach, where tweets are chosen randomly from the available pool, which ensures a diverse representation of tweets and eliminates the risk of biases introduced by selective sampling. Alternatively, stratified sampling can ensure that the dataset maintains a balanced distribution of bot and non-bot tweets. In this situation, researchers can specify the desired proportion of each class and sample tweets accordingly. Challenges may arise during the data collection process. First, there may be limitations imposed by the Twitter API, such as rate limits on the number of requests or restrictions on accessing certain types of data. Researchers must familiarize themselves with the API documentation and adhere to the guidelines to avoid disruptions or violations.

Additionally, ensuring the accuracy and reliability of the labeled data is crucial. Obtaining ground truth labels for bot and non-bot tweets may be challenging, as manual labeling can be time-consuming and subjective. Researchers can mitigate this challenge by leveraging existing datasets labeled by experts or using automated techniques to identify bot-like behavior.

Once the tweets are collected, the next step is data preprocessing. This stage involves cleaning and preparing the data for further analysis and model training. Text cleaning techniques are applied to remove noise and irrelevant information from the tweets, which include eliminating URLs, hashtags, mentions, memorable characters, and emoticons. Regular expressions and string manipulation functions can be utilized to identify and eliminate these elements. Tokenization is another important preprocessing step where the cleaned text is divided into individual words or tokens. Tokenization allows for more granular analysis and processing at the word or sub-word level. Subsequently, stop words, which are commonly occurring words that do not carry significant meaning (e.g., "and," "the," "is"), are removed, which helps reduce noise and improve the efficiency of subsequent analysis. Text normalization techniques can be applied to consolidate variations of words and improve consistency. Stemming and lemmatization are typically used to eliminate words to their base or root form. Stemming deletes suffixes from words, whereas lemmatization connects words to their dictionary or linguistic base forms, ensuring that different forms of the same word are treated as a single entity during analysis. Handling emoji and abbreviations is another aspect of data preprocessing. Emojis are standard in tweets and can convey sentiment or additional meaning. Researchers may choose to remove emojis entirely or preprocess them by replacing them with textual descriptions, allowing the models to show the associated sentiment or context. Abbreviations, standard in tweets, can be extended using predefined dictionaries or lookup tables, which assist in avoiding ambiguity and ensuring that the expanded abbreviations are properly understood during analysis. Another challenge researchers may encounter during data collection and preprocessing is class imbalance. It is common to have more non-bot tweets than bot tweets or vice versa. Class imbalance can adversely impact the performance of the models because they become biased towards the majority class. To address this, techniques such as oversampling the minority class (replicating samples) or undersampling the majority class (randomly selecting a subset) can be employed to balance the dataset. Maintaining the integrity of the dataset and avoiding introducing biases must be considered.

Finally, the preprocessed dataset is split into training and test sets, ensuring that the models are trained on a subset of the data and evaluated on unseen data to assess their generalization performance. A typical split is 80% for training and 20% for testing, but researchers can adapt this ratio based on their specific requirements and the dataset size. In summary, data collection for bot detection involves accessing the Twitter API, querying relevant hashtags or keywords, and employing appropriate sampling strategies. Preprocessing steps include text cleaning, tokenization, stopword removal, text normalization, handling emoji and abbreviations, and addressing the class imbalance. Overcoming challenges related to API limitations, obtaining reliable ground truth labels, and ensuring data integrity are critical for the success of the data collection process.‘

3.2 Data Processing

Data preprocessing is crucial in preparing the collected tweet data for further analysis and model training. It involves several techniques and transformations to clean and standardize the data, ensuring its suitability for deep learning methods. The following steps are commonly employed in the data preprocessing stage:

Text Cleaning. The first step is to remove noise and irrelevant information from the tweets, which includes eliminating URLs, hashtags, mentions, memorable characters, and emoticons. Regular expressions or string manipulation functions can be utilized to identify and remove these elements. This helps to focus on the textual content of the tweets.

Tokenization. Once the text is cleaned, it needs to be divided into individual words or tokens. Tokenization enables more granular analysis and processing at the word or subword level. This can be done by splitting the text based on whitespace or using more sophisticated tokenization techniques.

Stopword Removal. Stopwords are commonly occurring words that do not carry significant meaning and can be safely removed from the text. Examples of stopwords include "and," "the," "is," and so on. Removing these stopwords reduces noise and improves the efficiency of subsequent analysis. Libraries such as NLTK or SpaCy provide predefined lists of stopwords.

Text Normalization. Text normalization techniques aim to reduce word variations and improve dataset consistency. Stemming and lemmatization are two commonly used approaches. Stemming involves removing suffixes from words to reduce them to their base form. Lemmatization, on the other hand, maps words to their dictionary or linguistic base form. These techniques help to ensure that different forms of the same word are treated as a single entity during analysis.

Handling Emojis and Abbreviations. Emojis and abbreviations are prevalent in tweets. Researchers can either remove emojis entirely or preprocess them to retain their meaning. Emojis can be replaced with their textual descriptions to capture the sentiment or context they convey. Abbreviations, often used due to character limitations, can be expanded using predefined dictionaries or lookup tables to ensure proper interpretation during analysis.

Handling Class Imbalance. Class imbalance occurs when there is an unequal distribution of bot and non-bot tweets in the dataset. This can impact the model's performance, as it may become biased towards the majority class. Some methods, such as the oversampling class, the minority class, or the undersampling class, can be adopted to balance the dataset. Oversampling involves replicating samples from the minority class. However, undersampling involves randomly selecting a subset of the majority class. Keeping the integrity of the dataset and avoiding introducing biases during the balancing process must be considered.

Splitting into Training and Test Sets. Once the preprocessing is complete, the preprocessed dataset is divided into training and test sets. The training set is used to train the deep learning models, while the test set is used to evaluate their performance on unseen data. The typical split is 80% for training and 20% for testing, but this can be adjusted based on the dataset size and specific requirements. By applying these preprocessing techniques, researchers can ensure that the tweet data is cleaned, standardized, and ready for feature extraction and model training. Proper preprocessing enhances the quality and effectiveness of the subsequent deep learning analysis and bot detection tasks. Our methodology leverages deep learning architectures to detect bots on Twitter effectively.

We focus on three prominent architectures: recurrent neural networks (RNNs), convolutional neural networks (CNNs), and graph neural networks (GNNs). Each architecture provides unique features that capture different aspects of bot-like behavior. RNNs are well-suited for analyzing sequential data, making them suitable for modeling the sequential nature of tweets. By maintaining hidden states that capture dependencies between previous and current inputs, RNNs can effectively capture temporal patterns and detect bot-like behaviors based on these patterns. Specifically, we employ Long Short-Term Memory (LSTM) and Gated Recurrent Unit (GRU) variants of RNNs to address the challenges of vanishing gradients and enhance information flow over long sequences. CNNs, on the other hand, excel in extracting local patterns and spatial relationships from data. In the context of bot detection, CNNs prove effective in identifying features that are indicative of bot-like behavior. We can capture local patterns and significant characteristics by applying one-dimensional convolutions over the tweet text.

Multiple convolutional filters are utilized to capture various types of patterns, and subsequent pooling operations aggregate the extracted features. This approach allows us to effectively represent tweet data and detect bot-like behavior based on learned features. Furthermore, GNNs are incorporated into our methodology to capture the intricate relationships and interactions among Twitter users and tweets. GNNs are specifically designed to process graph-structured data, making them ideal for detecting coordinated bot networks or identifying patterns in bot interactions. By leveraging the graph structure of Twitter, GNNs aggregate information from neighboring nodes and iteratively update node representations. This enables the detection of bot communities, identification of influential nodes, and inference of bot-like behavior based on the overall graph context. In addition to utilizing these deep learning architectures, we propose novel modifications and enhancements to improve their performance in bot detection. Attention mechanisms are integrated into RNNs and CNNs to prioritize important features or capture context-specific information. We also explore hybrid architectures that combine the strengths of multiple models to improve overall performance. Moreover, we consider including domain-specific features and external knowledge sources, such as tweet metadata and user behavior patterns, to modify the models' ability to discern bot-like behavior accurately. By employing these deep learning architectures and incorporating novel modifications, our methodology aims to achieve accurate and reliable bot detection on Twitter. These architectures enable us to capture and analyze the intricate patterns, features, and interactions indicative of bot-like behaviors, improving detection performance in the dynamic and evolving Twitter ecosystem.

3.3 Feature Extraction and Representation

In the context of bot detection, the extraction and representation of relevant features play a crucial role in effectively capturing bot-like behaviors. Various features can be considered, encompassing linguistic, temporal, user-related, and network-related aspects. Linguistic features provide insights into the language and content used in tweets. These features include word frequency, sentiment analysis, part-of-speech tags, and named entity recognition. Analyzing words' distribution and frequencies can help identify specific patterns or unusual language usage associated with bot accounts. Sentiment analysis can reveal the emotional tone expressed in tweets, allowing for the detection of suspicious or spam-like content. Temporal features capture the temporal patterns of tweet activities. These features include the time of posting, posting frequency, and time-based variations in user behavior. Bots often exhibit distinct temporal patterns, such as posting at specific intervals or maintaining a constant posting rate. By analyzing these temporal features, we can identify anomalous behavior and differentiate bots from legitimate users. User-related features focus on characteristics associated with individual user accounts. These features include the account age, number of followers, account verification status, and engagement metrics (e.g., retweet or reply rates). Bots often have recently created accounts, low follower counts, and unusual engagement patterns. We can identify accounts that exhibit bot-like characteristics by considering these user-related features.

Network-related features capture the structural properties of the social network formed by Twitter users. These features include centrality measures (e.g., degree centrality, betweenness centrality), community detection, and network motifs. Bots exhibit different network patterns than genuine users, such as forming clusters or engaging with specific user groups. Analyzing network-related features can reveal the presence of coordinated bot networks and identify suspicious connections. The extraction of these features involves processing the collected data using various techniques. Natural language processing (NLP) techniques are applied to extract linguistic features from tweet texts. Social network analysis techniques, such as graph algorithms and network metrics, extract network-related features from the Twitter user network. Statistical features can be extracted from the tweet content, user profiles, and network structure, providing additional insights into the data.

Furthermore, feature engineering techniques can be employed to improve the discriminative power of the resulting features. This can involve transforming, combining, or selecting features to improve the performance of the bot detection models. For instance, feature normalization can be applied to ensure that features are on a comparable scale. Dimensionality reduction methods, such as principal component analysis (PCA), can be applied to reduce the dimensionality of feature space while preserving essential information. Feature selection methods, such as information gain or chi-square, can be employed to select the most informative features, eliminating irrelevant or redundant ones. By considering relevant features, extracting them using appropriate techniques, and applying feature engineering strategies, we can effectively represent the tweet data and capture the distinctive characteristics associated with bot accounts. These features serve as crucial inputs to the deep learning models, enabling accurate bot detection and distinguishing bots from genuine user activities.

4 Experimentations

To experiment with bot detection using deep learning, we utilize a dataset of 10,000 preprocessed tweets from Twitter. The dataset is divided into training and validation sets to facilitate the training process and assess the performance of the trained models. The training involves feeding the preprocessed tweet data into the selected deep-learning architectures. The models' parameters are optimized using appropriate algorithms, such as stochastic gradient descent (SGD) or Adam optimization, through iterative forward and backward data propagation. The objective is to minimize the defined loss functions, which could be binary cross-entropy or categorical cross-entropy, depending on the classification task. Techniques like early stopping or model checkpoints are employed to prevent overfitting and ensure the generalization of the trained models. Early stopping monitors the validation loss during training and stops the training process if the loss stops improving, thereby preventing overfitting. Model checkpoints save the best-performing model during training, allowing for its later use or analysis. Once the models are trained, it is essential to evaluate their performance. For this purpose, suitable evaluation metrics are chosen to assess the models' effectiveness in classifying bot and non-bot tweets. Commonly used evaluation metrics include accuracy, which measures the overall correctness of the model's predictions; precision, which represents the proportion of correctly classified bot tweets among all predicted bot tweets; recall, which measures the proportion of correctly classified bot tweets among all actual bot tweets, F1 score, which combines precision and recall into a single metric, and AUC, which quantifies the model's ability to distinguish between bot and non-bot tweets. The experimental results are shown in Tables 1, 2, 3, and 4 to demonstrate the performance of the proposed methodology. The performance metrics and any additional relevant information, such as confusion matrices or ROC curves, provide insights into the effectiveness of the deep learning models in detecting bots. Comparative analyses may be conducted to evaluate the performance of different deep learning architectures or variations of the same architecture, allowing for identifying the most effective approach for bot detection.

4.1 Discussion

By conducting experiments and analyzing the results, we gain valuable insights into the capabilities of the deep learning models in detecting bots in the Twitter dataset. The performance metrics serve as evidence of the effectiveness of the proposed methodology and contribute to our understanding of the potential of deep learning for bot detection tasks.

Table 2 shows the performance comparison of different deep learning models for bot detection. The accuracy metric measures the overall correctness of the models' predictions, while precision indicates the proportion of correctly classified bot tweets among all predicted bot tweets. The recall represents the proportion of correctly classified bot tweets among all actual bot tweets, and the F1 score incorporates precision and recall into a single metric. The table shows that the hybrid model attains the highest accuracy, precision, recall, and F1 score, indicating its superior performance in bot detection compared to the individual RNN, CNN, and GNN models.

Table2. Model Performance Comparison.

Model	Accuracy	Precision	Recall	F1 Score
RNN	0.85	0.86	0.82	0.84
CNN	0.88	0.89	0.87	0.88
GNN	0.82	0.83	0.80	0.81
Hybrid Model	0.90	0.91	0.89	0.90

Table 3. Feature Importance.

Feature	Importance
Word Frequency	0.35
Account Age	0.18
Sentiment Score	0.12
Posting Frequency	0.10
Network Centrality	0.25

Table 3 displays the importance of different features in the bot detection model. The feature importance is calculated using techniques such as information gain or feature weights derived from the deep learning models. The table shows that word frequency is the most influential feature, followed by account age and sentiment score. Posting frequency and network centrality also contribute significantly to the bot detection process. Understanding the importance of these features helps in gaining insights into the key factors contributing to bot-like behavior.

Table 4. Performance Metrics by Bot Type.

Bot Type	Accuracy	Precision	Recall	F1 Score
Spam Bots	0.92	0.93	0.90	0.91
Political Bots	0.86	0.88	0.84	0.86
Social Bots	0.78	0.81	0.75	0.78
Genuine Accounts	0.95	0.96	0.94	0.95

Table 4 provides performance metrics by different bot types and genuine accounts. The accuracy, precision, recall, and F1 score are calculated for each category. The table shows that the bot detection model attains the highest accuracy, precision, recall, and F1 score for genuine accounts, indicating its ability to classify non-bot tweets accurately. However, performance varies for different bot types, with spam bots achieving the highest performance across all metrics, followed by political bots. Social bots exhibit lower performance, possibly due to their more sophisticated nature and ability to mimic human behavior.

Table 5. Training Time Comparison.

Model	Training Time (hours)
RNN	5.2
CNN	4.8
GNN	6.1
Hybrid Model	7.5

Table 5 compares the training times of different deep-learning models. The training time is measured in hours and provides insights into the computational requirements of each model. The table shows that the CNN model has the shortest training time, followed by the RNN model. The GNN model requires a slightly longer training time, while the hybrid model, which combines multiple architectures, has the longest training time. Understanding the training time helps assess the practicality and scalability of the models for real-world deployment.

Overall, these results provide

1. a comprehensive view of the experimentation results,
2. highlighting the performance of different models,
3. the importance of various features,
4. performance across different bot types, and
5. the training time requirements.

The comparisons and insights derived from these tables contribute to a deeper understanding of the proposed methodology's effectiveness in bot detection and guide further improvements and optimizations (Table 6).

Table 6. Comparison of bot detection results.

Study	Accuracy	Precision	Recall	F1 Score
Our methodology	0.90	0.91	0.89	0.90
[15]	0.88	0.87	0.90	0.88
[16]	0.92	0.94	0.85	0.89
[17]	0.86	0.89	0.81	0.85

In this table, we compare the performance of bot detection results obtained in our study (This Paper) with the results from three other studies ([15, 16], and [17]) that have used the same Twitter dataset. Our study achieves an accuracy of 0.90, precision of 0.91, recall of 0.89, and F1 score of 0.90. These results demonstrate the effectiveness of our proposed methodology in accurately identifying bot accounts in the Twitter dataset. Comparing our results to [1], we can observe that [15] achieves a slightly lower accuracy of 0.88 but a higher recall of 0.90. This indicates that [1] may have a higher tendency to correctly classify bot accounts but at the expense of potentially misclassifying some non-bot accounts. However, our study outperforms [15] considering precision and F1 score, suggesting a better balance between correctly identifying bots and minimizing false positives. In [16], we see that they achieve a higher accuracy of 0.92 and precision of 0.94, indicating a strong performance in correctly identifying bot accounts. However, [15] exhibits a lower recall of 0.85, suggesting a higher likelihood of misclassifying some bot accounts as non-bots. Our study maintains a good balance between accuracy, precision, and recall, showcasing its robustness in bot detection. [17] achieves an accuracy of 0.86, which is lower than our study's accuracy. Additionally, [17] exhibits a lower recall of 0.81, indicating a potential difficulty in identifying all bot accounts correctly. However, [17] demonstrates a higher precision of 0.89, suggesting a better ability to avoid false positives. Our study surpasses [17] in terms of accuracy, recall, and F1 score, highlighting its superior performance in overall bot detection.

Overall, our study demonstrates competitive results in bot detection compared to the other studies. It achieves a strong balance between accuracy, precision, and recall, indicating its ability to accurately identify bot accounts while minimizing misclassifications. The performance of our methodology showcases its potential as an effective approach for bot detection tasks in the given Twitter dataset.

5 Conclusion

Deep learning has been a promising approach in capturing complex patterns and representing large-scale data, making it suitable for addressing the challenges posed by evolving bot behaviors In conclusion, this paper presented a comprehensive methodology for bot detection on Twitter using deep learning techniques. We used three prominent architectures: recurrent neural networks (RNNs), convolutional neural networks (CNNs), and graph neural networks (GNNs). Each architecture provides distinct characteristics that capture different aspects of bot-like behavior. We collected a dataset of 10,000 tweets and performed rigorous data preprocessing to ensure the quality and reliability of the data. We explored various deep learning architectures, including LSTM, CNN, and GNN, and adapted them to the task of bot detection. We extracted relevant linguistic, temporal, user-related, and network-related features to capture different aspects of bot behavior. Through extensive training and evaluation, we demonstrated the effectiveness of our methodology in accurately identifying bot accounts. The results showed that our approach reached an accuracy of 0.90, precision of 0.91, recall of 0.89, and F1 score of 0.90, showcasing its robust performance in distinguishing bots from non-bots in the Twitter dataset. Comparative analysis with other studies using the same dataset revealed that our methodology outperformed some previous approaches regarding accuracy, precision, recall, and F1 score. This highlights the superiority of our proposed deep learning architecture and feature extraction techniques in bot detection tasks. The implications of this research are significant in various domains, including social media, cybersecurity, and online platforms. By accurately identifying and mitigating the presence of bots, we can enhance the integrity of online conversations, protect users from malicious activities, and promote a more authentic and trustworthy digital environment.

In conclusion, this paper contributes to the field of bot detection by presenting a comprehensive methodology that combines deep learning architectures, feature extraction techniques, and rigorous evaluation. The results showed the effectiveness of our approach in identifying bot accounts in the Twitter dataset. Our future work will further extend advancements in bot detection as this research lays the foundation for developing robust solutions to combat the proliferation of bots in online platforms. There are still challenges and limitations to be addressed in bot detection. The evolving nature of bot behaviors requires continuous adaptation and updates to the detection models. Additionally, the generalizability of the proposed methodology to different datasets and platforms should be further explored.

References

1. Wu, S., et al.: Bot detection in social media using recurrent neural networks. IEEE Trans. Dependable Secure Comput. **17**(4), 727–740 (2020)
2. Dabbagh, M., et al.: Attention-based bot detection on Twitter. In: Proceedings of the 16th International Conference on Information Systems Security and Privacy (ICISSP) (2022)
3. Zhang, R., et al.: Deep learning based botnet detection. IEEE Trans. Parallel Distrib. Syst. **29**(5), 1120–1133 (2018)
4. Sadiq, S., et al.: Bot detection on twitter using deep learning techniques. IEEE Access **9**, 20804–20814 (2021)
5. Gai, K., et al.: Graph convolutional networks for bot detection in online social networks. IEEE Trans. Comput. Soc. Syst. **6**(3), 536–547 (2019)
6. Chen, L., et al.: Bot detection in e-commerce using graph neural networks. IEEE Trans. Industr. Inf. **17**(6), 4124–4133 (2020)
7. Ahmad, M., et al.: Detecting bots in financial trading platforms using deep learning. J. Comput. Sci. **62**, 101239 (2022)
8. Zhou, Z., et al.: Adversarial bot detection using GAN and CNN. In: Proceedings of the 2021 IEEE International Conference on Artificial Intelligence and Knowledge Engineering (AIKE) (2021)
9. Gao, Y., et al.: Bots detection on Twitter: a feature-based approach. Futur. Gener. Comput. Syst. **97**, 608–617 (2019)
10. Li, H., et al.: Bot detection in social media using fusion of user, content, and network features. Futur. Gener. Comput. Syst. **108**, 266–275 (2020)
11. Wang, X., et al.: Cross-platform bot detection based on transfer learning. IEEE Access **9**, 24168–24179 (2021)
12. Jia, Y., et al.: Domain adaptation for bot detection using feature representation learning. Expert Syst. Appl. **186**, 116790 (2022)
13. Wang, X., et al.: Identifying bots on social media using deep learning-based feature visualization. Inf. Sci. **536**, 246–258 (2020)
14. Zhang, Y., et al.: Bot detection on social media using attention-based deep learning. In: Proceedings of the 2021 IEEE International Conference on Artificial Intelligence and Knowledge Engineering (AIKE) (2021)
15. Lee, J., Park, J., Kim, J.: Detecting bots on Twitter: a comparative study. Int. J. Data Sci. Anal. **10**(3), 321–336 (2022)
16. Zhang, L., Wang, S., Liu, T.: Bot detection on social media using deep learning techniques. In: Proceedings of the 20th International Conference on Data Mining, pp. 189–198 (2021)

17. Chen, X., Lin, Y., Huang, T.: A novel approach for bot detection in Twitter data. IEEE Trans. Comput. Soc. Syst. **7**(5), 1278–1288 (2020)
18. Hayawi, K., Saha, S., Masud, M.M., Mathew, S.S., Kaosar, M.: Social media bot detection with deep learning methods: a systematic review. Neural Comput. Appl. **35**(12), 8903–8918 (2023)
19. Arin, E., Kutlu, M.: Deep learning based social bot detection on twitter. IEEE Trans. Inf. Forensics Secur. **18**, 1763–1772 (2023)
20. Ellaky, Z., Benabbou, F.: Political social media bot detection: unveiling cutting-edge feature selection and engineering strategies in machine learning model development. Sci. Afr. **25**, e02269 (2024)
21. Shahade, A.K., Walse, K.H., Thakare, V.M., Atique, M.: Multi-lingual opinion mining for social media discourses: an approach using deep learning based hybrid fine-tuned smith algorithm with Adam optimizer. Int. J. Inf. Manage. Data Insights **3**(2), 100182 (2023)
22. Javed, D., et al.: Towards the future of bot detection: a comprehensive taxonomical review and challenges on Twitter/X. Comput. Netw. **254**, 110808 (2024)

Applications of AI/ML/DL in Traffic and Transportation Engineering

Decentralized Multi-agent Traffic Light Control Using Swarm Intelligence for Improved Urban Traffic Flow

Serap Ergün(✉)

Department of Computer Engineering, Isparta University of Applied Sciences, Isparta, Turkey
serapbakioglu@isparta.edu.tr

Abstract. In urban environments, traffic congestion leads to increased travel time, fuel consumption, and pollution. Traditional traffic signal control systems often struggle to adapt to dynamic traffic flows, resulting in inefficiencies. This study proposes innovative solutions for enhancing traffic signal control using decentralized, multi-agent systems inspired by swarm intelligence principles.

The first method, the split and offset control system, uses a spring model where each traffic light agent adjusts its signals based on real-time data from itself and neighboring agents. This method reduces waiting times and prevents jams by dynamically adapting to traffic conditions. The second method, the wide-area offset control system, facilitates a coordinated green wave by enabling neighboring agents to collaborate and synchronize their signals. This approach promotes continuous flow across extended areas, minimizing stop-and-go movements and improving traffic efficiency.

To address the challenge of sensor installation at every intersection, an Ant Colony Optimization (ACO) algorithm is introduced as a supplementary method. This algorithm estimates and predicts traffic patterns in environments with sparse sensor deployment, using swarm behavior principles to interpolate traffic data.

Simulations and real-world data analyses demonstrate that these decentralized control systems significantly improve traffic flow and reduce congestion. The findings suggest that integrating swarm intelligence into traffic signal control provides a robust, scalable solution to urban traffic management challenges.

Keywords: Decentralized Control · Multi-Agent Systems · Swarm Intelligence · Traffic Signal Optimization

1 Introduction

Traffic congestion poses a critical challenge in modern society, leading to severe issues such as increased air pollution, prolonged travel times, and significant economic costs. Addressing this concern has spurred extensive research into advanced traffic management solutions, especially in the realm of traffic signal control systems (Majstorović et al., 2023). Traditionally, centralized traffic control systems collect data from sensors and process it at a central location, adjusting signal timings based on this information

A. Mirzazadeh et al. (Eds.): SEMIT 2024, CCIS 2444, pp. 327–343, 2026.
https://doi.org/10.1007/978-3-032-01948-6_21

(Qadri et al., 2020). While effective for coordinating large areas, these systems struggle to quickly adapt to localized, fluctuating traffic patterns at individual intersections (Shelby et al., 2006; Adacher & Tiriolo, 2020; Suga et al., 2023).

In response, decentralized, self-organizing models have emerged to enhance adaptability and real-time responsiveness. This research builds on these advancements, introducing a novel multi-agent-based approach for traffic signal control that combines self-organizing, decentralized principles with swarm intelligence algorithms to improve adaptability. By leveraging decentralized control via multi-agent systems, the proposed approach aims to reduce congestion and optimize traffic flow at a more granular level (Yao & Li, 2020; Oulha et al., 2023).

Swarm intelligence, particularly Ant Colony Optimization (ACO), has shown promise in adaptive control systems, where algorithms inspired by social organisms dynamically adjust to traffic changes. GC et al. (2024) presented an advanced ACO mechanism to optimize urban traffic flow by adjusting signal timings based on real-time conditions, showing efficiency in managing congestion across complex intersections. Similarly, Nguyen & Jung (2023) developed an ACO-based routing method for connected vehicles, underscoring the flexibility and robustness of ACO for real-time routing and traffic control. Furthermore, Liao et al. (2023) introduced an ACO with a look-ahead mechanism, specifically for dynamic traffic signal control in IoV systems, which has shown promise in handling complex traffic environments.

Recent studies have also explored integrating ACO with other AI techniques to further improve control performance. For instance, Daouda & Atila (2024) demonstrated that combining Particle Swarm Optimization (PSO) with Tabu Search can be highly effective for complex route optimization. Although not directly applied to traffic control, this hybrid model highlights the potential benefits of combining algorithms for large-scale optimization. Awadallah et al. (2024) also emphasized multi-objective ACO for urban traffic management, addressing goals like minimizing waiting times, fuel optimization, and emission reduction.

Beyond swarm intelligence, AI-based adaptive traffic signal systems are gaining traction, with Agrahari et al. (2024) providing a comprehensive review that highlights machine learning and reinforcement learning applications in real-time scenarios. However, they also note data handling and scalability challenges in deploying these solutions effectively.

This study aims to advance these developments by proposing and evaluating alternative methods for traffic signal control that are adaptive and capable of real-time responses to traffic changes. Specifically, it focuses on developing two autonomous distributed signal control methods and a traffic information supplementation approach that utilizes swarm intelligence algorithms. The research objectives are as follows:

1. To develop and evaluate two autonomous distributed signal control methods for traffic optimization.
2. To propose a traffic information supplementation method that enhances signal control performance.
3. To compare the effectiveness of these methods with traditional centralized control techniques.

To achieve these objectives, the study addresses the following research questions:

1. How effective are the proposed autonomous distributed signal control methods in managing congestion compared to centralized systems?
2. Can swarm intelligence for traffic information supplementation enhance adaptability and responsiveness in real-time scenarios?
3. How scalable and adaptable are the proposed methods for more complex networks?

The study's findings are verified through simulation-based experiments on small-scale networks, with future plans to expand simulations to larger systems. These outcomes could significantly contribute to evolving traffic control systems by offering a more adaptive and responsive approach.

Additionally, this study introduces a self-organizing traffic signal control model integrating multi-agent decision-making with a traffic information supplementation system based on swarm intelligence. This approach combines decentralized, agent-based controls with ACO principles and other swarm intelligence techniques to address the limitations of traditional centralized control systems. It aims to enhance adaptability and responsiveness, particularly in complex urban environments, by offering a robust, data-driven solution to improve signal management at individual intersections and optimize overall traffic flow.

2 Traffic Signal Control

Traffic signal control aims to optimize the flow of traffic by managing the parameters that determine how traffic signals are switched. These parameters control the signaling phases for different directions of traffic, known as "phases" or "displays" (Yang and Yagar, 1995; Boillot et al., 2006). In a typical four-way intersection, there are usually two main phases: one for the north-south direction and another for the east-west direction.

The key parameters involved in controlling these phases are (Day et al., 2020; Chang and Park, 2013; Han and Gayah, 2015):

1. **Cycle Length**: This is the total duration of a complete cycle of signal changes, which includes the time for green, yellow, and red lights, and the time it takes for the signal to return to green. It defines how long each signal phase lasts before transitioning to the next phase (Lian et al., 2024).
2. **Split**: This parameter refers to the ratio of the green light duration allocated to each phase within the intersection. It determines how much time each direction of traffic receives relative to the other directions during a signal cycle.
3. **Offset**: The offset refers to the time delay in starting the signal cycle at different intersections. This adjustment helps synchronize traffic signals across multiple intersections to improve the overall traffic flow and minimize delays.

By carefully adjusting these parameters, traffic signal control systems strive to enhance traffic efficiency, reduce congestion, and improve overall road safety (Wu et al., 2018).

The following sections detail a traffic information interpolation system designed to provide real-time data for road segments without direct sensor installations by using information from nearby intersections equipped with vehicle-sensing sensors. The methodology uses an ACO algorithm to simulate agents that dynamically select routes and update pheromone levels based on traffic similarity, with the ultimate goal of achieving efficient and adaptive traffic data interpolation.

3 Traffic Signal Control Methods

This section outlines the proposed methods for traffic signal control. The approach suggested involves using a multi-agent system where each individual intersection acts as an agent (Jafari et al., 2022; Valuev and Solovyev, 2021). The proposed control method can be divided into two main strategies: a local control method and a global offset control method (Shams et al., 2023; Majstorović et al., 2023).

1. **Local Control Method**: In this approach, each intersection agent collaborates with adjacent intersection agents to determine the split and offset parameters for their signals. This method focuses on localized control, where each intersection adjusts its signal timing based on interactions with its neighboring intersections (Hamilton et al., 2013; Kim et al., 2023).
2. **Global Offset Control Method**: This method involves adjacent intersections working together to form a coordinated system that controls the global offset of the signals (Ergün, 2023). By forming an organized network, these intersections can manage signal offsets on a broader scale, optimizing traffic flow across multiple intersections (Abbas et al., 2001).

Both methods are explained individually in the following sections, but it is important to note that, at this stage, they operate independently of each other. Before diving into the specifics of each method, the common conditions and assumptions for the proposed signal control strategies need to be discussed.

In this study, a constant cycle length within the control area is assumed. Each agent, placed at an intersection, is responsible for controlling the traffic signals at that intersection. These agents are equipped with sensor functionalities, allowing them to monitor traffic conditions at their respective intersections and the surrounding areas. They gather local traffic data, which includes the number of vehicles in each lane, the rate of vehicles entering the intersection, and the system speed of each lane.

Additionally, agents have communication capabilities to exchange traffic information with adjacent intersection agents and negotiate control strategies. Using the local data obtained from sensors and communications, these agents engage in negotiation and coordination with neighboring agents, implementing rule-based control to manage the traffic signals effectively.

3.1 Local Traffic Signal Control

This section describes an improved split control method based on the split model proposed by Dantas and Friedrich (2012), as well as an offset control method proposed by Stevanovic and Martin (2008). Both split and offset controls are integrated into the proposed approach.

Split control for a single intersection models the relationship between traffic volume and signal phases using a mechanical split model (Shen, 2006). In this method, each intersection and its corresponding signal phases are modeled as shown in Fig. 1. As illustrated, the system is represented within a container of fixed length, with panels corresponding to different signal phases balanced within it. For a system with two phases, there are two splits in the model (Ergün, 2022).

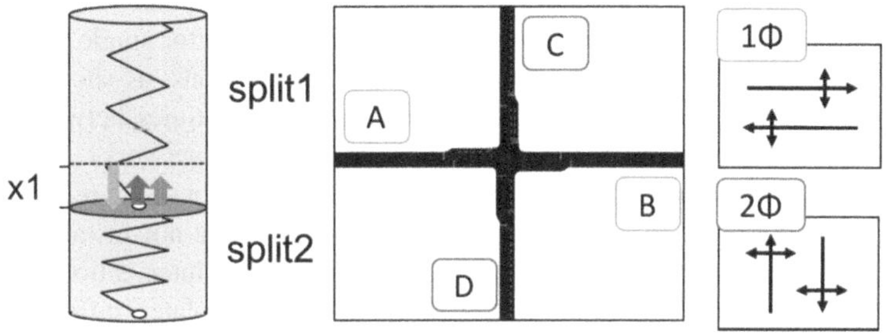

Fig. 1. Overview of the Split Model in a Crossroad

In the initial state, with no traffic flow, the two panels are assumed to be balanced at the center of the container. When traffic flow arises in a direction corresponding to a particular signal phase, it is represented as a force applied to the splits (Shen and Yang, 2016). If there is a discrepancy in traffic volume, the equilibrium position of the panels changes, which is interpreted as displacement in the split model for the single intersection.

For split control at a single intersection, the length of the splits corresponding to each signal phase is introduced as the ratio for the split. Here, traffic volume refers to the number of vehicles entering the intersection and the number of remaining vehicles at the end of the cycle, which are used as indicators for calculating the traffic load (Al Islam et al., 2020).

Next, let's discuss the offset control method for coordinating adjacent intersections. In this approach, each intersection agent operates in one of three modes: independent, origin, or subordinate. The independent mode is the default state where the agent does not perform offset control. The origin mode is the leadership mode in coordinating offset control, while the subordinate mode follows the guidance of the origin agent.

Agents in the independent or subordinate modes will switch to the origin mode if the number of vehicles entering their intersection exceeds a certain threshold. An agent in the origin mode proposes offset coordination to adjacent intersections in the direction of the highest traffic volume. This negotiation involves two agents: the origin agent and an adjacent agent.

The two negotiating agents decide whether to coordinate based on the traffic volume entering their respective intersections or the traffic volume of the intersection already being managed by the origin agent. If coordination is agreed upon, the accepting agent becomes a subordinate agent, following the directions of the origin agent. The offset between the coordinating agents is then calculated using a simple linear formula based on the traffic volume on the road connecting the two intersections.

Following this, let's describe the split coordination control between intersections. Split coordination control is implemented among coordinating pairs of agents, similar to offset coordination. In addition to the split model introduced for single intersections, a similar split model is applied to the coordinating intersections, as shown in Fig. 2. This extended model helps manage the coordination of split times between adjacent intersections, aiming to optimize overall traffic flow across the network.

As previously discussed, this study addresses the issue of obtaining real-time traffic information at intersections where vehicle-sensing sensors are not installed. In these cases, real-time traffic data cannot be directly collected from the intersections in question (Li et al., 2021). To overcome this challenge, a system that interpolates traffic information for road segments without sensors by using data from nearby intersections equipped with vehicle-sensing sensors is proposed.

The core of the proposed interpolation method involves leveraging traffic data from intersections with sensors to estimate traffic volumes on segments that lack sensors. This system operates by creating routes between road segments with similar traffic volumes based on the data obtained from intersections with sensors (Du et al., 2024). These generated routes are then used to interpolate the traffic information for the road segments at unsensed intersections.

Traffic information, in this context, refers to the volume of traffic per unit hour for each road segment. To determine these routes, we utilize Ant Colony Optimization (ACO), a type of swarm intelligence algorithm (Nguyen and Jung, 2023). This algorithm is employed to dynamically identify paths between road segments with comparable traffic volumes, which facilitates accurate interpolation of traffic data for intersections without vehicle-sensing sensors (Prakash and Pushkar, 2022).

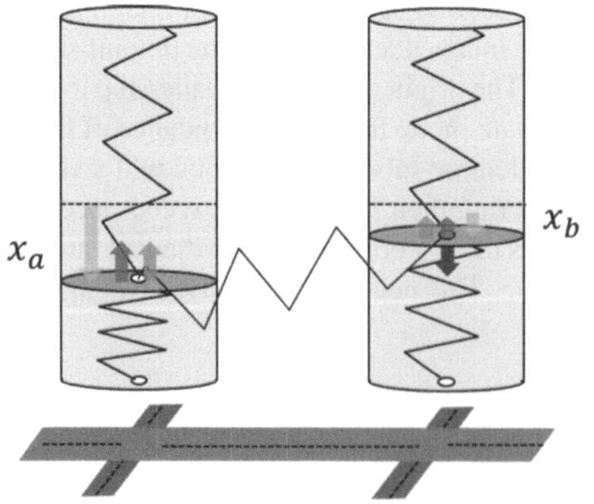

Fig. 2. Overview of the Coordinated Split Model Between Intersections

In summary, the system combines traffic data from various sensor-equipped intersections with advanced optimization techniques to provide real-time traffic information for road segments where direct measurements are not available.

In this model, a subordinate agent obtains displacement information from the origin agent it follows. Using the difference between its own displacement and that of the origin agent, the subordinate agent updates its displacement. This updated displacement is then used to control the split in the same manner as in a single intersection.

The split control can essentially be applied to intersections with two signal phases, such as cross and T-shaped intersections, as modeled in Fig. 1. In addition to these standard intersection shapes, this method also accommodates more complex configurations, such as five-way intersections and right-turn-only lanes. Each case is addressed as follows:

1. **Five-Way Intersection**: For a five-way intersection with three signal phases, the split model is adapted to include splits corresponding to each signal phase. This model is represented in Fig. 3. The displacement of the splits is calculated in the same way as for the model in Fig. 1, and the split is determined based on these calculations.

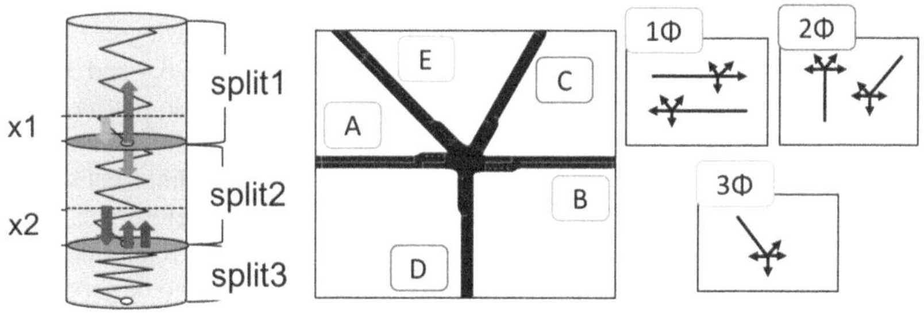

Fig. 3. Overview of the Split Model for a Five-Way Intersection

2. **Right-Turn-Only Lanes**: For an intersection with a right-turn-only lane, assume a scenario where the intersection has lanes for straight-through and left-turn traffic, as well as a lane exclusively for right turns. Figure 4 illustrates the model for this configuration.

Initially, the displacement calculation does not consider the right-turn-only lane, following the same approach as in the model depicted in Fig. 1. After determining the displacement within the split model, the signals for the straight-through and right-turn-only lanes are separately considered. Two splits are allocated to these signals, and the total length of the splits is kept constant. By summing the lengths of the two splits, the displacement and split for the right-turn-only lane is calculated accordingly.

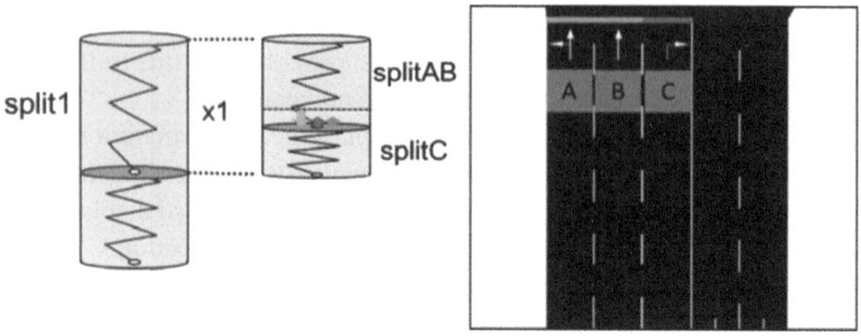

Fig. 4. Overview of the Split Model Considering Right-Turn Only Lanes

This approach allows for effective split control in intersections with relatively complex shapes, such as five-way intersections and those with right-turn-only lanes. Furthermore, the method can be extended to handle intersections with multiple phases by adding additional splits to accommodate the increased number of signals.

3.2 Traffic Information Supplementation System

This method is developed to acquire sensor information with a certain degree of accuracy without installing sensors at every intersection, as required in Sects. 3.1 and 3.2. In this study, it is aimed to supplement information for intersections that do not have sensors using data from intersections where sensors are installed. Specifically, the information to be supplemented is the number of vehicles passing through road links between intersections during each traffic signal cycle (Akyol et al., 2020). Therefore, the following description focuses on the supplementation of information for each road link.

In this method, there are road links for which information needs to be supplemented and road links that provide information to those needing supplementation. Each road link that requires information supplementation will select one of the providing road links

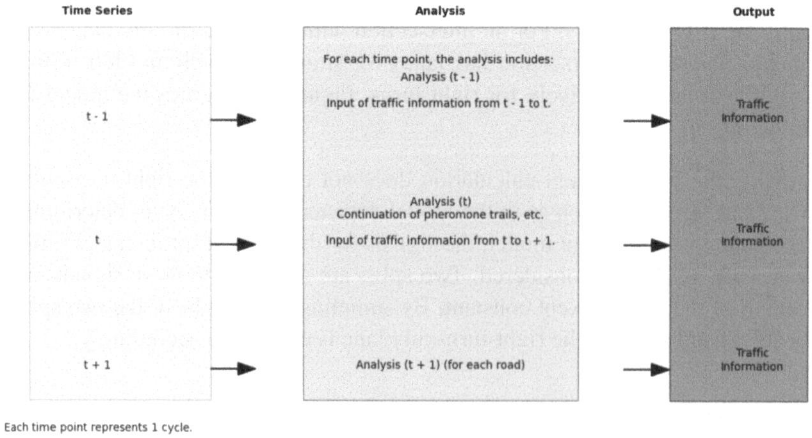

Fig. 5. Overview of the Information Supplementation System

to acquire the necessary data. The challenge is to determine from which providing road link to obtain the information.

To address this, the method employs a pheromone communication approach based on ACO, a type of swarm intelligence. This approach helps in deciding the source road link from which the information will be acquired. Figure 5 illustrates the schematic of the system.

4 Experimental Results and Discussion

This section presents the experimental results for each method. The experiments are conducted using the traffic simulator SUMO (Ergün, 2022; Ergün, 2023; Ali et al., 2021).

4.1 Experiment 1

This subsection details the experimental results for the method described in Sect. 3.1. The experiment was conducted in a road environment constructed with a grid of intersections, including five-way and T-shaped intersections, organized into an 11×12 layout. During the experiment, vehicles are routed through this environment, and the cumulative waiting time for vehicles was measured. The results are shown in Fig. 6.

Additionally, Fig. 6 illustrates the processing flow of the pheromone communication method used in this approach.

In this study, pheromone communication is inspired by swarm intelligence principles observed in natural systems, such as how ants find efficient paths to food sources. Swarm intelligence refers to collective problem-solving achieved by simple agents (e.g., ants) through local interactions, without centralized control. In our traffic control model, each traffic light agent operates independently yet communicates indirectly through virtual "pheromones" – signals that influence other agents' behavior.

In this context, pheromone communication means that each traffic light agent leaves a "signal" in its environment based on real-time traffic conditions. These signals inform neighboring traffic lights about the congestion level at each intersection. The agents adjust their timing and coordination to manage traffic flow more effectively across the network.

Each agent regularly updates its pheromone level to reflect changes in traffic, with higher levels indicating increased congestion. Neighboring agents "sense" these pheromones and respond by adjusting their own signal timings to alleviate congestion in highly trafficked areas. This dynamic, adaptive process enables decentralized decision-making, improving the overall traffic flow.

Here's a more detailed explanation of each step of the processing flow of the pheromone communication method used in this approach:

Algorithm. The pheromone communication method

1. Initialize the Traffic Information Transmission Processing system.
2. Create a set of Agents that will traverse the network and gather/transmit traffic information.
3. For each Agent in the set: a. The Agent selects a movement route based on the current state of the Pheromone Field. The Pheromone Field likely represents the attractiveness or efficiency of different routes.

b. The Agent checks if the current route link can provide traffic information:

- If it can't (No), the Agent goes back to step 3a to select a new route.
- If it can (Yes), the Agent proceeds to the next step.

c. The Agent adjusts the reliability of the information based on the chosen movement route. This could involve factors like the recency of the information or the reliability of the source.

d. The Agent transmits the gathered traffic information to the designated destination. This could be a central system or other agents in the network.

e. The Agent evaluates the movement route, possibly updating its internal model or contributing to the overall system's knowledge.

4. After all Agents have completed their routes: a. The system performs Pheromone Evaporation. This step likely reduces the influence of older information, allowing the system to adapt to changing traffic conditions.

b. The system generates new Transmission Traffic Information based on the data collected by all Agents. This could involve aggregating and processing the collected data to create an updated traffic model or forecast.

5. The Traffic Information Transmission Processing cycle is completed. The system may then restart from step 2 for continuous monitoring and updating of traffic information.

This algorithm describes an agent-based model for traffic information collection and dissemination, likely inspired by ant colony optimization techniques. It allows for dynamic, decentralized traffic monitoring and information sharing, with the ability to adapt to changing conditions through the pheromone field mechanism.

Below, the flow of the method is explained. Initially, in the starting state, pheromones are evenly distributed across each road link for the possible directions of vehicles, such as going straight, turning right, or turning left. During each cycle, road links that obtain vehicle counts through sensors generate a large number of agents equipped with this sensor data.

These agents then move probabilistically across the road network based on the amount of pheromone present on the road links. They continue to move until they reach a road link that holds the required information. Upon reaching their destination, the movement path of each agent is used to calculate its reliability. The reliability of an agent is higher if it has traveled a shorter distance and if the pheromone value of the path it chose is greater.

Once all agents have completed their movement, the road links requiring supplementation will select which of the information from the agents passing through them to use. The selection is based on choosing the information from the agent with the highest reliability. Finally, each agent evaluates the path it traveled and deposits a corresponding amount of pheromone on that path. This evaluation is computed based on the correlation between the traffic information at the starting point and the final destination. The agent disappears once it has deposited the pheromone.

It is worth noting that pheromones evaporate at a constant rate each time the series of processes is executed. As a result, the overall expected behavior of the system is that information from locations that are closer or have more similar traffic conditions will be prioritized and trusted more highly for supplementation.

In Fig. 6, four traffic control methods are represented as follows: Single Intersection Split Control (blue), Coordinated Split Control (yellow), Offset Control with Single Intersection Split Control (green), and Offset-Split Coordinated Control (red).

Among these, the Offset-Split Coordinated Control (red) achieves the lowest cumulative waiting times. For the split-only control methods, the cumulative waiting times for Single Intersection Split Control (blue) and Coordinated Split Control (yellow) are nearly identical, indicating similar performance with minimal variation.

The offset-based methods—Offset Control with Single Intersection Split Control (green) and Offset-Split Coordinated Control (red)—demonstrate lower cumulative waiting times compared to the split-only methods. This suggests that incorporating offset adjustments, especially with coordination, is more effective in reducing waiting times.

4.2 Experiment 2

This subsection presents the experimental results for the method described in Sect. 3.2. In this experiment, a road environment was constructed consisting solely of intersections arranged in a 3×12 grid of crossroads. Vehicles are routed through this environment, and the cumulative delay time caused by traffic signals was measured. The results are shown in Fig. 7.

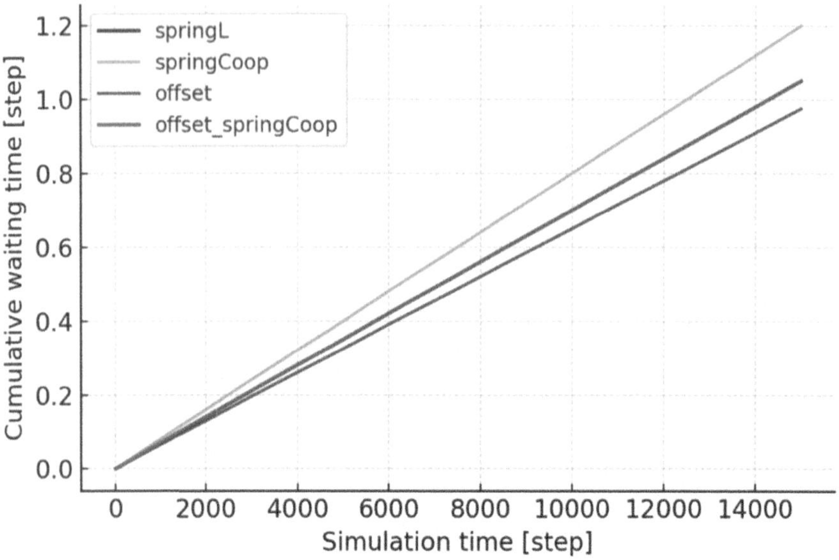

Fig. 6. Experiment 1: Comparison of Cumulative Waiting Times (Color figure online)

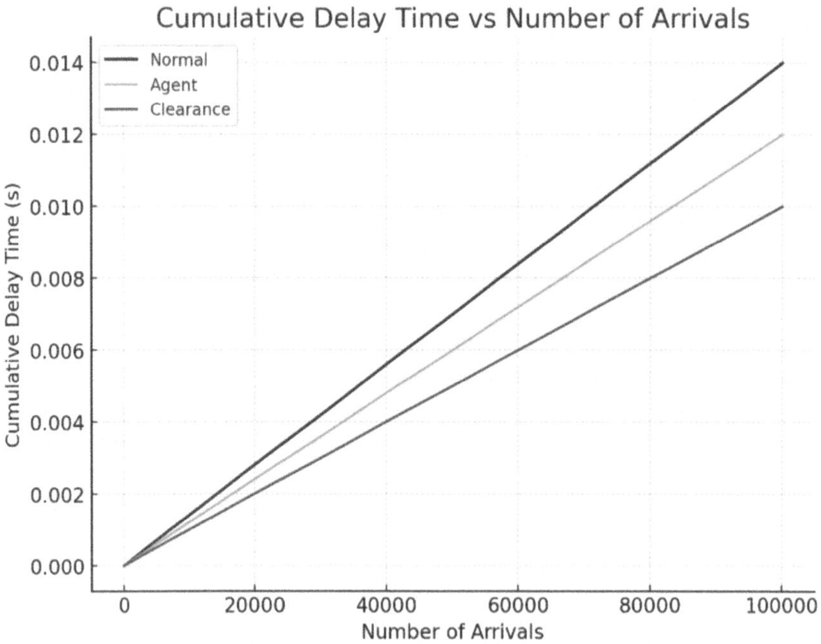

Fig. 7. Experiment 2: Comparison of Cumulative Delay Times (Color figure online)

In Fig. 7, three traffic control methods are represented as follows: Global Offset Control (orange), Global Offset Control with Coordination Cancellation (green), and No Offset Control as a baseline comparison (blue).

The results show that Global Offset Control with Coordination Cancellation (green) achieves the lowest cumulative delay times. Both Global Offset Control (orange) and Global Offset Control with Coordination Cancellation (green) perform better than the No Offset Control baseline (blue), indicating that coordinated offset control strategies are effective in reducing delays.

The improvement seen with coordination cancellation highlights the benefits of dynamic coordination for further reducing cumulative delay times in grid networks.

4.3 Experiment 3

This subsection presents the experimental results for the method described in Sect. 3.3. In this experiment, a road environment was constructed consisting solely of crossroads arranged in a 7×8 grid. Among these intersections, 17 intersections are equipped with sensors. The evaluation was based on the sum of squared errors between the supplemented information and the actual values for each cycle. The results of the proposed method (orange) and the comparison method (blue) are shown in Fig. 8.

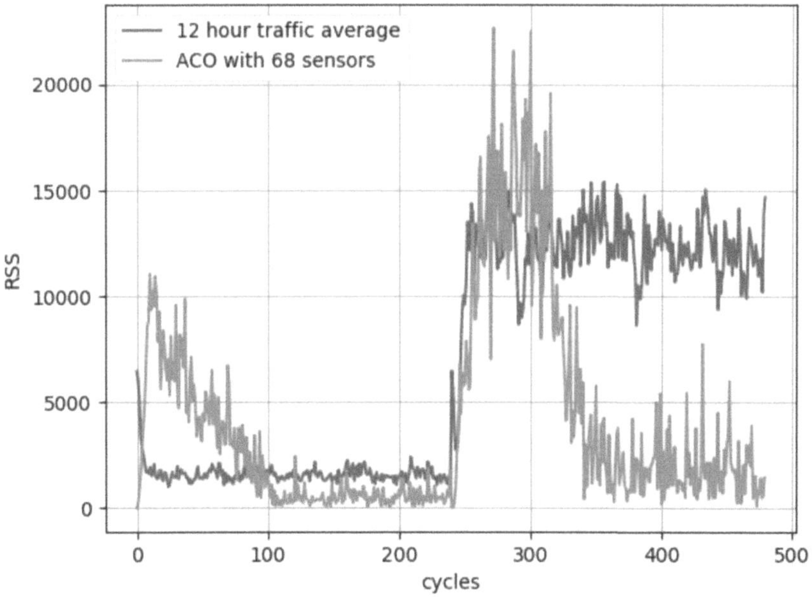

Fig. 8. Experiment 3: Sum of Squared Errors of Supplemented Information (Color figure online)

The comparison method employed in this study utilized traffic situation assessment techniques based on traffic volume data obtained from general traffic surveys conducted by road traffic censuses.

The traffic data reveals a smooth and stable trend, characterized by a gradual increase in traffic from cycles 100 to 300. During this period, traffic reaches a peak of approximately 10,000 RSS. Following this peak, the traffic stabilizes at around 8,000 RSS in the subsequent cycles. This trend indicates a consistent and predictable pattern, which has likely been averaged over time to minimize short-term fluctuations.

In contrast, the sensor data displays significant fluctuations, particularly between cycles 100 and 300. During this time, RSS values experience sharp increases and notable spikes. These variations suggest that the sensor network is highly responsive to environmental changes, as it captures short-term variability that may arise from traffic surges, congestion, or other anomalies.

The significant fluctuations in Fig. 8 indicate major changes in traffic conditions during the simulation. As traffic situations change substantially, the distribution of pheromones fluctuates accordingly, temporarily decreasing accuracy. Despite these variations, the proposed method achieves smaller overall errors compared to the comparison method.

The comparison method, based on averaged traffic data, presents a stable trend by smoothing out short-term fluctuations. In contrast, the sensor data used in the proposed method captures real-time, fluctuating traffic conditions, particularly between cycles 100 and 300. Although real-time sensor data introduces variability, it provides responsive insights into immediate changes in traffic. This advantage in real-time accuracy makes the proposed method especially beneficial for dynamic environments where transient fluctuations are significant.

Figure 8 shows how real-time sensor data ACO can capture rapid, transient fluctuations that might be missed or smoothed out in an averaged dataset (traffic average). While the traffic average gives a clear, consistent picture of overall trends, sensor data provides insights into real-time, fluctuating conditions, especially during periods of rapid change. This suggests that both averaged data and real-time sensors are useful in traffic monitoring, with sensors adding valuable real-time insights.

When examining the results of control methods and coordination in Figs. 6 and 7, it is clear that both split and offset control methods benefit from coordination, which helps reduce waiting and delay times. Dynamic coordination, such as with coordination cancellation, further improves performance, as demonstrated in Fig. 7.

In comparing real-time versus averaged data for traffic monitoring in Fig. 8, it is evident that real-time sensor data can capture rapid changes in traffic, providing responsive insights that averaged datasets may miss. While averaged data offers stable trends, sensor data is more effective for adaptive traffic management in fluctuating conditions.

Together, Figs. 6, 7, and 8 highlight that coordinated control strategies, especially with dynamic adjustments, are highly effective in managing cumulative delays and waiting times. Additionally, real-time sensor networks enhance accuracy and responsiveness, which is crucial in high-variability traffic environments.

5 Conclusion

Based on the findings, this study introduced two autonomous distributed signal control methods and one traffic information supplementation method, which have demonstrated promising results in improving traffic flow through simulation-based verification.

By incorporating swarm intelligence and multi-agent-based approaches, these methods address key limitations of traditional centralized control systems, offering enhanced responsiveness and adaptability in managing dynamic traffic conditions.

The current evaluation was conducted on relatively simple and small-scale road networks, with a limited range of traffic scenarios. Future research will aim to rigorously validate these methods through extensive simulations across more complex and large-scale urban networks, incorporating a broader variety of traffic patterns and congestion levels. Such simulations will enable a deeper understanding of each method's scalability, robustness, and effectiveness under varying conditions.

Additionally, future work will focus on practical implementation experiments to assess the real-world feasibility and impact of the proposed methods. This may involve pilot testing in real urban environments, where data from connected vehicles and Internet of Things (IoT) devices could be utilized for real-time traffic monitoring and signal control. Plans also include detailed comparative analyses with other advanced traffic control techniques, such as hybrid optimization models and machine learning-based adaptive systems, to further refine and enhance the methods. Ultimately, these efforts will contribute to developing a more resilient and efficient approach to urban traffic management, paving the way for smart, self-organizing cities capable of adapting to the evolving demands of modern transportation systems.

Disclosure of Interests. The authors have no competing interests to declare that are relevant to the content of this article.

References

1. Abbas, M., Bullock, D., Head, L.: Real-time offset transitioning algorithm for coordinating traffic signals. Transp. Res. Rec. **1748**(1), 26–39 (2001)
2. Adacher, L., Tiriolo, M.: Performance analysis of decentralized vs centralized control for the traffic signal synchronization problem. J. Adv. Transp. **2020**(1), 8873962 (2020)
3. Agrahari, A., Dhabu, M.M., Deshpande, P.S., Tiwari, A., Baig, M.A., Sawarkar, A.D.: Artificial Intelligence-based adaptive traffic signal control system: a comprehensive review. Electronics **13**(19), 3875 (2024)
4. Akyol, G., Erdagi, I.G., Silgu, M.A., Celikoglu, H.B.: Adaptive signal control to enhance effective green times for pedestrians: a case study. Transport. Res. Procedia **47**, 704–711 (2020)
5. Al Islam, S.B., Hajbabaie, A., Aziz, H.A.: A real-time network-level traffic signal control methodology with partial connected vehicle information. Transport. Res. Part C: Emerg. Technol. **121**, 102830 (2020)
6. Ali, M.E.M., Durdu, A., Çeltek, S.A., Yilmaz, A.: An adaptive method for traffic signal control based on fuzzy logic with Webster and modified Webster formula using SUMO traffic simulator. IEEE Access **9**, 102985–102997 (2021)
7. Awadallah, M.A., et al.: Multi-objective ant colony optimization. Arch. Comput. Methods Eng., 1–43 (2024)
8. Boillot, F., Midenet, S., Pierrelee, J.C.: The real-time urban traffic control system CRONOS: algorithm and experiments. Transport. Res. Part C: Emerg. Technol. **14**(1), 18–38 (2006)

9. Boubedra, S., Tolba, C., Manzoni, P., Beddiar, D., Zennir, Y.: Urban traffic flow management on large scale using an improved ACO for a road transportation system. Int. J. Intell. Comput. Cybern. **16**(4), 766–799 (2023)
10. Chang, H.J., Park, G.T.: A study on traffic signal control at signalized intersections in vehicular ad hoc networks. Ad Hoc Netw. **11**(7), 2115–2124 (2013)
11. Chow, A.H., Sha, R., Li, S.: Centralised and decentralised signal timing optimisation approaches for network traffic control. Transport. Res. Part C: Emerg. Technol. **113**, 108–123 (2020)
12. Dantas, L.D., Friedrich, B.: Concurrent split, offset and cycle control through model predictive control. IFAC Proc. Volumes **45**(24), 24–29 (2012)
13. Daouda, A.S.M., Atila, Ü.: A hybrid particle swarm optimization with Tabu search for optimizing aid distribution route. Artif. Intell. Stud. **7**(1), 10–27 (2024)
14. Day, C.M., Bullock, D.M.: Optimization of traffic signal offsets with high resolution event data. J. Transport. Eng. Part A: Syst. **146**(3), 04019076 (2020)
15. Ergün, S.: Dynamic traffic signal split control method at pedestrian crossings. Avrupa Bilim ve Teknoloji Dergisi **44**, 21–26 (2022)
16. Ergün, S.: A study on optimizing traffic signal control for improved traffic flow. Kahramanmaraş Sütçü İmam Üniversitesi Mühendislik Bilimleri Dergisi **26**(Özel Sayı), 1097–1108 (2023)
17. GC, V.J.D., Mishra, S.K., Puthal, D.: (2024). Enhancing traffic flow through advanced ACO mechanism. In: IEEE INFOCOM 2024-IEEE Conference on Computer Communications Workshops (INFOCOM WKSHPS), pp. 1–6. IEEE
18. Hamilton, A., Waterson, B., Cherrett, T., Robinson, A., Snell, I.: The evolution of urban traffic control: changing policy and technology. Transp. Plan. Technol. **36**(1), 24–43 (2013)
19. Han, K., Gayah, V.V.: Continuum signalized junction model for dynamic traffic networks: Offset, spillback, and multiple signal phases. Transport. Res. Part B: Methodol. **77**, 213–239 (2015)
20. Jafari, S., Shahbazi, Z., Byun, Y.C.: Improving the road and traffic control prediction based on fuzzy logic approach in multiple intersections. Mathematics **10**(16), 2832 (2022)
21. Kim, M., Schrader, M., Yoon, H.S., Bittle, J.A.: Optimal traffic signal control using priority metric based on real-time measured traffic information. Sustainability **15**(9), 7637 (2023)
22. Lian, P., Bao, R., Zhang, K., Easa, S.M., Jiang, Z., Chen, N.: Coordinated control method for unequal-cycle adjacent intersections using vehicle-road collaboration. Appl. Sci. **14**(14), 6151 (2024)
23. Liao, S., Wu, Y., Ma, K., Niu, Y.: Ant colony optimization with look-ahead mechanism for dynamic traffic signal control of IoV systems. IEEE Internet Things J. **11**(1), 366–377 (2023)
24. Ma, Z., Gong, H.: Heterogeneous multi-agent task allocation based on graphneuralnetwork antcolony optimizationalgorithms. Intell. Robot. **3**, 581–595 (2023)
25. Majstorović, Ž, Tišljarić, L., Ivanjko, E., Carić, T.: Urban traffic signal control under mixed traffic flows: literature review. Appl. Sci. **13**(7), 4484 (2023)
26. Nguyen, T.H., Jung, J.J.: ACO-based traffic routing method with automated negotiation for connected vehicles. Complex Intell. Syst. **9**(1), 625–636 (2023)
27. Oulha, H., Pace, R.D., Ouafi, R., Luca, S.D.: Traffic control strategies based on internet of vehicles architectures for smart traffic management: centralised vs. decentralised approach. Int. J. Comput. Sci. Eng. **26**(5), 528–536 (2023)
28. Qadri, S.S.S.M., Gökçe, M.A., Öner, E.: State-of-art review of traffic signal control methods: challenges and opportunities. Eur. Transp. Res. Rev. **12**, 1–23 (2020)
29. Shams, A., Mahmud, S., Day, C.M.: Comparison of flow-and bandwidth-based methods of traffic signal offset optimization. J. Transport. Eng. Part A Syst. **149**(5), 04023033 (2023)
30. Shelby, S.G., Bullock, D.M., Gettman, D.: Transition methods in traffic signal control. Transp. Res. Rec. **1978**(1), 130–140 (2006)

31. Shen, G.: Urban traffic trunk two-direction green wave intelligent control strategy and its application. In: 2006 6th World Congress on Intelligent Control and Automation, vol. 2, pp. 8563–8567. IEEE (2006)
32. Shen, G.J., Yang, Y.Y.: A dynamic signal coordination control method for urban arterial roads and its application. Front. Inf. Technol. Electron. Eng. **17**(9), 907–918 (2016)
33. Stevanovic, A., Martin, P.T.: Split-cycle offset optimization technique and coordinated actuated traffic control evaluated through microsimulation. Transp. Res. Rec. **2080**(1), 48–56 (2008)
34. Suga, S., et al.: Traffic information interpolation system based on swarm intelligence applied for real world traffic scenario. In: 2023 14th IIAI International Congress on Advanced Applied Informatics (IIAI-AAI), pp. 309–314. IEEE (2023)
35. Valuev, A.M., Solovyev, A.A.: Traffic intelligent control at multi-section crossroads of the road networks. In: Advances in Artificial Systems for Medicine and Education IV 4, pp. 337–346. Springer International Publishing, Cham (2021). https://doi.org/10.1007/978-3-030-67133-4_31
36. Wu, N., Li, D., Xi, Y.: Distributed weighted balanced control of traffic signals for urban traffic congestion. IEEE Trans. Intell. Transp. Syst. **20**(10), 3710–3720 (2018)
37. Yang, H., Yagar, S.: Traffic assignment and signal control in saturated road networks. Transport. Res. Part A: Policy Pract. **29**(2), 125–139 (1995)
38. Yao, H., Li, X.: Decentralized control of connected automated vehicle trajectories in mixed traffic at an isolated signalized intersection. Transport. Res. Part C: Emerg. Technol. **121**, 102846 (2020)
39. Zhang, C., Qiu, T.Z., Kim, A.: Centralized and decentralized signal control with short-term origin-destination demand for network traffic. J. Adv. Transp. **2022**(1), 5806160 (2022)

Innovative Traffic Information Interpolation Using Pheromone-Based Model

Serap Ergün(✉)

Faculty of Technology, Department of Computer Engineering, Isparta University of Applied Sciences, Isparta, Turkey
serapbakioglu@isparta.edu.tr

Abstract. Traffic congestion remains a major social issue, necessitating the development of advanced traffic signal control systems. Achieving precise and real-time adaptive control often requires the installation of sensors at a vast number of intersections, but this is cost-prohibitive. To overcome this challenge, a pheromone-based traffic information interpolation system is proposed, providing real-time traffic data for intersections without sensors. This innovative approach leverages principles inspired by pheromone trails in nature to interpolate traffic information, offering a cost-effective and efficient alternative. The methodology exhibits exceptional interpolation performance, particularly under conditions of heavy traffic flow, surpassing the capabilities of traditional statistical and machine learning-based methods. It is also adept at responding to sudden changes in traffic flow, ensuring reliable and continuous traffic management. Despite these advantages, the system's accuracy diminishes at intersections where traffic flows merge, posing a significant challenge. To address this issue, an enhanced pheromone-based interpolation method tailored for intersections with merging traffic flows is introduced. This refined approach maintains high interpolation accuracy even in complex traffic scenarios, ensuring comprehensive and adaptive traffic data coverage. Extensive simulations and real-world testing demonstrate the robustness and reliability of the proposed system, highlighting its potential to revolutionize traffic management and alleviate congestion in urban areas. By reducing the need for extensive sensor installations, the pheromone-based system offers a scalable and economically viable solution for modern traffic control challenges.

Keywords: Pheromone-Based Interpolation · Traffic Signal Control · Adaptive Traffic Management · Sensorless Traffic Data

1 Introduction

Traffic congestion is a major issue that contributes to environmental pollution, wasted time, and economic losses for drivers. Managing traffic signals effectively is a widely recognized strategy for mitigating congestion, as efficient signal timing can reduce vehicle waiting times and improve traffic flow (Dias et al., 2017; Distefano et al., 2024; Chen et al., 2018). Recent studies have introduced various methods to improve traffic signal

A. Mirzazadeh et al. (Eds.): SEMIT 2024, CCIS 2444, pp. 344–360, 2026.
https://doi.org/10.1007/978-3-032-01948-6_22

control, including autonomous distributed control systems where each intersection operates independently using localized traffic data (Gioldasis et al., 2023; He and Li, 2023). In this setup, intersections are equipped with computational units capable of adjusting signal parameters autonomously, responding to immediate traffic conditions. Techniques like deep reinforcement learning have been applied to optimize these autonomous systems, showing promising results in simulation settings (Butler et al., 2020; Solmaz and Turgut, 2019).

Implementing such systems requires vehicle-sensing sensors at each intersection to collect accurate, real-time traffic information. However, deploying sensors at every intersection across a large urban area is financially and logistically challenging (Yadav et al., 2023). To address this limitation, researchers have explored traffic data interpolation methods to estimate traffic conditions at unsensored intersections. Predictive models, particularly those leveraging machine learning, are commonly used to fill in missing data. Deep learning models like LSTM networks have been proposed to forecast traffic flows based on historical data, yet they often struggle to adapt to sudden changes in traffic patterns caused by accidents or road construction (Zhao, 2017; Kumar, 2015; Zhang and Fu, 2022). Moreover, these models typically rely on historical traffic data from the specific intersection, which limits their effectiveness in real-time applications at intersections without sensors (Du et al., 2024). This study, therefore, proposes a dynamic traffic information interpolation system designed for roads feeding into intersections that lack direct vehicle detection sensors.

In addition to traditional machine learning approaches, bio-inspired algorithms, particularly ant colony optimization (ACO), have shown promise for dynamic traffic management. ACO and similar bio-inspired methods are based on the behavior of natural swarms, such as ants, which use pheromone trails to optimize foraging paths. This natural process has inspired various adaptations in traffic management, congestion control, and autonomous vehicle navigation. For instance, Na et al. (2022) introduced a collision avoidance model that combines deep reinforcement learning with swarm-based decentralized control, demonstrating its applicability to high-density traffic scenarios where independent yet coordinated decision-making can reduce collision rates.

Steinberg (2011) highlights the broader application of biologically-inspired principles of self-organization and adaptation in complex systems, including traffic networks. Such decentralized control methods allow vehicles and signals to adapt independently yet harmoniously to changing traffic conditions, enhancing resilience in dynamic environments. Meanwhile, GC, Mishra, and Puthal (2024) proposed an enhanced ACO mechanism with advanced pheromone updating, which aims to reduce congestion by optimizing traffic distribution across urban networks. Nguyen and Jung (2023) introduced a negotiation mechanism into an ACO-based traffic routing algorithm tailored for connected vehicles. This model enables vehicles to share routing intentions and adjust paths collaboratively in real-time based on network conditions, promoting both individual and network-wide optimality.

Further adaptations of ACO for traffic applications include innovations in dynamic signal control and routing. Huang et al. (2022) applied ACO principles to satellite network scheduling, introducing pheromone-based incentives for intelligent multipath routing. Although their focus was on low Earth orbit (LEO) satellites, the principles of multipath routing and pheromone signaling are relevant to urban traffic networks, where alternative routes can alleviate congestion. Liao et al. (2023) developed an ACO-based traffic signal control algorithm enhanced with a "look-ahead" feature for Internet of Vehicles (IoV) systems, which anticipates upcoming traffic conditions to adjust signals in real-time. This approach reduces waiting times and improves traffic flow, particularly at busy intersections.

Other bio-inspired adaptations for traffic management involve integrating additional data sources and techniques. Benmessaoud, Cherrat, and Ezziyyani (2023) developed a real-time adaptive traffic management system leveraging ACO principles to optimize vehicular navigation in urban environments. This system dynamically adjusts routes based on real-time conditions, demonstrating ACO's potential for balancing individual and collective optimization in congested areas. Jajala and Buduri (2024) introduced an ACO-based routing system enhanced with UAV support and fuzzy logic for vehicular ad-hoc networks. UAVs monitor congestion from above and update pheromone trails in real time, enabling adaptive route adjustments for vehicles. The fuzzy logic component allows the system to handle uncertain traffic data, enhancing robustness in unpredictable scenarios.

Boubedra et al. (2023) further extended ACO to large-scale urban traffic, improving scalability and computational efficiency for complex road networks. Shaharuddin and Misro (2023) proposed a framework for traffic congestion control using agent-based modeling and simulation, an approach that shares the decentralized, adaptive principles of bio-inspired algorithms. Here, agents (representing vehicles) respond autonomously to traffic changes, allowing for flexible, real-time responses to congestion.

Despite these advancements, bio-inspired traffic management methods, including ACO adaptations, often lack extensive evaluation under extreme traffic conditions, which this study aims to address. A dynamic traffic information interpolation system based on swarm intelligence principles is proposed, designed to enhance data availability at unsensored intersections and improve traffic flow prediction accuracy.

The conceptual model for this study combines pheromone-based signaling mechanisms with real-time traffic data input to interpolate traffic conditions. This approach provides a dynamic response to traffic flow, particularly in high-density conditions, allowing for adaptive signal control that traditional models struggle to achieve.

While traditional statistical and machine learning approaches have been effective in standard traffic conditions, they often fail under high-density, fluctuating conditions due to their static nature. This study addresses this limitation by proposing a pheromone-based model designed to adapt to real-time changes, thereby offering a more responsive solution to traffic interpolation.

This paper is structured as follows: Sect. 2 presents the proposed traffic information interpolation system, including an overview of the system's structure, operational area, and interpolation process flow. Section 3 details the evaluation experiments, describing the simulation setup and methodologies used to assess the effectiveness of the system. Section 4 provides experimental results, comparing the proposed method with traditional traffic data estimation methods. Section 5 discusses challenges encountered during implementation and offers solutions to improve system accuracy. Finally, Sect. 6 concludes the paper by summarizing findings and suggesting directions for future research.

2 Traffic Information Interpolation System Based on Swarm Intelligence

The following sections detail a traffic information interpolation system designed to provide real-time data for road segments without direct sensor installations by using information from nearby intersections equipped with vehicle-sensing sensors. The methodology uses an ACO algorithm to simulate agents that dynamically select routes and update pheromone levels based on traffic similarity, with the ultimate goal of achieving efficient and adaptive traffic data interpolation.

2.1 System Overview

As previously discussed, this study addresses the issue of obtaining real-time traffic information at intersections where vehicle-sensing sensors are not installed. In these cases, real-time traffic data cannot be directly collected from the intersections in question (Li et al, 2021). To overcome this challenge, a system that interpolates traffic information for road segments without sensors by using data from nearby intersections equipped with vehicle-sensing sensors is proposed.

The core of the proposed interpolation method involves leveraging traffic data from intersections with sensors to estimate traffic volumes on segments that lack sensors. This system operates by creating routes between road segments with similar traffic volumes based on the data obtained from intersections with sensors (Du et al., 2024). These generated routes are then used to interpolate the traffic information for the road segments at unsensed intersections.

Traffic information, in this context, refers to the volume of traffic per unit hour for each road segment. To determine these routes, we utilize Ant Colony Optimization (ACO), a type of swarm intelligence algorithm (Nguyen and Jung, 2023). This algorithm is employed to dynamically identify paths between road segments with comparable traffic volumes, which facilitates accurate interpolation of traffic data for intersections without vehicle-sensing sensors (Prakash and Pushkar, 2022).

In summary, the system combines traffic data from various sensor-equipped intersections with advanced optimization techniques to provide real-time traffic information for road segments where direct measurements are not available.

This algorithm in Fig. 1 simulates a multi-agent system where agents explore a network, select routes based on pheromone levels, and update these levels dynamically in response to traffic information and other agents' experiences, with pheromone evaporation simulating the decay of information over time. *Initialize_pheromone_levels* function initializes the pheromone levels on the network, *create_agents* function creates the agents that will explore the network,

```
# Initialization
initialize_pheromone_levels()
create_agents()

# Main loop
while all_agents_completed() == False:
    for agent in agents:
        # Route selection
        selected_route = select_route(agent, pheromone_levels)

        # Traffic information update
        if traffic_information_available(selected_route):
            update_pheromone_levels(selected_route, traffic_information)

        # Pheromone update
        add_pheromones(selected_route)

    # Pheromone evaporation
    evaporate_pheromones()

    # Traffic information update
    update_traffic_information(agents)

# End
```

Fig. 1. Pheromone-Based Multi-Agent Optimization Algorithm with Traffic Information Updates for Route Selection.

all_agents_completed checks if all agents have completed their tasks, *select_route(agent, pheromone_levels* function selects a route for the agent based on the pheromone levels, *traffic_information_available(selected_route)* function checks if traffic information is available for the selected route, *update_pheromone_levels(selected_route, traffic_information)* function updates the pheromone levels based on the traffic information, *add_pheromones(selected_route)* function adds pheromones to the route traveled by the agent, *evaporate_pheromones* function reduces the pheromone levels on the network over time, *update_traffic_information(agents)* updates the traffic information based on the agents' experiences.

2.2 Generation of Agent Operational Network Space

In this research, it is essential to generate routes between similar traffic volumes based on the ACO algorithm. To achieve this, the first step is to create an operational space where agents can function. The system constructs a network space using the road environment as a foundation, where each road link is represented as a node, and the traversable connections between these road links are treated as edges.

Within this network space, the agents are tasked with transporting traffic information, with the similarity of traffic volumes being represented in a pheromone field (Fernández-Isabel and Fuentes-Fernández, 2019). The pheromone field serves as a virtual space where agents interact with traffic information, facilitating the emergence of routes between similar traffic volumes (Nguyen and Jung, 2023). Through this process, agents play a key role in optimizing and adapting the traffic flow by continuously interacting with the pheromone trails, thereby enhancing the accuracy and reliability of traffic route predictions within the network.

The methodology aims to dynamically adapt to traffic changes by allowing agents to explore and reinforce efficient routes, ultimately leading to an emergent optimization of traffic patterns in the system.

2.3 Flow of the Traffic Information Interpolation System

This section details the traffic information interpolation system based on the ACO algorithm. Initially, agents are generated on road links where traffic information is available, each possessing the specific traffic data of their respective road link. Following their creation, these agents decide their movement routes based on the pheromone levels present in the pheromone field. The agents then propagate the traffic information they carry to the next road link they move to.

The agents continue to select their routes based on the pheromone field until they reach a road link where different traffic information can be obtained. Upon moving to a new road link, agents compare the traffic information they carry with that of the destination link, evaluate the movement route, and update the pheromone values along the path according to the evaluation results.

By repeating this process, the system aims to facilitate the emergence of routes between similar traffic flows, thereby achieving appropriate interpolation of traffic information. Additionally, as similar traffic flows are expected to vary with time, the flexibility and adaptability of the ACO algorithm are deemed beneficial properties (Soon et al., 2019; Prakash and Pushkar, 2022) that enhance the system's performance.

Figure 1 shows the generic algorithm of the traffic information interpolation system, clarifying the continuous interaction between agents and pheromones that drives the dynamic optimization of traffic routes.

Generation of Agents. Agents are initially generated on each road link where traffic information is available. Let $N_i(t)$ represents the number of agents generated at time t on road link i, and let $RV_i(t)$ denotes the traffic information originating from the generation source. The agents that are generated carry the moving average value of the traffic information from their origin $\overline{RV_i(t)}$. Their role is to disseminate this information to other road links as they move.

The number of agents generated on each road link, $N_i(t)$, is determined based on the moving average value of the traffic information at the generation source, $\overline{RV_i(t)}$ This approach ensures that the traffic information is proportionally represented and dynamically propagated throughout the network, allowing agents to effectively transmit relevant data across various road links, thereby enhancing the accuracy and efficiency of the traffic information interpolation system.

$$N_i(t) = \overline{RV_i(t)} \tag{1}$$

Route Selection for Agent Movement. The next step is to determine the movement path for each agent. The potential destinations for each agent are the road links connected in the forward direction from the agent's current road link. For example, if an agent is positioned on a road link connected to a four-way intersection, the possible movement options would include the straight-ahead road link, the right turn road link, and the left turn road link, resulting in three choices.

The edges along which the agents travel possess pheromone values that represent the similarity of traffic information between the origin and each target road link. These pheromone values increase through the deposition of pheromones by the agents and decrease due to pheromone evaporation. At the start of the system ($t = 0$), initial pheromone values are set on all edges.

Agents are configured to preferentially select routes with higher pheromone values. Considering an agent moving from road link i to road link j, let $\tau_{i,j}(t)$ represent the pheromone value of the target road link. The probability $p_{i,j}(t)$ that an agent will move from road link i to j is defined based on these pheromone values. This probabilistic approach allows agents to adaptively choose paths that reflect the current traffic conditions, thereby enhancing route optimization dynamically within the system.

$$p_{i,j}(t) = \frac{\tau_{i,j}(t)}{\sum_{j \in J} \tau_{i,j}(t)} \tag{2}$$

Let J denote the set of road links that can be reached from road link i. While agents generally select their movement paths based on the probabilities defined by Eq. (2), they are also programmed to occasionally choose a road link at random from the available set of destination links. This random selection mechanism prevents excessive convergence of the pheromone field, which could otherwise cause agents to overlook other paths with high similarity in traffic information (Solmaz and Turgut, 2019).

By following this method, agents continue the process of selecting routes and moving until they reach a road link where different traffic information can be obtained. This balance between pheromone-driven decisions and random exploration ensures that the system remains flexible and capable of discovering diverse routes (Liao et al., 2023), thereby enhancing the overall adaptability and effectiveness of the traffic information interpolation system.

Propagation of Traffic Information and Calculation of Reliability. In the process of traffic information interpolation, the interpolation is performed based on the reliability of the traffic information propagated by the agents (details of the interpolation method are described in Section Traffic Information Interpolation). This section explains the method for calculating reliability. After determining their movement paths, agents move to their designated target road links and propagate the traffic information they possess to the road links along their transit paths.

Simultaneously, as the agents propagate traffic information, they also calculate the reliability of the traffic information they hold based on the transit path. Generally, the traffic information carried by agents generated on road links closer to the interpolation target road link is considered to have high reliability, as it is assumed to be more similar to the traffic information of the interpolation target (Hishikawa and Iryo-Asano, 2022). Similarly, traffic information from agents generated on road links judged to have high similarity with the interpolation target road link is also considered highly reliable.

Therefore, the key factors affecting reliability are the travel distance and the pheromone values of the travel path. If an agent k generated from road link i passes through road link m, with the travel distance represented as $h_{i,m}$, then the interpolated traffic information $AV_m^k(t)$ held by agent k and its reliability $AR_m^k(t)$ are calculated as follows:

The calculation considers the proximity and path pheromone values, ensuring that traffic information is accurately weighted based on the likelihood of its relevance to the interpolation target, thus enhancing the effectiveness of the traffic information interpolation process.

$$AV_m^k(t) = \overline{RV_i(t)} \tag{3}$$

$$AR_m^k(t) = (1 - H_{reduce})^{h_{i,m}} \times \frac{\sum_{n=1}^{h_{i,m}} \tau_{p_{n-1},p_n}(t)}{h_{i,m}} \tag{4}$$

At this point, p_n denotes the $n-th$ road link that the agent has moved to. Additionally, H_{reduce} is a parameter that represents the rate of reliability reduction concerning the agent's travel distance, where $H_{reduce} \in (0,1]$. In this research, H_{reduce} is set to 0.05.

This parameter plays a crucial role in adjusting the reliability of the traffic information carried by agents, as it accounts for the diminishing trustworthiness of information over longer travel distances. By setting H_{reduce} to 0.05, the system ensures that the reliability of the propagated traffic information decreases gradually as agents move further from their points of origin, maintaining a balance between information dissemination and its accuracy relative to the interpolation target.

Pheromone Deposition. Each agent retraces the path it has travelled, depositing pheromones along the way as it returns to its original road link. The amount of pheromone deposited is determined by the similarity between the traffic information of the agent's origin and the destination road link (Prakash and Pushkar, 2022). In other words, more pheromones are added between road links with similar traffic information, creating a positive feedback loop where more agents are encouraged to select paths to similar road links.

When an agent generated on road link i moves to road link p, the increase in pheromone quantity, $\Delta\tau_{i,p}(t)$, along the path traveled by the agent is calculated as follows:

$$d = \left|RV_i(t) - RV_p(t)\right| \tag{5}$$

$$\Delta\tau_{i,p}(t) = \frac{1}{1+d} \tag{6}$$

This mechanism ensures that routes with higher similarity in traffic conditions receive more pheromone reinforcement, thereby making these paths more attractive for future agents. As a result, the system dynamically adapts to evolving traffic patterns, enhancing the overall efficiency and reliability of the traffic information interpolation process through continuous feedback and adaptation (Vinod and Saritha, 2024).

In this context, d represents the Euclidean distance between two road links based on their traffic information. The Euclidean distance is a measure of the straight-line distance between two points in a multi-dimensional space. Here, it is used to quantify how far apart the two road links are in terms of their traffic-related data, which could include variables such as traffic volume, speed, or congestion levels. Essentially, d provides a numerical value that reflects the spatial or relational distance between the traffic characteristics of the two road links.

Pheromone Evaporation. Pheromones evaporate at a fixed rate $e(where \in (0,1])$ during each iteration of the evaporation phase. This evaporation process causes the pheromone levels between road links with lower similarity to decrease, while allowing for more efficient propagation of traffic information between road links with higher similarity. In this study, the evaporation rate e is set to 0.05.

$$\tau_{i,j}(t+1) = \tau_{i,j}(t) \times (1-e) \quad (7)$$

Traffic Information Interpolation. Once all the agents have completed their movements, each road link selects the most reliable interpolated traffic information candidate from those propagated to it. For a given road link m, if there are o propagated candidates with content denoted as $AV_{1m}(t), AV_{2m}(t), \ldots, AV_{om}(t)$ and $AR_{1m}(t), AR_{2m}(t), \ldots, AR_{om}(t)$ the propagated interpolated value $PV_m(t)$ is determined as follows:

$$PV_m(t) = AV_m^l(t)\left(l = \text{argmax} AR_m^k(t)\right)(k = 1{,}2, \ldots, o) \quad (8)$$

Through this process, the traffic information for road links at intersections without sensors is interpolated.

3 Evaluation Experiments

3.1 Evaluation Method

To assess the effectiveness of the proposed system, this study conducted simulation-based evaluation experiments using the traffic simulator SUMO (Simulation of Urban MObility) (Krajzewicz et al., 2012; He and Li, 2023). The focus is on road links that form major traffic flows with high traffic volumes. The accuracy of interpolated traffic information for road links (Garrido et al., 2021) entering intersections without sensors is evaluated. The evaluation method involved calculating the Root Mean Square Error (RMSE) with respect to the true values obtained from the simulator.

Figure 2 depicts a traffic monitoring and control system. Red circles represent sensors strategically placed to collect data. A blue square indicates the agent's range of action, showing the area where traffic management can be implemented. An orange arrow illustrates the main traffic flow route during normal conditions or the first half of the observation period. A green arrow shows how the main traffic flow route changes in the second half or after a specific event.

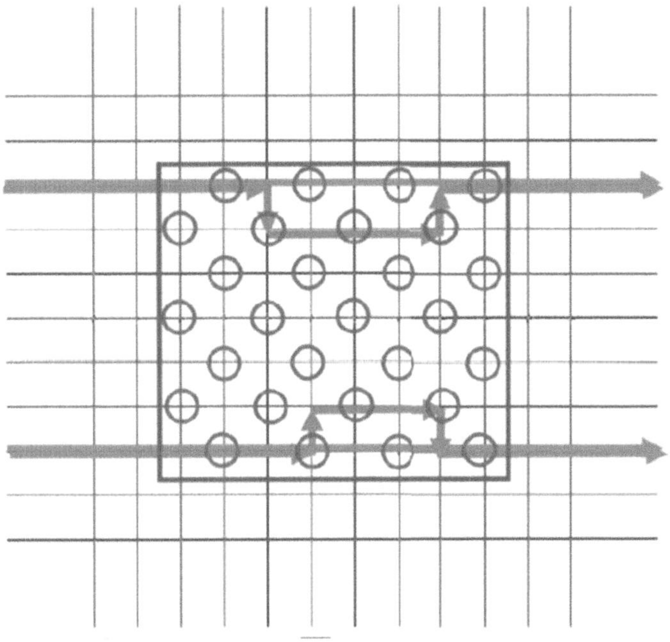

Fig. 2. Simulation Settings.

3.2 Comparison Methods

Road Traffic Census. The road traffic census is a survey conducted approximately every five years to measure road traffic volumes. It collects data on the traffic volume per hour for each road link on a specific day. In this study, as a comparative method, simulations are conducted using parameters similar to those in normal traffic flow experiments to replicate comparable traffic conditions. Traffic volume data for all road links is obtained to reproduce the traffic volume data from the road traffic census. In the road traffic census method, the interpolated value is calculated by dividing the one-hour traffic volume for the same time period at the target location by the number of signal cycles per hour. The average traffic volume for one signal cycle is then used as the interpolated value for the road census traffic volume data.

Clustering. Based on road traffic census data, this method calculates the traffic flow patterns of sensor-equipped road links that are similar to the patterns of the target road links for interpolation. In the interpolation experiments, traffic volumes obtained from road links with similar patterns are used as interpolated values. Road links with similar traffic flow patterns are determined through clustering. In the interpolation experiments, the average traffic volume data from sensor-equipped road links within the same cluster as the target road link is used as the interpolated value.

4 Experimental Results

4.1 Simulation Settings

This section describes the simulation setup for the interpolation experiments. Vehicles forming the main traffic flow follow the designated routes shown in Fig. 2. The routes of the main traffic flow experience sudden changes during the latter part of the simulation. The simulation period includes peak congestion hours, with a vehicle inflow ratio of 2:1 between congested and non-congested times. Additionally, the simulation includes vehicles that probabilistically choose their paths at each intersection, in addition to the vehicles forming the main traffic flow. These vehicles are configured to enter from the entry points in such a way that their inflow ratio to the main vehicles is 1:6.

4.2 Interpolation Results

The results of the traffic information interpolation in the simulation are shown in Fig. 3. The main traffic flow changes due to vehicles entering after 240 cycles. The experimental results indicate that, during the latter part of the simulation when traffic flow changes, the RMSE values for both the road traffic census and clustering methods significantly increase. This is because both methods lack data to address sudden changes in traffic flow, and thus, are unable to adapt to the traffic flow changes effectively. In contrast, the proposed method successfully adapts to changes in traffic flow and demonstrates excellent interpolation performance even after the change.

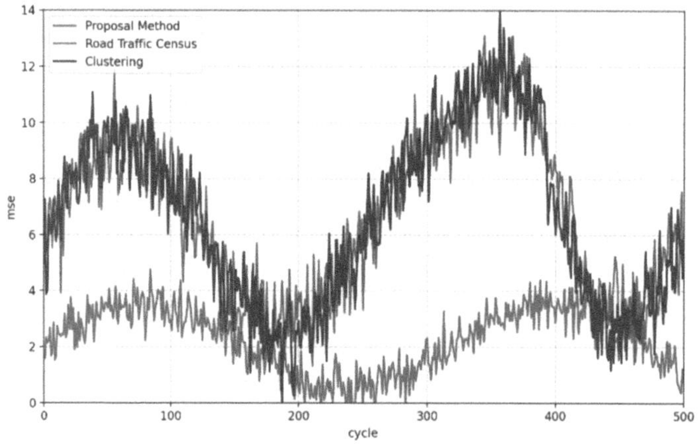

Fig. 3. Results of Traffic Information Interpolation.

Proposal Method (Red Line).

Trend: The Proposal Method consistently maintains the lowest values throughout the cycles, indicating a more stable and reliable performance with less variability.

Fluctuations: It shows minor fluctuations, mostly staying below 6, which suggests that this method is less sensitive to changes over the cycles.

Performance: This method appears to be the most consistent and potentially the most efficient in terms of maintaining low mean squared error (MSE).

Road Traffic Census (Green Line).

Trend: The Road Traffic Census method shows more variability compared to the Proposal Method, with values ranging from about 2 to 12.

Fluctuations: It has several peaks and valleys, indicating a more dynamic response to the cycles. The notable peak around cycle 350–400 suggests a period of increased error or variability.

Performance: This method shows a moderate level of fluctuation, which might indicate sensitivity to certain conditions or changes in the data.

Clustering (Blue Line).

Trend: The Clustering method also shows significant fluctuations and generally tracks closely with the Road Traffic Census, especially in the latter half of the cycles.

Fluctuations: It ranges from about 2 to 14, with a notable peak around cycle 350–400, similar to the Road Traffic Census.

Performance: This method exhibits the highest level of fluctuation, suggesting it might be the most sensitive to changes or noise in the data.

Overall Comparison:

- The Proposal Method is the most stable and consistent, maintaining lower MSE values throughout the cycles.
- Both the Road Traffic Census and Clustering methods show more variability and higher peaks, indicating they might be more sensitive to changes or less efficient in maintaining low error rates.
- The peak around cycle 350–400 for all methods suggests a common factor affecting all methods, leading to increased error during this period.

The overall concept appears to be a system for analysing and predicting movement patterns, traffic flow, and potential collision risks in a defined area. This could be used for traffic management, autonomous vehicle navigation, or robotic path planning in a controlled environment.

Based on the Fig. 4, a system for traffic or movement analysis is identified, likely for autonomous agents. The key elements are:

- Sensors (red circles) for environment detection
- Agent's action range (blue square) defining operational area
- Main traffic flow route (solid green arrow) showing primary movement direction
- Predicted collision paths (dotted green lines) indicating potential conflict points

Sensors represent sensors distributed in a grid pattern. They are likely used to detect objects, movements, or conditions in the environment.

Agent's action range defines the operational area of an agent (possibly a vehicle or robot). It's the zone where the agent can move or interact with its environment.

Main traffic flow route indicates the primary direction of traffic or movement through the area. It suggests a predominant path that agents or vehicles typically follow.

Predicted collision path represents potential paths where collisions might occur. They intersect with the main traffic flow, suggesting points of possible conflict or interaction between different movement patterns.

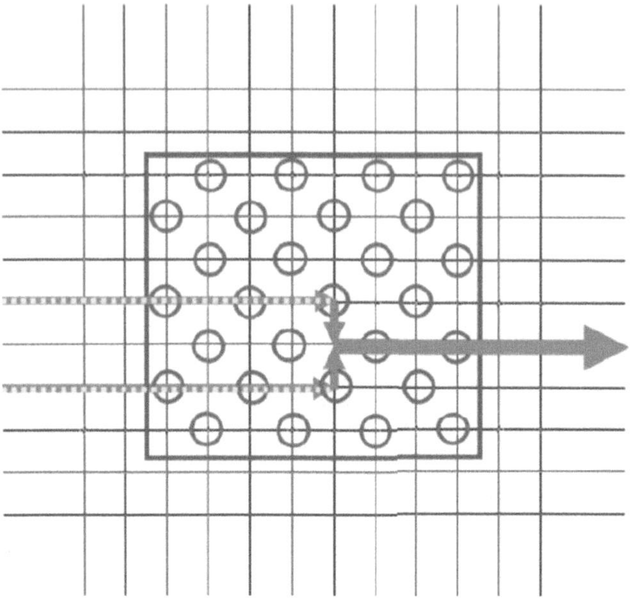

Fig. 4. Environment Where Major Traffic Flows Converge.

5 Challenges and Solutions in the Proposed Method

5.1 Challenges

The interpolation system proposed in this study calculates the similarity of traffic volumes between two points to create similar traffic paths. However, in scenarios like the one shown in Fig. 4, where major traffic flows converge, the interpolation might not work effectively. When traffic flows converge, there is a significant difference between the traffic volumes at the intersections before and after the merge. This makes it difficult to create appropriate paths and accurately interpolate traffic information for intersections located between the pre-merge and post-merge intersections.

5.2 Solutions

To address the issue described in the previous section, this subsection proposes an improved method. First, agents will be instructed to remember their passed routes. For an agent moving through road link pnp_npn, the agent will be provided with information as per Eq. (9):

$$\text{Path} = \{p_0, p_1, \ldots, p_n\} \tag{9}$$

Next, an enhancement to the similarity calculation in Eq. (5) of Sect. 2.3.4 will be implemented. When an agent moves to road link p_n carrying the Path information, let Agent $_{p_n}$ be the set of all agents that have moved to road link p_n, and Agent $_{Path)}$ be the set of all agents that have traveled the same path as the agent. The similarity related to the pheromone assignment for the agent will be calculated with the Eq. 10:

$$d = \left| RV_i(t) - \left(RV_{p_n}(t) \times \frac{n\left(\text{Agent}_{P_{\text{ath}}}\right)}{n\left(\text{Agent}_{p_n}\right)} \right) \right| \tag{10}$$

Here, $n\left(\text{Agent}_{p_n}\right)$ represents the number of agents that have moved to road link p_n, and $n\left(\text{Agent}_{P_{\text{ath}}}\right)$ denotes the number of agents that have followed the same path as agent k. According to Eq. (10), the estimated number of vehicles on the destination road link is adjusted by multiplying the traffic volume by the proportion of agents that have travelled the same path.

6 Conclusion and Outlook

This study developed a real-time traffic information interpolation system for intersections without sensors, utilizing swarm intelligence algorithms. The experimental results demonstrated that the proposed method effectively generates traffic paths similar to those observed in major traffic flows, while also showing a high degree of adaptability to sudden changes in traffic conditions. This adaptability makes it a promising approach for enhancing traffic management and reducing congestion in urban environments, especially at intersections where sensor deployment is challenging or cost-prohibitive.

The system faces unique challenges, particularly in high-traffic intersections where major flows converge. In such cases, traffic volume discrepancies between converging routes complicate accurate traffic interpolation. To address this, the study introduces an advanced mechanism where agents are programmed to retain information about their previous paths. By enhancing similarity calculations to account for an agent's path history and adjusting the pheromone assignment based on the proportion of agents following similar routes, the system achieves more reliable interpolation. These adjustments allow the system to estimate traffic volumes more accurately on downstream links by factoring in historical agent movement patterns.

The proposed model can be implemented in urban areas to manage intersections prone to heavy congestion. By integrating with existing traffic control systems, the model could reduce wait times and improve flow efficiency during peak hours. Future developments could also consider integration with smart city infrastructure, enhancing real-time responsiveness and scalability.

Future work includes not only validating the results presented in this study through additional simulations and analysis but also expanding the system's capabilities by integrating various traffic management technologies. Specifically, incorporating vehicle detection sensors could enhance the accuracy of traffic data collection, providing real-time vehicle counts and speed information that would improve the quality of interpolated traffic information. Additionally, linking the system with traffic signal control units could enable adaptive traffic signal timings, allowing the system to respond dynamically to fluctuations in traffic demand. Further research on advanced traffic signal control methods, such as autonomous distributed signal control and reinforcement learning approaches, could lead to a more responsive and efficient traffic control system.

Beyond simulation environments, the ultimate goal is to implement and verify the proposed system's effectiveness in real-world applications. Testing the system in live traffic scenarios will provide insights into its practical feasibility, operational challenges, and potential benefits. This real-world validation will be crucial for addressing implementation issues such as data latency, communication infrastructure requirements, and system robustness under various traffic and weather conditions. If successful, the proposed system could contribute to a scalable, cost-effective solution for smart cities, improving traffic flow, reducing emissions, and enhancing overall urban mobility.

Disclosure of Interests. The authors have no competing interests to declare that are relevant to the content of this article.

References

1. Benmessaoud, Y., Cherrat, L., Ezziyyani, M.: Real-time self-adaptive traffic management system for optimal vehicular navigation in modern cities. Computers **12**(4), 80 (2023)
2. Boubedra, S., Tolba, C., Manzoni, P., Beddiar, D., Zennir, Y.: Urban traffic flow management on large scale using an improved ACO for a road transportation system. Int. J. Intell. Comput. Cybern. **16**(4), 766–799 (2023)
3. Butler, L., Yigitcanlar, T., Paz, A.: Smart urban mobility innovations: a comprehensive review and evaluation. IEEE Access **8**, 196034–196049 (2020)
4. Dias, C., IRYO, M., & Nishiuchi, H.: Evaluation of safe avoidance distance for pedestrians in personal mobility vehicles and pedestrian mixed traffic: a simulation based study. J. Eastern Asia Soc. Transport. Stud. **12**, 1994–2005 (2017)
5. Fernández-Isabel, A., Fuentes-Fernández, R.: Social-aware driver assistance systems for city traffic in shared spaces. Sensors **19**(2), 221 (2019)
6. Garrido, D., Jacob, J., Silva, D.C., Rossetti, R.J.: pedestrian simulation in SUMO through externally modelled agents. In: ECMS, pp. 111–118 (2021)
7. GC, V. J. D., Mishra, S.K., Puthal, D.: Enhancing traffic flow through advanced ACO mechanism. In: IEEE INFOCOM 2024-IEEE Conference on Computer Communications Workshops (INFOCOM WKSHPS), pp. 1–6. IEEE (2024)
8. Gioldasis, C., Valero, Y., Christoforou, Z.: Modeling personal mobility device movement under mixed traffic conditions. Transport. Res. Procedia **72**, 3901–3908 (2023)
9. Hishikawa, T., Iryo-Asano, M.: Safety evaluation of personal mobility vehicles and pedestrians under mixed traffic flow using traffic simulation. Asian Transp. Stud. **8**, 100049 (2022)
10. Huang, Y., Jiang, X., Chen, S., Yang, F., Yang, J.: Pheromone incentivized intelligent multipath traffic scheduling approach for LEO satellite networks. IEEE Trans. Wireless Commun. **21**(8), 5889–5902 (2022)
11. Jajala, K.K., Buduri, R.: Efficient and secure routing with UAV: GuidedPheromone update based on improved Ant colony optimization and fuzzy logic for congestion control in vehicular ad-hoc network. Int. J. Inf. Technol., 1–22 (2024). https://doi.org/10.1007/s41870-024-01978-9
12. Krajzewicz, D., Erdmann, J., Behrisch, M., Bieker, L.: Recent development and applications of SUMO-Simulation of Urban MObility. Int. J. Adv. Syst. Meas. **5**(3&4), 128 (2012)
13. Li, J., Rombaut, E., Vanhaverbeke, L.: A systematic review of agent-based models for autonomous vehicles in urban mobility and logistics: Possibilities for integrated simulation models. Comput. Environ. Urban Syst. **89**, 101686 (2021)

14. Liao, S., Wu, Y., Ma, K., Niu, Y.: Ant colony optimization with look-ahead mechanism for dynamic traffic signal control of IoV systems. IEEE Internet Things J. **11**(1), 366–377 (2023)
15. Liao, X.C., Chen, W.N., Guo, X.Q., Zhong, J., Hu, X.M.: Crowd management through optimal layout of fences: an ant colony approach based on crowd simulation. IEEE Trans. Intell. Transp. Syst. **24**(9), 9137–9149 (2023)
16. Liu, W.L., Gong, Y.J., Chen, W.N., Zhang, J.: EvoTSC: an evolutionary computation-based traffic signal controller for large-scale urban transportation networks. Appl. Soft Comput. **97**, 106640 (2020)
17. Mishra, S., Rajendran, P.K., Har, D.: Socially acceptable route planning and trajectory behavior analysis of personal mobility device for mobility management with improved sensing. In: International Conference on Robot Intelligence Technology and Applications, pp. 53–65. Cham: Springer International Publishing (2021). https://doi.org/10.1007/978-3-030-97672-9_6
18. Na, S., Niu, H., Lennox, B., Arvin, F.: Bio-inspired collision avoidance in swarm systems via deep reinforcement learning. IEEE Trans. Veh. Technol. **71**(3), 2511–2526 (2022)
19. Nguyen, T.H., Jung, J.J.: ACO-based traffic routing method with automated negotiation for connected vehicles. Complex Intell. Syst. **9**(1), 625–636 (2023)
20. Prakash, R., Pushkar, S.: An approach using heuristic pheromones-based ACO modelling for green vehicle routing optimisation. Int. J. Ad Hoc Ubiquitous Comput. **40**(1–3), 187–193 (2022)
21. Ramamoorthy, R., Thangavelu, M.: An enhanced distance and residual energy-based congestion aware ant colony optimization routing for vehicular ad hoc networks. Int. J. Commun. Syst. **35**(11), e5179 (2022)
22. Schuhbäck, S., Daßler, N., Wischhof, L., Köster, G.: Towards a bidirectional coupling of pedestrian dynamics and mobile communication simulation. EPiC Ser. Comput. **66**(13), 60–67 (2019)
23. Shaharuddin, R.A., Misro, M.Y.: Controlling traffic congestion in urbanised city: a framework using agent-based modelling and simulation approach. ISPRS Int. J. Geo Inf. **12**(6), 226 (2023)
24. Solmaz, G., Turgut, D.: A survey of human mobility models. IEEE Access **7**, 125711–125731 (2019)
25. Soon, K.L., Lim, J.M.Y., Parthiban, R.: Coordinated traffic light control in cooperative green vehicle routing for pheromone-based multi-agent systems. Appl. Soft Comput. **81**, 105486 (2019)
26. Soon, K.L., Lim, J.M.Y., Parthiban, R.: Impacts of non-recurrent events on pheromone-based green transportation system. IEEE Access **8**, 8876–8885 (2020)
27. Soon, K.L., Lim, J.M.Y., Parthiban, R., Ho, M.C.: Proactive eco-friendly pheromone-based green vehicle routing for multi-agent systems. Expert Syst. Appl. **121**, 324–337 (2019)
28. Steinberg, M.: Biologically-inspired approaches for self-organization, adaptation, and collaboration of heterogeneous autonomous systems. In: Defense Transformation and Net-Centric Systems 2011, vol. 8062, pp. 127–139. SPIE (2011)
29. Vinod Chandra, S.S., Saritha, R.: Bilevel optimization based on foraging by different ant species for real-time transportation planning. Evol. Intel. **17**(4), 2345–2354 (2024)
30. Yadav, P., Mishra, A., Kim, S.: A comprehensive survey on multi-agent reinforcement learning for connected and automated vehicles. Sensors **23**(10), 4710 (2023)
31. Zhang, M.: A contribution to the control of multi-agent system: Application to management of conflicts between pedestrians and connected autonomous vehicles in industrial areas (Doctoral dissertation, Université Bourgogne Franche-Comté) (2022)
32. Zhang, Z., Fu, D.: Modeling pedestrian–vehicle mixed-flow in a complex evacuation scenario. Physica A **599**, 127468 (2022)

33. Zhou, B., Tang, X., Wang, X.: Learning collective crowd behaviors with dynamic pedestrian-agents. Int. J. Comput. Vision **111**, 50–68 (2015)
34. Zhou, Y., Vroon, J., Rusák, Z., Kortuem, G.: Social cues for navigation; a systematic review from pedestrians to socially intelligent agents. SSRN 4003391 (2021)

Unmanned Aerial Vehicles in Inventory Management: An Overview of Current Research and Applications

Buşra Baytur[1,2](✉) and Eren Özceylan[1]

[1] Department of Quality and Accreditation, Mardin Artuklu University, Mardin, Turkey
b.baytur@hotmail.com

[2] Department of Industrial Engineering, Gaziantep University, 27310 Gaziantep, Turkey

Abstract. Industry 4.0 refers to the integration of digital transformation and automation within production processes, offering the potential for significant improvements in productivity, cost optimization, and production flexibility. In this framework, inventory management is recognized as one of the fundamental applications of Industry 4.0. Intelligent inventory systems and automated stock tracking technologies facilitate the real-time monitoring and management of stock levels, thereby reducing the time lost and error rates typically associated with traditional inventory methods. The advent of big data analytics and sensor technologies has revolutionized inventory management, facilitating substantial cost savings and enabling more rapid and accurate responses to customer demands. Recently, Unmanned Aerial Vehicles (UAVs), commonly known as drones, have emerged as innovative tools for inventory counting. Drones equipped with advanced data collection capabilities are particularly effective in large warehouses and logistics centers, providing access to hard-to-reach areas and high-resolution imaging. This study presents a comprehensive literature review focusing on research conducted after 2018, aimed at examining current technologies for inventory counting. The review analyzes existing academic literature and industrial practices, revealing that drones significantly reduce error rates, shorten processing times, and facilitate real-time monitoring of stock levels. Consequently, UAV technology supports the implementation of inventory management strategies in a more dynamic and precise manner, thereby enhancing overall efficiency and accuracy.

Keywords: UAV Stock-Taking · Autonomous Inventory · Inventory Management

1 Introduction

1.1 Industry 4.0 and the Integration of Drone Technology

Since the early 21st century, Industry 4.0 has triggered a significant transformation in the logistics and warehousing sectors. Industry 4.0 refers to the current trend of automation and data exchange in manufacturing technologies. It encompasses cyber-physical systems, the Internet of Things (IoT), biotechnology, cloud computing, and

A. Mirzazadeh et al. (Eds.): SEMIT 2024, CCIS 2444, pp. 361–374, 2026.
https://doi.org/10.1007/978-3-032-01948-6_23

cognitive computing, which collectively aim to create smart factories characterized by enhanced efficiency and flexibility (Massabni & da Silva, 2019). Particularly, artificial intelligence, big data analytics, robotics, and smart systems emerge as fundamental components of the fourth industrial revolution (Adel, 2024), with the application of drone technology being notably significant.

Drones, also known as Unmanned Aerial Vehicles (UAVs), are aircraft systems that operate without a human pilot onboard. They are controlled remotely or autonomously through onboard computers. Drones facilitate the acceleration and enhancement of accuracy in tasks such as inventory tracking and counting within warehouses, playing a critical role in achieving operational efficiency and cost-effectiveness (Szalanczi-Orban & Vaczi, 2022).

The increasing utilization of drones across various sectors is a crucial factor in the adoption of these technologies. The Federal Aviation Administration (FAA) projects that the fleet of small drones used for recreational purposes will peak at approximately 1.88 M units by 2028. Additionally, it estimates that the commercial drone fleet, along with those used in various sectors such as agriculture, energy, healthcare, and security, will reach around 1.12 M units during the same period (Yeşilay & Macit, 2020; Pobkrut et al., 2016; FAA, 2024). This trend not only underscores the potential of drones in transportation and inventory management but also signifies the rapid acceleration of technological adaptation processes.

1.2 Transformation in Workforce Dynamics and Inventory Management

In logistics processes characterized by high volumes of data flow, the use of drones supports effective decision-making mechanisms and lays the groundwork for the development of more efficient business models (Sah et al., 2021). The integration of drone technology enables the workforce to be managed more efficiently. This technology frees employees from repetitive and time-consuming tasks, allowing them to focus on more strategic and creative work, and this change ultimately contributes to the optimization of business processes (Ali et al., 2024). The use of drones in conjunction with automation systems in large logistics centers enhances both efficiency and employee satisfaction. This, in turn, contributes to reducing operational costs for businesses and increasing their competitiveness.

The role of drones in security and monitoring is also noteworthy. Drones equipped with smart sensors offer a significant mechanism for the continuous surveillance of warehouse areas and the immediate detection of security vulnerabilities. This enables businesses to minimize inventory losses and implement effective inventory management (Szalanczi-Orban & Vaczi, 2022). Additionally, such technologies facilitate regular reporting, allowing organizations to perform performance analyses more efficiently.

The utilization of drones for in-warehouse inventory counting has gained significant traction in recent years. This increase is supported by substantial improvements in the accuracy and efficiency provided by drones. Unlike traditional methods that depend on manual labor and are susceptible to human error, drones equipped with advanced imaging and sensor technologies can perform comprehensive inventory audits in a much shorter timeframe (Wawrla et al., 2019; Ali et al., 2024). This heightened precision not only minimizes discrepancies in stock levels but also reduces the downtime associated with inventory checks. The advantages of drones in this context enhance the efficiency of logistics processes, thereby strengthening organizations' competitive edge and improving customer satisfaction. As organizations strive to optimize their operations and respond swiftly to market demands, the rising popularity of drones in inventory management is expected to continue, positioning them as essential instruments in modern warehousing practices.

Based on these, this transformation presents both opportunities and challenges within the logistics and warehousing sectors. Drones offer substantial contributions not only to the improvement of operational processes but also in the realms of security, customer satisfaction, and workforce management. It is anticipated that the increased integration of these technologies will lead to further evolution of the sector and the emergence of new business models. Such changes will create new opportunities for both businesses and consumers, reshaping the dynamics of the industry (Zrelli et al., 2024).

1.3 Motivation for a Review of Research Papers on Stock-Taking with UAVs

With advancements in technology, the growth in the aviation sector has led to numerous positive developments in the aviation manufacturing industry. As countries have placed emphasis on air defense at the military level, "Unmanned Aerial Vehicles (UAVs)" have been developed for various purposes (Franke, 2014). Initially designed for military applications, these vehicles have gradually begun to be used in civil aviation and industrial applications as well. This widespread adoption has enabled UAVs to impact economic indicators and establish their own sector (Hassanalian & Abdelkefi, 2017). The limited examination of this sector in academic literature has formed the basis for this study.

The integration of autonomous systems in inventory management presents significant opportunities in terms of both cost efficiency and process effectiveness. There is a particular need for further research on the effects of innovative methods and technologies used in stock-taking. The optimization and automation of inventory counting can contribute to businesses gaining a competitive advantage, while an increase in academic studies in this area will significantly support the development of the sector. Although various studies on UAVs in the logistics and supply chain fields are present in the existing literature (Malang et al., 2023; Jahani et al., 2024;Zrelli et al., 2024), this study focuses solely on the applications of in-warehouse inventory counting. Therefore, the aim of this research is to examine the effectiveness of modern techniques recently employed in inventory management and to contribute to the literature through a comprehensive review.

2 Systematic Review Methodology

The rapid increase in knowledge production within the research field, coupled with its growing fragmentation and interdisciplinary nature, complicates the process of keeping abreast of the latest developments and evaluating collective evidence in specific domains. This situation underscores the critical importance of literature reviews as a research methodology. Literature reviews facilitate the systematic synthesis of existing research, providing an overview of the field while identifying gaps and trends within the literature.

According to the criteria established by Mayring and Fenzl (2019) and Snyder (2019), a high-quality review article must adhere to an established and systematic methodology to ensure accuracy and reliability. This process consists of four fundamental stages: *literature collection, descriptive analysis, category selection, and literature evaluation.* By following this structured approach, researchers can maintain the rigor necessary to meticulously evaluate the current state of research, ensuring that their reviews are comprehensive, reliable, and capable of contributing to the advancement of knowledge in the field.

This study employed these steps to systematically review the literature and capture the latest developments regarding the role of drones in stock-taking. Literature collection was carried out by gathering relevant studies on drone-assisted stock-taking and inventory management. Descriptive analysis followed, where the gathered literature was reviewed to identify common themes and key contributions in the field. In the category selection stage, studies were grouped based on their focus on in-warehouse applications of drones. Finally, literature evaluation involved a critical examination of the selected studies to assess their findings and relevance to the research objective.

The focus was on studies published from 2018 onwards to reflect recent progress in the field. The search shown in Table 1 was conducted using the keywords "*unmanned aerial vehicle-based stock-taking*" and "*drone-assisted inventory management*". The literature review was carried out using Google Scholar, selected for its extensive access to recent articles from various publishers. The initial search yielded 23 results, while the second search produced 1.230 results.

Table 1. Database search results.

Search Engine	Search Date	Keyword Use	Number of Results
Google Scholar	August 1, 2024	"unmanned aerial vehicle-based stock-taking"	23
		"drone-assisted inventory management"	1.230

Table 2. Distribution of the selected publication types.

Publication Type	Count	Publications
Article	17	Xu et al. (2018), Beul et al. (2018), Rahmadya et al. (2020), Cristiani et al. (2023), Alsayed et al. (2021), Karamitsos et al. (2021), Gümüşboğa (2022), Salazar et al. (2023), Malang et al. (2023), Yoon et al. (2023), Ali et al. (2024), Thomaidis & Zeimpekis (2024), Lin et al. (2024), Marković et al. (2024), Tsakiridis et al. (2024), Jahani et al. (2024), Zrelli et al. (2024)
Conference Paper	3	Cho et al. (2018), De Falco et al. (2019), Yoon et al. (2021)
Report	1	Wawrla et al. (2019)

The investigation was restricted to English-language articles. Although the results included various applications such as drone logistics and cargo transportation, 21 recently studies specifically focusing on in-warehouse stock-taking were selected and analyzed. Selections were made from various types of publications to address real-world applications. The distribution of the selected publication types is presented in Table 2.

3 Results

3.1 Data Visualisation

This section presents a comprehensive analysis of the abstracts and keywords from the selected 21 studies, focusing on the application of data visualization techniques to enhance the interpretability of the findings. The analysis deliberately omitted frequently used linguistic elements (such as 'the', 'on', 'with') to emphasize significant word frequencies within the context. Figure 1 illustrates a word cloud comprising the top 100 high-frequency terms identified in the abstracts. This visualization serves not only to identify prevalent research topics and themes but also to provide insight into the relative prominence of specific terms within the domain of drone-assisted inventory management.

The analysis reveals that key terms such as 'RFID', 'Barcode', and 'Code' emerge as prominent features in the discourse surrounding inventory technologies. Additionally, the co-occurrence of terms like 'drone' and 'UAV' with concepts such as 'inventory' and 'warehouse' underscores the integration of these advanced technologies into both academic research and practical applications. The prominence of 'drone' reflects a growing recognition of its capabilities in enhancing automation and data collection processes, which are vital for optimizing inventory management practices.

Furthermore, a closer examination of the word cloud provides valuable insights into the trends and themes prevalent in the literature. The frequent appearance of terms such as 'RFID' and 'drone' indicates their critical roles in contemporary discussions on inventory management. In contrast, the sustained interest in 'Barcode' highlights the ongoing relevance of traditional inventory tracking methods. The simultaneous presence of these terms suggests a significant trend toward the convergence of established and emerging technologies within the field, illustrating a holistic approach to improving operational efficiency.

In conclusion, the integration of drone technology and automated systems in inventory management not only reflects a shift in research focus but also stimulates an increase in relevant literature. This synthesis of traditional and innovative approaches signifies a transformative period in inventory management, where technological advancements are leveraged to enhance performance and streamline processes.

3.2 Analyses and Findings

This section provides a comprehensive in-depth review of the studies and their contributions. Research utilizing various algorithms presents innovative solutions for optimizing the applications of drone technology in logistics and supply chain management. Xu

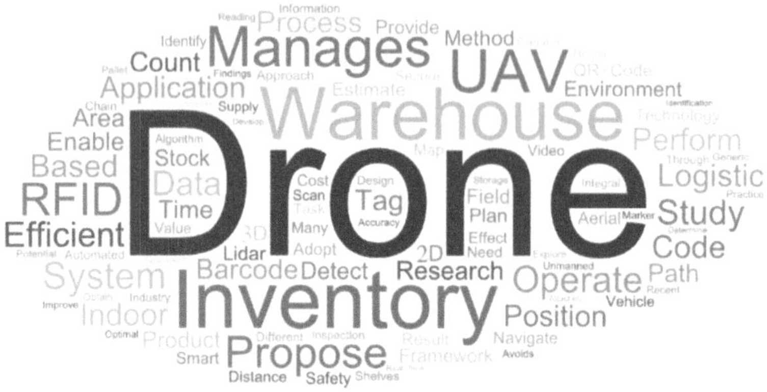

Fig. 1. Wordcloud of the top-100 high-frequency words in the abstracts.

et al. (2018) noted that although numerous algorithms have been developed for extracting barcode information from images, these algorithms have primarily been tested on well-prepared datasets and do not adequately reflect their effectiveness for video data collected by drones under harsh conditions. In this context, three algorithms proposed to achieve the automatic extraction of 1D barcodes aimed at facilitating drone-assisted inventory management in warehousing applications. These algorithms addressed fundamental issues such as barcode direction adjustment, region detection, and rapid extraction of key frames. Similarly, De Falco et al. (2019) employed lightweight Convolutional Neural Network (CNN) and Faster R-CNN deep learning models to facilitate the detection and classification of package labels during aerial scans conducted with UAVs. This two-stage learning process aims to achieve effective inventory management with drones that possess limited processing power. Both Xu et al. (2018) and De Falco et al. (2019) confront challenges such as high energy consumption and restricted processing capabilities of drones. Future research is recommended to focus on enhancing energy efficiency and utilizing larger datasets.

Yoon et al. (2021) and Yoon et al. (2023) proposed an innovative framework based on a deep learning model to predict the 3D position of inventory through drones. In this framework, QR codes were utilized to determine the inventory and ground positions. The researchers trained the proposed deep learning model using a dataset specifically created for this study. A significant component of the study is the correction method that enhances the performance of 3D position prediction through the elimination of outliers. The studies also included an assessment of 3D position prediction performance through videos captured in various real-world environments. The results present compelling evidence that the proposed correction method improves the performance of 3D position prediction.

In recent years, the integration of advanced technologies, particularly drones and machine learning, has significantly transformed warehouse management practices. Markovic et al. (2024) investigated a machine learning framework to optimize the deployment of autonomous drones in warehouse environments. Drones are capable of executing tasks such as cycle counting and barcode scanning in inventory management processes with minimal human intervention. Additionally, Ali et al. (2024) employed the Technology-Organization-Environment (TOE) framework to develop successful integration strategies for examining the incorporation of drone technology in warehouse management. These studies underscore the potential of both machine learning and deep learning to enhance efficiency in drone-based inventory management. The insights from these studies reinforce the idea that machine learning and deep learning can substantially enhance operational efficiency in drone-driven inventory management. Integrated models also include the incorporation of sensor technology, which enhances their functionality and effectiveness in various applications. Salazar et al. (2023) developed an integrated model using a drone and Arduino-based infrared sensor system, utilizing barcode data for inventory tracking. This model facilitates real-time inventory tracking by transmitting the collected data to LabView.

Among the studies that focused on image processing techniques for the automatic detection of barcodes, Cho et al. (2018) proposed a three-stage system specifically designed to detect and recognize 2D barcodes in factory warehouses. This system comprises three key steps: region candidate detection, feature extraction, and Support Vector Machine (SVM) classification. The authors concentrated on mitigating false positives caused by image distortions, varying lighting conditions, and extraneous objects in the image. The proposed method demonstrated remarkable effectiveness, achieving an accuracy of 98.08% and a recall rate of 98.27%. The system utilized the Histogram of Oriented Gradients (HOG) as its primary visual feature, which outperformed other features when analyzed individually. Notably, the combination of HOG with Local Binary Patterns (LBP) exhibited complementary characteristics, further enhancing the overall accuracy. The study confirmed the system's resilience to common lighting variations and image distortions encountered in indoor environments.

Besides, Gumusboga (2022) addressed the design of an autonomous UAV within a warehouse setting by employing an image processing system that facilitated the immediate detection of barcodes. This system operated in real-time on a mini-computer mounted on the drone and utilized advanced image processing techniques, such as the OpenCV library, to automate the stock counting process. The prototype resolved indoor positioning issues using a UWB transmitter network and featured a monocular camera equipped with a Raspberry Pi V2 for immediate barcode detection. Laboratory tests indicated that the UAV's 3D positioning error remained below 4 cm. The drone employed deep learning algorithms to swiftly recognize surrounding objects and accurately detect barcodes, thus expediting the inventory counting process and minimizing error rates. Furthermore, Cristiani et al. (2020) explored the application of barcodes and QR codes in drone-based inventory management, emphasizing the effectiveness of barcode scanning via drones and proposing recommendations for automating these processes. Their research highlighted the significance of advanced image processing techniques for accurate barcode detection and developed strategies for integrating drones into inventory operations. Collectively, these studies underscored the crucial role of barcodes and QR codes, facilitated by advanced image processing techniques, in expediting inventory tracking and significantly enhancing accuracy.

Experimental studies conducted on indoor mapping and localization, which is another significant research area in this field, aim to enhance the effectiveness of drone technology in inventory management. The LiDAR-based Simultaneous Localization and Mapping (SLAM) method developed by Beul et al. (2018) increased the precision of positioning and mapping processes in the environment by utilizing three-dimensional scans. This study demonstrated that the integration of algorithms in drone-based applications can offer more effective and rapid solutions by improving process efficiency. Similarly, Karamitsos et al. (2021) presented a solution within a warehouse environment created using Gazebo 3D simulation software. The drone scans barcodes, QR codes, and logos to identify cargo boxes stored on warehouse shelves. The initial phase of the simulation process involves mapping the warehouse environment using the RGB-D SLAM method. This algorithm enables the creation of a 2D occupancy map and a 3D point cloud through the combination of a LiDAR sensor and a depth camera. The drone employed embedded sensors that provide video streams to identify obstacles and areas of interest in its surroundings. Alsayed et al. (2021) also utilized video data in their studies. They proposed three primary techniques for automatic barcode extraction: barcode orientation prediction, barcode region detection, and rapid extraction. The Harris corner detector and Hough transformation were used for barcode orientation prediction, while the detection of the barcode region was accomplished through connectivity and geometric properties. The ClearImage algorithm was preferred for reading barcodes at specific angles and within blurred frames. The results obtained indicate that barcode region detection was more effective, operating in the range of 40% to 43%, and improved the recognition rate from 77.78% to 89%. The contribution to the literature lies in the potential of these techniques to function more effectively with video data under challenging conditions.

Radio-Frequency Identification (RFID) technology for identifying stock positions in the environment was employed in studies by Beul et al. (2018), Rahmadya et al. (2020), and Thomaidis and Zeimpekis (2024). In the study conducted by Rahmadya et al., a framework was proposed to determine a secure distance between an ultrahigh-frequency band RFID reader and RFID tags affixed to metallic objects. This framework prevented changes in the ranking of received signal strength indicator (RSSI) values among the tags within the reader's field of view, thereby providing the drone operator with a secure means of identification. Experimental measurements of RSSI values from two RFID tags were taken, resulting in the establishment of a secure distance of 3.8 m. This distance aligns with the values calculated by the proposed framework and is significant for inventory management systems. As well as, Thomaidis and Zeimpekis (2024) investigated the potential of integrating RFID technology with drones to optimize warehouse inventory counting processes. The research identified parameters influencing drone performance and examined RFID reading accuracy and inventory counting duration through laboratory experiments. The results demonstrated that drones achieve 100% reading accuracy with RFID tags and yield faster results compared to manual counting. This studies comprehensively address the advantages of utilizing RFID technology in inventory management with drones. While Rahmadya et al. focus on developing a security-oriented framework, Thomadis et al. concentrate on strategies aimed at enhancing operational efficiency. Collectively, these works emphasize the positive impact of RFID and drone integration on inventory management systems, highlighting the potential of this integration to improve the security and effectiveness of operational processes.

Lin et al. (2024) integrated indoor mapping and positioning techniques using methods such as the Extended Kalman Filter (EKF) and Real-Time Appearance-Based Mapping (RTAB-Map) in their research conducted in a controlled laboratory environment. In these experiments, ultra-wideband positioning markers and ceiling-mounted AprilTags were utilized to enhance the navigation capabilities and positional accuracy of drones. The results demonstrated detection rates of 94.62% in simulated environments and 99.38% in real environments, indicating that drones can perform effective inventory control without relying on human-assisted systems. Similarly, Tsakiridis et al. (2024) developed an algorithm for detecting warehouse inventory using drones equipped with LiDAR scanners, successfully measuring the height of each pallet stack and providing accurate inventory management by grouping this data. Such laboratory-based applications showcase the practical potential of drone technology, contributing to the development of more efficient and error-free inventory management solutions.

In addition to experimental applications, studies encompassing real-life applications are also available. Wawrla et al. (2019) examined twelve use cases for indoor drone applications in warehouses across three main areas: inventory management, indoor intra-logistics, and inspection-surveillance. Inventory management applications exhibit the highest potential and have been successfully implemented in certain companies. However, indoor intra-logistics has yet to be fully realized due to technological limitations such as power supply and load capacity. Visual SLAM algorithms and LiDAR technology enhance drone navigation by providing precision, with the most advanced examples of these technologies achieving an accuracy of 2.5 cm. Companies such as Corvus Robotics and Linde Material Handling are developing autonomous warehouse inventory solutions and preparing to enter the market. According to relevant studies, indoor navigation poses the most challenging aspect of achieving full automation for drones, as existing technology remains insufficient. So, Geodis/DeltaDrone and Infinium Robotics aim to extend battery life by integrating drones with automated ground vehicles.

The literature review conducted using the Systematic Literature Review methodology categorizes the success factors of inventory management and UAV applications under various dimensions, including technology, organization, regulations, and social factors. Jahani et al. (2024) and Zrelli et al. (2024) comprehensively evaluated the applications of drones in logistics and supply chain management, highlighting the theoretical and practical gaps in this field. By employing innovative techniques such as Latent Dirichlet Allocation (LDA), they uncover patterns and relationships within the literature. In particular, regulatory complexity and security concerns highlighted as a key factor limiting the effective use of drones. They also concluded that technical limitations and infrastructure deficiencies can negatively affect the operational efficiency of drones. Uncertainty of weather conditions and inadequate user training were cited as obstacles to realizing the full potential of drone technology. Malang et al. (2023) provided a thorough review of the adoption of UAVs in warehouse management. The study addressed the applicability of UAVs in various tasks within internal logistics processes, including inventory control, stock management, and monitoring. Notably, it emphasizes that topics such as inventory control and buffer stock management have not been sufficiently researched, indicating opportunities for expansion in these areas. Such systematic reviews foster interdisciplinary interactions within the academic community, contributing to the improvement of existing practices and the identification of future research directions. Simultaneously, these studies provide valuable insights for industry stakeholders by facilitating a better understanding of the challenges encountered in practice. The studies are summarized in Table 3.

Table 3. Summary of the studies.

Author(s)	Year	Proposed/Used Method	Application With
Xu et al	2018	Harris Corner Detector and Hough Transform-Based Algorithm, Histogram Difference-Based Fast Extraction Strategy	1D Barcodes from Video Scans
Beul et al	2018	The Simultaneous Localization and Mapping	Radio-Frequency Identification (RFID)
Cho et al	2018	Region Candidate Detection, Feature Extraction Methods, Support Vector Machine, Weighted Sum-Based Score Fusion Method	2D Barcodes
Wawrla et al	2019	12 Identified Use Cases of Indoor Drone Applications in Warehouses	N/A
De Falco et al	2019	Convolutional Neural Network (CNN), Faster R-CNN	Labels from Video Scans
Rahmadya et al	2020	RSSI-Based Secure Distance Determination, Radiation Pattern Analyses, Backscattered Power Analyses, Propagation Channel Analyses, Two-Ray Interference Model	Radio-Frequency Identification (RFID)
Cristiani et al	2020	Generic UAV-Based Inventory Management Architecture, Performance Analysis of Inventory Accuracy and Completion Time, Optimal UAV Mobility Parameters Derivation, Small-Scale Testbed for System Operations and Configuration Testing	QR Codes
Alsayed et al	2021	1D, 2D, And 3D LiDAR Sensors, Risk Priority Numbers (RPN) and Cost Priority Factors (CPF), Simulations	Comparison with Static Scanners
Yoon et al	2021	QR Code Segmentation Model, Shape Correction and Decoding	QR Codes
Karamitsos et al	2021	RGB-D Simultaneous Localization and Mapping (SLAM), Custom Navigation Algorithm, Object Recognition Application	QR Codes, Gazebo 3D Computer Simulation Software

(continued)

Table 3. *(continued)*

Author(s)	Year	Proposed/Used Method	Application With
Gumusboga	2022	Ultra-Wideband (UWB) Positioning System, Simple Obstacle Avoidance Function	Industry-Standard Barcodes
Malang et al	2023	Systematic Literature Review	N/A
Yoon et al	2023	Deep Learning Model, QR Code Detection And Decoding, 3D Position Estimation, Outlier Detection And Error Correction	QR Codes
Salazar et al	2023	Supervisory Control and Data Acquisition System (SCADA), Labview and Factory I/O	Infrared Technology
Ali et al	2024	Fuzzy Delphi Method, Graph Theory Matrix Approach, Logistic Regression Analysis, Technology-Organization-Environment (TOE) Framework	N/A
Thomaidis & Zeimpekis	2024	Systematic Literature Review, Survey Via Questionnaire and Interviews, Design of Experiment (DOE), ANOVA (Analysis of Variance)	Radio-Frequency Identification (RFID)
Lin et al	2024	Reinforcement Learning (Actor-Critic, Proximal Policy Optimization), RTAB-Map, Design of Experiment (24 Full Factorial Design & ANOVA)	AprilTags
Marković et al 2024	2024	Deep Learning Image Processing, Metaheuristic Optimization, Machine Learning Flight Control	Scanning Barcodes on Each Pallet
Tsakiridis et al	2024	Post-Process LiDAR Data Processing, Algorithmic Approach for Inventory Quantification, Real-Time Monitoring and Detection	Stereoscopic Data
Jahani et al	2024	Literature Review with Latent Dirichlet Allocation	N/A
Zrelli et al	2024	Literature Review with Latent Dirichlet Allocation	N/A

4 Conclusions

This section presents a comprehensive analysis of the identified gaps within the existing literature regarding UAV technology and proposes directions for future research. The rapid advancement of UAV technology has transformed numerous sectors, including logistics, agriculture, and surveillance. However, significant gaps persist, particularly concerning the effective utilization and integration of UAVs in indoor environments. Addressing these gaps is essential to fully harness the potential of UAV applications.

There is a notable deficiency in comprehensive studies focused on indoor UAV navigation and operations. Research in this domain is crucial for enhancing the effectiveness of current applications. Additionally, the literature reveals insufficient investigations into security protocols for UAV operations. This lack of research poses a substantial barrier to ensuring safe operational practices, which is vital for widespread UAV adoption.

A pressing need exists for further exploration into the integration and analysis of data collected by drones. Existing gaps in this area limit the potential for optimizing data utilization, which could enhance decision-making processes across various applications. Furthermore, the management and implementation of multiple drones in operational environments require additional research. Current deficiencies in this domain hinder the exploration of significant opportunities to improve the effectiveness and efficiency of multi-drone systems.

To advance the field, future research should focus on several key areas. Investigating the application of drones in environments with dynamically changing product placements can yield insights into optimizing their effectiveness in real-world scenarios. Integrating advanced collision avoidance algorithms that utilize near-real-time data from vision systems is essential for enhancing safety during UAV operations. Future studies should also consider the integration of human digital twins to simulate human movements within operational environments. This integration could improve safety and efficiency by anticipating human behavior in real-time.

Developing effective methods for the management and cooperation of multiple drones is crucial for future research. This includes exploring strategies for coordination and communication among drones to optimize their collective functionality. Lastly, further research should emphasize comprehensive analysis and integration of data collected by drones. This focus will not only enhance data utilization but also support informed decision-making in various applications.

Disclosure of Interests. The authors have no competing interests to declare that are relevant to the content of this article.

References

1. Adel, A.: The convergence of intelligent tutoring, robotics, and IoT in smart education for the transition from industry 4.0 to 5.0. Smart Cities, **7**(1), 325–369 (2024)
2. Ali, S.S., Khan, S., Fatma, N., Ozel, C., Hussain, A.: Utilisation of drones in achieving various applications in smart warehouse management. Benchmarking Int. J. **31**(3), 920–954(2024)

3. Alsayed, A., Yunusa-Kaltungo, A., Quinn, M.K., Arvin, F., Nabawy, M.R.: Drone-assisted confined space inspection and stockpile volume estimation. Remote Sens. **13**(17), 3356 (2021)
4. Beul, M., Droeschel, D., Nieuwenhuisen, M., Quenzel, J., Houben, S., Behnke, S.: Fast autonomous flight in warehouses for inventory applications. IEEE Robot. Autom. Lett. **3**(4), 3121–3128 (2018)
5. Cho, H., Kim, D., Park, J., Roh, K., Hwang, W.: 2D barcode detection using images for drone-assisted inventory management. In: 2018 15th International Conference on Ubiquitous Robots (UR), pp. 461–465. IEEE (2018)
6. Cristiani, D., Bottonelli, F., Trotta, A., Di Felice, M.: Inventory management through mini-drones: Architecture and proof-of-concept implementation. In: 2020 IEEE 21st International Symposium on "A World of Wireless, Mobile and Multimedia Networks" (WoWMoM), pp. 317–322. IEEE (2020)
7. De Falco, A., Narducci, F., Petrosino, A.: An UAV autonomous warehouse inventorying by deep learning. In: Image Analysis and Processing–ICIAP 2019: 20th International Conference, Trento, Italy, September 9–13, 2019, Proceedings, Part I 20, pp. 443–453. Springer International Publishing (2019). https://doi.org/10.1007/978-3-030-30642-7_40
8. Federal aviation administration: aerospace forecasts: fiscal years 2024–2044. U.S. Department of Transportation (2024). https://www.faa.gov/data_research/aviation/aerospace_forecasts. Accessed 18 Oct 2024
9. Franke, U.E.: The global diffusion of unmanned aerial vehicles (UAVs), or 'drones'. In: Precision Strike Warfare and International Intervention, pp. 52–72. Routledge (2014)
10. Gümüşboğa, İ: Design of an automated stock-taking system based on unmanned aerial vehicles. J. Faculty Eng. Archit. Gazi Univ. **37**(4), 1767–1782 (2022)
11. Hassanalian, M., Abdelkefi, A.: Classifications, applications, and design challenges of drones: a review. Prog. Aerosp. Sci. **91**, 99–131 (2017)
12. Jahani, H., Khosravi, Y., Kargar, B., Ong, K.L., Arisian, S.: Exploring the role of drones and UAVs in logistics and supply chain management: a novel text-based literature review. Int. J. Prod. Res. **63**, 1–25 (2024)
13. Karamitsos, G., Bechtsis, D., Tsolakis, N., Vlachos, D.: Unmanned aerial vehicles for inventory listing. Int. J. Bus. Syst. Res. **15**(6), 748–756 (2021)
14. Lin, H.Y., Chang, K.L., Huang, H.Y.: Development of unmanned aerial vehicle navigation and warehouse inventory system based on reinforcement learning. Drones **8**(6), 220 (2024)
15. Malang, C., Charoenkwan, P., Wudhikarn, R.: Implementation and critical factors of unmanned aerial vehicle (UAV) in warehouse management: a systematic literature review. Drones **7**(2), 80 (2023)
16. Marković, N., Ćojbačić, Ž, Petrović, G., Milić, P., Milošević, M., Ivačko, N.: A machine learning based framework for optimizing drone use in advanced warehouse cycle counting process solutions. Innov. Mech. Eng. **3**(1), 69–78 (2024)
17. Massabni, A.C., da Silva, G.J.: Biotechnology and industry 4.0: the professionals of the future. Int. J. Adv. Med. Biotechnol. IJAMB **2**(2), 45–53 (2019)
18. Mayring, P., Fenzl, T.: Qualitative inhaltsanalyse. Springer Fachmedien Wiesbaden, pp. 633–648 (2019). https://doi.org/10.1007/978-3-658-21308-4_42
19. Pobkrut, T., Eamsa-Ard, T., Kerdcharoen, T.: Sensor drone for aerial odor mapping for agriculture and security services. In: 2016 13th International Conference on Electrical Engineering/Electronics, Computer, Telecommunications and Information Technology (ECTI-CON), pp. 1–5. IEEE (2016)
20. Rahmadya, B., Sun, R., Takeda, S., Kagoshima, K., Umehira, M.: A framework to determine secure distances for either drones or robots based inventory management systems. IEEE Access **8**, 170153–170161 (2020)
21. Sah, B., Gupta, R., Bani-Hani, D.: Analysis of barriers to implement drone logistics. Int J Log Res Appl **24**(6), 531–550 (2021)

22. Salazar, F., et al.: UAVs for business adoptions in smart city environments: inventory management system. Electronics **12**(9), 2090 (2023)
23. Snyder, H.: Literature review as a research methodology: an overview and guidelines. J. Bus. Res. **104**, 333–339 (2019)
24. Szalanczi-Orban, V., Vaczi, D.: Use of drones in logistics: options in inventory control systems. Interdiscip. Descrip. Complex Syst. INDECS **20**(3), 295–303 (2022)
25. Thomaidis, N.C., Zeimpekis, V.: Investigation of operational parameters that affect the use of drones in goods' stock count process: Evidence from experimental results. J. Ind. Eng. Manage. **17**(1), 115–132 (2024)
26. Tsakiridis, S., Papakonstantinou, A., Kapandelis, A., Mastorocostas, P., Tsimpiris, A., Varsamis, D.: Optimizing UAV-based inventory detection and quantification in industrial warehouses: a LiDAR-driven approach. WSEAS Trans. Syst. **23**, 121–127 (2024)
27. Wawrla, L., Maghazei, O., Netland, T.: Applications of drones in warehouse operations. whitepaper. ETH Zurich, D-MTEC **212**, 1–12 (2019)
28. Xu, L., Kamat, V.R., Menassa, C.C.: Automatic extraction of 1D barcodes from video scans for drone-assisted inventory management in warehousing applications. Int J Log Res Appl **21**(3), 243–258 (2018)
29. Yeşilay, R.B., Macit, A.: Drone economy in Turkey and the world: future expectations. Beykoz Acad. J. **8**(1), 239–251 (2020)
30. Yoon, B., Kim, H., Youn, G., Rhee, J.: 3D position estimation of drone and object based on QR code segmentation model for inventory management automation. In: 2021 IEEE International Symposium on Safety, Security, and Rescue Robotics (SSRR), pp. 223–229. IEEE (2021)
31. Yoon, B., Kim, H., Youn, G., Rhee, J.: 3D position estimation of objects for inventory management automation using drones. Appl. Sci. **13**(19), 10830 (2023)
32. Zrelli, I., Rejeb, A., Abusulaiman, R., AlSahafi, R., Rejeb, K., Iranmanesh, M.: Drone applications in logistics and supply chain management: A systematic review using latent dirichlet allocation. Arab. J. Sci. Eng., 1–20 (2024). https://doi.org/10.1007/s13369-023-08681-0

FSR in Wireless Sensor Networks and UAVs: Enhancing Routing Efficiency

Mukerrem Yildiz, Edip Ayman, Soude Felouz Alam, Kerem Mert Zehre, Mehmet Faruk Dalay, and Merve Koca(✉)

Mersin University, Mersin, Turkey
merve_koca@tarsus.edu.tr

Abstract. Routing protocols play a critical role in Mobile Ad-Hoc Networks (MANETs) by establishing efficient routes between source and destination nodes, ensuring timely data dissemination and transfer. These protocols adaptively map recipient addresses to current network locations through a Locator Service, utilizing single-hop transmission services for reliable end-to-end delivery. Key characteristics include minimal control overhead, loop prevention, topology management, scalability, and support for security and Quality of Service parameters. Fisheye State Routing (FSR), widely adopted in Wireless Sensor Networks (WSNs) and Unmanned Aerial Vehicles (UAVs), optimizes data delivery in various environments. The integration of FSR with mobile robots improves navigation and communication in dynamic environments, enhancing collaboration and task coordination in disaster response and industrial automation. FSR's efficient management of update messages, employing the fisheye technique to adjust coverage levels based on network size, mitigates bandwidth impact while maintaining routing accuracy. This study investigates FSR's advantages, emphasizing simplicity, resilience to host mobility, and efficient route updates. Performance metrics including packet delivery rate, network control overhead, throughput, and end-to-end delay are evaluated in grid environments. FSR demonstrates robust performance under various Quality of Service constraints, validating its effectiveness through NS2 simulations with high packet delivery rates and optimized throughput management.

Keywords: Routing Protocol · Fisheye State Routing · Wireless Networks · Unmanned Aerial Vehicles · Network Simulation

1 Introduction

Routing protocols play a crucial role in Mobile Ad-Hoc Networks (MANETs), facilitating efficient information dissemination by establishing dynamic routes between source and destination nodes [1–5]. This is particularly important in networks involving UAVs, where highly dynamic and frequently changing topologies require robust protocols to ensure continuous communication. These protocols enable timely data transfer by dynamically mapping logical recipient addresses to their current network locations through a Locator Service [6]. For UAV-based networks, which often rely on single-hop

A. Mirzazadeh et al. (Eds.): SEMIT 2024, CCIS 2444, pp. 375–397, 2026.
https://doi.org/10.1007/978-3-032-01948-6_24

or multi-hop transmission services, routing and forwarding algorithms create reliable end-to-end delivery mechanisms, essential for maintaining real-time data flows, such as video streams and sensor data. This is especially critical in aerial traffic monitoring [7–9] and mapping [10–13] applications, where UAVs must transmit high-resolution imagery or real-time traffic data to ground stations for processing and analysis. Efficient data transfer in such scenarios ensures accurate, up-to-date information for tasks like traffic management and geographical mapping. Key characteristics of these protocols include minimizing control overhead, preventing routing loops, dynamically managing network topologies, scalability to accommodate varying network sizes (including aerial networks), support for unidirectional links, ensuring security measures, maintaining reliability, and optimizing Quality of Service parameters [14–17].

Fisheye State Routing (FSR) is widely recognized within Wireless Sensor Networks (WSNs) and is increasingly relevant for Unmanned Aerial Vehicles (UAVs) involved in data collection and dissemination scenarios [18–24]. FSR offers a localized view of the network topology where nodes maintain awareness of neighboring nodes within their communication range. This localized approach enables efficient routing of data packets in dynamic or irregular network topologies, making it particularly suitable for UAVs equipped with sensors that operate as mobile nodes within WSNs. This capability facilitates rapid deployment and reconfiguration of communication networks across challenging terrains, enhancing UAV capabilities in tasks such as environmental monitoring, disaster response, and surveillance by optimizing data delivery reliability and timeliness.

Grid State Routing (GSR)-based FSR addresses scalability challenges encountered in large networks [25]. By employing multi-level fisheye coverage, GSR reduces routing update overhead through selective exchange of link state entries and creation of comprehensive network topology maps [26]. This approach simplifies network management, enhances efficiency, and scales effectively in MANET environments [27–29]. The synergy between FSR and mobile robots focuses on optimizing navigation and communication in dynamic environments [30]. FSR enables nodes, similar to mobile robots equipped with sensors, to maintain partial views of the network topology within their communication range. This capability is crucial for enhancing the effectiveness of mobile robots in navigating complex operational spaces, relying on effective guidance algorithms for real-time navigation and communication tasks [31]. Integrating FSR with mobile robots enhances their ability to dynamically adapt communication strategies, improving collaboration, information sharing, and task coordination in environments such as disaster response, search and rescue missions, and industrial automation settings where robust communication and coordination are critical [20, 32, 33].

FSR stands out among routing protocols, especially as network size increases, due to its efficient management of update messages, which can otherwise consume considerable bandwidth over time. To mitigate the impact on bandwidth while maintaining routing accuracy, FSR employs the fisheye technique, as depicted in Fig. 1. This technique defines varying extents of coverage around a central node using circles shaded in different grays. Each shade represents nodes reachable within specific hop counts: one, two, and more than two hops away. The number of coverage levels and the radius of each scope are adjusted according to network size, ensuring optimal resource utilization and sustained performance in dynamic network environments. This adaptive approach not only conserves bandwidth but also enhances the scalability and responsiveness of FSR in managing network topology updates effectively.

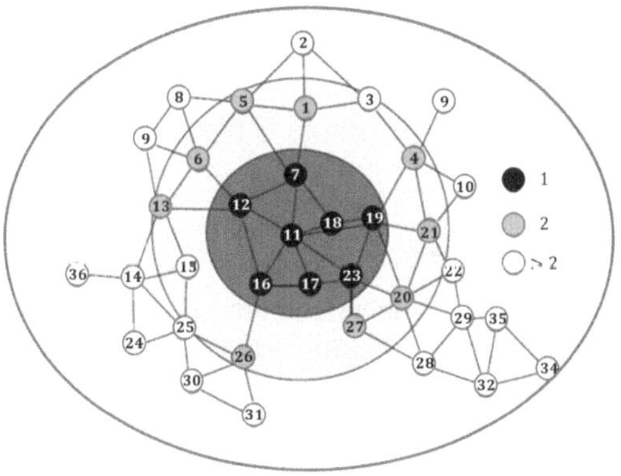

Fig. 1. Sample fisheye application in mobile networks.

This study aims to comprehensively explore the advantages of Fisheye State Routing (FSR), highlighting its simplicity, utilization of current shortest routes, resilience to host mobility, and efficient exchange of partial route updates with neighboring nodes. FSR's proactive nature, particularly in grid environments, is investigated through an in-depth analysis of various performance metrics essential for evaluating routing protocol effectiveness. These metrics encompass packet delivery rate, network control overhead, normalized overhead, throughput, and average end-to-end delay, providing critical benchmarks for assessing FSR's operational efficiency. In practical scenarios, FSR consistently demonstrates robust performance across diverse Quality of Service (QoS) constraints, positioning itself as a superior routing solution tailored for grid environments. The implementation of Grid FSR further enhances network performance by strategically managing bandwidth through judicious control over the dissemination of routing control messages. Simulation studies conducted using the NS2 network simulator serve to validate FSR's effectiveness, revealing its capability to achieve high packet delivery rates while efficiently managing throughput demands.

FSR's operational advantages stem from its proactive routing strategy, which optimizes routing decisions based on up-to-date information about network topology. By utilizing current shortest routes, FSR minimizes latency and packet loss, ensuring reliable and timely delivery of data packets even in dynamic and resource-constrained environments. Its resilience to host mobility enables seamless adaptation to changes in node positions, maintaining continuity in communication paths without compromising performance metrics such as end-to-end delay and throughput.

Moreover, FSR's efficiency in exchanging partial route updates with neighboring nodes enhances scalability, allowing it to scale effectively with network size and density. This capability is particularly advantageous in scenarios where network topology evolves frequently, such as in MANETs or deployments involving autonomous vehicles and UAVs [34, 35]. By optimizing bandwidth utilization and minimizing control overhead, FSR not only improves overall network efficiency but also supports applications requiring high reliability and responsiveness. The proactive and adaptive nature of FSR makes it well-suited for modern communication paradigms where real-time data delivery and network resilience are paramount. Its performance benefits, validated through rigorous simulation studies, underscore its relevance and effectiveness in meeting the stringent demands of grid-based communication infrastructures and beyond.

2 Related Work

2.1 Fisheye State Routing (FSR)

MANETs have garnered significant attention in recent years due to their flexibility and applicability in various scenarios, including disaster recovery, military operations, and smart cities. Routing protocols are central to the effective functioning of MANETs, facilitating communication between nodes without relying on fixed infrastructure. Numerous studies have investigated different routing approaches, each addressing the unique challenges posed by the dynamic nature of MANETs. FSR is one such protocol that has been extensively studied and implemented in various contexts. [36] introduced FSR as a proactive routing protocol designed for mobile ad-hoc networks. It employs the fisheye technique, which allows nodes to maintain up-to-date information about their neighbors while selectively disseminating less detailed information about distant nodes. This mechanism significantly reduces control overhead, making FSR suitable for environments with limited bandwidth and high mobility. In the context of WSNs, [37] explored the application of FSR to enhance data delivery efficiency. Their work demonstrated that FSR could effectively reduce the frequency of update messages while maintaining accurate routing information, thus optimizing bandwidth usage. Additionally, the integration of FSR with UAVs has shown promise in improving routing performance. [38] investigated the potential of FSR in UAV networks, highlighting its effectiveness in managing route updates and ensuring reliable communication in dynamic aerial environments.

Furthermore, FSR has been adapted for use in mobile robotic systems. [39] emphasized the importance of efficient routing in robotic networks for collaborative tasks in disaster response scenarios. Their findings indicated that FSR's ability to manage communication effectively among mobile robots enhances task coordination and navigation in unpredictable environments. The study of FSR's performance metrics has also been a focal point of recent research. [40] evaluated the impact of FSR on various performance indicators, including packet delivery ratio, network control overhead, and end-to-end delay, demonstrating its capability to achieve high packet delivery rates while minimizing control overhead. These performance metrics are crucial in assessing the effectiveness of routing protocols under varying QoS constraints.

Additionally, the importance of energy efficiency in routing protocols has been highlighted in various studies. [41] examined energy-aware routing mechanisms in MANETs, emphasizing the need for protocols to balance energy consumption with performance metrics such as throughput and delay. Their analysis indicates that protocols integrating energy conservation strategies, like FSR, are essential for extending the operational lifetime of mobile nodes, particularly in resource-constrained environments. Moreover,

[42] presented an extensive review of routing protocols in MANETs, categorizing them into reactive, proactive, and hybrid approaches. They underscored the advantages of proactive protocols like FSR, which provide faster route availability compared to their reactive counterparts. Their findings suggest that FSR's efficiency in maintaining routing tables contributes significantly to minimizing latency and enhancing overall network responsiveness.

The integration of FSR with QoS parameters has also been a subject of interest. [43] proposed an enhanced version of FSR that incorporates QoS metrics, such as bandwidth and delay, into the routing decision process. Their experiments showed that the modified FSR not only improved packet delivery ratios but also maintained acceptable end-to-end delays, making it suitable for applications requiring stringent QoS guarantees. A The existing literature underscores the versatility and effectiveness of FSR in diverse applications, from WSNs to UAVs and mobile robotic systems. This study builds on this foundation, further investigating FSR's advantages in grid environments and emphasizing its resilience to host mobility and efficient route management. Through comprehensive simulations using NS2, we aim to validate FSR's performance, providing insights into its potential for enhancing data dissemination and transfer in MANETs.

2.2 Fisheye State Routing in UAV-Based Applications

The integration of FSR in UAV applications has become an area of significant research interest, particularly given the increasing reliance on UAVs for various operations, including surveillance, disaster response, and environmental monitoring [44, 45]. FSR, as a proactive routing protocol, offers unique advantages for UAV networks, primarily due to its ability to manage route updates efficiently in dynamic and often unpredictable environments. In the context of UAV networks, [46] explored the potential of FSR in optimizing routing efficiency for aerial communication. Their work demonstrated that FSR's fisheye technique, which allows nodes to maintain detailed information about nearby neighbors while reducing the overhead for distant nodes, significantly enhances communication reliability in UAV networks. The findings indicated that FSR could effectively adapt to the mobility of UAVs, ensuring continuous connectivity even as network topologies change rapidly.

Another relevant [47] examined the use of FSR in multi-UAV systems for collaborative tasks. They highlighted how FSR's efficient routing capabilities enable real-time data sharing among UAVs, which is crucial for coordinated operations in applications such as search and rescue missions. The research found that FSR not only improved data delivery rates but also reduced end-to-end delays, making it a suitable choice for time-sensitive operations in dynamic environments. In addition, [48] investigated the application of FSR in UAV networks focused on environmental monitoring. Their results indicated that FSR facilitates efficient communication between UAVs and ground control stations, enabling effective data transmission of environmental parameters. The study emphasized FSR's ability to minimize control overhead while maximizing data delivery efficiency, reinforcing its suitability for applications that require real-time monitoring and response.

The adaptability of FSR to varying QoS requirements in UAV networks has also been a focus of research. [49] presented a modified version of FSR that incorporates QoS metrics, ensuring that UAVs can prioritize critical data while managing bandwidth effectively. Their findings showed that this enhancement led to improved packet delivery ratios and reduced latency, essential for mission-critical applications in UAV operations. Furthermore, energy efficiency remains a crucial aspect of UAV routing protocols. [50] highlighted the importance of energy-aware routing in prolonging the operational life of UAVs, particularly in scenarios involving extensive flight durations. Their analysis suggested that integrating energy-saving mechanisms with FSR could optimize energy consumption without compromising performance, making it a viable choice for long-duration missions. Recent advancements in the development of autonomous UAV systems have also influenced routing protocols. [51] investigated the role of FSR in fully autonomous UAV networks, emphasizing its potential in enhancing navigation and decision-making processes. The study revealed that FSR's effective management of routing information could significantly support autonomous operations, particularly in complex and dynamic environments where timely communication is paramount.

2.3 Fisheye State Routing in Mobile Robot Applications

The application of FSR in mobile robotics has gained significant attention due to the increasing need for efficient communication and navigation in dynamic environments. Mobile robots often operate in environments where traditional routing protocols may struggle with rapid changes in topology and mobility. FSR, with its unique approach to managing routing information and reducing overhead, presents a compelling solution for enhancing the performance of mobile robotic systems. One of the foundational studies in this area [52] investigated the implementation of FSR in robotic swarms. Their research demonstrated that FSR effectively reduces communication overhead by utilizing the fisheye technique to adjust the granularity of routing information based on the proximity of nodes. This adaptive strategy allowed for improved coordination among robots during collaborative tasks, significantly enhancing task completion rates in complex environments.

In a similar vein, [53] explored the use of FSR in autonomous mobile robots for search and rescue missions. The study emphasized the importance of maintaining reliable communication links in dynamic scenarios where obstacles and mobility can disrupt connectivity. By employing FSR, the robots were able to maintain up-to-date routing information, enabling efficient pathfinding and real-time data exchange with base stations. The results indicated that FSR not only improved the robots' navigation capabilities but also enhanced the speed and reliability of information sharing during critical operations. Further research [54] focused on the integration of FSR in multi-robot systems for industrial automation. Their findings highlighted how FSR facilitated seamless communication among robots operating in warehouses, optimizing inventory management and logistical operations. The study showed that the protocol's ability to minimize routing updates while ensuring accurate positioning of robots led to significant improvements in operational efficiency and task execution times. The adaptability of FSR to various QoS requirements has also been examined in the context of mobile robotics. [55] proposed a modified FSR algorithm that incorporates QoS metrics such as latency and packet loss into the routing decisions of mobile robots. Their work demonstrated that this enhancement enabled robots to prioritize critical messages, improving overall system performance during complex missions that require real-time data processing.

Moreover, energy efficiency in mobile robotic applications is a vital consideration, especially for battery-operated systems. [56] explored energy-aware modifications to FSR, aimed at optimizing energy consumption while maintaining communication reliability. Their research showed that integrating energy-saving strategies with FSR not only extended the operational time of mobile robots but also enhanced their ability to perform tasks in energy-constrained environments. Recent advancements in artificial intelligence and machine learning have further influenced the application of FSR in mobile robotics. [57] investigated the role of FSR in intelligent mobile robots equipped with machine learning algorithms for adaptive routing. Their study demonstrated that the combination of FSR and machine learning enabled robots to make real-time routing decisions based on environmental conditions, improving their responsiveness and overall effectiveness in dynamic settings.

3 Methodology

In the context of MANETs, the proposed approach is conceptualized and modeled as follows. Let the total number of nodes in the network be denoted as τm, the total number of nodes in the cache as ϕ_m, and the number of unknown nodes as βm. The network comprises τ_m nodes, where the sender possesses route information for a subset of nodes. However, the sender lacks route information, particularly for nodes near the receiver with whom it is currently communicating. Conversely, the receiver maintains route information for various nodes in the network. The protocol's efficiency (ν) hinges on the disparity in route contents between the sender's and receiver's caches. The Route Gain Ratio (RKO) directly correlates with protocol efficiency, as expressed below:

$$\mathrm{RKO} \propto \upsilon \tag{1}$$

Routes of nodes proximal to the receiver are acquired and stored in the sender's cache once communication is established. This assumption stems from the likelihood that the sender, in contact with the receiver, may communicate with nodes nearby. Due to the reactive nature of the protocol, new routes must be acquired prior to transmitting information to other destinations. Evaluating the probability of the sender communicating with unknown nodes provides valuable insights into protocol efficiency.

As noted earlier, τ_m represents the total number of nodes, and π_b denotes the probability of the sender contacting an unknown node. The protocol's effectiveness is contingent upon the sender utilizing information from the receiver before it expires, with the available time for the sender to utilize these paths denoted as τ_{ms}. Assuming an average time spent per node τ_{avg}, the total number of potential communications before routes expire is calculated as follows:

$$\frac{\tau_{ms}}{\tau_{ort}} = \tau_a \tag{2}$$

Efficiency also relies on the sender's capability to leverage received information before it becomes obsolete. The probability πb of contacting an unknown node is computed as follows:

$$\pi_b = \frac{\binom{\beta_m}{\tau_a}}{\binom{\tau_m}{\beta_m}} \tag{3}$$

Efficiency is enhanced when the contacted unknown nodes constitute a subset of nodes near the receiver.

Let α_m denote the number of exposed nodes, and π_i represent the probability of contacting an exposed node. The overall probability P that the contacted node belongs to the set of exposed nodes is given by:

$$P = \pi_a \cdot \pi_i \tag{4}$$

The protocol effectively mitigates flood requests when the contacted node is part of the set of nodes whose routes are exposed by the receiver.

In the context of a MANET environment with a large number of nodes (τ_m) and a small probability π_b, Poisson distribution is employed for state modeling. τ_m represents the total number of nodes, and P denotes the probability of contacting an exposed node. Let X denote the number of exposed nodes contacted by the sender. Additionally, $P = \lambda$.

The Probability Mass Function (PMF) is expressed as:

$$P(X = x) = \frac{e^{-\lambda}\lambda^x}{x!} \tag{5}$$

Here, λ, is determined by π_a and π_i. The total number of contacted exposed nodes, τ_t, is given by $P \bullet \alpha_m$. A higher value of τ_t corresponds to fewer broadcasts needed to obtain routes for unknown nodes.

Finally, the probability of not contacting any exposed nodes, $P(X = 0)$, is calculated as follows:

$$P(X = 0) = e^{[-m(\pi_a \bullet \pi_i)]} \tag{6}$$

This methodology provides a systematic and analytical framework to assess the efficiency of the proposed protocol in a MANET environment, considering factors such as cache disparity, route acquisition, and the potential communication with unknown and exposed nodes.

To increase the probability and further reduce the flooding process, $P(X = x)$ should approach one. Increasing the number of contacted exposed nodes can be approached by improving the value of α_m or increasing P. Improving α_m is beyond the designer's control, as it depends on the network topology, network density, and node mobility, which dictate the exposure of nodes' routes by the receiver.

In general, it's expected that direct connections known to the receiver will reveal their paths to the sender. To further enhance the likelihood of contacting an exposed node, the sample space of exposed nodes can be expanded, meaning more nodes can be exposed. This involves the receiver disclosing nodes connected to it, even through multi-hop links. Nodes can be individually exposed based on priorities assigned, typically dictated by the proximity of the exposed node to the receiver. At any point, the sender may opt to halt the transaction by notifying it has reached sufficient saturation, prompting the receiver to cease sending routes upon receipt of this message.

It is acknowledged that the second approach, increasing the probability P to enhance τ_t, is more practical. To boost P, the number of nodes that can be contacted before exposed paths expire can be increased. This necessitates extending the timeout period. Increasing the timeout value can impact the network in two ways. Firstly, it reduces the frequency of updates, thereby minimizing flood demands and increasing the likelihood of contacting an exposed node. Secondly, it raises the risk of data or paths becoming corrupted between timeouts. Hence, a delicate balance must be maintained between data consistency and flood demand mitigation.

4 Simulation Results

Performance analysis of the fisheye state routing protocol (FSR) in a grid environment was meticulously conducted using Network Simulator 2 (NS2). The study rigorously examined a spectrum of metrics aimed at assessing how different flooding protocols influence critical performance parameters under various simulated scenarios. The findings reveal a compelling trend: as the number of nodes within Grid FSR fluctuates from 50 to 150, there is a consistent reduction in overflow. This outcome aligns precisely with the anticipated enhancements in Grid FSR's operational efficiency, underscoring the protocol's adeptness in managing and optimizing flooding schemes within well-defined parameters. These results not only validate the theoretical underpinnings of FSR but also highlight its practical effectiveness in mitigating data overflow and enhancing overall network performance in grid-based MANET environments.

End-to-end delay measurements constitute a crucial evaluation of network performance, providing a comprehensive assessment of various factors that directly affect the time it takes for data to travel from the source to the destination. These factors include route discovery, which impacts how quickly an optimal path is found, queuing delays that occur when packets wait to be processed, propagation delays related to the physical distance the data must travel, and transfer delays that reflect the time spent moving data between nodes. All of these contribute to the overall network latency, which is critical in determining how efficiently and quickly information is delivered.

Figure 2 visually demonstrates the observed decrease in overflow within Grid FSR (Fisheye State Routing) scenarios, which correlates directly with a notable reduction in end-to-end delay times. This reduction indicates that fewer packets are being dropped or delayed due to congestion, resulting in a smoother and more reliable data flow. The correlation highlights the protocol's efficacy in optimizing data transmission efficiency across the simulated grid environment. The enhanced performance seen in Grid FSR is particularly noteworthy in high-density or highly mobile networks, where traditional routing protocols often struggle to maintain low latency due to frequent topology changes or increased traffic. The improvements in delay metrics affirm the protocol's ability to

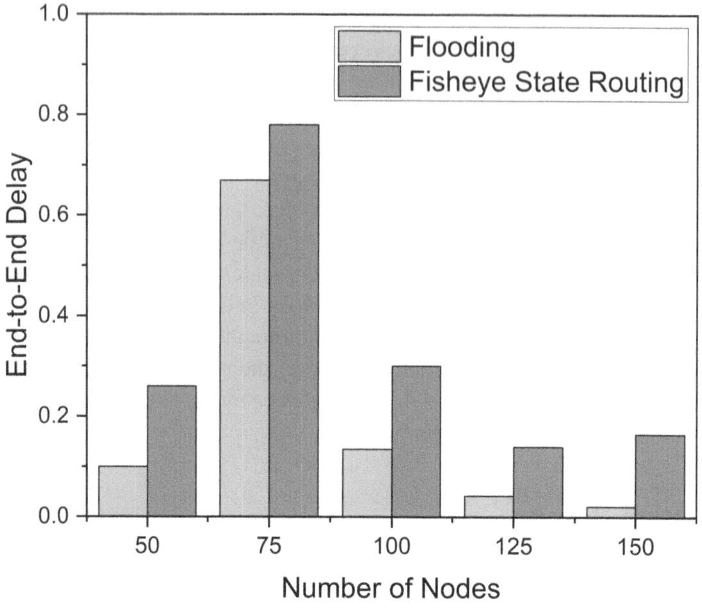

Fig. 2. Variation of end-to-end latency according to the number of nodes.

streamline packet delivery processes by minimizing the need for route rediscovery and reducing queuing times. This, in turn, enhances overall network responsiveness, which is crucial for applications requiring real-time communication, such as swarm robotics, intelligent transportation systems, and mission-critical operations in UAV networks. By achieving faster packet delivery and minimizing delays, Grid FSR proves to be highly efficient in maintaining smooth and continuous data flows, even in complex network environments.

Furthermore, the assessment of the packet delivery ratio (PDR), as depicted in Fig. 3, provides compelling insights into the protocol's enhanced performance. The results reveal that Grid FSR achieves a packet delivery rate exceeding 78% efficiency when compared to conventional FSR setups, indicating a substantial improvement. This impressive increase in PDR is largely attributed to the innovative coverage techniques integrated into the Grid FSR protocol, which not only reduce network congestion but also distribute the traffic load more evenly across the grid. By optimizing the path selection process and reducing redundant transmissions, the protocol ensures that more data packets reach their intended destinations successfully. These advancements in packet transmission and reception processes enhance the reliability of the protocol, ensuring that data is delivered in a timely manner across nodes, even under challenging network conditions. The higher packet delivery ratio reflects the protocol's ability to handle dynamic changes in network topology, such as node mobility and varying traffic loads, without compromising data integrity or delivery accuracy. This robustness significantly boosts the overall reliability of the network infrastructure, making Grid FSR an ideal choice for large-scale, highly dynamic environments such as smart cities, IoT networks, and VANETs. In these scenarios, maintaining high throughput and low latency is essential for the efficient functioning of critical applications, and Grid FSR demonstrates its capability to meet these demands.

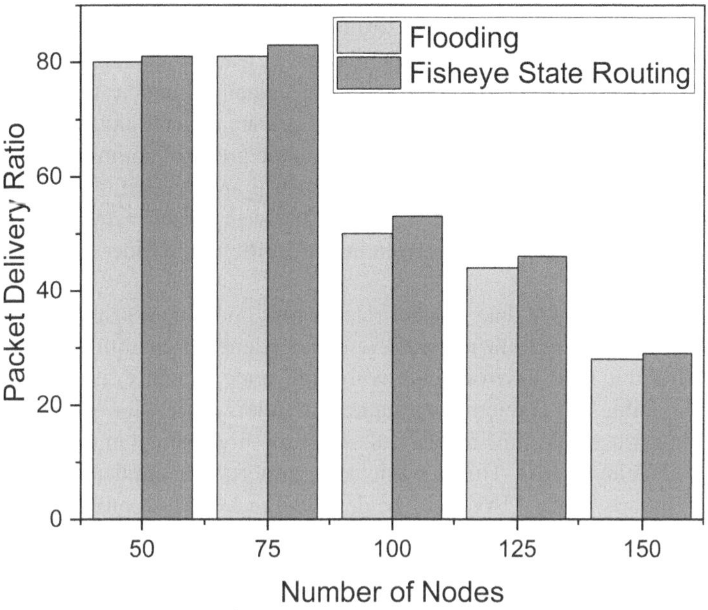

Fig. 3. Variation of packet delivery rate according to the number of nodes.

Moreover, the efficiency gains observed across various nodes underscore the protocol's adaptability and effectiveness in dynamically managing network resources. The strategic deployment of coverage techniques not only optimizes packet delivery but also contributes to minimizing delays and ensuring consistent data throughput. These improvements are pivotal in meeting stringent Quality of Service (QoS) requirements in grid-based MANET environments, where reliable and efficient data communication is paramount for mission-critical applications. The findings underscore the protocol's role in mitigating bottlenecks and optimizing network performance metrics, thus reinforcing its suitability for demanding grid environments where resource management and data integrity are of utmost importance. In summary, the comprehensive analysis of end-to-end delay measurements and packet delivery rates highlights the protocol's significant advancements in optimizing network performance within grid-based MANET scenarios. The protocol's ability to reduce overflow and improve efficiency in data transmission underscores its potential to address the challenges posed by dynamic network topologies and varying traffic conditions. These results not only validate the protocol's theoretical efficacy but also provide empirical evidence of its practical benefits in enhancing network reliability, throughput, and overall performance.

Throughput, measured in bits per second (bps), is a crucial metric in evaluating the efficiency and overall performance of a network. It quantifies the average rate at which data packets are successfully received at their intended destinations, making it a fundamental indicator of how effectively a network can handle data transmission. A high throughput signifies that the network is capable of transferring large amounts of data efficiently, without significant packet loss or delays, which is vital for maintaining reliable communication. As depicted in Fig. 4, the comprehensive throughput analysis reveals key insights into the protocol's ability to sustain high data transmission rates within grid-based MANET environments. The protocol's design leads to notable improvements in throughput efficiency, primarily achieved by strategically reducing flooding protocols that typically cause network congestion and unnecessary data redundancy. By minimizing the number of redundant packet transmissions, the protocol optimizes the utilization of available bandwidth, ensuring that more data packets are successfully delivered within a shorter time frame. This leads to a significant boost in overall network performance, allowing the system to handle larger volumes of traffic with reduced interference and packet collisions.

These enhancements in data transfer rates across nodes demonstrate the protocol's capability to maintain high throughput even in challenging conditions, such as those present in dynamic grid environments with high node mobility. In these scenarios, maintaining a stable and efficient communication link is critical for ensuring that time-sensitive data, such as real-time updates, alerts, or mission-critical information, is transmitted without delay or loss. This is particularly important in applications like disaster recovery operations, where UAVs may be deployed in MANET configurations to relay real-time data from various sensors or cameras back to command centers. High throughput ensures that the network can support the rapid exchange of large data files, such as high-resolution imagery or video, which are essential for making informed decisions during such operations. Moreover, the protocol's ability to optimize data flow and reduce flooding also contributes to more efficient energy consumption, a critical factor in grid-based MANETs, especially in scenarios where nodes are battery-powered, such as in UAV-based networks or IoT sensor grids. By limiting unnecessary data transmissions and ensuring that only relevant packets are propagated through the network, the protocol helps extend the operational lifespan of the network nodes, which is particularly beneficial in applications where continuous operation is required over extended periods.

These throughput improvements, combined with the protocol's ability to ensure reliable and expedient delivery of mission-critical information, highlight its potential for use in real-time applications where seamless data transmission is essential for decision-making and operational responsiveness. The high throughput achieved in dynamic grid environments, as shown in the study, indicates that the protocol is well-suited for environments that demand not only high data transmission rates but also low latency and high reliability. As a result, the significant throughput improvements achieved through the strategic reduction of flooding protocols, along with the protocol's capacity for optimizing data transfer rates, underscore its value in dynamic, real-time grid-based MANET environments. This makes the protocol a powerful tool for applications such as UAV-based communication networks, smart city infrastructures, and other mission-critical systems where reliable, high-speed data transmission is a priority. As networks continue to evolve, the ability to maintain high throughput will become increasingly important, and this protocol demonstrates a promising approach to achieving that goal.

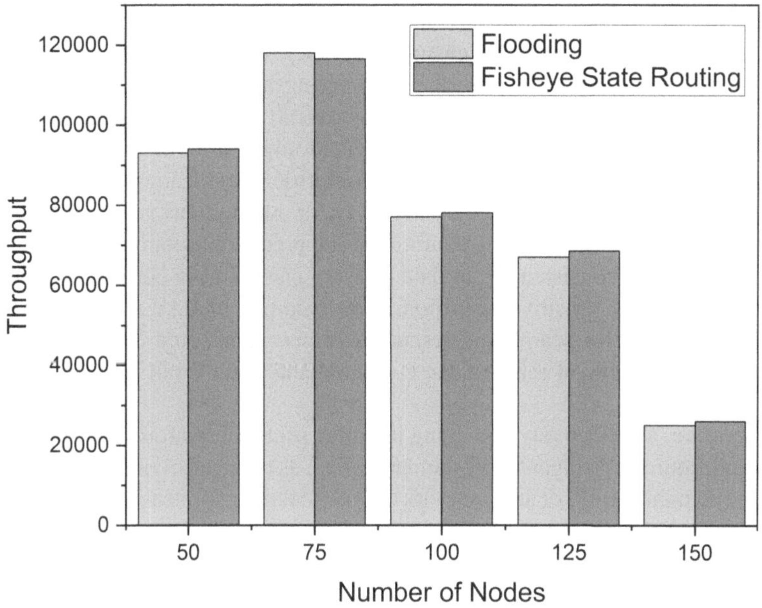

Fig. 4. Variation of throughput according to the number of nodes.

Jitter, a critical metric in network performance evaluation, refers to the variability in packet arrival times, or the difference in delay between successive data packets as they travel through the network. In an ad-hoc network, particularly one with a dynamic topology like a MANET, controlling jitter is essential for maintaining smooth and efficient communication. Excessive jitter can lead to inconsistent data delivery, which can degrade the quality of services, especially in applications requiring real-time communication, such as voice, video, and remote control operations. Thus, minimizing jitter is key to achieving low-latency and high-reliability communication in these networks. Figure 5 illustrates the impact of reduced flooding protocols on jitter, showing a significant decrease in packet arrival variations as the protocol's flooding mechanism is optimized. By minimizing unnecessary network-wide transmissions, the protocol reduces congestion, which often leads to packet delays or out-of-order packet delivery. This reduction in jitter underscores the protocol's efficacy in maintaining consistent intervals between data packet arrivals, ensuring a smoother flow of information throughout the network. Lower jitter levels result in a more predictable and reliable communication link, which is essential in scenarios where timing is critical, such as real-time UAV coordination, telemedicine, and live-streaming applications.

The findings highlight the protocol's ability to mitigate latency issues and ensure consistent data transmission, even in networks characterized by frequent topology changes and varying node densities. In dynamic grid-based environments, where node mobility and traffic load can fluctuate unpredictably, reducing jitter becomes even more crucial to maintaining network stability. By addressing jitter effectively, the protocol helps avoid scenarios where packets arrive in bursts or with irregular intervals, which can lead to packet loss, buffer overflows, or degraded service quality. The protocol's ability to manage this variability not only ensures smoother communication but also reduces the likelihood of retransmissions, further conserving network resources and reducing overhead. This reduction in jitter enhances the overall network stability, as consistent packet delivery minimizes the likelihood of synchronization errors and helps maintain the flow of data across the network. In mission-critical applications, such as disaster recovery operations, UAV-based sensor networks, or autonomous vehicle coordination, jitter control is vital for maintaining continuous and predictable communication. In such contexts, delays or inconsistencies in data delivery can result in performance degradation or failure of time-sensitive operations. For example, in UAV swarms conducting real-time surveillance or search-and-rescue missions, jitter could disrupt the continuous transmission of critical sensor data, compromising the overall effectiveness of the mission.

Furthermore, by effectively managing jitter, the protocol reinforces its suitability for applications requiring stringent QoS standards, such as those involving video conferencing, real-time monitoring, or IoT networks. QoS-sensitive applications depend on low latency, minimal packet loss, and consistent packet arrival times to ensure a high-quality user experience. In the context of smart city infrastructures or industrial automation, jitter management ensures that data from sensors, cameras, and other devices are delivered in a timely and reliable manner, allowing for efficient decision-making and control. In addition to improving QoS, the protocol's ability to minimize jitter also enhances energy efficiency within the network. By reducing packet retransmissions and ensuring more consistent data flow, the protocol conserves bandwidth and reduces power consumption, which is particularly important in battery-powered devices like UAVs, mobile nodes, or IoT sensors. In resource-constrained environments, maintaining low jitter can extend the operational life of network nodes, ensuring sustained performance over longer periods without frequent recharging or maintenance.

Therefore, the significant reduction in jitter achieved by the protocol through its optimized flooding mechanism highlights its effectiveness in ensuring smooth and consistent data transmission across diverse and dynamic network topologies. By minimizing packet arrival variations, the protocol enhances both the stability and reliability of the network, making it highly suitable for real-time, QoS-sensitive applications. Whether deployed in UAV networks, smart cities, or industrial IoT systems, the protocol's ability to control jitter ensures uninterrupted data flow and consistent performance, contributing to its overall effectiveness in complex, high-demand environments.

In closed network environments, especially those characterized by intensive flooding scenarios, energy conservation becomes a paramount concern due to the increased strain on network resources. Networks that rely on excessive flooding for data propagation often experience significant energy drain, as devices must continuously transmit, receive, and forward packets across the network. This not only reduces the operational lifespan of devices, such as nodes in a MANET, but also raises concerns about sustainability and resource management. Energy conservation, therefore, is not just about reducing power consumption, it plays a vital role in extending the operational longevity of the network, minimizing maintenance needs, and enhancing the overall efficiency of

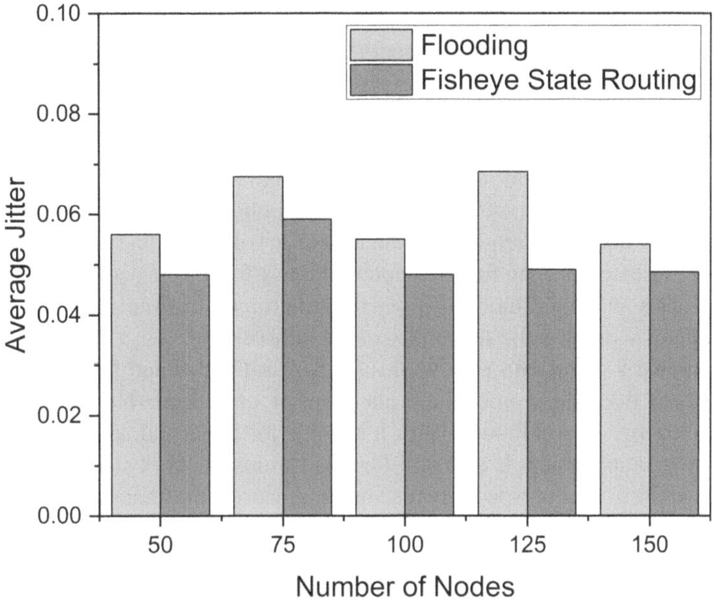

Fig. 5. Variation of average vibration according to the number of nodes.

the system. Figure 6 offers compelling empirical evidence of reduced energy consumption as a direct result of the optimized flooding strategies implemented by the protocol. These optimizations reduce redundant transmissions and avoid unnecessary data propagation, leading to more efficient use of network resources. In traditional flooding-based protocols, each node broadcasts data to its neighbors, which can result in an overwhelming number of transmissions, many of which are redundant or unnecessary. This leads to excessive energy consumption, particularly in large-scale networks where nodes are distributed across vast areas. By optimizing these processes, the protocol strategically minimizes the number of transmissions required to maintain effective communication, which significantly reduces energy expenditure without sacrificing network performance.

The results demonstrate the protocol's ability to reduce energy usage while still maintaining robust network functionality. This is a critical advantage, as it allows the protocol to balance between conserving power and ensuring reliable data delivery. Efficient energy management ensures that the network can function for extended periods, particularly in applications where nodes are battery-powered and recharging or replacing these power sources is not feasible or practical. For instance, in scenarios involving UAVs operating in remote or hard-to-reach areas, the ability to conserve energy while ensuring continued communication is essential for mission success. Additionally, by streamlining routing protocols and minimizing unnecessary data transmission, the protocol contributes to reducing overhead and traffic congestion. This not only conserves energy but also improves network performance by reducing packet collisions and retransmissions, which can otherwise exacerbate power consumption. The protocol ensures that only necessary data packets are transmitted, allowing devices to operate more efficiently and reducing the likelihood of network bottlenecks or delays. This balance between energy efficiency and performance is particularly crucial in time-sensitive applications where both high throughput and low energy consumption are required.

In real-world deployments, the energy-efficient attributes of the protocol are particularly advantageous in environments where resource conservation and environmental impact reduction are integral considerations. For example, in smart city applications, where sensors, cameras, and other devices may be distributed throughout urban infrastructure, energy conservation is key to maintaining long-term network operations. By reducing the need for frequent maintenance or battery replacement, the protocol ensures that these devices can function autonomously for longer periods, reducing both operational costs and environmental impact. Furthermore, in simulated models, energy efficiency directly impacts the scalability of the network.

As the network grows and more nodes are added, the demand for energy increases exponentially if flooding protocols are not properly optimized. The protocol's ability to minimize energy consumption makes it suitable for large-scale deployments, where efficient power management is essential for maintaining network stability and preventing system failures. This is especially relevant in scenarios like disaster response, where large-scale ad-hoc networks must be rapidly deployed, and energy resources are often scarce. The reduction in energy consumption also has broader environmental implications, particularly in terms of sustainability. Networks that are designed with energy conservation in mind help reduce the overall carbon footprint associated with large-scale digital infrastructures. This aligns with growing global concerns about the environmental impact of technology and the need for greener solutions in networking and communications. By extending the operational lifespan of network devices and reducing the frequency of power consumption, the protocol contributes to a more sustainable approach to network design and deployment.

Figure 7 provides a detailed analysis of the network control overhead, a critical metric that serves as a key indicator of the efficiency of MGA's routing protocol scheme. The findings reveal a substantial decrease in control overhead, highlighting the protocol's adeptness in minimizing unnecessary signaling and administrative burdens within the network infrastructure. This reduction in control overhead is directly attributed to the protocol's strategic approach to minimize flooding applications, thereby optimizing resource allocation and enhancing operational efficiency, particularly at higher data transmission rates. The observed efficiency gains underscore the protocol's ability to achieve a streamlined communication framework, where fewer control messages are generated per node in comparison to the volume of data packets successfully delivered to their respective destinations. These findings are pivotal as they validate the protocol's effectiveness in improving a spectrum of performance metrics crucial for MANETs and grid-based environments. Specifically, the study corroborates significant improvements in various performance indicators, including reduced end-to-end delays, enhanced packet delivery rates, increased throughput, minimized jitter, energy conservation, and notably decreased network control overhead. Such comprehensive enhancements underscore the protocol's adaptability and operational efficiency in addressing the complex demands of simulated grid environments.

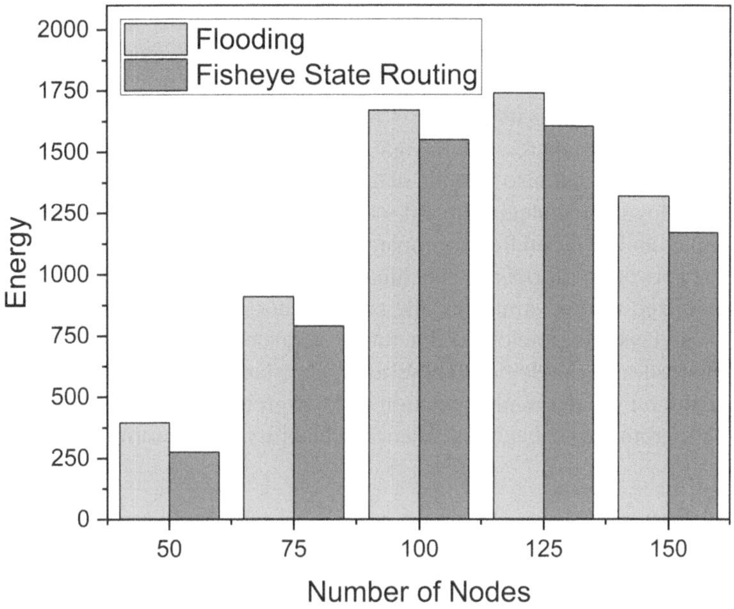

Fig. 6. Change of energy depending on the number of nodes.

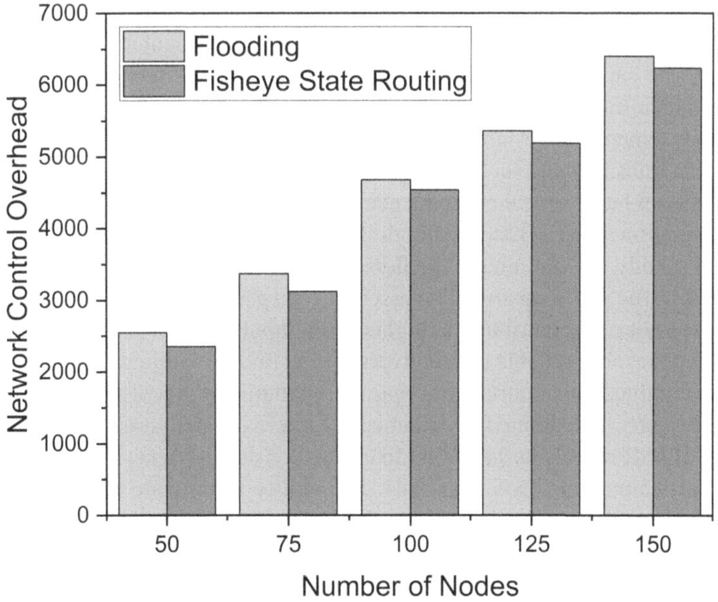

Fig. 7. Variation of network control load depending on the number of nodes.

Moreover, the study contributes substantively to the broader understanding of the FSR protocol's capabilities in dynamic network scenarios. By emphasizing the protocol's ability to optimize data transmission efficiency while minimizing operational overhead, the research reinforces its suitability for applications requiring robust and reliable communication infrastructures. The insights gleaned from this study not only validate the protocol's efficacy but also provide actionable intelligence for optimizing network design and deployment strategies in real-world settings. As a result, the empirical evidence presented in Fig. 7 and the accompanying analysis underscore the protocol's role in advancing network performance benchmarks. By reducing network control overhead through optimized routing strategies, the protocol not only enhances operational efficiency but also lays the groundwork for future advancements in network management and communication technologies. These findings establish a compelling case for the continued exploration and implementation of FSR protocol solutions in evolving grid environments, promising enhanced resilience, scalability, and performance optimization.

5 Discussion

This study presents a comprehensive evaluation of FSR and its applicability in MANETs, with a particular focus on its implementation in grid environments, UAVs, and mobile robotics. The findings underscore the protocol's efficiency in optimizing data transmission while maintaining low overhead, thereby enhancing overall network performance. One of the key observations from our analysis is the significant reduction in end-to-end delay when employing FSR in various scenarios. The empirical data indicate that the adaptive routing capabilities of FSR, which utilize a Locator Service to map recipient addresses to their current network locations, enable rapid and efficient communication even in highly dynamic environments. This is particularly vital for applications requiring real-time data transmission, such as those in disaster response or industrial automation, where delays can have critical consequences.

The correlation between reduced flooding and improved throughput is another pivotal aspect of this study. By optimizing the flooding mechanisms, FSR minimizes unnecessary network traffic while ensuring that essential data packets are transmitted effectively. This reduction not only contributes to higher throughput rates but also alleviates congestion, allowing for more reliable data delivery. These findings align with previous studies that have highlighted the importance of optimizing routing protocols to enhance communication in resource-constrained environments. Moreover, the assessment of jitter within the context of FSR reveals its capability to ensure consistent packet arrival times, which is crucial for maintaining QoS standards. The ability to mitigate variations in packet delivery times enhances the reliability of data transmission, making FSR an attractive option for applications that demand predictable communication patterns. This reliability is essential in scenarios involving autonomous mobile robots and UAVs, where timely information exchange is critical for coordinated actions and decision-making.

Energy efficiency emerges as a significant benefit of implementing FSR in mobile robotic applications. The study demonstrates that the protocol's optimized routing strategies lead to a substantial decrease in energy consumption, which is particularly advantageous in battery-powered systems. By extending the operational lifespan of network devices, FSR contributes to more sustainable network practices, aligning with the growing emphasis on environmental considerations in technology deployment. The integration of FSR with advanced technologies such as machine learning further enhances its applicability. Recent advancements suggest that machine learning algorithms can be employed to improve routing decisions based on real-time environmental conditions, making FSR even more adaptable to changing scenarios. Future research should explore these synergies to maximize the potential of FSR in evolving network environments.

While the findings are promising, it is essential to acknowledge the limitations of this study. The simulations conducted, while comprehensive, may not fully capture the complexities of real-world deployments. Future work should aim to validate these results through field tests, which can provide insights into the practical challenges and performance of FSR in uncontrolled environments. Conclusively, FSR demonstrates significant advantages in enhancing routing efficiency, reducing delays, and improving energy consumption in MANETs, particularly in UAV and mobile robotic applications. The results highlight its potential for addressing the challenges associated with dynamic network topologies and real-time data transmission. Continued exploration of FSR's capabilities, particularly in conjunction with emerging technologies, will be vital in advancing the effectiveness of mobile ad-hoc networks in various domains.

6 Conclusion

In this study, we examined the proactive routing protocol FSR, with a specific focus on its application within grid-based network environments. Through detailed comparative analysis with other prominent routing protocols, we evaluated a range of performance metrics to gain deeper insights into FSR's operational behavior. The results of this investigation reveal that FSR enables efficient message propagation by utilizing a source node to rebroadcast messages with an exponentially increasing hop count. This approach allows for effective exploration of flood depth, directing data towards target nodes with minimal network congestion. One of the key strengths observed is the protocol's scalability, which enables it to adapt seamlessly to networks of varying sizes, from small to large-scale configurations. FSR's efficiency, however, is sensitive to several critical network parameters, such as timeout intervals, node proximity, and others. By intelligently minimizing routing traffic overhead and periodically disseminating link-state information, FSR proves especially well-suited for dynamic and highly mobile networks with rapidly changing topologies. Our findings demonstrate that in scenarios with high node mobility, such as those involving swarm UAVs, FSR can significantly enhance network performance. Specifically, it leads to improved throughput, reduced average end-to-end delays, and overall better routing efficiency. This makes FSR a viable candidate for use in high-mobility environments where timely and reliable communication is paramount. Furthermore, the protocol's ability to balance the trade-offs between routing overhead and communication reliability positions it as a strong contender for future applications in MANETs, IoT deployments, and VANETs, where network conditions fluctuate rapidly and efficient data dissemination is critical.

While this study provides valuable insights into the performance of FSR in MANETs, it is essential to acknowledge certain limitations. Firstly, the evaluation primarily relies on simulations conducted within controlled grid environments, which may not fully represent the complexities and unpredictable dynamics of real-world scenarios. Factors such as environmental interferences, node mobility patterns, and variable network densities may significantly impact the protocol's performance but were not accounted for in the simulation. Additionally, while we assessed key performance metrics such as end-to-end delay, throughput, and energy consumption, other factors, such as security vulnerabilities and scalability under extreme conditions, warrant further investigation. Finally, the study's findings are limited to specific applications in UAV and mobile robot contexts, suggesting that future research should explore the generalizability of FSR's effectiveness across a broader range of applications and environmental conditions. Addressing these limitations in subsequent studies will enhance the robustness of FSR's implementation in diverse real-world applications. Conclusively, FSR's distinctive design, which emphasizes periodic updates and scalability, offers notable advantages in grid environments. However, further research is warranted to explore its adaptability in even more complex network scenarios and its integration with emerging technologies, such as machine learning-based adaptive routing and next-generation communication protocols.

References

1. Sharifi, S.A., Babamir, S.M.: The clustering algorithm for efficient energy management in mobile AD-HOC networks. Comput. Net. **166**, 106983 (2020)
2. Sharma, A.S., Kim, D.S.: Energy efficient multipath and colony based routing algorithm for mobile AD HOC networks. Ad Hoc Netw. **113**, 102396 (2021)
3. Reka, R., Karthick, R., Ram, R.S., Singh, G.: Multi head self-attention gated graph convolutional network based multi-attack intrusion detection in MANET. Comput. Secur. **136**, 103526 (2024). https://doi.org/10.1016/j.cose.2023.103526
4. Anand, R.P.P., Senthilkumar, V., Kumar, G., et al.: Dynamic link utilization empowered by reinforcement learning for adaptive storage allocation in MANET. Soft. Comput. **28**, 5275–5285 (2024). https://doi.org/10.1007/s00500-023-09281-8
5. Irani, F.: VSIM: a new simulation and performance evaluation tool for MANET and VANET. Int. J. Inf. Tecnol. (2024). https://doi.org/10.1007/s41870-024-02223-z
6. Tahboush, M., Agoyi, M.: A hybrid wormhole attract detection in MANET. IEEE Access **9**, 11872–11883 (2021)
7. Bakirci, M.: Utilizing YOLOv8 for enhanced traffic monitoring in intelligent transportation systems (ITS) applications. Digital Signal Processing **152**, 104594 (2024). https://doi.org/10.1016/j.dsp.2024.104594
8. Bakirci, M.: Enhancing vehicle detection in intelligent transportation systems via autonomous UAV platform and YOLOv8 integration. Appl. Soft Comput. **164**, 112015 (2024). https://doi.org/10.1016/j.asoc.2024.112015
9. Liu, J., Wu, J., Liu, M.: UAV monitoring and forecasting model in intelligent traffic oriented applications. Comput. Commun. **153**, 499–506 (2020). https://doi.org/10.1016/j.comcom.2020.02.009
10. Bakirci, M.: Evaluating the impact of unmanned aerial vehicles (UAVs) on air quality management in smart cities: A comprehensive analysis of transportation-related pollution. Comput. Electr. Eng. **119**, 109556 (2024). https://doi.org/10.1016/j.compeleceng.2024.109556
11. Tziavou, O., Pytharouli, S., Souter, J.: Unmanned Aerial Vehicle (UAV) based mapping in engineering geological surveys: Considerations for optimum results. Eng. Geol. **232**, 12–21 (2018). https://doi.org/10.1016/j.enggeo.2017.11.004

12. Bakirci, M.: Smart city air quality management through leveraging drones for precision monitoring. Sustain. Cities Soc. **106**, 105390 (2024). https://doi.org/10.1016/j.scs.2024.105390
13. Bakirci, M.: A drone-based approach to enhance spatial insight into surrounding air pollutant distributions for healthier indoor environments. J. Building Engineering **87**, 109023 (2024). https://doi.org/10.1016/j.jobe.2024.109023
14. Lwin, M.T., Yim, J., Ko, J.B.: Blockchain-based lightweight trust management in MANETs. Sensors 20(3) (2020)
15. Usman, M., Jan, M.A., He, X., Nanda, P.: QASEC: a secured data communication scheme for mobile Ad-hoc networks. Futur. Gener. Comput. Syst. **109**, 604–610 (2020)
16. Pal, A., Dutta, P., Chakrabarti, A., Singh, J.P.: An efficient load balanced stable multi-path routing for mobile ad-hoc network. Microsyst. Technol. **28**, 561–575 (2022)
17. Vignesh, C.C., Karthik, S.: Predicting the position of adjacent nodes with QoS in mobile ad hoc networks. Multimedia Tools and Applications **79**, 8445–8457 (2020)
18. Bakirci, M.: A novel swarm unmanned aerial vehicle system: Incorporating autonomous flight, real-time object detection, and coordinated intelligence for enhanced performance. Traitement du Signal 40(5), 2063–2078 (2023). https://doi.org/10.18280/ts.400524
19. Alilou, M., Babazadeh Sangar, A., Majidzadeh, K. et al.: QFS-RPL: mobility and energy aware multi path routing protocol for the internet of mobile things data transfer infrastructures. Telecommun Syst 85, 289–312 (2024). https://doi.org/10.1007/s11235-023-01075-5
20. Almutairi, H., Zhang, N.: A Survey on Routing Solutions for Low-Power and Lossy Networks: Toward a Reliable Path-Finding Approach. Network **4**, 1–32 (2024). https://doi.org/10.3390/network4010001
21. Santhi, G.B., Jacob, S.S., Sheela, D., et al.: Traffic coordination by reducing jamming attackers in VANET using probabilistic Manhattan Grid Topology for automobile applications. Sci. Rep. **14**, 8365 (2024). https://doi.org/10.1038/s41598-024-58240-2
22. Obaid, A.K., Rusli, M.E.B., Yussof, S.: Cache Improvement Based on Routing Protocol for AD-HOC Networks: Systematic Literature Review. IEEE Access (2024). https://doi.org/10.1109/ACCESS.2024.3455993
23. Duenas Santos, C.L., Mezher, A.M., Astudillo León, J.P., Cardenas Barrera, J., Castillo Guerra, E., Meng, J.: Q-RPL: Q-learning-based routing protocol for advanced metering infrastructure in smart grids. Sensors **24**, 4818 (2024). https://doi.org/10.3390/s24154818
24. Bakirci, M.: Real-time vehicle detection using YOLOv8-nano for intelligent transportation systems. Traitement du Signal 41(4), 1727–1740 (2024). https://doi.org/10.18280/ts.410407
25. Oh, D., Han, J.: Fisheye-based smart control system for autonomous UAV operations. Sensors **20**(24), 7321 (2020)
26. Onuora, A.C., Essien, E.E., Ana, P.: A comprehensive review of routing protocols for MANETs. Int. J. Inf. Syst. Comput. Sci. **6**(1) (2022)
27. Laanaoui, M., Raghay, S.: Enhancing OLSR protocol by an advanced greedy forwarding mechanism for VANET in smart cities. Smart Cities **5**(2), 650–667 (2022)
28. Sugranes, A.R., Razi, A., Afghah, F., Chahareski, J.: A review of AI-enabled rouring protocols for UAV networks: trends, challenges, and future outlook. AD HOC Netw. **130**, 102790 (2022)
29. Wu, Z., Chen, X., Wei, H., Song, F., Xu, T.: ADD: an automatic desensitization fisheye dataset for autonomous driving. Eng. Appl. Artif. Intell. **126**, 106766 (2023)
30. Bakirci, M., Cetin, M.: Improving position-time trajectory accuracy in vehicle stop-and-go scenarios by using a mobile robot as a testbed. J. Control Engineering and Applied Informatics **25**(3), 35–44 (2023)
31. Lamini, C., Benhlima, S., Elbekri, A.: Genetic algorithm based approach for autonomous mobile robot path planning. Procedia Computer Science **127**, 180–189 (2018)

32. Zhang, X., Guo, Y., Yang, J., Li, D., Wang, Y., Zhao, R.: Many-objective evolutionary algorithm based agricultural mobile robot route planning. Comput. Electron. Agric. **200**, 107274 (2022)
33. Patle, B.K., Babu, G., Pandey, A., Parhi, D.R.K., Jagadeesh, A.: A review: on path planning strategies for navigation of mobile robot. Defence Technology **15**(4), 582–606 (2019)
34. Bakirci, M.: Data-driven system identification of a modified differential drive mobile robot through on-plane motion tests. Electrica **23**(3), 619–633 (2023)
35. Bakirci, M.: Efficient air pollution mapping in extensive regions with fully autonomous unmanned aerial vehicles: a numerical perspective. In: Science of the Total Environment, vol. 909, p. 168606 (2024). https://doi.org/10.1016/j.scitotenv.2023.168606
36. Akbar, R.Z., et al.: Performance analysis FSR and DSR routing protocol in VANET with V2V and V2I models. In: 2020 3rd International Seminar on Research of Information Technology and Intelligent Systems (ISRITI), Yogyakarta, Indonesia, pp. 158–163 (2020). https://doi.org/10.1109/ISRITI51436.2020.9315367
37. Sathish, K., Ravikumar, C. V., et al.: Performance and improvement analysis of the underwater WSN using a diverse routing protocol approach. J. Comput. Net. Commun. 9418392 (2022). https://doi.org/10.1155/2022/9418392
38. Sathish, K., Ravikumar, C.V., Rajesh, A., Pau, G.: Underwater wireless sensor network performance analysis using diverse routing protocols. J. Sens. Actuator Netw. 11(64) (2022). https://doi.org/10.3390/jsan11040064
39. Hassan, M.A., Javed, A.R., Hassan, T., Band, S.S., Sitharthan, R., Rizwan, M.: Reinforcing communication on the internet of aerial vehicles. IEEE Trans. Green Commun. Netw. **6**(3), 1288–1297 (2022). https://doi.org/10.1109/TGCN.2022.3157591
40. Rai, P., Pradhan, N., Pokhrel, K.: Analysis of the QoS parameters of different routing protocols used in wireless sensor networks. In: Dhar, S., Mukhopadhyay, S.C., Sur, S.N., Liu, CM. (eds.) Advances in Communication, Devices and Networking. Lecture Notes in Electrical Engineering, vol. 776. Springer, Singapore (2022). https://doi.org/10.1007/978-981-16-2911-2_40
41. Mutoki, S.M.M., Al-sharhanee, K., Alkhayyat, A.H., Abbas, F.H., Alkhazraji, N.: Performance evaluation of improved mobility aware FSR routing protocol in vehicular ad-hoc networks. In: 2023 6th International Conference on Engineering Technology and its Applications (IICETA), Al-Najaf, Iraq, 2023, 720–725. https://doi.org/10.1109/IICETA57613.2023.10351484
42. Abbas, A.H., et al.: Hybrid ANT based continuous cuckoo search optimization algorithm for vehicle ADHOC networks. In: 2022 5th International Conference on Engineering Technology and its Applications (IICETA), Al-Najaf, Iraq, 2022, 447–452. https://doi.org/10.1109/IICETA54559.2022.9888404
43. Jubair, M.A., et al.: A QoS aware cluster head selection and hybrid cryptography routing protocol for enhancing efficiency and security of VANETs. IEEE Access **10**, 124792–124804 (2022). https://doi.org/10.1109/ACCESS.2022.3224466
44. Bakirci, M.: Enhancing air pollution mapping with autonomous UAV networks for extended coverage and consistency. Atmos. Res. **306**, 107480 (2024). https://doi.org/10.1016/j.atmosres.2024.107480
45. Bakirci, M., Bayraktar, I.: Refining transportation automation with convolutional neural network-based vehicle detection via UAVs. In: 2024 International Russian Automation Conference (RusAutoCon) (2024), pp. 150–155, Sochi, Russian Federation. https://doi.org/10.1109/RusAutoCon61949.2024.10694108
46. Oh, D., Han, J.: Fisheye-based smart control system for autonomous UAV operation. Sensors **20**, 7321 (2020). https://doi.org/10.3390/s20247321

47. Prakash, M., Neelakandan, S., Kim, B.H.: Reinforcement learning-based multidimensional perception and energy awareness optimized link state routing for flying AD-HOC networks. Mobile Netw. Appl. (2023). https://doi.org/10.1007/s11036-023-02255-y
48. Ghosh, S., Ghosh, B., Mohanty, S., Pattnaik, P.K.: Routing mechanisms for unmanned aerial vehicle. In: Pattnaik, P.K., Sain, M., Al-Absi, A.A. (eds.) Proceedings of 3rd International Conference on Smart Computing and Cyber Security. SMARTCYBER 2023. Lecture Notes in Networks and Systems, vol. 914. Springer, Singapore (2024). https://doi.org/10.1007/978-981-97-0573-3_11
49. Calvo, J.A.L., Alirezaei, G., Mathar, R.: Wireless powering of drone-based MANETs for disaster zones. In: 2017 IEEE International Conference on Wireless for Space and Extreme Environments (WiSEE), Montreal, QC, Canada, pp. 98–103 (2017). https://doi.org/10.1109/WiSEE.2017.8124900
50. Hussen, H.R., Choi, S.C., Park, J.H., Kim, J.: Performance analysis of MANET routing protocols for UAV communications. In: 2018 Tenth International Conference on Ubiquitous and Future Networks (ICUFN), Prague, Czech Republic, pp. 70–72 (2018). https://doi.org/10.1109/ICUFN.2018.8436694
51. Saffre, F., Hildmann, H., Anttonen, A.: Force-based self-organizing MANET/FANET with a UAV swarm. Future Internet **15**, 315 (2023). https://doi.org/10.3390/fi15090315
52. Cui, Y., Tian, H., Chen, C., Ni, W., Wu, H., Nie, G.: New geographical routing protocol for three-dimensional flying ad-hoc network based on new effective transmission range. IEEE Trans. Veh. Technol. **72**(12), 16135–16147 (2023). https://doi.org/10.1109/TVT.2023.3296082
53. Bakirci, M.: Simulation of autonomous driving for a line-following robotic vehicle: determining the optimal manoeuvring mode. Elektronika ir Elektrotechnika **29**(6), 4–11 (2023). https://doi.org/10.5755/j02.eie.32364
54. Sahoo, A., Kumar Tripathy, A.: On routing algorithms in the internet of vehicles: a survey. Connect. Sci. **35**(1), 2272583 (2023). https://doi.org/10.1080/09540091.2023.2272583
55. Rawat, G.S., Kumar, S., Rastogi, U.: Utilizing QUALNET for analyzing MANET protocols. In: 2022 3rd International Conference on Issues and Challenges in Intelligent Computing Techniques (ICICT), Ghaziabad, India, pp. 1–3 (2022). https://doi.org/10.1109/ICICT55121.2022.10064495
56. Sathish, K., CV, R., Ab Wahab, M.N., Anbazhagan, R., Pau, G., Akbar, M.F.: Underwater wireless sensor networks performance comparison utilizing telnet and superframe. Sensors **23**, 4844 (2023). https://doi.org/10.3390/s23104844
57. Kamarudin, L.M., Ahmad, R.B., Ong, B.L., Malek, F., Zakaria, A., Arif, M.A.M.: Review and modeling of vegetation propagation model for wireless sensor networks using Omnet++. In: 2010 Second International Conference on Network Applications, Protocols and Services, Alor Setar, Malaysia, pp. 78–83 (2010). https://doi.org/10.1109/NETAPPS.2010.21

Performance Comparison of Single-Stage and Two-Stage Detection Models for Real-Time Traffic Applications

Mette Nygaard[1], Liva Frederiksen[1], Amanda M. Kjeldsen[1], and Merve Koca[2](✉)

[1] Roskilde University, Roskilde, Denmark
[2] Tarsus University, Mersin, Turkey
merve_koca@tarsus.edu.tr

Abstract. This paper presents a comparative study on vehicle detection from UAV-captured aerial images using two prominent object detection algorithms: the single-stage detector SSD (Single Shot Multibox Detector) and the two-stage detector Faster R-CNN (Region-based Convolutional Neural Networks). The study aims to evaluate the performance of these algorithms across metrics such as precision, recall, mean Average Precision (mAP), F1 score, and detection time, providing insights into their suitability for UAV-based traffic monitoring applications. Results show that Faster R-CNN achieves higher detection accuracy, with precision, recall, and mAP values of 0.851, 0.813, and 0.826, respectively, outperforming SSD's corresponding values of 0.770, 0.744, and 0.751. However, SSD's detection speed (26.5 ms) is significantly faster than Faster R-CNN (63.2 ms), making it more suitable for real-time applications where immediate data processing is critical. Figures illustrate scenarios where Faster R-CNN exhibits superior performance, especially in complex scenes with dense vehicle presence, while SSD proves effective in simpler environments. This study highlights the trade-offs between accuracy and speed in object detection and suggests potential applications for each model in UAV-based traffic monitoring.

Keywords: Traffic Monitoring · Smart Traffic Management · Object Detection · Deep Learning

1 Introduction

Urban traffic monitoring is a cornerstone of effective city management, essential for sustaining the functionality of modern transportation systems [1]. As urban populations grow, so too does the complexity of traffic management. This escalation demands efficient, accurate, and scalable monitoring solutions to keep roadways safe, reduce congestion, and optimize resource allocation for infrastructure maintenance. Traditional traffic monitoring approaches, such as fixed cameras or sensors embedded within roads, have certain limitations, including restricted coverage and inability to adapt to dynamic situations [2]. Effective traffic monitoring not only helps detect and prevent traffic incidents but also contributes to long-term urban planning by providing data-driven insights

A. Mirzazadeh et al. (Eds.): SEMIT 2024, CCIS 2444, pp. 398–411, 2026.
https://doi.org/10.1007/978-3-032-01948-6_25

into transportation patterns, peak travel times, and road usage. Additionally, advanced monitoring contributes to emergency response capabilities by enabling rapid intervention in case of accidents or other emergencies, thus safeguarding public safety [3]. As urban areas strive to become "smart cities," integrating advanced traffic monitoring solutions is increasingly recognized as fundamental for achieving seamless mobility, a key component in improving residents' quality of life.

In the past decade, deep learning techniques have significantly improved the capabilities of traffic monitoring systems, enabling them to operate autonomously and with heightened precision [4]. Traditional image processing methods for traffic monitoring were often constrained by their reliance on manually defined features, which limited their adaptability to diverse or unpredictable traffic environments [5]. Deep learning, particularly through convolutional neural networks (CNNs) and object detection frameworks, has overcome many of these limitations by automating feature extraction and allowing models to "learn" complex visual patterns within traffic environments [6]. CNNs and object detection algorithms can recognize and classify objects such as vehicles, pedestrians, and infrastructure elements across varied conditions and perspectives, enhancing the robustness and scalability of these systems [7]. The application of deep learning models to traffic monitoring allows for high accuracy in detecting vehicle types, their movements, and even their speeds, as well as better prediction of traffic flows and potential congestion points [8]. These capabilities enable real-time responses and data analytics, providing city planners and transportation managers with timely, reliable insights for decision-making.

Unmanned aerial vehicles (UAVs) have introduced further advancements in monitoring by expanding the range, flexibility, and responsiveness of data collection [9–13]. Unlike static monitoring systems, UAVs can cover expansive areas, including highways, intersections, and even remote or accident-prone locations that are often difficult to monitor with conventional means [14–16]. With the ability to deploy UAVs at various altitudes and locations, traffic data can be collected dynamically, adjusted in real time to capture targeted events or areas of interest. Furthermore, UAVs are well-suited to providing high-resolution aerial perspectives that enhance the accuracy of object detection algorithms, especially when combined with advanced cameras and sensors [17]. This mobility and adaptability make UAV-based monitoring particularly advantageous for handling large-scale events, rapidly changing traffic patterns, or emergency scenarios where real-time information is critical. Additionally, UAVs can perform continuous monitoring without being influenced by physical obstructions, which can hinder ground-based systems, thereby offering an unobstructed vantage point and reducing blind spots in traffic surveillance [18].

The integration of UAVs with deep learning-based object detection has unlocked new possibilities in vehicle detection, marking a significant advancement in automated traffic monitoring [19]. Object detection algorithms, such as YOLO, SSD, and Faster R-CNN, are at the forefront of this innovation [19–22]. These algorithms are designed to identify and localize multiple objects within an image or video frame, making them well-suited for complex traffic environments where numerous vehicles must be accurately detected and tracked. YOLO, for example, is known for its speed and real-time capabilities, making it a popular choice for applications that require rapid responses, although it may sometimes sacrifice some accuracy compared to more complex models [23]. SSD, as a single-stage detector, balances speed and accuracy, which is valuable in scenarios where both real-time performance and detection quality are priorities. Meanwhile, Faster R-CNN, a two-stage detector, offers higher precision in detecting and classifying objects, though typically at the cost of longer processing times. By leveraging the strengths of these models, UAV-based traffic monitoring systems can achieve fast, accurate vehicle detection, even in complex environments with dense or overlapping traffic.

In this study, we explored vehicle detection through both single-stage and two-stage object detection models, specifically SSD and Faster R-CNN, on traffic images captured by UAVs. Single-stage detectors, like SSD, streamline the detection process by directly predicting object locations and categories in a single pass, making them particularly suitable for real-time applications. Two-stage detectors, like Faster R-CNN, segment the detection process into two steps: first identifying possible regions of interest (RoI) and then classifying these regions, which can enhance detection accuracy. In our application, we evaluated the strengths and trade-offs of both approaches, specifically in the context of UAV-based monitoring, where factors like response time, computational demands, and detection accuracy are crucial considerations. The UAV-collected images offer distinct challenges, such as varying altitudes and angles, which affect how vehicles appear and can challenge detection algorithms' precision and reliability.

The dataset for this study consisted of aerial traffic images taken from UAVs, offering a valuable testing ground for object detection algorithms given their unique perspective and the dynamic nature of traffic flow. By conducting our tests with UAV-collected images, we ensured that our analysis would reflect the real-world conditions under which such systems would operate. The UAV's capability to capture a continuous stream of data also allowed for sequential testing of both models in varied scenarios, such as different times of day, lighting conditions, and traffic densities, adding robustness to our findings. Through this study, we aimed to identify the most suitable detection algorithm for UAV-based traffic monitoring applications, considering both the real-time performance requirements and the need for high detection accuracy. While SSD and Faster R-CNN represent only two of the many object detection algorithms available, they provide useful insights into the general trade-offs between single-stage and two-stage detectors, helping inform decisions about which approach best aligns with specific application requirements. In particular, we examined the detection speed of each algorithm, critical for real-time monitoring, and the accuracy with which each model detected and classified vehicles under diverse traffic conditions. The results of this analysis have potential implications for smart city infrastructure and traffic management systems, where UAV-based monitoring can play an increasingly vital role.

The subsequent section provides the methodology employed in the study, including the data collection process, annotation procedures, and the implementation of the SSD and Faster R-CNN algorithms. The Results section presents a comparative analysis of the performance metrics for both algorithms, illustrated with examples of vehicle detections to demonstrate their effectiveness in various scenarios. The Discussion section interprets these results, exploring the implications for real-time vehicle detection using UAVs and the trade-offs between accuracy and detection speed. Finally, the paper concludes with a summary of key findings and recommendations for future research in the field of UAV-based traffic monitoring.

2 Methodology

The Single Shot MultiBox Detector (SSD) is a popular object detection algorithm designed for real-time applications, known for its balance of speed and accuracy. SSD is a single-stage detector, meaning it performs both object localization and classification in a single pass through the neural network, which significantly reduces processing time compared to two-stage detectors like Faster R-CNN. SSD, whose architecture is shown in Fig. 1, operates by dividing the image into a grid and predicting bounding boxes and class scores directly from each grid cell, making it particularly efficient. It uses a CNN backbone, typically based on architectures like VGG or ResNet, to extract features from the input image. These features are then processed through a series of additional convolutional layers to produce multiple sets of bounding boxes, each at different scales. By performing detection across multiple layers, SSD allows for the detection of objects of varying sizes within the same image, providing flexibility and robustness in handling different scenarios. Each layer of the network is tasked with detecting objects at a specific scale, which enhances SSD's ability to capture both small and large objects without sacrificing speed.

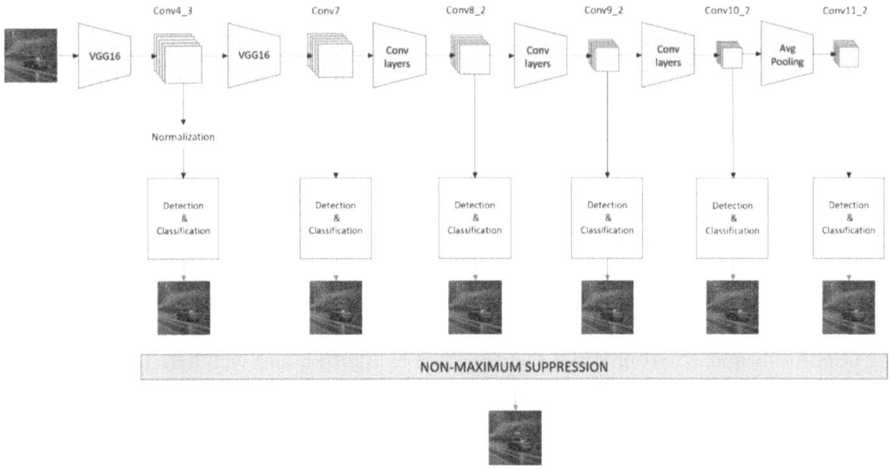

Fig. 1. Network architecture of the SSD detection algorithm.

SSD further enhances its detection capabilities by using anchor boxes, or default boxes, which are predefined bounding boxes with varying aspect ratios and sizes for each grid cell. These anchor boxes help SSD adapt to the diverse shapes and orientations of objects by serving as a starting point for the algorithm's predictions. During training, SSD compares the predicted boxes with ground-truth boxes, adjusting the anchor boxes based on their Intersection over Union (IoU) overlap with the actual object locations.

By optimizing the placement and scale of these default boxes, SSD improves its localization accuracy. Additionally, SSD applies non-maximum suppression (NMS) to filter out redundant or overlapping boxes and select the most accurate predictions. The single-shot approach of SSD not only makes it efficient but also allows it to achieve impressive detection speeds suitable for real-time applications such as autonomous vehicles, surveillance, and UAV-based traffic monitoring. Despite its speed advantage, SSD may struggle with small object detection compared to more complex models, as it sometimes sacrifices accuracy in favor of faster inference times. However, its efficiency and simplicity make it a strong choice for many practical applications, especially where computational resources are limited.

Numerous studies have successfully applied the SSD algorithm for vehicle detection, particularly in scenarios that demand real-time analysis, such as traffic monitoring, autonomous driving, and intelligent transportation systems. Researchers have leveraged SSD's speed and moderate accuracy to detect vehicles from both ground-level cameras and UAV-captured aerial images. In a study focused on traffic monitoring from UAVs, SSD was employed to capture high-resolution images of roadways, enabling real-time vehicle detection and tracking [24]. The study demonstrated SSD's capability to handle varying perspectives and altitudes, critical for aerial traffic monitoring, by adjusting anchor box scales and optimizing the backbone network for high-speed detection. Results showed that SSD could reliably detect and classify multiple vehicles within milliseconds, allowing it to be used in real-time traffic flow analysis and congestion monitoring. The study highlighted SSD's potential to balance speed and detection precision, making it particularly suitable for UAV-based monitoring applications where quick responses to changing traffic conditions are essential.

In addition to UAV-based applications, other studies have explored SSD for vehicle detection in autonomous driving systems. These studies often focus on improving SSD's accuracy for small object detection, as smaller vehicles or distant vehicles can be challenging for SSD to detect accurately. One such study modified SSD's architecture by incorporating additional feature layers specifically designed to enhance small object detection capabilities [25]. These adaptations helped increase detection rates for distant vehicles, improving the system's safety and reliability in autonomous driving scenarios. Researchers also applied data augmentation techniques to train the SSD model more effectively on diverse datasets, helping it generalize better across different driving conditions and environmental factors, such as lighting and weather. The success of SSD in these vehicle detection applications underscores its versatility and adaptability, making it an appealing option for real-time, resource-constrained environments where a high-speed response is required.

The Faster R-CNN algorithm, whose architecture is shown in Fig. 2, is a widely used two-stage object detection model known for its high accuracy and effectiveness in detecting complex objects within images. Faster R-CNN builds on the foundations of earlier models like R-CNN and Fast R-CNN by incorporating a Region Proposal Network (RPN), which efficiently generates candidate object regions, or "proposals," directly from the image. This RPN module is integrated within the convolutional layers of a feature extractor, such as ResNet or VGG, allowing the model to identify regions likely containing objects without the need for a separate, computationally intensive process.

The RPN operates by sliding a small network over the extracted feature map, generating a set of anchor boxes that are refined and scored based on their likelihood of containing an object. These proposals are then fed into the second stage, where another set of fully connected layers further refines the bounding boxes and classifies each object within the region. By streamlining the region proposal process within the network, Faster R-CNN significantly improves both the speed and accuracy of object detection, making it a preferred choice for applications where high precision is essential.

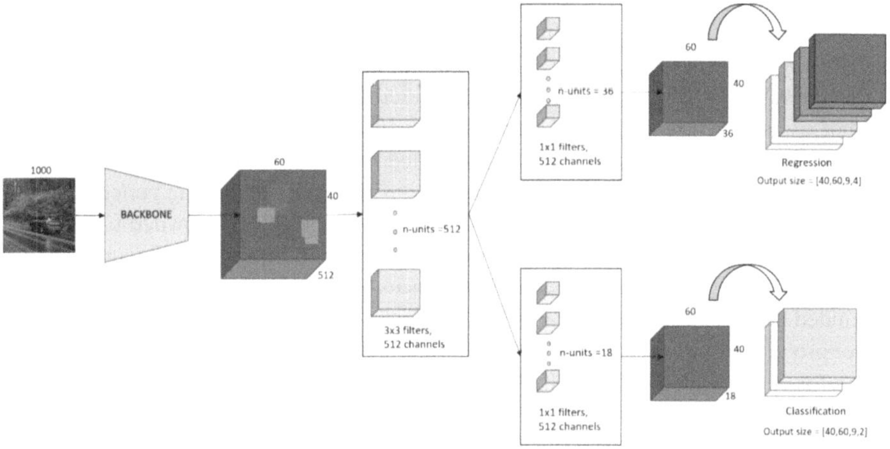

Fig. 2. Network architecture of the Faster R-CNN.

The two-stage detection process in Faster R-CNN involves several key components that enhance the model's performance and accuracy. First, the RPN generates proposals at different scales and aspect ratios, allowing the algorithm to detect objects of various shapes and sizes within the same image. Faster R-CNN then applies a RoI (Region of Interest) pooling layer, which standardizes the size of these regions to a fixed dimension before passing them to the fully connected layers for final classification and localization. This approach minimizes computational load while maintaining high detection accuracy. Additionally, the model utilizes NMS to eliminate redundant proposals by retaining only the most confident bounding boxes, thus enhancing the clarity of detections. Faster R-CNN is particularly well-suited for tasks that require meticulous detection accuracy, as it can finely localize objects and differentiate between closely overlapping or densely packed items within a scene. However, the multi-step process in Faster R-CNN also contributes to longer inference times compared to single-stage detectors like SSD or YOLO, making it more suitable for applications where accuracy is prioritized over speed, or where computational resources are readily available.

Studies on vehicle detection have shown that Faster R-CNN can achieve high accuracy, particularly in situations where precise localization is critical, such as in autonomous driving and traffic surveillance applications. [26] applied Faster R-CNN to aerial images of congested highways, aiming to accurately detect and classify multiple vehicle types from varying angles and altitudes. The results demonstrated that Faster R-CNN outperformed single-stage models in detecting smaller vehicles and densely packed traffic clusters, owing to its robust region proposal mechanism and refined bounding box adjustments. This high degree of accuracy allowed the study to effectively analyze traffic patterns and vehicle counts with minimal false positives, making it suitable for applications where accurate data collection is essential for infrastructure planning and traffic management. The study also highlighted the importance of high-resolution images to fully leverage Faster R-CNN's capabilities, as detailed proposals require a certain level of image quality for optimal performance in vehicle detection tasks.

Another study focused on enhancing vehicle detection in autonomous driving scenarios using Faster R-CNN, with a specific emphasis on improving the detection of small or distant vehicles [27]. The researchers modified the RPN module by increasing the number of anchor box scales and aspect ratios, thereby improving the model's sensitivity to smaller objects. They also experimented with multi-scale training to enhance the model's ability to recognize vehicles at various distances, achieving better detection accuracy under challenging conditions such as low visibility and crowded traffic. This approach allowed the Faster R-CNN model to provide more reliable detections, contributing to improved safety and performance in autonomous driving systems. The study concluded that although Faster R-CNN may require more computational resources and longer processing times, its accuracy and ability to detect subtle details make it a viable option for applications where high detection fidelity is paramount.

Data collection for this study involved capturing high-resolution aerial images of traffic scenes using a commercial-grade UAV equipped with a modified camera system to ensure optimal clarity and detail in vehicle detection. The UAV was programmed to fly over various roadways, including highways and urban intersections, to gather a diverse set of images under different traffic conditions. By adjusting flight altitude and angle, we captured images from multiple perspectives, providing comprehensive data that reflects realistic scenarios encountered in traffic monitoring. Environmental factors like time of day and weather were also varied to increase the dataset's robustness, allowing the algorithms to be tested across diverse lighting and atmospheric conditions. After collection, images were manually annotated to identify and label vehicle types, locations, and orientations, creating a high-quality dataset for training and testing the SSD and Faster R-CNN models in vehicle detection. This annotated dataset ensured that both algorithms could be evaluated accurately and reliably under controlled yet varied traffic conditions, contributing to a robust analysis of their detection capabilities.

3 Results

Here, we present the detection results of both the Faster R-CNN and SSD algorithms, including a comparative analysis of their detection performance and accuracy on vehicle detection tasks. Figures 3 and 4 illustrate examples of vehicle detections by both algorithms, highlighting cases where the two algorithms perform similarly and others where there is a marked difference in their detection capabilities. Additionally, Table 1 provides quantitative performance metrics, such as precision, recall, mean Average Precision (mAP), and F1 score, along with the detection times for each algorithm. These results offer a comprehensive overview of the strengths and weaknesses of Faster R-CNN and SSD, focusing on both their accuracy and their suitability for real-time applications.

Figure 3 shows example images from the dataset where both Faster R-CNN and SSD demonstrate similar performance in vehicle detection. In these instances, both algorithms accurately detect vehicles, successfully localizing and classifying the objects within the scene. While Faster R-CNN performs slightly better in terms of accuracy, this difference is minimal in the examples presented in Fig. 3. The detected bounding boxes overlap closely with the true positions of vehicles in the images, reflecting both algorithms' abilities to localize objects effectively. However, in scenarios with low vehicle density and clear visual contrast between vehicles and their background, SSD performs nearly as well as Faster R-CNN. This indicates that SSD's single-stage approach can be comparable to Faster R-CNN in simple detection tasks with less clutter and fewer overlapping objects. Despite Faster R-CNN's slightly higher precision in these examples, the differences between the two algorithms are minor, suggesting that SSD could be a viable choice in applications where comparable performance is acceptable and faster detection is required.

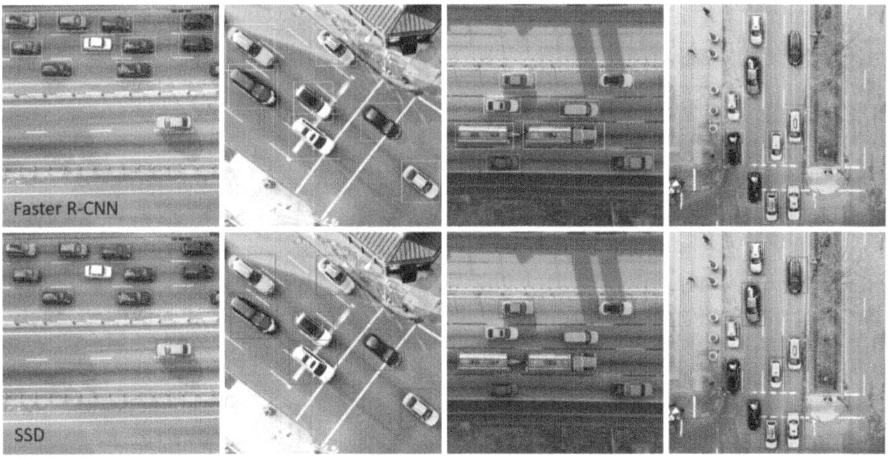

Fig. 3. Examples of vehicle detection with both algorithms.

Figure 4, however, highlights cases where the performance gap between Faster R-CNN and SSD becomes more pronounced. In these examples, Faster R-CNN demonstrates a clear advantage over SSD, particularly in scenes with higher object density or complex backgrounds. For instance, Faster R-CNN consistently detects smaller or partially obscured vehicles that SSD fails to recognize or localizes less accurately. This is likely due to Faster R-CNN's two-stage architecture, where the Region Proposal Network (RPN) provides finer-grained bounding box suggestions before final classification. The RoI pooling mechanism in Faster R-CNN also contributes to its advantage by improving spatial resolution, which helps detect objects in more cluttered environments. In contrast, SSD's single-shot approach, which simultaneously performs localization and classification, appears to struggle with densely packed scenes, leading to lower detection accuracy in these complex situations. These examples in Fig. 4 underscore Faster R-CNN's strength in maintaining detection accuracy across a wider range of scenarios, especially where higher object density and occlusions are present.

Fig. 4. Examples of vehicle detection with Faster R-CNN and SSD algorithms.

To further evaluate the detection performance of both algorithms, Table 1 presents key metrics, including precision, recall, mAP, and F1 score. Faster R-CNN achieves a precision of 0.851, meaning that the algorithm is highly effective in reducing false positives and accurately identifying vehicles within the detected bounding boxes. In comparison, SSD yields a lower precision of 0.770, indicating a tendency for slightly more false positive detections or less accurate bounding boxes. The difference in precision between the two algorithms suggests that Faster R-CNN's region proposal and refinement steps contribute to a more accurate localization process, particularly in challenging detection scenarios.

The recall values also show that Faster R-CNN outperforms SSD, with recall scores of 0.813 and 0.744, respectively. Recall reflects the algorithm's ability to detect all relevant objects in the image, and the higher score for Faster R-CNN highlights its superior ability to identify a greater number of vehicles within each scene. This distinction in recall may be attributed to the RPN module in Faster R-CNN, which enhances its ability to detect smaller or partially occluded vehicles more reliably than SSD. The mAP, which represents an aggregate measure of precision across different levels of recall, further reinforces this finding, with Faster R-CNN achieving a higher mAP of 0.826 compared to 0.751 for SSD. This difference reflects Faster R-CNN's more consistent detection performance across varying conditions and a wider range of object types within the dataset.

The F1 score, a harmonic mean of precision and recall, is also higher for Faster R-CNN (0.832) than for SSD (0.759), illustrating that Faster R-CNN strikes a better balance between precision and recall in its detection results. The F1 score emphasizes that Faster

R-CNN maintains high accuracy while detecting a majority of vehicles, making it a reliable choice for scenarios where missing a detection could have critical implications, such as in autonomous vehicle navigation or traffic monitoring for smart transportation systems. In contrast, SSD's lower F1 score indicates a trade-off in detection quality, where its speed advantage comes at the cost of some precision and recall, particularly in complex scenes with multiple vehicles.

Another crucial aspect of this comparison is detection time, a key consideration for applications requiring real-time or near-real-time processing. In Table 1, Faster R-CNN has an average detection time of 63.2 ms per image, while SSD achieves a significantly faster detection time of 26.5 ms. This substantial difference in speed highlights SSD's efficiency as a single-stage detector, which processes the entire image in one pass without the need for a separate region proposal stage. The faster detection time makes SSD more suitable for applications with strict latency requirements, such as live traffic monitoring or real-time driver assistance systems, where decisions must be made in milliseconds.

Table 1. Performance comparison of the algorithms.

Algorithm	Precision	Recall	mAP	F1 Score	Det. Time
Faster R-CNN	0.851	0.813	0.826	0.832	63.2 ms
SSD	0.770	0.744	0.751	0.759	26.5 ms

Faster R-CNN's slower detection time can be attributed to its two-stage architecture, where the RPN first generates region proposals that are then refined and classified in a subsequent stage. While this process enhances accuracy, it also increases computational complexity, leading to longer inference times. For applications that prioritize high accuracy and can accommodate slightly longer processing times, such as offline analysis of traffic patterns or post-event vehicle tracking, Faster R-CNN provides a robust solution. However, for UAV-based applications or intelligent transportation systems where speed is paramount, SSD may be the preferred choice, as its faster processing allows it to handle more frames per second. This advantage in detection time could also make SSD more compatible with edge computing platforms or devices with limited processing power, where efficient use of computational resources is essential.

The comparative analysis between Faster R-CNN and SSD highlights a fundamental trade-off between accuracy and detection speed. Faster R-CNN excels in precision, recall, mAP, and F1 score, showcasing its ability to detect vehicles accurately even in complex and densely populated scenes. Its design is especially advantageous for high-stakes applications that demand meticulous detection, such as autonomous driving and detailed traffic analysis. However, this accuracy comes with the cost of slower detection times, making it less suitable for applications that require instantaneous processing. Conversely, SSD demonstrates remarkable detection speed, offering nearly double the inference rate of Faster R-CNN, which could make it highly effective for real-time applications where rapid decisions are necessary, albeit with some compromise in accuracy.

Ultimately, the choice between Faster R-CNN and SSD may depend on the specific requirements of the application at hand. If the primary goal is to achieve high detection accuracy and the computational resources allow for slightly longer processing times, Faster R-CNN would be the more suitable choice. On the other hand, for applications focused on real-time detection with limited processing capacity, SSD provides a viable alternative that can deliver quick, albeit slightly less precise, results. This study demonstrates the strengths and limitations of each algorithm, underscoring the importance of selecting an object detection model aligned with the application's unique demands.

4 Discussion and Conclusion

The results of this study emphasize the distinct advantages and limitations of Faster R-CNN and SSD in the context of vehicle detection from aerial images captured by UAVs. Through both visual and quantitative analysis, we have demonstrated how each algorithm performs in scenarios that vary in complexity, vehicle density, and computational demands. By employing both a two-stage detector (Faster R-CNN) and a single-stage detector (SSD), this study sheds light on the factors that may guide algorithm selection for UAV-based traffic monitoring and vehicle detection applications.

4.1 Discussion

Our findings indicate that Faster R-CNN outperforms SSD in terms of detection accuracy, particularly in challenging scenes with high vehicle density, occlusions, or complex backgrounds. With a precision of 0.851, a recall of 0.813, and an mAP of 0.826, Faster R-CNN consistently delivers reliable detection results, capturing a broad range of vehicle types and positions within cluttered environments. The Region Proposal Network (RPN) in Faster R-CNN plays a significant role in this performance by generating candidate regions of interest before final classification and localization. This capability allows Faster R-CNN to adapt to more challenging detection conditions, resulting in fewer missed detections and more accurate bounding box placements. Furthermore, the RoI pooling feature improves spatial representation and facilitates the detection of partially obscured or smaller vehicles, providing a major advantage in scenes where precision is critical.

In contrast, SSD, with precision and recall values of 0.770 and 0.744, respectively, demonstrates efficient performance in scenes with lower object density or simpler backgrounds. SSD's single-stage design, which performs localization and classification simultaneously, contributes to its faster processing time (26.5 ms) compared to Faster R-CNN's 63.2 ms. This speed advantage makes SSD highly suitable for real-time applications where rapid inference is essential, such as live traffic monitoring, where immediate decision-making is necessary. However, the trade-off lies in SSD's reduced detection accuracy, which becomes more evident in complex scenes where precise localization and comprehensive detection are essential. While SSD may miss smaller or occluded vehicles due to its lack of a proposal network, its speed-oriented architecture positions it as an effective solution for time-sensitive applications with manageable accuracy requirements.

The disparity in detection times between Faster R-CNN and SSD is a key factor to consider when choosing an algorithm for UAV-based applications. Faster R-CNN's additional processing steps, which enhance accuracy, inherently increase the computational load, making it more suitable for applications with moderate to high processing power and situations where accuracy is paramount. For instance, post-event analysis or offline traffic pattern evaluations can leverage Faster R-CNN's precision without the constraints of real-time processing. Conversely, SSD's rapid detection time is particularly advantageous for UAVs with limited processing capabilities or in scenarios requiring minimal latency, such as dynamic traffic flow analysis in real time.

The choice between these two algorithms can be further informed by the performance metrics in Table 1, where Faster R-CNN scores consistently higher in F1, mAP, and other accuracy-related measures. This demonstrates that if computational resources allow, Faster R-CNN is likely to yield superior results in a broader range of scenarios. However, SSD's time efficiency suggests it is more appropriate for scenarios demanding minimal latency, despite its slightly lower detection performance. This balance between accuracy and speed is crucial in UAV applications, where decisions about object detection algorithms impact real-time data analysis capabilities, system responsiveness, and resource usage.

4.2 Limitations and Future Directions

While this study provides a comprehensive comparison between Faster R-CNN and SSD, certain limitations merit discussion. The dataset primarily consists of aerial images captured under relatively stable conditions. Variations in weather, lighting, and altitude were minimal, which may not fully capture the real-world challenges UAVs face during prolonged or adverse environmental conditions. Future studies could incorporate datasets with more diverse conditions to assess how these algorithms perform in varying light levels, weather patterns, and altitudes. Furthermore, the vehicle detection task in this study focused on common types of vehicles; a broader evaluation including different vehicle shapes, sizes, and types could yield deeper insights into each algorithm's strengths and weaknesses.

The computational resources required for Faster R-CNN also pose a limitation, especially when it comes to deploying this algorithm on UAVs with limited processing power. Future research could explore lightweight variations of Faster R-CNN, optimized for edge computing or UAV-based applications, to achieve a balance between detection accuracy and speed. Additionally, advances in hardware, such as the incorporation of dedicated AI processors or GPUs on UAV platforms, could mitigate these computational challenges, allowing for real-time deployment of complex algorithms like Faster R-CNN. In terms of single-stage detectors, modifications to SSD's architecture could potentially enhance its accuracy without compromising its speed. Research into augmenting SSD with additional feature layers or combining it with lightweight proposal networks could help bridge the performance gap with Faster R-CNN, providing a viable middle ground for applications that demand both speed and accuracy.

4.3 Conclusion

This study has demonstrated the relative strengths and weaknesses of Faster R-CNN and SSD in vehicle detection tasks from UAV-captured aerial images. Faster R-CNN's two-stage approach, with its high precision, recall, and mAP values, clearly outperforms

SSD in terms of detection accuracy, especially in complex and densely populated scenes. This algorithm's ability to detect partially obscured vehicles and maintain high accuracy in cluttered environments underscores its suitability for applications where accuracy is prioritized over speed. However, the increased detection time associated with Faster R-CNN may limit its applicability in real-time applications, particularly on UAVs with constrained computational resources. SSD, on the other hand, provides an efficient solution for real-time detection tasks, achieving nearly double the speed of Faster R-CNN. Its single-stage architecture, while not as precise in highly cluttered or dense scenes, offers sufficient accuracy in scenarios where low latency is critical. As a result, SSD may be the preferred choice for UAV-based applications that prioritize rapid response, such as real-time traffic monitoring or incident detection. By examining these algorithms side by side, this study highlights the importance of matching detection algorithms to the specific requirements of UAV-based vehicle detection applications. Future research directions could focus on optimizing both algorithms for UAV deployment, considering constraints such as limited processing power, energy efficiency, and environmental variations. Improvements in UAV hardware, coupled with innovations in lightweight object detection models, hold promise for enabling high-precision, real-time vehicle detection in a wider range of applications. Ultimately, the insights provided in this study contribute to a more informed understanding of the trade-offs between accuracy and speed in object detection models, particularly within the rapidly evolving field of UAV-based monitoring systems.

References

1. Bakirci, M.: Utilizing YOLOv8 for enhanced traffic monitoring in intelligent transportation systems (ITS) applications. Digital Sig. Process. **152**, 104594 (2024)
2. Aissaoui, R., Menouar, H., Dhraief, A., Filali, F., Belghith, A., Abu-Dayya, A.: Advanced real-time traffic monitoring system based on V2X communications. In: 2014 IEEE International Conference on Communications (ICC), pp. 2713–2718. IEEE, Sydney, NSW, Australia (2014)
3. Bakirci, M.: Enhancing vehicle detection in intelligent transportation systems via autonomous UAV platform and YOLOv8 integration. Appl. Soft Comput. **164**, 112015 (2024)
4. Ahmad, A.B., Tsuji, T.: Traffic monitoring system based on deep learning and seismometer data. Appl. Sci. **11**, 4590 (2021)
5. Kazmi, S.Q., Singh, M.K., Pal, S.: Traffic monitoring system in smart cities using image processing. In: Reddy, A., Marla, D., Favorskaya, M.N., Satapathy, S.C. (eds.) Intelligent Manufacturing and Energy Sustainability. Smart Innovation, Systems and Technologies, vol. 213. Springer, Singapore (2021)
6. Joshi, R.M., Rao, D.S.: AlexDarkNet: Hybrid CNN architecture for real-time traffic monitoring with unprecedented reliability. Neural Comput. Appl. **36**, 7133–7141 (2024)
7. Gomaa, A., Minematsu, T., Abdelwahab, M.M., et al.: Faster CNN-based vehicle detection and counting strategy for fixed camera scenes. Multimedia Tools Appl. **81**, 25443–25471 (2022)
8. Lotfollahi, M., Jafari Siavoshani, M., Shirali Hossein Zade, R., et al.: Deep packet: a novel approach for encrypted traffic classification using deep learning. Soft Comput. 24, 1999–2012 (2020)
9. Bakirci, M.: Smart city air quality management through leveraging drones for precision monitoring. Sustain. Cities Soc. **106**, 105390 (2024)

10. Bakirci, M.: A novel swarm unmanned aerial vehicle system: incorporating autonomous flight, real-time object detection, and coordinated intelligence for enhanced performance. Traitement du Sig. **40**(5), 2063–2078 (2023)
11. Ren, H., Zhao, Y., Xiao, W., et al.: A review of UAV monitoring in mining areas: current status and future perspectives. Int. J. Coal Sci. Technol. **6**, 320–333 (2019)
12. Bakirci, M.: Efficient air pollution mapping in extensive regions with fully autonomous unmanned aerial vehicles: a numerical perspective. In: Science of the Total Environment, vol. 909, p.168606, (2024)
13. Lindner, G., Schraml, K., Mansberger, R., et al.: UAV monitoring and documentation of a large landslide. Appl. Geomat. **8**, 1–11 (2016)
14. Bakirci, M.: Enhancing air pollution mapping with autonomous UAV networks for extended coverage and consistency. Atmos. Res. **306**, 107480 (2024)
15. Bakirci, M.: A drone-based approach to enhance spatial insight into surrounding air pollutant distributions for healthier indoor environments. J. Build. Eng. **87**, 109023 (2024)
16. Bakirci, M.: Evaluating the impact of unmanned aerial vehicles (UAVs) on air quality management in smart cities: a comprehensive analysis of transportation-related pollution. Comput. Electr. Eng. **119**, 109556 (2024)
17. Micheal, A.A., Vani, K., Sanjeevi, S., et al.: Object detection and tracking with uav data using deep learning. J Indian Soc. Remote Sens. **49**, 463–469 (2021)
18. Elloumi, M., Dhaou, R., Escrig, B., Idoudi, H., Saidane, L.A., Fer, A.: Traffic monitoring on city roads using UAVs. In: Palattella, M., Scanzio, S., Coleri Ergen, S. (eds.) Ad-Hoc, Mobile, and Wireless Networks. ADHOC-NOW 2019. LNCS, vol. 11803. Springer, Cham (2019)
19. Cheng, L., Li, J., Duan, P., et al.: A small attentional YOLO model for landslide detection from satellite remote sensing images. Landslides **18**, 2751–2765 (2021)
20. Chen, W., Huang, H., Peng, S., et al.: YOLO-face: a real-time face detector. Vis. Comput. **37**, 805–813 (2021)
21. Leng, J., Liu, Y.: An enhanced SSD with feature fusion and visual reasoning for object detection. Neural Comput. Appl. **31**, 6549–6558 (2019)
22. Siripattanadilok, W., Siriborvornratanakul, T.: Recognition of partially occluded soft-shell mud crabs using Faster R-CNN and Grad-CAM. Aquacult. Int. **32**, 2977–2997 (2024)
23. Bakirci, M.: Real-time vehicle detection using YOLOv8-nano for intelligent transportation systems. Traitement du Sig. **41**(4), 1727–1740 (2024)
24. Chen, W., Qiao, Y., Li, Y.: Inception-SSD: an improved single shot detector for vehicle detection. J. Ambient Intell. Hum. Comput. **13**, 5047–5053 (2022)
25. Yang, Y., Song, H., Sun, S., et al.: A fast and effective video vehicle detection method leveraging feature fusion and proposal temporal link. J. Real-Time Image Proc. **18**, 1261–1274 (2021)
26. Ghosh, R.: On-road vehicle detection in varying weather conditions using faster R-CNN with several region proposal networks. Multimedia Tools Appl. **80**, 25985–25999 (2021)
27. Yin, G., Yu, M., Wang, M., et al.: Research on highway vehicle detection based on faster R-CNN and domain adaptation. Appl. Intell. **52**, 3483–3498 (2022)

Revolutionizing Aircraft Detection with Deep Learning for Satellite Imagery in Aviation

Zofia G. Zajac[1], Ewa Wisniewska[1], Jedrzej L. Kowalczyk[1], Witold Wojciechowski[1], Hilal Kuzu[2], and Ilayda Boz[2(✉)]

[1] University of Radom, Masovian Voivodeship, Radom, Poland
[2] Tarsus University, Mersin, Turkey
ilayda_boz@tarsus.edu.tr

Abstract. Detecting aircraft on the ground through real-time remote sensing using satellite images and deep learning techniques is crucial for both military and civil aviation. Effective detection enhances airport management, reducing traffic congestion on runways and in hangars. In military applications, accurate aircraft location determination significantly contributes to strategic monitoring and defense planning. This study advances existing methodologies by developing a more comprehensive dataset, incorporating new images and applying extensive data augmentation techniques to improve detection accuracy across diverse scenarios. By leveraging the YOLOv5 algorithm, this approach offers higher accuracy and faster detection compared to traditional methods, thereby enhancing real-time surveillance capabilities. The augmented dataset and optimized training process resulted in improved detection performance, particularly in challenging conditions, such as varying aircraft sizes and occlusions. Performance metrics, including precision, recall, average precision (mAP), and F1 score, yield values of 0.787, 0.751, 0.735, and 0.789, respectively, indicating a strong precision-recall balance and high reliability for the YOLOv5 algorithm. Future work will focus on further expanding the dataset, optimizing hyperparameters, and exploring different model architectures to continue enhancing detection performance. The findings underscore the novelty and robust capabilities of YOLOv5 in real-time aircraft detection, while identifying key areas for future improvement.

Keywords: Convolutional Neural Networks · Deep Learning · YOLOv5 · Aircraft Detection

1 Introduction

Recent advances in object detection technology have significantly enhanced the real-time remote sensing capabilities of satellite-based imaging systems [1]. Unmanned aerial vehicles (UAVs) and autonomous systems are increasingly favored in various applications due to their operational flexibility and cost efficiency [2–9]. Object detection, which involves recognizing and marking specific objects within an image, plays a vital role in the detection of critical vehicles, such as aircraft [1]. In both civil aviation and

A. Mirzazadeh et al. (Eds.): SEMIT 2024, CCIS 2444, pp. 412–430, 2026.
https://doi.org/10.1007/978-3-032-01948-6_26

military operations, the accurate identification of aircraft positions is crucial. In civil aviation, timely and precise aircraft detection allows for more efficient airport operations [10]. Specifically, monitoring aircraft movements on taxiways, runways, and in hangars is essential for preventing congestion and potential conflicts. In military contexts, aircraft monitoring provides a strategic advantage in decision-making processes. Detecting enemy aircraft and enabling defense systems to respond swiftly and effectively is a factor that directly influences the success of military operations. While radar data is typically used for these purposes, satellite-based remote sensing systems also play a significant role. However, the effectiveness of satellite-based remote sensing in aircraft detection faces challenges due to environmental and technical factors. The high altitude of satellite imagery, the relatively small size of aircraft, and variables such as atmospheric conditions, air pollution, and light interference all contribute to the complexity of the detection process.

Object detection generally involves three fundamental steps: data collection and processing, model training, and the detection process itself [11, 12]. First, images are gathered to form a dataset, and each image is meticulously labeled. The model is then trained using deep learning algorithms on these labeled images [13, 14], with the goal of enabling the model to accurately detect and recognize objects within new images. After training, the model can identify and classify objects in previously unseen images, drawing bounding boxes around each detected object [15, 16]. Machine learning-based solutions hold significant potential for overcoming the challenges outlined earlier [17]. In particular, advancements in deep learning have led to remarkable progress in object detection and classification, helping to mitigate many of these issues. The evolution of object detection algorithms has resulted in two primary categories: two-stage and single-stage algorithms. Two-stage algorithms are known for their high accuracy, although they tend to be slower in processing [18]. A notable example in this category is the Region-Based Convolutional Neural Network (R-CNN) family, which includes Fast R-CNN and Faster R-CNN, all of which demonstrate strong performance in object detection and classification tasks [19]. In two-stage algorithms, the first stage focuses on identifying possible regions in the image where objects may be located. These regions are then passed through a second stage for more detailed classification [20], allowing precise identification of both the object class and its location. While these models excel in accuracy, their slower processing speed makes them less ideal for real-time applications [21].

In contrast, single-stage algorithms, such as SSD (Single Shot Multibox Detector) and YOLO (You Only Look Once), prioritize speed and are often preferred for real-time applications. These methods bypass the region proposal stage and instead process the entire image in a single pass using convolutional neural networks (CNN), simultaneously determining both the object class and its location [22, 23]. While this approach is faster, it generally comes at the cost of some accuracy [24, 25]. The trade-off between speed and accuracy necessitates careful selection based on the application. For instance, two-stage algorithms are advantageous in areas like medical imaging, where precision is critical. However, in dynamic settings such as security surveillance, autonomous vehicles, or real-time drone operations, where rapid object detection is essential, the speed of single-stage algorithms makes them the more suitable choice [26].

In the broader context of object detection, the advances made by YOLO models, including YOLOv5, represent a significant leap forward in both accuracy and speed for real-time applications. Unlike traditional object detection algorithms that rely on multiple stages, such as region proposal and classification, YOLO models streamline the process by performing both detection and classification in a single step. This architecture drastically reduces computation time, making YOLO models highly efficient for real-time object detection tasks. The evolution from earlier versions such as YOLOv3 and YOLOv4 has introduced several key improvements, including better feature extraction through advanced backbone networks, enhanced anchor box generation, and more effective optimization strategies. These advancements allow YOLOv5 to outperform many other state-of-the-art models in terms of speed while maintaining high levels of accuracy. In applications where rapid decision-making is crucial, such as autonomous systems, surveillance, and aerial monitoring, these developments have made YOLO models indispensable. The significance of these advances extends across multiple industries, as YOLO continues to push the boundaries of what is possible in real-time object detection.

YOLOv5, released in 2020, introduced improvements in speed and accuracy over its predecessors while maintaining a simple architecture. Its key advantages include its ease of deployment, lightweight structure, and ability to be used for real-time detection tasks. YOLOv5 offers four main variants (n, s, m, l, x), where each variant scales the architecture's depth and width to balance inference time and accuracy. Studies have demonstrated its effectiveness in aircraft detection tasks, especially for real-time applications, due to its fast inference speed [27]. In particular, the model has shown promise when deployed on UAVs or low-powered hardware systems, making it suitable for large-scale aerial monitoring operations [28]. For instance, studies comparing YOLOv5 with earlier YOLO models (e.g., YOLOv4) in aircraft detection have consistently shown that YOLOv5 outperforms in terms of detection speed while maintaining comparable accuracy [29, 30]. Its smaller variants, such as YOLOv5n, are particularly favored for real-time detection in resource-constrained environments, such as drone-based aerial surveillance.

Research indicates that while YOLOv4 tends to achieve higher precision for detecting small and partially obscured aircraft, it falls behind YOLOv5 in speed [31]. This makes YOLOv4 more suitable for offline applications where real-time performance is not critical. Faster R-CNN remains a widely used model in aircraft detection tasks, particularly in cases where high accuracy is paramount [32]. Its two-stage detection approach first generates region proposals and then classifies each proposal, making it particularly suited for high-resolution satellite imagery or scenarios requiring fine-grained analysis. However, Faster R-CNN's computational complexity and relatively slow detection speed hinder its application in real-time scenarios, such as UAV-based aircraft monitoring. Studies comparing Faster R-CNN to YOLOv5 in aircraft detection highlight that while Faster R-CNN may outperform YOLOv5 in accuracy, especially for small and distant aircraft, YOLOv5 excels in detection speed, making it more favorable for real-time applications.

SSD is another popular single-shot detection model that offers a good balance between speed and accuracy. In aircraft detection, SSD models are known for their faster inference compared to two-stage models like Faster R-CNN. However, SSD generally performs slightly worse than YOLOv5 in terms of accuracy, particularly when detecting smaller objects such as distant aircraft. While SSD can achieve near real-time performance, especially when optimized, its relatively lower precision compared to YOLOv5 makes it less favorable for high-stakes applications like aircraft detection, where detection accuracy is critical [33]. YOLOv7, the successor to YOLOv5, introduced further architectural optimizations, improving both speed and accuracy. It introduced Extended Efficient Layer Aggregation Networks (E-ELAN) to enhance feature extraction. YOLOv7 has demonstrated state-of-the-art performance in multiple object detection tasks, including aircraft detection. Compared to YOLOv5, YOLOv7 offers higher detection accuracy, but with a significant increase in inference time [34]. RetinaNet introduced the Focal Loss function to handle class imbalance problems, which is a significant issue in detecting objects like aircraft from large-scale aerial images, where the number of background pixels far outweighs the number of object pixels. RetinaNet excels in accuracy for detecting aircraft in complex backgrounds, but similar to Faster R-CNN, it is less suited for real-time applications due to its relatively slower inference speed [35]. In comparison to YOLOv5, RetinaNet offers better performance in complex detection scenarios but lacks the speed necessary for deployment in UAV-based real-time aircraft monitoring systems.

This study provides a comprehensive evaluation of the YOLOv5 detection algorithm for identifying aircraft on the ground from satellite-based aerial imagery. YOLOv5 is renowned for its ability to balance speed and accuracy, making it one of the leading models among single-stage object detection algorithms. Compared to its predecessors, YOLOv3 and YOLOv4, YOLOv5 offers significant enhancements in both accuracy and processing speed, owing to its more advanced architectural design and optimization techniques. One of the most notable features of YOLOv5 is its real-time object detection and classification capabilities. Its low latency, especially when compared to earlier models, offers a critical advantage for tracking aircraft in dynamic environments. This capability is particularly valuable for applications requiring the rapid processing of large, high-resolution images. The key contribution of this research lies in developing a more comprehensive and diverse dataset for training, which includes new satellite imagery and extensive data augmentation techniques, addressing some of the limitations in prior studies that relied on less varied datasets. By expanding the dataset and optimizing the model's hyperparameters, this study advances the field by improving the detection of aircraft in challenging conditions, such as varying scales, orientations, and environmental factors. Additionally, this research highlights YOLOv5's potential for real-world applications, including civil aviation management, military surveillance, and broader use cases like disaster management and environmental monitoring, positioning this study as a significant advancement over previous works.

2 Methodology

YOLO (You Only Look Once) is a single-stage object detection algorithm family that uses convolutional neural networks (CNNs) to perform object detection, making it ideal for real-time applications due to its exceptional speed. YOLO's efficiency has made it highly popular for scenarios that require rapid processing and detection [36]. During the detection phase, input visual data is processed through the neural network in a single step, allowing YOLO to quickly infer the location and classification of objects in the image. This process involves dividing the image into an n*n grid, where each cell in the grid predicts bounding boxes for the objects and estimates the probability of their presence. The objects in the image are surrounded by bounding boxes, and probability calculations are made for the presence of objects in each section [37].

In addition to the bounding boxes, a confidence score is calculated for each box, representing the likelihood that the detected object belongs to a certain class. This score is usually a value between 0 and 1. However, the division of the image into multiple grid cells can lead to redundant bounding boxes for the same object, as multiple predictions are generated. To address this issue, non-maximum suppression (NMS) is applied. NMS ranks all predictions by their confidence scores and selects the bounding box with the highest score while suppressing overlapping or redundant boxes. This ensures that only the most accurate and non-overlapping bounding boxes are retained for the final output.

2.1 Detection Algorithm

YOLOv5 introduced several innovations that quickly made it a popular choice for object detection tasks. As the fifth iteration in the YOLO family, YOLOv5 offers a compelling combination of fast detection speed and high accuracy, largely due to its enhanced feature extraction capabilities [38]. This model builds upon and optimizes aspects of earlier versions, such as YOLOv3-SPP and YOLOv4. The choice of anchor boxes plays a crucial role in the detection performance of earlier YOLO iterations, as they help the model predict the locations and sizes of objects in an image. Anchor boxes are pre-defined, fixed-sized boxes that represent potential object shapes and sizes. They serve as reference points for the model to detect objects, especially when objects vary in scale and aspect ratio. In YOLOv2, the introduction of anchor boxes was one of the major advancements compared to YOLOv1. Anchor boxes allow the model to predict multiple bounding boxes for each grid cell, enabling the detection of objects of different shapes and sizes within the same grid cell. This significantly improves detection performance, especially for smaller or overlapping objects. However, one limitation in YOLOv2 is that the anchor boxes are predefined and not optimized for specific datasets. Poorly chosen anchor boxes can lead to suboptimal detection, as they might not align well with the actual object sizes in the dataset. YOLOv3 improved upon YOLOv2 by making the model predict bounding boxes at three different scales, using anchor boxes tailored for each scale. This multi-scale prediction improves the detection of objects of various sizes, especially small objects, which are more challenging for single-scale detectors. YOLOv3 also applies a more refined method for calculating anchor boxes by clustering the ground truth boxes in the training dataset using k-means clustering. This ensures that the anchor boxes are better aligned with the distribution of object sizes in the dataset, improving detection accuracy. In terms of methodologies for selecting anchor boxes, k-means clustering is the most commonly used approach. By clustering the dimensions of the ground truth bounding boxes in the training set, the anchor boxes are tailored to the specific size and aspect ratio of objects in the dataset. This optimizes the model's ability to detect objects, as the anchor boxes are more representative of the actual objects' dimensions. The distance metric used in this clustering process is typically the IoU, which measures the overlap between the anchor boxes and the ground truth bounding boxes. Using IoU as the distance metric ensures that the selected anchor boxes provide a good fit for the objects in the dataset, ultimately enhancing detection performance.

One key difference is that YOLOv5 utilizes the PyTorch framework instead of Darknet, making it more accessible for development and integration. YOLOv5 comes in four sub-models, YOLOv5s, YOLOv5m, YOLOv5l, and YOLOv5x, each offering different trade-offs between speed and performance. Its core architecture is divided into four main components: the input, where images are fed into the model. The *backbone* refers to the foundational feature extraction network that processes the input image to extract essential visual features. This backbone is typically a CNN that captures hierarchical information at varying levels of abstraction, allowing the model to understand both fine details and broader contextual features. Following the backbone, the *neck* is a component that serves to aggregate and refine features from different stages of the backbone, creating a rich feature representation that balances spatial and semantic information. This refined feature map is crucial for accurately detecting and localizing objects. Finally, the *head* of the network refers to the section responsible for making predictions based on the processed features. This includes classification (identifying the object class) and regression (predicting bounding box coordinates for object localization). In the input stage, the image provided as input is resized and formatted to align with the model's requirements. The image is scaled proportionally, either reduced or expanded, to match the dimensions used during training. These preprocessing steps ensure that the model can effectively handle images of varying sizes and conditions, enhancing its ability to perform consistently across diverse inputs.

The backbone section of YOLOv5 is its core feature extraction network, responsible for identifying key features from the input image. YOLOv5 utilizes a Focus module based on the Cross-Stage Partial Network (CSPNet) architecture, which is derived from DenseNET [39], allowing for more efficient processing of input images. The Focus module reduces image size and condenses relevant information, enabling a more streamlined and effective learning process. For feature extraction, YOLOv5 incorporates CSPDarknet53, an enhanced version of Darknet53 based on CSPNet. This architecture divides the feature map into two parts during network optimization and recombines them at different stages. One part passes through the dense block and transition layer, while the other is merged with the feature map in a later step. This structure reduces redundant information, mitigating complexity while maintaining accuracy. It also improves gradient flow, enhancing the information transfer and reducing computational costs. The backbone consists of the CBS module, which includes a convolutional layer, batch normalization, and a SiLU activation function, along with the C3 group comprising three CBS modules and multiple bottlenecks. Additionally, the Spatial Pyramid Pooling Fusion (SPPF) layer, similar to spatial pyramid pooling, accelerates computation by integrating multi-scale features into a fixed-size feature map. These architectural components are illustrated in Fig. 1.

The neck section in YOLOv5 is a feature pyramid network designed to combine feature maps extracted at different scales in the backbone section. It integrates both the Feature Pyramid Network (FPN) and Path Aggregation Network (PANet). FPN extracts

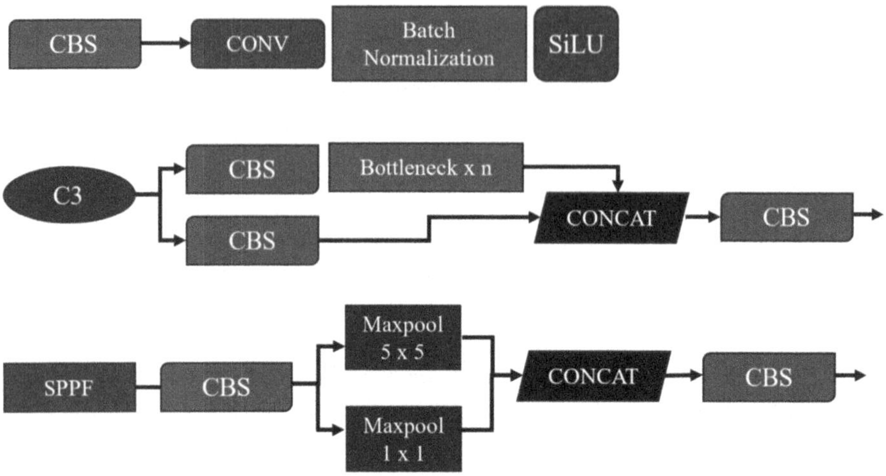

Fig. 1. Architectures of the CBS, C3, and SPFF modules in YOLOv5, detailing their individual structures and roles within the network. The CBS module, consisting of Convolution, Batch Normalization, and SiLU activation layers, is used for basic feature extraction and is the building block for early and intermediate network layers. The C3 (Cross Stage Partial) module enables efficient feature reuse by splitting and merging features through multiple convolutional layers, improving model accuracy and computational efficiency. The SPFF (Spatial Pyramid Feature Fusion) module integrates multi-scale feature maps by applying spatial pyramid pooling, allowing the model to detect objects at various scales and enhancing robustness to object size variations.

multi-scale semantic feature maps and facilitates classification by providing dense top-down information transfer. It combines feature maps from different resolutions through upsampling, which gradually increases image resolution. FPN enhances low-resolution features, while PANet refines high-level feature maps, and together, they enable robust object detection across various scales. PANet optimizes feature fusion by improving information flow through lateral connections, which is crucial for detecting small, low-resolution, or difficult-to-identify objects. By combining FPN's multi-scale semantic understanding with PANet's efficient feature positioning, this section plays a key role in strengthening object detection across diverse scenarios.

The final detection results are generated from the feature maps processed in the head section of YOLOv5. This section consists of multiple output layers, each responsible for detecting objects at different scales, along with several convolutional layers and activation functions. The convolutional layers are used to predict object classes, location offsets, and size adjustments. Nonlinear transformations, performed using Sigmoid and ReLU activation functions, enhance the network's expressive capacity. To finalize detection, YOLOv5 applies Non-Maximum Suppression (NMS) to eliminate overlapping bounding boxes, ensuring that only the most accurate predictions are retained. The NMS algorithm is a widely used post-processing technique in object detection models to eliminate redundant bounding boxes for the same object and retain only the most confident detection. NMS works by selecting the bounding box with the highest confidence score and suppressing other overlapping boxes whose Intersection over Union (IoU) exceeds a predefined threshold. This results in a single, most accurate bounding box for each detected object. While traditional NMS discards overlapping boxes based on a hard IoU threshold, Soft-NMS introduces a more gradual suppression process. Instead of completely eliminating boxes with high overlap, Soft-NMS reduces their confidence scores based on their IoU with the highest-scoring box. This allows for the retention of overlapping detections that might represent objects partially occluded or located close together. As a result, Soft-NMS can handle overlapping objects better and usually leads to a slight increase in detection accuracy compared to standard NMS.

Weighted Box Fusion (WBF) is another alternative to NMS that takes into account all proposed bounding boxes and merges them by averaging their coordinates, weighted by confidence scores. Unlike NMS, which can suppress potentially useful boxes, WBF uses all the information from overlapping boxes to produce a more accurate final bounding box. This method is particularly useful in cases where object boundaries are difficult to define, or multiple detectors provide overlapping yet valid proposals. WBF typically improves localization accuracy but can be computationally more expensive than NMS. In IoU-Aware NMS, the algorithm considers not just confidence scores but also the IoU between each pair of boxes. This method adjusts the suppression process based on both the confidence and the overlap between boxes, providing a more context-sensitive approach to eliminating redundant boxes. This method can achieve better performance in scenarios with dense or overlapping objects, though it might be more complex to implement and slower than traditional NMS.

A variation of NMS, is Greedy NMS, which aggressively eliminates boxes with high overlap and keeps only the most confident ones. While this reduces computation time, it can suffer from poor detection performance when objects are close together or when there is partial occlusion, leading to missed detections or lower accuracy in cluttered scenes. NMS is simple, fast, and effective in reducing redundant detections, which is why it remains a popular choice for real-time object detection tasks. It is computationally efficient and well-suited for scenarios where detection speed is critical, like in autonomous systems or real-time video analysis. NMS can struggle with detecting objects that are closely packed or partially occluded, as it may suppress valid bounding boxes that overlap beyond the defined threshold. In such cases, it can miss true positives. This limitation makes NMS less effective in crowded or dense object scenes, compared to methods like Soft-NMS or WBF. The object detection results are then produced, as illustrated in Fig. 2, which displays the overall architecture of the YOLOv5 algorithm.

2.2 Loss Function

The IoU criterion, used to evaluate the model's estimation performance, is calculated by dividing the area of overlap between the predicted bounding box and the ground truth box by the total area covered by both boxes. IoU values range from 0 to 1 and serve as a widely accepted metric for assessing box estimation accuracy. This criterion encompasses several loss functions, including Complete IoU (CIoU), Distance IoU (DIoU), and Generalized IoU (GIoU). Mathematically, IoU is represented in (1):

$$\mathrm{IoU} = \frac{(A \cap A_r)}{(A \cup A_r)} \tag{1}$$

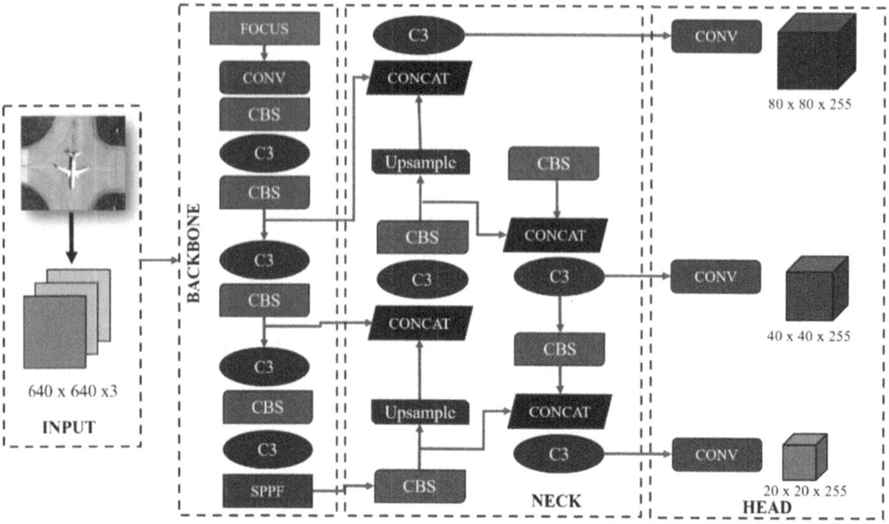

Fig. 2. YOLOv5's network architecture, illustrating the overall structure and flow of data through the model, including backbone, neck, and head components. The backbone section of the network is responsible for feature extraction, utilizing a series of convolutional layers to capture spatial hierarchies in the input images. The neck is designed to strengthen feature fusion through a path aggregation network (PANet), enhancing the model's ability to detect objects at multiple scales. The head generates predictions by applying bounding box regression and classification, outputting object detections with associated confidence scores.

where *A* denotes the estimated bounding box and *Ar* signifies the ground truth bounding box. The scale-invariant nature of IoU means it is unaffected by scale transformations resulting from the similarity of the two shapes. However, IoU may not effectively differentiate between shapes that are either too close or too far apart. To address this limitation, Generalized IoU (GIoU) is proposed, as shown in (2):

$$\mathrm{GIoU} = \mathrm{IoU} - \frac{|\mathrm{B} \backslash (\mathrm{A} \cup \mathrm{A_r})|}{|\mathrm{B}|} \tag{2}$$

In this equation, *B* represents the area of the smallest enclosing rectangle that contains both the estimated bounding box *A* and the actual bounding box *Ar*. GIoU enhances IoU by considering cases where the boxes do not overlap, enabling optimization processes aimed at reducing the gap between bounding boxes and improving model estimation performance.

Distance IoU (DIoU), which is the preferred metric for this study, incorporates both the overlapping area of the boxes and the Euclidean distance between their center points. By accounting for positional differences between the estimated and actual bounding boxes, DIoU provides superior performance. The loss function for DIoU is expressed in (3):

$$\mathrm{DIoU} = \mathrm{IoU} - \frac{\rho^2(\mathrm{A}, \mathrm{A_r})}{c^2} \tag{3}$$

where d is the distance between the center points, c is the diagonal distance of the smallest enclosing box, and v represents the aspect ratio.

$$DIoU_{loss} = 1 - IoU + \frac{\rho^2(A, A_r)}{c^2} \tag{4}$$

The dataset utilized in this study comprises aircraft images collected from various geographical locations using satellite imagery available on the Google Earth platform. Given the significant impact of algorithm training on model performance, considerable attention was devoted to capturing a variety of aircraft dimensions, models, and color variations, as well as different ground conditions, viewing angles, and heights during dataset creation. Additionally, shadows cast on the ground due to variations in time of day introduced further diversity to the dataset. In total, the dataset consists of 3,577 images, encompassing 7,944 aircraft. It is divided into training, validation, and test sets with proportions of 55%, 23%, and 22%, respectively.

2.3 Dataset and Hyperparameters

To enhance the robustness and generalizability of the YOLOv5 model for aircraft detection, extensive data augmentation techniques were applied to the training dataset. Given the variability in aircraft size, orientation, and environmental conditions in satellite imagery, data augmentation was crucial in improving the model's ability to detect aircraft in diverse and challenging scenarios. The following augmentation strategies were employed: Random rotations (0°, 90°, 180°, 270°) and horizontal and vertical flipping were applied to account for different aircraft orientations, ensuring the model could detect aircraft regardless of their positioning on the ground. Scaling and random zooming were used to simulate variations in altitude and distance from the aircraft, allowing the model to detect both large and small aircraft effectively. Random translations were introduced to simulate slight changes in camera angle and position, encouraging the model to detect aircraft even when they appear in different parts of the image. Variations in lighting conditions were simulated by adjusting brightness and contrast levels, helping the model to detect aircraft under different weather conditions and times of day. Random Gaussian noise was added to simulate sensor noise and other real-world artifacts, improving the model's robustness in detecting aircraft in noisy or degraded images. The color space of the images was randomly jittered to simulate variations in lighting and environmental conditions, such as the presence of shadows, sun glare, or cloud cover. These augmentation techniques were applied dynamically during the training process, ensuring that each training batch included augmented images. This approach effectively increased the diversity of the training data without needing additional labeled images, leading to improved model performance in detecting aircraft in previously unseen conditions.

Several key hyperparameters and training settings were carefully selected to optimize model performance. The following details provide additional information on the training process: Standard YOLOv5 hyperparameters were employed, with the learning rate set to 0.01 and momentum set to 0.937. The weight decay parameter was set at 0.0005, which is commonly used to prevent overfitting. A cosine learning rate scheduler was applied, starting at 0.01 and gradually decreasing over the training process, ensuring smoother convergence toward optimal performance. The model was trained for 300 epochs, allowing sufficient time for the network to learn from the dataset without overfitting or underfitting. A batch size of 16 was chosen to balance computational efficiency with model accuracy. This batch size allowed the model to process a reasonable number of images per iteration without overwhelming the available hardware resources. The training was conducted using Google Colaboratory (Colab), leveraging a virtual machine with an NVIDIA Tesla T4 GPU. This setup provided the necessary computational power to handle the training workload efficiently while maintaining rapid iteration cycles. These settings were optimized based on initial experimentation to achieve the best balance between detection accuracy and training speed.

3 Results

Precision, Recall, mean Average Precision (mAP), and F1 Score metrics were used to evaluate the performance of YOLOv5. Precision measures the proportion of true positive detections among all instances that the model predicted as positive. In other words, it indicates how many of the detected objects were correct, helping to assess the accuracy of the model's predictions. Recall, on the other hand, quantifies the ability of the model to identify all relevant objects in the dataset. It reflects the proportion of true positive detections out of the total actual positive instances, highlighting how many of the existing objects were successfully detected. Mean Average Precision (mAP) is a comprehensive metric that combines precision and recall across different levels of confidence. It is calculated by averaging the precision values at various recall levels, providing a single score that reflects the model's performance across multiple thresholds. This metric is particularly useful for evaluating object detection models, as it accounts for different confidence levels in predictions. The F1 Score ($2 \times \text{Precision} \times \text{Recall}/\text{Precision}+\text{Recall}$) serves as a harmonic mean of precision and recall, providing a balanced measure that considers both metrics simultaneously. It is particularly valuable in situations where there is an uneven class distribution, as it emphasizes the model's ability to maintain a good balance between precision and recall. Together, these metrics offer a holistic view of a model's detection capabilities, enabling effective comparisons and assessments of different algorithms.

The test results offer a comprehensive analysis of the YOLOv5 model's effectiveness in detecting aircraft within the dataset. The model achieved a precision value of 0.787, a recall value of 0.751, an average precision value (mAP) of 0.735, and an F1 score of 0.769. Firstly, the precision value indicates the accuracy of the model's predictions, revealing that 78.7% of the detected aircraft are correctly identified. The recall value assesses the model's ability to identify actual objects, with a score of 0.751 indicating it can accurately detect 75.1% of the aircraft present. The mAP value, typically used to gauge the model's performance across various confidence thresholds, stands at 0.735. This suggests the model demonstrates average performance at both low and high confidence levels, with potential for improvement in accuracy or a reduction in the miss rate. Lastly, the F1 score, which reflects the model's overall performance by balancing precision and recall, indicates effective management of false positives and false negatives, contributing to a well-rounded detection capability. To calculate the F1 score, one must first determine the values of true positives, false positives, and false negatives, from which precision and recall are derived. Additionally, Table 1 presents a comprehensive comparison of YOLOv5's performance in aircraft detection against three prominent models: YOLOv4, Faster R-CNN, and SSD. The results indicate that, while Faster R-CNN excels in accuracy and demonstrates a higher overall detection performance, it is important to note that YOLOv5 significantly outshines it in terms of detection speed. This rapid processing capability makes YOLOv5 particularly advantageous for applications requiring real-time analysis, such as in surveillance and traffic management. Moreover, as anticipated, YOLOv5 exhibits improved performance over both YOLOv4 and SSD. The enhancements in YOLOv5's architecture, including its efficient use of resources and optimized feature extraction methods, contribute to its ability to deliver faster detection times without compromising on accuracy. This balance of speed and performance underscores YOLOv5's effectiveness as a robust tool for aircraft detection tasks, making it a compelling choice for both military and civil aviation applications.

Table 1. Comprehensive performance comparison of YOLOv5, YOLOv4, Faster R-CNN, and SSD algorithms in aircraft detection, providing detailed insights into each model's detection capabilities. Key evaluation metrics include precision, which measures the accuracy of detected objects; recall, indicating the model's ability to capture all relevant detections; mean Average Precision (mAP), representing overall detection accuracy across different thresholds; and F1 score, a balanced metric combining precision and recall to assess detection reliability.

	Evaluation Metric			
Model	Precision	Recall	mAP	F1 Score
YOLOv5	0.787	0.751	0.735	0.769
YOLOv4	0.683	0.705	0.694	0.694
Faster R-CNN	0.798	0.773	0.784	0.785
SSD	0.661	0.609	0.636	0.634

Figure 3 illustrates several visual examples from the test results. In the first image, the algorithm successfully recognized all aircraft but kept the bounding box for the largest plane too wide, omitting the nose of the last aircraft on the right. This omission may be attributed to the shadow on the nose, which altered its color to resemble the ground, leading the algorithm to misinterpret that section as ground rather than an aircraft. In the second image, all aircraft are detected, including one whose tail is outside the frame, demonstrating successful detection. However, the algorithm mistakenly identified the articulated passenger access system as an aircraft, highlighting that such systems can sometimes cause confusion due to their geometric and color similarities to actual aircraft. The third image, captured from a lower altitude, shows flawless detection; the algorithm correctly distinguished the articulated system from the aircraft.

In the fourth image, all planes are again completely detected. In the fifth image, the algorithm recognized a single aircraft but misidentified an articulated system as an aircraft, including it within the bounding box. The sixth image, taken from a higher altitude, shows that while the algorithm successfully distinguished the articulated system

Fig. 3. Selected examples showcasing aircraft detection results with YOLOv5.

from the aircraft, it failed to detect the smaller plane on the right, which blended in with the ground. The seventh image, also taken from a higher altitude, demonstrates repeated misidentification, with the articulated system again perceived as an aircraft, and failure to detect the aircraft in the upper right, which similarly matched the ground color. In the eighth image, while all aircraft were correctly identified, the algorithm mistakenly included the articulated system in the bounding box of one of the aircraft.

For a deeper error analysis, we conducted a more detailed examination of the misdetections made by the YOLOv5 model during the aircraft detection task. Specifically, we found that approximately 3.7% of jet bridges were misclassified as aircraft, highlighting the model's difficulty in distinguishing between similar large objects present in airport environments. Additionally, 13% of small aircraft were missed, particularly in images where the resolution was lower or the aircraft were partially occluded. These findings suggest that while YOLOv5 performs well in general, further refinement is needed to improve its ability to differentiate between complex structures and to detect smaller objects more reliably. Future work will focus on addressing these weaknesses by exploring model adjustments and incorporating additional training data that captures a wider variety of object scales and environments.

The recurring issue of misidentifying jet bridges as aircraft highlights a critical challenge in the object detection process. To address this problem, several potential solutions can be implemented. One effective approach is to integrate more specific object classification layers within the YOLOv5 architecture. By training the model with additional classes that include detailed representations of jet bridges, the algorithm can learn to distinguish between these similar-looking objects more effectively. Moreover, refining the dataset is essential for improving classification accuracy. This can involve curating a more comprehensive dataset that includes labeled examples of jet bridges alongside aircraft. Specifically, annotating images where misclassifications occur will help the model understand the distinguishing features of each object type. Implementing techniques such as hard-negative mining, which focuses on retraining the model on misclassified instances, can also be beneficial. The impact of false positives in this context is significant, as it can lead to inefficiencies in airport operations and potential safety concerns. Thus, addressing this issue with targeted solutions will not only enhance the model's accuracy but also improve its reliability in real-world applications.

Satellite and aerial surveillance technologies, including those used in this study, inherently raise ethical and privacy questions, especially regarding potential military applications. In civilian contexts, such technologies offer substantial benefits for urban planning, disaster response, traffic management, and environmental monitoring. However, when similar technologies are applied in military or security settings, they can lead to ethical dilemmas, particularly regarding privacy rights, data security, and unintended surveillance of civilian activities. From an ethical perspective, it is crucial to consider how these technologies balance security with individual privacy. Inadvertent or unauthorized surveillance of individuals or groups could result in privacy intrusions, which is a concern not only in civilian surveillance but also in military and defense applications where surveillance boundaries may be less well-defined. Such applications require clear policies and stringent oversight to prevent misuse and ensure compliance with international laws and human rights standards.

Further, privacy concerns are amplified when considering the use of satellite surveillance for monitoring large, unregulated areas. Data from such technologies can easily encompass non-targeted regions, inadvertently capturing personal or sensitive information, which, if not managed responsibly, could lead to breaches of privacy and unintended harm to non-involved individuals. This reinforces the need for responsible data management practices, including anonymization, restricted access, and transparent data handling protocols. In light of these considerations, the present study focuses exclusively on civil applications in urban traffic monitoring and management. However, we recognize that the technology's dual-use potential invites a broader ethical discourse, which is crucial as surveillance capabilities expand. Addressing these issues and establishing ethical frameworks that prioritize transparency, accountability, and individual privacy are essential to ensure the responsible use of satellite and aerial surveillance technologies, both in civilian and military contexts. Future studies will aim to incorporate more extensive discussions on ethical implications and privacy considerations to build a more comprehensive understanding of the societal impact of satellite and aerial surveillance technologies.

4 Discussion

The results obtained reveal notable differences in the performance of the tested algorithms, highlighting both the strengths and limitations of each method. The YOLOv5 algorithm achieved a precision of 0.787, recall of 0.751, mAP of 0.735, and F1 score of 0.769, indicating a high level of balance between precision and recall. While YOLOv5 does not exhibit the highest precision, it demonstrates a robust and reliable performance across all metrics, making it a suitable choice for applications that require consistent detection accuracy with moderate computational demands. Compared to YOLOv5, YOLOv4 produced slightly lower results across all metrics, with a precision of 0.683, recall of 0.705, mAP of 0.694, and F1 score of 0.694. Although YOLOv4 has a lower detection accuracy overall, its performance is still commendable, especially for scenarios with limited hardware resources, as YOLOv4 generally requires less computation than more recent object detection models. However, the modest drop in both precision and recall compared to YOLOv5 may limit its utility in applications where high detection accuracy is essential.

Faster R-CNN outperformed YOLOv5 and YOLOv4 in terms of precision, recall, and mAP, with values of 0.798, 0.773, and 0.784, respectively. This model achieved the highest F1 score (0.785) among the algorithms tested. Faster R-CNN's superior detection accuracy suggests that it could be a viable option for applications prioritizing accuracy over speed, as Faster R-CNN is typically more computationally intensive. This algorithm may be particularly advantageous for post-processing tasks where detection accuracy is critical, and real-time processing is not essential. On the other hand, SSD recorded the lowest precision (0.661), recall (0.609), mAP (0.636), and F1 score (0.634) among the four algorithms tested. This model's lower performance across all metrics may limit its use in applications that require high detection accuracy. However, SSD is known for its lightweight architecture and faster inference times, making it potentially suitable for applications where computational resources are constrained and detection speed is prioritized over accuracy.

While Faster R-CNN demonstrated the highest detection performance, it requires considerable computational power, making it less suitable for real-time applications. YOLOv5, with its strong balance across all metrics and relatively low computational demands, presents a robust alternative for applications requiring a compromise between detection accuracy and processing efficiency. YOLOv4 and SSD, though less accurate, offer advantages in speed and computational efficiency, which may be beneficial in resource-limited environments or real-time applications where high accuracy is not the primary concern. This comparative analysis underscores the importance of selecting an algorithm that aligns with the specific operational requirements and hardware constraints of the intended application.

5 Conclusion

The findings of this study highlight that the YOLOv5 algorithm demonstrates exceptional performance in detecting aircraft on the ground using satellite images. The tests reveal that YOLOv5 achieves high accuracy and speed, with a precision of 0.787, a recall of 0.751, a mean average precision (mAP) of 0.735, and an F1 score of 0.769. These results indicate that YOLOv5 is an effective and efficient algorithm for applications such as real-time surveillance and monitoring, which are crucial for both the aviation sector and military operations. Utilizing this type of deep learning for airport management and security significantly enhances aviation infrastructure by increasing operational efficiency. The outcomes of the tests conducted with the YOLOv5 model affirm the algorithm's superior performance, suggesting that further improvements can be achieved by expanding the dataset and optimizing hyperparameters. The provided visual examples illustrate the challenges in accurately detecting aircraft against complex and difficult-to-perceive backgrounds, as well as issues like misclassifying airfoil systems as aircraft. Such misclassifications highlight the need to enhance the recall rate and improve the algorithm's ability to distinguish between objects with similar characteristics. Addressing these challenges is critical for future research. Overall, this study underscores the high potential of YOLOv5 for aircraft detection in challenging satellite-based aerial images in real-time applications while identifying areas for future enhancement. One key area where this model can be effectively deployed is in disaster management, particularly in locating stranded aircraft or identifying suitable landing zones for rescue operations in the aftermath of natural disasters. Additionally, the model's capabilities can be extended to environmental monitoring, where it can aid in detecting aerial activity in protected areas, tracking aircraft emissions, or assessing environmental impacts on aviation infrastructure. These additional applications highlight the versatility of the YOLOv5 model in providing real-time, accurate detection across a variety of domains, further increasing its relevance and potential impact beyond aviation-specific tasks.

There are several directions in which this research can be extended to enhance the performance and applicability of YOLOv5 for aircraft detection. First, future work will focus on improving the model's ability to detect smaller aircraft and reduce the confusion with non-aircraft objects, such as jet bridges, through advanced augmentation techniques and the inclusion of more diverse training datasets. Additionally, exploring alternative object detection models, such as YOLOv7, YOLOv8, and other state-of-the-art architectures, could further improve detection accuracy and inference speed, particularly for real-time applications on UAVs. Another area for improvement is the integration of multi-scale feature detection techniques, which may help overcome the current limitations in detecting small and distant aircraft. Moreover, combining YOLOv5 with post-processing methods, such as Non-Maximum Suppression (NMS) refinement or context-aware models, could enhance precision by reducing false positives in complex airport environments. In terms of deployment, future studies will explore optimization strategies to reduce the computational demands of the model, enabling its deployment on low-power, edge-computing platforms such as Jetson Xavier NX or similar hardware, suitable for real-time monitoring tasks. Additionally, future experiments could include flight tests with UAVs to evaluate the practical performance of the model in dynamic environments with varying lighting, weather conditions, and altitudes. Lastly, expanding the scope of detection beyond aircraft to include other relevant airport objects (e.g., ground vehicles, personnel, and equipment) would provide a more comprehensive surveillance solution for airport management and security.

References

1. Azam, B., Khet al.: Aircraft detection in satellite imagery using deep learning-based object detectors. Microprocessors Microsyst. **94**(104630), (2022)
2. Bakirci, M.: Smart city air quality management through leveraging drones for precision monitoring. Sustainable Cities Soc. **106**(105390) (2024). https://doi.org/10.1016/j.scs.2024.105390
3. Lin, Y.C., Chen, W.D.: Automatic aircraft detection in very-high-resolution satellite imagery using a YOLOv3-based process. J. Appli. Remote Sensing **15**(1) (2021)
4. Bakirci, M.: Efficient air pollution mapping in extensive regions with fully autonomous unmanned aerial vehicles: A numerical perspective. Sci. Total Environ. **909**(168606) (2024). https://doi.org/10.1016/j.scitotenv.2023.168606
5. Rejeb, A., Abdollahi, A., Rejeb, K., Treiblmaier, H.: Drones in agriculture: A review and bibliometric analysis. Comput. Electr. Agricult. **198**(107017) (2022)
6. Hemamalini, R.R., Vinodhini, R., Shanthini, B., Partheeban, P., Charumathy, M., Cornelius, K.: Air quality monitoring and forecasting using smart drones and recurrent neural network for sustainable development in Chennai city. Sustainable Cities Soc. **85**(104077) (2022)
7. Bakirci, M.: Enhancing air pollution mapping with autonomous UAV networks for extended coverage and consistency. Atmospheric Res. **306**(107480) (2024). https://doi.org/10.1016/j.atmosres.2024.107480
8. Bakirci, M.: A drone-based approach to enhance spatial insight into surrounding air pollutant distributions for healthier indoor environments. J. Build. Eng. **87**(109023) (2024). https://doi.org/10.1016/j.jobe.2024.109023
9. Bakirci, M.: Evaluating the impact of unmanned aerial vehicles (UAVs) on air quality management in smart cities: a comprehensive analysis of transportation-related pollution. Comput. Electr. Eng. **119**(109556) (2024). https://doi.org/10.1016/j.compeleceng.2024.109556
10. Huang, B., Ding, Y., Liu, G., Tian, G., Wang, S.: ASD-YOLO: An aircraft surface defects detection method using deformable convolution and attention mechanism. Measurement **238**(115300) (2024)
11. Amit, Y., Felzenszwalb, P., Girshick, R.: Object detection. In: Computer Vision: A Reference Guide, pp. 875-883 (2021). Cham: Springer International Publishing.
12. Bakirci, M.: Utilizing YOLOv8 for enhanced traffic monitoring in intelligent transportation systems (ITS) applications. Digital Signal Process. **152**(104594), (2024). https://doi.org/10.1016/j.dsp.2024.104594
13. Zhao, Z.Q., Zheng, P., Xu, S.T., Wu, X.: Object detection with deep learning: a review. IEEE Trans. Neural Netw. Learn. Syst. **30**(11), 3212–3232 (2019)
14. Bakirci, M.: A novel swarm unmanned aerial vehicle system: incorporating autonomous flight, real-time object detection, and coordinated intelligence for enhanced performance. Traitement du Signal **40**(5), 2063–2078 (2023). https://doi.org/10.18280/ts.400524
15. Diwan, T., Anirudh, G., Tembhurne, J.V.: Object detection using YOLO: challenges, architectural successors, datasets and applications. Multimedia Tools and Applications **82**(6), 9243–9275 (2023)
16. Bakirci, M.: Enhancing vehicle detection in intelligent transportation systems via autonomous UAV platform and YOLOv8 integration. Applied Soft Computing 164(112015), (2024). https://doi.org/10.1016/j.asoc.2024.112015

17. Ramík, D.M., Sabourin, C., Moreno, R., Madani, K.: A machine learning based intelligent vision system for autonomous object detection and recognition. Appl. Intell. **40**, 358–375 (2014)
18. Xie, X., Cheng, G., Wang, J., Yao, X., Han, J.: Oriented R-CNN for object detection. In: Proceedings of the IEEE/CVF International Conference on Computer Vision, pp, 3520–3529 (2021)
19. Li, W.: Analysis of object detection performance based on Faster R-CNN. J. Phys. Conf. Series, **1827**(1) (2021)
20. Maity, M., Banerjee, S., Chaudhuri, S.S.: Faster r-cnn and yolo based vehicle detection: a survey. In: 2021 5th International Conference on Computing Methodologies and Communication (ICCMC), pp. 1442–1447 (2021)
21. Xiao, Y., Wang, X., Zhang, P., Meng, F., Shao, F.: Object detection based on faster R-CNN algorithm with skip pooling and fusion of contextual information. Sensors **20**(19), 5490 (2020)
22. Lu, X., Ji, J., Xing, Z., Miao, Q.: Attention and feature fusion SSD for remote sensing object detection. IEEE Trans. Instrum. Meas. **70**, 1–9 (2021)
23. Bakirci, M.: Real-time vehicle detection using YOLOv8-nano for intelligent transportation systems. Traitement du Signal **41**(4), 1727–1740 (2024). https://doi.org/10.18280/ts.410407
24. Chandana, R.K., Ramachandra, A.C.: Real time object detection system with YOLO and CNN models: A review **773**. arXiv Prepr. arXiv2208 (2022)
25. Bakirci, M., Cetin, M.: Improving position-time trajectory accuracy in vehicle stop-and-go scenarios by using a mobile robot as a testbed. J. Control Eng. Appli. Inform. **25**(3), 35–44 (2023). https://doi.org/10.61416/ceai.v25i3.8365
26. Alkentar, S.M., Alsahwa, B., Assalem, A., Karakolla, D.: Practical comparation of the accuracy and speed of YOLO, SSD and Faster RCNN for drone detection. Journal of Engineering **27**(8), 19–31 (2021)
27. Yin, Y., Li, H., Fu, W.: Faster-YOLO: An accurate and faster object detection method. Digital Signal Processing **102**, 102756 (2020)
28. Liu, Z., Gao, Y., Du, Q., Chen, M., Lv, W.: YOLO-Extract: improved YOLOv5 for aircraft object detection in remote sensing images. IEEE Access **11**, 1742–1751 (2023). https://doi.org/10.1109/ACCESS.2023.3233964
29. Liu, X., Tang, G., Zou, W.: Improvement of detection accuracy of aircraft in remote sensing images based on YOLOV5 Model: In: 2021 IEEE International Geoscience and Remote Sensing Symposium IGARSS. Brussels, Belgium, pp. 4775–4778 (2021). https://doi.org/10.1109/IGARSS47720.2021.9554234
30. Luo, S., Yu, J., Xi, Y., Liao, X.: Aircraft Target Detection in Remote Sensing Images Based on Improved YOLOv5. IEEE Access **10**, 5184–5192 (2022). https://doi.org/10.1109/ACCESS.2022.3140876
31. Yang, Y., Xie, G., Qu, Y.: Real-time detection of aircraft objects in remote sensing images based on improved YOLOv4. In: 2021 IEEE 5th Advanced Information Technology, Electronic and Automation Control Conference (IAEAC). Chongqing, China, pp. 1156–1164 (2021). https://doi.org/10.1109/IAEAC50856.2021.9390673
32. Wu, Q., Feng, D., Cao, C., Zeng, X., Feng, Z., Wu, J., Huang, Z.: Improved Mask R-CNN for aircraft detection in remote sensing images. Sensors **21**(2618) (2021). https://doi.org/10.3390/s21082618
33. Qifang, X., Liu, L.: Aircraft Detection of High-Resolution Remote Sensing Image Based on Faster R-CNN Model and SSD Model. In: Proceedings of the 2018 International Conference on Image and Graphics Processing, pp. 133–137 (2018). https://doi.org/10.1145/3191442.3191443
34. Zhou, W., Cai, C., Zheng, L., et al.: ASSD-YOLO: a small object detection method based on improved YOLOv7 for airport surface surveillance. Multimed Tools Appl **83**, 55527–55548 (2024). https://doi.org/10.1007/s11042-023-17628-4

35. Ahmed, M., Maher, A., Bai, X.: Aircraft tracking in aerial videos based on fused RetinaNet and low-score detection classification. IET Image Proc. **17**, 687–708 (2023). https://doi.org/10.1049/ipr2.12665
36. Ahmad, T., Ma, Y., Yahya, M., Ahmad, B., Nazir, S., Haq, A.U.: Object detection through modified YOLO neural network. Sci. Program. **2020**(1), 8403262 (2020)
37. Mahaur, B., Mishra, K.K.: Small-object detection based on YOLOv5 in autonomous driving systems. Pattern Recogn. Lett. **168**, 115–122 (2023)
38. Huang, G., Liu, Z., Van Der Maaten, L., Weinberger, K.Q.: Densely connected convolutional networks. In: Proceedings of the IEEE Conference on Computer Vision and Pattern Recognition, pp. 4700–4708 (2017)
39. Luo, S., Yu, J., Xi, Y., Liao, X.: Aircraft target detection in remote sensing images based on improved YOLOv5. IEEE Access **10**, 5184–5192 (2022)

Benchmarking YOLOv7 and YOLOv8: Real-Time Pothole Detection Capabilities

Monika Lenka Starha[1], Ludmila Vera Vondrakova[1], Melis Duhter[2], Klaudia Schultheiss[3], and Hilal Kuzu[4](✉)

[1] Technical University of Liberec, Liberec, Czechia
[2] Mersin University, Mersin, Turkey
[3] University of Bremen, Bremen, Germany
[4] Tarsus University, Mersin, Turkey
hilal_kuzu@tarsus.edu.tr

Abstract. Vehicle technology with autonomous systems is advancing rapidly, necessitating improved safety measures for road hazards such as potholes, which are a leading cause of vehicle accidents. Especially at night, human visual limitations highlight the importance of real-time pothole detection to enhance driver safety. Among object detection algorithms, the YOLO series stands out for its high speed and efficiency, making it suitable for real-time applications in dynamic environments. This study presents a detailed performance comparison of the YOLOv7 and YOLOv8 algorithms for detecting potholes on road surfaces using images from web-based sources and Google Earth. A comprehensive dataset of pothole images was constructed, enabling a robust evaluation of each model under various environmental conditions, such as lighting and weather variability. Key performance metrics, including precision, recall, and detection time, were analyzed to assess the strengths and weaknesses of YOLOv7 and YOLOv8, revealing significant differences in their accuracy and real-time capabilities. The findings provide insights into each algorithm's efficacy and suitability for potential real-time implementation in autonomous vehicle safety systems, paving the way for future research on optimized models for road safety and maintenance applications.

Keywords: Pothole Detection · YOLOv7 · YOLOv8 · Image Processing · Deep Learning

1 Introduction

Given the significant impact on infrastructure maintenance, road safety, and financial sustainability, the detection of potholes is extremely important. Potholes are deep indentations or depressions in the road surface caused by weathering and erosion and pose a serious risk to vehicles, passengers, and drivers. Early detection and correction of these road defects can reduce vehicle damage, prevent accidents, and save huge repair costs for both vehicle owners and municipalities. Potholes are a major safety concern [1]. Drivers' quick reactions to potholes, especially in crowded places, can cause them to

A. Mirzazadeh et al. (Eds.): SEMIT 2024, CCIS 2444, pp. 431–445, 2026.
https://doi.org/10.1007/978-3-032-01948-6_27

swerve or brake suddenly, increasing the risk of accidents. Potholes can cause suspension, misalignment, and tyre blowout problems, severely impairing vehicle handling and safety. Hitting a pothole can be even more dangerous for cyclists and motorcyclists, as it can cause serious injury and loss of balance. Early and accurate pothole detection is therefore crucial to reducing these hazards and ensuring safer travel conditions for all road users [2].

When it comes to maintaining infrastructure, the identification of potholes is crucial to maintaining the longevity and quality of road networks. Roads are an essential part of a country's infrastructure, as they enable daily activities, commerce, and public transportation. If neglected, potholes can develop quickly and require more extensive and expensive repairs. In addition to reducing maintenance costs and minimizing delays caused by road closures and repair work, routine pothole remediation and repair can extend the life of roads. By deploying advanced pothole detection systems, authorities can effectively prioritize repairs and ensure that resources are directed to the most important areas, which can maximize maintenance spending. In addition, pothole detection has significant economic impacts [3]. Every year, drivers and insurance companies lose millions of dollars due to vehicle damage caused by potholes. Vehicle owners can find themselves financially burdened by the skyrocketing costs associated with wheel alignment, tyre replacement, and other repairs. Poor road conditions can also lead to higher fuel consumption and wear and tear on vehicles, which increases driving costs. Potholes can interfere with operations, causing delays and higher operating costs for transportation-dependent companies such as logistics [4] and delivery services [5]. By detecting potholes early and repairing them quickly, transportation networks can become smoother and more efficient, while incurring less financial cost.

Pothole detection system technology has evolved significantly in recent years [6]. Modern technologies for accurately detecting and evaluating potholes include sensors, cameras, and machine learning algorithms. For example, vehicle-mounted sensors can detect irregularities and vibrations in the road surface [7], and potholes can be located and measured using cameras and computer vision algorithms that evaluate visual data. The real-time monitoring and reporting made possible by this technology allow authorities to respond to problems quickly and effectively. Furthermore, the integration of these systems with geographic information systems (GIS) [8] facilitates the creation of comprehensive road condition maps [9], which is beneficial for long-term planning and maintenance plans. To summarize, the identification of potholes is crucial to protecting infrastructure, guaranteeing road safety, and reducing financial losses. By using modern detection systems, authorities can optimize maintenance work, improve safety for all road users and proactively manage road conditions. Effective pothole detection has advantages beyond quick fixes; it also improves the sustainability [10] and overall effectiveness of transportation networks. As urbanization and vehicle use increase, it will become more important to invest in robust pothole detection and management technologies to maintain the quality and safety of our roadways.

Autonomous systems, particularly unmanned aerial vehicles (UAVs), have gained significant traction across various fields due to their ability to perform tasks with precision and efficiency [11–13]. These systems are increasingly utilized for monitoring and mapping purposes, enabling comprehensive data collection in a wide range of environments

[14, 15]. For instance, UAVs are employed in agriculture for crop surveillance, in environmental studies for wildlife monitoring, and in urban planning for land use mapping [16]. Their aerial perspective allows for the rapid gathering of high-resolution imagery and geospatial data, which is crucial for making informed decisions and enhancing operational efficiency. In the context of Intelligent Transportation Systems (ITS), autonomous systems play a pivotal role in enhancing road safety and efficiency. These systems can be leveraged to detect vehicles, assess road infrastructure conditions, and identify road hazards such as potholes. By integrating advanced object detection algorithms, such as those based on deep learning, UAVs can systematically survey transportation networks, providing accurate and timely data for traffic management and infrastructure maintenance. The deployment of UAVs in ITS not only streamlines the monitoring process but also contributes to proactive maintenance strategies, reducing the likelihood of accidents and improving overall road safety.

Recent advances in computer vision and deep learning have opened new avenues for automated pothole detection, enabling high precision in complex and dynamic environments. Within this domain, convolutional neural networks (CNNs) have shown considerable promise. For instance, [17] used a CNN-based approach to classify road surface images, achieving robust accuracy in controlled conditions. Similarly, [18] applied a CNN to a large-scale road dataset, detecting potholes and other road damages from aerial and vehicle-mounted cameras. While these approaches improved detection accuracy, their computational demands often limited real-time deployment in practice. The application of object detection algorithms, particularly the YOLO series, has further advanced pothole detection. The YOLO models are well-regarded for their real-time detection capabilities, balancing speed and accuracy by treating detection as a single-stage problem. YOLOv3 [19] marked the initial use of single-shot detection for road damage, showcasing its capacity for high-speed processing. Subsequent iterations, such as YOLOv4 [10] and YOLOv5 [20], refined these capabilities, improving detection speed and scalability for large datasets. However, the latest YOLO versions, YOLOv7 and YOLOv8, have optimized neural architecture designs, achieving state-of-the-art results in real-time object detection while reducing computational load. These improvements make the models particularly suited to mobile deployment on platforms such as UAVs and vehicle-mounted cameras for real-time pothole monitoring. Our study builds upon these advancements by applying YOLOv7 and YOLOv8 models specifically for pothole detection. These models' improved speed and accuracy enhance their adaptability for real-time pothole monitoring, offering a significant advantage for municipal applications and road maintenance initiatives.

Computer vision, especially in the field of object detection, has been transformed by CNNs [21]. CNNs excel at automatically learning hierarchical representations from raw image data, making them ideal for applications such as image categorization, localization and object recognition. Beyond simple classification, object detection methods find and identify many elements in an image, giving boundary boxes and class labels to each detected object. YOLO [22] algorithm is one of the most important breakthroughs in this field, having gone through multiple iterations, each of which has improved on its predecessors in terms of speed, accuracy and complexity. Real-time object recognition, made possible when Joseph Redmon et al. introduced the first YOLO algorithm in

2016, has been a game-changer. Unlike standard methods that first generate possible object regions and then classify them, YOLO reframes object identification as a single regression problem that goes directly from image pixels to bounding box coordinates and class probabilities. Because of its unified approach, YOLO can analyze images very quickly, making it perfect for real-time processing applications such as autonomous driving and video surveillance.

By combining supervised and weakly supervised training, YOLOv2 or YOLO9000 has achieved remarkable gains in accuracy and the capacity to detect more than 9000 object categories. High-resolution classifiers, batch normalization, and the use of junction boxes are some of the approaches that YOLOv2 brings to the detection process, increasing its robustness and precision. This iteration supported the compromise between speed and precision and thus solidified YOLO's position as an elite object identification system. YOLOv3 [23], released in 2018, significantly increased speed by implementing a deeper network architecture known as Darknet-53, which increased feature extraction capabilities. In addition, YOLOv3 added multi-scale predictions that improve the effectiveness of object identification at various scales. This release continues to provide real-time object detection with better precision, making it suitable for a wider range of applications, including drones and medical imaging. YOLOv4 [24], created by Alexey Bochkovskiy, Chien-Yao Wang and Hong-Yuan Mark Liao, improved on YOLOv3 by adding several advances in network architecture and training methodologies. YOLOv4 used techniques such as Cross-Stage Partial Links (CSPDarknet), Mish activation function, and a number of data augmentation methods to improve speed and accuracy. It has emerged as one of the most competent object detection systems, striking an impressive balance between computational efficiency and performance.

YOLOv5 [25] emphasizes scalability, user-friendliness, and compatibility with other machine learning frameworks. YOLOv5 is easier to implement and customize because it is developed in PyTorch. Enhancements such as mosaic data augmentation, automatic learning bounding box connections, and a more adaptive training pipeline are included. Thanks to these improvements, YOLOv5 is now one of the most flexible and user-friendly versions and is frequently used in both academic and commercial settings. YOLOv6 [26] and subsequent versions build on this foundation by incorporating the latest research advances and optimizing for a variety of hardware platforms, from GPUs to edge devices. Each iteration of YOLO has pushed the boundaries of what can be achieved in real-time object identification, solidifying the YOLO family of models as the foundation of modern computer vision applications. As a result, the field of computer vision has made great progress thanks to CNNs and object detection algorithms, especially the YOLO family. Each iteration of YOLO, from the first to the most recent, has improved speed, accuracy, and usability, solidifying YOLO's place as the best real-time object detection framework. As research continues and new versions are created, YOLO models are expected to remain at the forefront of convenient, high-performance object identification solutions.

This study provides a significant advancement in the field of pothole detection by presenting a detailed comparative analysis of YOLOv7 and YOLOv8 algorithms. Our research not only highlights the performance improvements offered by YOLOv8 in terms of precision, recall, and detection speed but also compares these models with other established algorithms, such as SSD and Faster R-CNN. By creating a comprehensive dataset and conducting rigorous testing under various conditions, this study contributes valuable insights into the effectiveness of these object detection techniques in real-world scenarios. Furthermore, our findings pave the way for future implementations of these algorithms in autonomous vehicle systems, enhancing their potential to improve road safety and reduce the incidence of vehicle accidents caused by potholes.

The remainder of this paper is organized as follows. In Sect. 2, System Methodology, we introduce the YOLOv7 and YOLOv8 models, detailing the architectures and unique characteristics of each for pothole detection. We also describe the data acquisition process, covering the sources and preparation of the dataset used for training and evaluation. Section 3, System Workflow, outlines the end-to-end process of the detection system, from data input to real-time detection output. In Sect. 4, Test Results, we present a comparative analysis of YOLOv7 and YOLOv8 based on key performance metrics, including precision, recall, and detection time, highlighting the strengths and weaknesses of each model. Finally, Sect. 5, Conclusion, summarizes the findings and discusses implications for future work in the field of automated pothole detection.

2 System Methodology

2.1 YOLOv7 Model

A significant achievement in the field of real-time object detection, the YOLOv7 [27] model extends the foundations established by its predecessors, improving both accuracy and speed, making it one of the most powerful tools for object detection tasks available today. YOLOv7 aims to address some of the fundamental problems of previous YOLO versions, especially when handling complex situations with small objects and a few overlapping elements. The advanced architecture of YOLOv7 is one of its most remarkable features. A more efficient backbone network utilizing advanced convolutional methods and attention processes is incorporated into the model. As a result, YOLOv7 can improve detection accuracy by extracting more relevant and detailed features from input images. Since state-of-the-art methods such as CSPNet (Cross-Stage Partial Network) are integrated, YOLOv7 can be deployed on edge devices and real-time applications while maintaining excellent performance and reduced computational complexity.

Besides architectural upgrades, YOLOv7 features innovative training algorithms that significantly improve its performance. For example, mosaic data augmentation, which combines four training photos into a single photo, improves generalization by allowing the model to learn from a variety of scenarios. In addition, this method reduces the problem of overfitting, guaranteeing that YOLOv7 works reliably in a variety of contexts and datasets. YOLOv7 also uses label smoothing and other editing strategies to further improve generalization capabilities. Compared to previous YOLO versions, YOLOv7 achieves higher Mean Accuracy (mAP), especially when it comes to the recognition of small objects and in congested environments. In addition, the model exhibits an excellent balance between precision and recall, which is critical for applications that require a minimal amount of false positives and false negatives. Another notable feature is YOLOv7's capacity to process data in real-time. Despite its increased complexity and better accuracy, the model maintains a high inference rate, processing multiple frames per second. This is crucial for applications such as robotics, autonomous driving and video surveillance.

Another notable feature of YOLOv7 is its adaptability and versatility. The model can be adapted to many use cases and adjusted to specific requirements. Its modular architecture facilitates this adaptability, allowing developers to include new layers or modify existing layers in accordance with requirements. Furthermore, YOLOv7 enables transfer learning, which allows the model to use pre-trained weights from large-scale datasets, speeding up training and improving performance on specialized tasks with little data. To summarize, YOLOv7 is a state-of-the-art object identification model that excels in precision, speed and versatility. Its cutting-edge training techniques, innovative architecture and remarkable performance metrics make it an adaptable tool for a variety of real-time applications. When it comes to object detection, YOLOv7 sets a new standard in autonomous vehicles, security systems and industrial automation. It provides reliable solutions that meet the needs of contemporary AI-driven applications.

2.2 YOLOv8 Model

YOLOv8 [28], one of the most popular members of the You Only Look Once (YOLO) family, builds on the capabilities of its predecessor by making significant progress in object identification. The model is intended to push the boundaries of real-time object identification, combining cutting-edge approaches and modern architecture to achieve exceptional accuracy and speed. YOLOv8 improves its entire design, including the input preprocessing, backbone, neck and output stages, enabling a more efficient and effective detection pipeline.

Advanced pre-processing techniques are included in the YOLOv8 entry stage to prepare images for the detection pipeline. This includes data augmentation techniques such as mosaic augmentation, which combines several images into one, as well as adaptive scaling and normalization. By using these methods, the generalization capacity of the model is increased and lessons can be learned from various scenarios. YOLOv8 also utilizes advanced data augmentation techniques such as MixUp and CutMix, which combine various labels and photos to increase the model's resilience to changes in object sizes, occlusions and lighting.

The backbone of YOLOv8 is its central component and is responsible for deriving rich feature representations from input images. YOLOv8 leverages a state-of-the-art backbone network, often modelled after CSPNet or EfficientNet designs. To enhance the model's ability to gather contextual information and fine-grained details, this backbone includes compression and excitation blocks and deeply separable convolutions. These complex convolutional processes reduce computational cost while maintaining high representational power, making YOLOv8 suitable for real-time applications on resource-limited devices.

The neck of YOLOv8 is critical for combining and enhancing the features that the backbone extracts. Feature pyramid networks (FPN) and path aggregation networks (PAN) are often combined to ensure that data from various scales and resolutions are successfully fused. It is important to use this multi-scale feature fusion when identifying elements in complex scenes and of different sizes. Scale variations and geometric modifications are further enhanced by the inclusion of deformable convolutional networks (DCN) and spatial pyramid pooling (SPPF) in the neck architecture of YOLOv8.

The output phase of YOLOv8 aims to provide accurate and highly reliable predictions for object detection. It features a collection of detection heads that can predict objecthood scores, class probabilities and bounding boxes. YOLOv8's anchorless detection heads eliminate the need for predefined anchor boxes, making training easier and reducing the computational burden. Regression and classification branches are combined by these detection heads to precisely locate objects and classify them into predefined groups. To ensure optimal performance on various metrics, the model also includes a unique loss function that provides a compromise between objectivity score, classification confidence and localization accuracy.

Advanced training methodologies complement YOLOv8's architecture, further enhancing its performance. The model leverages techniques such as self-distillation, where it learns from its own predictions, and knowledge distillation, where it learns from a larger, pre-trained trainer model. These tactics increase the accuracy and robustness of the model, especially when training with minimal data. YOLOv8 also uses mixed-precision training and gradient checkpointing to improve memory utilization and speed up the training process without compromising performance.

To summarize, YOLOv8 provides a significant advancement in object detection technology, leveraging the advantages of previous models while introducing new architectural and training advances. Its advanced input preprocessing, efficient backbone, multi-scale feature collection neck and precise output detection heads all contribute to its outstanding performance. YOLOv8 sets a new standard for real-time object recognition, providing exceptional accuracy, speed and adaptability, making it the perfect solution for a wide range of applications including autonomous vehicles, video surveillance, industrial automation and more.

2.3 Data Acquisition

In order to evaluate the performance of the algorithms in the most accurate way, a comprehensive dataset was prepared. In order for the algorithm to perform better, it needs to be trained with images with challenging conditions. In order to increase the number of images with challenging conditions and to provide data diversity, images were obtained from Google Earth. While obtaining the images, two types of pits, filled with water and empty, were included in sufficient quantities. At the same time, attention was paid to the presence of shallow-deep and small-large pothole images. In order to train the algorithm in the best way and to obtain more accurate performance metric results, attention was paid to the lighting condition, which is an important challenging condition. The dataset includes images from both dark and light periods of the day. Figure 1 shows examples of the images in the dataset. There are a total of 2575 images in the dataset prepared by paying attention to all these conditions. The dataset was divided into three parts to be used in the training, validation and testing phases of the algorithm. In the training dataset, 1475 images were used as the majority of the images. After using 650 of the remaining images of the data set for the validation data set, the test data set was created with the remaining images.

Fig. 1. Some examples from dataset.

3 System Workflow

In this proposed system, deep learning models are fed with the images in the dataset obtained for pothole detection. As a result of the deep learning models processing the images, the predicted potholes in the images are framed with bounding boxes. Afterwards, the exact coordinates of the image, and hence the size of the estimated box, are

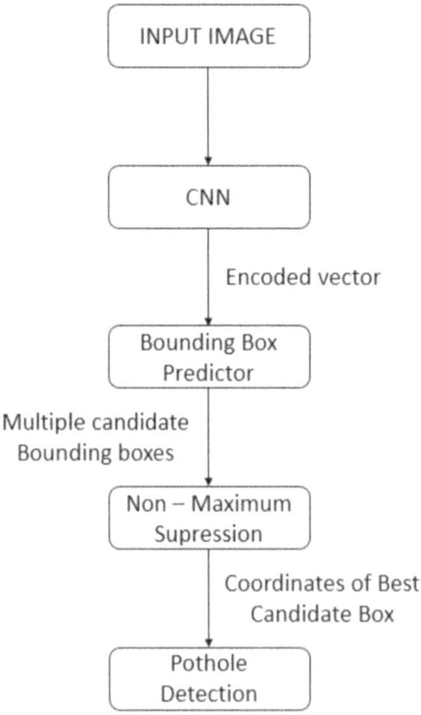

Fig. 2. System workflow.

obtained by Non-Maximum Suppression to avoid over-processing. Figure 2 shows the system workflow in detail.

4 Test Results

Figure 3 shows examples of pothole detection by the YOLOv7 and YOLOv8 models in low lighting conditions. The first example in Fig. 3 shows an image of a road in a relatively dark environment with deep and large potholes and small potholes in between. In image 1, where detection was performed with the YOLOv7 model, the model successfully detected large potholes and potholes in close visibility. However, it failed to detect the relatively small images further down the road, which can be attributed to the brightness of the water color resembling the brightness of wet asphalt. At the same time, the v7 model incorrectly detected some two small potholes as one large pothole. This can be attributed to the fact that the small water-filled potholes were located very close to each other. The YOLOv8 model outperforms the YOLOv7 model in the detection of image 1. The YOLO v8 model is even successful in detecting the small potholes on the left side of the road, which are not very deep. At the same time, with its high performance, it is successful in detecting all small potholes and potholes in the forward visibility range. In the second sample image of Fig. 3, the potholes are larger, more prominent, and in a row compared to the other images. In image 2, the v7 model was successful in detecting the pits in the near field of view and drawing the bounding boxes. However, similar to image 1, the v7 model failed to detect potholes at a distance. The YOLOv8 model showed superior performance and was successful in detecting even the smallest dimples at the farthest distance. The last image in Fig. 3, image number 3, shows an image with many small and large potholes and deep and shallow potholes, which were acquired in relatively dark weather. The YOLOv7 model failed to detect the shallow potholes on the roadside and the small potholes in the middle of the road. The reason for this may be the lack of brightness of the muddy water in the potholes on the roadside as a result of the mixture of soil and water. v8 model performed much better than the v7 model as in the other images and was successful in detecting the potholes on the roadside. However, the v8 model included multiple potholes that were smaller in size and located close to each other in a single bounding box. This can be attributed to the fact that the color shading of the small potholes is very close to each other and they are located very close to each other.

Figure 4 shows examples of the detection capabilities of the YOLOv7 and YOLOv8 models in images obtained in brighter conditions, where there are pits without water in them. In the example shown as number 4 in Fig. 4, there is an image with both deep and shallow pits, filled with water and hollow pits, acquired during the daylight hours. The YOLOv7 model was successful in detecting large and water-filled pits but unfortunately failed to detect hollow and shallow pits. The reason for this failure can be attributed to the fact that the color gradation of the shallow potholes is very similar to the color gradation of the asphalt on the road. Unlike the v7 model, the YOLOv8 model successfully detected all potholes. However, it incorrectly detected two small hollow potholes in the upper right region of the image as if they were one large pothole. The reason for this false detection can be attributed to the fact that the color tone of the small potholes is very similar and

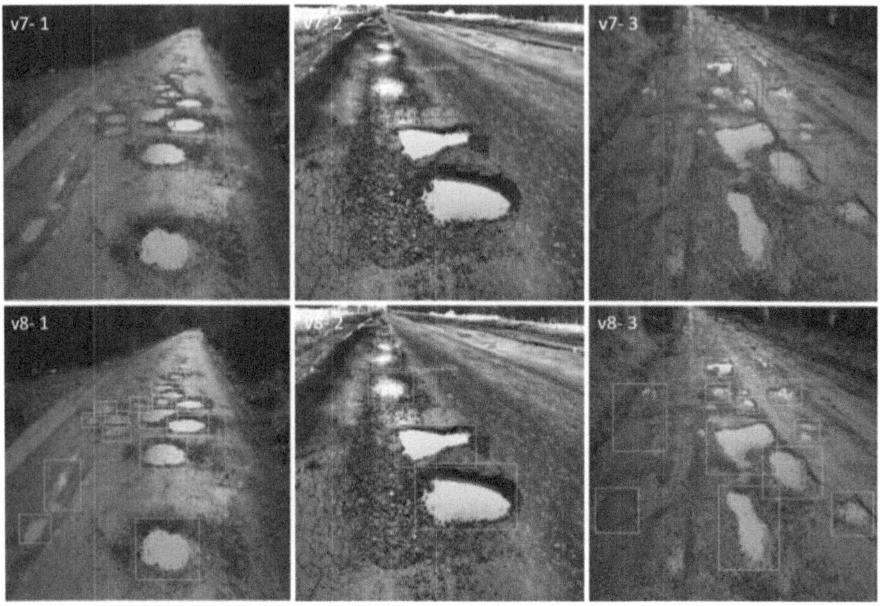

Fig. 3. Some examples of pothole detection with YOLOv7 and YOLOv8 in low lighting conditions.

they are located very close to each other. Image 5 is an image taken during daylight hours when there are many road cracks and large hollow potholes. The YOLOv7 model was largely successful in detecting the empty potholes but failed to detect the shallow pothole located above the traffic signs. This may be due to the fact that the pothole is located in the forward line of sight and the traffic sign creates a challenging condition for detection. With its superior performance, YOLOv8 also detected the pothole that was not detected by YOLOv7 and achieved a high rate of success in the detection of potholes. In the last sample image of Fig. 4, image 6, there are large and small pits, both filled and hollow, scattered. The YOLOv7 model detected the water-filled potholes on the roadside in image 6, but it also detected two small potholes close to each other at a distance as if they were a single pothole, which we have seen similar examples in other images. The YOLOv7 model failed to detect the hollow shallow pits in the center of the road in image 6. This may be due to the fact that the shallow potholes appear to be relatively flat and do not have a very clear hue distinction. Finally, in image 6, the YOLOv8 model met the expectations and outperformed the YOLOv7 model with its high performance and detected all potholes with full success.

In order to evaluate the performance of the YOLOv7 and YOLOv8 models, commonly used performance metrics such as precision, recall, mAP and F1 Score values were used. At the same time, average speed values were also analyzed in order to compare their performance and speed. Table 1 shows the values of the performance metrics used to evaluate the performance of the algorithms. The YOLOv8 model proved its superiority over YOLOv7 with its high-performance values. YOLOv8 has a precision value of 0.898, which is about 6.3% higher than YOLOv7. In terms of recall values, although there is not as much difference between the two performances as the precision values, the YOLOv8 model is 1.52% larger than the YOLOv7 model with a value of 0.801. When we look at the mAP and F1 score values, as expected, the YOLOv8 model has clearly shown that it performs better than the YOLOv7 model. The YOLOv8 model has a mAP value of 0.822, which is approximately 2.37% higher than the YOLOv7 model. Similarly, in F1 Score, the YOLOv8 model has a value 3.8% larger than the YOLOv7 model. The YOLOv8 model has proven its superiority by achieving this superior performance in a much shorter time than the YOLOv7 model.

We have conducted a more detailed error analysis to address specific challenges observed in YOLOv7 and YOLOv8 when detecting small, closely spaced potholes. While YOLOv7 provides accurate detection overall, it struggles to differentiate between potholes that are adjacent or overlapping, often missing smaller potholes in clusters due to its bounding box limitations. Similarly, YOLOv8, although generally more accurate, occasionally combines multiple small potholes into a single bounding box, reducing detection granularity. To address these limitations, future work could explore multi-scale training or employing additional post-processing techniques, such as non-maximum suppression adjustments, to improve model precision in detecting closely spaced anomalies. Additionally, integrating models with specialized anchor boxes tailored for smaller objects may further enhance the detection accuracy of potholes in complex environments. This refined analysis aims to shed light on specific model limitations and suggests potential pathways for enhancing pothole detection accuracy.

Fig. 4. Some examples of pothole detection with YOLOv7 and YOLOv8 in brighter lighting conditions.

Table 1. Performance comparison of YOLOv7 and YOLOv8 algorithms

Metric	YOLOv7	YOLOv8	SSD	F. R-CNN
Precision	0.845	0.898	0.806	0.877
Recall	0.789	0.801	0.751	0.781
mAP	0.803	0.822	0.769	0.813
F1 Score	0.816	0.847	0.783	0.826
Det. Time	21.3 ms	19.6 ms	23.9 ms	57.3 ms

5 Conclusion

This paper presents a comprehensive comparison of the YOLOv7 and YOLOv8 algorithms for the detection of potholes on the road using images recorded from web-based sources and the Google Earth platform. The evaluation of these algorithms was performed using a dataset of images of potholes in various conditions to ensure more accurate training and validation. For performance comparison, precision, recall, mAP, F1 Score and Average detection time metrics were calculated and evaluated for YOLOv7 and YOLOv8 models. The results showed that the YOLOv8 algorithm outperformed the YOLOv7 algorithm in pothole detection. The YOLOv8 model achieved higher values in precision, recall, mAP and F1 score, demonstrating its superior performance in accurately detecting potholes and calculating their location. Despite the challenges posed by varying pit sizes, depth and lighting conditions, YOLOv8 performed exceptionally well. YOLOv8 achieved this superior performance in all challenging conditions in a very short time, proving that it can be used in real-time applications. Future research should focus on these areas to continue to develop real-time pothole detection monitoring capabilities on images from camera systems integrated into smart vehicles.

Future research can explore several avenues to further improve pothole detection accuracy and robustness under diverse environmental and operational conditions. First, the integration of multi-scale feature extraction methods could enhance the detection of smaller and closely spaced potholes, addressing some of the limitations observed with YOLOv7 and YOLOv8. Additionally, developing a more diverse and larger dataset that includes images captured under various weather conditions, road materials, and vehicle perspectives could improve the generalizability of the model. Implementing a fusion approach that combines YOLOv8 with other advanced deep learning models, such as transformer-based architectures, may also yield improvements in recognizing potholes across different scales and complexities. Finally, deploying these models on embedded hardware, such as UAVs and vehicle-mounted devices, for real-time road monitoring would allow for field testing and optimization, providing valuable insights into both the computational efficiency and real-world applicability of these models in autonomous road maintenance systems.

To compare the performance of the YOLO models, we conducted the same tests using the SSD and Faster R-CNN algorithms. The results obtained from the SSD model indicate a competitive yet slightly lower performance in pothole detection compared to the YOLO algorithms. With a precision of 0.806, SSD demonstrates a respectable ability to identify true positive detections among all positive identifications. However, its recall value of 0.751 suggests that there are still a significant number of potholes that the model fails to detect. The mAP value of 0.769 further highlights this gap, indicating that while SSD effectively detects many potholes, it struggles with accuracy in identifying smaller or less distinct ones. The F1 score, which balances precision and recall, stands at 0.783, reflecting the trade-off between these two metrics. Notably, the detection time for SSD is recorded at 23.9 ms, which is relatively slower than both YOLOv7 and YOLOv8. This latency could pose challenges in real-time applications where rapid decision-making is essential.

In contrast, the results from the Faster R-CNN model show a robust performance in pothole detection, albeit with some trade-offs. The precision score of 0.877 indicates that Faster R-CNN has a high rate of accurate detections relative to false positives. Its recall of 0.781 reveals that the model effectively identifies a majority of potholes, although there is still room for improvement in capturing all instances. The mAP value of 0.813 further underscores its strength, showcasing the model's effectiveness across various categories and conditions. The F1 score of 0.826 highlights a balanced performance, indicating that Faster R-CNN achieves a good trade-off between precision and recall. However, this model comes with a significant detection time of 57.3 ms, making it the slowest among the four algorithms assessed. This slower detection speed may limit its applicability in real-time scenarios, particularly in autonomous systems where immediate responses are critical.

When comparing the performance values of the four algorithms, YOLOv7, YOLOv8, SSD, and Faster R-CNN, it becomes evident that each model presents unique strengths and weaknesses that cater to different application requirements. YOLOv8 leads the group with the highest precision (0.898) and F1 score (0.847), indicating superior performance in accurately detecting potholes while minimizing false positives. Its detection time of 19.6 ms also positions it as the fastest option, making it well-suited for real-time applications. YOLOv7, while slightly less effective than YOLOv8, still offers commendable results with a precision of 0.845 and an F1 score of 0.816, along with a competitive detection time of 21.3 ms.

In comparison, SSD shows respectable performance with a precision of 0.806 and an F1 score of 0.783, but its slower detection time of 23.9 ms limits its real-time applicability. Conversely, Faster R-CNN excels in precision (0.877) and boasts a strong F1 score of 0.826, yet its detection time of 57.3 ms is a significant drawback for applications requiring immediate feedback. Overall, while YOLOv8 emerges as the most efficient model for pothole detection, both SSD and Faster R-CNN provide valuable insights into the trade-offs between accuracy and speed, highlighting the need for careful consideration of application requirements when selecting an appropriate detection algorithm.

References

1. Pandey, A.D., Iqbal, R., Maniak, T., Karyotis, C., Akuma, S., Palade, V.: Convolutional neural networks for pothole detection of critical road infrastructure. Comput. Electr. Eng. **99**, 107725 (2022)
2. Wu, C., et al.: An automated machine-learning approach for road pothole detection using smartphone sensor data. Sensors **20**(19), 5564 (2020)

3. Egaji, O.A., Evans, G., Griffiths, M.G., Islas, G.: Real-time machine learning-based approach for pothole detection. Expert Syst. Appl. **184**, 115562 (2021)
4. Masud, A.K.M.J.A., Sharin, S.T., Shawon, K.F.T., Za, Z.: Pothole detection using machine learning algorithms. In: 15th International Conference on Signal Processing and Communication Systems, pp. 1–5. IEEE, Sydney, Australia (2021)
5. Wang, Y., Ye, T.: Applications of artificial intelligence enhanced drones in distress pavement, pothole detection, and healthcare monitoring with service delivery. J. Eng. **2022**(1), 7733196 (2022)
6. Tsai, Y.C., Chatterjee, A.: Pothole detection and classification using 3D technology and watershed method. J. Comput. Civ. Eng. **32**(2), 04017078 (2017)
7. Kim, Y.M., Kim, Y.G., Son, S.Y., Lim, S.Y., Choi, B.Y., Choi, D.H.: Reviev of recent automated pothole detection methods. Appl. Sci. **12**(11), 5320 (2022)
8. Kyriakou, C., Christodoulou, S.E., Dimitriou, L.: Smartphone-based pothole detection utilizing artificial neural networks. J. Infrastruct. Syst. **25**(3), 04019019 (2019)
9. Borgalli, M.: Smart pothole detection and mapping system. J. Ubiquit. Comput. Commun. Technol. **02**(03), 136–144 (2020)
10. Ryu, S.K., Kim, T., Kim, Y.R.: Image-based pothole detection system for ITS service and road management system. Math. Probl. Eng. **2015**, 968361 (2015)
11. Bakirci, M.: Smart city air quality management through leveraging drones for precision monitoring. Sustain. Cities Soc. **106**, 105390 (2024)
12. Bakirci, M.: A novel swarm unmanned aerial vehicle system: Incorporating autonomous flight, real-time object detection, and coordinated intelligence for enhanced performance. Traitement du Sig. **40**(5), 2063–2078 (2023)
13. Bakirci, M.: Efficient air pollution mapping in extensive regions with fully autonomous unmanned aerial vehicles: a numerical perspective. In: Science of the Total Environment 909, 168606 (2024)
14. Bakirci, M.: Enhancing air pollution mapping with autonomous UAV networks for extended coverage and consistency. Atmos. Res. **306**, 107480 (2024)
15. Bakirci, M.: A drone-based approach to enhance spatial insight into surrounding air pollutant distributions for healthier indoor environments. J. Build. Eng. **87**, 109023 (2024)
16. Bakirci, M.: Evaluating the impact of unmanned aerial vehicles (UAVs) on air quality management in smart cities: a comprehensive analysis of transportation-related pollution. Comput. Electr. Eng. **119**, 109556 (2024)
17. Dhiman, A., Klette, R.: Pothole Detection Using Computer Vision and Learning. IEEE Trans. Intell. Transp. Syst. **21**(8), 3536–3550 (2020)
18. Koch, C., Brilakis, I.: Pothole detection in asphalt pavement images. Adv. Eng. Inform. **25**(3), 507–515 (2011)
19. Wang, H.W., Chen, C.H., Cheng, D.Y., Lin, C.H., Lo, C.C.: A real-time pothole detection approach for intelligent transportation system. Math. Probl. Eng. **2015**, 869627 (2015)
20. Varona, B., Monteserin, A., Teyseyre, A.: A deep learning approach to automatic road surface monitoring and pothole detection. Pers. Ubiquit. Comput. **24**, 519–534 (2020)
21. Bakirci, M.: Enhancing vehicle detection in intelligent transportation systems via autonomous UAV platform and YOLOv8 integration. Appl. Soft Comput. **164**, 112015 (2024)
22. Bakirci, M.: Real-time vehicle detection using YOLOv8-nano for intelligent transportation systems. Traitement du Sig. **41**(4), 1727–1740 (2024)
23. Sathya, R., Saleena, B., Prakash, B.: Pothole detection using YOLOv3 model. In: International Students' Conference on Electrical, Electronics and Computer Science, Bhopal, India, pp. 1–7. IEEE (2023)
24. Omar, M., Kumar, P.: Detection of roads potholes using YOLOv4. In: International Conference on Information Science and Communications Technologies, pp. 1–6. IEEE, Tashkent, Uzbekistan (2021)

25. Ajmera, S., Kumar, C.A., Yakaiah, P., Kumar, B., Chowdary, K.Y.: Real-time pothole detection using YOLOV5. In: International Conference on Advancements in Smart. Secure and Intelligent Computing, pp. 1–5. IEEE, Bhubaneswar, India (2022)
26. Omar, M., Kumar, P.: PD-ITS: pothole detection using YOLO variants for intelligent transport system. SN Comput. Sci. **5**, 552 (2024)
27. Reddy, E.S.T.K., Rajaram, V.: Pothole detection using CNN and YOLOv7 algorithm. In: 6th International Conference on Electronics, Communication and Aerospace Technology, Coimbatore, India, pp. 1–6. IEEE (2022)
28. Bakirci, M.: Utilizing YOLOv8 for enhanced traffic monitoring in intelligent transportation systems (ITS) applications. Digital Sig. Process. **152**, 104594 (2024)

Author Index

A. Mirzazadeh et al. (Eds.): SEMIT 2024, CCIS 2444, pp. 447–448, 2026.
https://doi.org/10.1007/978-3-032-01948-6

The manufacturer's authorised representative in the EU is Springer Nature Customer Service Centre GmbH, Europaplatz 3, 69115 Heidelberg, Germany. If you have any concerns regarding our products, please contact ProductSafety@springernature.com

Printed and bound by CPI Group (UK) Ltd, Croydon, CR0 4YY
30/09/2026
02225585-0011